JFK

JFK

COMING OF
AGE IN THE
AMERICAN
CENTURY,
1917–1956

FREDRIK
LOGEVALL

RANDOM HOUSE

NEW YORK

Copyright © 2020 by Fredrik Logevall
Maps copyright © 2020 by David Lindroth Inc.

Published in the United States by Random House, an imprint and division of
Penguin Random House LLC, New York.

RANDOM HOUSE and the HOUSE colophon are registered trademarks
of Penguin Random House LLC.

Excerpt from poem by Jacqueline Kennedy reprinted by permission of Ambassador Caroline
Kennedy c/o the John F. Kennedy Presidential Library and Museum, Boston, Massachusetts.

LIBRARY OF CONGRESS CATALOGING-IN-PUBLICATION DATA

Names: Logevall, Fredrik, author.
Title: JFK / Fredrik Logevall.
Other titles: John Fitzgerald Kennedy
Description: New York : Random House, 2020– | Includes bibliographical references
and index. | Contents: [Vol. 1] Coming of age in the American century, 1917–1956
Identifiers: LCCN 2020003488 (print) | LCCN 2020003489 (ebook) |
ISBN 9780812997132 (v.1 ; hardcover) | ISBN 9780812997149 (v.1 ; ebook)
Subjects: LCSH: Kennedy, John F. (John Fitzgerald), 1917–1963. | Kennedy, John F.
(John Fitzgerald), 1917–1963—Family. | Legislators—Massachusetts—Biography. |
United States. Congress. Senate—Biography. | New England—Politics and government—
20th century. United States—Politics and government—1945–1989. | Massachusetts—
Biography. | Presidents—United States—Biography.
Classification: LCC E842 .L.555 2020 (print) | LCC E842 (ebook) |
DDC 973.922092 [B]—dc23
LC record available at https://lccn.loc.gov/2020003488
LC ebook record available at https://lccn.loc.gov/2020003489

Printed in the United States of America on acid-free paper

randomhousebooks.com

9 8 7 6 5 4 3 2 1

First Edition

Book design by Jo Anne Metsch

FRONTISPIECE: Jack Kennedy in Hyannis Port, early 1940s.

For Danyel

CONTENTS

PREFACE

E arly one morning in August 1939, twenty-two-year-old Jack Kennedy
looked out his window at the Hotel Excelsior, in Berlin, not far from the
Reich Chancellery, and caught a glimpse of things to come: on the
street below, Nazi storm troopers marched by. A rising senior at Harvard, Kennedy was nearing the end of an extraordinary seven-month
study-abroad adventure, one that had included stints working in the U.S.
embassies in London (where his father was the ambassador) and Paris, as
well as travels to a dozen countries in Europe and the Middle East. At each
stop, he'd used his father's connections to meet with local officials and
U.S. diplomats, asking questions, taking notes, and forming a picture of a
world in crisis.[1]

Now he was in Germany's capital, the nerve center of Nazi power. Rumors were rife that Hitler's armies were readying to invade Poland. Kennedy, a skeptic by nature, wasn't sure—the German dictator might be
bluffing—but he felt unease as he took in the atmosphere of tense expec-
tancy in the city. At every turn, he saw evidence of fearsome Nazi propaganda at work as the authorities bombarded Berliners with supposed
proof of heinous behavior by the contemptible Poles.[2] So relentless was
the barrage, Kennedy suggested in a letter to his friend Lem Billings on

August 20, that German officials might be hemming themselves in, unable to back down even if they wanted to. Moreover, Jack wondered, did Hitler grasp that Britain and France, allied to Poland, were likely to show greater resolve this time than they had mustered during the Munich negotiations the previous year, when they had meekly let the Führer seize part of Czechoslovakia? "England seems firm this time," he wrote to Billings, "but as that is not completely understood here the big danger here lies in the Germans counting on another Munich then finding themselves in a war when Chamberlain refuses to give in."[3]

The following evening, shortly before midnight, came staggering news via Berlin radio: Germany and the Soviet Union, longtime bitter foes, would sign a nonaggression pact, with details to be worked out in Moscow in two days. Though many ordinary Germans were relieved—surely the Poles would now succumb without a fight, and the conflict would be resolved in much the same nonviolent way as the Czech crisis the previous year—seasoned diplomats, privy to official thinking in Warsaw and Paris and London, knew better.[4] They recognized that the Nazi-Soviet deal, by isolating the Poles, made war more likely, not less. When Jack visited the U.S. embassy shortly before his departure from the city, Alexander Kirk, the chargé d'affaires and senior officer (Ambassador Hugh Wilson had departed several months prior), asked him to take a secret message back to Ambassador Kennedy in London: Germany would invade Poland within a week.[5]

The invasion came on September 1. By then Jack was back in London, joining his parents and eight siblings at the ambassadorial residence in Knightsbridge. On September 3, he and his mother, Rose, along with two of his siblings—older brother Joe Junior and younger sister Kick—were in the visitors' gallery of the House of Commons when Prime Minister Neville Chamberlain somberly affirmed what he had just announced in a radio broadcast: Britain was at war with Germany. Jack's worry as expressed to Lem Billings two weeks before had been borne out. Ambassador Joseph Kennedy, an unbending supporter of Chamberlain's failed efforts to avert war through a policy of appeasement, had been moved almost to tears by the prime minister's mournful radio address. His wife felt the same as she took in Chamberlain's remarks in the Commons.[6]

For Jack, however, another speaker on this historic day left the deepest impression. Standing before the Commons as the incoming First Lord of the Admiralty, Winston Churchill summoned his compatriots to the glorious endeavor ahead: "Outside, the storms of war may blow and the lands may be lashed with the fury of its gales, but in our own hearts this Sunday morning there is peace." Jack watched transfixed as Churchill declared, "Our hands may be active, but our consciences are at rest."[7]

A photo shows the three Kennedy siblings—vibrant and handsome—on their way to the Houses of Parliament:

The trio understood that they were eyewitnesses to history. But they had no inkling of how much the war that was just beginning would transform the world and their place in it. In five years, Joe Junior would be erased from the picture, killed in action, and Kick's husband would also perish, mere weeks after their wedding. Joe Senior's public career would be destroyed. The war would also tear asunder the European-led international order, as Jack saw up close when he returned to the Continent in mid-1945 as a twenty-eight-year-old journalist and decorated veteran. Germany had capitulated, and its ally imperial Japan was ravaged, close to defeat. Much of Berlin, including the Excelsior, lay in ruins. Two Allied powers, the Soviet Union and the United States, stood supreme, eyeing each other warily as they began to fill the geopolitical vacuum left by the war. When Kennedy came back again in 1948, as a junior congressman, Kick, too, was gone, and the Soviets and Americans were locked in a tense Cold War, with Berlin a focal point. This superpower confrontation was still ongoing when now-President Kennedy returned yet again, in June 1963, and declared, before a rapturous audience of more than a million in West Berlin, "Ich bin ein Berliner." Five months later, he met his death, felled by an assassin's bullet while riding in an open-air limousine in Dallas.

World War II occupies a central place in this book, the first of two volumes on the life and times of John F. Kennedy. Born in 1917, during one world war and at the dawning of the American Century, he came of age in a second world war, then rose all the way to the presidency, only to be cut down at forty-six while leading a United States that stood at the zenith of its power. He was a man of privilege and wealth who endured chronic ill health and pain as well as immense personal tragedy, and whose storybook life captivated millions of people—not merely in the United States but abroad, not merely in death but in life. Known for his handsome looks, cool and graceful demeanor, and persistent womanizing, Kennedy was gifted and flawed, as a politician and as a person, and his thousand days in the White House saw missteps as well as successes. But through his magnetic leadership and inspirational rhetoric, he elevated Americans' belief in the capacity of politics to solve big problems and speak to society's highest aspirations, while in foreign affairs he showed it was possible to move from bitter hostility toward the Soviet Union to coexistence. The public responded. By the middle of 1963, close to 60 percent of Americans claimed that they had voted for Kennedy in 1960, although only 49.7 percent had actually done so. After his death, his landslide grew to 65 percent. Kennedy's average approval rating of 70 percent while in office puts him at the top among post-1945 American presidents, and later generations would rate his performance higher still.[8]

Despite Kennedy's larger-than-life status, few serious biographies of him have been attempted, and there exists virtually no full-scale biography, one that considers the full life and times and makes abundant use of the massive archival record now available—some of it only recently declassified.[9] The White House period must of course loom large, and will take up the bulk of volume 2, but so, too, do Kennedy's pre-presidential and pre-congressional years demand our attention.[10] For Kennedy, as for most of us, his teens and twenties were the years when his personality and worldview took shape. His war experience, in particular, had a profound effect on his outlook and his career trajectory, informing a political philosophy he would carry with him always.[11]

There's another reason why the early years of John Kennedy warrant close scrutiny. To a greater degree than with most public figures, the man known universally by his initials has been swept away by mythology. The JFK legend has obscured the real-life Kennedy, the workaday Kennedy, rendering him opaque and inscrutable. To recapture him, one must examine him when he was young and untried, still finding his way in his large and competitive Irish Catholic family and in the world, still learning what he was about. Within these pages, therefore, is a portrait of the full man—his relationships, his experiences, his ideas, his writings, his political aspirations. It's an effort made easier by the vast correspondence the Kennedy family conducted from the start of the 1930s through World War II, much of which survives and is now open for research at the John F. Kennedy Library, in Boston.[12] Kennedy himself was a prolific letter writer at key points in his life, and he kept diaries and notebooks during many of his travels. A number of his college papers survive, as does his senior thesis, which was published as a widely praised book, *Why England Slept*, in 1940, soon after his graduation and the fall of France, when he was only twenty-three.

Of course, any serious attempt to re-create Kennedy's world as he experienced it requires suspending as much as possible the knowledge of how it all turned out, and resisting the urge to see in this freshman essay or that wartime letter seeds of his later greatness. Only by so doing can one hope to play it straight, to look the man right in the eye, not up in adulation or down in disdain.

No less important, the work of biography requires bearing in mind that Kennedy was a product of his time and place. Context matters—a lot. And there's a payoff here, indeed a double payoff: situating Kennedy within the wider setting of the era and the world helps us better comprehend not only his rise but his country's rise, first to great-power status and then to superpower status. In fact, a principal theme of this book is the degree to which Kennedy's life story tracks with major facets of America's political and geopolitical story. The charged debate between "isolationists" and "interventionists" in the years before Pearl Harbor; the tumult of the Second World War, through which the United States emerged as a global colossus; the outbreak and spread of the Cold War; the domestic politics of anti-Communism and the attendant scourge of McCarthyism; the growth of television's influence on politics—each of these seminal events and developments can be grasped more clearly through the lens of John F. Kennedy's life and career. The same holds for the period to be examined in the volume still to come, when additional topics come to the fore: civil rights; the arms race and the prospect of nuclear Armageddon, made vivid during the tense days of the Cuban Missile Crisis; the revival of affirmative government as a precursor to the Great Society; the descent into Vietnam (for which Kennedy, despite his early and prescient misgivings about seeking a military solution there, would bear considerable responsibility); and the space program.

The more we understand Kennedy and his coming of age, in short, the more we understand the United States in the middle decades of the century. I am struck in this regard by historian and Kennedy adviser Arthur M. Schlesinger Jr.'s remark, in his memoirs, *A Life in the 20th Century:* "For my generation, four dates remain indelibly scarred on memory, four occasions when none of us can forget where and how we heard the staggering news: Pearl Harbor, the death of Franklin Roosevelt, the death of John Kennedy, the landing of men on the moon."[13] All four moments are, in their way, pivotal to the story I'm telling here. Though Kennedy did not live to see the moon landing, his initial commitment to the lunar project made it happen.

A second theme, captured in the image of the college-age Kennedy crisscrossing Europe and the Middle East in the lead-up to World War II, concerns his pronounced international sensibility. He was, from the start, a man of the world, deeply inquisitive about other political systems and cultures, comfortable with competing conceptions of national interest. This was partly an outgrowth of his Irish heritage and the sensibility of his parents, and in particular his mother, who looked outward, beyond the nation's shores. Partly, too, it resulted from his expansive reading as a bedridden child and teenager, which tilted toward European history and statecraft, and from his coursework in prep school and college. Most of all, the internationalist ethos emerged from Kennedy's travels during and after his college years—in addition to his grand excursion in 1939, there were substantial trips in 1937, 1938, and 1941. These trips broadened his horizons, as did his subsequent combat experience in the South Pacific. An interventionist well in advance of Pearl Harbor—in contrast to his father and older brother, who argued until the Japanese attack for keeping America out of the struggle, whatever the cost—Jack came out of the war committed to the proposition that the United States must play an ongoing leadership role in world affairs, working in concert with other nations. Thereafter, he held firmly to this view.

Herein lies a third theme: on matters of politics and policy, JFK was always his own master. His father, deeply influential in the lives of his children, was a towering figure in young Jack's life, modeling how he expected his second son to behave, not least in his brazen philandering. But there was always the sense that Jack stood somewhat apart from his large and close-knit family—he was of the unit but also outside of it. He was the family reader, the daydreamer, the introspective son, the one who relished words and their meaning, who liked poetry. Alone among the older kids, he had a romantic imagination, a feel for the things of the spirit, for the intangibles in human affairs. (It's what drew him to Churchill, a man whose appeal Joe Senior could never grasp.)[14] For years Jack resisted his father's exhortations to work harder in school, to apply himself; when he finally buckled down, in his junior year at Harvard, it was for his own reasons. Whereas Joe Junior always parroted his father's views on policy matters, Jack broke with the patriarch at key junctures, especially in the realm of foreign policy. He saw a more complex and crowded world than did the older man, and *Why England Slept* was partly a rebuke of Joe Senior's isolationist position. Later, in the early stages of the Cold War, Jack embraced a strident anti-Soviet position that his father loudly rejected. On domestic policy, Congressman and then Senator Kennedy was consistently to Joe Senior's left, though still a centrist within the Democratic Party as a whole.

Nor does the evidence support the claim, common in books as well as documentary films, that Jack Kennedy became a politician because his father decreed it, following the death of Joe Junior, his golden firstborn, in 1944. In reality, Jack was musing about seeking elected office at least two years earlier, in early 1942. His boyhood had been imbued by the political legend of his beloved grandfather John "Honey Fitz" Fitzgerald, and he relished hearing stories about the feats and foibles of earlier generations of Irish Catholic pols in Boston. In college he gravitated toward the study of government, and a later flirtation with law school was in part a manifestation of his deep interest in politics. No doubt the father's relentless advocacy after Joe's death was an additional spur, and it's interesting to speculate about which path Jack might have selected had his brother returned from the war alive. But he had his own reasons for choosing politics, and of the two brothers he could arguably claim the stronger credentials for the endeavor—as Joe Junior grasped all too well. During Jack's initial campaigns for the House (in 1946) and the Senate (in 1952), Joe Senior played an important role, not least in keeping his checkbook open at all times. Contrary to legend, however, he never drove campaign strategy, in either race. The son, never much impressed with his father's political acumen, preserved the key decision-making slot for himself. In the epic 1952 nail-biter against Republican Henry Cabot Lodge Jr., the paramount subordinate family part was played not by Joe Senior but by Jack's twenty-six-year-old brother, Robert.

Ultimately, the Kennedy who emerges in these pages is not the callow young man of our imaginations. At least not in the main, and at least not after he graduated from college. He could be vain and self-centered, could be heedless of friends, heedless of women. He cheated on his wife, Jackie, before their wedding, and he cheated on her afterwards. To him, as to others in his wealthy family, people were often viewed as interchangeable. (Which did not keep him from showing deep loyalty to a chosen few— namely, to his male friends and to his core staff, who repaid the loyalty in full.)[15] But that was not the sum total of the man. Behind the handsome face and the winsome smile was an insatiably curious individual, a poised and discerning analyst who treated serious things seriously yet largely avoided—thanks to his highly developed sense of irony and the absurd, and his self-deprecating wit—the trap of self-importance.[16] His historical sensibility and his recurring health travails taught him that life was capricious and fraught, but he didn't take from this that he should use his family's fortune to pursue a path of pure indulgence. On the contrary, these hardships deepened his determination to follow his parents' exhortation, issued regularly to their kids, to contribute to society, to believe in something greater than themselves and to act accordingly.

Signs of this emerging seriousness were evident early; he was no late bloomer, as is often suggested. Already in his undergraduate papers, Kennedy grappled with questions concerning political leadership that would fascinate and vex him to the end of his days. Is it possible for democratic leaders to respond nimbly and effectively in times of national or international crisis? How can policymakers reconcile their sense of the nation's interests with the fickle demands of their constituents? What is the nature of political courage? ("Unless democracy can produce able leaders," he wrote in one college essay, "its chances of survival are slight.") In letters home from the South Pacific in 1943, he expressed doubts about the efficacy of military leadership and about war as an instrument of policy that would deepen in the years ahead. "The war here is a dirty business," he wrote to his ex-girlfriend Inga Arvad. "We get so used to talking about billions of dollars and millions of soldiers, and thousands of casualties begin to sound like drops in the bucket. But if those thousands want to live as much as my PT boat crew, the people deciding the whys and wherefores had better make mighty sure that all this effort is headed for some definite goal and that when we reach that goal we may say it was worth it." In late 1951, following two lengthy overseas trips covering much of the world, he revised his easy Cold War verities and told a nationwide radio audience that the Communist threat "cannot be met effectively by merely the force of arms. It is the peoples themselves that must be led to reject it, and it is to those peoples that our policies must be directed." Democratic ideals, he was saying, mattered more than military power. This, too, was a theme to which he would return often, including as president.[17]

Even that most celebrated of Kennedy appeals, "Ask not what your country can do for you—ask what you can do for your country," from the 1961 inaugural, had early roots. It had been drilled into him at Choate, his prep school alma mater. When, in 1946, he returned to the school to give an address, he urged the students to be engaged citizens and to answer the call to public service.[18] On the stump that year, in his first election campaign, he elaborated the argument, sounding tones that seem especially resonant in our own time. Beware lazy cynicism about politics and politicians, the skinny twenty-nine-year-old candidate implored audiences, for the survival of democracy depended on having an informed and active citizenry, committed to reasoned discourse and accepting of good-faith bargaining between the parties. He employed the language of empathy, emphasizing Americans' shared dreams and shared destiny as a people. Neither then nor later was Kennedy above bare-knuckle politics or partisan sparring, but he grasped already in this first race that compromise is necessary to a well-functioning democracy, and that civility in the public realm prevents dehumanization and helps us see political opponents as adversaries, not enemies. His 1956 book, *Profiles in Courage*, is an ode to the art of politics, to the hard and vital work of governing in a system of conflicting pressures and visions.

Perhaps it's this abiding faith in his nation and its democratic politics that explains most fully the enduring hold of John F. Kennedy's legacy. From his earliest days as a politician right to the end in Texas, Kennedy summoned the narrative of American hope as he challenged people to believe in a better society at home while embracing the nation's leadership position abroad. It was a capacious vision, one that rejected the parochial nationalism of his father and extolled the promise of public activism. Today, whether we question this governing philosophy or yearn for its rebirth, we still see Kennedy as the dynamic young figure who seized the mantle of leadership, and we wonder what might have been had he lived.[19] We'll never know, no matter how much we imagine. But we can learn much about this singular and surprising life, and about the nation and the world in which he came of age, if we delve deeply into who he really was.

PART
I

FOUNDATIONS

TWO FAMILIES

John F. Kennedy's birthplace, at 83 Beals Street in Brookline, Massachusetts, is today a national historic site. To a modern visitor the home feels confined, with a compact kitchen and modest-size bedrooms, but in the fall of 1914, when Joseph Kennedy bought the house to raise what he and his wife, Rose, hoped would be a large family, it seemed ideal, situated as it was on a pleasant street in a middle-class neighborhood made up of people like themselves, who had ambitions but not much cash, who sought a good address as proof they had arrived—or were arriving. The trolley to Boston was but a short walk away, and St. Aidan's Roman Catholic Church and the Edward Devotion public school were nearby. To finance the purchase, Joe borrowed $2,000 for the down payment and took a mortgage for the remaining $4,500.[1]

The street, named after the wealthy speculator who originally bought the land, had been laid out only two decades earlier, during the streetcar boom of the 1890s. In the years thereafter, a variety of tightly packed brick-and-timber tract homes popped up on both sides of the street, behind sidewalks and tastefully planted maple trees. But with the economic downturn of 1910, construction stopped, and in 1914, number 83 was the last house in the row, beyond which stood a succession of empty plots to the next corner. With a gabled roof and a large white front porch where toddlers could play, the five-year-old home boasted three bedrooms on the second floor and two more on the third, while the kitchen featured a large black-iron coal-and-gas stove.[2]

Brookline in 1914 was one of the wealthiest municipalities in the Northeast, which surely added to its allure for the young Joe Kennedy. He could not yet afford to live in the pricier neighborhoods south of Boylston Street, with their grand homes and manicured gardens along gently winding streets, but at least he and Rose were now residents of the town. For the better part of a century, many of the biggest names in Boston society had kept summer homes in Brookline. Over time, some opted to make the quiet summer town their year-round residence, adopting the

The first family home, and Jack's birthplace, 83 Beals Street, Brookline.

English model of an aristocratic elite rooted in the country, the better to separate themselves from the seamy underside of industrialization and the influx of immigrants. The Lowells, Cabots, Sargents, Amorys, Codmans, and other prominent families all came, creating a larger concentration of Brahmins than in perhaps any other town in the region.[3] As the money flowed in, Brookline acquired more urban services than most surrounding towns; by the 1850s, it had one of the best school systems in New England, as well as an excellent public library; by the turn of the century, there were sewers and telephone lines. Although the town housed a sizable working-class population to serve the needs of the wealthy and had a growing middle class, 36 percent of the town's residents were wealthy enough to employ live-in domestic servants.[4]

History does not record whether Joe and Rose, on their first evening in that new home, reflected on how far their respective families had come since their grandparents arrived from Ireland six decades before. Joe in particular was not the introspective sort. But they needed no one to tell them that they were benefiting from improvements in the lot of Irish Americans scarcely imaginable to that earlier generation.

II

Patrick Kennedy wasn't thinking that far ahead in October 1848 when he made his way on foot—so it is said—from Dunganstown, a town in southwest County Wexford, along the River Barrow, down to New Ross, six miles away, to board a ship to Liverpool and from there, he hoped, to the New World.[5] He was just trying to escape an Ireland that was three years into a catastrophic famine.

In 1845, following an unusually wet summer, a mysterious blight caused the potato crop to fail. The disease had crossed the Atlantic on ships bound for European ports and thence reached Ireland, carried across the Irish Sea by rain and wind. Desperate farmers and peasants tried to stop the scourge by cutting off the blackened leaves and stalks, only to find that the tubers had rotted completely. For a time farmers assumed it was a fluke event, a one-off, but early in 1846 the deadly fungus reappeared, and by the end of that summer more than 90 percent of Ireland's potato crop was gone. By early October, many Irish towns reported having not a single loaf of bread or pound of grain to feed their residents. A harsh winter followed, with cold rains and snow, and in 1847 potato yields were a fraction of what they had been in 1844.[6]

This might have been less of a problem had not the potato been such a staple of the Irish diet. Introduced to Ireland in the late sixteenth century, it became in time critically important. More than half of the population of eight million relied on it as their main source of nourishment; upwards of a third, including the poorest of the poor, survived on it almost exclusively. The potato was an ideal subsistence food for Irish peasants, since it was highly nutritious (the Irish were among the tallest and most fertile people in Europe, if also perhaps the most impoverished) and since impressive yields could be had on small plots of land and even in poor conditions. Except when the crop failed. As conditions deteriorated, hunger spread, then starvation. Some families took to the road, wandering from village to village, hoping forlornly that someone would take them in. Others waited in their cottages, shared their remaining morsels, and died quietly, one by one. Many who avoided starvation succumbed to typhus, which spread rapidly among the weakened population.

All told, about one million people died between 1846 and 1851 from starvation or disease, a figure amounting to 13 percent of Ireland's population. The effects were most severe in the west and southwest—in Mayo and Clare and Kerry, people died by the tens of thousands—but Wexford, too, suffered greatly. "Deaths from famine had been numerous . . . caused by the utter want of food," reported the Wexford *Independent* in January 1847, and one shopkeeper wrote that "the young and old are dying as fast as they can bury them, [for] the fever is rageing here at such arate that there are in healthy in the morning knows not but in the Evening may have taken the infection."[7]

The worst of the suffering might have been avoided had British authorities been more attentive or compassionate. But Parliament's response was piecemeal and inadequate, confirming for many Irish what they could expect from their alien oppressors across the Irish Sea. For centuries the English had exploited them, maltreated them; why should it be any different now? Many London observers believed that the famine was God's work and endorsed the view of Charles Trevelyan, the director of government relief, that Ireland's "great evil" was not famine but "the selfish, perverse and turbulent character of the people."[8] In the summer of 1847, an officially sanctioned soup kitchen program fed almost three million people, suggesting what kind of relief could be mobilized by the British state, but the program was shut down that fall. Under an Irish Poor Law Extension Act, Parliament shifted the burden of famine relief away from central government to local Irish communities, who would ostensibly raise their own tax funds for poor relief. A clause in the law stipulated that any head of household renting more than a tenth of a hectare of land would be ineligible for public assistance. Some tenants starved to death rather than give up land to their landlord; many others abandoned their farms, accepted relief, and, faced with extreme poverty, chose the route of emigration. All told, two million Irish men and women, the majority of them Catholic and from the south and west of the country, fled for points overseas during the decade following the famine's outbreak. The vast majority ended up in the United States.[9]

The less fortunate were the first to leave, but they were not the *least* fortunate in most cases, because the journey required some savings or other assets that could be converted into cash. In the words of economic historian Cormac Ó Gráda, "In the hierarchy of suffering the poorest of the poor emigrated to the next world; those who emigrated to the New World had the resources to escape."[10]

Twenty-six-year-old Patrick Kennedy was among the latter. His exact reasons for leaving remain a mystery, but as the third-born son he knew that even if conditions improved, he would have little chance of inheriting the family farm—or of gaining access to any other parcel of land, for that matter. True, the Kennedys were comparatively well-off in Dunganstown, and had been spared the worst of the famine, but even so, the future for someone in Pat's position was bleak. So he set his sights on the far side of the Atlantic, on "the States," that strange and wondrous place so often discussed at family gatherings. America offered hope to people like him, and, what's more, there were already substantial numbers of Irish in the United States to welcome the newcomers to its shores. Pat surely knew as well that conditions on the ships to New York or Boston or Philadelphia were less brutal than on those bound for Quebec, a destination that, moreover, had the disadvantage of being under British rule. (In 1847, an estimated 30 percent of those bound for British North America perished on board or shortly after their arrival in Quebec.) A ticket to Australia, also under British dominion, was too pricey to consider.[11]

Still, the voyage to America, typically lasting a month and costing $17 to $20 (the equivalent of $550 to $650 today), including provisions, was arduous enough. Often, the ships were barely seaworthy; always, they were dangerously overcrowded. Only in fair weather were passengers allowed on deck, and often not even then. The steerage below was cramped—a grown man could not stand without stooping—and unsanitary, and in short order the illnesses that the Irish had fled were sweeping through the crammed holds. Typhus was especially pervasive. Water soon turned foul and could be forced down only with the addition of plentiful amounts of vinegar. Food supplies dwindled, and the stench from the privies became overpowering. Day after day the misery raged on, often in rough weather that created its own misery and stress. Mortality rates were high. As nerves frayed and tempers flared, fights broke out, sometimes leaving the combatants a bloodied mess. Single women faced their own agony: the threat of assault by rapacious sailors.[12]

It took a healthy disposition and a dose of good luck to survive the passage on these "coffin ships" with mind and body intact. Patrick did. Even upon arrival at port in East Boston (or Noddle's Island, as it was known, which was still accessible from the mainland only by ferry), his challenges were just beginning. Immigrant Boston was a forbidding land. As he emerged from the shadowy steerage, blinking in the daylight, then crossed over the gangplank onto the brimming dock, Pat would have been met by a motley mix of hucksters and con men, eager to take advantage of the disoriented newcomers by promising pleasant lodgings that often turned out to be squalid and windowless, or well-paying jobs that in reality were backbreaking and might pay one dollar for a fourteen-hour workday.

But at least there were jobs to be had, and in Boston no one, not even the most destitute, starved to death. Indeed, East Boston at midcentury was experiencing a boom of sorts, largely because of the shipbuilding that went on there and because it provided transatlantic shipping companies with a deepwater port. One of these companies, the Cunard Line, employed many of the new arrivals as carpenters and dockhands as it built piers and warehouses on the waterfront. Others found work in Donald McKay's shipyard, maker of the world's finest clipper ships, beautifully finished and furnished and built for speed. (In 1854, the *Flying Cloud*, at seventeen hundred tons, made the trip from New York to San Francisco, by way of Cape Horn, in eighty-nine days, eight hours, the fastest on record.*) Pat Kennedy, having learned the skills of coopering (barrel and

---

* The record would stand, for a sailing ship, for 135 years, until 1989.

cask making) in Wexford, found work at Daniel Francis's cooperage and brass foundry on Sumner Street, which made mostly shop castings and whiskey barrels, the latter destined for the taverns that were popping up like mushrooms all over Irish Boston. Soon he was working twelve-hour days, seven days a week. (Like other immigrants, he quickly discovered that in America the workday was longer than anything he had experienced in Ireland.)[13]

He also found time to marry. Bridget Murphy, another recent arrival from County Wexford, became Pat's wife in September 1849, in a ceremony at Holy Redeemer Church.[14] They bought a modest house on Sumner Street, proof positive that Patrick had established genuine job security and a decent wage. Their first child, Mary, was born in 1851, followed by Joanna in 1852, John in 1854 (who died of cholera before his second birthday), Margaret in 1855, and Patrick Joseph, called "P. J." so as not to be confused with his father, in early 1858.

All the while, Pat Kennedy maintained his grueling work schedule until, one autumn day, he could do it no more. In November 1858, ten months after the birth of P. J. and nine years after stepping ashore in Boston, Pat died, at age thirty-five, with a wife and four young children, leaving behind no documents or portraits. The immediate cause was either cholera or consumption, but years of punishing work, every day of the week, surely took their toll on his immune system, made him susceptible to infection and then unable to fight it off. The first of this clan of Kennedy men to set foot in America, he was the last to die in anonymity.[15]

III

It says something about the experience of Irish-born men in Boston at this time that so many of them died young, leaving large numbers of children to be raised by their mothers. According to one estimate, the average Irishman of Patrick's generation survived only fourteen years in the New World.[16] The congested and unsanitary conditions in which many of them lived was a factor—often they made do in cellar apartments in the North End or Fort Hill that offered little light or air and were prone to flooding; it was not unheard of for a hundred people to share one sink and privy—since they made the community a prime target for every scourge and disease. Cholera hit the Irish sections of the city hard in 1849, and there were regular outbreaks of smallpox and tuberculosis. Add to that the extremely long hours in physically taxing jobs in the quarries or on the docks and it becomes easy to see why so many met their end prematurely. Three Irish Americans who in due course would reach the pinnacle of the political scene in Boston—Martin Lomasney, James Michael Curley, and one of John F. Kennedy's grandfathers, P. J. Kennedy—all lost their fathers in childhood. Kennedy's other grandfather, John F. Fitzgerald, had barely reached adulthood before his father passed on. (His mother had already died.)[17]

The constant stream of new arrivals strained Boston's resources well past the limit. In 1847 the city built two hospitals on Deer Island, in the harbor, to treat "Foreign Diseased Paupers"; both were soon swamped with patients, almost all of them Irish. Acute needs remained. A health inspection committee visiting a teeming Irish area near the harbor in 1849 found horrible conditions (perhaps colored by prejudice on the part of its members):

> In Broad Street and all the surrounding neighborhood . . . the situation of the Irish is particularly wretched. . . . This whole district is a perfect hive of human beings, without comforts and mostly without common necessaries; in many cases, huddled together like brutes, without regard to sex, or age, or sense of decency; grown men and women sleeping together in the same apartment, and sometimes wife and husband, brothers and sisters, in the same bed. Under such circumstances, self-respect, forethought, all high and noble virtues soon die out, and sullen indifference and despair, or disorder, intemperance and utter degradation reign supreme.[18]

The description speaks to one overriding characteristic of the Boston Irish: their ballooning numbers. In 1800, the city counted little more than a thousand Irish. By 1830 the figure had risen to eight thousand. But in 1847 alone, 37,000 came ashore. (This in a city that, according to an 1845 census, had a total of 114,366 residents.) Many others traveled overland to the city from Canadian ports. On just one spring day that year—April 10—one thousand Irish overwhelmed the port of Boston. By the early 1850s Irish-born Catholics made up a quarter of Boston's population, and Reverend Theodore Parker remarked that in a single decade Suffolk County had become a "New England County Cork," and the city of Boston "the Dublin of America." Catholic churches soon dotted the landscape in Irish Boston, each becoming the unifying center for its neighborhood, around which community life revolved. In 1860, on the eve of the Civil War, the city's Irish-born population stood at 45,991.[19]

If there was strength in numbers, young Bridget Kennedy could be forgiven for not seeing it as she contemplated her new life as a single mother. The Boston in which she and her compatriots had arrived was already more than two centuries old, and it possessed a reputation and civic identity that could terrify the newcomer.[20] Everywhere she turned, she saw evidence of anti-Irish and anti-Catholic prejudice. Anglo-Saxon Bostonians, steeped in anti-papist rhetoric that coursed deep into their colonial past, saw the immigrants as crude and clannish and uncivilized, prone to crime and public drunkenness. These residents regularly posted "No Irish Wanted" notices when making hires, and excluded even the small band of well-educated, professional Irish Catholics from the city's rigidly defined and tightly restrictive financial hierarchy. Being Irish and Catholic was an occupational handicap at midcentury that few could overcome.[21]

Even women who worked as maids, as Bridget Kennedy had done, found themselves under suspicion. "Though Bostonians could not do without the Irish servant girl, distrust of her mounted steadily," historian Oscar Handlin wrote. "Natives began to regard her as a spy of the Pope who revealed their secrets regularly to priests in confession." Soon there were newspaper ads like the one for "a good, reliable woman" to care for a two-year-old in Brookline, then a Yankee enclave. The person hired would not have any washing or ironing duty, but the post had one iron-clad requirement: "Positively no Irish need apply."[22]

Politically, too, the Irish found themselves frozen out. In the early 1850s, the reactionary Know Nothing movement (so named because its adherents would feign ignorance when asked about the organization) swept the immigrant-heavy Eastern Seaboard and became, for a time, an unstoppable force in Massachusetts. With an ideology rooted in anti-Catholicism and opposition to immigrants, the party sought to extend the period for naturalization and the right to vote from the then-current five years to twenty-one years, and ran candidates under the motto "Americans must rule America." In the state election in 1854, two out of three Massachusetts voters backed Know Nothing candidates, with the result that the party took all but a handful of legislative seats as well as the gov-

ernor's office and the Boston mayor's seat. In short order, the state legislature put forth a program of "Temperance, Liberty, and Protestantism,"
which mandated among other things that Protestant hymns and the
King James Bible be used in public schools, and which deprived Catholics
of the right to hold public office because of their supposed allegiance to
Rome.[23]

The bigotry of the Know Nothings prompted Abraham Lincoln, an
up-and-coming Illinois politician, to despair to a friend in 1855, "Our
progress in degeneracy appears to me to be pretty rapid. As a nation we
began by declaring that *all men are created equal.*' We now practically read
it 'all men are created equal, *except negroes.*' When the Know-Nothings
get control, it will read 'all men are created equal except negroes, *and foreigners, and Catholics.*' "[24]

The Know Nothing surge in American politics proved short-lived,
thanks to Lincoln's rapidly growing Republican Party, but Know Nothing
sentiments continued to hold sway in Massachusetts state politics for
many years to come, and kept the Irish population away from elected office. The nativist press duly chronicled the alleged lawlessness and chronic
alcoholism and disease in Boston's immigrant neighborhoods, and state
voters approved laws mandating literacy tests that were designed to keep
Irish from the polls. Catholics were discriminated against in hospitals and
were prohibited from burying their dead in public cemeteries. Hundreds
of impoverished Irish in poorhouses and asylums were deported back to
Liverpool on the grounds that they were a drain on the public purse.[25]

At the same time, the Irish experienced tensions with other immigrant
blocs—the Germans, the Scots, the English, the Canadians—who saw
their wages diminish on account of the throngs of unskilled newcomers.
As John F. Kennedy would later remark about the era of immigration lasting into the early 1900s, "Each wave disliked and distrusted the next. The
English said the Irish 'kept the Sabbath and everything else they could lay
their hands on.' The English and the Irish distrusted the Germans who
'worked too hard.' The English and the Irish and the Germans disliked the
Italians; and the Italians joined their predecessors in disparaging the
Slavs." From time to time in later years, after the influx of Italian immigrants to Boston in the 1890s, noises were made about the Irish and Italians banding together against the Yankees, but unity proved elusive—the
economic and social tensions were simply too deep.[26]

Under different circumstances, the newcomers might have responded to these restrictions by striking out for greener pastures elsewhere in the United States. But few Irish had the training or the skills to feel confident they could make it out there in the great unknown. Some could not read; others lacked the skills needed to settle on the rural frontier. There was also the simple matter of Boston's geography, different from that of almost every other major American city in that it was substantially water-locked. To venture out from areas where most immigrants lived required the payment of tolls or fares, which, however modest, were prohibitive for a people struggling to eke out an existence. (As late as 1858, bridges leaving the city charged tolls even for pedestrians.) Most of all, perhaps, this was a place to which they could relate, with an established Irish community—with recognizable faces, a neighborhood parish, an Irish-run saloon.[27]

Moving was in any event out of the question for a young widow with a brood to raise. So Bridget Kennedy hunkered down and set about doing what needed to be done. In June 1860, a year and a half after Pat's passing, a Boston census taker reported that she had personal effects worth $75, a respectable sum in the neighborhood at that time. To help make ends meet, she took in boarders occasionally, including Mary Roach, eighteen, who looked after the Kennedy children. Details regarding Bridget's employment are sketchy, but it seems she worked as a hairdresser and housecleaner before becoming the proprietor of a notions shop near the waterfront in East Boston that in due course started also carrying groceries and baked goods, even some liquor.[28]

Bridget loved her daughters, but P. J., as the lone son, was the measure of all things. She and the girls coddled him and worked to keep him on the straight and narrow. Determined to give him the opportunity for a better life, Bridget saved every penny she could in order to send him to Sacred Heart, a school run by the Sisters of Notre Dame. Quiet and reserved, with fair skin, blue eyes, and wavy brownish-red hair to go with a sturdy build, the boy was ambitious and blessed with a quick and agile mind, but book learning left him antsy; he lasted in school only until his early or mid teens. He then went to work as a dockhand on East Boston's busy waterfront, but although he had the strength for physical labor, he lacked the temperament. The hard-drinking, brawling ways of his co-workers left him cold, and, with his mother's constant encouragement, he aspired to bigger things. Each month he put away part of his earnings and kept on the lookout for an opportunity.

One day it came: a saloon in Haymarket Square was losing money and had been put up for sale. P. J. pounced and acquired it for next to nothing. Before long the enterprising and self-possessed young man, now in his early twenties, turned the tavern into a profitable business, specializing in offerings of lager beer. He carefully plowed the profits back in, becoming part owner of two additional taverns and expanding into whiskey importation and distribution. A teetotaler like his son after him (he did not wish to be associated with the stereotype of the blustering and bellicose Irish drunkard), Kennedy was a popular saloonkeeper, and he looked the part, with his stocky physique and swooping handlebar mustache. His patrons appreciated his friendly and unassuming manner and his willingness to help new arrivals find lodging and work, to straighten out misunderstandings with the police, to find legal assistance and arrange bail. Most of all, he had the great saloonkeeper's ability to listen, to absorb the constant babbling without complaint, to laugh with the jokesters and commiserate with the down-and-out.[29]

Owning the taverns also gave Kennedy something else: political influence. As a neighborhood social center, a refuge in the cold and impersonal urban environment, the corner saloon was where the Irishman could stop on his way home from work and rest his tired body, forget his troubles, and tell a tall tale or two while delaying the return to his often dingy tenement apartment, teeming with children and boarders. Invariably, the chatter touched on social issues, and the tavern became a key center of political activity, its owner often a notable figure in the community, second only to the parish priest in power and prestige. Soon Kennedy knew who was running for office, knew the campaign strategies and shenanigans, knew who had dirt on whom. Small wonder, then, that he and many other saloon owners became ward bosses who built their political power through jobs and favors.

With each passing year, the political discussions in the taverns shifted more and more away from the remembered grievances of Ireland and toward local concerns. No longer did England's serial transgressions against their beloved Emerald Isle generate the most fervor among the men who hunched over the bar; now it mattered more whether fares could be reduced on ferries linking East Boston to the mainland, and whether Boston's new sewage system would fully encompass Irish neighborhoods. The attachment to Eire and its beauty remained, but America was home now to these men, many of them naturalized citizens who had fought for the Union in the Civil War. They saw meaning in politics and found a home in the Democratic Party, and they flocked to its banner. Kennedy, his influence rising, became a leader of Boston's Ward Two and, in 1884, at age twenty-six, was appointed precinct officer. Two years later, just shy of his twenty-eighth birthday, he won a seat in the state House of Representatives.[30]

IV

P. J. Kennedy's success was one sign among many that the Irish had arrived in Massachusetts politics. The sheer numbers tell the tale, just as farsighted Yankee Protestants had long feared. By the mid-1870s, with the second generation now in adulthood, with the birth rate high and the mortality rate waning, and with more transplants arriving from the motherland by the week (emigration slowed after the end of the famine, but it never disappeared), Irish Americans represented more than a

Patrick Joseph "P. J." Kennedy,
circa 1878, in his youthful,
pre-mustachioed days.

Mary Augusta "Mame"
Kennedy, date unknown.

third of Boston's population of 300,000 and were fast approaching 50 percent.[31] The Beacon Hill bluebloods might retain control of the financial and cultural institutions and the social pecking order, but the political contest was a different story. The Boston Irish were electing state legislators and city aldermen, and in 1882 one of their own, Patrick Collins, was elected to the U.S. Congress. Two years after that, Hugh O'Brien became the city's first Irish and first Catholic mayor. Meanwhile, ward bosses such as Kennedy and the legendary Martin "the Mahatma" Lomasney wielded great power in their areas, as did the cocky John F. Fitzgerald, the rakish ruler of the North End, who in time would become P. J.'s in-law.[32]

As Kennedy prospered in business and politics, he also found success in his personal life. He began courting Mary Augusta Hickey, a tall, handsome woman with stately grace and formidable intelligence who was two years his senior and hailed from an affluent Irish family in Brockton, then an upscale suburb. Her Irish-born father, James, was a prosperous businessman, and her three brothers had all done well: Charles was the mayor of Brockton, Jim was a police captain, and John, a graduate of Harvard Medical School, was a doctor in nearby Winthrop. If any family can be said to have represented the so-called lace-curtain Irish (solidly middle class, and to be distinguished from the down-at-the-heels "shanty" Irish), it was the Hickeys. On Thanksgiving eve 1887, P. J. and Mary Augusta ("Mame," he called her) were married at Sacred Heart Church. A little over nine months later, on September 6, 1888, they had their first child, Joseph Patrick Kennedy. In 1891 followed Francis Benedict, who died of diphtheria about a year later, then Mary Loretta, in 1892, and Margaret Louise, in 1898.

Bridget Kennedy, for her part, lived long enough to see her son find success in the world in which she had struggled to survive, and to see his first son born into it. She died in her home in December 1888, at age sixty-seven.[33]

Her daughter-in-law, it turned out, was much like her in one respect: she was intensely ambitious for her son. Just as P. J. had been the star in his family firmament, so Joseph would be in his, the child on whom Mary Augusta lavished her primary attention. "My Joe," she called him as she immersed herself in his daily life, doting on him, engaging him on his school activities, and reminding him that his uncle John had gone to Harvard. Joe felt the bond, rushing home from the local parish school every day to have lunch with her. "He missed me," Mary Augusta remembered delightedly years later, after he had begun to make his mark on Boston society. "He missed me and wanted to hurry home and see me again."[34]

Initially, the family resided at 151 Meridian Street, in the business district of East Boston, a three-story dark-red brick house, which we would today call a townhouse and which was near one of P. J.'s taverns. But before long they moved up—in both senses of the word—to a large house at 165 Webster Street, an elegant, tree-lined avenue on Jeffries Point, overlooking the harbor, with a backyard that sloped down to the water. Young Joe had the run of the place, the Irish servant girls treating him like a young prince and his sisters constantly deferring to him. "I thought he was a god," Margaret said of her brother many years afterwards. "I'd be thrilled even if he asked me to put something away for him—anything, just as long as he noticed me." Loretta, meanwhile, remarked on the authority Joe seemed to possess within the family, even at a young age. In this largely female world, he was the pivot around which all things circled, an arrangement he took to be the normal order of things.[35]

The details of Joe Kennedy's boyhood are largely lost to us, in part because in later years he showed little interest in talking about it. He offered few clues as to the nature of life within the household, or about his relationships with his sisters, though in adulthood he corresponded with them via letters and phone calls and backed them financially.[36] Never one to look back, Joe was also keen to hide the fact that he had grown up in a life of privilege, wanting for nothing and with advantages others did not have. ("Joe did not come in on a raft," his niece Mary Lou McCarthy would subsequently remark. "His life was very comfortable."[37]) To admit such a thing would be to admit that he might not be fully responsible for his own success, and this was something Kennedy was loath to do. A devotee in his boyhood of Horatio Alger Jr. books, he loved their up-from-nothing, against-all-odds theme and came firmly to believe that anyone with God-given talents who worked hard could achieve great things. Kennedy never said or implied he was a child of poverty or that he faced undue hardships growing up, but he did push the narrative that his success was entirely his own.[38]

Young Joe looked up to his father, and recalled with satisfaction being allowed to tag along with him to campaign rallies and torchlight parades. He took pride in being the son of one of East Boston's most prominent figures, someone who had achieved rare distinction in business and politics. He admired his father's shrewdness and talent for organization, could see the respect he carried in the community. Yet there was also a sense, no doubt encouraged by his strong-willed mother, Mary Augusta, that he should set his own sights higher, that his father's success, however great, was too bounded, too local. And indeed, P. J. Kennedy, for all his determination to make good, did not have a driving ambition to extend his influence beyond his corner of the city. A mediocre public speaker with scant interest in chatting up voters on street corners, Kennedy preferred to wield his political power from behind the scenes. His tenure in the state house was undistinguished, and he achieved little after being elected to the state senate in 1892. After two one-year terms in the upper chamber, he stepped aside. East Boston was the heart of his political world; being ward boss was his calling.[39]

Mary Augusta felt differently. Although she was proud of her husband's accomplishments and of her Irish roots, she also chafed at them, aware that among the "proper" Bostonians against whom she measured herself and her family—the Yankee Protestants of Beacon Hill and the Back Bay—parochial politics of the type her husband practiced was not altogether honorable. And she was less willing than P. J. to accept the unwritten regulations of the social game: *equal but separate.* She wanted something more for her Joe, wanted him to be on equal footing with the Brahmins who ruled Boston society, wanted him to go to Harvard, not the Jesuit-run Boston College or Holy Cross, where the lace-curtain Irish typically sent their sons. She urged him to introduce himself as "Joe" rather than "Joe Kennedy," the better to hide his Irish heritage.[40] One detects her strong influence behind the couple's decision to send the boy, upon his completion of the seventh grade in parochial school in 1901, to Boston Latin, the oldest and most distinguished public school in the country, whose alumni included five signers of the Declaration of Independence (Franklin, Hancock, Hooper, Paine, and Samuel Adams) as well as Cotton Mather, Ralph Waldo Emerson, and Henry Ward Beecher. By the start of the twentieth century, most upper-class Protestants no longer sent their sons to Boston Latin—they preferred the even more exclusive Northeast prep schools now dotting the landscape—but it was still a forbidding Yankee institution, and even the preternaturally confident Joe must have felt some butterflies on his first day, September 12, as he boarded the ferry that would carry him across the canal and into an environment wholly new to him.[41]

The curriculum was classical and rigorous, focused on preparing students for the Harvard entrance examinations. Six years of Latin were compulsory, as were six years of science, math, and English, five years of history, and four years of French. In this hothouse atmosphere, Joe struggled. Though he did not lack for brains—he possessed a fine analytical intelligence and a superior memory—his transcript shows a string of C's and D's and failing grades in elementary French, elementary physics, and advanced Latin. So poorly did he perform in the classroom that he had to repeat his senior year. Curiously, these dismal results did not seem to dampen the boy's ego, at least in any lasting way. He looked with scorn on the bookish and humorless types who grubbed for grades and focused his energies instead on the social realm and on athletic pursuits.[42]

Tall, trim, and physically graceful, Joe excelled on the sports field. He captained the tennis team, played basketball, and became proficient as well at military drill, a high-status activity at the school. When, as a colonel, he led the Boston Latin team to victory in a citywide drill competition, he became a heroic figure on campus. But it was on the baseball diamond that Joe really dazzled. A superb line-drive hitter, he maintained an astonishing .667 batting average as a senior, a feat that earned him the Mayor's Cup for batting in the city high school league, and gave him a trophy in a ceremony presided over by his future father-in-law, Mayor John F.

Joe Kennedy during his senior year at Boston Latin.

Fitzgerald. In subsequent years, Joe would recall individual games in perfect detail, and offer highlights to any listener who made the mistake of showing even a modicum of interest.[43]

Then as now in American high schools, athletes were accorded more than their share of respect. Add to this Joe's self-assurance, indefatigable energy, and good looks—he had strikingly blue eyes, gleaming white teeth, and brownish-red hair to go with an athletic build—and it's no surprise that he was popular with the faculty and with fellow students. In the span of a few glorious weeks in the fall of 1907, he was reelected manager of the football team (*The Boston Globe* had the story, along with a large photo), elected senior class president, and named captain of the baseball team. Many years later, he called Boston Latin "a shrine that somehow seemed to make us all feel that if we could stick it out we were made of just a little bit better stuff than the fellows our age who were attending what we always thought were easier schools."[44]

Perhaps so, but to our modern sensibility, it still surprises that the boy with the awful grades, who had to repeat a year and who was Irish Catholic to boot, would be admitted into the Harvard College class of 1912. But so he was. Joe's rousing success in extracurricular endeavors no doubt helped, as did the fact that Boston Latin was a feeder school, sending more students to Harvard—twenty-five, half of the graduating class—than did any other high school in the country, public or private. That Harvard took more public school graduates and more Catholics (and Jews) than did Yale or Princeton may have mattered as well.[45] And the admissions office was surely aware that the boy with the spotty record happened to be the son of one of Boston's leading political figures.

V

And so, on the first day of October 1908, Joseph Patrick Kennedy headed across the Charles River and onto the grounds of the most prestigious university in the country. Though physically outside the city, in neighboring Cambridge, Harvard at the start of the century was at the epicenter of "proper Boston"; as a calling card to the city's privileged elite, the university was more important than either occupation or address. The nineteenth-century Yankee and alumnus Edmund Quincy, whose father had been president of the college, expressed the prevailing sentiment: "If a man's in there," he remarked, tapping his Harvard Triennial Catalogue, with its full list of graduates, "that's who he is. If he's not, who is he?"[46]

Joe understood the point, as did his mother, who had dreamed of this moment since the day he was born. He knew, she knew, her husband knew, that Joe's grandmother had been a servant, her first name so common and obviously Irish that the patrician women called their female servants "our Bridgets." Yet now here he was, however improbably, a Harvard man. If Joe felt nervous about what lay ahead, he didn't show it.

Academically, he saw no reason to worry, given that Boston Latin was widely known to be more demanding than anything Harvard could throw at him. The rigid curriculum of the former gave way now to an elective system in which there were no core requirements and no need even to select a major. With the barest of effort, one could avoid difficult subjects and choose a path of least resistance. Kennedy did. Though he had a good head for numbers, he took no math or science but instead concentrated in government and economics, with a smattering of humanities courses thrown in.

As at Boston Latin, academics at Harvard mattered less to Joe than did the goings-on outside the classroom. He rarely opened a book unless it was required for class. But this time he would have a much harder time scaling the social and sporting peaks of the school. Like the journalist Walter Lippmann, who was two years ahead of him in the class of 1910, he did not fully realize how many Harvards there were, and how little they overlapped.[47] There was the Harvard of the privileged young men from proper families such as the Cabots, Bancrofts, Winthrops, Welds, Lodges, and Saltonstalls, with their "final clubs" such as the Porcellian, the A.D., and the Fly, who might or might not go to class and aimed only for a "gentleman's C" average. There was the Harvard of athletes; the Harvard of intellectuals intent on an academic career; the Harvard of socialites focused mostly on having a good time and securing a gig on Wall Street; the Harvard of iconoclastic outsiders looking to find their way; and the Harvard of public school graduates, many of whom commuted from home every morning and returned home every night.[48]

Joe Kennedy was firmly in the last group, even though he lived in residence in Harvard Yard. It didn't take him long to realize that, despite the fact that freshmen were thrown together in the dormitories and dining halls in the Yard, sharp class distinctions defined the social environment. Being accepted into the right organization was the coin of the realm for many students, and the Catholic Joe, like the Jewish Lippmann, would never be tapped for membership at the elite ones—or even come close.

It was not for lack of trying. Where another student with his profile might have avoided the pursuit for fear of being rejected, or simply seen it as a lost cause, Joe charged ahead. When one door closed in his face, he knocked on the next. It was his nature to be irrepressible, not to mention ultracompetitive; both attributes would serve him well in his business activities in the years ahead, but at Harvard they did not get him through the narrow gate to a top final club. He had the wrong surname, the wrong family background, the wrong religious denomination. Perhaps, too, the very aggressiveness of his pursuit hurt his cause; he simply tried too hard, and lacked the finesse to hide it. Joe did gain membership to other university groups, including the Hasty Pudding Club and, in his senior year, Delta Upsilon, a lesser club where even Jews and scholarship boys were welcome, but for the rest of his life it stung him that no emissaries from the "Porc" or the Fly ever showed up at his door, depriving him of the recognition he most craved. (Franklin Delano Roosevelt, class of 1904, likewise never forgot being passed over by the Porcellian.) In the ultimate determination of in or out at Harvard, Joe Kennedy was out.[49]

On the athletic field, too, Kennedy experienced disappointment. Like many who had starred in high school, he had the sudden, unnerving realization in college that he was merely ordinary. Superior talents were all around him. Though he suited up for baseball his first three years, and remained a potent hitter, his fielding and baserunning were liabilities, and he never made the varsity squad until late in his junior year; although he earned a coveted letter, he played in only four games and had seven at-bats.[50] He did not try out for the team as a senior.

All in all, then, Joe Kennedy's Harvard experience was a mixed one. Continuing his lax approach to his studies, he did just well enough to squeak by, earning mostly C's and not a single A.[51] Sporting success eluded him. And despite all-consuming effort, he failed to grab hold of the college's most desired status symbol, membership in a top final club, which left him envious and scornful. On the flip side, he had his degree and would always be a Harvard man. Gregarious and bright, he proved quite popular among those classmates who didn't mind his social climbing. And he made some connections with elite Bostonians that would prove useful going forward.

Most notable of all, it was during his Harvard years that Joe positioned himself as the leading suitor of Rose Fitzgerald, the mayor's daughter.

VI

They had first met many years before, as children, when the Kennedys and the Fitzgeralds vacationed at Old Orchard Beach, Maine. A newspaper photo from that year shows Joe, age seven, and Rose, age five, standing a few feet apart, but in later years neither could recall this initial encounter. And there might have been other fleeting meetings, since, after all, their fathers were prominent political figures who occasionally brought their firstborn to campaign events.

Then again, P. J. Kennedy and John F. Fitzgerald ("Fitzie" to many, or "Johnny Fitz," or, somewhat later, "Honey Fitz") were also rivals of sorts, so perhaps the opportunities for chance encounters were fewer than one might imagine. Like the Kennedys, the Fitzgeralds were now second-generation Irish Americans. But where P. J. was restrained and unflashy, even a little severe, Fitzgerald was merry and pugnacious and dashing, a dynamo who could pontificate on any subject at machine-gun speed, the words gushing forth at a rate that astonished first-time listeners.

In other ways too, the two men were polar opposites. Kennedy was systematic in his climb to power, pragmatic and calculating, working patiently behind the scenes and considering his every move carefully. Fitzgerald, on the other hand, was the prototypical gate-crasher, glad-handing and histrionic and bombastic, inclined to shoot first and ask questions later. Short of stature at five feet, five inches, with a large, round face, blue eyes, and sandy hair parted down the middle, he was a natty dresser who reveled in his Irishness and refused to follow the guidelines of any party strategy. A buffoon to some, he had street smarts in spades, and a keen political antenna, and he vowed always to "work harder than any-one else." And so he did. Ever smiling in photographs, he took on a gloomy look when crossed, his brow furrowed, and didn't mind in the slightest when told it made him look a bit like Napoleon.[52]

Born in the North End in 1863 to Thomas Fitzgerald, a grocer, and Rosanna Cox Fitzgerald, who hailed from County Wexford and County Cavan, respectively, young John excelled in his studies and attended Boston Latin, one of the first Irishmen (if not the first) to gain admission. Intending to become a doctor, he enrolled at Harvard Medical School but dropped out before the end of his first year when his widowed father died suddenly and he had to support his siblings. Soon Fitzgerald began his ascent up the greasy pole of politics, first as a member of the Boston Common Council, then as a state senator (where he served alongside P. J. Kennedy), then as a U.S. congressman representing the Ninth District for three terms, then, beginning with his election on December 12, 1905, as Boston's mayor, under the slogan "Bigger, Better, Busier Boston."[53]

That he had a gift for politics no one doubted. It was said that Honey

Fitz was the first and most expert practitioner of the "Irish switch"—shaking the hand of one person while talking to another and smiling at a third. An oft-told story had it that he could talk with a person for fifteen minutes, at a rate of two hundred words a minute, barely letting the person get a word in, then pat the fellow on the back and say how much he'd loved the conversation. Night after night he was on the go, seemingly indefatigable, often taking in two, even three dinners in a single evening—one account estimated that in just his first two years as mayor Fitzgerald attended twelve hundred dinners, fifteen hundred dances, and two hundred picnics and delivered three thousand speeches.[54] This seems implausible, but even if the estimate overshoots by half, one is left with an almost superhuman level of activity. Then again, this is a man who would go to parties with spare collars in his back pocket so that he could dance all night and still appear fresh. On his fiftieth birthday he celebrated by sprinting a hundred yards at 7:00 A.M., running a quarter mile at nine, wrestling at noon, and boxing at one.[55]

In 1889, Fitzgerald had married his second cousin Mary Josephine ("Josie") Hannon, of Acton, Massachusetts, whose parents hailed from County Limerick. Slender and petite, with soft brown hair and an erect bearing she would keep into her tenth decade, Josie was bashful and retiring, the antithesis of her husband. A daughter, Rose Elizabeth, arrived in July 1890, and five more children followed. Rose was born in the North End, the center of her father's political power, in the family's first home, at 4 Garden Court Street. There followed a stint in a big, rambling house in West Concord, twenty-five miles northwest of Boston, but in 1904 Honey Fitz, wanting to be closer to the action, bought a fifteen-room Italianate home with mansard eaves on Welles Avenue in Dorchester, just south of Boston. Inspired by her father's lessons and their frequent excursions to see the city's many landmarks, Rose became deeply interested in history. She was a stellar student, blessed with a sharp intelligence and a prodigious memory. From her mother, meanwhile, she inherited a deep religious faith and a serene disposition.[56]

From the beginning, "Rosie" was the apple of her father's eye, and he in turn became the dominant figure in her life, notwithstanding his frequent absences. "Rose was like her father for all the world," a childhood friend commented years afterwards. "She was always quoting her father—in fact, we used to call her 'Father Says.'"[57] From a young age,

John "Honey Fitz" Fitzgerald and Mary Josephine
"Josie" Fitzgerald, circa 1889.

Rose accompanied Fitzgerald on political trips (in 1897, at age seven, she met President William McKinley in the White House), and she developed a deep and lasting love of politics that neither her mother nor her siblings nor even her future husband—for all his political ambition for himself and his sons—remotely shared. She relished it all, not merely the campaign rallies, with their blaring brass bands and blizzards of confetti, but also the backroom strategizing and the secret maneuvering that made election victories happen and governing take place. "She damn well knows all the nuts and bolts of politics," her son Jack's press secretary Pierre Salinger would marvel decades later, after watching her in action in two campaigns. "She knows how to get votes out, how you make the phone calls, raise money, and all that; and as a speaker, she's an absolute spellbinder."[58]

Over time, Rose began taking on some of her mother's political duties. With her deep shyness, Josie Fitzgerald hated the ceremonial rounds she was expected to make as a political wife; when she relented and took part, her distaste was palpable and she came off as cold and forbidding. Rose, starting in her mid-teens, stepped in, acting as hostess and greeter at myriad Honey Fitz campaign events and joining him at banquets, ship launches, and building dedications. She became, indeed, a kind of substitute wife. She loved every minute, and won accolades from the press for her precocity and striking beauty. There was something regal about her bearing, observers remarked, owing to her perfect posture and the sureness of her movement. Her skill at piano accompaniment came in handy, too, at many of these mayoral events, as her father loved nothing more than to unleash his Irish tenor and belt out "Sweet Adeline" whenever it was requested, and often when it wasn't.

In June 1906, Rose graduated from Dorchester High. Not yet sixteen, she was the youngest person ever to graduate from the school, and ranked third in a class of 285. Petite and graceful, she had shiny black curly hair and a winning smile, and she radiated poise as she strode across the stage at graduation. On hand to award her the diploma was none other than her father, the mayor, brimming with pride, the moment captured by a photo that ran in *The Boston Post* the following day. "Most Beautiful Girl Graduate?" blared the headline, no doubt with encouragement from the mayor.[59]

VII

Rose seemed to have the world in her hand, and she soon had another reason to be thrilled: she found love. That same summer, back at Old Orchard Beach in Maine, she and Joe Kennedy met properly for the first time. Though their encounter was brief, she was smitten by his energy and athletic good looks.[60] That fall, he invited her to a dance at Boston Latin. She wanted desperately to say yes but turned down the invitation, because her father "refused to let me go. He disapproved of a girl of sixteen going around to dances in strange places and meeting people who might cause trouble."[61] Undaunted, Rose and Joe carried on a nominally secret relationship that school year while she took college preparatory classes at Dorchester High and attended lectures about European culture and languages at the Lowell Institute, in Boston. He would meet her after lectures and walk her (almost) all the way home, or they would arrange to rendezvous at friends' parties.

"During that last year at Dorchester High, and the following year," Rose recalled, "Joe and I managed to see each other rather often. Less

The Kennedys and the Fitzgeralds vacationing in Old Orchard Beach, Maine, in 1907. P. J. is second from left, Rose is third from left, Honey Fitz is fourth from left, and Joe is second from right.

often than we would have liked, but more often than my father was aware of." Joe's class book in his graduation year at Boston Latin punningly predicted that he would "earn his living in a very round-a-bout way. He will run the flying horses at 'Severe' beach [a reference to the carousel at Revere Beach]; on every horse there will be a pretty Rose—that is where the Rose Fitz."[62]

Rose's father had other ideas. Though a union of his daughter with Joe Kennedy would bring together two of the most prominent Irish families in Boston and generate lavish press attention, Fitzgerald frowned on the relationship. Perhaps he felt Joe wasn't good enough for his daughter, or perhaps he sensed even then that the young man would not be a true and devoted partner. And perhaps, too, Fitzgerald's own low-wattage rivalry with P. J. Kennedy influenced his thinking, as he seemed much more keen on another Harvard-educated Irish Catholic suitor, Hugh Nawn, the handsome son of a wealthy Dorchester contractor. (Rose liked Hugh well enough but thought he lacked Joe's charisma.) Whatever the case, when Rose's ardor for Joe refused to cool, Fitzgerald took a more dramatic step:

in 1908 he shipped her and her sister Agnes off to a Sacred Heart convent in the Netherlands.

Her father's decisions regarding her education frustrated Rose to no end. He had already quashed her desire to attend Wellesley College, to which she had been admitted—too secular, he determined, and besides, at seventeen she was too young to matriculate. Now he was shipping her abroad, and to a convent. Ever the dutiful daughter, however, Rose took the decisions with minimal complaint. Her letters home indicate that she profited in important ways from the experience, not least by cultivating the cosmopolitan interest she had in the world outside the United States. Her proficiency in French improved considerably, and she studied German as well. The convent's strictly regimented schedule did not keep the two girls from traveling to various parts of the Continent and reporting home rapturously about their experiences. To her surprise, Rose found that she did not mind the devotional emphasis and strict routines of the school.[63]

She didn't mention in her letters home that she kept Joe Kennedy's photo on the table in her room, or that she missed him terribly. The feeling was mutual. For Joe, Mayor Fitzgerald's opposition to him only sweetened the prize, only made him more determined to have what he considered the prettiest, most famous Catholic girl in the city. Upon Rose's return to the United States in mid-1909, she and Kennedy picked up right where they had left off, though their meetings were sporadic, as Rose spent the next academic year in New York at the Academy of the Sacred Heart, a girls' boarding school (which would become Manhattanville College).[64] Only in 1910, with her return to Boston, could the romance fully resume, with carefully planned meetings in Harvard Yard, in friends' homes, and in the Christian Science church, where no one would think to look for them. When, in January 1911, Rose had her coming-out with a splashy debut party at her parents' home, Joe was present, as were his parents and some four hundred other guests, including every notable Democratic politician in the city. The press was there, too, of course, reporting the following day that the lovely debutante was the belle of Irish Boston, looking sublime in her white chiffon dress.[65]

Eventually, her father relented in his opposition to Joe Kennedy's courtship. He could see her determination, and furthermore he had to acknowledge, however grudgingly, that Joe brought a lot of attractive attributes to the table—education, ambition, affability, good looks, and a

Rose Fitzgerald in 1911, the year of her
official debut to Boston society.

kind of superhuman stamina that could rival Fitzgerald's own. In addition, Kennedy was already making impressive moves in his young career. On leaving Harvard, he had set his sights high, aiming to crack Boston's financial institutions, still tightly controlled by the Yankee Protestants. That is to say, he went into banking. From a young age and right through college, he had shown a talent for profit-making enterprises, and he grasped early on that power came from money.* He had a head for numbers, and had made useful contacts while at Harvard with students whose families controlled the city's leading banks. Besides, as he later told an interviewer, "Banking could lead a man anywhere, as it played an important part in every business."[66]

* In the summers before and after his final year at Harvard, Joe invested in a sightseeing bus, the *Mayflower*, with his friend Joe Donovan. While Donovan drove, Joe narrated. In two seasons, running from late spring to early fall, the partners cleared several thousand dollars each.

Upon his graduation, in 1912, Kennedy got himself appointed as a state bank examiner, a position that allowed him to see bank records and books throughout the greater Boston area and to learn how the banks operated and made their money. From there he cleverly maneuvered his way into the presidency of East Boston's Columbia Trust, a small bank his father had helped found in the mid-1890s. At just twenty-five, he was reportedly the youngest bank president in the state, perhaps in the country. And he was determined to make good. Commuting daily by train from the family home in Winthrop (P. J., after losing a race for street commissioner in 1908, had pulled up stakes and moved the family to a rambling home in this coastal enclave), Joe put in long hours and made use of every possible family connection to breathe new life into a trust company that had been losing assets. Often he skipped lunch or made do with crackers and milk at his desk.

Joe was popular with the immigrants who made up the bulk of the bank's clientele. Eschewing the stodgy, standoffish reserve of many bankers, he mingled and joked with his clients, many of them poor, and earned their respect with his friendly demeanor and his efforts on their behalf. Strong personal relations with customers were key to business success, Kennedy preached to his staff, and he modeled the message. Stories were legion of his helping clients in desperate economic circumstances who had been turned down by other banks. Less commonly reported was that he always kept an eye on the bottom line—he could be as quick as any banker in calling a loan or foreclosing a mortgage.[67]

The strenuous efforts paid off: in short order Kennedy, an instinctive businessman for whom dealmaking came easily, boosted deposits and brought in new business for Columbia Trust. Within six months he had increased the bank's holdings by 27 percent. Even Honey Fitz had to tip his hat.[68]

For his part, Fitzgerald soon had bigger things to worry about. For years, his mayoralty had been dogged by charges of corruption, with sworn testimony of payoffs and cronyism. Then, in 1913, a fellow Democrat named James Michael Curley announced that he would challenge Fitzgerald's quest for reelection. An unscrupulous and silver-tongued demagogue, Curley, who at six feet and two hundred pounds dwarfed his opponent, learned that Fitzgerald had been carrying on with a curvaceous blond cigarette girl named Elizabeth "Toodles" Ryan, whom he'd met in a hotel bar. Curley sent a letter to Josie threatening to make the affair public if her husband did not withdraw as a candidate. When Honey Fitz refused to get out of the race, Curley announced publicly that he would give a series of high-profile lectures, including "Great Lovers in History: From Cleopatra to Toodles" and "Libertines: From Henry VIII to the Present Day." In short order, Fitzgerald's office announced he would not be running after all. A ditty began making the rounds: "A whiskey glass and Toodles' ass / made a horse's ass / out of Honey Fitz."[69]

In late December 1913, newspapers began speculating about a possible engagement between Rose Fitzgerald and Joseph Kennedy. The official announcement came on June 20, 1914, after Joe presented Rose with a flawless two-carat diamond he had purchased at discount from a Harvard classmate who had entered his family jewelry business.

One week later, Franz Ferdinand, archduke of Austria-Hungary, was assassinated in Sarajevo, at the hands of a sixteen-year-old Bosnian Serb nationalist. At first, few Americans paid much attention—the crisis seemed no worse than those that had preceded it in the Balkans since 1908 and been resolved peacefully. But this time the Austrians, urged on by their ally Germany, sought to crush the Serbs for good, and the result was a cascade of events that led, in early August, to the start of the First World War. As armies across Europe mobilized, the United States, under President Woodrow Wilson, declared its neutrality, a position the nation would steadfastly maintain for another two and a half years.[70]

On October 7, 1914, in the midst of a war-induced financial downturn, Rose and Joe were married. Cardinal William O'Connell presided, and Honey Fitz gave the bride away. Acceding to Rose's wishes, her parents kept the reception small (a prudent move, perhaps, in view of her father's recent scandal), whereupon bride and groom honeymooned in Philadelphia (where they took in the first two games of the World Series between the Boston Braves and the Philadelphia Athletics) and White Sulphur Springs, West Virginia, where they spent their days riding, golfing, and playing tennis. On Sunday, October 25, they returned to Boston, and that Wednesday, the twenty-eighth, they moved to the sturdy and unassuming house on Beals Street.[71]

On July 25, 1915, nine months to the day after they returned from the honeymoon, Rose gave birth to the couple's first child, Joseph Patrick

Kennedy Jr. An exuberant Honey Fitz reported of his first grandson that "his mother and father have already decided that he is going to be president of the United States."[72] Twenty-two months after that, on May 29, 1917, on the heels of America's fateful entry in the war, came child number two. His parents named him John Fitzgerald Kennedy.

CHILDISH THINGS

ohn Fitzgerald Kennedy's birth in May 1917 coincided with a turning point in American and world history, the effects of which would reverberate through the decades and have immense implications for Kennedy's life and career, right down to his death in Dallas forty-six years later. On April 6, the United States entered the First World War, a move that, all the combatant nations agreed, mattered enormously for a struggle that was then deep into its third bloody year, with no end in sight. In May, Congress passed the Selective Service Act to raise an army for the war effort, and by June the first American troops had arrived in France. Upheaval in Russia, meanwhile, had forced Tsar Nicholas II to abdicate, ending centuries of tsarist rule and causing that nation's war effort to all but collapse. A liberal provisional government took over and pledged to keep Russia in the fight, but turmoil festered, and on April 16 Vladimir Ilyich Lenin, leader of the revolutionary Bolshevik Party, arrived in Petrograd (St. Petersburg) to a tumultuous reception after a decade in exile. Within months, Lenin's Bolsheviks would seize power and take Russia out of the war.[1]

U.S. entry into World War I marked the real start, it may be said, of the

American Century, which would last through the end of the twentieth century and into the twenty-first, and during which the United States would emerge as the greatest power—in economic, political, and military terms—the world had ever seen.[2] The Russian Revolution, for its part, would shape global politics in profound ways long after the Bolsheviks consolidated control of the huge Russian landmass and then proclaimed a still larger Union of Soviet Socialist Republics. In time, the United States and the USSR became superpowers and were pitted in a decades-long Cold War in which decisions in Washington and Moscow dominated international politics. Writing of the long epoch that drew to a close with the end of that Soviet-American confrontation in the late 1980s, historian Eric Hobsbawm called it "a world shaped by the impact of the Russian Revolution of 1917."[3]

If all this was still in the future when Joseph and Rose Kennedy's second child made his entrance into the world in the upstairs master bedroom at 83 Beals Street shortly after 3:00 P.M. on the afternoon of May 29, some sagacious observers could see the general outline of things to come.* Three-quarters of a century before, in 1835, the French analyst Alexis de Tocqueville had already foreseen the day when the United States would stand astride much of the world, on account of its geographic advantages and potential for growth.[4] By the turn of the century such assessments were routine, for the young nation was an economic and demographic steamroller.[5] The United States already had 200,000 miles of railway track in 1900—more than all of Europe—and was the world's largest producer of wheat, coal, and iron. A single industrialist, Andrew Carnegie, produced more steel than the whole of England put together. At the outbreak of war in 1914, the American share of world manufacturing stood at 32 percent (up from 23.6 in 1900), as compared with Great Britain at 13.6 percent (down from 18.5 in 1900). Over the previous half century, since the end of the Civil War, the U.S. economy had grown faster than any economy had ever grown before—by an astronomical margin—fueled in good part by the arrival of millions of enterprising immigrants

---

* The evening edition of *The Boston Globe* on the day of the birth indicated the momentousness of the time. Separate headlines on page 1 announced that the British had lost three ships in the latest fighting, that the U.S. government was going after draft opponents, that the French had scored a major victory near Verdun, and that veterans of the American Civil War were calling on the nation's young men to repeat their example ("Message of the boys of '61 to boys of '17: 'We carried the flag then, you carry it now' ").

who, uneducated and poor though they might be, had ambition, energy, and intelligence in abundance.[6]

Yet the United States in 1914 was still a young upstart waiting in the wings of history, a kind of apprentice member of the great-power club. And for the better part of three years, President Woodrow Wilson kept his nation out of the European conflagration. At first he did so by issuing a proclamation of neutrality—the traditional U.S. policy toward European wars—and he asked Americans to refrain from taking sides, to exhibit "the dignity of self-control," to be "impartial in thought as well as in action."[7] But standing apart proved easier said than done, for Wilson no less than for ordinary Americans. A longtime Anglophile, he soon came to share the British conviction that a victory by the Central powers (Germany, Austria-Hungary, and Italy) would destroy free enterprise and the rule of law. If Germany won the war, he prophesied, "it would change the course of our civilization and make the United States a military nation." Several of Wilson's chief advisers and diplomats—notably his close aide Colonel Edward House; ambassador to London Walter Hines Page; and Robert Lansing, a counselor in the State Department who later became Wilson's secretary of state—held similar anti-German views, which often translated into anti-German policies.[8]

U.S. economic ties with the Allied powers of Britain, France, and Russia also rendered neutrality a near-impossible proposition. Britain had long been one of the nation's leading customers, and early in the fighting it flooded the United States with new orders, especially for munitions. Sales to the Entente—which dwarfed those to the Central powers—helped pull the American economy out of a recession induced by the outbreak of the struggle.[9] Much of this trade was financed by private American banks, which extended loans totaling $2.3 billion to Britain and France during the neutrality period. Germany received only $27 million over the same span. The Wilson administration, which initially opposed these transactions on the grounds that they compromised the nation's neutrality, came to see them as necessary to America's economic health.[10]

All the while, the war raged on. For Joe Kennedy, the news of blood-filled trenches only solidified the argument for keeping America out of the war. From the time the first shots were fired in 1914, he determined that this was a European struggle that should be fought by Europeans, and he held to that position tenaciously thereafter. As an Irish American, moreover, he had no desire to suit up for a defense of the British Empire, and he scoffed at the claims by Britain's propagandists and their U.S. allies that this was an epic existential struggle to save civilization from German barbarism.

A scene from Kennedy's parents' home in coastal Winthrop, Massachusetts, at the start of July 1916 is emblematic of his thinking. He had invited some Harvard friends for a weekend at the beach, and the conversation soon turned to the Battle of the Somme, then just getting under way in northern France. All the pals were ebullient about the Allied offensive and the heroism of the British and French soldiers.* But not Kennedy. In Rose's recollection, he initially just listened to his guests' exuberant chatter and didn't say much. "He merely shook his head with sadness." Then, unable to restrain himself any longer, he launched in, saying their "whole attitude was strange and incomprehensible to him." As he saw it, thousands of young men were about to be mowed down, their lives barely begun, "cut off from the world of their parents and their memories, cut off from their dreams of the future." And all to capture a piece of territory. "He warned his friends [that] by accepting the idea of the grandeur of the struggle, they themselves were contributing to the momentum of the senseless war, certain to ruin the victors as well as the vanquished."[11]

That evening, after a hasty breakup of the gathering, Kennedy went upstairs and, with Rose, checked on the sleeping Joseph Junior, who was just shy of his first birthday. "This is the only happiness that lasts," he said softly, then walked away.[12]

The remark gets at a core aspect of Kennedy's worldview, one that would condition his approach to not only this world war but the one still to come. Cynical about human nature, he tended to see international problems not in moral or geopolitical terms but on the basis of economics; even more, he judged such matters according to what they meant for him per-

---

* Of the 3,500 Americans who volunteered to go to the front as ambulance drivers during the period of U.S. neutrality in 1914–17, some 450 were undergraduates or alumni of Harvard. They included novelists Charles Nordhoff ('09) and John Dos Passos ('16) and poets e. e. cummings ('15), Robert Hillyer ('17), and Archibald MacLeish, LL.B. '19. Alan Seeger ('10), whose poem "I Have a Rendezvous with Death" would become a favorite of John F. Kennedy's (and whose nephew, the folk singer and activist Pete Seeger, would be a classmate of Kennedy's), joined the Foreign Legion in August 1914 and was killed on July 4, 1916, just as the Somme offensive began and as Joe Kennedy entertained his friends in Winthrop. Ultimately, more than eleven thousand Harvard men would serve in the war, including during the period of American belligerency; 373 died in service, of whom 43 had not yet graduated.

sonally and for his family. This mindset inclined him toward isolationism in foreign policy, and it opened him to charges of myopia and selfishness.

But there was also power in Joe Kennedy's analysis that summer day in Winthrop. He might have been a minority of one at this particular gathering, but many thoughtful and informed Americans in 1916 shared his deep skepticism about the supposed "grandeur of the struggle" and his opposition to the United States' becoming directly engaged in the fighting. However much the war correspondents might romanticize the "terrible beauty" and "glorious purpose" of the Somme fighting, Kennedy grasped the sordid truth: it was wretchedness. On the first day alone, the British lost almost twenty thousand soldiers, some 30 percent of them behind their own lines on account of artillery fire. By the time the battle ended, Britain and France had suffered 600,000 dead or wounded to earn only 125 square miles; the Germans had lost 400,000 men. At Verdun that same year, 336,000 Germans perished, and at Passchendaele, in 1917, more than 370,000 British men died to gain about forty miles of mud and barbed wire. Ambassador Page grew sickened by what Europe had become—"a bankrupt slaughter-house inhabited by unmated women."[13]

In the presidential election of 1916, Kennedy cast a heartfelt vote for Woodrow Wilson, whose campaign slogan was both a boast and a promise: "He kept us out of war!" The rallying cry worked, and Wilson was narrowly reelected. But the promise proved short-lived. Long convinced that the United States could no longer isolate itself from international power politics, Wilson believed that he alone occupied the best position to mediate a fair settlement and stop the bloodshed. At the same time, he feared that only if the United States became a belligerent could he be assured of a seat at the negotiating table.[14] He was still grappling with this dilemma when Germany, in a desperate bid to upset the military balance, commenced total submarine warfare on February 17, 1917. All ships in war zones were now fair game. Two days later, Wilson broke off diplomatic relations with Berlin.

When war came two months later, Kennedy expressed no enthusiasm. The surge of patriotic fervor that even many former opponents of intervention experienced eluded him. Unlike most of his Harvard friends, Kennedy did not enlist, but on June 5, one week after John's birth, he reported to his local polling place and completed his registration card. It soon became clear that he would get no exemption for marriage or fatherhood,

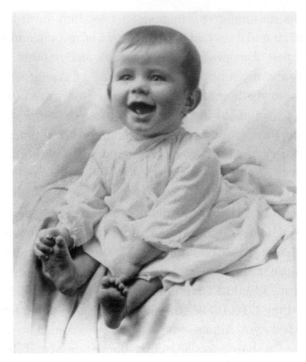

A happy Jack at approximately
six months, in fall 1917.

but an "industrial exemption" might be possible, provided he had a job that qualified. In September 1917, Joe jumped at the offer to become assistant general manager of the Fore River Shipyard, in Quincy, ten miles south of Boston, which had been contracted to produce destroyers for the war effort.[15]

Kennedy knew little about shipbuilding, but he was a quick study and nothing if not industrious, frequently putting in seventy-hour workweeks and often sleeping in his office. Colleagues marveled at his stamina, and Rose and the family seldom saw him except on Sundays. When, to his astonishment, his draft board in February 1918 informed him he had been classified Class 1 and might be called for military service, Kennedy appealed immediately for a deferment "on industrial grounds" and included with his appeal a lengthy letter in which he laid out his responsibilities at Fore River.[16] His superiors vouched for him, and the effort worked. He never received a deferment, but neither was he called for the draft, and he remained at Fore River till the end of the war.

That end came sooner than many anticipated, and the American contribution was considerable. Allied victory in the Second Battle of the Marne, northeast of Paris, in July 1918 stopped all German advances, and in the massive Meuse-Argonne offensive that followed, more than a million American soldiers joined French and British units in six weeks of ferocious combat along much of the Western Front, beginning with a U.S. strike northward toward Sedan on September 26. More than 26,000 Americans died in the ensuing struggle, and another hundred thousand were wounded—making it the bloodiest campaign in American history to this day—before the Allies gained the upper hand. For Germany, there was no escape. Its submarine war and ground operations had been stymied, its exhausted troops and cities were mutinous, and the kaiser had abdicated. Allied Austria and Turkey were giving up the fight. The Entente powers, meanwhile, had the luxury of endless American troop reinforcements and arms shipments. Peace became essential, and the Germans accepted an exacting armistice. It went into effect on the morning of November 11, 1918, at the eleventh hour of the eleventh day of the eleventh month.[17]

No one can fully calculate the costs of the war, but the magnitude is clear enough: the belligerents counted some ten million soldiers and a roughly equal number of civilians dead and twenty million people wounded, eight million of them permanently disabled. Fifty-three thousand U.S. soldiers perished in battle. The economic damage was immense as well, which helps to explain the pervasive starvation Europe endured in the winter of 1918–19. Economic activity on much of the Continent withered, and transport over meaningful distances was in some countries almost impossible. The German, Austro-Hungarian, Ottoman, and Russian empires disappeared, and for a time it seemed the Bolshevik Revolution would spread westward into the heart of a weak and weary Europe. "We are at the dead season of our fortunes," wrote one young British observer, the economist John Maynard Keynes. "Never in the lifetime of men now living has the universal element in the soul of man burnt so dimly."[18]

II

For the Kennedys, as for many other Americans, the final months of the war had been a blur as they grappled with a more immediate menace: the influenza pandemic that swept the earth in the summer and fall of 1918 and would kill more than twice as many as the Great War itself—somewhere between fifty and a hundred million people. In the United States, nearly 700,000 people died. (Among U.S. soldiers in Europe, the disease claimed more lives—63,000—than did the fighting.) It was an illness like no other. People could be healthy on Monday and dead by Wednesday evening. Some died quickly, experiencing a rapid accumulation of fluid in the lungs that caused them to literally drown. Others lingered before succumbing to secondary bacterial infection. Mortality rates were highest for those in their twenties and thirties.[19]

The first cases were identified in the American Midwest in the late winter of 1918, and some of the soldiers shipping out to Europe in large numbers unknowingly carried the virus in their lungs. The disease appeared on the Western Front in April, then made its way to Spain, where it killed so many people—some eight million—that it became known as the Spanish flu. There followed a midsummer lull, after which a second, deadlier form of the illness began spreading to various points of the globe, and in September the disease rampaged down the East Coast of the United States, from Boston to New York to Baltimore and beyond. That month, more than twelve thousand Americans perished.

Joe Kennedy was given the task of managing the impact of the crisis at Fore River. With scores of the company's workers falling ill, he converted shipyard dormitories into infirmaries, hoping to isolate the ailing and prevent further contagion. He stayed put in Quincy for days on end, no doubt partly in order to avoid the risk of contaminating his family. In addition to Rose, Joe Junior, and John, there was now also Rose Marie (later Rosemary, or, to the family, Rosie), born on September 13. "She was," Rose recalled, "a very pretty baby and she was sweet and peaceable and cried less than the first two had, which at the time I supposed was part of her being a girl." A clipping in Rose's scrapbook included the line "A brilliant future is predicted for the baby."[20]

In October, the pandemic reached maximum ferocity, hitting almost every corner of the world. In the United States that month, 200,000 perished. Then suddenly, in November, for reasons that remain murky, the crisis eased, and by early 1919 the pandemic was over. With India alone suffering as many as seventeen million deaths, and Samoa losing more than a fifth of its population, it was, in historian Roy Porter's words, "the greatest single demographic shock mankind has ever experienced."[21] The war was partly responsible for spreading the disease, but so were advances in shipbuilding that for several decades had facilitated global travel and made the world smaller.

The Kennedys survived the epidemic intact, but the long hours and the stress took their toll on Joe, who developed an ulcer and suffered a physical breakdown in late 1918, requiring several weeks of recuperation at a "health farm." For Rose the absence was not much of a change, for her husband hadn't been around much during his years at Fore River. Even before that—indeed, from the beginning of their marriage—he had worked brutally long hours at Columbia Trust, including on weekends. Usually he came home at night, but not always. On those occasions, Rose did not question where he had been—or why. "Joe's time was his own," she remarked in her memoirs, "as it had been and always would be: School and college had once taken much of it before, and now it was business."[22]

Only business? Rose was too discreet to say, but the careful words suggest she had some inkling of what she was getting when she married him, knew there was an area of his life that she would not be a part of, a compartment she could not enter. Of their pre-marriage days, biographer David Nasaw writes, "At Harvard and after graduation, Joe remained faithful to Rose in the way that men of his generation and class remained faithful to their best girls. He did not court any other marriageable women, but neither did he remain chaste until his wedding day." Afterwards, it seems, the pattern continued. Which is to say, Joe did not give up being a womanizer. He had affairs, lots of them, with secretaries, stenographers, waitresses, actresses, and others.[23] How much this surprised his wife—if it did at all—we don't know. She was well aware that her father had been untrue to her mother, and that many of the other politicians and celebrities she met during her years as Honey Fitz's hostess and sidekick had likewise cheated on their wives. Even so, and even though she was highly adept at suppressing or ignoring things that made her unhappy (and certainly did not record them for posterity), it can't have been easy on those occasions when evening came and no husband appeared.

The sheer quietude of those evenings, even when Joe was home, was undoubtedly a shock to Rose's system. No longer was she the belle of Catholic Boston, written about in the press, attending balls, traveling internationally, meeting famous people, appearing alongside her effervescent father at this or that lavish banquet or campaign rally or ship launching, or in a box on opening night at the theater. She'd loved that life, and even though marriage and domesticity brought their own pleasures, it's hard to imagine that a wave of nostalgia did not wash over her from time to time. Her new existence gave her scant opportunity to exercise her formidable and capacious intelligence, her passion for politics, and her wide-ranging curiosity about the world.[24]

All around her she could see the gains that women were experiencing in American society. In August 1920, the Nineteenth Amendment gave women the right to vote, and though they remained excluded from local and national political realms, they found increased opportunities for making their voices heard through a plethora of civic, religious, and voluntary groups and clubs.[25] More women were entering the job force as well, albeit in positions men seldom sought—nursing, teaching, and clerical work. Fashions were changing as new fabrics and dyes allowed for more self-expression and less restrictive cuts. Hemlines moved up and necklines crept lower. Corsets went in the trash or in a box in the attic. The boundaries between appropriate and unacceptable behavior for women blurred as drinking, smoking, and frankness about sex became fashionable. Whereas in 1915 most middle- and upper-class young women had to be chaperoned during social engagements, by a decade later they engaged in unsupervised dating, in which a fellow "asked out" a woman and spent money on her. Rose gave little overt indication that she longed for full access to this new world—it conflicted in key respects with the conservative version of Catholic womanhood to which she and her mother adhered—but in a moment of candor she acknowledged that "life was flowing past."[26]

Only once that we know of was there a seeming rupture. The details are sketchy, but according to relatives, in early 1920, heavily pregnant with her fourth child—Kathleen would be born on February 20—Rose abruptly moved back to her parents' home on Welles Avenue in Dorchester. Joe's constant work and frequent absences were too much, the emotional deprivation too draining. Even when Joe was home, a part of him was not really there, as he refused to talk about work and no longer shared his dreams or plans with her, as he had done during the many years of courtship. She felt isolated, she told her parents, and ached for more. Honey Fitz and Josie had long had their doubts about their son-in-law and his ruthless ambition, but they were not thrilled by the new arrangement. After three weeks, Honey Fitz told his daughter that, in so many words, she had made her bed and must lie in it. The kids needed her, and so did her husband. "You've made your commitment, Rosie," he told her, "and you must honor it now. What is past is past. The old days are gone. [But] you can make things work out. I know you can."[27]

Rose complied and, after attending a church retreat, returned to Beals Street, determined to fulfill her duties as wife and mother. If her subsequent unambiguous defense of the marriage in this period—"[You] never heard a cross word, we always understood one another and trusted one another and that was it"—doesn't exactly have the ring of truth, it's almost certainly the case that Rose gave little thought to divorce. Her deep Catholic faith proscribed it. Moreover, church teachings provided a measure of comfort, instructing her that all spouses faced pressures, especially in child-rearing, and that there was true nobility in marital sacrifices.[28]

III

And indeed, there were plenty of good times in these years, too. Often on Saturday evenings, Joe and Rose would attend the symphony in Boston. At Harvard he had developed a deep interest in classical music, and she had studied composition and performance during her school year in Holland. They relished taking in live concerts as well as playing records at home on the family Victrola. At other times Rose would sit down at the piano in the living room and play popular songs, with Joe and the children or family friends joining in with the words. On Sundays they piled the kids into the family Model T and drove the ten miles to Winthrop to visit Joe's parents. And on weekday mornings, Rose took pleasure in taking the children on excursions in the neighborhood, pulling Rosemary in a kiddie car and holding little Jack (as they called him) by the hand while Joe Junior walked alongside.[29] They would stop in a store or two—the five-and-ten in Coolidge Corner was particularly exciting for the boys—and at St. Aidan's Church, on Freeman Street, to instill in the children the idea, she later said, that "church isn't just for Sundays and special times on the calendar but should be part of daily life."[30]

And so it was. Rose insisted that her children observe the important Catholic rituals, starting with baptism in the days after birth and then, as they grew, First Confession, First Holy Communion, and Confirmation. Before and after meals and before bed, she guided them in prayer. She made sure they never traveled without a rosary in their pocket. Every

Sunday, without fail, and on First Fridays, the family attended Mass, and they were in the pews as well on the Holy Days of Obligation—the Epiphany on January 6, the Assumption of the Blessed Virgin Mary on August 15, All Saints' Day on November 1, and so on. The boys served as altar boys, and the girls wore veils and carried prayer books.[31]

Joe, meanwhile, could show his tender side, surprising Rose with flowers or a loving note. At the birth of each child, he gave her a thoughtful, often expensive gift. And whenever a child became ill, this workaholic father would become instantly engaged. Jack's fragile health was a special concern. His birth, in May 1917, had been uncomplicated—Dr. Frederick L. Good, a Boston obstetrician who was summoned along with his nurse to the Kennedy home for the delivery (he would deliver each of the Kennedy children, and a few of the grandchildren after that), pronounced the baby healthy and handsome. But from an early point, little Jack was sickly and frail. Rose tried hard to build up his strength, to no avail. In February 1920, at age two years, nine months, he contracted scarlet fever, mere days after Kathleen's birth. A leading cause of childhood death in those years, the illness also could have serious aftereffects (kidney disease, rheumatic heart disease, arthritis), and it was highly contagious, a potential disaster in the tight confines of a family home. With the local Brookline hospital refusing to take patients with contagious illnesses, Kennedy enlisted his father's and his father-in-law's help to get little Jack admitted to Boston City Hospital, even though he was not a Boston resident.

"By the time he got there," Rose remembered, "Jack was a very, very sick little boy." Unable to visit him because she was adhering to the custom of the day to remain in bed for three weeks after childbirth, Rose dispatched Joe, who for two months changed his schedule so he could spend each afternoon and evening at his son's hospital bedside.[32] The situation was acute, and Joe feared the worst. For several agonizing days, Jack hovered between life and death. But eventually he pulled through, aided in no small part by the treatment he received from the attending physician, Dr. Edward Place, widely acknowledged as the nation's leading authority on measles and scarlet fever. In early July, Joe penned a heartfelt note of thanks to Dr. Place, "for your wonderful work for Jack during his recent illness." He added that he had "never experienced any serious sickness in my family previous to this case of Jack's, and I little realized what an effect such a happening could possibly have on me. During the darkest days I felt that nothing else mattered except his recovery."[33]

At one point during the harrowing episode, Kennedy pledged—to God, or to himself, or both—that if Jack lived, he would give half of his fortune to the Church. When his son did recover, he wrote a check for $3,740, half of his liquid assets (on paper he was worth infinitely more), to the Guild of Saint Appollonia, which had been formed a decade before to provide free dental care to the city's Catholic schoolchildren. Jack, for his part, so endeared himself to the nurses with his sweetness and vulnerability that two of them would later pay him a visit at home. "He is such a wonderful boy," nurse Sara Miller wrote in a letter to Joe. "We all love him very much." Nurse Anna Pope agreed some weeks later: "Jack is certainly the nicest little boy I have ever seen. . . . I'm afraid I asked for too much when I asked for Jack's picture but he was so lovable and such an excellent little patient, everyone loved him. I felt very lonesome when I left him." Upon being discharged, Jack was sent away for several weeks of convalescence at the Mansion House Hotel, in Poland Springs, Maine, as there was worry he might still be contagious. Only in May, three months after falling ill and near his third birthday, did he return home to Brookline. His nurse reported that he had been "an excellent little patient" and that, after meeting his baby sister at last, he appeared "very happy."[34]

By this stage the Kennedys were on the move. The previous year, Joe had taken a management position with Hayden, Stone and Company, a leading stockbrokerage firm with offices in Boston and New York. From the start, he thrived, learning market operations and the intricacies of insider trading (not then illegal, but widely considered unethical) from Galen Stone, the portly and mustached co-founder, who became his mentor. With his zest for hard work and his skill at juggling numbers and accounts, Kennedy did well for the company and for himself, investing in stocks on the side and buying and selling real estate, all the while expanding his connections in the financial world. In one case, he learned from Stone that the Pond Creek Coal Company, whose board of directors Stone chaired, was about to be acquired by Henry Ford. Before the plan was made public, Joe bought fifteen thousand shares at $16, mostly with borrowed funds; when news of Ford's plans broke, Pond Creek skyrocketed, and Kennedy promptly sold, netting more than half a million dollars.[35]

As socially ambitious as ever, Kennedy dressed for success, ordering tailored suits and custom-made shirts, and he joined first the Woodland Golf Club and then the Middlesex Club, the oldest Republican club in New England (though he kept his Democratic affiliation). And he moved his family to a new Brookline home, at 131 Naples Road.[36] The anticipated further expansion of his family made a change of address imperative, but it mattered as well that the new residence was in a fancier neighborhood, with grander houses on bigger plots, more suitable for a man of his station. This home, for which he paid $16,000, sat on an acre, had twelve rooms, high ceilings, a formal entry, curved bay windows, plus an icebox and a washing machine. The Beals Street house they sold to Joe's loyal assistant and confidant Edward "Eddie" Moore and his wife, Mary, who, with no children of their own, became fixtures at Naples Road, chipping in to help as needed, including as babysitters to the ever-growing brood of Kennedy children.

Rose was delighted with the relocation. She loved the splendor of the new residence, reminiscent as it was of what she had had as a teenager in Dorchester, yet it was close enough to Beals Street that she still knew her way about the neighborhood. Most of all, it had the space her growing family needed. She turned the large wraparound front porch into a playroom, separating the children with folding partitions—"two, three or four of them as the situation at the time indicated. That way they could be with each other and entertain one another for hours at a time with a minimal risk that they would push one another down or stick one another with something sharp or perhaps pile heavy objects inside or on top of the baby carriage."[37] Soon pregnant again, she delivered Eunice in July 1921. Patricia followed in May 1924, and then Robert in November 1925, Jean in February 1928, and finally Edward (named for Eddie Moore) in February 1932.

To manage her ever-expanding family, Rose relied not merely on full-time domestic help but on a detailed cataloging system in which she kept index cards and index tabs listing illnesses, treatments, and measurements for each child. She became an "executive," as she herself put it, overseeing the kids' clothes and their daily exercise and managing a complex operation of maids, nurses, and cooks:

> I had to be sure there were plenty of good-quality diapers on hand, and that they were changed as needed and properly washed and stored for us. . . . There was also the daily supply of bottles and nipples to be cleaned and sterilized. I didn't do much of it myself, but I had to make sure it was done properly, and on a schedule that didn't interfere with another vital schedule. If nursemaids were in the

kitchen boiling bottles and nipples and preparing "formulas" and pureeing vegetables (there were no canned baby foods then) when the cook needed the stove and some of the same utensils to prepare supper, there could be a kitchen crisis, sharp words and bruised feelings and, from a management point of view, a precipitous drop in morale and efficiency.[38]

In later years Rose would be faulted for what some saw as a severe and overly clinical approach to child-rearing, one focused on "efficiency" and order rather than on love and affection. It's true that she doled out hugs and kisses sparingly, and placed a premium on presentation—proper attire, proper grammar, proper posture. She obsessed about the children's weight, especially the girls'. It may be, as some have suggested, that she dealt with her husband's philandering by isolating herself emotionally from her family—and, in part, physically as well, through frequent traveling vacations without her husband and children. Five-year-old Jack's memorable rebuke, when his mother prepared to depart for a six-week trip to California with her sister Agnes, is telling: "Gee, *you're* a great mother to go away and leave your children all alone!"[39]

Telling behavior—but only to a degree. It bears noting that Rose herself was the source for Jack's comment, in her diary entry for April 3, 1923, and also that she used it to underscore the young boy's wit and precociousness. In her memoirs, moreover, she acknowledged that Jack's comment wounded her, and that she felt miserable the next day as the kids gathered on the porch to see her off. "They looked so forlorn, and when I kissed them good-bye I had tears in my eyes," she wrote. But then: "After I was down the street a way I suddenly realized there was something I had forgotten and I came back—to find them all laughing and playing on the porch, apparently not missing me much at all. I resumed my journey with an easy conscience."[40]

To some extent, at least, an "executive" approach to her task was necessitated by her circumstances. She had five children in six years, from 1915 to 1921, and two more by the end of 1925, with two more still to come after that. Oldest daughter Rosemary, moreover, showed signs of being slow to develop and required extra attention. Rose was effectively a single parent most of the time, as her husband's work not only kept him in the office until all hours but took him out of town for days, even weeks, on end. The family finances allowed her to have much more domestic help than most mothers of the era—as she herself readily acknowledged—but even so, the logistical demands were extraordinary, especially given her commitment to the then-current ideal of achievement-oriented child-rearing. The right kind of mothering, this Victorian notion held, could set a child on a lifelong path of personal and social significance. From this ideal flowed movements like Republican Motherhood, centered in New England and urging women to be highly engaged with their offspring and to raise patriotic sons who would enter public service.[41]

Even Rose's practice of withholding physical affection from her children, so jarring to our modern sensibility and no doubt to many parents at the time, had expert support behind it. With her characteristic hunger for learning, Rose avidly studied the "scientific" child-rearing recommendations of the era and tried to follow them. Eleanor Roosevelt and countless other women did the same. L. Emmett Holt's bestselling study *The Care and Feeding of Children: A Catechism for the Use of Mothers and Children's Nurses*, which made him a kind of Dr. Spock figure of his day, warned mothers against coddling children or playing with them or displaying a lot of affection toward them. Babies, he wrote, should be kissed only on the cheek or forehead, "but the less even of this the better." Feeding and sleeping schedules should be highly regimented, and children ought to be weighed at standardized intervals. (The data should be collected on, yes, index cards.) They should also get plenty of fresh air and exercise. Rose followed each of these recommendations, and she took to heart as well Holt's emphasis on dental hygiene. Healthy teeth were imperative to good health and good looks, he declared, and mothers should not fall into the trap of thinking they could delay proper dental care for their offspring. Rose hired an orthodontist to straighten out the children's teeth, and she insisted on toothbrushings after every meal.[42]

It wasn't just Holt. A survey of magazine articles focusing on motherhood between 1910 and 1935 found that the writers considered "too much love" to be the greatest threat to a child's welfare. And John B. Watson, in his influential book *The Psychological Care of Infant and Child* (1928), built on Holt's theories to argue for a stern, controlling, discipline-centered parenting style and to warn against too much maternal affection toward the children. Kissing and hugging, he noted, should be avoided to the greatest extent possible. "If you must, kiss them once on the forehead when they say good night. Shake hands with them in the morning."[43]

IV

With a live-in staff that freed her from some of the basic caregiving for the younger children, Rose could focus her attention on the intellectual and social development of the older ones. In addition to outings to points of interest in Brookline, including the public library on Washington Street, she took them on regular visits to see Boston's historic sites, much as Honey Fitz had done with her when she was little. (Often she would rattle off improvised math challenges en route: "What is two plus two, subtract three, then add two?") Rose was adamant that "they should know history and especially the history of their own country," and on their excursions to landmarks she would explain what had happened at the spot and why it mattered, encouraging questions and discussion so the kids would re-member. "I was determined about this, and I may have overdone it a little since there can be too much even of a good thing," she recalled. "In any case they did learn, their interest developed with the years, and I suspect that this may be one reason why as adults they wanted to serve the coun-try in public life."[44]

Jack in particular seemed to be fascinated by history, and by the world generally. His curiosity was insatiable. Rose noticed it during these day trips, and also when she read to him in the evenings. He loved adventure stories of all kinds—*Sinbad the Sailor, Black Beauty, Peter Pan*—and was especially fond of *Billy Whiskers,* a picture book series by Frances Trego Montgomery featuring a mischievous goat that marries and has two "kids." Rose found the illustrations crude and harsh, but Jack adored the tales. When he learned in one story that Billy stopped in the Sandwich Islands on his way across the Pacific, Jack asked his mother to get infor-mation on this mysterious-sounding place, which she duly did, pulling out the family atlas so Jack could see for himself. Another time, when she read to the older children the Easter story of Christ's entrance into Jeru-salem on a donkey, shortly before the Crucifixion and Resurrection, Jack piped up: "Mother, we know what happened to Jesus Christ, but what hap-pened to the donkey?"[45]

With his quick wit and irreverent spirit, Jack resembled his maternal grandfather, Honey Fitz, which may explain why the two got on so well. A frequent visitor in these years, "Grandpa Fitz" would take the two older boys for hours at a time, to a sporting event or to the swan boats in the Public Garden, or to the State House where he had formerly been a sena-

Rose with her five children, circa 1922. From left: Eunice,
Rosemary (in foreground), Kathleen, Jack, and Joe Junior.

tor. The boys loved his sense of fun, his infectious love of learning, his
sheer delight at being in their presence. (By contrast, their other grandfather, P. J. Kennedy, "wouldn't let us cut up or even wink in his presence,"
Jack remembered.) They never tired of hearing the old man's well-worn
stories, listening with rapt attention and pleading, "Tell that one again,
Grandpa!"[46]

The fifty-nine-year-old Fitzgerald had ample time for his grandsons because his once-storied political career had sputtered. In 1916, two years
after the Toodles scandal forced his withdrawal from the mayor's race,
he'd won the Democratic nomination for the U.S. Senate, but he was defeated in the general election by Republican Henry Cabot Lodge. In 1918
he rebounded to claim a seat in Congress, representing the Tenth District,
only to be forced out after seven months when a congressional investigation found evidence of voter fraud. Yearning for one more shot at the
limelight, Honey Fitz announced in 1922 that he would challenge Lodge
a second time for the Senate, then abruptly switched his candidacy to the
race for governor. One of Jack Kennedy's earliest memories was touring
the Boston wards with his grandfather, who invariably let loose his pat-

ented rendition of "Sweet Adeline" and chatted up anyone and everyone. The crowds loved him, but it was not enough: Honey Fitz lost by a wide margin. His political peak had passed.[47]

Jack remained frail and prone to sickness, in contrast to his robust and physically imposing older brother. But he did well enough academically at the local Edward Devotion School to enter second grade (under Miss Bicknell) at age six, a year ahead of most kids his age. And he had charm in abundance, not to mention a taste for mischief. Admonished by his mother to get serious in school, he breezily replied, "You know, I'm getting on all right, and if you study too much, you're liable to go crazy." That same fall, 1923, Jack and Joe Junior were caught shoplifting false mustaches from a shop, this after they formed a club in which they initiated new members by sticking pins into them. On an eatery sign reading "No dogs allowed in this Restaurant," they scribbled "Hot" before "dogs." On another occasion in 1923, soon after a family vacation, Jack confessed to his father, "Well, here I have been home only a few hours and the cops are chasing me already." He had teased a little girl who had promptly gone to tell a policeman on him, whereupon Jack had raced home and hidden in the cellar until nightfall.[48]

It was all standard high jinks for two energetic youngsters, but for the family "executive," Rose Kennedy, it suggested the need for a more structured environment. The point was brought home when Joe Junior cajoled Jack into racing around the block on their bikes in opposite directions and a collision occurred, sending Jack to the hospital for twenty-eight stitches. Another time she caught the two boys in the cellar, surrounded by empty milk bottles they had purloined from the neighborhood in order to resell. She opted to transfer them from Edward Devotion School to the private Noble and Greenough Lower School (soon thereafter renamed Dexter), six blocks from home, which fielded sports teams and where "there would be after-school supervised play" until 4:45 in the afternoon.[49]

The principal of the school, Miss Myra Fiske, had interviewed the boys in the spring of 1924 and liked what she saw. She noted Jack's precocious intellect and wrote that she was "very glad that we decided to take this little John Kennedy. He is a fine chap." That fall the brothers enrolled and instantly entered an elite world, a Brahmin bastion where Catholics were rare and blacks and Jews unknown. "We were probably the first and only ones who were Catholics," Jack later reflected, which may have been an exaggeration but not by much.[50]

A well-groomed Jack in his Dexter
School picture in 1925.

Inevitably, the taunting and bullying soon followed. "Almost everybody was a Protestant," schoolmate Augustus Soule recalled. "I think there was a sort of snobbery, which the children adopted. I think that in those days the upper crust Boston families, of which there were a great number sending their children to the school, were very down on the Irish. . . . To be Irish and Catholic was a real, real stigma—and when the other boys got mad at the Kennedys, they would resort to calling them Irish or Catholic." Sometimes the fists started flying. Joe, older and bigger than his brother, not to mention more pugnacious and combative, seemed to take the encounters in stride, even challenging older boys to fight on occasion. Jack took a different tack, betting on his brother to win the scraps using a popular schoolyard currency. Soule again:

> In those days, marbles: that was the big thing. You always carried a little bag of marbles in your pants pocket. And I can remember going back to my father and saying, "I need some more marbles."
> "What happened to the ones you had?" he'd ask.
> "Well, I lost them all in a bet."
> "With whom?"
> "I bet with Jack Kennedy."
> It's an indelible memory I have: Joe fighting and getting all bloody, and Jack going around, betting marbles very quietly. To my mind that illustrates how completely different the two brothers were![51]

For all the ostracism they suffered, however, both Joe and Jack liked the school. They played sports and eventually earned starting slots on the football team, with Joe as a bruising fullback and Jack as the lithe and scrappy quarterback.[52] They had dedicated and able teachers. Miss Fiske, much beloved by the students, would gather them all together for assembly each morning, and they would recite in unison the school motto ("Our best today, better tomorrow"), followed by Lincoln's Gettysburg Address or his second inaugural address, or a passage from literature or the Bible.[53]

With his lively wit and natural interest in history, Jack became Miss Fiske's special pet. One day he asked her to take him to the historic sites of Lexington and Concord, and offered to get his father's Rolls-Royce for the occasion. "I don't think Rose came," Fiske recalled many years later. "All the boys turned out to see the famous Rolls-Royce. And when it came it was a dilapidated old Ford! Jack never got over how the other boys hooted him—something had happened to the Rolls-Royce!"[54]

V

That Jack could even offer the luxury automobile for an after-school excursion says something about the family's finances at mid-decade. In actuality, Joseph P. Kennedy owned not one Rolls but two, and his fortune was growing by the day. After leaving Hayden, Stone at the start of 1923 (though highly successful at the firm, he felt certain, no doubt rightly,

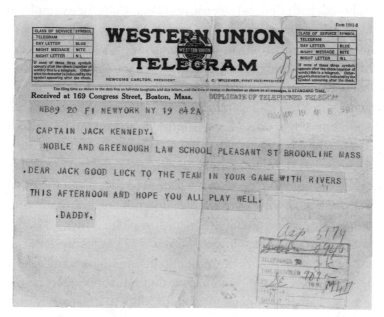

Telegram to "Captain Jack Kennedy" from his father, May 19, 1926, prior to a Dexter football game. The message reads: "Dear Jack, good luck to the team in your game with Rivers this afternoon, and hope you all play well. Daddy."

that as an Irish Catholic he would never make partner), he had struck out on his own, down the hall from his old firm, on Milk Street in Boston's financial district, behind a door marked "Joseph P. Kennedy, Banker." At thirty-four, he was in business for himself, with only Eddie Moore, his genial and devoted factotum, and accountant E. B. Derr on his staff. "It's so easy to make money in this market," Kennedy told a Harvard friend. "We'd better get it before they pass a law against it."[55]

And so he did. His timing was exquisite, as the economy was emerging full-force out of the postwar doldrums. Farmers struggled and would do so through the end of the decade, but the automobile industry zoomed ahead and the manufacturing sector gained enormously from new technologies—electric motors, aluminum, synthetic materials—that allowed for a proliferation of new consumer goods. The expansion of the economy also gave Americans more discretionary income to spend on the new appliances, as well as on restaurant meals, beauty products, and movies. By the late 1920s, the United States produced nearly half of the world's industrial goods and ranked first among exporters—by 1929, it was responsible for nearly one-sixth of global exports. One in every five Americans now had a car. More and more American companies were looking abroad, with General Electric and Coca-Cola, for example, investing heavily in Germany and with several U.S. firms challenging British companies for control of Middle East petroleum.[56]

To a degree fully evident only after the fact, the Great War had altered the global power balance as the United States challenged a prostrate and divided Europe for world leadership. During the course of the war, financial predominance had crossed the Atlantic from London to New York as Europe's international debts skyrocketed and the United States became the world's largest creditor nation. By the time the shooting stopped, America's gross domestic product was equal to that of all the European states together. Old World leaders took due notice, and oriented themselves to the prospect of a new American-led global order. In the geopolitical arena, however, Washington punched below its weight, and the postwar peacemaking effort proved difficult—the bitter and protracted battle between Woodrow Wilson and his domestic opponents resulted in the Senate's rejecting American membership in the newly founded League of Nations. The result preserved the notion (artificial, it would turn out) of a Euro-centered world, and cheered those—like Joseph Kennedy—who wanted the United States to stay out of foreign political entanglements, out of fear that they would encroach on American sovereignty and threaten its way of life. Even many of those who wanted U.S. membership in the League took the defeat in stride, seeing it as a minor bump on the road to growth and prosperity.[57]

Wall Street reflected the growing popular optimism, though the boom market was still some years off when Joseph Kennedy established his business. Under Galen Stone's tutelage, he had learned to use inside information to minimize risk and maximize return; with his lack of sentiment and skill with numbers, he became savvy at market schemes that, while then still legal, were considered by many to be disreputable. A favorite tactic was the stock pool, in which a few traders banded together to buy shares of inactive stock and trade them back and forth to create the appearance of a boom and thus draw in less adroit investors. At an agreed-upon top price, the pool would "pull the plug" and leave the duped investors holding the bag as the stock sank back to its real market value. An elaboration of the maneuver added the option of short selling the stock on its way down.[58]

Decades later, after his sons became prominent political figures, critics would charge that much of Joe Kennedy's investment capital during the 1920s came from bootlegging operations undertaken with mob figures in what was, after all, an era of Prohibition. (The Eighteenth Amendment, ratified by the states in 1919 and put into effect the following year, prohibited the manufacturing, transportation, and sale of alcohol within the United States.[59]) No solid evidence ever accompanied these claims, and careful research by Daniel Okrent and David Nasaw has failed to turn up any.* Moreover, as Nasaw notes, the notion of Kennedy as bootlegger runs contrary to what we know about the man. He always moved cautiously in his business affairs, always placed a premium on achieving and maintaining the appearance of respectability. As an Irish Catholic outsider in the WASP financial world, he understood all too well that his opponents were watching him closely, hoping he would trip up; he needed to watch his every step. Though not averse to playing at the margins of le-

---

* The bootlegger myth may have been fed by the fact that he made a killing importing Haig & Haig and Dewar's Scotch after Prohibition's repeal, in 1933. Indeed, even before the formal repeal, Kennedy, having secured distribution rights from the British distillers, stockpiled thousands of cases of liquor in his newly created Somerset Importers warehouses. (The shipments came in legally under "medicinal" licenses issued in Washington.) (Whalen, *Founding Father,* 136.)

gality, or to taking financial risks when the situation warranted, he took care not to cross over into unlawful territory—he had too much to lose.[60]

By the end of 1925, Joseph P. Kennedy was a millionaire several times over. A vow he had made upon graduating from university—that he would make his first million by thirty-five—had been realized and surpassed.[61]

Yet he was dissatisfied. Almost on a daily basis, he received reminders that he and his family would never be fully accepted among "proper Bostonians"—even if in material terms he had long since left his patrician Harvard friends in his wake. He saw it in the treatment his boys received at school, in the barriers that would keep his daughters from being invited to the right debutante parties when they came of age, in the glass ceiling he had come up against at Hayden, Stone. When he rented a summerhouse for the family above a rock-studded beach in Cohasset, fifteen miles southeast of Boston, he found pointed evidence of Brahmin prejudice. Many of Boston's elite families passed the summers there, and made it clear they wanted nothing to do with the Irish American newcomers. The community's matrons snubbed Rose, and Joe was blackballed when he applied for membership in the Cohasset Country Club.[62]

A different man would have brushed aside the disappointments, secure in the knowledge that they paled next to his extraordinary financial accomplishments and his large and handsome family. But Joe Kennedy could never rationalize things that way. His pride wouldn't let him. Beneath his proud and bullish bravado was a deeply insecure man, whose sense of self-worth was so intimately connected to success that even minor defeats or rejections—the social slights at Harvard, the country-club snubs—left deep and lasting wounds. It didn't matter how many triumphs he achieved along the way. "Goddamn it! I was born here," he exclaimed in an interview, referring to Boston, his frustration rising with each word. "My children were born here. What the hell do I have to do to be an American?"[63]

He wanted out: wanted out of Boston's constrictive social environment, wanted to move the family to a more open and meritocratic place, a place where he was spending more and more of his time anyway—namely, New York City. Boston was "no place to bring up Catholic children," he later said. Perhaps not, but his very Catholic wife frowned at the idea. Rose Kennedy had moved schools several times as a child herself and had found the experience difficult; she didn't want the same thing for her kids. And Boston was her town. She cherished its rich history, its status as the cradle of the American Revolution, and she knew her way around its landmarks as few others did. But her husband persisted, and it was her habit to defer to him on matters of consequence. ("The architect of our lives," she revealingly called him.) She found herself softening. She realized she liked Manhattan on her visits there to see Joe, and enjoyed the Broadway shows they took in. When an outbreak of poliomyelitis—the same disease that crippled Franklin Roosevelt in 1921—broke out in Massachusetts in September 1927, and the Dexter School announced it would not reopen before October, Rose took it as a sign and relented: New York it would be.[64]

On September 27, 1927, the Kennedy family, numbering nine strong and traveling in a specially hired railway car, made its way south to Riverdale, a leafy part of the Bronx overlooking the Hudson River. There they settled in a rented stucco house at the corner of Independence Avenue and 252nd Street. Not far away stood the Wave Hill estate, once lived in by both Mark Twain and Theodore Roosevelt. Rose had advocated for Riverdale because it resembled Brookline in key respects: a suburb with excellent schools that were within walking distance of home. On September 28, the day after their arrival, the school-age kids enrolled at the private, nonsectarian Riverdale Country School.[65]

VI

Perhaps Rose Kennedy had one additional motivation in agreeing to the move: she hoped she and the children would see more of Joe, who was increasingly ensconced in the New York financial world. It was not to be. Barely had they settled in when her husband began spending much of his time in Hollywood, to pursue a growing side business in the movies. Years before, while still president of Columbia Trust, Kennedy had remarked to an associate, "We must get into the picture business. This is a new industry and a gold mine." By early 1920, while at Hayden, Stone, he'd had a hand in a variety of production and distribution efforts, and in short order had gained control of a chain of thirty-one New England theaters. His timing, again, was superb: in total capital investment, the motion picture industry was fast becoming one of the nation's largest. Some twenty thousand theaters dotted the country, ranging from the modest small-town venue with a hundred seats to the luxurious urban "picture palaces," with their baroque lobbies and a thousand or more padded seats. In 1922, movies drew some forty million viewers weekly; by 1929 the number approached a hundred million—this at a time when the nation's population was 122 million and weekly church attendance was sixty million.[66]

Yet it struck Kennedy that it was a poorly run industry, anarchic and wasteful and lacking a structure, and tailor-made for someone like him, with an eye for numbers and for profits. In 1926 he bought a struggling company called Film Booking Offices and was soon churning out highly profitable Hollywood potboilers at the rate of two or three per month. Artistic distinction mattered not a whit—Kennedy's sole concern, as producer, was whether the film would make money. Westerns and melodramas predominated, with titles such as *The Dude Cowboy* and *Red Hot Hooves*, featuring no-name actors or over-the-hill stars. (He also tried in vain to sign baseball star Babe Ruth.) Budgets seldom exceeded $30,000.[67]

As he had with the Boston Brahmins, Kennedy expressed private contempt for Hollywood elites while at the same time compulsively seeking their acceptance. In early 1927, he hit upon the idea of bringing the top studio heads to Harvard for a lecture series on the film industry. The dean of the business school signed off, as did President A. Lawrence Lowell, and the invitations went out. Though many of the tycoons were not on speaking terms—a few were even suing each other—the prestige of speaking at the nation's leading university won them over, just as Kennedy had predicted. One after another they accepted the invitation and soon began descending on the campus, barely able to hide their awed enthusiasm. "I cannot begin to tell you how it impresses me, coming to a great college such as this to deliver a lecture, when I have never even seen the inside of one before," gushed an emotional Marcus Loew. Other giants, including Alfred Zukor and Harry Warner, spoke in similar terms. For Kennedy the endeavor was a smashing personal success that secured his standing as a leading new fixture on the Hollywood scene.[68]

Rose was aware, in broad outline, of Joe's film work (to the delight of the Kennedy children and their stupefied friends, he would screen first-run motion pictures from a projector set up in the family living room), and she assumed he would run his growing empire from New York City. And indeed, Kennedy maintained the main FBO office at 1560 Broadway, off Forty-sixth Street, in Manhattan. But more often than not he was out west, sometimes for weeks at a time. And not just for business. "In those days," film writer Cy Howard would later observe,

> Hollywood was the perfect place for an Eastern banker to have an affair. Separated from the East Coast by three days on a train, there was little worry of the accidental encounter between a wife and a mistress in a restaurant or on a street corner. Beyond that, there was the nature of the film industry, which provided dozens of Hollywood producers just like Joe with the perfect cover for spending their time with any number of beautiful actresses that just happened to work for them. You see, the film industry was actually the cover, allowing men to take their mistresses to dinners or even to parties, providing a form of legalized whoring.[69]

Kennedy took full advantage, seeing a steady stream of actresses and dancers.

In November 1927, soon after the family's move to Riverdale, Kennedy met Gloria Swanson, Hollywood's reigning screen siren and the most powerful woman in the industry. The first actress to turn down a million dollars for a role, she and her films were subjects of feverish discussion in beauty parlors and church picnics across the country. A younger, more sophisticated version of Rose—they had the same dark hair, luminous skin, and petite figures—the twenty-eight-year-old captivated Kennedy with her street smarts and vivacity and her low, sultry voice. "Together we could make millions," he assured her one night over dinner. Swanson, well aware of Kennedy's reputation as one of the shrewdest moneymen in Hollywood and taken with his energy and good looks, agreed to let him manage her financial interests, which were a mess after several years of overspending and dubious investing.[70]

Soon they became lovers. In her memoirs, Swanson recalled the first time they had sex, in a Palm Beach, Florida, hotel in February 1928 (just as Rose Kennedy was preparing to give birth to daughter Jean back in Boston). "Since his kiss on the train, I had known this would happen. And I knew, as I lay there, that it would go on. Why? I thought. We were both happily married with children. . . . All arguments were useless, however. I knew perfectly well that whatever adjustments or deceits must inevitably follow, the strange man beside me, more than my husband, owned me." There followed many "intimate hours together" at Kennedy's rented house on Rodeo Drive in Beverly Hills, after which "Joe would have one of his horsemen [often the ubiquitous Eddie Moore] drive me home."[71] Mesmerized with Swanson as with no lover before, Kennedy led a split life, between his wife and family on the one hand, and his Hollywood megastar, the ultimate trophy mistress, on the other. Not completely split, however—Swanson and her husband on one occasion traveled with Rose and Joe in Europe (the two women shopped together at the exclusive Paris couturier Lucien Lelong), and she was a guest of the Kennedy family in their home.[72]

Swanson tried to resist the European excursion, but it was pointless. "When his mind was made up," she later wrote, "there was not a big enough lever in the world to move him. I might argue all day, but I knew he would only out-argue me." So she agreed to "throw a shawl over my scarlet letter and have tea with his wife and my husband and the vicar, doubtless, not to mention the press."[73]

Rose Kennedy would always deny that her husband had anything other than a professional relationship with Swanson. According to Eunice Kennedy Shriver, her mother didn't even hear rumors about the affair until the 1960s, and then waved them off. The claim of ignorance seems hard to believe. More likely, Rose knew about the romance while it was going on but chose to suppress it, to pretend it wasn't there. "Mrs. Kennedy had this amazing knack for shutting out anything she did not want to know or face or deal with, and conversely of actually believing what she wanted to believe," an employee in the household recalled. Perhaps some small part of Rose even condoned the relationship, or at least understood it, in view of what appears to have been her highly circumscribed view of what constituted proper sexual behavior for a devout Catholic—in essence, outside of procreation, intercourse should be sharply limited, in both frequency and duration—and her knowledge that it conflicted with her husband's sex drive.[74]

For his part, Joe Kennedy knew that his philandering was wrong, that adultery was contrary to God's word. But he also believed in confession and the forgiveness of sins. So he went on straying from the marriage bed. Obsessively focused on winning, on conquest, he always wanted more, more, more—in all areas of life. A journalist who knew him speculated that for Kennedy, a mistress was "another thing that a rich man had—like caviar. It wasn't sex, it was part of the image . . . his idea of manliness."[75]

Never, it seems, did Kennedy seriously consider leaving Rose for another woman, not even for Gloria Swanson. The actress hints in her memoirs that he contemplated forsaking Rose for her, but the notion is far-fetched.[76] She was a huge catch, one of the most alluring women in the entire world, and dating her gave Kennedy prestige in Hollywood and—even more so—among his astonished Harvard friends. But he spent less time with her than he might have if the affair were as important to him as Swanson wanted it to be. For Kennedy, family was ultimately sacrosanct, even if he often had an odd and callous way of showing it. His preferred arrangement, common enough among men of his station, was having a wife at home and girlfriends away from home. By the fall of 1929 the affair had run its course, and Kennedy was readying to leave Hollywood and the film business behind—$5 million richer, thirty pounds lighter, and fighting an ulcer.[77]

He needed to rein himself in, he understood, needed to return to the more buttoned-up Northeast, to his wife and kids. Earlier in 1929, P. J. Kennedy had become deathly ill, at age seventy-one. (Mary Augusta had died in 1923.) Joe had spent several days by his father's bedside in Boston in the final days; when P. J. seemed to rally, the son took it as a sign he could return to California, only for death to come on May 18. Nor did he travel back from Hollywood for the funeral (he sent Rose and Joe Junior in his place), a decision he regretted instantly. Never the introspective sort, Kennedy nonetheless understood that, having turned forty and with his father now gone, he needed to get his priorities in order, lest he lose his family. He had to be home, and home was not the wild west of glitzy young Southern California.[78]

And besides, even with his gargantuan work ethic, Kennedy found it hard to give sufficient attention from Los Angeles to the chattering stock ticker in New York. Now, as he gradually transitioned back to the East, he could afford to do that. He sensed big things were in the offing on Wall Street and made a major decision, one that went against the crowd and the consensus of expert opinion: he got out. Guy Currier, a well-connected and flamboyant lawyer to whom Kennedy often turned for advice, had warned him that the stock market seemed inflated, edgy, precarious, the danger signs flashing all around. Kennedy, predisposed toward pessimism, agreed, and he systematically went about liquidating much of his vast portfolio, even as the bankers and industrialists and traders around him stayed bullish. When prices began falling in September 1929, he stood at a safe distance. He remained there when the bottom fell out on October 29, Black Tuesday.[79]

One of Kennedy's Harvard classmates, historian Frederick Lewis Allen, captured the moment in his classic work *Only Yesterday:*

> The big gong had hardly sounded in the great hall of the Exchange at ten o'clock Tuesday morning before the storm broke out in full force. Huge blocks of stock were thrown upon the market for what they would bring. Five thousand shares, ten thousand shares appeared at a time on the laboring ticker at fearful recessions in price. Not only were innumerable small traders being sold out, but big ones, too, protagonists of the new economic era who a few weeks before had counted themselves millionaires. Again and again the specialist in a stock would find himself surrounded by brokers fighting to sell—and nobody at all even thinking of buying.[80]

VII

It is tempting to see the Kennedy marriage in this period as little more than an elaborate masquerade, or at best as a sterile collaboration between two people who felt little for each other but were stolidly committed to raising successful children. The temptation should be resisted. If (as some authors assert) the Kennedys' relationship had become largely sexless by the end of the decade, and if they kept aspects of their emotional lives from each other, it is also true that they maintained a strong bond. The letters between them (especially those from Joe) attest to that fact. There was affection in their long talks about their children, and comfort in their shared history and rituals. Joe was proud of Rose as a dedicated mother and as an intelligent and talented wife, and she admired and treasured his deep commitment to the kids' welfare and his interest in their many activities and accomplishments.[81]

Still, the tensions in the marriage in the late 1920s were real enough, visible not only to the household staff but to the older children as well, who knew full well that their father carried on with other women. Joe's long absences in California (and Palm Beach, where he liked to spend time in winter), combined with Rose's own weeks-long travels, meant that for significant stretches, the Kennedy children had to make do with surrogate parents, whether in the form of the staff or the ever loyal Eddie and Mary Moore. Did young Jack resent the marital discord in this period, and his mother's absences? The record is unclear, but surely he did, at least to a degree.[82] Any child would. Some later authors would see in Rose's trips proof of her emotional sterility and lack of maternal love, and of her "managerial" approach to parenting. But though it's true that she always withheld a part of herself, did not let motherhood consume her, and at times stood slightly apart from the whirlwind of family activity, can one really blame her? She had eight children, with one more to come, and was married to a serial adulterer, one who thought nothing of occasionally bringing a mistress home for dinner. Maintaining a separate identity was for her a form of self-preservation. To numerous contemporary observers, including her son Jack, Rose was the glue that held the family together. As one close friend told a biographer, "Joe provided the fire in the family, but Rose provided the steel, and still does."[83]

Decades later, Jack offered a revealing and generous summation of his mother: "She was a little removed and still is, which I think is the only way to survive when you have nine children. I thought she was a very model mother for a big family."[84]

Whatever the strains he felt at home after the move to New York, Jack appears to have adjusted reasonably well to the new surroundings, and to Riverdale Country School. His teachers described him as bright, confident, and personable, while friends remembered him as popular, athletic, and girl crazy. In sixth grade, Jack received excellent grades in his history bimonthly reports (with scores consistently in the nineties) and won the school's commencement prize for best composition. "Far be it from the Kennedys to spoil their children," Harold Klue, one of his social studies teachers, recalled. "They were taught to do for themselves and think for themselves."[85]

Jack, for one, certainly didn't think he was being spoiled. Although at one time or another all of the Kennedy kids hit their father up for an increased weekly allowance, no effort would be quite as stylish as Jack's "Plea for a Raise," issued to "My Mr. J. P. Kennedy" sometime during the first year in New York, and invoking a phrase from I Corinthians 13:

My recent allowance is 40¢. This I used for aeroplanes and other playthings of childhood but now I am a scout and I put away my childish things. Before I would spend 20¢ of my ¢.40 allowance and in five minutes I would have empty pockets and nothing to gain and 20¢ to lose. When I am a scout I have to buy canteens, haversacks, blankets, searchlidgs [sic], ponchos, things that will last for years . . . and so I put in my plea for a raise of thirty cents for me to buy scout things and pay my own way more around.[86]

The appeal worked: "Mr. J. P. Kennedy" granted the increase.

In the seventh grade, Jack's grades slipped into the average range. "Creditable," his generous headmaster noted of his overall performance, while a classmate recalled that Jack's main concern that year seemed to be "getting a date for the Saturday afternoon movie."[87] (Like many twelve-year-old boys, he was shy around girls—according to family lore, he could barely bring himself to speak to them when they started calling the house.) Perhaps, too, the disruption caused by another move affected his academic performance: in May 1929 the family moved to a twelve-room colonial on Pondfield Road in Bronxville, a one-square-mile village close to Riverdale. Central Manhattan was fifteen miles to the south. Joe paid $250,000 for the mansion (about $3.7 million today), named Crown-lands, which sat on six acres of lush lawns and boasted a grass tennis court, a five-car garage, and gardener's as well as chauffeur's cottages. Joe Junior, Jack, and eventually Bobby rode the bus to school in Riverdale, while the girls attended the public Bronxville School.

Crownlands, however, was not Joe's most important home purchase of the period. After their humiliating snubbing in Cohasset, the family had spent several summers fifty miles to the south, in Hyannis Port, on the Cape Cod peninsula. A small hamlet next to the larger town of Hyannis, Hyannis Port comprised about a hundred well-built, roomy, shingled or clapboard houses, separated from one another by manicured hedges or low stone walls. It was not yet the fashionable place it would become, and was far less of a summer destination for Boston's elites than Cohasset or Bar Harbor or Newport, but it nevertheless had several things in its favor: good railway access, sandy beaches, a Catholic church, a golf club that was willing to accept Joe Kennedy as a member, and a yacht club where Joe Junior and Jack, and the other children as they grew older, could learn to sail and race. Best of all, Hyannis Port contained no concentration of "proper Bostonians" who would look down their noses at the upstart Irish Catholic Kennedys. And it gave

Rose the Massachusetts anchor she desperately missed—and wanted. The family rented Malcolm Cottage, a rambling three-gabled house on Marchant Avenue, with white wooden shingles and black shutters, wide porches, two and a half acres of sloping lawn where the kids could play, a tennis court, and a private beach with a superb view of Nantucket Sound. A breakwater poked out to the left to protect against the battering of the ocean waves.

In 1928, Joe purchased the property in his and Rose's names and immediately commissioned an addition that more or less doubled the home's size and gave them fifteen rooms and nine baths, plus an RCA sound theater (unheard of in a private residence at the time) in the basement. It would become, more than any other residence, what the Kennedys meant when they spoke of "home," the place where Joe, newly returned to the

Eight little Kennedys in a row: Jean, Bobby, Pat, Eunice, Kathleen, Rosemary, Jack, and Joe Junior, in Hyannis Port, August 1928.

East Coast, would, during days of ceaseless activity, set about molding his children.[88]

For the two oldest boys in particular, Hyannis Port would take on far more meaning than the Bronxville house ever would. For their days of living at home during the academic year were rapidly coming to a close. Boarding school beckoned.

THREE

SECOND SON

They were born less than two years apart, and before all the others. And they were boys in a male-centered household. Just as their father and their grandfathers had held privileged perches in their own homes growing up, so Joe Junior and Jack had pride of place among their siblings. But they were not equals. Joe Junior, or Young Joe, as he was sometimes called, held the position of primacy as the eldest. In his facial features and dark hair he was a Fitzgerald, but in physique and temperament he resembled his father—rugged and combative, gregarious and dynamic, with a captivating smile, a hot temper, and a cocksure, competitive spirit, in contrast to the quieter, more introspective, more Rose-like Jack. Aware from an early age that, as the first son, he had a special burden as the bearer of the family's aspirations, Joe exuded a sense of responsibility that made him seem older than his years. Earnest and goal-oriented, he was determined to live up to the exacting standards his father and mother set for him.

If Young Joe had any doubts about his standing in the family, his parents wiped them away. The father saw him as an extension of himself, while Rose determined early on that her hearty and handsome firstborn was the son destined for greatness. For a long time it was inconceivable to either parent that their sickly second son could be as smart as, or even smarter than, his brother, never mind that the most cursory look at their respective letters home from school would suggest as much. (In an interview half a century later, Rose acknowledged that testing had indicated Jack had the higher IQ, but she said she didn't believe it, either at the time of the test or subsequently.[1]) When Joe Junior was little, author Doris Kearns Goodwin has written, mother and father would break into radiant smiles at the mere sound of his voice calling or talking. "From all accounts, this was clearly a child of love. Emotions resonated between young Joe and his parents that none of the others would ever know, that none of the others would ever forget."[2]

As he grew older, Joe Junior would assume the role of paternal stand-in during Joe Senior's many absences. He did not hesitate to dole out discipline. "It was not the father they were afraid of," said one family acquaintance, "it was Joe Junior. The real reason they didn't sneak a smoke here and there was that they were afraid he would find out and beat the hell out of them." But he could be loving and kind as well, patiently teaching the younger kids on the athletic field and in the pool. It meant the world: when Joe came home from school, it was not uncommon to see one or more of the younger children running to give him a hug and a kiss as if he were their father and not their brother. To little Bobby he became a hero figure. "My brother Joe took the greatest interest in us," Bobby later said. "He taught us to sail, to swim, to play football and baseball."[3]

The closeness between father and son was evident at the dinner table. More than mere meals, the Kennedy family suppers were seminars, in which Joe Senior quizzed his male progeny on the great international and domestic issues of the day. (Money and business were the only taboo subjects: "Big businessmen are the most overrated men in the country. Here I am, a boy from East Boston, and I took 'em. So don't be impressed.") Initially, he directed his questions largely to his eldest son, who more often than not parroted the father's views; when Jack became old enough, he, too, was invited to participate, though usually only after his brother had spoken. "What do you think, Jack?" the father would say. "Give us your opinion." Later, Bobby entered the mix. In this chauvinist culture, the girls were expected to listen respectfully while father and sons engaged, although Kirk LeMoyne "Lem" Billings, Jack's closest friend and a frequent dinner guest, recalled that Kathleen (or "Kick" as everyone but her

Jack and Joe Junior in their Sunday best, Brookline, 1919.

mother called her), who was "bright and on the ball" and "more like Jack in many ways," regularly joined the conversation.[4] When Joe Senior was out of town, Rose led the discussion, often from a prepared list of questions with an emphasis on literature and history, and again directing queries first at the two older boys:

"There are enormous dust storms sweeping through the Great Plains. Those poor people are breathing in dust and soot. What would you do if you were in their situation?"

"Poor Amelia Earhart is still missing. It's been weeks. It seems impossible they haven't found her. Where do you think she could be, children?"[5]

The meals could be tense times for friends of the children who were invited to stay. Would Mr. or Mrs. Kennedy turn to them to request a penetrating reflection? What if they didn't understand the question, or didn't know the first thing about the topic under discussion? One such friend, Harry Fowler, had come to the home with the illusion that summer was for fun and relaxation. "My lord, this is a nice summer afternoon," he remembered thinking as he sat with the family at lunch. "What in the hell is Mrs. Kennedy doing anyway?"[6]

In truth, the pals needn't have worried about being called on; they were nonplayers in these seminars. Mr. Kennedy in particular made clear that he was interested only in what his own sons had to say. His concern was molding them into the young men he wanted them to be; their friends were merely a distraction. When one of Jack's schoolmates, new to the experience, made the mistake of asking a question, he was answered "rather curtly, as though [Mr. Kennedy] did not want to be bothered." By contrast, any query from his sons, no matter how inconsequential, would elicit from the father a full and expansive answer, and often a return question.[7]

If the visitors begrudged the dismissive treatment, they also frequently remarked on Joseph Kennedy's devotion to his children's welfare and his commitment to parenting. More than most fathers of his generation, who tended to be remote figures in their households, Kennedy was deeply involved in child-rearing, especially after his return from Hollywood.[8] In contrast to the more emotionally distant Rose, Joe was tactile and warm—Jean, number eight in the birth order, later referred to him as "cozy." He almost never talked down to the kids, and was quick to forgive when they did wrong, quick to accept and move on when they failed to live up to his expectations. All the same, he didn't spoil them. Even when he was away on business trips, the children sensed they were on his mind as he penned innumerable letters, encouraging them, guiding them, offering them tips on self-improvement, but seldom trying to force on them a particular career choice or life philosophy. Or at least not fully—because his own heroes were not artists or poets or philosophers but men of action, Kennedy took it for granted that his children would likewise gravitate in that direction. Above all, he preached that Kennedys always stood together, come what may—the family against the world. The kids, for their part, adored him and talked of him constantly. When he arrived home, they crowded around the door to greet him. When they had problems, they usually consulted him before their mother.[9]

"He was never abusive, never wounding toward any of his children, but he had a way of letting us know exactly what he expected of us," wrote Edward (known to all as Teddy and later Ted), the youngest, in his affecting 2009 memoir *True Compass*. In one conversation, the father used phrasing "so concise and vivid" that his son could still recall the exact words sixty-five years later: "You can have a serious life or a nonserious life, Teddy. I'll still love you whichever choice you make. But if you decide to have a nonserious life, I won't have much time for you. You make up your own mind. There are too many children here who are doing things that are interesting for me to do much with you." Never, Ted emphasized, was his father's love for him in question: "We knew that we could always come home, that we could make mistakes, get defeated, but when all was said and done, we would be respected and appreciated at home."[10]

Jack grasped that Joe Junior's primogeniture gave him a stature within the brood that he himself could never attain. Yet he chafed against it just the same. He would have understood, if not entirely accepted with regard to his own case, psychologist Alfred Adler's comment on the drama of birth order: "The mood of the second-born is comparable to the envy of the dispossessed with the prevailing feeling of having been slighted. His goal may be placed so high that he will suffer from it for the rest of his life, and his inner harmony be destroyed in consequence. This was well expressed by a little boy of four, who cried out, weeping, 'I am so unhappy because I can never be as old as my brother.'" Henry James, whose age gap with his older brother, William, was similar to Jack's vis-à-vis Joe, wrote that William "had gained such an advantage of me in his sixteen months' experience of the world before mine began that I never for all the time of childhood and youth in the least caught up with him or overtook him."[11]

Alone among the siblings, Jack tried to challenge Young Joe's primacy. Though weaker and smaller, he was canny enough to constitute a threat in his brother's eyes, even if he seldom got the upper hand in their physical encounters. There were fierce fights on the living room floor that left the younger kids cowering in terror or running upstairs. (Bobby would be especially distraught, crying, his hands over his ears.) Invariably, Jack ended up pinned and humiliated. They would go toe-to-toe on the athletic field, where Joe's greater size and strength usually overcame Jack's fortitude and physical coordination. Frequently outgunned, Jack would utilize the classic weapons of the weak: cunning and audacity. Years later,

Rose recalled a typical incident in Hyannis Port in which Jack, having finished his dessert, swiped Joe's from his plate and took off running, stuffing it in his mouth with his brother in hot pursuit, before he was finally forced to jump into the water to avoid being caught and pummeled, knowing what awaited him when he got out.[12]

When asked decades afterwards if anything had really troubled him in childhood, Jack could think of only one thing: his big brother. "He had a pugnacious personality," he said of Joe. "Later on it smoothed out but it was a problem in my boyhood."[13]

Far from working to ease the rivalry between his sons, Joe Senior stoked it. "Remember that Jack is practicing at the piano each day an hour and studying from one-half to three-quarters of an hour on his books so that he is really spending more time than you are," he wrote the older boy in July 1926.[14] When the two of them fought, he refused to intercede, viewing the competition, even when physical, as instilling toughness they would need in spades as they made their way in the world.

II

Did Jack resent the favoritism his parents showed toward his brother? One guesses he did, at least somewhat. According to Lem Billings, however, Jack found it fairly easy to forgive the partiality, because he never felt unfairly treated and because he treasured the space and relative anonymity his status as the second son provided. It allowed him to develop his natural inquisitiveness, to lose himself in his reading and thereby escape, if only momentarily, the fever-pitched intensity of life in the Kennedy family. Confident that he matched or outshone his older brother in mental ability, and confined to his bed by frequent maladies, Jack cultivated an intellectual prowess that no one else in the family really had, and this proved irritating to Joe Junior, who expected to be the best in everything.[15]

Words and their meanings interested Jack. He was the only one in the family, his sister Eunice said, "who looked things up," the one who "did the best on all the intellectual things and sort of monopolized them." Rose remembered that "he gobbled books," and "not necessarily the ones I had so thoughtfully chosen for him from the PTA- and library-approved lists." More than any of his siblings, he internalized his mother's mantra that reading constituted "the most important instrument of knowledge." Biography, history, tales of adventure and chivalry—these were his genres, as he devoured Robert Louis Stevenson and Sir Walter Scott and read and reread Macaulay's *Lays of Ancient Rome*. The cadences of historical prose appealed to him, and he had a first-rate memory of what he read, often able to recall scenes and quotations with astonishing accuracy, even decades later. "He had a strong romantic and idealistic streak," Rose said. "In fact, he was inclined to be somewhat of a dreamer. I often had the feeling his mind was only half occupied with the subject at hand, such as doing his arithmetic homework or picking his clothes up off the floor, and the rest of his thoughts were far away weaving daydreams. . . . I remember him in his boyhood reading and rereading his copy of *King Arthur and the Round Table*."[16]

One also detects from an early point a sense of ironic self-awareness and detachment concerning the Kennedy clan's peculiarities that his older brother entirely lacked. Jack could be at once of the family and apart from it. In a family that prized punctuality, he was habitually late. Notwithstanding his mother's obsessive focus on order and decorum, he was sloppy, forgetful, irreverent—and grew more so over time. In the winter of 1932, when two friends picked him up from the Bronxville train station, he remarked sardonically, "I want to stop by the house for a minute, and check the nursery and see if there's anybody new in the family." He came out and exclaimed, "By God, there is!" (It was Teddy, born on February 22.)[17]

As Rose later put it, from boyhood on, Jack "thought his own thoughts, did things his own way, and somehow just didn't fit any pattern. Now and then, fairly often in fact, that distressed me, since I thought I knew what was best. But at the same time that I was taken aback, I was enchanted and amused. He was a funny little boy, and he said things in such an original, vivid way." At least compared with his three brothers, a friend noted, Jack was "neither pushy nor calculating." Another acquaintance expanded on the point, describing Jack as "a loner, a self-contained person. It may be that in the intensely competitive family situation he withdrew somewhat into himself, learned to keep his own counsel, and put a layer of insulation between himself and other people."[18]

"Unquestionably," historian Herbert Parmet would write, "the introspective second son was the one who resembled his father least of all."[19]

Yet Jack was also plainly devoted to his family, and fiercely loyal. He cared about what his parents thought, and during his prep school years cherished his vacation visits home. His father was now around much more, having left Hollywood behind, and his parents' marriage seemed stronger, even with his continued serial womanizing. (Rose Kennedy in her memoirs describes the early 1930s as a golden time, as she and Joe spent long hours with each other, walking hand in hand along the shore at the Cape or through the Bronxville woodlands.) Meanwhile, Jack formed a special bond with Kick, three years younger, who possessed a quick, self-deprecating sense of humor much like his own (Joe Junior's was more biting and sarcastic) and whose radiant charm and free-spiritedness he found enchanting. He enjoyed spending time with his other younger siblings as well—upon Teddy's birth he asked his parents if he could be named the godfather, and was granted his wish. (He had less luck with another suggestion: that the boy be named George Washington Kennedy, since he shared a birthday with the first president.) When Teddy got a little older, it was Jack who taught him how to ride a bicycle and sail.[20]

What's more, for all the differences with Young Joe and all the intense competition between them, the two brothers shared a common vitality and mutual affection. From an early age they were each other's number-one playmate, and they had innumerable adventures together—in Brookline, in New York, in Hyannis Port, and later in prep school and college.* From his brother Jack learned how to sail—how to be an effective crewman, how to shift ballast in a jib, how to secure the advantage in tight races. Joe Senior recalled that his two oldest boys "were out in sailboats alone here in Hyannis Port when they were so small you couldn't see their heads. It looked from shore as if the boats were empty." The boys christened their first boat the *Rose Elizabeth*, after their mother, and spent endless hours tinkering with it and learning to sail it with consummate skill and speed. As competitive as they could be with each other, they fought much more fiercely as a team against outsiders, whether on the sporting field or in the schoolyard.[21]

---

* One escapade didn't go quite as planned. Joe and Jack determined that the roof of the Bronxville home would be ideal as a jumping-off point for a parachutist. They made a parachute from sheets and ropes and generously invited the son of the family chauffeur to share in the fun. They helped him on with the chute, then helped him off the ledge. Fortunately, a bad ankle sprain was the only damage.

A letter from Jack to his mother on Choate letterhead,
February 1932. The P.S. reads: "Can I be Godfather to the baby."

Years later Jack would write:

I have always felt that Joe achieved his greatest success as the oldest
brother. Very early in life he acquired a sense of responsibility
towards his brothers and sisters and I do not think that he ever forgot it. . . . He would spend long hours throwing a football with
Bobby, swimming with Teddy and teaching the younger girls how to
sail. . . . I think that if the Kennedy children amount to anything
now or ever amount to anything, it will be due more to Joe's behavior and his constant example than to any other factor. He made the
task of bringing up a large family immeasurably easier for my father
and mother for what they taught him, he passed on to us and their
teachings were not diluted through him but strengthened.[22]

Those parental teachings centered on the importance of education, of avoiding idleness, of respecting public service, of loyalty to family. But more than anything, they were about winning. The point, Joe Senior insisted time and again, was not to play well, to compete for the sake of competing, but to defeat all comers, to secure the top prize. Even good sportsmanship paled in comparison. "We want no losers around here, only winners," he proclaimed. From the time the children were six or seven years old, Joe and Rose entered them in swimming and sailing races, taking care to put them in different categories so they didn't have to race each other. Always, Joe exhorted them to reach the finish line first. "The thing he always kept telling us was that coming in second was just no good," remarked Eunice, who became an excellent sailor and all-around athlete. "The important thing was to win—don't come in second or third, that doesn't count, but win, win, win." Small wonder that the Kennedys took on the reputation within the Hyannis community of being graceless competitors, of being willing to do anything to prevail. Though not an accomplished sailor himself, Joe Senior would follow his kids' boats and make note of deficiencies he saw in performance or effort. Any slacker would be subjected to a stern talking-to at dinner in front of the family and sent in disgrace to eat alone in the kitchen.[23]

"My husband was quite a strict father," Rose later acknowledged. "He liked the boys to win at sports and everything they tried. If they didn't win, he would discuss their failure with them, but he did not have much patience with the loser."[24]

One of Jack's friends, Paul Chase, remembered seeing—and hearing— Mr. Kennedy's win-at-all-costs approach up close. "Several times, Jack asked me to crew for him when he could not find anyone else. Once we lost badly and caught a half-hour lecture from the old man on our return to shore. He said he had watched the race and that he was disgusted with both of us. There was no sense, he claimed, in going into a race unless you did your damnedest to win, an endeavor at which we had failed miserably. He was really angry with us."[25]

Chase's anecdote hints at the possibility of a more benign assessment of Joe Kennedy's relentlessness: that it was less about winning than about expending maximum effort in the attempt. The Kennedy kids were expected to always work harder than anyone, Robert Kennedy later wrote, even if others in the competition were more talented. " 'After you have done the best you can,' he used to say, 'the hell with it.' "[26]

The house in Hyannis Port.

Visitors to the Hyannis Port home marveled at the sheer orchestration of daytime activity. Here the summers were not holidays, filled with lassitude and soaking in the sun. Joe could not abide his offspring lounging around, even briefly, and he insisted on a packed schedule. His wife felt the same. Each evening, she posted a schedule of events for the following day—moving from tennis to golf to swimming to sailing, sometimes with professional instructors alongside. On a bulletin board next to the dining room she pinned articles from magazines and newspapers that she wanted her kids to read, and she scattered special lamps throughout the house to encourage reading.* Friday night was movie night in the basement, with its twenty-seven-seat theater. Saturdays were taken up with more sporting activities, and another movie or a game of charades after dinner. The younger children, supervised by a nurse, were forbidden from riding their bikes off the property; the older ones, watched over by a governess, were expected to be in the house when the lights went on at dusk. All had to be seated at the dining table five minutes before mealtimes, with

* Always a strict grammarian and champion of decorous speech, Rose hoped that through extensive reading her children would learn the essential mechanics of written expression. She was disappointed in the results: "To my distress most of them seemed to be afflicted with deafness about the proper uses of 'who' and 'whom,' 'I' and 'me,' 'shall' and 'will,' 'may' and 'can.' They split infinitives with abandon, and put in commas or left them out as the spirit (an evil spirit) moved them, and they ended sentences with prepositions." (RK, *Times to Remember*, 113.)

dinner served promptly at 7:15 each evening. Rose had clocks placed in each room so no one would be late.[27]

Though the Kennedys were one of the richest families in America, guests encountered few signs of ostentatious wealth or conspicuous consumption. Quite the contrary: "We each had a napkin," Teddy later related, "and that napkin was expected to last the entire week. If it suffered any stains—which of course is what napkins are designed to do—too bad." The furniture in the house was comfortable but mostly ordinary; the bicycles and sporting equipment were often weathered and beaten, meant to be used until they fell apart. On birthdays the children could expect to receive no more than one or two gifts, none of them extravagant. Their weekly allowances were kept small.[28]

In subsequent years the suggestion would be made that the close-knit Kennedys practiced an insular solidarity and didn't mix much with the other families of Hyannis Port, many of them Protestants from Pittsburgh. Lem Billings, for one, didn't deny the claim, but he questioned whether anti-Catholic prejudice played much of a role. "The children were invited certainly to every party there was in Hyannis Port and there was no problem about the mixing of the Pittsburgh Protestant children and the Catholic Kennedy children," Billings said. "I know that when I used to visit the Kennedys I knew a lot of the boys and girls in Hyannis Port better than they did, because I'd been raised with them in Pittsburgh, but this didn't mean they weren't invited to whatever went on. I don't think they probably went as often as they could have, because it was a very self-sufficient family. They had everything they needed at home. They had their own movies; they had all their own athletic facilities."[29]

Always, the culture of competition dominated among the children. "Which one of us is the best looking?" visitors would be asked. "Who is the funniest?" "Whose outfit do you prefer?" Seemingly friendly "touch" football games on the family lawn would turn into fierce, bruising affairs, much to the astonishment of unsuspecting guests. The gentle pleasure of skipping stones would become competitive, as would seeing whose seashell floated out the farthest into Nantucket Sound. If the family was waiting for a car and had a few minutes to kill, someone would come up with a game to play. Even board games and charades would be hotly contested. At the ages of twelve and ten, respectively, Joe Junior and Jack started winning local sailing races, and they did not let up. Eunice would soon do the same. Patricia, for her part, became an accomplished golfer. At times, Joe Senior got into the athletic act, taking on his sons in sports in which he knew he would prevail. An excellent low-handicap golfer who regularly shot in the low and mid-eighties, he would challenge Joe and Jack and beat them every time. In tennis, too, he always won comfortably, until one day when Joe Junior, then in his mid-teens, nearly bested him. That was the end of the father-son tennis matches—Kennedy preferred to hang up his racket rather than lose to one of his boys.[30]

Years later, one weary weekend visitor outlined the "Rules for Visiting the Kennedys":

> Anticipate that each Kennedy will ask what you think of another Kennedy's (a) dress, (b) hairdo, (c) backhand, (d) latest public achievement. Be sure to answer "terrific." This should get you through dinner. Now for the football field. It's "touch," but it's murder. If you don't want to play, don't come. If you do come, play, or you'll be fed in the kitchen and no one will speak to you. Don't let the girls fool you. Even pregnant, they can make you look silly. Above all, don't suggest any plays, even if you played quarterback at school. The Kennedys have the signal-calling department sewed up, and all of them have A-pluses in leadership. . . . Run madly on every play, and make a lot of noise. Don't appear to be having too much fun, though. They'll accuse you of not taking the game seriously enough.[31]

As a philosophy of life, winning was of course problematic. On some level, Joe and Rose understood as much. Their eldest daughter, Rosemary, pretty and round-faced and sweet-natured, with a lovely smile that dimpled her cheeks, could never compete in the family's do-or-die ethos. A mere sixteen months younger than Jack, she had been slow to crawl and then to walk. Reading and writing were difficult for her—for a long time, she scrawled her letters from the right side of the page to the left. Like Joe Junior and Jack, she had entered Edward Devotion School, but at the end of kindergarten her teachers determined that she would not be promoted to first grade but would instead repeat the year. This time she passed, with a C, but the struggles went on. She couldn't balance herself on a bicycle or throw a ball or steer a sled like the others. At the dinner table, she struggled to manage a knife, so her meat was served precut. The intricacies of sailing eluded her; alone among her siblings, she did not have her own boat. Her parents consulted a stream of experts, including the head of the psychology department at Harvard and a specialist in Washington, D.C. "Each of them told me she was retarded," Rose recalled, "but what to do about her, where to send her, how to help her seemed an unanswered question. . . . I had never heard of a retarded child."[32]

For a time the parents opted for what was then an enlightened approach, in the form of what today would be called "mainstreaming." They determined Rosemary would be sent to regular school, not institutionalized in the draconian way common for the "feebleminded" (as they were then labeled) of the era. When conventional schooling proved unworkable—there were few schools in the United States then for children with special needs—they opted for homeschooling, with hired tutors and with Rose in the supervisory role. Progress was slow and fleeting. Rosemary learned to write but did not progress beyond block letters. Rose avoided using cursive in her letters to her daughter and refrained from sprinkling in French expressions when speaking to the other children, for fear of making Rosemary feel disaffected. At her insistence, Rosemary was included in most social activities, including dances at the Yacht Club, where Joe Junior and Jack, if they saw her sitting by herself, were to make sure she kept dancing, even if it cut into their own fun.[33]

Years afterwards, Rose would express guilt that her preoccupation with Rosemary may have made her neglectful of Jack, so close to his sister in age. "When his sister was born after him, it was such a shock, and I was frustrated and confused as to what I should do with her or where I could send her or where I could get advice about her, that I did spend a lot of time going to different places or having her tutored or having her physically examined or mentally examined, and I thought he might have felt neglected." She expressed no similar worry about Kathleen or Eunice, born after Rosemary, who evidently could make do with less mothering than a son could.[34]

In September 1929, not long before her eleventh birthday, Rosemary was sent away to the Devereux School, in Berwyn, Pennsylvania, which provided specialized instruction for intellectually challenged students. She struggled to adjust to being away from home, and it did not help that the school discouraged parental visits. In mid-November, her father received his first letter and replied right away. "I cannot tell you how excited and pleased I was to get your letter," he enthused. "You were a darling to write me so soon." He filled her in on family goings-on and told her that

Gloria Swanson would soon send her a letter and a photo, then nudged her to work hard in her studies: "I was very glad to see a lot of improvement in the report card, and I am sure that within the next couple of months it will be even better." It didn't happen. Though Rosemary adapted somewhat to the social environment of the school, she plateaued academically—she lacked confidence, her teachers reported, and had difficulty concentrating on any but the simplest tasks. Even elementary concepts eluded her. The parents hoped for improved performance when she returned to Devereux for a second year in 1930, and then for a third in 1931; each time they were disappointed.[35]

III

As the 1920s ended and Young Joe and Jack entered their teenage years, their father assumed a key role in their educational development, while Rose remained in charge of the girls and Bobby. Rose had wanted her sons to attend Catholic schools, but Joe thought that if they were to compete in the political world, they needed to be with boys from prominent—which meant Protestant—families. "There is nothing wrong with Catholic schools," he later said. "They're fine. But I figured the boys could get all the religion they needed in Church, and that it would be broadening for them to attend Protestant schools." Only such a school, he felt, could make his sons the kind of men he wanted them to be—and, at the same time, pave their path to Harvard.[36]

But which school should it be? Kennedy consulted widely, including with Russell Ayers, a Harvard classmate who taught history and coached baseball at Choate and who encouraged him to send his boys there. Choate was a highly respected private boarding academy, one that sent many of its graduates to the Ivy League (especially Yale) and had students from forty states and several foreign countries, but it wasn't the elite of the elite among New England prep schools.[37] The scions of New York money went there—Paul Mellon, son of Gilded Age robber baron Andrew W. Mellon, was a graduate—while the true blue-blood families sent their sons to the older and more prestigious St. Mark's, St. Paul's, or Groton. Joe Kennedy's wealth was too new, and his lineage too Irish, to be fully acceptable to these schools.[38] At Choate, the Kennedy sons were more likely to be accepted, and it had the further advantage of being closer to

Bronxville—sixty-five miles away, in Wallingford, Connecticut—than the other schools.

"My only hesitancy about doing it," Kennedy wrote C. Wardell St. John, the Choate assistant headmaster (and double cousin of the headmaster), in late April 1929, "is I realize that when the boys go away now to school, they are practically gone forever, because it is three years there and then four years at college, and you realize how little you see of them after that. I may be selfish in wanting to hold on for another year at least. . . . However I am talking the matter over with his mother and will try to come to a decision and make out the applications as you suggest." A few days later, Kennedy wrote Ayers to say, "I have definitely made up my mind to send them to Choate, provided I can get them in."[39]

That September, Joe Junior enrolled at Choate. After a rough start, he adjusted and became a model student, making up with hard work what he lacked in natural aptitude. ("Joe is better at facts than at imagination," one teacher wrote of him.) Soon he was a standout on the athletic field as well, suiting up for football, wrestling, hockey, and crew. "He has been one of the most livable boys in the whole house," his housemaster wrote at the conclusion of the spring 1930 term, "and he accepted discipline—not nearly as frequently necessary in the latter portion of the year—with more grace and manliness than any other boy."[40]

Initially, Jack was set to follow his brother and enroll in 1931, in the third form (or freshman year); then it was determined he would start a year sooner, in September 1930.[41] But then the plan changed again, likely on account of Rose's advocacy—she suspected Choate of having a Protestant bias. That fall, Jack was dispatched instead to Canterbury, an all-boys Catholic boarding school in New Milford, Connecticut, that aspired to prepare students not just for Catholic colleges but for the Ivy League.[42]

He showed up, without a uniform, on September 24, 1930, one of thirty-two new students. For the first time in his life he was on his own, in an alien, forbidding place. The campus was bleak, with nondescript buildings scattered about and a stone church at its center. The Housatonic River ran nearby. Just how Jack felt upon being deposited here instead of with his brother down the road in Wallingford is unclear; perhaps a part of him wanted to strike out alone, or imagined so. "It's a pretty good place but I was pretty homesick the first night," he acknowledged in a letter to his grandfather Honey Fitz soon after arriving. "The swimming pool is great even though the football team looks pretty bad. You have a whole lot of religion and the studies are pretty hard. The only time you can get out of here is to see the Harvard-Yale and the Army-Yale [games]. This place is freezing at night and pretty cold in the daytime." To encourage his mother, he noted in another letter, "We have chapel every morning and evening and I will be quite pius [*sic*] I guess when I get home."[43]

Soon he began suffering one malady after another—hives, fevers, lightheadedness, upset stomach, pink eye. The school infirmary became a second home. One wonders if some of these ailments were exacerbated by—if not rooted in—the shock of being away from home, by the pressure to match his brother's achievements, and by the need to live up to the Kennedy family credo, which decreed that you never gripe too much, never say you miss your parents or siblings. ("My knees are very red with white lumps of skin," he wrote in a letter home, "but I guess I will pull through.") Jack's letters detail his problems with fatigue and with keeping his weight up—he hovered around 117 pounds, not exactly brawny in a thirteen-year-old boy—and the challenges his comparatively small stature presented on the athletic field: "Football practice is pretty hard and I am the lightest fellow about on the squad. My nose my leg and other parts of my anatomy have been pushed around so much that it is beginning to be funny." Lest his parents think him weaker than his brother, he pointedly reminded them, after describing feeling dizzy and weak to the point of almost blacking out in chapel, that "Joe fainted twicc in church so I guess I will live."[44]

To his mother, Jack wrote, "I have hives, that is a sickness which everything begins to itch. My face ~~had~~ hands knees and feet. I also have a cold. Outside of that I am O.K. When ever I go out the Doc jumps ~~one~~ on me for not wearing enough all the other boys arent either." Then again, Jack added, his spelling questionable at best, some classmates had it worse: "One fellow who cracked his head to pieces and broke his collor bone sledding was one of them. They patched up his arm and then let him out two days later. He was a little fellow in the first form two days later he was down with pnemonia. They should not have let him out because he was weak and white. The other boy went to the infirmary with a slight cold and then he got pnemonia." About his eyesight, Jack added, "It has gotten worse and everything is a blur at over eight feet but if you ~~do~~ want me to wait till Easter I will if you think it best."[45]

Rose Kennedy's index cards from the fall of 1930 indicate that Jack lost weight steadily between October and early December. At her request,

Nelson Hume, the headmaster at Canterbury, arranged for the boy to be seen by a local physician named Schloss, who prescribed a special drink for weight gain. "Jack tells me that he has about finished the tonic that Dr. Schloss gave him," Hume informed Joe Kennedy in January 1931, adding that, as headmaster, he was taking a personal interest in Jack's health: "I am going to take immediate charge of the question of increasing Jack's weight myself." Increased dairy consumption was deemed to be the key, and Hume informed Mr. Kennedy that Jack would be given milk to drink all throughout the day.[46]

If such protracted ailments would send most parents today racing to the school to provide succor to their child, the Kennedys were not such parents. The record suggests that Rose and Joe paid but one visit to Canterbury during their son's time there. Few thought this all that unusual at the time (though we can note that the parents of Jack's fellow student and future brother-in-law Sargent Shriver, who did not suffer similar health problems, came to see their son on numerous weekends in the first year). Joe and Rose did write frequently to Jack, and also communicated via mail with his teachers and with the school administration.[47]

Little by little, the young teenager acclimated to campus life. Academically, he did better in some subjects than others. In English, where the class read one of his favorite authors, Sir Walter Scott, he earned his best grade, a 95. In math he scored a 93, followed by 80 in history, 78 in science, and 68 in Latin. (Foreign languages would forever be a struggle for him.)[48] One senses in his letters a restive momentum, a nascent intellectualism, and an ear for rhetoric. "We are reading *Ivanhoe* in English," he wrote his father, "and though I may not be able to remember material things such as tickets, gloves and so on I can remember things like Ivanhoe and the last time we had an exam on it I got a ninety eight." Then an elegant wrap-up: "There goes the bell and that is not just a form of finish because it really did ring." He wrote of hearing a visiting speaker give "one of the most interesting talks that I ever heard, about India," and in another letter he implored his father, one year after the Wall Street crash, to sign him up for a subscription to "Litary Digest because I did not know about the Market Slump until a long time after." He added, "Please send some golf balls."[49]

Latin class presented a special problem: "Today we had a latin test. I handed in my paper the last one and I thought he had it because I gave it to him. He was also handing out some corrected papers so he must have handed out mine because I have not seen it around and I cant convince him that I gave it to him so he gave me a zero which pulls my mark down to about 40 and so I guess my average will be very very low this month. In all my other subject after the first weeks bad start I am doing pretty well but the first week counts ⅕ so my average will be around 69 or maybe higher. What a mess!"[50]

Like other thirteen-year-old boys, Jack puzzled over the alterations to his voice. At choir practice, he thought he sounded like the family dog: "My voice must be changing, because when I go up it sounds as if Buddy is howling. I go up another note and Buddy is choking. Another note and Buddy and me have gasped our last."[51]

Then, in April, soon after spring break, came a sudden onset of crippling abdominal pains. Joe Kennedy dispatched a nurse and a surgeon to attend to him, and they soon pinpointed the cause: appendicitis. Jack underwent an appendectomy at nearby Danbury Hospital. Though it was normally a routine procedure, there were unspecified complications, and recovery proved slow. At the beginning of May it was decided that Jack would not return to school but would convalesce at home in Bronxville, with tutors paying periodic visits. He made up the missing work and passed his examinations, but the ordeal marked the end of his lone experience in a Catholic school. For his father had, in the interval, arranged for a fall transfer to Choate.[52]

IV

How Jack Kennedy felt about the decision, and about the prospect of being reunited with his hard-driving brother, is unknown, but there is no record of an objection. In any case, before he could matriculate at Choate he had to pass the qualifying examinations. He got by in math and English but failed his Latin test by eight points. He was allowed to sit for a makeup, but it meant a summer of preparation and home tutoring in Hyannis Port. The tutor, Bruce Belmore, was impressed by his pupil and wrote to Wardell St. John that Jack was "a fine chap. He will be a credit to Choate." When September rolled around, however, Jack found he had misplaced the notice telling him when to appear for the Latin exam, prompting Rose to cable the school from Hyannis. On the afternoon of October 2, 1931, Jack signed in at Choate and retook the test. This time he passed, and took his place in the third form.[53]

One imagines the scene as Jack arrived in the family's chauffeured Rolls-Royce, laden with luggage that his brother helped him carry up the stairs in Choate House, the rambling brown-shingled, three-story structure where all third-formers lived. He got his first look at the elm-shaded campus, modeled on Eton and situated in the rolling New England countryside, with playing fields, tennis courts, stables, chapel, infirmary, and library. Young Joe, one speculates, showed him around, schooling him about the culture of the place, about the social pecking order among the students, about which teachers to hope to get and which to pray to avoid. They would have eaten together in the dining hall that first evening, whereupon Joe patted his kid brother on the back and headed out in the fall evening air, back to his friends and his dorm, and Jack headed to the headmaster's home for a welcome party.

Mrs. Kennedy had by then already advised the headmaster, George St.

On the beach in Hyannis Port, September 1931. From left: Bobby, Jack, Eunice, Jean, Joe, Rose, Pat (in front of Rose), Kick, Joe Junior, and Rosemary.

John, that her younger son would need more watching than the older boy. "As a matter of fact," she said of Jack, "he hates routine work, but loves History and English—subjects which fire his imagination. Again let me thank you for your interest and patience with Jack. He has a very attractive personality—we think—but he is quite different from Joe for whom we feel you have done so much."[54]

St. John, an austere, balding pipe smoker who came from a family of teachers and farmers and had worked his way through Harvard, assured Rose early in the term that everything seemed in order. Jack, he told her, "sits at a nearby table in the Dining Hall where I look him in the eye three times a day, and he is fine." His wife, Clara, sent her own letter to Mrs. Kennedy: "Everyone likes your boy, and he is rapidly making a real place for himself in the life of the school," joining with the other third-formers in having ice cream and singing around the piano.[55]

Before long, however, the assessment would change. George St. John, exacting and pedantic, ran the school like a personal fiefdom, with strict regulations not merely for students but for their teachers, who were expected to do double duty as housemasters and live with the boys, and who had to obtain St. John's permission if they wished to marry. Everyone was under his control. He could be generous in spirit as long as his authority was not questioned, and he cared deeply for his charges. ("If a single boy is lost," he liked to say, "the school is too large by one.") A devout Episcopalian Anglophile, St. John would also remark, "We save a boy's soul at the same time we are saving his algebra," and he promised parents that the school would provide excellent teaching, rigorous exercise, and "manly discipline." To go into town required the dean's permission, and only seniors could go to the movies. The dress code was rigidly enforced—all students wore jackets and ties to class, and suits (with stiff-collared white shirts, in the style of the day) to dinner.[56]

Into this regimented, bounded environment stepped young Jack Kennedy, absentminded, untidy, casual in manner and appearance. After just a week, his housemaster, Earl "Cap" (or "Cappy") Leinbach, would write, "Jack has a pleasing personality, and is warmly received by all the boys in the house, but rules bother him a bit." There were early squabbles with the assigned roommate, Godfrey Kaufmann Jr., whose father owned *The Washington Star* and who objected to Jack's penchant for turning their shared closet into a garbage heap and leaving books strewn about the room. Leinbach had to intervene, and things improved, but the two boys continued to spar regularly—at one point they drew a white chalk line down the center of the room that neither was permitted to cross. (Even so, they regularly got in trouble for conversing long past lights-out at night—with the light still on.)

The handsome, blue-eyed Leinbach, who had been a military intelligence officer in World War I and whose beautiful southern wife all the boys fancied, took Jack under his wing and became a kind of mentor. He liked the young man's wit and vitality, while Jack was impressed by Leinbach's military courage—during the war he had apparently made a daring escape from his German captors shortly before he was to be taken out and shot. By the end of the first month Leinbach could report a "gradual improvement" in Jack's attitude, noting that "Jack found it irksome to settle down, is naturally active and impulsive, but he has responded and is now exceedingly cooperative. He is in all respects a fine citizen."[57]

Headmaster St. John was less convinced. Not long after Clara St. John reported to Mrs. Kennedy that Joe Junior "is established as one of the 'big boys' of the school on whom we are going to depend," her husband informed Mr. Kennedy that the younger brother's results "are not yet commensurate with the standard we set for him. . . . His problem is still one of application." Joe Senior responded in kind, acknowledging that, while Jack had abundant natural talent, he was "careless in applying it." He urged the headmaster to prod his son, to keep him under strict watch, lest Jack allow this cavalier approach to get the better of him.[58]

St. John's solicitous attitude toward the Kennedy parents may have had something to do with a hope that they would respond with a contribution to the school's coffers. There was irony here, inasmuch as he was wary of Catholic climbers such as Joe Kennedy and didn't much want their kids at his Episcopal school. But there were bills to pay, and the Kennedys had wealth. When St. John hinted coyly of the need for a sound motion picture projector, Joe Kennedy got the message: he sent the school a high-end model costing $3,500, thus earning the headmaster's gratitude and cementing his commitment to keeping a watchful eye on the sons. "We'll try to show our appreciation, our sheer gratitude, in every way we know," St. John wrote Kennedy. "I'm keeping close to Jack."[59]

Still, to the headmaster and his teachers, Jack went on being a square peg who didn't fit in the round hole they had assigned him. He seems to have determined early on that he would not seek to match, much less exceed, his brother's exploits, and he viewed with bemused detachment the vaunted Choate values and Choate ways that Joe Junior worked so hard to embody. Jack's irresponsibility in this sense likely reflected his bid to preserve his individuality, to create a sense of self. Joe worked indefatigably to maintain his grades (which in the end were not that much higher on average than his brother's); Jack seemed to make a point of hardly studying. Joe was noted for his laser-like focus; Jack, his teachers complained, suffered from an "inability to concentrate effectively." Joe respected hierarchy and kowtowed to the rule makers and the enforcers; Jack brooked authority and poked fun at the conceit that lay behind it. Joe maintained a neat personal appearance, to the approving eyes of the Choate faculty; Jack was casual, slovenly, raffish—charmingly nonconformist, a different crowd might say.[60]

Then again, these dichotomies don't give the full picture. Behind Jack's insouciance lay the angst of living in the shadow of a brother who was accumulating accolades left and right, and—perhaps—a tacit admission that victory in the sibling rivalry lay beyond reach, at least for now. (*You can't lose if you don't compete.*) And underneath the slacker mien existed a pronounced bookishness and an intense curiosity about the world—as well as knowledge about it. Jack's friend Ralph "Rip" Horton noticed that whenever a group of boys got together to listen to the popular radio quiz show *Information Please,* most of them could answer only a few questions, but Jack whizzed through more than half. "How do you know all this stuff?" they'd ask. "I guess I read a lot," came the reply, neither boastful nor falsely modest.[61]

"Jack read a great deal but not to the point that he was burdensome about it," Horton remembered. "I think he could read quite fast, and, yes, he read a great deal but not ostentatiously. . . . He seemed to absorb what he read much better than the rest of us. He also, which I think is rather indicative of his future, always read *The New York Times*. He read that every single day from cover to cover, and I think that gave him a great insight into the political scene and international activities which he was so interested in."[62]

Horton, who hailed from New York City, also saw other sides to his new friend: "He was a boy of many interests. He liked sports, he liked roughhousing, he liked to be sloppy, he liked to play golf, he liked girls. But he would never stick to anything, would never give himself over entirely to anything. He loved to come to New York to see me."[63]

In other words: a fairly typical fourteen-year-old. The picture of an

unconventional Jack Kennedy, going against the grain at a highly structured, tradition-bound prep school, should not be overdrawn. Careless
and inattentive, chafing against rules, he still sought to fit in, to be popular, to win acceptance among his peers, to gain his parents' approval.
Athletics were a means to that end, and Jack's letters home in the first
year reveal his dogged pursuit of sporting success. Results were meager.
To his father he expressed confidence that he would make the basketball
team and play alongside his brother, but he crashed out in the tryouts.
Even more dispiriting, gridiron success eluded him. Football was where a
Choate boy could most easily gain campus recognition, but whereas
Young Joe did, Jack was simply too light and willowy to withstand the
rigors of the game, and had to content himself with playing below the
first-team level, on one of the school's lower teams.[64]

Only in golf, where Jack could put his excellent hand-eye coordination
to good use, did he make the squad, though not the top-six unit. And golf
was a minor sport at the school and, as such, small consolation for a boy
who had internalized his father's win-at-all-costs mentality, who understood all too well that his fragile constitution looked pathetic next to the
sturdy, irrepressible Joe Junior—not least in his father's eyes. In a letter in
December 1931, Jack made much of playing football in foot-high snow
that turned to ice, and then cautioned his father against thinking his
brother was all that tough:

> The first thing [Joe] did to show me how tough he was was to get sick
> so that he could not have any thanksgiving dinner. Manly Youth. He
> was then going to show me how to Indian wrestle. I then through
> him over on his neck. Did the sixth formers lick him. Oh Man he was
> all blisters, they almost paddled the life out of him. He was rough-
> housing in the hall, a sixth former caught him, he led him in and all
> the sixth formers had a swat or two. What I wouldn't have given to
> be a sixth former. They have some pretty strong fellows up there if
> blisters have anything to do with it.[65]

The letter was further proof, if such was needed, that the fourteen-
year-old, coming to the end of his first term at Choate, was feeling the
pressure to perform, to measure up, to meet his father's approval. Though
Jack and Joe led largely separate lives at the school, moving in different
circles, living in different dorms, seeing each other only occasionally, the

older boy was ever present in his brother's mental world, as the shining star in the family firmament, the golden child, the one who could do no wrong in the eyes of his parents or Choate's administration and faculty.

But it was not to be forever. In eighteen months, Jack knew, big brother would graduate from this place and move on to his next success. The burden would be lifted, at least to a degree. Still, as the Choate community prepared to scatter for Christmas break 1931, young Jack Kennedy continued to grapple with his core dilemma: how to be true to his own sensibility and make his own way in the world while remaining a Kennedy, with all that that implied.

FOUR

JACK AND LEM

As he had at Canterbury, Jack Kennedy suffered myriad health problems during his four years at Choate. And, as they had been then, diagnoses were usually elusive. He missed classes, probably more of them than any other boy in his year, which hardly helped his grades. In one six-day stretch in early 1932, Clara St. John, the headmaster's wife, sent five separate updates to Rose Kennedy.

January 20: "Keeping Jack in the Infirmary . . . because he does not yet seem to be entirely himself."

January 21: "Jack is up and dressed . . . regaining his pep. . . . He will be himself again after another 24 hours of taking things easy at the Infirmary."

January 22: "The weather is so unpleasant we don't dare run the risk of releasing Jack."

January 23: "Don't be discouraged with me for writing that Jack is still in the Infirmary! We are in no way troubled about him but he still has quite a cough. . . . We are starting Kepler's Malt and Cod Liver Oil [as per Rose's request]. I will see that his House Master will follow him up on it."

January 25: "You will rejoice with us [that] Jack is being allowed to go out into this glorious sunshine today. We are so glad."[1]

Mr. and Mrs. Kennedy, already frustrated by their second son's lack of discipline, took a detached approach to the maladies, accustomed as they were to his constant trips to the infirmary. "What concerned us as much [as his ailments], or more," Rose revealingly remarked years later, "was his lack of diligence in his studies; or, let us say, lack of 'fight' in trying to do well in those subjects that didn't happen to interest him." Whereas Joe Junior breezed along, having "no trouble at all" operating within Choate's tightly regulated system, "Jack couldn't or wouldn't conform. He did pretty much what he wanted, rather than what the school wanted of him."[2]

Her husband tried to gently curb the boy's careless ways. In April 1932 he wrote:

In looking over the monthly statement from Choate, I notice there is a charge of $10.80 for suit pressing for the month of March. It strikes me that this is very high and while I want you to keep looking well, I think that if you spent a little more time picking up your clothes instead of leaving them on the floor, it wouldn't be necessary to have them pressed so often. Also, there are certain things during these times which it might not be a hardship to go without, such as the University hat. I think it would be well to watch all these expenditures in times like these, in order that the bills will not run too high.[3]

With Jack's grades sinking fast in the spring of 1932, especially in French and Latin, Cappy Leinbach instituted a strict new regimen whereby Jack had to repeat to him his French and Latin vocabularies every evening and could not leave his room during study period. The two also worked together on algebra. Leinbach assured headmaster George St. John that he was doing all he could to help his immature—though undeniably likable—young charge: "What makes the whole problem difficult is Jack's winning smile and charming personality. I have to literally stifle an impulse to rebuke him with a grin, for he does meet each challenge with the most absurd and yet ingenious pretexts for not doing what is expected. . . . The inescapable fact [is] that his actions are *really* amusing and evoke *real* hilarity." Among other high jinks, the boy stole a life-size cardboard cutout of Mae West from the Wallingford cinema and slipped it into his bed, much to Leinbach's shock during room inspection the next morning.[4]

Then again, the room inspection was often frustrating for the former military man. "Whenever Jack wants a clean shirt or a suit," Leinbach reported to St. John, "it is necessary for him to pull every shirt or suit out of the drawer or closet, and then he *does not 'have time'* to put them back. His room is inspected night and morning *every day,* and I always find the floor cluttered up with articles of every description. When he sees me enter the room, he will at once start to put everything in order. He does it willingly and often remarks, 'I never get away with anything in this house!'"[5]

Leinbach's prodding no doubt helped prevent more serious disciplinary problems, but failed to turn the young pupil into an academic success, despite periodic predictions that a breakthrough was imminent. In May 1932, after Clara St. John relayed Rose Kennedy's request that Jack not be forced to have a summer tutor (with Teddy having just been born, she had nine kids to care for, and said she could not also oversee a tutor arrangement), director of studies Frank Wheeler replied, "Jack Kennedy has a high IQ, and is one of the most undependable boys in the third form. . . . I don't see how we can by any means guarantee he won't have to have a tutor. We could relieve her of all worry if she would send him to the summer session."[6]

The headmaster appealed accordingly to Joe and Rose, and they agreed to enroll Jack in summer session, in order to "make up his deficiencies" from the first year. He did the required remedial work, but no more. (At session's end, his algebra teacher complained of his sloppy habits in the subject and his "careless attitude toward academic work in general.")[7] Jack's well-established willingness to settle for the minimum passing grade, and to wait until the last possible moment to study for a test, remained intact through all four years at the school, and he racked up one middling grade after another. His Latin score went from 62 at the end of the first year to 69 at the conclusion of the second, whereupon he could mercifully end his longtime struggle with the language.* Four years of

---

* Headmaster St. John informed Joe Kennedy in June 1933: "Jack wishes to drop Latin, and we are entirely in agreement with that desire, unless you have some strong reason for wishing him to continue in the subject. The boy is perfectly capable of doing good work in it, but he does not like it or 'see the sense in it'; and there are plenty of other subjects that furnish equal training in logical thinking and accuracy." (St. John to JPK, June 27, 1933, Choate School Archives.)

French yielded a cumulative average of 67. ("There is actually very little except physical violence that I haven't tried," his exasperated French teacher reported to the headmaster at the end of the first year. "His papers are chaotic, and he invariably forgets books, pencil, or paper.") In math, he mustered a 69.67. Chemistry and biology bored him. Even in English and history, his preferred subjects, he hardly blazed a trail, usually scoring in the seventies and low eighties. His final rank at the school placed him sixty-fifth in a class of one hundred ten.[8]

Of course, such metrics hardly ever tell the full story, confusing as they do motivation and diligence with aptitude. Jack Kennedy's teachers, like those at his previous schools, saw his potential, his intelligence, his way with words, his ability to absorb information quickly and accurately from the printed page. Harold L. Tinker, his fifth-form English teacher, gave Jack a low overall grade but thought highly enough of his papers to conclude that he was a gifted writer, who made up for his poor spelling and erratic punctuation with an exceptionally good vocabulary and who ought to consider a literary career.[9] Tinker also found that Jack, when engaged, often grasped the insights of a novel or a poem—he was partial to Robert Frost—more fully than his classmates, and he was impressed by the young man's expansive knowledge of world affairs. History teacher Russell Ayers remarked in the fall of 1933 that Jack possessed "one of the few great minds" he had ever had in history class. Teachers and friends alike noted his interest in, and knowledge of, diplomatic history and contemporary world affairs, as well as his excellent memory, which enabled him to recite poems at considerable length. Courteney Hemeney, who taught English and history, later said of Jack that "he understood the reading even when he hadn't read it and always wrote fluently and incisively." And, though he was "not as steady as his brother Joe, there were flashes of brilliance."[10]

Such evidence of Jack's potential only frustrated Joe Kennedy, whose concern was his second son's insouciance and lack of application. He poured out his worries in a letter to St. John in the late fall of 1933, soon after visiting the school and seeing Jack play in a football game. Things had reached "a very critical stage," Kennedy wrote, and Jack "certainly is not on the right track. The observations that I made [in speaking with Jack] are not much different than I made before, that the work he wants to do he does exceptionally well, but he seems to lack entirely a sense of re-

The Choate junior football team, fall 1933. Jack is in the first row, second from right.

sponsibility, and that to my way of thinking must be developed in him very quickly, or else I am very fearful of the results." Feeling the need to underscore the point, Kennedy added, "The happy-go-lucky manner with a degree of indifference that he shows towards the things that he has no interest in does not portend well for his future development." But hope was not lost: "I feel very, very sure that if responsibility can be pushed on his shoulders, not only in his studies but in other things, that he may decide to observe them. He has too many fundamentally good qualities not to feel that once he got on the right track he would be a really worthwhile citizen."[11]

St. John got Kennedy's permission to share and discuss the letter with Jack. The conversation was productive, the headmaster reported to Kennedy, and he saw little reason for deep concern: "The fact of the matter is that I cannot feel seriously uneasy or worried about Jack. The longer I live and work with him, and the more I talk with him, the more confidence I have in him. I would be willing to bet anything that within two years you will be as proud of Jack as you are now of Joe."[12]

II

In one essay that year, Jack pondered how a Christian God could allow evil in the world, and how true justice could be achieved when people were born into such widely varying circumstances. Does God in fact "render to everyone his just due," Jack asked, given the vast disparities in the human condition?

> A boy is born in a rich family, brought up in [a] clean environment with an excellent education and good companions, inherits a foolproof business from his father, is married and then eventually dies a just and honest man. Take the other extreme. A boy is born in the slums, of a poor family, has evil companions, no education, becomes a loafer, as that is all there is to do, turns into a drunken bum, and dies, worthless. Was it because of the [rich] boys abylity that he landed in the lap of luxery, or was it the poor boys fault that he was born in squalor? The answer will often come back "The poor boy will get his reward in the life hereafter if he is good." While that is a dubious prospect to many of us, yet [there is] something in it. But how much better chance has [the] boy born with a silver spoon in his mouth of being good than the boy who from birth is surrounded by rottenness and filth. This even to the most religious of us can hardly seem a "square deal." Thus we see that justice is not always received from "The Most Just" so how can we poor mortals ever hope to attain it.

The young Kennedy, himself a son of privilege, was professing here that he saw little reason why the less fortunate should put much stock in the traditional Christian promise of a heavenly reward for a life well lived. Maybe such a reward would indeed be forthcoming, he allowed, but inequalities of condition and opportunity made the task of living a morally upright life much more daunting for those born into poverty and despair. In sum, injustice in the world remained a problem for which the Bible offered few answers.[13]

It was a core philosophical position, staked out at sixteen, in the midst of the Great Depression, from which the grown-up Jack Kennedy—congressman, senator, president—would never waver.

Kay Halle, a wealthy socialite friend of Joe Senior's, got a sense of

Jack's precocity when, accompanied by the father, she visited him in a hospital room where he was laid up with one malady or another. It was her first encounter with him, and it made an impression. "Jack was lying in bed, very pale, which highlighted the freckles across his nose. He was so surrounded by books I could hardly see him. I was very impressed, because at that point this very young child was reading *The World Crisis*, by Winston Churchill." Halle did not indicate whether Jack had all six volumes of this epic mega-history of World War I in the hospital room that day, and one wonders, too, what he made of Churchill's interpretation of the war, so different from his father's. Whereas the elder Kennedy still clung to his view that the Great War had been a colossal waste, sacrificing millions of young men for no good reason, Churchill, though critical of many aspects of British and Allied strategy, extolled leaders and fighting men who set duty and sacrifice before self-interest, who were driven by something bigger than themselves, and whose cause was entirely just: "Every man a volunteer, inspired not only by love of country but by a widespread conviction that human freedom was challenged by military and Imperial tyranny."[14]

Author Barbara Leaming suggests that Jack's reading of *The World Crisis* initiated his lifelong fascination with and admiration for Churchill (later in adolescence he read and loved the Englishman's massive million-word biography of Marlborough, the great military commander, statesman, and Churchill ancestor) and also spurred a deep and lasting interest in the question of how wars begin—and how to prevent them.[15] This seems right, and there can be no doubt that, given his growing interest in international affairs, Jack in this period followed current global politics as well—the climb to power in 1933, during his second year at Choate, of Adolf Hitler and his National Socialist Party in depression-ravaged Germany; the deepening crisis of confidence in France and Britain; and the growing tensions in East Asia as a rising Japan flexed its muscles.

With respect to domestic affairs, on the other hand, including the widespread dislocation and deprivation caused by the Great Depression, one doesn't see the same level of engagement from young Jack—notwithstanding his probing fifth-form paper on injustice. To a considerable extent, the cloistered Choate existence kept the students isolated from the outside world. Then again, from his daily *New York Times* Jack would have been aware of the devastating effects of the economic downturn on his fellow Americans. Given his superior recall, he might even have known some specifics: that between 1929 and 1933, the gross national product declined by half; that 100,000 businesses in that period shut their doors; that corporate profits fell from $10 billion to $1 billion; that by the time of the presidential election of 1932, a quarter of the nation's workforce was unemployed, while millions more worked only part-time; and that there was no national safety net: no unemployment compensation, no welfare system, no social security.

On home visits, too, Jack would have observed up close his father's deepening gloom over the state of the nation. This was something new, for over the previous dozen years Joe Kennedy had shown scant sustained concern about political developments—he'd been too busy making money and producing movies. Even the historic candidacy of fellow Catholic Alfred E. Smith, the Democrats' choice for president in 1928, had failed to excite him. Although still a Democrat by party affiliation (if more from inheritance than conviction), Kennedy had profited handsomely from the "Coolidge prosperity" of mid-decade, and he had felt strongly that Herbert Hoover stood a better chance than Al Smith of keeping the good times going. (He may also have been embarrassed by the informality of Smith's campaign style, adhering in core respects to the stereotype of the crude Irish pols of Joe's Boston youth.)[16]

The stock market crash and subsequent Depression changed him. Though his vast fortune remained intact and indeed grew, thanks to his expertly timed withdrawal from the stock market prior to the crash and his adept short selling afterwards (in 1935 his wealth would be estimated at $180 million, or $3.6 billion today), he now saw the future in bleak, self-centered terms, fearing a radical upheaval that might bring down the social and economic order and scuttle everything he had built for his family. His political philosophy, such as it was, remained inchoate and cynical—basically, acquiring and maintaining power were all that really mattered—but he intuited that whereas in the twenties business had been supreme, the thirties would be the decade of government, with the reformers running the show, and that he needed to shift his attention accordingly. He saw the limits of his long-held belief that money brought power; real power, he now saw, rested in politics.[17]

Kennedy hitched his hopes to one man, Franklin Delano Roosevelt, the governor of New York and Democratic candidate for president in 1932. The history between the two men reportedly went back to World War I, when, as manager of the Fore River shipyard, Kennedy negotiated testily with Roosevelt, then assistant secretary of the Navy, over the fate of two Argentine dreadnoughts completed before the war but returned to the Fore River yard for premature repairs. (Kennedy, so the story goes, refused to deliver the vessels until payment was received; Roosevelt objected and, when Kennedy stood firm, dispatched Navy tugs to tow away the ships.)[18] Now, a decade and a half later, Kennedy, having seen up close the flaws in the economic system that had made him rich, willed himself to believe that Roosevelt, more than the ineffectual Hoover, represented capitalism's best hope against revolution from below. And there was cold opportunism, too: Kennedy speculated that FDR would win and that through him he might himself find an entrée into politics. Roosevelt, for his part, saw in Kennedy not only a means of building up his presidential war chest, but a rare and formidable ally in the world of finance.[19]

"Roosevelt was a man of action," Kennedy told a journalist later. "He had the capacity to get things done. . . . Long before the campaign, long before his name was even seriously considered, I went out to work for him. I think I was the first man with more than $12 in the bank who openly supported him. I did this because I had seen him in action. I knew what he could do and how he did it, and I felt that after a long period of inactivity we needed a leader who would lead." To another reporter he said, "I wanted [Roosevelt] in the White House for my own security and for the security of our kids, and I was ready to do anything to elect him."[20]

They were a fascinating pair, so similar in some ways, so contrasting in others. Both were intelligent and egotistical men, skilled in the art of concealing their true motives behind guileless masks. Both were impatient with intellectual debate over abstract ideas and theories. (At Harvard, where they were eight years apart, they had been content to scrape by in their classes and to prioritize the social dimensions of collegiate life.) Both were hearty and outgoing, adept at attracting talented and dedicated subordinates, yet were not known for maintaining deep friendships— or being true to their wives. The differences were equally telling. Where Kennedy was fervent and single-minded, Roosevelt was cool and urbane, content to operate on myriad levels at once. Kennedy viewed the human condition in dark, fatalistic terms, whereas Roosevelt usually saw reasons for optimism even in the most difficult circumstances; he had the greater faith in the power of democratic ideals. Kennedy's intellect, though formidable, had a narrow character, and he was uncomfortable with doubt; Roosevelt, with his more capacious sensibility, liked to entertain differing points of view. Most striking of all, whereas for Kennedy his children were always supreme, Roosevelt seemed at times more responsive to his constituency—his "national family"—than to his own offspring.[21]

Thus began a marriage of convenience, one that was never free of mutual suspicion but that for a time, in the early and mid-1930s, also featured a degree of affection, or at least commonality based on a shared sense of humor and an appreciation of each other's talents and achievements. Kennedy poured money and time into Roosevelt's campaign in 1932, contributing ideas to the candidate's speeches on the economy and calling wealthy Democrats to urge them to make donations. He also helped persuade newspaper magnate William Randolph Hearst to break the deadlock at the Democratic National Convention that threatened an early FDR win. Kennedy then accompanied the candidate on a whistle-stop train tour to the western states in September, voicing robust support as Roosevelt called for greater government involvement in combating the economic crisis through "a new deal for the American people." On election night, Kennedy put on a lavish victory party that took up two floors of the Waldorf Astoria, in New York, with Roosevelt's theme song "Happy Days Are Here Again" blaring through the night. In the weeks thereafter, he laid on the flattery: in one telegram he informed FDR that a nun at his daughter Rosemary's convent school had declared the new administration to be "like another Resurrection." (Roosevelt, perhaps recalling what had occurred immediately before the previous Resurrection, replied vaguely with a thank-you for the "awfully nice telegram.")[22]

There had been signs during the campaign of what would become two pronounced features of Joe Kennedy's public persona in the years to come: his cultivation of the press and an obsessive interest in image-building. The right sort of publicity, his Hollywood years had taught him, could endow a person with fame as well as prestige; consequently, he made friends among the reporters who covered Roosevelt and took every chance to chat them up. "He liked being with the press more than he liked being with the politicians," said Ernest Lindley, a correspondent who two years earlier had penned the first Roosevelt biography. "He liked the repartee."[23]

Kennedy hoped to be appointed secretary of the Treasury in the new administration, but, to his intense frustration, there would be no offer of any kind for more than a year after the inauguration, in large part because of opposition at the White House, especially from the gnarled, gnomish, chain-smoking chief secretary, Louis Howe, who loathed the idea of bringing on a man he considered an unscrupulous Wall Street denizen. His pride wounded, Kennedy turned privately critical of Roosevelt—in letters, phone calls, and face-to-face meetings, he unloaded on FDR for his ingratitude and callousness—only to fall under the spell of the president's mesmerizing charm whenever they met and leave each encounter pledging his undying support. In 1934, after being passed over a second time for the Treasury slot and turning down an offer to become the U.S. representative to Ireland, he agreed to head up the Securities and Exchange Commission, a newly created entity designed to regulate stock exchanges, meaning that the notorious stock speculator would now be the cop on Wall Street's corner.[24] Presidential aides objected to the appointment for that reason, but Roosevelt held firm. Set a thief to catch a thief, he reasoned.[25]

III

As much as anything, what comes through in the accounts of Jack's Choate years is his lively wit. It's a theme in contemporaneous assessments and in subsequent oral histories, and it's there in his own letters to family and friends. Headmaster St. John, hardly one of the young man's great champions in this period, acknowledged Jack's gift for satirizing mundane everyday developments and mining them for laughs.[26]

The sense of humor and the charm go a long way toward explaining Jack's most conspicuous talent during his four years in Wallingford: his ability to make friends. Not everyone took to him—a few classmates thought him glib and cavalier. For the most part, however, and even before his brother graduated in 1933 (in a blaze of glory: he won the Harvard Trophy, awarded to the graduating student who best combined sportsmanship and scholarship), Jack was broadly popular, at least among the boys in his year.[27] "With Jack," said Seymour St. John, the headmaster's son, who would later take over that position himself, "nobody really admired what he did or respected what he did, but they liked his personality. When he flashed his smile, he could charm a bird off a tree."[28] From the start, Jack never lacked for pals, many of whom were drawn in by his irreverence and easy laugh, and by his lack of ostentatiousness despite his family's wealth. An early companion was Rip Horton, whose family ran a major dairy business in New York City. On occasion the two teens ventured into Manhattan together, with Horton procuring passes that got them into speakeasies and other clubs.

Another acquaintance was Al Lerner, from New York City, who in time would become known as Alan Jay Lerner and who, with Frederick Loewe, would write some of Broadway's most beloved musicals, among them *Brigadoon, My Fair Lady,* and *Camelot.* The last would be a favorite of Jack's and would become, with its famous "one brief shining moment" line, a sobriquet for his presidency.

But it was Lem Billings who became Jack's closest friend, a distinction he would keep for the rest of Kennedy's life. They met toward the end of spring semester in 1933, while working on the school yearbook, *The Brief.* Handsome and bespectacled, with curly blondish hair and a piercing nasal voice, Billings was tall and strong at six-two and 175 pounds, not all that coordinated but big enough to play first-team football and be a regular on the crew team. With ancestors on his mother's side who had arrived in America aboard the *Mayflower* in 1620, Lem was the son of a prominent Pittsburgh doctor who had recently died unexpectedly and left almost nothing behind, having lost his fortune after the Wall Street crash. Like Jack, Lem followed in the footsteps of a more celebrated brother who carried his father's name: Frederic "Josh" Billings Jr. was president of his Choate class of 1929, chairman of the student council, editor in chief of the yearbook, and captain of the football team; later he was an athletic and academic standout at Princeton and a Rhodes Scholar. The two "second sons" soon bonded. In a postcard to Lem from Hyannis Port that summer, Jack closed with "I'll see you next fall, which is a damn sight too near for comfort."[29]

Their friendship deepened when they returned to school in September. They shared a love of practical jokes and gossiping, as well as an instinct for flouting authority. "Jack had the best sense of humor of anybody I've known in my life," Billings remembered. "And I don't think I've known anybody who was as much fun."[30] Together, they delighted in mocking pomposity and self-importance and blind conformism, all qualities found in abundance on the Choate campus. But they were also powerfully dependent on each other. In Lem, Jack found a loyal, intelligent confidant and caretaker of sorts as he battled through his ailments, while Lem relied on Jack not just for unconditional friendship but for stability following his father's sudden death. They found they enjoyed each other without ri-

Lem and Jack, winter 1934.

valry. Over winter break that year, Jack invited Billings to Palm Beach, playground of the wealthy, where Joe Senior had recently paid $115,000 for a six-bedroom, two-story oceanfront vacation home on North Ocean Boulevard, complete with pool and tennis court.[31]

Lem would become a fixture at the various Kennedy houses in the years to come. He noticed early on that the family seemed to lack a true sense of place, of belonging. "They really didn't have a real home with their own rooms where they had pictures on the walls or memorabilia on the shelves," he remarked years afterwards, "but would rather come home for holidays from their boarding schools and find whatever room was available." Upon arrival Lem would hear Jack say to his mother, "Which room do I have this time?" Yet Billings found himself drawn to the Kennedys just the same—to their intense vitality, their open-mindedness, their frantic activism. "With them, life speeded up." He loved the informality among the siblings and their penchant for playful teasing, and marveled at their deep loyalty to one another. So frequently did Billings visit that young Teddy for a time thought he was a member of the family. "I was three years old before it dawned on me that Lem wasn't one more older brother," Teddy said, adding that Lem kept more clothes in the Hyannis Port home on a continual basis than Jack did.[32]

Joe Kennedy could sense the bond Billings had not just with Jack but with all the Kennedy kids. A few years later, he sent the young man a letter: "Dear Lem, This is as good a time to tell you that the Kennedy children from young Joe down should be very proud to be your friends, because year in and year out you have given them what few people really enjoy. True Friendship. I'm glad we *all* know you.—JPK."[33]

Jack in many ways dominated the friendship. He enjoyed teasing and needling people, and often his closest friend became the target of his barbs. Soon Lem had a string of nicknames such as "LeMoan," "Pneumoan," and "Delemma," and soon Jack's letters to him opened with the greeting "Dear Unattractive" or "Dear Crap." One letter, from April 1934, began, "Received your very uninteresting post card."[34] Most of the time Lem took the taunts in stride, but not always—on occasion he took offense at perceived slights. Jack, for his part, could sometimes get angry, too, especially over suggestions that he treated his friend unfairly. When Lem got upset over a mix-up concerning an invitation to the Palm Beach home, Jack let him have it:

> Of all the cheap shit I have ever gotten this is about the cheapest. You were invited down on Thanksgiving when the family was not coming. But then you were too busy and you and Rip [Horton] were going to St. Lawrence. Then you decide to come down as Rip was going to. But by that time, the family had decided to come down. Then you get hot in the arse because there may not be room enough, not forgetting that there was room enough at Thanksgiving but you didn't want to come until Rip decided he wanted to come. . . . Then I heard from dad saying it was okay. That was the situation: as regards the cheap shit you are pulling, you can do what you want. . . . If you look at this thing you will see you are not so fucking abused.[35]

Author David Pitts summarizes the dynamic well: "Like many close attachments, their friendship was complicated, and neither boy likely fully understood its nature or limitations at this time in their lives. Lem was clearly the more emotionally involved. He needed Jack and Jack knew it. But it also was apparent that Jack needed Lem, too. In the early years, they tested each other, as boys are prone to do, each seeking dominance."[36]

Seymour St. John, who would see the two boys together on his visits home from Yale, where he was an undergraduate, wrote perceptively that "their schoolboy banter was humorously critical, devil-may-care, which gave them a protective veneer and a sense of security." There was mutual dependence, St. John went on, and Lem "was ready to follow and applaud Jack in every escapade." The notorious school disciplinarian, J. J. Maher, the housemaster of their West Wing dorm, whom Jack in particular detested, was less forgiving of the boys' friendship, complaining to the headmaster of their self-centered, "silly, giggling inseparable companionship." An unyielding disciplinarian, the bachelor Maher was a compact, muscular figure who doubled as the school's first-team football coach and prided himself on being stronger and faster than any member of his team. He proved an irresistible target for the two boys' antics, such as the time when, late in the evening, they noisily began carrying Jack's trunk down the stairs to the basement after a vacation. An incensed Maher came flying out of his room, roaring at them for making a racket and reminding them that such work should be done not at night but in the morning. Jack duly apologized, and they resumed the work the next morning—before sunrise. Maher was furious, much to the boys' amusement.[37]

IV

In January 1934, soon after the Christmas break, Rose Kennedy wrote the school to ask if Jack could be permitted to travel to Providence, Rhode Island, to attend a dance with Rosemary. "The reason I am making this seemingly absurd request is because the young lady is his sister and she has an inferiority complex." George Steele, the dean of students, readily consented. "I appreciate thoroughly how much it would mean to you and Jack's sister to have him accept. . . . I know Jack will want to do this for Rosemary."[38]

Rosemary, age fifteen, was by then in her second year at the Convent of the Sacred Heart School, Elmhurst, in Providence. Her parents, hoping that a new environment would spur her academically, had transferred her from the Devereux School in the fall of 1932. As before, progress was slow and intermittent, her limited attention span thwarting teachers' efforts to educate her; as before, she craved her family's approval and attention. "Thank you very much for the lovely letter you sent me," she wrote her parents in the spring of 1934, perhaps with help from the nuns, her penmanship and grammar similar to those of a ten-year-old. "I got three bottles of perfume, but it is allright. I am satisfied. I like the handkerchief lot. . . . I cannot thank you enough for everything you have done to make Elmhurst so happy. Thanking you again for your kindness."[39]

Jack never got the chance to go to Rhode Island, for suddenly he again fell ill—this time ominously so. He had skinned his knee in Palm Beach playing tennis with Billings, and it became infected. Whether for that reason or another, he began feeling terrible. By early February he had been transported to New Haven Hospital. His condition deteriorated further and, according to Billings, he "came very close to dying." Rumors spread among the students that Jack was at death's door; heartfelt prayers were issued in the school chapel. Leukemia seemed a possibility, but doctors ruled it out. "It was some very serious blood condition," Billings recalled, which seems as exact a diagnosis as any. Headmaster St. John got swept up in the emotion of the moment, telling Joe Senior that "Jack is one of the best people that ever lived—one of the most able and interesting. I could go on about Jack!" To Jack himself St. John wrote with warmth and emotional attachment: "I think of you over and over, and wish I had you under my own roof; but I am grateful you are in such good scientific care."[40]

As was her pattern, Rose did not visit her son during the weeklong ordeal, choosing to stay put in Palm Beach. (Her husband did come to the hospital, as did Eddie Moore.) Not once during his four years at Choate did she come to Connecticut—even with all his illnesses. She did, however, take numerous solo vacations during those four years, and she also accompanied Joe Senior on trips to Europe. (Between 1929 and 1936 she went abroad seventeen times.) How Jack felt about her absence during his myriad infirmary stays goes unrecorded, but we can guess that it stung. We can imagine that some part of him wished she had come even once to the annual Mother's Day at the school, held in the spring each year, or had made the two-hour drive from Bronxville on some other occasion. If Rose's distance had the compensating advantage of making him more self-reliant, more independent, that was small consolation.[41]

Rose did maintain close written contact with the school and hospital staff during the crisis. "Jack's sense of humor hasn't left him for a minute, even when he felt most miserable," Mrs. St. John reported to her as the situation began to improve. When he had his first meal "after what must have seemed to him a terribly long time . . . he said to me, 'It was just as well that they decided to give me breakfast; if they hadn't, I think the nurse would have come in pretty soon and looked in my bed and not been able to see me at all!' "[42]

As soon as his symptoms abated, Jack was sent down to the family home in Florida for several weeks of rest and recuperation. While there, he kept up with his schoolwork with the help of a tutor, and sent the St. Johns a handwritten letter of thanks for their "numerous kindnesses" while he was in the hospital. He returned to school after Easter break. His weight, which had gone down to 125 pounds, was back up to 140. Exams soon followed, and he acknowledged to his mother that, although "I did not come out with flying colors, still I passed which is in itself a small accomplishment." To his father he bemoaned the rainy spring weather and the fact that "Mr. Maher came back from his holidays looking blacker than ever."[43] Taskmaster Maher, for his part, conceded in his housemaster's report that "to say that I understand Jack is more an expression of fond hope than a statement of fact." His young pupil was "such a complete individualist in theory and practice that the ordinary appeals of group spirit and social consciousness . . . have no effect." Jack's basic approach, Maher continued, was to say, "I'm a lively young fellow with a nimble brain and a bag full of tricks. You'll spoil my fun if I let you, so here I go; catch me if you can." The housemaster expressed hope that the "silly game" had lost its zest and that the young man was learning to distinguish between "liberty and license."[44]

Then, in June, with the school year just completed, another illness, leading to yet another hospitalization. This time it was determined that Jack should be sent to the famed Mayo Clinic, in Rochester, Minnesota, in the hope of finding out, once and for all, what plagued him. Neither parent accompanied him; instead the honor fell to Eddie Moore. Jack was miserable, not least because he knew that Lem Billings was in Hyannis Port with the rest of the Kennedys enjoying the summer sun. (As it happened, Lem scalded himself in the Kennedys' shower and was himself laid up in the hospital for three weeks.)[45] Humiliating pokes and prods by the Mayo staff came in quick succession, and he wrote a string of letters to Billings describing his ordeal. Many were lewd. "I'm suffering terribly out here and I now have gut ache all the time," read one missive. "I'm still eating peas and corn for food and I had an enema given by a beautiful blonde. That, my sweet, is the height of cheap thrills."[46]

"Here I am in the hottest place, except the Kennedys' shower, in the country," he wrote after learning of Lem's scalding. "A fellow stuck his finger up my rectum today and I, much to my embarrassment, burst out laughing. That rather upset the mgmt. of the whole place. How are you feeling? I hope you are having a pleasant stay. . . . They ask me the most personal questions, and I am blushing terribly especially when they ask me the color of my stool. They also gave my penis a *tremendous* jerk and I began to giggle coyly."[47]

Sex was never far from the seventeen-year-old's mind. "My virility is being sapped. I'm just a shell of the former man and my penis looks as if it has been through a wringer." The nurses were "very tantalizing and I'm really the pet of the hospital . . . and let me tell you, the nurses are almost as dirty as you, you filthy minded shit." Exhibiting even at this age a chauvinistic view of women, he boasted that one of the nurses "wanted to know if I would give her a workout," but, to his disappointment, she failed to return to his room.[48]

The adolescent boasting and obscenity were surely employed to cover what must have been a deeply trying experience. Here he was, half a continent from home, surrounded by strangers and subjected to an endless string of tests, each one seemingly designed to damage his dignity. Yet his letters give little evidence of self-pity or of the other emotion that many teenagers in his condition—or adults, for that matter—would feel, namely, fear. He was sick and hurting but wouldn't admit it, not even perhaps to himself. Instead he stood detached, a ceaseless observer of his own life, his letters suffused with his characteristic stoicism and a dark and richly inventive sense of humor. "I only had two enemas today and feel kind of full," he informed Billings on June 30. But finally there was hopeful news: "They have found something wrong with me at last. I don't know what but it's probably something revolting like piles or a disease of my vital organ." No definitive diagnosis was in fact ever made that summer, but the doctors concluded he suffered from allergies as well as from spastic colon (known today as irritable bowel syndrome) or, more seriously, from colitis, which, if true, would explain why it was hard for him to gain weight and could generate worse problems if the colon bled or became ulcerated. Jack returned home with orders to follow a proper diet and also to take steps to relieve emotional stress, at the time thought to be a major contributor to the condition.[49]

He would have only a few weeks in Hyannis Port that summer, but he was determined to make the most of them. He loved this place more than any other, not least for the opportunity it gave him to be out on the water in Nantucket Sound. He had become, by this point in his young life, a highly skilled racing skipper, with a reputation for boldness and cunning and for catching his opponents by surprise. He and Joe Junior, one observer noted, went for "split-second timing at the start, recklessness at the windward buoy, disregard for the risk of a tiny misjudgment." They carried full canvas while rival skippers reefed, possessed a deft touch at the tiller, and were adept at picking up the hint of a breeze in light winds. In the early years, the boys used two cleverly named sixteen-footers in the Wianno junior class—*Tenovus*, followed, after the birth of Teddy, by *Onemore*—and in 1932 Joe Senior added to the fleet, buying a used twenty-five-foot Wianno senior with a small cuddy for overnight trips. Jack named her *Victura* ("something to do with winning"), and she became the vehicle for his greatest successes.[50]

V

In the fall of 1934, Jack returned to Choate for his senior year. He and Lem Billings roomed together. Headmaster St. John had allowed it, over J. J. Maher's warning—prescient, time would reveal—that mischief would follow. That Jack and Lem would even ask to be roommates is fascinating, in view of what their summer correspondence had revealed: for Lem, this was more than a friendship. At some point over the previous year he had fallen in love with Jack. At first content with the relationship being purely platonic, he found it harder and harder to restrain himself, even though he was pretty sure his feelings were not reciprocated.[51]

But how should he proceed? Unwilling to risk a termination of the friendship by openly stating his feelings and admitting that his sexual attractions were directed to boys and, in particular, to Jack, he opted to drop a hint. The unspoken tradition at Choate, borrowed from British private schools, was for boys who wanted to have sexual encounters with other boys to exchange notes written on toilet paper (which could be flushed or even swallowed to avoid a paper trail). In early June, Lem had sent such a note to Jack—no doubt after much agonized indecision. The note does not survive, and we don't know what precisely it said, but we have Jack's response. "Please don't write to me on toilet paper anymore," he wrote from his hospital bed later that month. "I'm not that kind of boy." As if to assuage any embarrassment on his friend's part, or cover his own, or both, he devoted the rest of the letter to his medical condition and his sagging manhood.[52]

Whether Jack had any prior inkling of Lem's interest in him is unclear. His letters from the period suggest he took Lem to be a ladies' man like himself. A year before, in June 1933, in his very first letter to Lem, he wrote, "Please give my best to Pussy [Brooks, a girl from Pittsburgh whom Lem knew] and take it easy on the women." And certainly, a single incident of this nature at an all-boys prep school does not say all that much about a person's sexual orientation. Yet there were periodic hints that Lem might be cut from a different cloth. Earlier in 1934, the two boys had ventured to Harlem in full evening dress to find a prostitute, in order to lose their virginity in the same evening to the same woman. Jack went into the room with the woman he had selected, while Lem—as he recalled later—waited uncomfortably by the door. When Jack came out, he had to coax his friend into going into the room, where, it seems, Lem did not lose his virginity.[53]

On another occasion, Jack and Lem and an alumnus of the school, Pete Caesar, left a Choate evening social with two girls, Olive Cawley and Pussy Brooks, and drove to a nearby farm. En route, the quintet noticed they were being followed by one of the school's cars. On Jack's suggestion, Pete and Pussy remained in the car while the other three dashed off unseen. When the campus cops arrived, they merely found an alumnus necking with his girl and drove on. Jack and Olive, meanwhile, had found a remote corner of a barn, and Lem planted himself in a haystack in another barn and waited quietly for everyone to finish.[54]

Having been rebuffed by Jack in no uncertain terms, Lem backed off and, it seems, never made the proposition again. He could only watch as Jack became increasingly infatuated with Cawley, a pretty and vibrant brunette who hailed from New York City and attended the private Kimberley School, in New Jersey.[55] But it's telling that Jack, contrary to what one would expect of a straight man in that era, did not break off the friendship. Even after it became incontrovertibly clear in later years that Lem was gay, the two remained close. "Jack was a hell of a forgiving guy," their friend Rip Horton said. "He was terribly understanding." Journalist Charles Bartlett, who befriended Jack and Lem after the Second World War, said much the same thing: "I liked Lem and saw that he was a good friend of Jack's. Jack was not a judgmental type of guy. He accepted his friends without passing judgment on them."[56]

The truth was that Jack enjoyed spending time with Lem, valued his friendship. The perspicacious Seymour St. John, in an interview half a century later, saw Lem as a tragic figure whose identity over time became entirely wrapped up in Jack Kennedy and his family, "who had nothing really to hold onto" until he found Jack. After that, "anything Jack did, he would follow right along with him and be the stooge." But St. John also perceived the positive side of the friendship, not least for Jack, who could count on his friend to be the jester, to lift his spirits when he might otherwise have sunk into despair, with his chronic ailments and his ongoing rivalry with Joe Junior. "It was Billings's loyalty that helped [Jack] to emerge from his adolescent trials with his confidence in himself strengthened rather than broken," St. John said.[57]

Now, as they entered their final year (Lem could have finished in 1934, but, as if to demonstrate Seymour St. John's point, he stayed on an extra year in order to be with Jack and their friends), they were determined to have a good time. Maher, sensing trouble, put them in a room right next to his own.[58] The trouble came soon enough. Jack had brought with him from Hyannis Port a pristine old Victrola and a bunch of records, and in short order their room became the hangout spot for a dozen friends. Maher informed the headmaster of the noise and messiness, and before long George St. John stood before the student body in the long, formal English dining hall and spoke of a small group of selfish, pleasure-loving troublemakers who seemed intent on destroying the peace of the school. They were "muckers," the headmaster said, nothing more than muckers, and he would not stand for it.[59]

Perfect, Jack and his buddies thought as they listened: *muckers!* The name fit them to a tee. The group promptly went into Wallingford and shelled out $12 each for a small gold charm in the shape of a shovel and engraved with the initials CMC, for Choate Muckers Club. (Another meaning of *mucker* was someone who, in the days before automobiles, shoveled horse manure off the streets.) Their subsequent antics were misdemeanors at worst—sneaking off school grounds for milkshakes and playing music after hours. Alcohol was never in the equation, and neither was smoking. For Spring Festival they planned to have each member arrive at the dance pulling his date on a shovel, then have photographs taken outside next to a manure pile, shovels in hand.[60]

St. John was furious when he learned of the scheme. At lunch in the dining hall, he read off the Muckers' names, accused them of undermining Choate's morals and integrity, and ordered them into his study. There he expelled them and ordered them to clear out of their rooms and prepare to depart the school. The astonished boys trudged back to their dorms and fretted about how to tell their parents, only to be called back into the headmaster's study and informed that he had changed his mind: they would not be expelled after all. But there would be no more club, he told them, no more shenanigans, and they would be kept at school over the Easter break.[61]

At St. John's request, Joe Kennedy and Lem's mother, Romaine, traveled to the school to discuss the crisis. Their sons were the ringleaders, he told them, and he wanted them, as parents, to understand the seriousness of the situation. During the Kennedys' session, father and son nodded politely at the headmaster's stern words, and Jack expressed contrition. Mr. Kennedy professed to be appalled by the club's actions, but inside he questioned what all the fuss was about. Himself an outsider in this elite Episcopalian milieu, he wondered if George St. John's rumored anti-Catholicism played a role in his overheated approach to the affair. (For there was a third meaning of *mucker:* a lowly Irish Catholic immigrant who worked to clear the swamps of Boston's Back Bay.) When St. John interrupted their conversation to take a phone call, Joe leaned over and whispered to Jack, "My God, my son, you sure didn't inherit your father's directness or his reputation for using bad language. If that crazy Muckers Club had been mine, you can be sure it wouldn't have started with an *M!*"[62]

Jack with three fellow "Muckers" on a street in Wallingford.
From left: Ralph Horton, Lem Billings, Butch Schriber, and Jack.

One detects a sense of entitlement in how both Kennedys—father and son—reacted to the Muckers affair, a sense that the rules didn't fully apply to Jack, and that St. John couldn't really touch him. More than that, in Joe Kennedy's handling of the episode there's a strong whiff of fatherly pride. Well aware of his reputation for being a domineering, overbearing presence in his children's lives, he worked to instill in them—and especially the boys—a certain irreverence and independence of mind. When Young Joe graduated from Choate in 1933, his father, upon the recommendation of Harvard Law School professor Felix Frankfurter, dispatched him to the London School of Economics to spend a year studying with Harold Laski, the distinguished socialist theorist and economist, before matriculating at Harvard. Laski's political and economic philosophies were far from Kennedy's own, but he reasoned that a sustained period under the Briton's tutelage would broaden Joe Junior's intellectual range and hone his ability to defend a more conservative position. Nor was this a newfound philosophy: visitors to the Kennedy home had long noted that during the mealtime seminars, Mr. Kennedy never pushed Joe or Jack or the other children to adopt his positions, but encouraged them to adopt and defend their own points of view.[63]

But being informed and opinionated was not enough—commitment and responsibility were essential, too. In this regard Jack remained for his father a source of worry, no less at the end of the Choate years than at the beginning. In letter after letter that final year (penned, mind you, while he headed a major new government agency in Washington), he nudged and cajoled his second son, urging him to finish, as he put it, in "a blaze of glory." A missive from December 1934 gives the flavor:

> After long experience in sizing up people, I definitely know you have the goods and you can go a long way. Now aren't you foolish not to get all there is out of what God has given you and what you can do with it yourself? After all, I would be lacking even as a friend if I did not urge you to take advantage of the qualities you have. It is very difficult to make up fundamentals you have neglected when you were very young, and that is why I am urging you to do the best you can. I am not expecting too much, and I will not be disappointed if you don't turn out to be a real genius, but I think you can be a really worthwhile citizen with good judgment and understanding.[64]

In the wake of the near expulsion in the spring, Choate gave three of the troublemakers an opportunity to meet with a Columbia University psychologist, Prescott Lecky. Jack, perhaps at his father's urging, accepted the offer. Lecky reported that he found the young man to be very able, "but definitely in a trap, psychologically speaking. He has established a reputation in the family for thoughtlessness, sloppiness, and inefficiency, and he feels entirely at home in the role." When Lecky asked him if he expected to succeed in the world with this attitude, Jack had no answer. "He thinks of himself as a self-reliant, intelligent, and courageous boy," Lecky continued, "but he has never recognized the difficulty he will have in maintaining those definitions unless he sacrifices the defense devices that he has built up through the years. He does not worry about his sloppiness, he says, and has never been neat in his life; but it is obvious that he must worry sooner or later, or give up the definitions he values most."

More than anything, Lecky determined, the source of Jack's troubles could be found in the rivalry with Joe Junior. "My brother is the efficient one in the family," Jack told him, "and I am the boy who doesn't get things done. If my brother were not so efficient, it would be easier for me to be efficient. He does it so much better than I do." Lecky concluded that "Jack is apparently avoiding comparison and withdraws from the race, so to speak, in order to convince himself that he is not trying."[65]

It was an astute appraisal of a young man who had yet to find his way. Lecky was surely right that the sibling rivalry and the inferiority complex that resulted from his second-son status helped explain Jack's anti-establishment flair and slacker ways. Then again, one could go too far with the notion. Perhaps a part of Jack was simply following in the foot-steps of his father, a similarly indifferent student during his days at Boston Latin thirty years before.

Whatever the case, as Jack prepared to depart Choate that spring of 1935—aged eighteen, tall and wiry, with an angular, handsome face and a mop of hair that resisted all efforts at control—he could take a certain satisfaction from his four years at the school. His health travails had been at times all-consuming and, partly for that reason, his academic performance seldom went beyond middling. But he experienced a freedom he had never had before, especially after his brother's departure at the mid-point. He met a lifelong friend in Lem Billings and enjoyed the conviviality of a large circle of other pals. What's more, he learned during his Choate years how to get along on his own, independently, even in the face of ad-versity, and saw the degree to which he could use his charm and sense of humor to his advantage. "In any school he would have got away with some things, just on his smile," George St. John conceded. "He was a very likeable person, very lovable." One measure of that: despite ranking barely above the median in his class, Jack Kennedy was voted by his class-mates "most likely to succeed." No doubt the result owed a good deal to the Kennedys' immense wealth, well known on campus, and to the ener-getic efforts of the ex-Muckers, led by Billings, to round up votes for their leader, but it also resulted from Jack's popularity among his fellow stu-dents.[66]

The vote was Jack's final poke in the eye to the Choate establishment, and it must have annoyed the school's leaders to see their exasperating Mucker recognized in this way. But they could see the promise in the lad, more so than in his accomplished older brother, who lacked his creative intelligence. "Jack has a clever, individualist mind," George St. John had told Mr. Kennedy some time before. "It is a harder mind to put in harness than Joe's. . . . When he learns the right place for humor and learns to use his individual way of looking at things as an asset instead of a handicap, his natural gift of an individual outlook and witty expression are going to help him. A more conventional mind and a more plodding and mature point of view would help him a lot more right now; but we have to allow, my dear Mr. Kennedy, with boys like Jack, for a period of adjustment . . . and growing up; and the final product is often more interesting and more effective than the boy with a more conventional mind who has been to us parents and teachers much less trouble."[67]

Assistant headmaster Wardell St. John had a similar inkling. "Jack has it in him to be a great leader of men," he wrote at the end of spring term, "and somehow I have a feeling that he is going to be just that."[68]

It was, time would reveal, a most penetrating pair of assessments.

FRESHMAN YEARS

O n September 25, 1935, eighteen-year-old John F. Kennedy boarded the French ocean liner *Normandie,* along with his parents and his sister Kathleen (Kick). They were bound for England. The previous spring, Jack had applied for admission to Harvard and Princeton, and had been accepted to both.[1] On his Harvard entrance examination he had scored 85 in both English and history, which were considered honors grades at the time.[2] But, contrary to expectations, he leaned against following brother Joe to their father's alma mater and instead hoped to join Lem Billings and Rip Horton at Princeton. His father did not say yes or no, but he insisted that Jack postpone college in order to spend a year at the London School of Economics, as his brother had, under the tutelage of the left-wing economist Harold Laski.

Kennedy's motivation was the same as it had been for his older son: exposure to Laski's socialist ideas would encourage Jack's intellectual independence and sharpen his ability to defend a more conservative position. It had worked the first time around (though there was a doubtful moment—much to Jack's amusement, his brother came back from London fleetingly spouting quasi-socialist ideas), and the father saw no reason it could not succeed again. Laski, he said afterwards, was "a nut and a crank. I disagreed with everything he wrote. We were black and white. But I never taught the boys to disapprove of someone just because I didn't like him. They heard enough from me, and I decided they should be exposed to someone of intelligence and vitality on the other side."[3] It was a philosophy that spoke well of Kennedy's confidence in his sons, and also of his recognition that politics had taken a leftward turn under the weight of the Depression and that his sons needed to understand this new world. It didn't hurt that Laski had been a dazzling instructor at Harvard and thus was conversant with America and its politics, or that he was in regular correspondence with such leading lights as Franklin Roosevelt, Walter Lippmann, Felix Frankfurter, and Oliver Wendell Holmes Jr., or that he was considered by some to be the most articulate man who ever lived. Finally, the LSE's cosmopolitan outlook and student body would instill in the boys a better grasp of other cultures. (When he learned that Joe Junior was rooming with an American, Kennedy recommended that he "keep your contacts with the foreigners as much as possible. You have Americans to live with the rest of your life.")[4]

Later it would be said that Jack went to London only because his father forced him to, but in reality he was intrigued by the prospect of having a European experience, and traveled willingly. Already the previous fall, during his final year at Choate, he had written to his parents of his desire to go to England and of his recognition that he needed to improve his academic performance in order to make it happen: "LeMoyne and I have been talking about how poorly we have done this quarter, and we have definitely decided to stop any fooling around. I really do realize how important it is that I get a good job done this year if I want to go to England. I really feel, now that I think it over, that I have been bluffing myself about how much real work I've been doing."[5]

Still, Mr. Kennedy's wishes drove the ultimate decision. "My father wanted me to see both sides of the street," Jack later said.[6]

That fifteen-year-old Kick was along for the voyage was an added bonus for him. It had been decided that she would take time away from her studies at Sacred Heart Convent, a Catholic all-girls boarding academy in Noroton, Connecticut, to spend a year at an affiliated Sacred Heart Convent school in Neuilly-sur-Seine, an affluent suburb of Paris, thus repeating the kind of educational experience her mother had had as a girl. Rose had struggled in vain to harness Kick's free-spirited ways, and she thought her daughter altogether too popular with boys, who were prone to distracting Kick from her schoolwork. The solution: ship her overseas for an extended period in a convent, where she might also absorb French language and culture.[7]

Kick adored her two older brothers, but she was especially fond of Jack. The two enjoyed a good-natured teasing relationship, with a penchant for clever repartee that greatly amused their friends. Jack, the family reader, would rib Kick for her ostensibly shallow interests; she would poke fun at his vanity and his skinny frame. But the bond was deep. "She really thinks you are a great fellow," his father had informed Jack a few months before. "She has a love and devotion to you that you should be very proud to have deserved. It probably does not become apparent to you, but it does to both Mother and me. She thinks you are quite the grandest fellow that ever lived, and your letters furnish her most of her laughs at the Convent."[8] Jack, for his part, treasured Kick's open, intelligent, irreverent personality, so similar to his own, and sought her approval of the girls he brought home. His own friends, meanwhile, invariably fell in love with Kick on first meeting—though not conventionally beautiful, she was cute and feminine, with rich auburn hair, and her effervescence and easy charm made her irresistible to a steady stream of suitors.

Jack and Kick shared a lively interest in people and what made them tick, and could talk endlessly about their shared social experiences. "After parties," one friend remembered, "Kathleen liked nothing better than to sit up in her bathrobe with Jack, talking into the middle of the night about the personality of everyone who was there. They were so close at times I thought of them as twins."[9]

The close connection between brother and sister was evident in their written correspondence, both then and later. During the Muckers affair at Choate, Jack had given Kick the highlights via letter, whereupon she promptly fired off a congratulatory telegram to him and Lem Billings: DEAR PUBLIC ENEMIES ONE AND TWO ALL OUR PRAYERS ARE UNITED WITH YOU AND THE OTHER ELEVEN MUCKS. WHEN THE OLD MEN ARRIVE SORRY WE WON'T BE THERE FOR THE BURIAL.[10] The Choate staff had intercepted the telegram, adding to Jack's troubles. Joe Senior scolded her and said she had added "fuel to the fire." Jack, too, was upset with his sister, but only momentarily. It was the sort of missive, after all, in both tone and content, that he himself could have dashed off if the situation were reversed.[11]

That summer at Hyannis Port, the two siblings were again thick as thieves, taking off at a moment's notice in a family car (Jack now had his license) to dance at the Yacht Club or see a movie at the Idle Hour Theatre, or to have ice cream at the Rexall Drugstore, where the family kept a tab. If they got home late, they would pull into the driveway quietly, headlights off, and sneak into the house on tiptoes, shoes in hand. In the morning, Kick would find a note next to her pillow from her mother: "Next time be sure to be in on time."[12]

II

Now here they were, bound for Europe together. It was the first time for both. And what a means of transportation they had! The *Normandie* was the greatest of all ocean liners (arguably to this day), the largest and fastest passenger ship afloat. Her maiden voyage had taken place just a few months earlier, during which she set a transatlantic speed record, covering Le Havre to New York in just four days, three hours, and fourteen minutes, at an average speed of thirty knots. Her lavish interiors, finished entirely in the Art Deco style, featured spectacular entryways and staircases, as well as a 305-foot-long dining room with silver walls and twenty-four-foot gold ceilings, a room larger than the Hall of Mirrors at Versailles, able to seat seven hundred guests at 157 tables. Other amenities included indoor and outdoor pools, a theater, a chapel, a winter garden, and an open-air tennis court. The Kennedys were enthralled, as Rose made clear in her diary, though Jack's devouring of the French delicacies caused grumbling from one quarter. "The food here is very pimp-laden," he wrote Billings, "and my face is causing much comment from the old man, and it is getting damned embarrassing. He really rang the bell when after helping myself to a dessert that was oozing with potential pimps he said my face was getting to look like yours."[13]

The Kennedys were to disembark at Plymouth, on England's south coast, but bad weather compelled the captain to make straight for Le Havre, in Normandy. From nearby Dieppe the family then boarded a small craft for a rough crossing to Newhaven, in East Sussex. "Everyone ill except Joe, Jack, and Kick all of whom stayed on upper deck in rain freezing to death," Rose wrote in her diary.[14]

Jack, Joe, Rose, and Kick aboard the SS *Normandie,*
September 25, 1935.

Upon arrival in London they settled in at Claridge's hotel, in Mayfair, just off Grosvenor Square and the shops of Bond Street. It was an eventful time to be in Europe. A British election was fast approaching, and there were rising tensions on the Continent. Earlier in the year, German leader Adolf Hitler had warned that rival powers should get used to dealing with Germany on an equal footing—in March he announced the existence of a German Luftwaffe (air force) and ordered the conscription of all able-bodied men aged nineteen or over. Both were violations of the Versailles Treaty—the most consequential of a series of treaties imposed by the Allies on the defeated powers at the end of World War I—and caused acute consternation in European chancelleries. The Soviet Union and France responded by signing a treaty of friendship and mutual support. In September, shortly before the Kennedys set sail from New York, Hitler imposed the Nuremberg Laws, in which Jews were denied the rights of German citizenship and marriage, and extramarital relations between Jews and "Aryans" were prohibited. The swastika became the official flag of Germany. On October 2–3, Benito Mussolini's Italy invaded Abyssinia (Ethiopia), a clear breach of the League of Nations' sanctions against aggression.[15]

For informed observers at the time, and for legions of historians later, these were deeply ominous developments, proof positive that the fragile international order was foundering. Coming out of the Great War, the Allied leaders, led by Woodrow Wilson, had championed a new way of conducting world affairs, with the end of secret diplomacy and bilateral deals and the creation of the League of Nations to settle geopolitical crises and head off interstate violence. Disarmament efforts would make the world safer and contribute to the avoidance of another destructive general war. Much to Wilson's dismay, the U.S. Senate had rejected American membership in the League—the centerpiece of his vision for the postwar world—but under the subsequent Republican administrations, U.S. officials nonetheless participated discreetly in League meetings on a range of issues.[16] Hitler's accession to power in 1933 scuttled the disarmament talks—he walked out of them in short order, rendering further efforts moot, and the World Disarmament Conference adjourned indefinitely. Mussolini's invasion of Abyssinia, meanwhile, brought sharp verbal condemnation from the world's powers but little more. Italy swiftly resigned from the League and drew closer to Nazi Germany.[17]

How much Jack took note of these machinations is unclear. He read the daily newspapers and (following his mother's example) clipped articles that interested him. But mostly he devoted his early efforts in London to penetrating the city's social scene. The LSE intrigued him, but he did not take to Harold Laski, finding him humorless and self-important and his socialist ideas impractical and narrow.[18] Suddenly the prospect of spending an academic year—or even a term—under this man seemed like a nightmare. Seemingly on cue, another mystery ailment arrived, placing Jack in the hospital and leaving physicians confounded once again. He was jaundiced and had joint pain, and his blood count was off, but he was not fully symptomatic of anything. The doctors settled on hepatitis as the likely diagnosis, but without conviction. "They are doing a number of strange things to me," he wrote Lem from his bed, "not the least of which is to shove a tremendous needle up my cheeks. Today was most embarrassing as one doctor came in just after I had woken up and was reclining with a semi [erection] on due to the cold weather. His plan was to stick his finger under my pickle and have me cough. His plan quickly changed however when he drew back the covers and there was 'JJ Maher' quivering with life." (Jack had named his penis after his detested Choate housemaster.) The "very sexy" night nurse, meanwhile, "is continually trying to goose me so I always have to be on my guard."[19]

In time, much would be made of Jack Kennedy's exposure to the famous Laski's teachings. Jack himself talked up the connection, presumably in order to enhance the impression of his academic credentials. References would be made by political operatives to the "term" he spent at the LSE. In fact, he lasted in London all of a month before returning to the United States, his parents feeling his health could be better monitored from there.* Tellingly, he informed Billings in a letter that "Dad says I can go home if I want to." Not only that, but the elder Kennedy signed off on his son's request to enroll late at Princeton. (The school granted his appeal.) On October 21, 1935, Billings received the good news via wire: ARRIVING PRINCETON THURSDAY AFTERNOON; HOPE YOU CAN ARRANGE ROOMING.[20]

Billings was thrilled. He wired back: NOTHING COULD POSSIBLY SOUND BETTER. SO HURRY HOME. And he did have accommodation for his friend, though admittedly it wasn't much: a dumpy two-bedroom apartment that he shared with Rip Horton on the fourth floor of South Reunion Hall. The main bathroom was in the basement, seventy-two steps away, and the flat had long since seen its best days. It had but a single radiator and a lone cramped closet. But it was cheap, and it offered a splendid view of ivy-covered Nassau Hall, the oldest building on campus, dating to 1756, when the university was known as the College of New Jersey.[21]

If Jack felt let down by his new digs, he didn't show it. Never one to live with the ostentation his family wealth afforded him, he entered college with the same casual, even sloppy, manner of dress and lifestyle he had

---

* It is not clear whether, prior to departure, Jack joined his parents for their visit to Winston Churchill's country home, Chartwell, in Kent. "[He is] almost seventy—a pleasant, talkative, country gentleman, probably the most versatile whom I have ever met," Rose jotted in her diary of the future prime minister, who would become a bitter antagonist of her husband. "Has a studio in his garden where he often goes + paints for recreation whatever interests him." (U.d., box 1, RK Personal Papers.) (In actuality, Churchill was just turning sixty-one.) Churchill, upon learning of Jack's illness, wrote to Joe, "I am deeply grieved at your anxiety about your son, and earnestly trust it will soon be relieved." (Maier, *When Lions Roar,* 13.)

followed at Choate. He happily bunked on a spare cot in Billings's small bedroom. He was aware, moreover, that the spartan arrangement was made necessary by his friend's financial constraints. Though he could belittle Lem in letters (in a way Lem never dared do to him), Jack was also deeply loyal. He worried about his friend's money problems, and pledged to help him out. "Your financial worries have upset me," he wrote from London, "as Princeton would not be awfully jolly without your sif [syphilis] covered face." He offered Billings $500 and added, "I won't need it. You can pay me after you get out of college. You then would not have to borrow from that old Prick Uncle Ike [Lem's uncle]. Let me know about this, and wether [sic] you need it, because I won't be needing it."[22]

The reunion of the three ex-Muckers was a happy one, and soon they were enjoying weekends in New York City, ninety minutes away by train. About his studies, however, Jack remained as lackadaisical as ever, if not more so. He barely cracked open his books. Princeton as an institution disappointed him—it seemed dismayingly similar to Choate in his mind, a kind of overgrown boarding school more than a university, palpably insular and oppressively Protestant. "I think he was a little disenchanted with the country-club atmosphere of Princeton," a friend recalled. Nor did it help that he soon fell ill again. He could drag himself to class, but barely, and the jaundice from London returned—his complexion, an observer noted, took on a yellowish-brown hue, "as though he'd been sunbathing."[23] Already on November 11, barely two weeks after Jack's arrival, his father wrote him an affectionate letter, suggesting that they monitor his health until Thanksgiving and then make a determination about whether he could remain in school: "After all, the only consideration I have in the whole matter is your happiness, and I don't want you to lose a year of your college life (which ordinarily brings great pleasure to a boy) by wrestling with a bad physical condition and a jam in your studies. A year is important, but it isn't so important if it's going to leave a mark for the rest of your life. . . . You know I really think you are a pretty good guy and my only interest is in doing what is best for you."[24]

III

Thanksgiving came and went and Jack did not improve. He was sent to Peter Bent Brigham Hospital, in Boston, for tests and observation. (TELL

A 1935 Christmas card from three Princeton roommates, with a
greeting inspired by the lead song in the new Fred Astaire/Ginger Rogers
film, *Top Hat:* Rip [Ralph Horton], Leem [Lem Billings], and Ken [Jack].

US WHAT TIME TO ARRIVE FOR THE FUNERAL, Billings and Horton cabled
him on December 10.) The doctors there were mystified, however, which
prompted the university physician to write to the dean: "You are probably
familiar with the interesting case of John Fitzgerald Kennedy, [class of]
'39. We have been in touch with his doctors ever since he came here and
it now appears advisable for him to withdraw from the university for the
purpose of having such examinations and treatment as his condition

may require in the hope that he will improve sufficiently to return as a Freshman next fall."[25]

And thus ended Jack Kennedy's tenure as a Princeton man, six weeks after it began. He would not return. The prospect of being laid up in Boston seemed dreadful, but he couldn't quibble with his father's argument that it was imperative "to arrive at a definite conclusion regardless of how much time it takes because we must settle this matter once and for all on this occasion." The physicians got to work. "They are doing quite a number of things," the young patient wrote his parents from his hospital bed, "but I am rather a difficult subject."[26] A flood of letters to Billings followed—witty, obscene, uninhibited, gossipy, unflappable, and suffused with a striking vitality that his mother had noticed in his language ever since he was a small child.

January 18, 1936: "My blood count this morning was 3500. When I came it was 6,000. At 1500 you die. They call me '2,000 to go Kennedy.' "[27]

January [undated]: "[It is] the most harrowing experience of my storm-tossed career. They came in this morning with a gigantic rubber tube. Old stuff, I said, and I rolled over thinking it would be stuffed up my arse. I didn't know whether they thought my face was my ass or what but anyway they shoved it up my nose and down into my stomach. Then they poured alcohol down the tube, me meanwhile going crazy as I couldn't taste the stuff and you know what a good stiff drink does to me."[28]

January 27: "They haven't told me anything, except that I have leukemia, and agranalecencytosis [presumably he meant agranulocytosis, a rare blood disorder]. Took a peak [sic] at my chart yesterday and could see that they were mentally measuring me for a coffin. Eat, drink, and make Olive [Cawley], as tomorrow or next week we attend my funeral."[29]

January 27: "Flash! Got the hottest neck ever out of Hanson Saturday night. She is pretty good so am looking forward to bigger and better ones. Also got a good one last night from J. so am doing you proud. Gave up Bunny Day, I must admit, as a failure." (In an earlier letter he had boasted that he would soon "climb" her "frame.")[30]

Though playful in these missives, Jack could be cruel toward Lem in a way that betrayed his sense of entitlement. "I don't know why you and Rip are so unpopular with girls," he scoffed in one, signing off with one of his nicknames: "You're certainly not ugly looking exactly. I guess they're [sic] is just something about you that makes girls dislike you on sight. I was figuring it out this morning. . . . It certainly is too bad. I guess you are just not cut out to be a ladies man. Mr. Niehans even has a girl, and so has Ike England. Frankly, my son, I'm stumped. Well send me my belt you prick right away, Regards, Ken."[31]

Yet there was a tenderness in the letters, too, a vulnerability that Jack hated to reveal but that Billings undoubtedly picked up on, however couched it was in Kennedy's devil-may-care personal style. Still smitten with Olive Cawley, who had been named the first Peanut Festival Queen in Montclair, New Jersey, and was about to embark on a modeling career in New York, he asked Lem for help: "Am coming to you for advice on the Cawley situation—should I ask her after this deliberate slight?" (Olive had not replied to his most recent letter.) "It's your roomie who is asking and he's also asking you to leave my writing paper alone. That writing paper was a present from one of my feminine admirers, a woman who worships the very air I breathe," he said of Mrs. Billings, "but who unfortunately has a son with bad breath." The barb no doubt stung the easily wounded Billings, but he always sensed his friend's underlying devotion to him. Rip Horton saw this side of Jack, too. "[He] was very light, very witty, a particularly loyal good friend who cherished old friendships very, very much," Rip subsequently said. Sometimes, Horton added, Jack went to greater lengths to maintain the relationships than the friends did.[32]

Lem offered his own assessment: "I think it's interesting," he told an interviewer, "because I, frankly, haven't had another friend whom I've known as long as Jack Kennedy. . . . There must have been something about him that kept people wanting him to be their friend through all the years. Much more interesting is why Jack wanted to keep all these friends, since his mind and interests did grow, let's face it, at a much faster clip than any of his contemporaries."[33]

When Billings forfeited his scholarship at Princeton due to poor grades, Jack was quick to offer his sermonizing take. "It's too damn bad about losing your scholarship," he lectured, "but here is my advice. You have been a damn fool—spending money you didn't have, taking week-ends you shouldn't have, and generally fooling around." Jack did not deny that he was partly to blame, but he admonished his friend that only hard work could salvage the situation. "If you decide to go on a vacation you can come [to Palm Beach] as we have plenty of room. However, you have been a terrific ass, and unless you come around now, you haven't a chance. If you do good work now, maybe you can get the scholarship back."[34]

The exhortation worked; Lem put in the necessary effort to reclaim the scholarship.

Beyond the misdiagnosis of leukemia, the Boston doctors reached no conclusions, and in February 1936 Jack was dispatched to Palm Beach to convalesce. His father was there, still waiting to be tapped for a major job within the Roosevelt administration. He had concluded a successful tenure as head of the Securities and Exchange Commission and hoped now to get a bigger role—a cabinet position, certainly, and ideally Treasury secretary. Roosevelt's shift to the left in 1935—he created the Works Progress Administration, a massive employment and infrastructure program, and signed into law the Social Security Act—did not concern Kennedy, or if it did he refrained from saying so. On the contrary, he paid Arthur Krock of *The New York Times* $5,000 to gather together scattered notes into a short book with a snappy title, *I'm for Roosevelt*, that offered a rich man's fawning endorsement of the New Deal and a second FDR term and would be published under Kennedy's name in time for the 1936 presidential election. Businessmen should be grateful to Roosevelt for saving capitalism, the book argued, and it credited the president for every economic advancement since 1933.[35]

To head off complaints that the book was a mere attempt at gaining a senior post in Washington, Kennedy included a humble and disingenuous disclaimer at the outset: "I have no political ambitions for myself or my children and I put down these few thoughts about our President, conscious only of my concern as a father for the future of his family and my anxiety as a citizen that the facts about the President's philosophy be not lost in a fog of unworthy emotion."[36]

Barely had Jack arrived in Florida when his father determined that he needed fresh air and physical labor to build up his strength. (Jack had other ideas: "The girls are few and far between," he lamented to Billings early on, "but speaking of between, I expect I shall get laid shortly.") On Krock's recommendation, he arranged for his son to travel to the Jay Six Cattle Ranch, in Benson, Arizona, for several weeks of hard work in warm weather. It was a dramatic change for the East Coast urbanite, but the labor—making adobe bricks, rounding up cattle, fixing fences—seemed to have its desired effect.[37] Jack's health improved dramatically, and he soon found time for extracurricular adventures across the border in Nogales. "Got a fuck and suck in a Mexican hoar-house [*sic*] for 65¢, so am feeling fit and very clean," he reported to Billings in a letter entitled "Travels in a Mexican Whore-house with Your Roomie." He enthused, "What a thing of beauty my body has become with the open air, riding horses and Mexicans."[38]

One detects more than a bit of artistic license in these carnal boasts as our protagonist works to project an image of macho health—vigorous, outdoorsy, athletic, virile—that stands in contrast with the more fragile reality. "I think he was making it up," one college friend later said of the sexual bragging of this period in the mid-1930s. "That was the masculine ethic. And I think he made up three-quarters of it. And I don't hold it against him." Jack was telling his friends, telling himself, what kind of man he sought to be and could be. He projected an image of himself as a lothario well before he actually became one.[39]

Before returning to the East Coast, Jack headed for Hollywood, where he claimed he met and bedded a gorgeous movie extra. "The best looking thing that I have seen," he bragged to Lem. "I will show you her picture when I get in."[40] There followed a summer in Hyannis Port filled with fun and frolic with the rest of the Kennedy clan—Joe Junior, 21, Rosemary, 17, Kathleen, 16, Eunice, 15, Pat, 12, Bobby, 10, Jean, 8, and Teddy, 4—and a stream of visitors, who as always looked with astonishment at the packed event schedule and manic family energy. Relatives came, too, including the three children of Rose's sister Agnes and her husband, Joseph Gargan: Mary Jo, Joey, and Ann. (Agnes would die suddenly of an embolism in September, at age forty-three; in subsequent years, the Gargan kids would spend their summers on the Cape, effectively raising the size of Joe and Rose's brood to an even dozen.) If Jack did not hold quite the esteem in his younger siblings' eyes that the mature and responsible Joe Junior did, he had their affection for his witty individualism and for the attention he paid to them—not least Rosemary. As Eunice remembered, he quietly made sure his mentally challenged sister was not left out at parties: "Jack would take her to a dance at the club, and would dance with her and kid with her and would make sure a few of his close pals cut in, so she felt popular. He'd bring her home at midnight. Then he'd go back to the dance."[41]

Much time was spent on the water that summer, in innumerable sailing competitions. Together Joe Junior and Jack raced from Edgartown, on Martha's Vineyard, to Nantucket and back to Hyannis Port. At the end of

August, Jack won a major solo race, the 1936 Atlantic Coast Champion-ships, with a margin of victory—four minutes—that astonished other sailors. No doubt it helped that the ever competitive Joseph P. Kennedy employed a Scandinavian maintenance expert that summer to look after the family's boats in order to make sure each was in tip-top racing shape.

Jack also found time to do something else: reapply to Harvard. He pre-ferred it over the smaller, more cloistered Princeton, he had decided, and it was where his father always wanted him to go. Young Joe, too, urged him to join him in Cambridge. Now entering his third year, Joe had expe-rienced disappointments at Harvard—he'd been passed over by the elite final clubs and had yet to find glory on the football field—but he liked his courses in government and had a coterie of friends who appreciated his endless energy and ebullience. Women were a preoccupation and, follow-ing his father's example, he played the field with abandon, preferring showgirls over coeds. (The former were less likely to latch on, he said, less likely to make demands.) On one occasion he escorted to a Harvard dance the budding film star Katharine Hepburn, who accepted his invitation on the condition that her mother also join.[42]

Jack wrote from Hyannis Port on July 6:

Gentlemen, I am writing in regard to my entering Harvard this fall, in the class of 1940. I presented an application to enter Harvard . . . last year to enter with the class of 1939 which was accepted. My plans changed, and I decided to go abroad to the London School of Economics for a year. . . . After my return from [Florida] I went out to Arizona returning a week ago. After seeing my physician who said he thought it would be perfectly all right for me to attend college next year, I decided to present my application to Harvard. If there is any other information desired, I should be glad to communicate with you or go to Boston to discuss the matter.[43]

To be on the safe side, Jack submitted a similar letter to Princeton. But within three days Harvard's dean of freshmen replied with the good news: he was in.[44] In his roundabout way, Jack had had what in today's parlance would be referred to as a gap year between high school and college, and he arrived in Cambridge in August a year older than most freshmen and two years older than a few. He stood six feet tall and weighed 149 pounds, and felt as good as he had in years.

IV

The Harvard that Jack Kennedy entered in the fall of 1936 was still what it had been when his father matriculated three decades before, and when his great-grandfather Patrick Kennedy stepped ashore in nearby East Boston sixty years before that: the oldest, most richly endowed, and most prestigious university in the nation. Jack's arrival coincided with the institution's three hundredth anniversary and all the attendant celebrations. (On September 18, fifteen thousand alumni, including Franklin Roosevelt, joined delegates from five hundred universities around the world for a day of speeches and celebration in Harvard Yard.)[45] But there was scant evidence of smug self-satisfaction that fall in the presidential office of James B. Conant. Since becoming Harvard's leader three years before, Conant, a gaunt and bespectacled chemist whose descendants arrived in the Massachusetts Bay Colony in 1637 but whose father was a lowly photoengraver from Dorchester, had set about making the institution more meritocratic, more academics-focused. His predecessor, the aristocratic and conservative A. Lawrence Lowell, had taken office in 1909, soon after Joe Senior matriculated, and over the next quarter century had done much to enhance Harvard's architectural glories as well as its already robust reputation for exclusion: he set quotas on Jewish admissions, kept the small number of black freshmen out of Harvard dorms, and refused Marie Curie an honorary doctorate on account of her sex. When a senior professor was revealed to be a homosexual, Lowell not only demanded his prompt resignation but urged him to use a gun to "destroy himself."[46]

Conant was no strict egalitarian, but he recognized that Harvard needed to change, needed to prioritize scholarly over social distinction. Rival institutions in the Midwest and California were on the rise, and it was no longer unheard of (if still rare) for major professors to turn down chairs at Harvard. Standards of faculty promotion were too lax, Conant determined, and the college was filled with "mediocre men" who were not doing first-rate original research. He set about toughening hiring and tenure standards for faculty and redressing what he saw as the "exclusively eastern orientation" of the student body (some 90 percent of the students came from states along the Eastern Seaboard) by offering Harvard National Scholarships to notably talented applicants from the Midwest and Far West who might not otherwise be able to afford the annual tuition of $400 or the additional $700 for room and board. "Many boys without financial resources are potentially future leaders of the professions, of business, and of public affairs," Conant declared. "The country needs their talents and character." Much to the delight of Irish, Italian, and Jewish day students from middle- or lower-class backgrounds who commuted by subway from their homes in greater Boston, he set aside the ground floor of Dudley House so that these boys would have somewhere to eat their brown-bag lunches.[47]

The journalist Theodore H. White, class of 1938 and one of the commuters, thrilled at Conant's reforms. "Excellence was his goal as he began shaking up both faculty and student body," White would recall in his captivating memoir *In Search of History*, before quoting approvingly from the president's address to the freshmen in August 1934: " 'If you call everyone to the right of you a Bourbon and everyone to the left of you a Communist, you'll get nothing out of Harvard,' he said to us. And he went on to explain that what we would get out of Harvard was what we could take from it ourselves; Harvard was open, so—go seek."[48]

All the same, college life went on much as it had before. Students continued, as always, to subcategorize themselves—no less under Conant than under his predecessors—and the hierarchies of privilege remained firmly in place. Theodore White identified three categories: white men, gray men, and meatballs. The white men were the "white shoe" prep school grads of prominent name—White's own class contained two Roosevelts, a Hearst, a Rockefeller, a Morgan, a Saltonstall, and, a tad apart, a certain Joseph Kennedy Jr.—many of whom adhered to the timeworn maxim of the Harvard gentleman: "Three C's and a D, and keep out of the newspapers." The gray men were the products of public schools, "sturdy sons of the middle class." They played football and baseball and hockey, edited the *Crimson* and the *Lampoon*, and ran for student government. (Among the gray men in White's year was Caspar Weinberger, later to be Ronald Reagan's secretary of defense.) At the bottom of White's classification was his own group, the meatballs—scholarship boys and day students, many of them Italian, Jewish, or Irish. "We were at Harvard not to enjoy the games, the girls, the burlesque shows of the Old Howard, the companionship, the elms, the turning leaves of fall, the grassy banks of the Charles," White wrote. "We had come to get the Harvard badge, which says 'Veritas,' but really means a job somewhere in the future, in some bureaucracy, in some institution, in some school, laboratory, university, or law firm."[49] For these students, social life at Harvard was a closed book—they emerged from the subway station in Harvard Square in the morning, went to class, and were whisked away on the evening train.

Within the groups could be found further distinctions. In Anton Myrer's novel *The Last Convertible,* set in the same period, the blandly lovable narrator, George Virdon, a solidly middle-class product of a public high school who is at Harvard only because of a scholarship, describes the particular snobbery of the "St. Grotlesex" men—that is, the graduates of St. Mark's, St. Paul's, Groton, and Middlesex—who "by and large kept to themselves, dined and hung out at their exclusive final clubs, took a very casual attitude toward classes and grades, and very nearly constituted a college within the college. A Groton man sat next to me in a course on the Hapsburg Empire and never said a single word to me. Not one. It wasn't that he cut me, exactly—I don't think he ever even saw me. Some, like me, can accept it with equanimity and go their way. For others . . . it eats away at the vitals like acid: they may suppress it, but they never get over it."[50]

A few students defied categorization. For White, the outstanding example in his class was the brilliant Arthur M. Schlesinger Jr., whose father was on the faculty in history and who somehow mingled with the meatballs as easily as with the gray and white men. With his intellectual precocity and ravenous curiosity, Schlesinger asked only that people be interesting. "How could one not be friendly to dear Teddy White, himself the most loyal and sentimental of old friends?" Schlesinger wrote in his own memoirs of his friend's description.[51]

Jack Kennedy likewise would skirt White's taxonomy when he arrived at Harvard two years later. According to family wealth and academic pedigree, Kennedy should have been in the top group, but his private school, though prestigious, was not "St. Grotlesex." (In Myrer's formulation, the men from larger prep schools such as Andover, Milton, Exeter, and Choate were "better mixers" than those from St. Grotlesex, though they still tended to separate themselves from the groups below them.) More important, Kennedy was an Irish Catholic in what was still a bastion of WASP privilege. He, too, was a kind of outsider, and it generated in him a palpable detachment, an aloofness resulting from his uncertainty about where he really belonged. It also made him more accepting of other outsiders, of whatever stripe, made him inclined to take people for who they were. At Choate he had moved easily among boys from different backgrounds; his best friend, Lem Billings, was a middle-class scholarship student from Pittsburgh. At Harvard as well, Kennedy's circle of acquaintances would be wide, even if made up mostly of gray men and white men. His best friend would be Torbert "Torby" Macdonald, himself a hybrid: a middle-class Irish Catholic from suburban Boston who had gone to Andover and who commuted from home his freshman year.

Daily routines were complicated for the students of that era, as Schlesinger recalled. Wristwatches had to be wound on a nightly basis, as battery-powered watches were still to come. Garters held up socks, and all shoes had laces, the loafer being deemed unacceptable. When there was writing to do, students filled fountain pens from inkwells—the ballpoint pen was not yet a thing. There were no televisions, no electric blankets, no air-conditioning. Manners, meanwhile, were more formal, and few Harvard students sported beards or crew cuts. Caps were seldom seen except among self-identified proletarians. The women of Radcliffe all wore skirts, and were forbidden from appearing hatless in Harvard Square.[52]

Then as now, Harvard housed most of its freshmen in Harvard Yard, the symbolic heart of the university, a pastoral green oasis of twenty-two acres set apart from the frenetic bustle and noise of the Square. Here were located, in addition to the dorms, two dozen classroom and administration buildings of diverse character, massed around quadrangles and courtyards, with diagonal walking paths dissecting the expansive lawns and a canopy of mature elms that provided a sense of enclosure. Entry came by way of two dozen gates scattered about the perimeter. Jack was assigned a single in Weld Hall, mere steps from the Widener Library, the crownpiece of the largest university library system in the world, its imposing pillars and gray facade dominating the Yard. From its colonnade he could look across the treetops to the gilt face and black hands of Memorial Hall. Whether the young man darkened the library's doorways much in that first year is questionable—unlike Teddy White, Kennedy *was* in college to enjoy the games, the girls, and the burlesque shows. He scraped by in his freshman classes, earning C's in English, French, and history and a B in economics, but academics were a secondary concern, suggesting that the gap year had not done much to focus his scholastic energy.[53]

No, for Kennedy college was about athletics and skirt chasing, in varying order. He dreamed of football glory, of scoring touchdowns on crisp autumn afternoons, and lined up with a hundred other freshmen for tryouts by the Charles River. Varsity was out of the question, but he made the freshman squad through intense effort—he induced Torby Macdonald to throw passes to him for long hours after practice—though his scrawny frame was a liability, especially in an era when one played both offense and defense. He was a talented receiver (the most adept on the team, his coach said in a postseason review) and he knew how to tackle but was too skinny to block effectively. "Jack was a big, tall string bean," one of his coaches remembered. "He didn't look much like an athlete. You could blow him over with a good breath. He didn't have the physique for football. The game was too much for his build."[54]

Moreover, Jack's extracurricular pursuits affected his athletic ambitions as much as they impaired his academics. When his coach learned of a weekend of debauchery at Hyannis Port involving Jack and some teammates and several girls, he promptly demoted the player he (rightly) deemed responsible, namely Jack. "The fucking football situation has now gotten out of hand," Jack complained to Billings, "as the coaches found out about our little party and I am now known as 'Play-boy' . . . I have been shoved down to the third team."[55]

He had greater success in swimming and golf, both minor sports at Harvard. He was strong in the backstroke, even besting the reigning Harvard champion in that discipline on one occasion in the team tryouts. The scrapbook of John Sterling Stillman, a classmate who would serve as an assistant secretary of commerce in the Kennedy administration, includes programs from freshman-team swim meets in Jack's first year, when the team went undefeated and was deemed the strongest in the school's history. His participation in the three-hundred-yard medley team was credited with helping Harvard defeat Dartmouth College on March 6, 1937. He hoped to be added to the varsity squad for the big contest against archrival Yale later in the month, but was laid up in the infirmary in the days before the meet, and not even Macdonald smuggling steaks and shakes into his room in an effort to keep his weight up was enough—Jack lost by three seconds in the team tryouts to Richard Tregaskis, later of World War II reportorial fame for his book *Guadalcanal Diary*. In golf as well, Kennedy made the freshman squad, while in his sophomore year he also won distinction in sailing—he and Joe Junior, as members of the Harvard Yacht Club, each sailed a boat to victory to win the McMillan Cup for Harvard.[56]

"I had Jack Kennedy on my Harvard teams for three years," swim coach Hal Ulen recalled, "and I remember him very vividly. He was a fine kid, frail and not too strong, but always giving it everything he had. He was more of a team man than an individualist and, in fact, was so modest that he used to hide when news photographers would come around to take pictures of the team."[57]

The university suited him, he determined. He took to the general atmosphere of the place, to the quiet grace of the Yard, to the Charles and its grassy banks, to the history, the traditions. As a dormitory Weld Hall was nothing special, but he liked its central location and got on well with his housemates. The university's proximity to Boston and to various nearby women's colleges were also pluses, and even Harvard Square had a respectable assortment of restaurants and bookstores, certainly as compared with Princeton.

As at Choate, Jack operated in brother Joe's shadow, but he did not seem to be unduly troubled by the fact. The two-year gulf between them, so wide in childhood and adolescence, now seemed to narrow. They got on well, and saw each other regularly. When the time came in April 1937 to select a residence for the following fall, Jack chose Winthrop House, partly because it was the house favored by Harvard athletes but also because his brother lived there. At the same time, Jack insisted on cutting his own path, a point noted by Joe's tutor, the six-foot-eight Canadian transplant John Kenneth Galbraith, then a young lecturer in economics. Of Joe, Galbraith remarked that he was "slender and handsome, with a heavy shock of hair and a serious, slightly humorless manner. He was much interested in politics and public affairs," and "would invariably introduce his thoughts with the words 'Father says.'" (Rose at the same age had done the same with Honey Fitz.) Jack, on the other hand, was also "handsome but, unlike Joe, was gregarious, given to varied amusements, much devoted to social life and affectionately and diversely to women. One did not cultivate such students."[58]

That seems harsh—surely some such students, if they showed aptitude and latent promise, were worthy of cultivation. But it's true that our gangly nineteen-year-old gave few hints in his first year of college of the accomplishments to come. He made no notable impression in the classroom and lost badly in his bid to become president of the freshman class. (He was eliminated on the first ballot.) His greatest distinction was gaining the honor to serve as chairman—and master of ceremonies—of the

Freshman Smoker, a party for the freshman class held in Memorial Hall at the end of spring term. It was a big affair, with a guest list of more than a thousand; his brother had run the event two years before. Here Jack did prove his worth, arranging ample free food, tobacco, and ginger ale and putting together what some called the most impressive Smoker in Harvard's history, with forty entertainers, including two jazz orchestras as well as the Dancing Rhythmettes, and appearances by baseball stars Dizzy Dean and Frankie Frisch.[59]

The night's headliner was Gertrude Niesen, a prominent torch singer and actress. It says something about Jack Kennedy that, although a mere college freshman, he was not shy about directing wisecracks at a high-profile entertainer many years his senior. It started during the rehearsal and went on throughout the day, Jack's quips just cascading out of him and Niesen responding in kind. "She was giving it back and Kennedy was giving it to her in humor, and it was a very, very funny two hours, and it was a tremendous night," one classmate remembered. "He didn't take Gertrude Niesen seriously and she didn't take him seriously. It just worked very well. . . . And by eight or nine o'clock when the performance went on, I think we were all pretty well along in the evening, and Gertrude Niesen was just enjoying the hell out of it, and Jack Kennedy was joking with her the whole time." To another classmate, the Smoker "was Jack's first visible sign of being outstanding, the first time that people recognized him for being a little different from us."[60]

All the while, he put in the necessary work to get through his classes—if barely in some cases. ("Exam to-day so have to open my book to see what the fucking course is about," he wrote Billings.[61]) Few papers survive, but his effort for his French F class, ten pages in length and written half in English and half in French, offers fascinating insight into his thought processes and the man he was becoming.[62] For his topic, Jack selected Francis I, the French ruler of the first half of the sixteenth century. He chronicled Francis's rise to the top, stressing the key role played by the young monarch's cunning and ambitious mother in that ascent as well as his penchant for philandering from his early twenties on. "Ambitious, spoiled, possessed of an unbounded vitality and a physique capable of tremendous physical activity, he was the pride and personification of his age," Jack wrote. "His lusty interest in life took many forms, the chase, war, and women."

Women were one of the dominating interests in his life and he had many affairs. Unlike his contemporary across the channel, Henry VIII, he did not marry for reasons of the heart or the fulfillment of passion, but married for reasons of state and thus missed going down in the history books [as a lover]. Francis's marriages, definitely political, took up little of his time. He kept his first wife Claude, daughter of Louis XII, busy producing children, most of whom died while he continued his "amours guerreuses" with women like Le Foix. He knew women's place, however, and except for his mother and his sister, they never assumed a position of great influence, at least until his later life.[63]

Was there something of the young Jack Kennedy in this portrait? In all likelihood, yes. Moreover, Jack admired Francis's bold political leadership and military ambition. "Hardly on the throne, he had reached in a short time the zenith of his fortunes," he noted, though as it turned out his grip on power was tenuous, and in time would be overcome by the "methodical machine" of Charles V, resulting in Francis's disastrous defeat at Pavia in 1525. Thereafter, the king more and more experienced a life of "distractions, living with his thousands of courtiers and living from one chateau to another."

I have tried to give a picture of Francis's character and age. In studying his career it seems almost a pity that he could not have died at Pavia, as his career was an anticlimax [after that], although it had traces of glory. Francis was a man with an intense vitality for life: he was superficial but with some deep appreciations and as such was the perfect personification of the Renaissance. . . . On France he had written his signature in chateaux. He understood the technique of the architect, as patron and as connoisseur. We find the true spirit of the reign of Francis, at least the best part of it, in the Chateau of Chambord. It was a living monument of all that was great in his reign. His life was not futile. It served its purpose, that of jolting France out of Medievalism.[64]

The course instructor, Halfdan Gregersen, was underwhelmed. The French grammar was spotty at best, and for historical detail Jack relied too heavily on a few secondary sources. Gregersen gave the paper a

D-plus.[65] (Seven or eight decades later, in an era of less demanding grading, the paper would have merited a B– or a B.)

V

Undistinguished though Jack Kennedy's freshman-year academic performance was, his father, himself an academic mediocrity during his Harvard days, was pleased with what he saw. "I am impressed with the almost complete turnaround you have made in yourself in the last year," he wrote to his son in February 1937, brushing aside Rose's concerns that the boy was spending too much time in nightclubs. "You know I always felt that you had great possibilities and I think you are now starting to avail yourself of them." Kennedy encouraged his sons' skirt chasing and gallivanting about town, and welcomed their determined pursuit of athletic success. Schoolwork had its place, too, he believed, but mostly as a means to an end—power and social status. Jack was taking full advantage of his extracurricular opportunities, as he should. Moreover, he was doing so at Harvard, where Joe Senior had always wanted him to be. "Got a letter from J.P. purring on my shoulder," Jack wrote to Lem soon after. "He is really worshipping at my feet these days."[66]

At the same time, Mr. and Mrs. Kennedy urged their older children to broaden their horizons, to learn about the world. Over Christmas break in Palm Beach, Joe Senior expressed fears that a European war was coming and urged his second son to tour the Continent while he still could. "You ought to plan on seeing Europe before the shooting starts," he told him.[67] Jack, who had intended to spend the summer of 1937 racing his sailboat off Cape Cod, quickly warmed to the idea. At Harvard he had developed a particular interest in European history (during his four years he would take courses from prominent historians such as Roger Bigelow Merriman and William L. Langer), and he wanted to see the Continent up close. He would take his car, he determined, and would bring along a friend. Inevitably, the friend turned out to be Lem Billings. Joe Kennedy arranged with Mrs. Billings that he would pay Lem's fare, on the understanding that Lem would pay back at least a portion of the amount after his graduation from Princeton.

They set off from New York on June 30, 1937, aboard the SS *Washington*. Also making the trip was Jack's Ford, a convertible with a fold-down top that he bought on installment (with help from his father) early in his freshman year. More important for posterity, Jack also packed a small leather-bound notebook given him by Kick and bearing the title "My Trip Abroad," in which he jotted down notes as the mood struck him. His first entry was true to form: "Very smooth crossing. Looked pretty dull the first couple of days but investigation revealed some girls—chiefly Ann Reed. Had cock-tails with the Captain who knew Sir Thomas Lipton and thus grand-pa. The chief source of interest was General Hill and his rather mysterious daughter. He was a congressman, she might have been anything."[68]

The two friends stayed up all night to be sure to catch a passing glimpse of Jack's ancestral Ireland, but decided it had not been worth it, Lem remembered, as "it necessitated sleeping the entire next day." Upon docking at Le Havre, they took off in the Ford, bound first for Mont-Saint-Michel and then for Rouen, where the cathedral impressed them mightily. From there they motored on to Beauvais, some fifty miles north of Paris, bunking for the night in a spartan little inn called La Cotelette. Thus was established a pattern they would follow for much of the trip: days spent seeing architectural treasures and historic landmarks, followed by nights in modest hotels—Lem's budget would allow no more. "This is another side of Jack's character," a grateful Billings recalled. "He was perfectly happy to live at places for forty cents a night, and we ate frightful food . . . but he did it [because] that was the only way I could go with him."[69]

Initially, Lem had the greater interest in the cathedrals and monuments, but Jack, too, was drawn in, albeit more by the historical dimensions than by the aesthetics. "Up at 12:00," reads his diary entry for July 8. "Wrote letters had lunch got our money and the medicine for Billings 'mal d'estomac' after much trouble—Then to Soissons—saw the Chemin des Dames—one of the great scenes of fighting during the war. Also saw the cathedral that had been bombed—then to Rheims where we looked at the cathedral and to the Hotel Majesty (1.00 for room for 2)—My French improving a bit + Billings' breath getting very French. Went to bed early—General feeling seems to be there will not be another war."[70]

The next day, after arriving in Paris:

July 9—Rheims, Chateau-Thierry, and Paris. The general impression seems to be that Roosevelt—his type of government—would not succeed in a country like France, which seems to lack the ability of seeing a problem as a whole. They don't like [Premier Léon] Blum as he takes away their money and gives it to someone else. That to a Frenchman is *tres mauvais*. The general impression also seems to be that there will *not* be a war in the near future and that France is much too well prepared for Germany. The permanence of the alliance of Germany and Italy is also questionable. From there [Rheims] we went to Chateau-Thierry picking up two French officers on the way. Arrived in Paris around eight. By mistake in French, invited one of the officers to dinner but succeeded in making him pay for it. Looked around and got a fairly cheap room for the night.[71]

The readiness of the French to exploit American tourists got under the boys' skin, and they took to parking the car around the corner from a prospective hotel in order to keep the proprietor from getting ideas and squeezing a higher rate out of them. When the car lights needed fixing, Jack felt certain the repair shop had fleeced him. "Got another screwing— these French will rob at every turn," he noted sourly.[72] Still, he and Lem loved the City of Light, and stayed out late at Moulin Rouge and other nightspots. At Catholic Mass at Notre-Dame on July 13, the eve of Bastille Day, Jack secured a seat near the front (thanks to an assist from the U.S. embassy, where his father had contacts), in the same row as the French president, while the Episcopalian Billings sat in the far back. The next day they took in the Paris Exposition, where the modern aircraft on display transfixed Jack—this was the future of warfare, he intuited, the future of geopolitical power.[73]

All the while, Lem marveled at his ever inquisitive friend's penchant for asking the locals for their views on Hitler and the German threat, on whether a war was coming and, if so, whether France could win. The responses varied, but a common theme was that the newly constructed Maginot Line (a string of concrete fortifications and weapon installations erected by the French government in the northeast in order to deter an invasion) would keep the country safe. Jack also picked up a copy of John Gunther's book *Inside Europe,* which became his bedside reading as they pressed on southward, in the direction of the Spanish frontier.[74]

"Walls very high but beautiful inside," Jack wrote after visiting Blois. "Saw Wall of the Conspirators where 1500 were hung and also the place where Charles XIII bumped his head and died. Finally thrown off the walls and continued to Chenonceau, built on the water, which is also very impressive. . . . Drove through to Angouleme, thru Tours to Poitiers, both deserted towns, and spent the night for 10 francs each." Here they found a less tourist-friendly atmosphere than they had expected, and experienced difficulty getting traveler's checks cashed. "Very impressed by the little farms we have been driving thru," Jack wrote. "America does not realize how fortunate they are. These people are satisfied with very little and they have very little as it is really a very conservative country, at least outside Paris."[75]

VI

Even before leaving America's shores, the two Ivy Leaguers had talked of visiting Spain, which was in the throes of a civil war between General Francisco Franco's fascist rebels and a republican government in Madrid. It was a nonstarter, as they themselves knew—their passports were marked "Not good for travel in Spain." Still, they made a vain attempt to cross the border just south of Saint-Jean-de-Luz; the police turned them back. They did get a glimpse of the border town of Irún, which had been bombed by the rebels, and in the ensuing days Jack took every chance to talk with refugees and take notes on what he heard. Their harrowing tales left their mark. In particular, he recoiled from a story of an imprisoned father, starving after being kept without food for a week, being brought a piece of meat and eating it, then being shown his son's body with a piece of flesh cut out of it.[76]

The tales of barbarism offered by the refugees took on added credence for Jack and Lem when they attended a bullfight in Biarritz. "Very interesting but very cruel," Jack wrote, "especially when the bull gored the horse. Believe all the atrocity stories now as these southerners, such as these French and the Spanish, are happiest at scenes of cruelty. They thought funniest sight was when horse ran out of the ring with his guts trailing." Billings in his trip diary echoed the point, but later acknowledged that perhaps he and his friend couldn't appreciate the finer aspects of the sport: "Of course, we didn't understand this temperament at all, and were disgusted by it."[77]

Then it was on to Italy, with stops in Toulouse, Carcassonne, Marseilles, Cannes, and Monte Carlo en route. Jack, reading Gunther, kept pondering the Spanish situation. "Not quite as positive about Franco victory," he recorded from Toulouse. "Shows that you can easily be influenced by people around you if you know nothing, and how easy it is to believe what you want to believe." But the ultimate outcome in Spain, he went on, depended in large part on what the outside powers, in particular Germany, Italy, and Russia, chose to do.[78]

Lem took notice of his friend's ponderings and saw in them something new: while Jack on the trip was the same witty, fun-loving, and girl-crazy millionaire's son he had always been, Billings told a later interviewer, he now showed a new seriousness of purpose and "more of an interest and more of a desire to think out the problems of the world and to record his ideas than he did two years before at Choate." Harvard had had an effect, as had seeing the Old World up close. "What I'm trying to say," Billings observed, "is that there was a noticeable change in Jack Kennedy in the summer of 1937."[79]

The powers of observation were on display also in Mussolini's Italy. Jack had no affinity for fascism, but he was struck by the lively atmosphere on the country's streets and by the attractiveness of its people. "Fascism seems to treat them well," he remarked after two days. In Milan, the two stayed in an inn owned by a Fascist veteran of the Abyssinian campaign, "which he said was easy to conquer but uncomfortable." Pictures of Mussolini were everywhere, but Jack wondered, "How long can he last without money and is he liable to fight when he goes broke?" They took in Milan's vast cathedral, and saw Da Vinci's crumbling *Last Supper* at the Dominican monastery Santa Maria delle Grazie. Soon thereafter, Jack completed *Inside Europe*, observing that "Gunther seems to be more partial to Socialism and Communism and a bitter enemy of Fascism." But the question remained: "What are the evils of Fascism as compared to Communism?"[80]

On August 5, the Americans and their convertible arrived in Rome. The first night, they snuck into the Colosseum, only to find a big crowd already there. "Very impressive by moonlight," Jack noted, though he would soon decide that "the Italians are the noisiest race in existence. They have to be in on everything, even if it's only Billings blowing his nose." While in the Italian capital, the two boys attended a "fantastic"

Mussolini rally, witnessing firsthand Il Duce's strutting style, and visited the Vatican, where through Joe Kennedy's connections they met senior Church leaders, including Cardinal Eugenio Pacelli, whom they had earlier heard preach at Notre-Dame, in Paris.[81]

Jack also talked his way into a meeting with Arnaldo Cortesi, the *New York Times* correspondent in the city, in order to learn more about European geopolitical developments. Cortesi told him war was unlikely, given that "if anyone had really wanted war there had been plenty of excuses for it. . . . Said Europe was too well prepared for war now—in contrast to 1914." Jack came away energized by the encounter and scribbled notes about the nature of fascism, the relationship to socialism, and the possibility of a major military clash. "Would Fascism be possible in a country with the economic distribution of wealth as in the US? Could there be any permanence in an alliance of Germany and Italy—or are their interests too much in conflict?"[82]

There followed the obligatory visits to Florence, which disappointed Jack (though he was awed by Michelangelo's *David*), and Venice, where they met up with American friends, including Al Lerner, from Choate days, who was now also in Jack's year at Harvard. Photos survive of the suntanned Jack and Lem with the pigeons in Piazza San Marco, and there's also this cryptic entry in Jack's diary for August 15, concerning a date he had with a girl on which his pal tagged along for a ride on a gondola: "Billings managed to make a gay threesome. Billings objects to this most unjust statement."[83]

VII

Only one significant destination remained on the great summer odyssey of 1937: Hitler's Germany. In hindsight, with our knowledge of the ghastly conflagration that was to come, it looms as the most important part of the trip, but even at the time, Jack Kennedy gave it pride of place on the itinerary. He understood, as perhaps did Lem, that Europe's future as well as the world's rested in large measure on the German leader's ambitions. The previous March, Hitler had unabashedly flouted the Versailles Treaty by sending troops into the Rhineland, which had been designated a demilitarized zone. The Western powers stood by. In August

1936 he ordered compulsory two-year military service, and that November he intervened with German air power on the side of fellow fascist Franco in the Spanish Civil War. Again the Western governments did little. All the while, Hitler engaged in intimidation of his country's neighbors, especially those with German-speaking populations along the borders of the Reich, and set his sights on bringing Austria, the land of his birth, into the German fold.

Departing Italy on August 16, the boys motored their way north, through the Brenner Pass and thence to Germany by way of Austria and a youth hostel in Innsbruck. Upon arrival in Munich, the cradle of National Socialism, where Hitler had gotten his start with his failed Beer Hall Putsch of 1923 and where the buildings were now festooned with Nazi flags and pictures of the Führer, Jack recorded his view that the German dictator "seems as popular here as Mussolini was in Italy, although propaganda seems to be his strongest weapon."[84]

The vibe in Bavaria felt wrong from the start, ominously so, in the boys' minds. Both experienced a sense of foreboding as the days passed. "We had a terrible feeling about Germany and all the 'Heil Hitler' stuff," Lem remembered. He and Jack found the Germans arrogant beyond measure, eager to show these Americans how superior they were. "Got up late and none too spry," Jack scribbled in his diary early on. "Had a talk with the proprietor who is quite the Hitler fan. There is no doubt about it that these dictators are more popular in the country than outside due to their effective propaganda." To Jack, it seemed doubtful that the Nazi regime had any real answer for the country's core problems: too few resources for too large a population, and too many rival powers working—singly and in coordination—to keep German ambitions in check.[85]

Jack's skepticism stood in contrast with the assessment offered by his brother Joe three years before, in 1934, when he visited Germany during his LSE year and was swept up in the Nazi mania. Hitler's murderous intentions were then less obvious to outsiders, and one could make allowances as well for Joe's tender age (he had yet to turn nineteen), but his words are nonetheless jarring, especially given that he had already then decided on a political career. He wrote to his father:

Hitler came in [to power]. He saw the need of a common enemy. Someone of whom to make the goat. Someone, by whose riddance the Germans would feel they had cast out the cause of their predicament. It was excellent psychology, and it was too bad that it had to be done to the Jews. This dislike of the Jews, however, was well-founded. They were at the heads of all big business, in law, etc. It's all to their credit for them to get so far, but their methods had been quite unscrupulous. . . . As far as the brutality is concerned, it must have been necessary to use some, to secure the wholehearted support of the people, which was necessary to put through this present program.

"As you know," Joe Junior continued, "[Hitler] has passed the sterilization law which I think is a great thing. I don't know how the Church feels about it, but it will do away with many of the disgusting specimens of men which inhabit this earth." Overall, he summarized, the Nazi program had created "a remarkable spirit which can do tremendous good or harm, whose fate rests with one man alone."*[86]

Having had their fill of Munich, Jack and Lem drove on to Nuremberg. The quality of the German roads awed them—especially the new autobahns, the world's first interstate highways—and Jack insisted on picking up hitchhikers and quizzing them on the state of affairs and their views of the Nazi regime. In Nuremberg they learned that Hitler would be holding a rally in the city three days hence; they contemplated staying around for it (and later regretted not doing so) but once again found the haughtiness of the people hard to take. They hit the road again—"Started out as usual except this time we had the added attraction of being spitten on," as Jack laconically put it in his diary, without further details—and made their way for England via Holland, Belgium, and finally the port of Calais.[87]

Time was now of the essence, as Jack wanted desperately to get to London to see Joe Junior and Kick before they returned to America. He made it in time, shopping with Kick rather than joining his brother on a visit with Harold Laski. He also met with his mother in Southampton, dutifully complimenting her on her latest Parisian fashion purchases and helping himself to what Lem in his diary referred to as a "mix of tomato juice & plenty of chocolate."[88] Back in London, he developed a bad case of hives,

* Joe Senior responded that he was "very pleased and gratified at your observations of the German situation. I think they show a very keen sense of perception, and I think your conclusions are very sound." (JPK to JPK Jr., May 4, 1934, box 21, JPK Papers.)

Jack with Dunker, the dachshund he and Lem bought for $8 at a
stop on the road to Nuremberg, and which Jack intended as a gift for
Olive Cawley. Soon after this photo was taken, Jack started wheezing
and sneezing; a German doctor determined he was allergic to dogs.
In Utrecht, someone agreed to buy Dunker for $3.

perhaps from the chocolates, prompting a frantic search by Billings for a
doctor who would pinpoint the problem. One physician after another was
stumped, until suddenly one morning the hives disappeared as fast as
they had arrived. Soon after, the two young men embarked on the journey home to the United States, with a stop in Scotland on the way.

It's tempting in hindsight to attach weighty importance to lengthy jaunts like the one Jack Kennedy and Lem Billings had in the summer of 1937. To do so isn't always wise. The two were in most respects the same young men after the two-and-a-half-month trip that they had been before. Still, the adventure left an impression. In Jack's case, his international sensibility, encouraged by his mother from the time he was a young boy, deepened, and one is struck as well by the increasingly sophisticated nature of his queries as the journey progressed, until by the end they were as serious-minded, if not yet as well developed, as those of professional journalists and diplomats. His determination to form independent judgments rather than simply echo his father's assessments or give in to lazy isolationist clichés about "foreigners" grew stronger. Most portentously, one sees in the young Kennedy that summer an emerging capacity and willingness to view world affairs in contextual, dispassionate terms—a contrast with his father, who tended always to view the outside world mostly in terms of what it meant for himself and his family.[89]

As it happened, this tendency on the part of Joseph P. Kennedy to personalize all public policy issues would soon land him in a heap of trouble, and in time cause a further separation in the worldviews of father and son.

PART
II

WARTIME

PREVIOUS PAGE: The flag from PT 109, replaced in July 1943, the month before the boat was sunk.

OUR MAN IN LONDON

On March 1, 1938, six months after John F. Kennedy left England in total anonymity to return for his sophomore year at Harvard, his father arrived on British shores to great fanfare. Newsreel cameras were there to record the event, just as they had been there for his departure from New York aboard the SS *Manhattan* six days before. "All of the children, except Jack [sick in Cambridge], were there to see me off, but I couldn't get to them," the father recalled. "Newspaper men, casual well-wishers, old friends and strangers by the thousand, it seemed to me, pressed into my cabin until we all nearly suffocated." Only with extreme effort did he make it to the deck to bid farewell to his brood.[1]

The reason for the hoopla: Joseph P. Kennedy had been named U.S. ambassador to Great Britain and was there to take up his post. He would present his credentials to King George VI at Buckingham Palace in a few days, and would hold early meetings with Prime Minister Neville Chamberlain and Lord Halifax, the foreign secretary. His family would follow him to London in short order. For journalists on both sides of the Atlantic, it was an irresistible story: the dynamic Irish Catholic Wall Street tycoon with the huge and handsome family taking the helm in London—the headlines practically wrote themselves. The *New York Times* society page even published the travel times for the remaining Kennedys—Rose and most of the children would sail on March 9, readers were informed, and Joe Junior and John would follow in June, at the conclusion of Harvard's spring term.[2]

It was a moment of triumph for the forty-nine-year-old Kennedy, the pinnacle of his public career to that point, and the climax of his five-year quest to land a prominent position in Franklin D. Roosevelt's government. Time and again during those years, Kennedy had believed that a senior cabinet appointment was in the offing, only to see his hopes dashed. Instead he had made do with second-tier positions, first as director of the SEC and then, in 1937, as the first head of the U.S. Maritime Commission. In both positions, he earned high marks with the public and the press alike—in September 1937, *Fortune* magazine made him the subject of a flattering cover story. But it was not enough. Kennedy wanted more, felt he deserved more after all he had done for this president and this White House. He had brought in $150,000 in donations for FDR's 1932 campaign, including $25,000 of his own money, and had published a gushing campaign book, *I'm for Roosevelt*, in time for Roosevelt's reelection effort in 1936. He'd helped FDR's son Jimmy build a successful insurance company in Boston and brought Jimmy and his wife along on a European vacation. When, in 1933, Father Coughlin, a Detroit-based Catholic priest and radio personality, built up a mass following with his fiery weekly sermons bashing capitalism and New Deal social programs alike (later he veered into anti-Semitism and pro-Nazism), Kennedy used his influence within the Catholic hierarchy to shackle him, joining with prominent bishops to isolate Coughlin and prevent him from gaining Vatican support.[3]

Beyond that, Joseph Kennedy had been a close associate of the president, advising him on finance-related policy issues and socializing with him—with regularity, Roosevelt would slip away from the White House for an evening at Marwood, Kennedy's twenty-five-room rented mansion in the Maryland countryside, in order to sip martinis and watch the latest Hollywood movies in the basement theater. Sometimes the president stayed overnight.[4]

It bears underscoring just how unusual it was for a Wall Street chieftain, a member of the nation's economic super elite, to be in the administration's corner. But Kennedy fit the bill. Though he occasionally expressed private concerns about Roosevelt's leftward turn in domestic policy in mid-decade, he refrained from expressing his misgivings publicly. Wall

Street bigwigs called him a traitor to his class (a charge they also leveled against FDR); he ignored them. The president had gotten the economy going again in his first term, Joe believed, and for that he deserved steadfast backing. He offered no dissent to FDR's powerful summation of his New Deal philosophy in his second inaugural, in January 1937: "The test of our progress is not whether we add more to the abundance of those who have much; it is whether we provide enough for those who have too little."[5]

"We've got to do something for old Joe, but I don't know what," Roosevelt told Jimmy not long after the 1936 election.[6] The president knew that Kennedy longed to be Treasury secretary, but that was a nonstarter: Roosevelt had no interest in moving his trusted ally and Dutchess County neighbor Henry Morgenthau Jr. from the post, and moreover he considered Kennedy too temperamental and thin-skinned, too filled with brooding resentments, too inclined to go his own way on policy, for such a prominent cabinet job. (A skeptic could reply that others in the cabinet had precisely those attributes.) As much as he valued Kennedy's camaraderie and often shrewd policy advice, and admired his managerial talents, he also mistrusted him as an implacable and power-hungry schemer out for his own interests. Yet the president understood at the same time that an unhappy Kennedy was a vocal and vengeful Kennedy, a Kennedy prone to running his mouth in a detrimental way to everyone within earshot, not least journalists. The Maritime Commission posting bought some breathing space, but Roosevelt knew it was just a matter of time before Kennedy resumed his efforts. Sure enough, in mid-1937 Kennedy began spreading the word around Washington that he had a new position in mind for himself: ambassador to the Court of St. James's.

The idea had been building in his mind for some time. The ambassadorial post in London was the most important overseas political posting in the American government, and the growing possibility of war in Europe only added to its cachet. In glamour terms, too, the job had no peer among U.S. positions abroad—it was the top of the social ladder. Through this appointment Kennedy would show those Boston Brahmins that he could get there without their help, that he would indeed be their social superior, and would secure tremendous societal preferment for himself and his children. On top of that, he would be the first Irish Catholic ambassador to Great Britain, a delicious irony in its own right. Most enticingly of all, the posting had long been a stepping-stone to greater things—the list of past ambassadors to London included five presidents, four vice presidents, and ten secretaries of state. Perhaps if he performed creditably in London, the Treasury posting, if not something still greater, could yet be his. When, in the fall of 1937, it became clear that Robert Bingham, the current ambassador, would have to resign on account of illness, Joe stepped up his campaigning. If he could not have the Treasury, he told Jimmy Roosevelt, he wanted London.[7]

Jimmy duly reported the exchange to his father, who on first hearing it threw his head back and "laughed so hard he almost toppled from his wheelchair." Surely Kennedy must be joking. The man had never shown much interest in, or knowledge of, international affairs, and he seemed by temperament spectacularly unsuited for the byzantine world of great-power diplomacy. Frank and profane, he did not "do nuance," yet he would be entering a world in which nuance was everything, in which people moved discreetly, meticulously, speaking in terms that concealed as much as they revealed, for the words would be written down by note-takers during or immediately after the meeting. Impatient with ceremonial events and rituals, Kennedy would have his calendar filled with them. His supreme self-confidence and conviction that he always knew best would count for little in a job in which he was only the spokesman for those in Washington who had the real power. He would have to practice consummate discretion, would have to submerge his ego for the greater good, would have to surrender his right to express personal opinions except in total privacy—could anyone possibly think Joe Kennedy would or could do so?[8]

The more he thought about it, however, the more Roosevelt saw advantages in the appointment. To begin with, Kennedy fulfilled a principal requisite for the job: he was rich. The ambassador to London would be expected to entertain on a grand scale while on a meager annual salary of $17,500 and an even more pitiful annual allowance of $4,800. Most entertainment costs would have to be paid out of pocket, which the mega-wealthy Kennedy could easily do. In addition, Kennedy already maintained personal relationships with leading British financiers, several of whom had hosted him on a visit to London in 1935; by all accounts he got on well with them. A shrewd negotiator and a skilled analyst who would not be swayed easily by ideology or fervor, he could also be counted on to be a trustworthy eavesdropper on the mounting rumors of war, a straightforward reporter of what he heard—and in the best listening post in Europe. Finally, there was the enchanting image of an Irishman at the Court of St. James's, which appealed to FDR's penchant for the whimsical gesture and which also had a more strategic element, in that it could score points for FDR with Irish Catholic voters, an important bloc in several states. As an Irish American, moreover, Kennedy would be less likely than his Anglophile predecessors to fall under the sway of the urbane and smooth-talking English. Roosevelt harbored a simmering dislike of what he saw as the imperiousness of British officials toward their American cousins, and he wanted an emissary who would deal unsentimentally and clearheadedly with his hosts. Kennedy could be that man.[9]

Top White House advisers were of two minds when they learned that Roosevelt might actually nominate Joe Kennedy to the post. Many of them resented Kennedy for his outspoken ways and for his habit of criticizing the president behind his back. They disliked his air of superiority, his certainty that he knew more than they did about the economy and business, and they suspected that his professed loyalty to the administration was skin-deep—his only allegiances were to his family and to his own advancement. "Don't you think," Morgenthau asked the president, "you are taking considerable risks by sending Kennedy who has talked so freely and so critically against your Administration?" FDR didn't disagree, but for this very reason he and some aides saw the attraction of getting the man away from the domestic press and shipping him overseas. "Kennedy is too dangerous to have around here," Roosevelt told Morgenthau, even as he assured his Treasury secretary that he had "made arrangements to have Joe Kennedy watched hourly and the first time he opens his mouth and criticizes me, I will fire him."[10]

On December 9, 1937, *The New York Times* broke the news that Kennedy would succeed Bingham. It was still unofficial, but friends expressed their enthusiasm and the Boston press churned out adulatory spreads detailing his life story and rise to prominence. Rose Kennedy voiced her appreciation privately in a letter: "My dear Mr. President, I do want to thank you for the wonderful appointment you have given to Joe. The children and I feel deeply honored, delighted, and thrilled, and we want you to know we do appreciate the fact that you have made possible this great rejoicing." Her husband, meanwhile, began assembling the publicity team he would take with him to London—Eddie Moore, of course, plus longtime aides Jim Seymour and Harvey Klemmer and, as press liaison, Harold Hinton, a reporter on leave from *The New York Times*. He also called his sister Loretta and asked her to locate all the old Boston Irish friends of their father's and urge them to be on the dock in New York to see him off.[11]

Only one discordant note could be heard within Kennedy's circle. Boake Carter, one of the nation's leading radio commentators and a fierce New Deal critic, wondered if his friend was really suited for a diplomatic position in which he would be taking orders from Washington and mostly conveying information back and forth from the State Department to the British Foreign Office. Kennedy assured him he was, but Carter remained skeptical. With uncanny foresight, as it would turn out, he predicted that if Kennedy took the post, he would return to the United States a defeated man, his reputation in tatters, with any hope of higher office forever dashed.[12]

Kennedy waved aside Carter's concern, but he felt at least a twinge of foreboding, joking with journalists after arriving in London that he hoped they would be "down to see me off when I'm recalled." To Jimmy Roosevelt he wrote, "I may not last long over here, but it is going to be fast and furious while it's on." These doubting prognostications had a theatrical quality to them—Kennedy would never have accepted the posting if he really believed his chances of success were so low—but there was honesty in them, too.[13] A Cassandra by nature, Kennedy had long since operated on the principle that disaster was just around the corner. Add in the ominous state of world politics in early 1938 and his own lack of diplomatic experience and it's easy to understand his trepidation. Within days of Kennedy's arrival in England, Hitler completed his annexation of Austria, in explicit violation of the Versailles Treaty but in keeping with Hitler's blueprint for a new Greater Germany. Immediately he began targeting Czechoslovakia, locked between the upper jaw of Silesia and the lower jaw of Austria and with an ethnic German population in the Sudeten borderlands that he had long cultivated.* German-Italian relations were growing ever warmer, meanwhile, as Hitler and Mussolini prepared to meet at the Brenner Pass to discuss collaboration in the event of war. And in Asia the forces of imperial Japan, having moved southward from Manchuria (which the Japanese had seized in 1931–32), captured key portions of China, including the cities of Beijing and Shanghai. In Spain, the civil war raged on, with Italian troops as well as German weapons and aircraft bolstering Franco's rebels.[14]

---

* The Sudetenland was a mountainous, horseshoe-shaped territory tucked inside the northern, western, and southern borders of Czechoslovakia. It contained a German-speaking minority of 3.25 million people.

It all placed tremendous pressure on the year-old British government of Neville Chamberlain, and meant a baptism by fire for the new American ambassador. Still, Kennedy got off to a strong start. "The U.S.A.'s Nine-Child Envoy," one British tabloid dubbed him as he rode a wave of favorable early press coverage—facilitated, without doubt, by his energetic publicity operation in the embassy. Journalists seemingly could not get enough of this candid, unconventional diplomat with the blazing blue eyes, athletic build, and handsome family. "Jolly Joe," they called him, and "the Father of America." Everything he did made news. A number of articles lauded Kennedy's unpretentiousness in declining to wear knee breeches in presenting his credentials to the king (his secret reason: he was bowlegged and thought the attire would accentuate the fact) and in ending the practice of presenting socially ambitious American debutantes at court.[15] Others marveled at his chummy banter and his habit of putting his feet up on his desk during meetings with reporters. In a special stroke of luck, Kennedy, on his first round of golf in England, hit a hole-in-one on the 128-yard second hole at the Stoke Poges course, in Buckinghamshire. Within hours, the accomplishment was front-page news all over Britain—the Sunday *Observer* even announced a competition for the best poem about the feat—and Kennedy conjured up a quip he would use repeatedly in the early months: "I am much happier being the father of nine children and making a hole in one than I would be as the father of one child and making a hole in nine." His older sons, though, sent a deflating wire: DUBIOUS ABOUT THE HOLE IN ONE.[16]

II

The wire came from Harvard, where the spring semester was now in full swing. Joe Junior, having failed in his final attempt to win a letter in football, was hard at work on a senior thesis on American organizations and the Spanish Civil War, and he looked forward to graduating in May. Jack was halfway through sophomore year. His Old World sojourn with Lem Billings the previous summer had matured him and deepened his interest in European politics and history, but that fall Jack, like many Harvard sophomores then and since, had attached primary importance to two nonacademic rituals of second year: the move into the college "house" where he would live for the next three years, and the attempt to gain admission into one of Harvard's elite final clubs.

The house system was in fact quite new, the result of philanthropist Edward Harkness's vision of creating at Harvard something akin to the residential colleges at Oxford and Cambridge. President A. Lawrence Lowell liked the idea and persuaded Harkness to part with $13 million to make it happen. Under the resulting plan, undergraduates spent their final three years at the university living not in traditional dormitories but in houses, seven of which were newly built neo-Georgian "river houses" overlooking Boston from the banks of the Charles, with masters, resident tutors, common rooms, libraries, and dining halls (which had table service and printed menus, and to which students wore jackets and neckties). Their names evoked Harvard's history—Dunster, Eliot, Kirkland, and Leverett honored former presidents, while Adams, Lowell, and Winthrop recognized families long involved with the college.[17]

At Winthrop House, Jack roomed with Torby Macdonald, his good friend from freshman year. For their valet they hired, on a part-time basis, George Taylor, a cheerful, cigar-chomping African American whose calling card read "The Gentlemen's Gentleman" and who also worked in the same capacity for Joe Junior. Taylor soon found himself picking up after Jack, who maintained his sloppy ways and left clothes strewn all over the floor. "One time he was changing his clothes to go out," Macdonald remembered, "heaving his things into a heap in the middle of the floor. I told him to watch the way he was throwing things around our room because it was getting to look like a rummage sale. 'Don't get too sanctimonious,' Jack countered. 'Whose stuff do you think I'm throwing mine *on top of?*'"[18]

Torby soon figured out Jack's system of dressing: he would simply put on whatever articles of clothing he spotted first upon getting up in the morning. More often than not it would be a baggy tweed jacket, wrinkled khakis, unmatched socks, and scuffed shoes. This disheveled manner of dress would remain a hallmark well into adulthood.[19]

Macdonald would in short order become, in historian Herbert Parmet's words, "Harvard's counterpart to Lem Billings"—or, more accurately, the number-two man behind Lem in Jack's pantheon of friendships. Like Jack a second son who had to fight for recognition within his Irish Catholic family, Torby hailed from Malden, Massachusetts, where his par-

ents were schoolteachers and his father also coached the high school football team. A stellar athlete who excelled in football, baseball, and hockey
during his school days at Andover, Torby found success on the playing
fields of Harvard as well. (He showed his talent early, posting fourth-
quarter runs of sixty and twenty yards in the freshman game against
Yale, and would find an honored place in the school's football hall of
fame.) What drew him and Jack together, however, was their shared sense
of humor and their irreverence. They showed a proclivity for matching
wits in a rapid-fire and wickedly humorous way that their Winthrop
mates found irresistible. "Torby Macdonald was [Jack's] foil," one of these
friends recalled, "because Torby was a very brilliant person, and Torby
and he would have a dialogue with a laugh a second for four or five minutes at a time, and the rest of us would just sit there and enjoy it."[20]

Most of all, Jack and Torby shared a similar outlook on life and a sense
of trust. Born a mere eight days apart, they simply clicked. Friends could
see it, as could family members—including Kick, with whom Torby
promptly fell head over heels in love. Torby appreciated Jack's unpretentiousness and his disinclination to flaunt his family name, while Jack valued Torby's steadfastness and good cheer—and his status as an emerging
Crimson football star. Yet any friendship with Jack Kennedy had limits, as
Lem Billings had long since learned. When Macdonald, on one occasion,
overheard Joe Junior lambasting his brother, he intervened on Jack's side,
only to learn that, among the Kennedys, family always came first: "Jack
whirled on me and told me off in no uncertain terms for butting into a
family affair. I never did it again."[21]

Jack and Torby's Catholicism greatly lengthened the odds that either
of them would be chosen for a final club. Long the center of Harvard social life, final clubs had changed little since Joe Senior's day—they were
places where gentlemen took their meals, drank, and socialized. As before, clubmen were invited to the leading debutante parties on Beacon
Hill and in Brookline; as before, they defined the social hierarchy of the
college. Despite intense and continuous effort, Joe Senior had failed in his
quest to get membership, as had Joe Junior, who had had to content himself with admission into the Hasty Pudding Institute, the university's
famed theatrical society (to which Jack was also accepted). Joe Senior and
Joe Junior had both been stung by their failure, and it looked likely that
Jack would suffer the same fate. Classmate Jimmy Rousmanière later said:

There are eight final clubs at Harvard. Each of them elects ten to fifteen in a class, so there's only a hundred members accepted out of a class of a thousand. . . . All of October of the sophomore year is sort of rushing season, and you get invited around every night for three weeks. They would invite perhaps a hundred people and finally find 15 that probably would like to join a particular club, and be acceptable—and I don't think Jack Kennedy's name ever got on that 15 list! The power of the Boston alumni was still so great—and they didn't like Joe Kennedy or Honey Fitzgerald.[22]

But Jack had a couple of things going for him. To begin with, he had won kudos and a measure of renown for his chairmanship of the Freshman Smoker the previous spring. A rousing success, the event was still being talked about six months afterwards. In addition, Jack possessed a subtle social intelligence that his father and brother lacked, and he used his likability to excellent effect. Though no less determined than Joe Junior to win admission into a final club, he wore his ambition more lightly, and exuded more charm. He was also politically shrewder, and showed it by focusing his effort on the Spee Club, whose president, Ralph Pope, had expressed opposition to the anti-Catholic bias prevalent within Harvard institutions.[23]

Two years earlier, the Spee leaders had taken a pass on Joe Junior, whom they considered too pushy, and they now said no to Torby Macdonald, who, with his fondness for drink, seemed likely to solidify rather than weaken Irish Catholic stereotypes, and whose family was poor to boot. They might have rejected Jack as well had not two eminently viable friends, the blue-blooded Rousmanière and William C. Coleman Jr., the Episcopalian son of a Republican judge in Baltimore, made a pact that they would join only as a package with Jack. Pope took notice, and he liked what he saw in the younger Kennedy. "By the time you could say something," Pope remembered, "he had a question or a remark about it, which went right to the heart. You never had to fool around or wonder, 'What the hell does he mean?' " Pope signed off, "just for that reason— that we needed somebody with some sense in the place. We were a bunch of lightweights." He said to the delighted trio, "O.K., if you guys want this three-man deal, we want it too. We'll take you all."[24]

Jack had achieved what was previously unachievable for a Kennedy:

admission into the inner sanctum of establishment power, a Harvard final club.

III

The Spee's handsome Georgian building, at 76 Mount Auburn Street, became Jack Kennedy's second home for the remainder of his time at Harvard, his refuge, his place away from parental and professorial supervision and, when he so chose, from his roommate and his brother. He took many of his meals and did much of his socializing within the club's ivy-covered walls and in short order was made assistant treasurer of the club and elected to its board of governors. From the club's high-ceilinged, dark-paneled library, with its Hogarth prints, he wrote letters on the club's stationery to family and friends and read for his courses. Intellectually, too, the Spee helped shape him, as mealtimes were an opportunity for wide-ranging discussion among self-confident young men able to discourse openly, freed from the masters and tutors of their Harvard houses. Contrary to Ralph Pope's "lightweights" lament, the club was not without meritorious distinction, counting among its members Blair Clark, the

Members of the Spee Club in their distinctive blue and yellow English-style regimental ties, spring 1938. Kennedy is in the top row, fourth from right.

head of *The Harvard Crimson*, the college newspaper, as well as Cleveland Amory, another *Crimson* editor. "The Spee had a damn good membership in those days," recalled a member of the rival A.D. Club.[25]

Ironically, some contemporaries were of the view that the glory days of the final clubs were over. To them, the old Harvard of stark social stratification, clubmen, and "gentleman's C's" was fading away, on account of the new house plan as well as President Conant's emphasis on scholarly rather than social distinction. Arthur Schlesinger Jr., two years ahead of Jack in the class of 1938, predicted in *The Harvard Advocate,* the undergraduate literary magazine, that the house plan, together with the influx of midwestern students and public school graduates, would transform the social dimensions of the university and effectively kill the final clubs, or at least banish them to the margins of Harvard life. "With a wave of Harkness's hand," Schlesinger wrote, "their chief excuse for existence— the pleasant living they provided—vanished," for the houses provided facilities that were superior in all respects: comfort, convenience, and overall magnitude. "The clubs will probably persist," he went on, "vain and exclusive little organisms, sustained by sons who join the clubs of their fathers, looking from within like the distillations of the best in Harvard life but from without like fragile soda water bubbles; yet the day is in sight when they will stop being very important even to the five per cent who now turn to them for refuge."[26]

Decades later, Schlesinger would ruefully admit that his prediction had left out one key element: "the power of snobbery."[27] The university was becoming less homogeneous, more democratic, but the clubs remained in place and kept their standing atop the social order. Jack Kennedy was a proud clubman, certainly, thrilled with his new status and seemingly content with a gentleman's C average in his coursework. He did pull off a B in sophomore year in Professor Bruce Hopper's government class, New Factors in International Relations: Asia, but managed only a C in Modern Government, co-taught by William Y. Elliott and Arthur Holcombe, and in Introduction to Art History, with Wilhelm Koehler. He declared government as his concentration, and his main reading showed a tilt toward politics, history, and economics, with a list that included, among other books, Guy Stanton Ford's *Dictatorship in the Modern World,* Gilbert Seldes's *Sawdust Caesar,* Calvin Hoover's *Germany Enters the Third Reich,* Herman Finer's *Mussolini's Italy,* Marx and Engels's *Commu-*

nist *Manifesto,* Lenin's *State and Revolution,* and Charles Beard's *The Economic Basis of Politics.*[28]

In an English course on public speaking taught by Frederick Clifton Packard Jr., Jack earned a C. In a fascinating voice recording from that class uncovered by Harvard archivists in 2017, we hear the familiar voice and speech pattern, but with a more pronounced Boston accent, speaking in confident tones about Supreme Court justice Hugo Black and the recent revelation that Black had been a member of the Ku Klux Klan for almost two years in the 1920s. "Whether Mr. Black's appointment to the Court was the correct one is hard to say," the twenty-year-old declares early on. "It was evidently done in the heat of presidential anger at the conservative element who did not back Mr. Roosevelt's court plan. . . . He evidently had his reasons and he went forward as he saw them."[29]

The grades don't tell the full story, of course. They seldom do. Surely it reveals something about Jack Kennedy's interests and aspirations that he chose for his topic in the class the Hugo Black controversy, whereas most of his classmates—at least those also captured on the recording—selected more mundane topics, such as sourdough bread, book collecting, and how to find a wife. Payson Wild, the acting master of Winthrop House and Jack's instructor in Elements of International Law, remembered him as one who "really did have the ability to think deeply and in theoretical terms," and to ponder big questions such as "Why do people obey?" In their one-on-one tutorials, Wild was impressed with the young man's thoughtful and substantive analysis of the Aristotelian and Platonic political theories, and with how quickly he grasped the essentials of Hobbes, Locke, and Rousseau and the social contract theory of the state. Wild felt certain that Jack "had basically the deep interest, that there was in him a basis for all the pragmatic interests and concerns that he showed later on, which he had to show."[30]

Wild also tutored Joe Junior, finding him less substantial intellectually than his brother. His mind was less creative. But Joe seemed already then to be the gregarious would-be politician: "He would call out under my window, 'Hi, Dr. Wild. I'm coming.' But Jack would never do that. He'd come up in a much quieter way."[31]

Notwithstanding his growing interest in political matters, Jack steered mostly clear of the debates then roiling Harvard about the New Deal and Roosevelt's activist government. Perhaps in part because the president was an unpopular man in the Yard—when he drove through Harvard Square during the 1936 campaign, FDR was booed lustily by students whose wealthy parents hated his liberal policies—Jack appears to have shunned altogether the Young Democrats and the Harvard Liberal Union, and there's no evidence that he ever spoke out publicly in favor of Roosevelt's reforms.[32] The president, it seems, did not stir anything in him emotionally, either then or later. Still, Jack was proud of his father's service in the administration, and he backed the comprehensive governmental effort to help the mass of Americans suffering extreme hardship in the Depression. He endorsed, one close friend recalled, "what the New Deal was trying to accomplish and that that was what government should do where it could."[33] This was Joe Senior's view, too: unlike many Wall Street financiers, the elder Kennedy believed strongly in the state's role in lifting up the downtrodden.

That autumn of 1937, the brothers were honored to host their father as the featured speaker in the Winthrop House Thursday evening lecture series. Late in arriving to the hall on account of sports practice, the two, according to head waitress Deedee de Pinto, hung back, not wanting to cause a stir. "Then the housemaster said, 'Go on, boys, say hello to your father.' They went up and both boys kissed him," with no evident hesitation about showing such affection in public. John Kenneth Galbraith, then a Winthrop tutor, remembered "an absolutely wonderful talk, filled with anecdotes about [Kennedy's] days in the unregulated stock market, telling what he personally knew of bucket shops, wire houses and pools," and concluding with his role in "leading the raid as SEC policeman" that shored up the foundation of the capitalist system. Throughout, Galbraith was struck by the self-assurance, showmanship, and physical vitality that emanated from the lectern, and he concluded, "Kennedy was so ebullient and so successful in his presentation that even if his son had not become President, I would have remembered that night."[34]

Jack's health, meanwhile, continued to be better than it had been during his prep school years and his Princeton interlude but less good than it should have been. He went on suffering bouts of vague maladies. There were periodic trips to the infirmary and more than occasional missed classes. During fall football season, in which he suited up for the junior varsity team but saw little playing time, he suffered a debilitating back injury, though it did not prevent him from swimming that winter for Harvard against Penn, Columbia, Princeton, and Dartmouth.[35] In February

The Harvard swim team in 1938. Kennedy is standing, third from left.

1938, he paid a brief return visit to the Mayo Clinic, in Minnesota, to undergo tests relating to ongoing stomach and colon problems, and at the end of the month he found himself in the Harvard infirmary with a bad case of the flu. An intestinal infection followed in March that compelled a stay of several days in New England Baptist Hospital. His weight dropped through the spring, in spite of the ice cream machine his friends installed for him at the Spee Club.[36]

All the while, the astonishing Kennedy energy and vitality kept him going. Torby Macdonald marveled at the ceaseless activity, not least when it came to women. They gravitated toward Jack more than ever, drawn in by his winning smile and wry sense of humor, and by a lighthearted, peppery flirtatiousness that never seemed to cross the line into vulgarity or predatory encroachment. His relationship with Olive Cawley having sputtered to an end with his failed pursuit of her virginity, he now made up for lost time.[37] Housemates would watch in wonderment as one or another Boston waitress came calling at Winthrop House. Or they'd see him zoom by on Memorial Drive or Garden Street in his Ford convertible, accompanied by a young woman from Radcliffe or Wellesley or Mount Holyoke or another of the women's colleges in the area—seemingly a different girl each time.

His success with the opposite sex bemused him, at least in the early going. After all, he said to Billings, he wasn't much better looking than other guys. The explanation, he went on, had to be in his personality. Billings, when asked by an interviewer long afterwards, saw a combination of factors: "Whenever he was home, there was always a girl around—usually it was a different girl each time. Almost, without exception, every girl he showed any interest in became very fond of him. I think the reason for this was that he was not only attractive but also he had tremendous interest in girls. They really liked him and he was very, very successful. This was important to him because he wanted to be successful in this area. He really enjoyed girls."[38] Like father, like son, in other words—and like older brother.

When Boston seemed too confining, Kennedy and Macdonald would drive to Smith or Vassar for double dates, taking turns behind the wheel. (Whenever Torby drove, Jack would snooze, astonishing his friend with his ability to fall asleep almost at will.) Or Jack would take a weekend jaunt to New York City, where he'd meet up with Lem Billings and Rip Horton and head to the fashionable Stork Club, on East Fifty-third Street. "In those days, that was the place to go," Billings later said, "and the Stork Club was very anxious to attract young people. They particularly encouraged young models and pretty girls to come there, and they made things easier for the boys who brought pretty girls. . . . There were presents for the girls and champagne. Of course we were very careful never to have more than one drink each while we were there—we couldn't spend any more than that. Jack didn't mind spending on the same basis as I did. Jack wasn't much of a drinker, so it wasn't any hardship to take one drink. He liked to dance very much."[39]

"Jack certainly never made anyone conscious of his wealth," Macdonald related. "In fact there were times when he had a disconcerting lack of consciousness about it himself. Once we double-dated a couple of girls and dined in a rather expensive Boston restaurant. When the bill came it amounted to something like $12. Jack dug into his pockets and came up with exactly nothing. I checked my wallet and found eight one-dollar bills. We had to borrow from the girls to get out of the place."[40]

If not in his spending habits, Jack Kennedy's sense of entitlement manifested itself in other ways. He was a notoriously reckless driver, with a fondness for putting the pedal to the floor and maneuvering quickly even in tight spaces. On one occasion in Allston, across the river from Cambridge, near the gray-arcaded horseshoe of Harvard Stadium, he got into a row with a woman after he backed into her car. Subsequently, he told Lem, the woman reported him to the police, "saying I had leered at her after bumping her four or five times, which story has some truth although I didn't know I was leering." Instead of taking the heat, Jack pretended he had loaned the car to Billings and urged him to agree. "Tell [the officer] you come from Florida if he asks for your license—also you're sorry and you realize you should not have done it, etc. . . . You write him a gracious letter and admit it," he instructed. Lem, dutiful as always, went along.[41]

IV

Jack studied hard for his finals in the spring semester, hoping, he told friends, to finish with a flourish and make the dean's list. He must have known it was a nonstarter—he simply had too much ground to make up in too many classes. He did find success outside the classroom, teaming up with brother Joe to carry Harvard to victory in the McMillan Cup sailing race, off Cape Cod, defeating nine other college teams in the process. Soon after that, the brothers joined their ambassador father, who had returned from London to attend Joe Junior's graduation, on his voyage back to England. That summer, Joe Junior was to serve as secretary to his father while Jack would watch and learn and chip in as needed until the start of fall semester.[42]

The home visit had been a frustrating one for the ambassador. He had hoped to not only attend his firstborn's graduation from Harvard but receive an honorary degree from the university. Friends had lobbied hard on his behalf but were turned down, on the grounds that an ambassadorship was an insufficient mark of distinction. The rejection stung all the more because two years prior, Kennedy had failed in his bid for a place on the Harvard Board of Overseers, running tenth among a dozen candidates. (Only the top five won a seat.) Associates tried in vain to console him by saying it was an honor merely to get on the ballot; he angrily insisted that only anti-Catholic bias could have caused the result. Now, with the refusal of an honorary degree, he felt doubly aggrieved, especially after *The New York Times,* quoting "authoritative sources," indicated the bestowal would be forthcoming. To save face, Kennedy felt compelled to "refuse" what had not been offered to him and further announced he would miss

Joe's commencement in order to spend time in Hyannis Port with his ailing son Jack who, if he'd taken ill, certainly didn't show it in the McMillan Cup. His petulance provoked mockery in the White House. "Can you imagine Joe Kennedy declining an honorary degree from Harvard?" Franklin Roosevelt chortled upon hearing the news.[43]

"It was a terrible blow to him," Rose Kennedy later acknowledged. "After all those expectations had been built up, it was hard to accept that he wasn't even in the running. . . . Suddenly he felt as if he were once again standing in front of the Porcellian Club, knowing he'd never be admitted."[44]

No wonder he looked forward to being back in Britain. There the press praised his every move, there the political leaders seemed more enamored of his performance than the Roosevelt administration at home was. From the start, Kennedy had won plaudits in London for his forthright and gregarious style and his close associations with Neville Chamberlain's year-old Conservative government. Though Chamberlain held a low opinion of the United States and its president—he viewed FDR as an untrustworthy dilettante who was overly fearful of his own electorate—he and Kennedy (who had first met earlier in the decade) hit it off immediately, with the American giving full support to the prime minister's efforts to head off a European war by whatever means necessary.[45] Like Kennedy a self-made businessman who fancied himself a pragmatist, the prim, austere, silver-haired Chamberlain shared with the American a pessimistic worldview and a tendency to see the world in economic terms—Hitler, he believed, wanted primarily to have equal economic participation in Europe, and would cease his aggressive behavior once he had it. For both men, peace was a precondition for commerce and trade and thus for prosperity. For both, Communism represented a far greater danger than fascism. Kennedy soon became more than a mere ambassador: he became a trusted colleague to Chamberlain and Foreign Secretary Halifax, a man with whom they could confide freely and openly.[46]

An early letter to Arthur Krock bespoke Kennedy's enthusiasm for the prime minister. "Chamberlain's speech last Thursday was a masterpiece," he enthused. "I sat spellbound in the diplomatic gallery and heard it all. It impressed me as a combination of high morals and politics such as I have never witnessed. . . . All this means, as I size it up, that there will be no war if Chamberlain stays in power with strong public backing, which he seems to be acquiring by the day."[47]

Kennedy also paid visits to Lord and Lady Astor at their palatial country estate at Cliveden, on the Thames in Buckinghamshire, which became known to critics as a favored meeting ground of Tory aristocrats determined to keep Britain out of war, through concessions to Germany if necessary. The "Cliveden Set," left-wing journalist Claud Cockburn dubbed them, and though it would be too much to say that Kennedy was a dupe of the group—his basic outlook on world affairs had been formed long before his first visit to Cliveden—the discussions around the Astors' dining table were intoxicating and gave him additional fodder for his claims. The American-born Lady Astor, originally from Virginia and now in her early sixties, radiated charm and glamour and fierce intelligence, as well as a pugnacious insistence on defending Hitler's Germany against criticism and on the need for a strong Germany to act as a counterweight to Stalin's Russia. The first woman to sit in the House of Commons, she was also known as one of the leading hostesses in all of Britain, with a knack for befriending the leading lights of the moment, such as T. E. Lawrence, George Bernard Shaw, and Mahatma Gandhi. She took to Ambassador Kennedy immediately, and he to her. They were kindred spirits, ebullient and forthright, whose conservative views, it may be said, came naturally to them; after all, they had a lot to conserve.[48]

"The march of events in Austria made my first days here more exciting than they might otherwise have been, but I am unable to see that the Central European developments affect our country or my job," Kennedy wrote to Krock, summarizing his noninterventionist stance. Economics, he went on, were determinative: "The more I talk with people . . . the more convinced I am in my own mind that the economic situation in Europe, and that includes Great Britain, is the key to the whole situation. All of the playing house they are doing on the political fronts is not putting people back to work and is not getting at the root of the situation. An unemployed man with a hungry family is the same fellow whether the swastika or some other flag floats above his head."[49]

In his first major speech as ambassador, weeks in preparation and delivered before the Pilgrims Society on March 18—mere days after the German annexation of Austria—Kennedy pleased his audience by pronouncing false the idea that the United States would never fight a war unless its home territory was directly threatened. His listeners were quiet, however, when he said "the great majority" of Americans, "appalled by the prospect of war," were opposed to entering any kind of "entangling alliances." And they were positively glum when he predicted that his country might well remain neutral in the event of a general war. Unbeknownst to the audience, Kennedy's original wording, rejected by the State Department, had been still more provocative: the United States, that version read, had "no plan to seek or offer assistance in the event that war—and I mean, of course, a war of major scope—should break out in the world."[50]

In retrospect, with our awareness of what lay in store, the words seem naive, shortsighted, stingy. It bears remembering, however, that at the time, in the late winter of 1938, Kennedy's speech was fully in line with majority opinion in the United States. Most Americans embraced some form of "isolationism," the key elements of which were an aversion to war and deep opposition to alliances with other nations. A 1937 Gallup poll found that nearly two-thirds of respondents thought American participation in the First World War had been a mistake. (Kennedy had held firmly to this view, it will be recalled, even at the time of U.S. entry in 1917; he never wavered from it.) Americans, this perspective held, had been tricked into intervening by clever British propaganda and by the machinations of U.S. arms merchants and bankers. Only a small minority of isolationists were actually sympathetic to fascism, and some were prepared to work with other nations to help China in its war against Japan. Some favored robust U.S. involvement in the Western Hemisphere to protect the nation against great-power threats. (In this sense the term was somewhat of a misnomer.) But all questioned whether the United States should be compelled to do what Europeans themselves appeared unwilling to do: block Nazi Germany. Isolationist sentiment tended to be strongest in the nation's heartland and among those of Irish or German ancestry, but it was a nationwide phenomenon that cut across ethnic, socioeconomic, party, and sectional lines, and was given voice by *Time* magazine and by the Hearst newspapers.[51]

The Harvard diplomatic historian William L. Langer, with whom Jack took a course, marveled at the shift in popular attitudes since 1917, when so many people had bought Woodrow Wilson's argument that the United States had a duty to make the world "safe for democracy." Langer said, in a book he wrote with S. Everett Gleason, "Americans, having once believed, erroneously, that war would settle everything, were now disposed to endorse the reverse fallacy that war could settle nothing."[52] The British philosopher and historian of ideas Isaiah Berlin made the same point differently: the United States of the 1930s, he wrote, was where "a great social experiment [the New Deal] was conducted with an isolationist disregard of the outside world."[53]

Popular culture reflected the national mood. Ernest Hemingway, for example, argued in *Esquire* in mid-decade, "They wrote in the old days that it is sweet and fitting to die for one's country. But in modern war there is nothing sweet nor fitting in your dying. You will die like a dog for no good reason. . . . Of the hell broth that is brewing in Europe we have no need to drink. Europe has always fought, the intervals of peace are only Armistices. We were fools to be sucked in once on a European war and we should never be sucked in again."[54] A similar theme was expounded in Dalton Trumbo's *Johnny Got His Gun* and William March's *Company K*, as well as in Lewis Milestone's hugely popular film adaptation of Erich Maria Remarque's novel *All Quiet on the Western Front*. The journalist and historian Walter Millis added seeming heft to the claim that involvement in World War I had been pointless with his 1935 bestseller *Road to War: America, 1914–1917*.[55] Efforts to push back against this narrative, including by such luminaries as Walter Lippmann—Americans, he wrote, were being "duped by a falsification of history . . . miseducated by a swarm of innocent but ignorant historians, by reckless demagogues"— were only partly successful.[56]

Kennedy also found support for his views in the writings of the well-known historian Charles A. Beard, who in a series of books and articles pushed the argument that the United States should steer clear of any involvement in Europe's looming crisis. A single lengthy sentence in *The Open Door at Home*, published in 1934, captured the essence:

> By cultivating its own garden, by setting an example of national self-restraint (which is certainly easier than restraining fifty other nations in an international conference, or beating them in war), by making no commitments that cannot be readily enforced by arms, by adopting toward other nations a policy of fair and open commodity exchange, by refraining from giving them any moral advice on any subject, and by providing a military and naval machine as adequate as possible to the defense of this policy, the United States may realize maximum security, attain minimum dependence upon governments and conditions beyond its control, and develop its own resources to the utmost.[57]

Joe Kennedy would not have changed a word.

Franklin Roosevelt, consummate politician that he was, had no desire to get ahead of public opinion. By heritage and upbringing a thoroughgoing internationalist, Roosevelt as a young man had thrilled at cousin Theodore's Cuban exploits and relished debating global issues with his Harvard classmates. As assistant secretary of the Navy from 1913 to 1920, and as James M. Cox's running mate on the losing Democratic presidential ticket in 1920, he championed robust U.S. involvement in world affairs. Membership in the League of Nations, Roosevelt argued, sounding at times more Wilsonian than Wilson himself, was critical to the nation's security and to world peace. It dismayed him that the Senate determined otherwise and rejected League membership. Gradually, however, during the second half of the 1920s, Roosevelt's internationalism faded, at least in terms of public expression. His eyes now on the White House, he shifted his position to align with popular sentiment and, in the 1932 election, assured voters that he opposed American membership in the organization. In his reelection campaign four years later, he went further: "We shun political commitments which might entangle us in foreign wars. . . . We seek to isolate ourselves completely from war."[58]

It came as no surprise, then, that in mid-decade the president signed a series of neutrality acts by which Congress outlawed the kinds of contacts that had compromised American neutrality during World War I. The Neutrality Act of 1935 banned the export of weapons and ammunition to either side in a military conflict, and also empowered the president to warn American citizens against traveling on ships flying belligerent flags. The Neutrality Act of 1936 renewed these provisions and also outlawed loans to belligerents; such arrangements, lawmakers argued, could give the United States a large monetary interest in a conflict's outcome. And in 1937, with global tensions ratcheting up and the Spanish Civil War raging, Congress passed a still more stringent Neutrality Act, this one introducing a cash-and-carry principle: warring nations wishing to trade with the United States would have to pay cash for their nonmilitary purchases and carry the goods from American ports on their own ships.[59]

By the end of 1937 FDR had begun to signal a tougher line. In a major speech in Chicago that October, he called for an "international quarantine" against the "epidemic of world lawlessness" and warned that U.S. national security was at stake. But he still moved gingerly. When the quarantine notion elicited condemnation in Congress and from some quarters of the press, he backed off. (Isolationist lawmakers had threatened him with impeachment.) Neither Roosevelt nor Secretary of State Cordell Hull, a courtly Tennessean and former congressman, objected to the thrust of Kennedy's draft Pilgrims Society speech; they merely found its tone too rigid, especially at a time when U.S. journalists were clamoring for a firmer American response to "the German rape of Austria."[60]

Nor did the White House at this point object to Kennedy's supportive assessment of Chamberlain's strategy vis-à-vis Germany. Here, too, hindsight can distort. Time would reveal the British prime minister's shortcomings—his limited imagination, his tendency toward wishful thinking, his smug and hubristic self-confidence, his hunger for flattery and sensitivity to criticism, his distrust of public opinion, his stubborn belief that Hitler was amenable to individual persuasion and judicious concession. But it is well to remember that Chamberlain was no foreign policy naïf: he disliked Hitler and all that Nazi ideology represented, and he had been among the first, in 1934, to push for British rearmament, albeit in limited form. It should be borne in mind, moreover, that here, in the early months of 1938, the policy of appeasement—in essence, making concessions to Germany and to a lesser extent Italy in order to avert the outbreak of war—had broad support in British officialdom.

At the core of the policy was the belief, widely held among British analysts, including those on the left, that Germany had legitimate grievances with the harshly punitive Versailles Treaty of 1919. A modest redrawing of frontiers on the Continent was justifiable, these observers held, especially if this involved bringing adjacent German-speaking minorities within the Reich. (Even Winston Churchill, certainly no fan of Chamberlain's approach, was willing to consider adjustments to the borders of Czechoslovakia, a view he was later happy to keep hidden.) In addition, the appeasement policy flowed from a conviction that Britain in 1937–38 had a weak hand, with commitments that massively exceeded its resources as it strove to protect far-flung interests in East Asia, Africa, the Mediterranean, and continental Europe, and with allies who were not dependable. A rearmament program was under way, but in piecemeal fashion (mostly in the development and production of fighter planes) as policymakers fretted that the soaring costs associated with it could not be sustained without wrecking a fragile national economy hit hard by the world economic crisis that followed the U.S. stock market crash in 1929.

Civil defense efforts were also behind schedule, with a mere sixty fire pumps in place for the whole of London.

The public, meanwhile, recalling the horrors of the Somme and Passchendaele and influenced by a wave of anti-war memoirs and literature in the 1920s, shuddered at the thought of a return to the carnage and registered its opposition to military conscription and to policies likely to lead to war. The dominions also counseled peace. And if all that was not enough to condition Chamberlain's approach, the Chiefs of Staff told him that Britain was in no condition to fight in 1938—the rearmament program needed more time. Alliance blocs could be pursued in the interval, certainly, but, given their role in the outbreak of war in 1914, did it really make sense to tie oneself to one of them?[61]

Roosevelt got all of this, and he saw value as well in Kennedy's being able to use his close ties to Chamberlain to get valuable intelligence on British thinking at the highest levels. What got under FDR's skin was something else: his ambassador's tendency, evident from his first days in the post, to go it alone and do end runs around the State Department, to speak his mind too much and to write letters directly to prominent U.S. financiers, journalists, and select members of Congress. Discretion seemed a foreign concept to him, just as the skeptics had feared. As a diplomat, Kennedy was supposed to be the eyes and ears of his government, but he seemingly could not resist also being the mouth, peppering the letters with sharp views on policy. He marked them "Private and Confidential," as if this guaranteed they would in all cases be read only by the recipient. Inevitably, word got around, leading to speculation that Kennedy was intent on using his position to advance his own career, specifically with an eye toward the 1940 Democratic presidential nomination.

"Will Joe Kennedy Run for President?" asked a May 21, 1938, article in *Liberty* magazine by the respected correspondent Ernest Lindley. Variations of the question were heard often in the press that spring. That Roosevelt had yet to announce his own plans for 1940 only added to the intrigue. Arthur Krock, who had drafted Kennedy's pro-Roosevelt campaign book in 1936 and was widely known to be an unofficial publicist for the family (he may indeed have been on retainer to Kennedy, without acknowledgment to his readers or to his bosses at *The New York Times*), could hardly contain his enthusiasm in his column: "Here is Kennedy back again, the rage of London, the best copy in the British press, his counsel steadily sought by statesmen of the country to which he is accredited, his influence manifest and powerful in all matters in which the United States has an interest in Great Britain. . . . Here he is back again, undazzled by such a taking up socially and officially as no American perhaps has known abroad since Franklin's day."[62]

Interior secretary Harold Ickes, whose dislike of the ambassador ran deep, speculated in his diary on the Kennedy-Krock effort: "I have been told that Krock is going to take some time off to devote himself to spreading the Kennedy-for-President gospel. There is probably no doubt that Kennedy is spending a great deal of money to further his Presidential ambitions. He has plenty of it and he is willing to spend it freely. Neither is there any doubt that he is making a good deal of headway in conservative quarters."[63]

Roosevelt, annoyed by the burst of speculation and by the brazen opportunism it seemed to signify, rejected the option of recalling Kennedy—that would accomplish little except to give the nation's most prominent Irish Catholic two years at home in the United States to cause mischief before the election. It could also alienate the Irish American electorate in key Northern states in the lead-up to the vote. Far better to keep Kennedy overseas but to clip his wings. Accordingly, Roosevelt allowed his press secretary, Steve Early, to leak copies of Kennedy's "Private and Confidential" letters to the *Chicago Tribune*, which ran the story on June 23 under the headline "Kennedy's 1940 Ambitions Open Roosevelt Rift." The ambassador, furious at what he saw as presidential backstabbing, immediately denied any claims on high political office. When he complained to FDR about the leak, the president artfully pretended innocence.[64]

"In this way he assuaged my feelings and I left again for London," Kennedy later wrote of the exchange, "but deep within me I knew that something had happened."[65]

SEVEN

THE AMBASSADOR'S SON

ater, after everything went wrong, after his public career lay in ruins and it seemed he might have destroyed his sons' political prospects, too, people would look back on this moment, in early July 1938, as the high point of Joseph P. Kennedy's storied life. On the brilliant summer day when the ship carrying the three Kennedy men docked at Plymouth, anything seemed possible for the American tycoon-turned-diplomat and his two beaming sons. Kennedy faced troubles in the Roosevelt White House, true, and there were looming dangers in European power politics that were sure to test his mettle and his judgment, but both challenges were in their way testimony to his success: he had earned the wrath of some in the administration, and the irritation of the president himself, in large part because serious journalists now spoke of him as a legitimate, if longshot, Democratic candidate for president in 1940, should FDR decline to run for a tradition-shattering third term; and he had established himself, in his short time as ambassador, as a close outside associate of Neville Chamberlain's government.

Now, moreover, with his eldest sons at last on British soil, the ambassadorship was fully and gloriously a family affair, as all eleven members were together in one place for the first time (excepting major holidays)

The Kennedy men upon arrival in Southampton, July 2, 1938.

since Joe Junior left for Choate nine years before, in 1929. Joe, freshly minted Harvard graduate, planned to work for a spell at the embassy and then embark on a year-long tour of Europe before entering law school; Jack would stay until the start of fall semester at Harvard. As the handsome trio rode the train up to London, they knew what awaited them: a joyous reunion of father and mother, ages forty-nine and forty-seven, and their nine children, from Joe at twenty-two to little Teddy at six.

The family's residence—the imposing six-story, thirty-six-room ambassadorial mansion at 14 Prince's Gate, which J. P. Morgan had donated to the U.S. government soon after the Great War—certainly made a winning impression. Located in fashionable Knightsbridge, just off Hyde Park and within easy walking distance of the embassy at Grosvenor Square, the home had been dilapidated when Joe Kennedy first arrived, in March. He quickly ordered a major renovation, to be paid for with his own funds. The final bill ran to $250,000 ($4.5 million in today's dollars). In advance of his family's arrival, he also purchased plentiful amounts of Maxwell House coffee, sweets, canned clam chowder, Jergens lotion, and Nivea cream. Through the Paris embassy he arranged for cigars, fresh produce, and fine wines to be sent from France. In May, five hundred bottles of Pommery & Greno champagne arrived from Rheims, to be served at official functions. Though Kennedy himself seldom drank, he knew many of his dinner guests would; he did not wish to be unprepared.[1]

Rose Kennedy, meanwhile, directed a permanent staff of twenty-three house servants and three chauffeurs, and an additional reserve of twenty part-timers for official functions. She was a subject of endless fascination in the British press, as were the children, who for the first time in their lives found themselves in the glare of publicity. The morning papers would regularly post pictures of one or another Kennedy child out and about in London: Teddy and Jean watching the changing of the guard at Buckingham Palace; Kick bringing home-baked cookies to a children's hospital; Bobby and Teddy on their first day of school. The American press, too, got in on the act. President Roosevelt, Henry Luce's *Life* magazine enthused, "got eleven ambassadors for the price of one. Amazed and delighted at the spectacle of an Ambassadorial family big enough to man a full-sized cricket team, England has taken them all, including extremely pretty and young-looking Mrs. Kennedy, to its heart."[2]

Eighteen-year-old Kick in particular took London society by storm, her vibrancy and exuberance obvious to all concerned, not least journalists. "The whole family is taking to London life with the ease of the proverbial ducks to the pond," said the London *Times*. "But it is Kathleen especially who is about everywhere, at all the parties, alert, observant, a merry girl who when she talks to you makes you feel as if you were seeing it all for the first time too." Interested in seemingly everything and everyone, and highly skilled in the art of conversation, Kick would talk with all comers, regardless of station, cheerfully expounding on any manner of topics, never boastfully but in a genial and charming way that her English hosts found enchanting. "It was," her mother said, "as if everything that made Kathleen what she was came together in London."[3]

Rosemary, on the other hand, now nineteen, remained a subject of parental concern. Years of effort to find an educational environment that would enable her to advance intellectually had yielded sparse results—she remained at a fourth-grade level, despite attending five schools in six years. No less than before, she struggled to retain information and to read social cues. "You could talk to Rosemary," said one family acquaintance, "but you could never have a conversation. She talked like a ten-year-old—just chattering all the time." A letter she wrote to her parents in 1936, while attending a school in Brookline, the town of her birth, indicated her communication level: "Jack is taken me to the next dance. He is going to take me in his new car. . . . I gave Jack $1 he didn't ask for it either. 2 cents I paid for his papper. . . . Lots of love kisses your darling daughter."[4]

In Eunice's recollection, "Mother was worried about Rosemary in London. Would she accidentally do something dangerous while Mother was occupied with some unavoidable official function? Would she get confused taking a bus and get lost among London's intricate streets? Would someone attack her? Could she protect herself if she were out of the eye of the governess? No one could watch out for Rose all the time."[5]

Kick, Rose, and Rosemary, in formal gowns, before their presentation at the Court of St. James's, May 11, 1938.

Nonetheless, her mother determined that Rosemary and Kick would both be presented at court, which they were on May 11. Although the actual presentation took mere seconds, it required elaborate preparation—the selection of the dresses and the fittings, the practice walks and curtsies—and adherence to strict rules. Presented in pairs before the seated King George VI and Queen Elizabeth, each woman performed a slow, sweeping curtsy to the king, then slid three steps to the right and did the same thing to the queen, then glided farther to the right and exited out a side door. With her parents watching anxiously, Rosemary carried it off, though not before losing her balance momentarily. Mrs. Kennedy, who traveled to Paris to buy her own dress for the occasion, found the whole experience "glamorous beyond belief."[6]

Rose loved London, loved being the wife of the ambassador, loved the garden parties, the formal dinners, the tennis at Wimbledon, the weekends at Blenheim Palace, the lavish balls given by Lady Astor for, among others, the king and queen. Diary entries show Rose's admiration for the upper-class English and their ways, for their "perfect manners" and "more exact enunciation," and her gratitude for the embrace they offered her and her family. "We became practically public property," she enthused decades afterwards. "I almost began to feel that we had been adopted as a family, by the whole British people."[7] She worried incessantly about whether she truly fit in—it horrified her to realize that she was the only one wearing tweeds during a Sunday lunch with the royals—but relished her sudden rise to the highest ranks of British society. A weekend at Windsor Castle was "one of the most fabulous events" of her life, she later wrote. Her husband agreed: as the two of them lounged in their suite in the castle tower, glasses of sherry in hand, he is said to have remarked, "Well, Rose, it's a hell of a long way from East Boston!"[8]

If Joe's wandering eye during these excursions pained her, she did her best not to show it; she had long since made her peace with his flings. It seems they had a kind of arrangement: she would look the other way, and he would avoid embarrassing her. Certainly his modus operandi in London had not changed. *Work hard and play hard*, Kennedy told his sons, and he led by example. Discretion proved somewhat easier here than in the United States, however, as his lovers now were not actresses and showgirls but aristocratic British women who had their own incentive for secrecy. Aide Harvey Klemmer marveled at the ambassador's detailed accounts of his conquests, especially given the individuals involved. "His name was connected to various women all the way to the top," Klemmer recalled. "Once he said the queen was one of the greatest women in the world. He wanted even that left to speculation, when there was absolutely nothing."[9]

Jack, too, seized on the chance to acquaint himself with British society. Soon after their arrival, he and Joe Junior attended a magnificent embassy dinner in honor of the Duke and Duchess of Kent; other guests included Winston Churchill and Interior Secretary Ickes. With Kick's debutante season still going strong, the brothers had no end of opportunities for evening fun, and they took full advantage. Jack in particular made a winning impression on his hosts, whereas Joe Junior could come off as caustic and hard-edged, his humor lacking the finesse and sense of irony prized by the English. He didn't wear well. At evening balls, Joe would cut in on dance partners just a tad too aggressively and thereby raise eyebrows. William Douglas-Home, the thirteenth Earl of Home and one of Kick's myriad British suitors, got to know both brothers that summer. He later said of Jack, "He was age 21, very young, and very interested in everything. I mean, not only in politics, but the thing that struck you about him was that he was so vital about everything. . . . He was interested, always interested. He would never have a deep political discussion without jokes at the same time. He had a very highly developed sense of humor. Joe was probably more serious than he was."[10]

Deborah "Debo" Mitford, the youngest of the famous Mitford sisters and a friend of Kick's, concurred: Jack and Kick were "very generous in outlook and very funny. That was what was so marvelous about Jack—he was able to laugh at himself. No politician I've ever known was like that. . . . Like Kick, he was an absolute fount of energy, enthusiasm, fun, and intelligence, all the things that make people want to become them."[11]

On July 11, Jack and some of his elite British pals went to the House of Commons for the chance to hear Winston Churchill in action. Since his early teenage years Jack had been fascinated by Churchill's books and speeches, astounded by his oratorical brilliance, his mastery of the written word, his deep sense of history; now, for the first time, Jack would be on hand as the hunched, gruff figure rose slowly from his seat to give what everyone expected would be another bravura performance. It always was when Churchill spoke—such was the power of his language and his delivery that even his detractors were keen to hear him; often, the signal that he was about to speak caused a minor commotion in the lobbies as members rushed into the chamber. Yet Jack was conflicted as he took in the scene in the visitors' gallery that midsummer day.[12] Drawn though he was to Churchill's charisma and eloquence, Jack felt ambivalent toward him, for Churchill represented a worldview distinctly at odds with his father's, not least with respect to how to handle the fascist powers.

Jack Kennedy's friends, too, felt that hesitation. They admired Churchill for all the reasons Jack did, but they had learned from their parents to distrust his supposedly reckless and unprincipled character and his seeming glorification of war. That summer the young men, including Jack, debated Churchill's newest book, *Arms and the Covenant,* a collection of his speeches since 1932 that would be published in the United States under the title *While England Slept: A Survey of World Affairs, 1932–1938.*

In particular, remembered Andrew Cavendish, who was two years Jack's junior and would go on to marry Debo Mitford, the friends sparred over one pointed exchange in the book: Churchill's accusation, in his speech "The Locust Years" (November 12, 1936), that British leaders had allowed the nation to "drift" while the Germans steadily rearmed, and the riposte by Stanley Baldwin, the prime minister at the time, that the electorate would not have countenanced a major rearmament effort at the time, and that any such effort would have brought the left to power, with disastrous consequences for Britain. This Churchill-Baldwin flap posed large questions for the young men about the role of leadership in a democracy. Should a leader pursue a course of action that, however meritorious on strategic or ethical grounds, might cause his political downfall? How much should public opinion matter in policymaking? Should a leader take care not to get too far ahead of the electorate, as Baldwin seemed to argue, or was Churchill right to insist that he must speak his mind, must educate the public, whatever the consequences to his own political standing?[13] Jack's thesis at Harvard would center on these questions, as would his 1956 book, *Profiles in Courage.*

At the end of July, the Kennedys decamped for the South of France, where Rose had rented a villa in Cap d'Antibes, near Cannes. She and eight of the kids arrived first, and Joe Senior and Kick joined a few days later. There followed numerous lazy days at the house or at the nearby Hôtel du Cap-Eden-Roc—whose guests that season included Marlene Dietrich, the Duke and Duchess of Windsor, and tennis star Bill Tilden—and evenings that harked back to the Hyannis Port ritual: everyone seated around a long rectangular dining table, with Mr. Kennedy directing the discussion like a "master conductor" (in the words of Dietrich's thirteen-year-old daughter, Maria).[14]

Louella Hennessy, the family's ebullient longtime nanny, remembered one particularly stormy afternoon at the villa during which Jack gave an impromptu history lesson to his younger siblings, all of them seated in a row in front of the fireplace. With references to Hannibal, Caesar, and Napoleon, he lectured to them about the rise and fall of nations—how they gained stature and wealth, how they maintained and expanded their might, how they eventually squandered it all. The United States had joined the ranks of the great powers, Jack went on, but it differed from the rest, for it was a republic and a democracy. The task for America would be to maintain its high position, learn from the mistakes of other great nations, and at the same time preserve its way of life, its freedoms. "As I listened to Jack," Hennessy said, "I thought with amazement, 'Why, he's only 21. Imagine him caring about these things.'"[15]

II

If Ambassador Kennedy had hoped to be able to ride out the European crisis in the Mediterranean idyll, it was not to be. By mid-August 1938 Adolf Hitler seemed poised to plunge the Continent into war by marching on Czechoslovakia. Whereas the Austrians (or at least the dominant Nazi Party) had acquiesced to the German takeover, the Czechs resisted. They had a security treaty with France and another with the Soviet Union, and they were determined to make a stand. Already the previous spring, Hitler and his generals had discussed plans for an attack; now he ordered the army to prepare for an October invasion. All the while, German propaganda trumpeted the complaints of Sudeten Germans and the urgent need to bring them into the fatherland. Under pressure from the State Department, Kennedy cut short his holiday and returned to London on August 29. Jack flew with him and thereby got a front-row seat as the Chamberlain government hemmed and hawed in fashioning a response.

All around him Jack could see signs of mounting British trepidation—and attempts at preparation. How things had changed, he thought, since the family's departure for the French Riviera just a month before. Air-raid shelters had been hastily dug in Hyde Park, anti-aircraft guns were going into place along the Embankment, and there were sandbags ringing crucial London buildings to protect basement windows. Office windows above were crisscrossed with white tape. The first evacuees from British cities were gathered up and transported to the countryside. The Royal Air Force was put on full alert, and the Royal Navy mobilized. It seemed impressive on initial glance, but to Jack it amounted to a sad pretense of readiness. Sandbags and white tape—was that really what Britain had to offer?[16]

In a draft of a speech intended for an audience in Aberdeen, Scotland, Ambassador Kennedy asked whether his listeners could conceive of "any dispute or controversy existing in the world which is worth the life of your son, or of anyone else's son? Perhaps I am not well informed of the terrifically vital force underlying all the unrest in the world, but for the life of me I cannot see anything involved which could remotely be considered worth shedding life for." It was a perfect encapsulation of Kennedy's political philosophy, and it brought a swift reply from Cordell Hull's State Department: the section must be expunged. No American representative could issue such an open invitation to Nazi aggression. "The young man needs his wrists slapped rather hard," a dismayed FDR muttered upon seeing the draft, an odd wording, since Kennedy was only six years his junior. The president privately parodied Joe by remarking, "I can't for the life of me understand why anybody would want to go to war to save the Czechs." But Roosevelt would do no more than grouse, and indeed hoped himself that some means could be found to preserve the peace.[17]

Neville Chamberlain desperately sought the same thing. His mistrust of Hitler had grown over the summer, but he stubbornly clung to the belief that the Führer had limited objectives and would be open to compromise. To believe otherwise was to believe that the German leader actually wanted war, and this seemed to the prime minister's rational mind impossible, given especially the epic catastrophe that was the First World War. In this sense the prime minister was not merely "buying time," as some historians have claimed, not merely putting off the day of reckoning until British capabilities had improved—he aimed to avoid war altogether. And certainly, he insisted, Czechoslovakia was not worth the price of a major military conflict. In a radio address to the British people, Chamberlain uttered words that tracked closely with Kennedy's prohibited Aberdeen remarks: "How horrible, fantastic, incredible it is that we should be digging trenches and trying on gas-masks here because of a quarrel in a far away country between people of whom we know nothing."[18]

The Paris government, under Prime Minister Édouard Daladier, a former history teacher from Provence who led the Radical Party (a centrist party despite its name), felt the same, even if it could not claim that Czechoslovakia was "far away." In the French view, Czechoslovakia's boundaries had been arbitrarily drawn up after World War I and lacked historical validity, and in any event France did not have the military capacity to defend the Czechs against German assault. When Soviet leader Joseph Stalin signaled that if the French and the British defended the Czechs he would help them, the response came quickly: *Thanks, but no thanks.*[19]

The solution, devised in London and enthusiastically backed by Joseph Kennedy—who was a fixture at 10 Downing Street and in the Foreign Office through much of September—was to appeal to Hitler's civilized judgment by agreeing to the transfer of the Sudetenland to Germany, thereby depriving him of the motive for additional revision of the Versailles peace settlement. Or so the argument went. On September 15, three days after Hitler denounced the Czechs in a fiery, semi-hysterical speech at Nuremberg, Chamberlain met with the German leader at Berchtesgaden to talk terms. (Much to Hitler's surprise, the Englishman had not insisted on a neutral site, or even a location on the Rhine, which would have cut the travel time in half.) He received a frosty reception but in effect affirmed his government's unwillingness to oppose the breakup of Czechoslovakia. A second meeting, at Bad Godesberg on the twenty-second, yielded no agreement, whereupon Chamberlain returned to London and impressed upon the Cabinet his view that Hitler "would not deliberately deceive a man whom he respected with whom he had been in negotiation." He also stressed the vital necessity of compelling the Czechs to submit, lest German bombers fill the skies over Britain, raining down their death and destruction.[20]

Kennedy encouraged the prime minister in this notion, his view influenced by a supposed expert he had befriended, the famed aviator and avowed isolationist Charles Lindbergh. More than a decade had passed since Lucky Lindy's epic solo transatlantic flight, but he retained a hero status among many Americans—in name recognition, he ranked second only to Roosevelt. Germans, too, admired him deeply, and beginning in 1936 Lindbergh paid several visits to Germany to inspect the fledgling Luftwaffe up close, touring factories and military bases, including some that had never been seen by an American. His hosts carefully screened where he could go and what he could see, and he came away awed, both by the military buildup and by what he saw as the vitality and orderliness of the country. Subsequently, Hermann Göring, the Luftwaffe's commander in chief, decorated Lindbergh with the Service Cross of the German Eagle, "by the order of the Führer." When Lindbergh met Kennedy at the Astors' home in May 1938, the two immediately hit it off, the normally reclusive flier finding in Kennedy someone witty and straightforward who shared his general take on things.[21]

Now he was back in London at Kennedy's urgent request, landing on September 20. The next day at the U.S. embassy, he delivered a relentlessly alarmist oral report on the state of British and French air power vis-à-vis Germany's. Kennedy asked him to commit his assessment to paper, which Lindbergh duly did the following day, a copy going also to 10 Downing Street at Kennedy's directive. The Luftwaffe's strength now exceeded that of the other European powers combined, the memo read; if unleashed over Britain, it could inflict sixty thousand casualties in a single day. French and British leaders must therefore resist war and "permit Germany's eastward expansion," lest they, too, be attacked: "For the first time in history, a nation has the power either to save or to ruin the great cities of Europe. Germany has such a preponderance of war planes that she can bomb any city in Europe with comparatively little resistance. England and France are too weak in the air to protect themselves."[22]

In his diary entry for that day, Lindbergh summarized what he had told Kennedy. "The English are in no shape for war. They do not realize what they are confronted with. They have always before had a fleet between themselves and their enemy, and they can't realize the change aviation has made. I am afraid this is the beginning of the end of England as a great power. She may be a 'hornet's nest' but she is no longer a 'lion's den.'" Another entry continued the theme: "I cannot see the future for this country. . . . Aviation has largely destroyed the security of the channel, and [Britain's] superiority of manufacture is a thing of the past."[23]

Lindbergh's analysis, we now know, was grievously off. The Luftwaffe in late 1938 was far less formidable than he claimed, its capacity limited to supporting German ground forces in continental European operations. It had not yet developed a fleet of long-range four-engine bombers capable of doing real damage to more distant targets such as London. In late 1937, subordinates had informed Göring that no German bombers could "operate meaningfully" over England; at most, they could have a "nuisance effect." The situation was little different ten months later.[24]

How much Lindbergh's misapprehension influenced Chamberlain's approach is hard to say. At most, it seems, it reinforced a strong inclination the prime minister already had.[25] Yet so swiftly were events moving that it seemed war might result after all. On Friday, September 23, the Czech government ordered general mobilization; Hitler mocked the action and again demanded the handover of Sudeten territory. Hostilities seemed imminent as all over London people were being fitted for gas masks. (On Sunday the twenty-fifth, Joe Kennedy heard a van cruising slowly through Grosvenor Square with a loudspeaker, urging people not to delay in getting their masks.) If the Führer launched an invasion and France declared war in response, His Majesty's Government would have to follow suit. British officialdom threatened to fracture, with Alfred Duff Cooper, First Lord of the Admiralty, and Conservative MP Winston Churchill urging a stiffening of the policy. As described by Joe Kennedy in a phone conversation with Cordell Hull, the split was between those in the Cabinet who advocated "peace at any price" and those who did not "want to take any more back talk from Hitler," as they "would have to fight anyhow."[26]

Chamberlain, firmly in the first group, on the twenty-ninth flew for a third meeting with Hitler, this one in Munich and with France's Daladier and Italy's Mussolini also present. In the early hours of the following day came the news: an agreement had been reached whereby Hitler would get the Sudetenland in exchange for a promise to stop there and respect the sovereignty of the remainder of Czechoslovakia. Chamberlain returned home to a hero's welcome, announcing that he had achieved "peace for our time." Because of the prime minister, editorial writers gushed, peace had been preserved, and thousands of young men would live. *The Spectator* nominated him for the Nobel Peace Prize. In Paris, Daladier was likewise greeted by cheering crowds. The Czechs had not been consulted.[27]

Only later would another effect become known: Hitler's foes within his own military, believing him to be a deranged warmonger dragging the nation into a conflagration for which it was not prepared, had planned to move against him if Paris and London stood firm and the Führer launched an invasion of Czechoslovakia. Now they were rendered immobile by another easy and bloodless victory. The plot might well have come to nothing anyway, but a chance was lost. Not for five years would Hitler face another serious internal challenge to his rule.[28]

III

Jack Kennedy missed the denouement of the Czech crisis, having returned in early September for his junior year at Harvard.* But he followed events closely from afar, devouring press accounts and radio reports whenever he could. (When Hitler delivered his Nuremberg address on September 12—the first one that Americans could follow live—Jack

A nattily attired Jack on board the liner *Bremen*, returning to the United States for the start of junior year at Harvard.

tuned in from the family home in Hyannis Port.) Though he didn't yet know it, he would devote his senior thesis to these very developments, with particular focus on British decision-making in the years leading up to the Munich agreement.

Harvard friends indeed noticed a more serious-minded and diligent Jack Kennedy that autumn as he upped his game in the classroom, despite a heavy course load (he took six classes), and raised his average to a B. In Government 9a, with A. Chester Hanford, Jack impressed with his active and discerning participation in class and his capacity for independent thought, though Hanford found it curious that the

---

* Upon disembarking in New York, Jack had his first-ever informal press conference. There to greet him were not only Lem Billings but also a gaggle of reporters keen to know about his father and the European crisis. Jack offered reassuring words, predicting there would be no war and Americans would not have to be evacuated. How dire could the situation be, he said, if the ambassador had opted to keep eight of his children in Europe? (Swift, *Gathering Storm*, 82.)

grandson of Honey Fitz Fitzgerald showed so little interest in state and local politics as compared with national affairs and foreign relations.

Arthur Holcombe, an erudite senior member of the faculty who had been around long enough to teach both Joe Senior and Joe Junior and now had Jack as well, came away impressed by the young man. "He stood out among the group he lived with," Holcombe later said. All of them saw a college education as "much more than studying things. They were interested in life. But Jack was more interested in ideas than most men who have the means of doing whatever they wish when they're in college. He had a genuine interest in ideas, there's no question about that." In Holcombe's Government 7 class, which focused on Congress, each student had to produce a research paper on an individual member of the House of Representatives, studying that lawmaker's methods and assessing accomplishments and failures as objectively as possible. Holcombe assigned Jack the upstate New York Republican Bertrand Snell, known chiefly for representing the electric power interests in his district. The result, Holcombe found, was a "masterpiece," based on "a very superior job of investigating," though admittedly the young man had certain advantages: during Christmas vacation, "he goes down to Washington, meets some of his father's friends, gets a further line on his congressman and on Congress."[29]

Jack's rooming arrangement at Winthrop House, meanwhile, had changed: he and Torby moved into a larger quad unit together with two football players, Charlie Houghton and Benjamin Smith (who would later fill Jack's seat in the U.S. Senate when he was elected president), who were dismayed by Jack's astonishing untidiness but otherwise found him to be a congenial and engaging roommate. "Jack was a very stimulating person to live with," Houghton recalled. "Very argumentative in a nice way. He questioned everything. I think the depth of his curiosity was shown in that he'd challenge anything you said. He had the best sense of humor of all the Kennedys."[30]

Donald Thurber, a fellow government major, likewise saw in Kennedy someone who was not content with the pat answer, who was willing to challenge assumptions and to ask, "What makes you think so?" "You got the impression that here was a mind that was learning from other people, and that longed to learn from other people—he would regard them as sources of information and knowledge to fill out his own." Nor could Kennedy be considered a mere lothario intent on having a good time, Thurber continued. "I knew plenty of playboys. I could spot a playboy on the other side of the room. Jack didn't fit into that mold at all—he was someone who played hard when he played, but his motivation was a serious one—you got the idea that he'd already decided life was a pretty serious proposition, even though it wouldn't have to be, with lots of money and so on. But it was going to be a serious proposition."[31]

To be sure, the desire for extracurricular fun had not dissipated. Kennedy wrote to Billings that fall about parties and sexual conquests, and about Harvard's superiority over Princeton in football. "Dear Billings: Yours of the 19th received and horseshit noted. Numerous Harvard varsity men have been quoted as saying, 'Four tough games in a row—Thank God we're playing Princeton.'" He instructed Billings to get a date for the Harvard-Yale game on November 19, "as we're going to have a party in Bronxville." With the rest of the Kennedys overseas, the three family homes could be—and not infrequently were—perfect settings for myriad undergrad debaucheries.[32]

In personal appearance he remained as casual as ever, often showing up to class with wrinkled pants and mismatched socks, his tie askew. And he gave few outward signs of personal wealth, despite the fact that he had become, on his twenty-first birthday the previous spring, a millionaire, gaining access to a trust fund established for him by his father a decade before. (He also received on his birthday two $1,000 checks from his father, for meeting a challenge to refrain from picking up smoking or drinking; even afterwards, indeed to the end of his life, Jack seldom touched tobacco or alcohol, apart from the occasional cigar or daiquiri.) Jack showed limited interest in luxury goods, or in material possessions generally; with respect to those belongings he did have he was, like many children of privilege, nonchalant, losing golf clubs and tennis rackets and suitcases with abandon, much to his mother's annoyance.[33]

He also fell in love, in a way he never had before. Her name was Frances Ann Cannon, a ravishingly beautiful North Carolina textile heiress and former Sarah Lawrence student who turned the heads of all the men in Winthrop House. Charlie Houghton took her out first and then Kennedy moved in, entranced by her looks, her sense of humor, her southern drawl, and her inquisitive mind and interest in politics. Soon her name started popping up in Kennedy's letters to Billings, and friends wondered if she might be the one, especially after he followed her to Mardi Gras in New Orleans. There, at the Comus Ball, Cannon's friend Jane Suydam (née Gaither Eustis) laid eyes on Jack for the first time. "He was standing there in the call-out section, very tanned, wearing white tie and tails," she remembered. "He was unbelievably handsome. He had this remarkable animal pull. The impact on me was overwhelming." Jack's friends had somewhat the same reaction upon meeting Frances Ann. Rip Horton, for one, thought her the most beautiful girl Jack had ever dated and recalled thinking after one double date, "My God, why doesn't Jack marry this girl?"[34]

Later Kennedy would contemplate that very thought, even though he surely knew the chances of a union were slim—his Catholicism was unacceptable to Ann's family, as was her Protestantism to his. For the moment, though, his priorities were directed elsewhere—namely, to getting himself back to Europe as soon as possible. His family was there, and so was the geopolitical action, notwithstanding the lull following the Munich agreement. The summer of motoring around the Continent with Lem had fired Jack's imagination, had made him hungry for more, so he asked his Harvard dean for permission to take a semester's leave in the spring of 1939 in order to spend it in Europe. He pledged to take along a stack of books on political philosophy and to do groundwork—in consultation with his Winthrop House tutor, Bruce Hopper—on a senior thesis dealing with some aspect of diplomatic history and international law. The dean, impressed by Jack's apparent seriousness of purpose, approved the request.

IV

Jack Kennedy had additional motivation for wanting to return to Europe: his father was in political trouble. In the immediate aftermath of the Munich Conference, with popular euphoria surging in Britain, Ambassador Kennedy had taken every opportunity to hail the bargain. He felt vindicated, all the more so when Franklin Roosevelt expressed satisfaction with the outcome. Upon learning that there would be a Munich meeting, FDR had sent Prime Minister Chamberlain a two-word telegram: GOOD MAN. When the deal was subsequently struck, the president pronounced himself pleased that war had been averted. Privately, however, he brooded about the rising Nazi threat and the inherent dangers in trying to appease an untrustworthy dictator. Munich could come to take on new and unwelcome connotations, the president suspected.[35]

Sure enough, before long the wave of relief in Britain began to ebb, and uncomfortable questions came to the fore: Had peace been purchased at a shameful price? Why had Czechoslovakia, the one democratic state in Central Europe, been left high and dry? And wouldn't Adolf Hitler soon resume his blackmail, demanding ever more from his Western adversaries? In the British Cabinet, long-simmering tensions erupted full bore, with Duff Cooper resigning in protest over the prime minister's openness to "the language of the mailed fist," while in Parliament scattered voices rose up in support of Winston Churchill's indictment of the Munich pact. "We have sustained a total and unmitigated defeat," the great orator, then an ordinary MP, declared in a remarkable speech in the House of Commons on October 5.

> All is over. Silent, mournful, abandoned, broken, Czechoslovakia recedes into the darkness. . . . We are in the presence of a disaster of the first magnitude which has befallen Great Britain and France. Do not let us blind ourselves to that. . . . What I find unendurable is the sense of our country falling into the power, into the orbit and influence of Nazi Germany and of our existence becoming dependent upon their good will or pleasure. . . . [The British people] should know that we have passed an awful milestone in our history, when the whole equilibrium of Europe has been deranged, and that the terrible words have for the time being been pronounced against the Western democracies: "Thou art weighed in the balance and found wanting." And do not suppose that this is the end. This is only the beginning of the reckoning. This is only the first sip, the first foretaste of a bitter cup which will be proffered to us year by year unless, by a supreme recovery of moral health and martial vigor, we arise again and take our stand for freedom as in the olden time.[36]

The key point for Churchill was Hitler's fundamental unappeasability. Everything flowed from this reality. He called instead for a strategy of deterrence, to be achieved substantially through a "Grand Alliance" with the Soviet Union. How realistic this notion was in the context of 1938 is debatable, especially given the profound mistrust of Soviet Communism and of Stalin's leadership within British and French officialdom. Moreover, Stalin could have intervened substantially on Czechoslovakia's behalf only if his troops were permitted to cross Romanian or Polish soil—both unlikely to happen. (Churchill's ideas, it bears noting, sometimes look better in hindsight than they did in their time.) Quite possibly, the Western powers had already missed their best chance for deterrence through their acquiescence to Hitler's wholesale violations of the Versailles Treaty over the previous five years. They had done nothing to keep Nazi Germany from becoming militarily powerful, and now they found themselves with few cards left to play.

Then again, their hand may not have been as bad in the early autumn of 1938 as Neville Chamberlain (and his later defenders) insisted. For one thing, in Czechoslovakia they had a willing and capable partner, one possessing a well-equipped army of forty-two divisions as well as robust border fortifications defending against a German onslaught of up to forty-four divisions.[37] For another, in both Britain and France, military authorities exaggerated their vulnerability to air power ("The bomber will always get through," former prime minister Stanley Baldwin famously said), though they failed to see that if their own military preparedness would benefit from a delay in the onset of hostilities, so would Germany's. If Britain in 1938 did not yet possess the aircraft and radar system necessary to defend against a German aerial war, neither did the Nazis have the Channel airfields or the planes to wage such action. A year hence, it could in fact be said—though it was not clear then—that Britain would be relatively weaker vis-à-vis Germany than it was when Chamberlain boarded his plane for Bavaria. As historian Ian Kershaw puts it, "The balance of forces had, in fact, in some respects by 1939 tipped somewhat towards Germany."[38]

Whatever the case, Chamberlain held his ground, insisting to all comers that Munich had been a shining example of statesmanship. "I sincerely believe that we have at last opened the way to that general appeasement which alone can save the world from chaos," he wrote to the Archbishop of Canterbury. To his mostly docile Cabinet, Chamberlain said he believed Hitler would now be willing to enter into disarmament deals, which in turn would lift Britain's tremendous economic burden. True, he acknowledged to Joe Kennedy, Hitler might not keep his word, but to date there was no compelling reason to doubt that he would. Secretary Halifax, tall, spare, courteous, and with a reputation for intellectual brilliance—to this day his long, saturnine face stares down quizzically from the wall of the Great Hall at All Souls College, Oxford—was characteristically conflicted, his ability to see every question from every angle inducing a kind of analytical paralysis. He sensed that the Munich deal would prove humiliating and horrible yet deemed it preferable to a potentially unwinnable war on behalf of a Czech state to which Britain had no formal treaty obligation. Most of his colleagues agreed with him.[39]

Kennedy, for his part, dismissed the carping of critics and remained steadfast in his support of the prime minister. In a carefully prepared Trafalgar Day speech before the Navy League on October 19, drafted over two weeks by Harold Hinton and Harvey Klemmer, he hailed the Munich accord and told his audience that it made no sense to emphasize the differences between dictatorships and democracies, since, "after all, we have to live together in the same world whether we like it or not."[40]

An uproar ensued. Get along with dictators? Did he really mean that? In London, the foes of appeasement took offense, since the address summarized succinctly the position of Chamberlain and his Cabinet. In other world capitals analysts wondered if Kennedy's remarks signaled a major change in U.S. policy, since they went directly against Roosevelt's assertion in Chicago the previous year that bandit nations should be "quarantined." American journalists wondered the same thing and further asked why the State Department would approve so provocative a speech. (The answer given: Kennedy had prefaced his claims by stating that his call for coexistence between dictatorships and democracies was merely an expression of his own view.) Influential columnist Walter Lippmann faulted Kennedy for his lack of ambassadorial discretion and for airing his private views publicly, and *The Washington Post* said he was dragging American diplomacy into an appeasement position. To quell the firestorm, the White House had FDR give his own perspective on the matter: "There can be no peace if national policy adopts as a deliberate instrument the threat of war."[41]

But Roosevelt would do no more, such as summon his London ambassador back to Washington or shift American policy in a sharper anti-Nazi direction. Increasingly exasperated with Kennedy and his unhelpful pronouncements, he still saw personal and political advantages in keeping him right where he was, an ocean away. FDR also felt hemmed in politically—he had seen his domestic strength slip after an economic downturn in 1937 and his failed Supreme Court–packing plan, and he remained intimidated by isolationist strength in Congress (more so than he should have been, no doubt—polls showed clearly that the public was more resolute against the dictatorships than were the noisy naysayers on Capitol Hill). More and more, conservatives in his own party were willing to join with Republicans to thwart reform legislation.[42] Indications were, moreover, that the upcoming midterm elections would be a disaster for Democrats, as indeed they were—the Republicans picked up eighty-one seats in the House and eight in the Senate, and they captured thirteen governorships. Our retrospective knowledge that Roosevelt won four successive presidential elections seduces us into thinking he was at all points a political juggernaut, when in fact he faced numerous periods of vulnerability. The fall of 1938 was one such time.

Nevertheless, Kennedy felt he had been stabbed in the back by FDR's statement. "I am so god-damned mad I can't see," he told Senator James Byrnes of South Carolina, adding that he hoped Byrnes would seek the 1940 Democratic nomination. But the ambassador understood on some level that he'd committed a massive blunder with the Trafalgar Day speech, and that he stood triply indicted: he had fashioned a statement with which a great many people found fault; had admitted doing so on the basis of much forethought; and had opted to make the statement in public, in a high-profile lecture. Accustomed to receiving mostly laudatory treatment from the press up to this point in his career, he now stood accused in some quarters of secretly siding with the fascists, of being Chamberlain's pawn, and of subversively undermining his president. He admitted he was "hardly prepared, despite years in public office, for the viciousness of this onslaught."[43]

V

Then came Kristallnacht. In the late hours of November 9–10, following the fatal shooting of a German embassy official in Paris by a German Jewish refugee distraught over the deportation of his parents, a state-sanctioned pogrom was launched all over Germany—synagogues were set ablaze, apartments were wrecked and furniture demolished, Jewish men, women, and children were beaten, and some eight thousand Jewish shops and businesses were destroyed by rampaging Nazi hordes. The shattered glass of the shop windows gave a name to the horror: Crystal Night, or Night of Broken Glass. Nearly a hundred Jews were killed, by official figures (the true count was almost certainly higher), and thirty thousand Jewish men were arrested and sent to concentration camps, where they were viciously maltreated and let go only after promising to leave Germany. Hitler had approved the unleashing of the mobs at the urging of his propaganda minister, Joseph Goebbels, the hope being that it would speed up Jewish emigration. The German government then confiscated the insurance money due to the Jews for the property damage and imposed on them a gargantuan one-billion-mark fine for, as Hermann Göring put it, "their abominable crimes, etc."[44]

Appeasers who previously had been able to avert their eyes from instances of anti-Jewish violence in Germany—there had been waves in 1933 and 1935, and another one after the takeover of Austria, earlier in 1938—now found that much harder to do. The savagery of the Nazi regime had been laid bare. Ambassador Kennedy, for one, was appalled by the images in the press, though seemingly as much because of the diplomatic implications as out of concern for the victims. "This last drive on the Jews in Germany has really made the most ardent hopers for peace very sick at heart," he wrote to Charles Lindbergh on November 12. "It is more and more difficult for those seeking peaceful solutions to advocate any plan when the papers are filled with such horror. So much is lost when so much could be gained."[45]

Joseph Kennedy's attitude toward Jews is not easy to decipher, even at eight decades' remove. He was not a hardcore anti-Semite in the way of, say, Henry Ford or the "radio priest" Father Charles Coughlin, attributing all evils to Jews and believing them genetically predisposed to being sinister and morally defective. Beginning in Hollywood in the 1920s and continuing through his career, Joe worked closely and effectively with Jews, often saying to them, "I'm an Irish Catholic; I know what it's like to be discriminated against." He admired and tried to emulate financier Bernard Baruch, interacting with him affectionately through the 1930s, and he tried repeatedly to convince Harvard to confer an honorary degree on Justice Louis Brandeis. In the early and mid-1930s he was on friendly terms with Felix Frankfurter and Henry Morgenthau. But Kennedy bought into anti-Semitic prejudices that were common (though by no means universal) among Americans of his station, and that were rife, for example, among the career officers in FDR's State Department. It was a casual anti-Semitism, marked by indifference and lack of imagination, and it had deeply pernicious effects. Kennedy took for granted the social exclusion of Jews in elite America, in his America. At Harvard in the 1920s, President A. Lawrence Lowell had sought to maintain quotas on Jewish admissions. (Yale and Princeton were even more restrictive.) In

Bronxville, the Kennedys resided in a community proud of its exclusion of Jewish residents. In tony Palm Beach, Jews were kept out of the most prestigious clubs, a situation that pertained also in Boston. On top of all that, Joe Kennedy had come of age in an Irish Roman Catholic milieu that distrusted Jews theologically, socially, and culturally.[46]

As his troubles deepened in late 1938, Kennedy grew more bitter, holding Jewish writers, columnists, and reporters responsible for the harsh press response to his Trafalgar Day speech—never mind that his non-Jewish press critics were far more numerous—and telling friends that the Jews of America were trying to manipulate the nation into war with Germany, a war likely to ensnare his sons. Roosevelt, he believed, was too much under the influence of Jewish advisers. In meetings with his German counterpart in London, Herbert Von Dirksen, Kennedy expressed admiration for Germany's impressive growth under the Nazis and for the living standards now enjoyed by the German people. In one dispatch, dated June 13, Dirksen told superiors in Berlin that Kennedy "understood our Jewish policy completely; he was from Boston and there, in one golf club, and in other clubs, no Jews had been admitted for the past 50 years." When Harvey Klemmer returned from a visit to Germany, he told Kennedy of the alarming actions he had witnessed, including Nazi storm troopers molesting Jews in the streets and painting swastikas on windows. In Klemmer's recollection, Kennedy looked at him and replied, "Well, they brought it on themselves."[47]

Yet there is little reason to doubt Kennedy's later claim that the Kristallnacht violence genuinely pained him. In the days thereafter, he urged the Chamberlain government to embrace a large-scale Jewish rescue by facilitating the emigration of German Jews to territories in Africa and the Western Hemisphere, under the joint administration of the United States and Britain. The scheme, which never moved beyond the conceptual stage, would require an enormous number of transport ships as well as massive financial resources, but Kennedy insisted it could be done. The press took notice, perhaps with an assist from the ambassador's publicity team. "What Mr. Kennedy has managed to do," *The New York Times* reported, "is the talk of diplomatic circles in London at the moment." But the moment did not last. The State Department, which had not been consulted and which was rife with anti-Semitic sentiments, took scant notice; American Jewish leaders kept their attention focused mostly on Palestine; and the White House, suspecting that Kennedy merely sought a means to reclaim the political momentum following his Trafal-gar Day debacle, didn't bother to respond.[48]

How Rose felt about Joe's ambassadorial troubles, or about the deep-ening European and world tensions, is a mystery. Though she had a deep and abiding interest in history—and knew more of it than her husband did—her letters from this period are for the most part silent on politics. In the years to come, she would pen innumerable "round-robin" letters to her scattered children, some of them running multiple single-space type-written pages in length. Lucid and well organized, they offered perceptive and sometimes witty observations about the goings-on within the Ken-nedy clan, but nary a word about the pressing affairs of the day. Her let-ters to Joe would be the same: several paragraphs detailing what the children were up to, then a throwaway sentence at the end noting that a speech he'd given had been well received in the press.

In her diary, she sometimes went further, though not by much. On September 15, with Chamberlain en route to the first meeting with Hitler, she recorded: "everyone ready to weep for joy and everyone confident the issues will be resolved." She added her pride that "Joe has been on hand constantly and has aided [Chamberlain] by his presence. Feel that he has given great moral support."[49]

Ever more marginalized within the administration, Joe drew suste-nance from his family. Joe Junior, back in London after a tour of European cities—Prague, Warsaw, Leningrad, Stockholm, and Berlin—offered his father full support and expressed enthusiasm for what he had seen in Ger-many. "They are really a marvelous people," Young Joe wrote to a friend, "and it is going to be an awful tough thing to keep them from getting what they want. Dad, as you know, got quite a lot of unfavorable comment in the U.S. press for his speech in trying to get along with the dictatorship. Makes me sore that all the rest of the people are trying to get everyone against the dictatorships. If we are not ready to fight them, we might as well get along with them." Joe lauded his father for trying to find a means for Jews to get out of Germany, while privately agreeing with his claim that American Jews were trying to undermine U.S. neutrality.[50]

In a journal entry on November 21, Joe Junior wrote, "I don't think [Dad] is too crazy about the job at this point and the other day spoke about quitting. He is afraid that they are trying to knock him off at home, and may make a monkey out of him in some diplomatic undertaking." An-other entry, from early December, continued the theme: "Dad is rather tired of his work. He claims that he would give it up in a minute if it wasn't for the benefits that Jack and I are getting out of it and the things Eunice will get when she comes out next spring. He doesn't like the idea of taking orders and working for hours trying to keep things out of his speeches which an ambassador shouldn't say. He also doesn't like the idea of sitting back and letting the Jewish columnists in America kick his head off. The papers have made up a pile of lies about him, and he can't do anything about it but claims that he is going to let a few blasts when he gets back there in a few days."[51]

The letter and diary entries are three examples of many that show Young Joe, twenty-three years old and a college graduate, remained in lockstep with his father's worldview, unwilling or unable even to consider separating himself from the older man's positions, however controversial. One looks in vain in Joe Junior's writings from the period for any sign of independence, any indication that the ambassador had overstepped, had misread the geopolitical situation. It's all one way: Dad knows best.

Jack, meanwhile, tried to direct his parents' attention in a more positive way: the Broadway premiere of Cole Porter's musical *Leave It to Me!*, starring Sophie Tucker and featuring several references to the Kennedys. (Upon learning that her husband has been named ambassador to the Soviet Union, Mrs. Leora Goodhue, played by Tucker, exclaims, "If only those sneaky Kennedys hadn't grabbed London first!") Jack attended on opening night and could hardly fail to hear the warning amid the levity: Ambassador Goodhue is recalled to Washington when he gives a speech calling for nations to get along. Still, Jack gave the performance a thumbs-up: "It's pretty funny and jokes about us get by far the biggest laughs whatever that signifies," he wrote to his parents.[52] To his father he offered a half-hearted and convoluted endorsement of the Trafalgar Day address: "While it seemed to be unpopular with the Jews, etc., [it] was considered to be very good by everyone who wasn't bitterly anti-fascist, although it is true that everyone is deadly set against collective security and don't seem to have a very accurate conception of England's position, due to the type of articles that have been written."[53]

As it happened, father and son would spend the Christmas holidays together, in Palm Beach, while the rest of the Kennedys stayed behind in Europe, skiing in St. Moritz. In Florida the ambassador sat naked by the pool, lathered in cocoa butter, and took calls from associates around the country. A parade of visitors also stopped in, among them Arthur Krock,

Walter Winchell, and "Colonel" Robert McCormick, editor and publisher of the staunchly isolationist *Chicago Tribune*. Far from walking back his endorsement of the Munich agreement, Joe crowed to Winchell that his decision to push Lindbergh's grim analysis of Germany's air strength on the British leadership had influenced Neville Chamberlain's decision to work harder for a deal with Hitler.[54]

One wonders what went through Jack's mind as he heard the elder Kennedy's pontifications that holiday season. Very much his father's son, he was at the same time more inclined than either Joe Senior or Joe Junior to keep an open mind on difficult international questions, to see both sides. He had a detachment and an ironic worldview that father and brother both lacked, and it inclined him toward a more noncommittal stance. At Harvard, meanwhile, his discussions inside and outside the classroom had given him a sense of why isolationism might prove untenable for the United States, why the appeasing of dictators might be both morally and strategically bankrupt and might only postpone the day of reckoning. Though isolationism was dominant among the students, the faculty were more mixed in their views. Jack's Winthrop House tutor, Bruce Hopper, who would have considerable influence on his intellectual development in the year and a half to come, had little patience with the appeasers—on Armistice Day every November, Hopper, a charismatic and authoritative speaker, would don his World War I coat and lecture to students on the vital importance of collective security and of confronting international threats head-on. Democracy, Hopper would insist, had to be defended not just by enunciating principles but by standing up and fighting.[55]

Hopper introduced Jack to the flamboyant and brilliant British historian John Wheeler-Bennett, a cane-carrying, monocle-wearing expert on Germany (and, incongruously, on the U.S. Civil War) who was in the early stages of penning a book on the Czech crisis. A lecturer at the University of Virginia that fall, Wheeler-Bennett was a spellbinding public speaker, whom Harold Macmillan, who would later be prime minister during the Kennedy administration, once called "one of the best talkers" he'd ever met. At Hopper's invitation, Wheeler-Bennett visited Cambridge and gave a talk on Munich and appeasement in Hopper's Government 18 class. After the lecture, Jack introduced himself and asked for a one-on-one meeting, and Wheeler-Bennett remembered being impressed by the "most pleasing, open countenanced, blue-eyed young man." The following afternoon, during a two-hour conversation along the Charles, with Win-throp and the other houses spread out next to them, golden and mellow in the late-day sun, the Briton impressed upon Jack the importance of considering "the imponderables of the human spirit" when assessing world affairs, and to consider carefully how one should balance principle with power in making policy. Jack, thrilled by the opportunity for sustained discussion with this erudite visitor, duly took down Wheeler-Bennett's suggestions for books to read.[56]

As 1938 turned into 1939 and Jack Kennedy prepared to join his father in London after Harvard's midyear exams, he knew what much of the rest of the world knew: that for a Europe in danger, Munich had provided but a breathing spell. The real crisis waited darkly in the wings.

EIGHT

THE OBSERVER

The day dawned clear and cold in the Italian capital. The Kennedy family, ten strong, was up with the sunrise, as were the two governesses and Mr. and Mrs. Moore. They dressed quickly in their Sunday best, jockeying for position in front of the mirror, gobbled down some breakfast, then piled into waiting limousines. Their destination was St. Peter's Square, where in a few hours they were to witness that rare and wondrous thing, especially to a Catholic: a papal coronation. It was March 12, 1939.

The Kennedys had been counting down the hours to this moment ever since President Roosevelt approved Joe's request to be the official American representative at the event. No president had ever sent an emissary to a papal coronation, and Joseph Kennedy relished being the first. To make the experience still more special, he and Rose had met the new pope previously—Cardinal Eugenio Pacelli, who took the designation Pius XII, had visited their home in Bronxville during a U.S. tour three years before, while serving as Vatican secretary of state, and Joe had met with him again on a subsequent visit to Rome in 1938. Now he would become pope, and Joe was determined to witness the event. The children should be there, too, Joe decided, so he brought them—without asking anyone's permission. Only Joe Junior, who was touring Spain and feared he would be denied reentry if he left the strife-torn country, did not come, much to his mother's disappointment.[1]

The square, majestic and graceful in the morning light, with its four-deep colonnades and its Egyptian obelisk rising in the center, was already packed with people at seven thirty when the four limousines pulled up, their American and papal flags flapping gently in the chilly breeze. The Kennedy contingent were ushered through the throng to their seats, in a prime location reserved for dignitaries in the outside portico of the basilica, near the equestrian statue of Charlemagne. Originally the Kennedys had been assigned two seats, for the ambassador and his wife, but hasty arrangements were made to expand the number to fourteen. Count Galeazzo Ciano, the Italian foreign minister and Mussolini's son-in-law, was livid upon learning that his assigned seat had been taken by a Kennedy child. He threatened to leave the basilica at once. More shuffling occurred, and Ciano ended up next to Joe, on the far end of the family.

The next morning, the pope held a private meeting with the Kennedy entourage in the anteroom of his papal apartment, and two days after that, on the morning of March 15, he celebrated his first papal Mass, a private one in a small red-walled chapel. The Kennedys were there, minus Rose, who had left for a long-scheduled appointment with, of all people, her dressmaker in Paris. While the rest of the family watched, seven-year-old Teddy, smartly turned out in a blue suit with a white rosette on his left arm, received, from the pope, his first Communion.[2]

It all made a profound impression on Ambassador Kennedy, whose dispatch to the State Department praised this "most saintly man" and his "extensive knowledge of world conditions. He is not pro-one country or anti-another. He is just pro-Christian. If the world hasn't gone too far to be influenced by a great and good man, this is the man."[3] Jack Kennedy likewise came away impressed, not least by the experience of receiving Communion from the pope. He, too, had met the man previously, during his summer 1937 European tour with Billings. He had liked Pacelli then, and he liked him now. At the same time, Jack couldn't resist making gentle fun of the unctuous undertones of the encounter. "Pacelli is now riding high," he wrote to Lem Billings a few days later, "so it's good you bowed and groveled like you did when you first met him. . . . They want to give dad the title of duke which will be hereditary and go to all his family which will make me Duke John of Bronxville and perhaps if you suck around sufficiently I might knight you."[4]

The Kennedys, minus Joe Junior, at the Vatican, March 13, 1939. From left: Kick, Pat, Bobby, Jack, Rose, Joe, Teddy, Eunice, Jean, and Rosemary.

Neither Jack nor his father failed to pick up on the palpable unease among the foreign dignitaries in Rome—the coronation occurred at an uncertain moment in history, under the shadow of war, and with the Mussolini government playing a significant role. And indeed, hardly had little Teddy received his Communion and the March 15 Mass ended when there came shocking news from the north: at six o'clock that morning, the German army had crossed the Czech border. By 9:00 A.M., forward units had entered Prague, and by day's end the rump of Czechoslovakia had ceased to exist. Adolf Hitler had now gotten what he wanted from the start: the conquest of not just the Sudetenland but Moravia and Bohemia as well. (Slovakia would become a German puppet state.) Immediately after the Munich agreement, the previous fall, he had expressed regrets about signing, claiming to subordinates that he had allowed himself to be hemmed in by "that senile old rascal" Chamberlain and had thereby squandered the chance to crush the Czechs in one fell swoop. ("If ever that silly old man comes interfering here again with his umbrella, I'll kick him downstairs and jump on his stomach in front of photographers," he had fumed.) Now the deed was done, and that very evening the Führer entered a sullen Prague in triumph.[5]

News of the conquest sent Neville Chamberlain into despair. Initially he tried to hold together the elements of his grand design, but within forty-eight hours he had shifted course. Appeasement was dead, the prime minister understood, at least as it had been practiced until now, and the Munich agreement was in tatters. (Hitler, he said privately, was "the blackest devil he had ever met."[6]) Lord Halifax, the foreign secretary, agreed. Both men grasped that by taking for the first time territory where the majority of the inhabitants were not German, Hitler had made resoundingly clear that he intended to do more than simply revise the provisions of the 1919 Versailles settlement. No longer could he be considered a conventional statesman out to right past injustices, especially with reports flowing in that he had designs on Poland next. In a speech in Birmingham, his home turf, on March 17, Chamberlain came off like a principled businessman who had been wronged—"I am convinced that after Munich the great majority of the British people shared my honest desire that the policy should be carried further, but today I share their disappointment, their indignation, that these hopes have been so wantonly shattered"—even as he also hinted at a new policy: "Is this the last attack upon a small State, or is it to be followed by others? Is this, in fact, a step in the direction of an attempt to dominate the world by force?"[7]

Across the Channel in Paris, Prime Minister Édouard Daladier could only nod knowingly when he learned of the invasion. Always more suspicious of Hitler's ambitions than was his British counterpart, Daladier had long believed the Führer would never be content with the Sudetenland and intended to devour Czechoslovakia, and moreover that his word could never be counted on. "Within six months," the dapper and diminutive Frenchman had predicted five and a half months earlier, right after the Munich agreement, "France and England would be face to face with new German demands."[8]

On March 31, soon after Hitler seized Memel (Klaipeda), a Lithuanian port on the Baltic that the League of Nations had declared an autonomous territory, Chamberlain announced a decision that would have hugely important ramifications: in the event that Germany threatened Poland's independence, he told Parliament, Britain and France would "feel bound to lend the Polish Government all support in their power." It marked the shift from appeasement to deterrence, though with the ultimate objective unchanged: to head off war. Tellingly, however, neither British nor French policymakers seriously considered making the Soviet Union a component of the deterrence strategy and thereby confronting Hitler with the prospect of a two-front war. Given only a few hours' advance notice of Chamberlain's declaration, angry Kremlin officials took it as further evidence that their Western counterparts were not to be trusted and perhaps hoped ultimately to see Germany and the USSR come to blows and bleed each other white.[9]

Ambassador Kennedy, upon learning of the prime minister's startling announcement, called FDR, who was at his presidential retreat in Warm Springs, Georgia. The president was asleep but called back ninety minutes later. Chamberlain's plan was a good one, he told Kennedy, but it probably meant war. Would this be an opportune time to call for a world peace conference? Roosevelt asked. Probably not, Kennedy replied—better to wait until official, as well as popular, responses in Germany and Italy to the Anglo-French move could be better gauged.[10]

II

By this point Jack Kennedy had arrived in Paris, where he hoped to serve a monthlong stint working at the U.S. embassy under Ambassador William C. Bullitt. Since departing the United States five weeks before, he had spent his time—apart from the excursion to Rome—in London, accompanying his father to lunches and dinners and other functions, all the while pining for Frances Ann Cannon.[11] He met with the king and took tea with the twelve-year-old Princess Elizabeth. He also worked part-time in the embassy, handling correspondence and occasionally representing his father at minor local events. (Here he followed in his brother's path, and also in that of John Quincy Adams, an aide during the ambassadorship of his father, John Adams, in the 1780s.) His letters show little evidence of father-son separation on the preferred strategy vis-à-vis Germany. If anything, Jack was the more sanguine, telling Lem Billings in late March, "Everyone thinks war is inevitable before the year is out. I personally don't, though Dad does."[12]

Now in Paris, spring had sprung, the daffodils and irises in the Jardin du Luxembourg bursting forth and the magnolias on the Champ de Mars in radiant bloom. The cafés were full. Jack thrilled at being there, and he took a liking to Bullitt, a wealthy Philadelphian and bon vivant who had been a cheerleader for the Bolshevik Revolution before turning rabidly anti-Communist during a stint as the first U.S. ambassador to the Soviet Union. Stylish and self-important, Bullitt was voted "most brilliant" in his Yale class of 1912, spoke fluent French and German, and made an immediate winning impression upon arriving in Paris in 1936—his hosts loved his flair and his linguistic prowess and considered him a man of superior judgment and taste. In short order he developed close ties to top French policymakers, even attending cabinet meetings, and—like Joe Kennedy in London—he kept the White House informed of the goings-on in the government. "Bullitt practically sleeps with the French cabinet," the cantankerous interior secretary, Harold Ickes, noted in his diary.[13] Initially supportive of appeasement—like Kennedy, he had been deeply influenced by Charles Lindbergh's depiction of an invincible Luftwaffe—Bullitt did a one-eighty in the winter of 1939; by the time Jack arrived in Paris in late March, the ambassador was espousing a hard-line anti-German position. Hitler, he told Roosevelt, was a madman with boundless ambition.[14]

Whereas his father had developed a chilly relationship with Bullitt, largely on account of a deep mutual competitive jealousy, Jack was charmed by his host and delighted in his company. "Bullitt has turned out to be a hell of a guy," he wrote to Billings. "Live like a king up there as Offie [Carmel Offie, Bullitt's private secretary] + I are the only ones there + about 30 lackies." The ambassador had "about 10 barrels of Munich beer in the cellar + and is always trying, unsuccessfully, to pour Champagne down my gullett." By day, Jack helped modestly with basic clerical work but mostly spent his time reading incoming cables and memoranda, even though Offie considered some of them "none of his business." Ever inquisitive, the young man asked questions about the functioning of the diplomatic process and about the meaning behind this or that missive, and he impressed both Bullitt and Offie with what would be a lifelong fascination with raw documentation. With his ready smile and insouciant manner, Jack masked how much knowledge he absorbed, and how swiftly.[15]

"Was at lunch today with the Lindberghs and they are the most attractive couple I've ever seen," he confided to Billings in early April, without giving away what he thought of Charles Lindbergh's pro-German sympathies or his gloomy analysis of the Anglo-French readiness for war (if he even knew about them). Anne Morrow Lindbergh, in particular, charmed him: "She takes a rotten picture and is really as pretty as hell and terribly nice." Her husband didn't return the compliment, writing in his diary of the luncheon that there were "probably forty people there, including some of society's greatest bores."[16]

On April 28, Jack and the rest of the embassy staff tuned in to Hitler's two-hour, twenty-minute speech to the Reichstag, which was occasioned by Franklin Roosevelt's message two weeks before in which he asked for Hitler's assurance that he would desist for the next twenty-five years from attacking a list of thirty nations. In exchange, FDR said, Washington would play its part on behalf of disarmament and equal access to world markets and raw materials. Hitler rejected the offer, his voice dripping with sarcasm, to the delight of his roaring audience, and he also took the opportunity to renounce Germany's nonaggression pact with Poland and to renew German claims to the seaport of Danzig.* "Just listened to Hitler's speech which they consider bad," Jack wrote to Billings right afterwards. He himself was less concerned, he went on, for if the German leader hoped to go after Danzig or all of Poland, "the time would have been a month ago before Poland and England signed up. That he didn't shows a reluctance on his part so I still think it will be OK. The whole thing is damn interesting and if this letter wasn't going on a German boat and if they weren't opening mail could tell you some interesting stuff."[17]

This was Jack's pattern during that spring of 1939: he tended in his correspondence to underestimate both the German dictator's bellicosity and, more generally, the seriousness of European tensions and the likelihood of war. He also seems to have misjudged the shift in the popular mood that had occurred in France and especially Britain during the seven months he had been back in the United States. The Munich agreement had created a split in British opinion that persisted into the new year, but little by little the appeasers found themselves losing the battle for public support. The fall of Prague on March 15 effectively killed the debate, giving the lie to Chamberlain's twin claims, upon returning from Bavaria,

---

* Danzig (later Gdansk), located at the mouth of the Vistula River on the Baltic Sea, was an ethnically German port city that had been taken from German control after World War I and made a League of Nations "free city," one that would be represented abroad by the newly reconstituted nation of Poland. Danzig and the so-called Polish Corridor along the Vistula ensured Poland's access to the Baltic but also divided East Prussia from the rest of Germany.

that he had brought "peace for our time," as well as "peace with honor." Together with the final defeat of the Republican side in the Spanish Civil War, culminating in the fall of Madrid in late March, it created in a great many Britons the conviction that the fascists could be stopped only by military force. Sooner or later, the battle would come. Moreover, many felt, Britain was now more ready to fight than it had been the previous fall, its rearmament program having made significant strides in the interval. To some observers, war might even be something to look forward to, if it helped wash away the malaise they felt had permeated British and European society since the decade began.[18]

All this is no doubt more clear in hindsight than it was at the time, but even so, Jack's failure to detect the transformation in popular attitudes is striking, especially given his own Anglophilia, evident from a young age but now given more opportunities for full expression. The upper-class British credo "Work hard, play hard, socialize hard" came naturally to him, he realized, and he admired the qualities often associated with "posh" Englishmen: cleverness, wit, irony, understatement, detachment, indirection, coolness under fire, self-possession. The actor David Niven was a modern archetype, while an earlier one was Queen Victoria's Whig prime minister Lord Melbourne—at least as rendered by David Cecil in his absorbing, gossipy biography *The Young Melbourne*, which appeared in Britain in early 1939 and which Jack devoured that spring. In Cecil's hands, Melbourne becomes for the young Kennedy a fascinating, altogether charming figure, indeed a kind of model for life: sophisticated and wittily idiosyncratic, poised and nonchalant, curious about people and what made them tick, skeptical of received wisdom and hostile to ideologues, susceptible to the pleasures of the flesh yet at the same time appealingly devoted to queen and country.[19]

"Life had taught him . . . always to relate thought to experience, to estimate theory in terms of its practical working," Cecil wrote of Melbourne, a description that fit Jack's vision of himself. And though more egalitarian than Melbourne, and more committed to an activist, democratic politics that would use established institutions and principles to benefit the common people (in British terms, a Tory position more than a Whig one), Jack certainly would have identified with Cecil's description of the broader upper-class milieu: "The ideal was the Renaissance ideal of the whole man, whose aspiration is to make the most of every advantage, intellectual and sensual, that life has to offer." Melbourne's own assertion that "things are coming to a pretty pass when religion is allowed to invade the sphere of private life" would likewise have appealed to Jack for its skeptical urbanity.[20]

Of Melbourne's carnal pursuits Cecil wrote, "His animal nature and his taste for women's society united to make him amorous, and natural tendency had been encouraged by the tradition of his home. Already, we gather, he had sown some wild oats. Like the other young men of his circle he thought chastity a dangerous state, and he seems early to have taken practical steps to avoid incurring the risks attendant to it." Jack, of course, knew all about this "tradition" from his own home.[21]

Cecil's succinct summation of the young Melbourne worked equally well for the young Kennedy: "He was a skeptic in thought; in practice a hedonist."[22]

Rose Kennedy, in explaining to a later interviewer the reasons for her second son's (and, palpably, her own) affinity for things English, spoke of his "Boston accent which is very much akin to the British, and then he responded to the British love of culture and literature and all that sort of thing."

> Most of the people in government circles and most of the people who had big houses and who entertained over there, were people whose families had been in government, and they had not only interest in government, in history and in politics, but they had had them for generations and so they were probably more cultured than the people were here, where most, or many, had started in very humble beginnings. And I think Jack responded to all that because he did like literature, and he did appreciate it, and then he was interested in government, and of course, he did enjoy seeing all the beautiful homes, because they were connected more or less to history. If you went away for the weekend, you'd see a house that had been there for hundreds of years. . . . There were different souvenirs of the years they had spent in government in those houses, and all those things Jack responded to, and so he did enjoy himself [there] as did we all, I think. And then of course it was more or less akin to Boston, because Boston is in a great part British, the people there are of British-Irish heritage, much more than they are in New York, for instance.[23]

III

In early May, Jack returned to London to attend a dinner party his parents were hosting for the king and queen, who were departing shortly on a royal visit to the United States and Canada. Then he headed off for Eastern Europe and the Middle East. His father helped arrange the itinerary and made the necessary contacts, and he received logistical help as well from Carmel Offie in the Paris embassy.[24] "Am now in Warsaw," Jack reported to Lem Billings early in the trip.

> It's been damn interesting and was up in Danzig for a couple of days. Danzig is completely nazified, much heiling of Hitler, etc. Talked with the Nazi heads and all the consuls up there. The situation up there is very complicated, but roughly here it is:
>
> 1st. The question of Danzig and the corridor are inseparable. They [the Germans] feel that both must be returned. If this is done then Poland is cut off completely from the sea. If [the Poles] return just Danzig . . . [the Germans] could thus control Polish trade, as by means of guns they could so dominate Gdynia that they could scare all the Jew merchants into shooting their trade thru Danzig. However, aside from the dollar + chits angle—which is only secondary— there is the question of principle. The Germans don't give a good god damn what happens to Poland's trade—and they told me frankly that the best thing for Poland would be to come into a customs union with Germany.

But the Poles had other ideas, Jack continued. "Poland is determined not to give up Danzig and you can take it as official that Poland will not give up Danzig and 2nd that she will not give Germany extra-territoriality rights in the corridor for the highways. She will offer compromises but never give it up. What Germany will do if she decides to go to war—will be to try to put Poland in the position of being aggressor—and then go to work. Poland has an army of 4,000,000 who are damn good—but poorly equipped."[25]

From there Jack pushed on to Russia, which struck him as "crude, backward, and hopelessly bureaucratic." His airplane en route had a broken window, which seemed to bother no one on board, and he had to sit on the floor. In Moscow he dined with Charles "Chip" Bohlen, the slim and handsome second secretary at the U.S. embassy—upon whom he made a favorable impression with his "charm and quick mind"—and he also visited Leningrad and the Crimea.[26] Then it was on to Turkey (a steamer ship brought him to Istanbul), Greece, Egypt, Palestine, Lebanon, Bulgaria, Romania, and Yugoslavia.[27] At each stop Jack penned for his father a detailed assessment of the local political situation. The historian James MacGregor Burns, who in the late 1950s saw these missives (regrettably, most were subsequently lost or stolen), remarked on their cool detachment and shrewd, balanced analysis—and poor spelling.[28]

We do have one of these evaluations, the report from Jerusalem, and a remarkable document it is. Subtle and penetrating, and free of any hint of anti-Semitism, the letter shows Kennedy's growing maturation as a thinker—and, no doubt, his many years of accumulated knowledge as a reader of history and international affairs, often from a sickbed. In particular, we see his grasp of the complex nature of the Arab-Jewish conflict in Palestine, and his understanding of the role of history in shaping the current tensions. Behind the official assertions of the two sides, we read, "are fundamental objections which, while they are not stated publicly, are nevertheless far more important."

On the Jewish side there is the desire for complete domination, with Jerusalem as the capital of their new land of milk and honey, with the right to colonize the Trans-Jordan. They feel that given sufficient opportunity they can cultivate the land and develop it as they have done in the Western portion. The Arab answer to this is incidentally that the Jews have had the benefit of capital, which had the Arabs possessed, equal miracles could have been performed by them. Though this is partly true, the economic set up of [Arab] agricultural progress with its absentee landlords and primitive methods of cultivation, could not under any circumstances probably have competed with the Jews.

There are hints, too, of Jack's emerging anticolonialism ("After all," he reminds his father, "Palestine was hardly Britain's to give away") and more than hints of his insistence on the need to pursue a realistic, pragmatic outcome, one resisting propaganda from either side. "It is useless to discuss which has the 'fairer' claim. The important thing is to try to work out a solution that will work." For Jack, this could be achieved only through the creation of "two autonomous districts giving them both self-government to the extent that they do not interfere with each other and that British interest is safeguarded. Jerusalem, having the background that it has, should be an independent unit. Though this is a difficult solution yet, it is the only one that I think can work."

Even then, the report concludes, it might well not be enough, especially given the deep splits within both groups:

> There is the strongly orthodox Jewish group, unwilling to make any compromise, who wished to have a government expressing this attitude, there is the liberal Jewish element composed of the younger group who fear these reactionaries, and wish to establish a very liberal, almost communistic form of government, and there are the in-betweens who are willing to make a compromise. . . . As for the Arabs, while most of them are heartily sick of the whole business which is playing hell with their economic life, yet so strong is the hold of the Mufti by reason of his religious grip and because of the strength of the new nationalism, that it is going to be extremely difficult to effect a solution without bringing him back.[29]

On his final night in Jerusalem, Jack received an up-close demonstration of the seriousness of the conflict when thirteen bombs exploded in the Jewish section; all of them, he reported to his father, were detonated by the Jews themselves. "The ironical part is that the Jewish terrorists bomb their own telephone lines and electric connections and the next day frantically phone the British to come and fix them up." His Majesty's representatives, Jack thought, responded with alacrity and skill; he felt his admiration for the British way of doing things deepen still further.[30]

IV

By June 1939 Jack was back in London, working by day in the embassy and hitting the parties and clubs by night, often in the company of sister Kick and a small entourage of British friends. He now saw in a way he had not before that Britain was girding for war. Some weeks earlier, the Chamberlain government had introduced conscription, and Anglo-French military staff talks had commenced to consider how best to wage a three-year war with Germany. The Oxford Union debating society's famous King and Country resolution from 1933 ("This House will in no circumstances fight for its King and Country") was overturned and expunged from the union's minute book. Ordinary Britons dug air-raid shelters in their back gardens. Chamberlain and Halifax still hoped Hitler would back down, or at least agree to negotiate without threats. The signing by Germany and Italy, in May, of the bombastically named Pact of Steel undermined the Englishmen's hopes of detaching Italy from Hitler's clutches, and they saw no option but to reaffirm publicly that if Germany attacked Poland, the British government would honor the guarantee to come to Poland's support. The French vowed likewise.

The irony was rich: after refusing the previous summer to make a guarantee to Czechoslovakia, a country ready to fight and holding alliances with France and the Soviet Union, Chamberlain and Daladier were now issuing one to a country that, as their own military leaders made clear to them, was geographically exposed and militarily ill-equipped and could not be effectively assisted in the event of a German invasion, with the result that she would likely hold out only a few weeks. Why would Hitler be deterred in such a situation?[31]

Joseph Kennedy thought the Anglo-French guarantee would do little except increase the likelihood of war—a war, moreover, that Germany would win, and that the United States should have no part of. He was adamant on this point, if anything more so than he had been the previous year. Increasingly, however, as spring turned into summer, Kennedy's pessimism rubbed Britons—including many leading political figures—the wrong way. In June, at a dinner in London in honor of the visiting Walter Lippmann (whose book *The Good Society* Jack Kennedy was reading that summer, at the urging of Bruce Hopper), Winston Churchill heard the columnist recount a meeting he had had with Kennedy earlier that day. The Western powers stood no chance against the mighty German war machine, the ambassador had insisted, which meant that Britain had no option but to concede to Hitler control over Eastern and Central Europe. "All Englishmen in their hearts *know* this to be true," Kennedy had declared, "but a small group of brilliant people has created a public feeling which makes it impossible for the government to take a sensible course."

Churchill, who had sat glumly brooding through the meal up to that point, exploded in fury. Kennedy was a timorous and naive man, he charged, an Anglophobe on account of his Irish heritage, whom Roosevelt, in a lapse of judgment, had foolishly selected for this vitally important post, and who was an impediment to British-U.S. cooperation. The author and diplomat Harold Nicolson, also at the table that evening, marveled at the scene as Churchill sat hunched, "waving his whiskey and soda to mark his periods, stubbing his cigar with the other hand," as he insisted that Britain would stoically endure whatever the Germans threw their way and repay the destruction with interest. Even should Germany prevail in the encounter, he went on, it would still have to tangle, sooner or later, with the most powerful nation of them all, the United States. "It will then be for you, for the Americans," he told Lippmann, "to preserve and to maintain the great heritage of the English-speaking peoples." Churchill then urged him to use his influential column to get his compatriots to "think imperially" and maintain their time-honored commitment to holding high "the torch of liberty." Lippmann, who prided himself on not being swept off his feet easily, came away mesmerized by the Englishman's colossal gift for language and oration and by his obvious leadership qualities, which Lippmann decided exceeded even those of the great and charismatic Theodore Roosevelt.[32]

What Joseph Kennedy never understood—it's a key explanation for his failure as ambassador—was that for many Britons, fighting had become a matter of dignity, even as they were under no illusions as to the heavy price it would extract. The concept of honor in international affairs was foreign to Kennedy; all that mattered was survival. Because Munich had been about such self-preservation, he saw no reason for Chamberlain or anyone else to be ashamed of it, and he continued in mid-1939 to regard Hitler as a responsible statesman with whom one could do business. War would be catastrophic, which meant that realism consisted of doing whatever was necessary to keep the peace. Jack, on the other hand, though pragmatically inclined like his father, had a greater feel for the things of the spirit, for the intangibles that often moved people. He understood, from his avid childhood reading about the deeds and misdeeds of past leaders, that respect and credibility mattered greatly in human affairs; they always had and they always would. His professors Bruce Hopper and Payson Wild had further impressed this notion on him. More directly, Jack, upon his return to London, could see the change in the young Englishmen he and Joe Junior and Kick met with socially: many of them now spoke of going after the Germans with guns blazing, come what may.[33]

One of these friends was David Ormsby-Gore, 5th Baron Harlech, whom he met through Kick and who would be Britain's ambassador to Washington during the Kennedy administration, remaining a close confidant until the end. Like Jack a second son who found sanctuary in books as a youngster, the slim and sharp-nosed Ormsby-Gore, who often wore a silk scarf tied insouciantly around his neck, was independent-minded and fun-loving, and blessed with a formidable intelligence. He was also extremely well connected, his father having been a member of Parliament for twenty-eight years and his mother being the granddaughter of Lord Salisbury, a prime minister under Queen Victoria and towering figure in the Conservative Party. In their early encounters, Jack seemed to Ormsby-Gore to be cut from the same cloth as him: fascinated by politics and statecraft, more an observer than a pontificator, and more a social animal than a sober student of world affairs. They soon developed a deep mutual affection. "He was very thin, wiry-thin with, I don't know how to describe it, this energy exuding from him," Ormsby-Gore remembered of his friend. Underneath the party persona, however, the young Englishman detected a more serious dimension, "because of course he was preparing his thesis—it was a longer than normal thesis."[34]

It was true: Jack had indeed decided on a topic for his upcoming Harvard thesis project. Bruce Hopper had reminded him in their spring correspondence that, with his travels and his father's position, he had an unmatched chance to study history in the making. Jack agreed. Partly on account of his intense discussions with his British friends the previous summer, he had developed a fascination with Great Britain's policies, and in particular with how it had gotten itself into such a predicament. How had it squandered the advantages it held after the Great War, when the empire stood supreme and the Royal Navy patrolled the world's seas? Where had the Chamberlain appeasement policy come from, and how would one assess its soundness? Shouldn't the British have been more prepared for the rise of Hitler's Germany?[35]

Jack had the thesis very much in mind when, in July, he left London and crossed the Channel again. He wanted to see Germany up close and to gauge the likelihood of war. This time he traveled with his Harvard roommate Torbert Macdonald, who had come over to Europe with the Harvard track team. Torby would have preferred to linger in London, for he was in love with Kick Kennedy and hoped to spend time with her. But at Jack's insistence they made their way for Munich, where they met up with Byron "Whizzer" White, a former all-American halfback from Colorado and now a Rhodes Scholar at Oxford. (Much later, under President Kennedy, White would be appointed to the Supreme Court.) Before their departure, Jack and Torby had been warned by Ambassador Kennedy to keep their heads down and stay out of trouble, but at the tomb of the Nazi hoodlum-martyr Horst Wessel the three Americans were accosted by local storm troopers who heckled them and threw rocks at their car (presumably because it bore British license plates). "Our first thought was to lay into them," Macdonald recalled, "but Jack, even though he was as sore as the rest of us, led us in a diplomatic retreat." The incident left the three Americans shaken. "If this is the way these people feel," Jack said, maybe war was inevitable.[36]

Some days later, having parted ways with White, Jack and Torby rented a car in Paris, intending to drive to the Riviera, where the Kennedy family had again rented a vacation villa near Cannes. Traveling at high speed south of Paris, Jack lost control of the vehicle—a jalopy that seemed to have a mind of its own and continually bucked to the right—and flipped it over. The car skidded on its roof for thirty feet, and the luggage was strewn about the pavement. Upside down in the compartment, Jack turned to his friend and calmly remarked, "Well, pal, we didn't make it, did we?"[37]

But eventually they did, meeting up with numerous Kennedys in the South. Kick was there, fueling Macdonald's hopes, but she soon crushed them by making clear she was not interested in a romance. (She had fallen hard for William "Billy" Cavendish, the Protestant Marquess of Hartington and heir to the dukedom of Devonshire, and brother of Jack's friend Andrew Cavendish.) That revelation sent the young men venturing north again, on August 12, bound once more for Germany. Rose noted in her diary that "they would like to go to Prague, but we are told no one is allowed to go there."[38] Undaunted, Jack headed for Vienna, while Torby split off to go to Budapest. Jack got into Prague with an assist from the U.S. embassy, but the diplomat responsible, George F. Kennan, was none too pleased to have to do it, recalling some years later:

In those days, as the German forces advanced like encroaching waves over all the borders of Bohemia, no trains were running, no

All smiles in Cannes, in early August 1939, as the war clouds gather.
Back row: Kick, Joe Junior, Rosemary, Rose, and Teddy.
Middle: Jack, Eunice, Joe, and Pat. Front: Bobby and Jean.

planes were flying, no frontier stations existed. Yet in the midst of
this confusion we received a telegram from the embassy in London,
the sense of which was that our ambassador there, Mr. Joseph Kennedy, had chosen this time to send one of his young sons on a fact-
finding tour around Europe, and it was up to us to find means of
getting him across the border and through the German lines so that
he could include in his itinerary a visit to Prague.

We were furious. Joe Kennedy was not exactly known as a friend
of the career service, and many of us, from what we had heard about
him, cordially reciprocated this lack of enthusiasm. His son had no
official status and was, in our eyes, obviously an upstart and an ignoramus. The idea that there was anything he could learn or report
about conditions in Europe which we didn't already know and had
not already reported seemed (and not without reason) wholly absurd. That busy people should have their time taken up arranging
his tour struck us as outrageous. With that polite but weary punc-
tiliousness that characterized diplomatic officials required to busy

themselves with pesky compatriots who insist on visiting places they have no business to be, I arranged to get him through German lines, had him escorted to Prague . . . and with a feeling of "that's that," washed my hands of him.[39]

Kennan could be forgiven for his annoyance at having to play host to a college student at this moment in time, with tensions in Europe running close to the boiling point. Even so, his pomposity—never far below the surface with Kennan—got the better of him. His young guest was no ignoramus. Quite the contrary, Jack's letters that spring and summer—to Billings, to his father, to others—reveal a penetrating and analytical mind at work, as well as a historical knowledge honed through immersion in books. Not all of the letters were carefully constructed—he often wrote in an emotive stream and showed a weakness for gossip and the crude put-down, suggesting he was not thinking as an aspiring politician with an eye to posterity—but invariably they contained telling insights about the local scene. The report to his father from Jerusalem in June was on par—in content if not in presentation—with what a veteran diplomat might produce.

V

History was on Jack Kennedy's mind that summer as Europe's crisis deepened. From Winston Churchill's *The World Crisis* and from course readings at Harvard, he understood how easily miscalculation and stubborn pride could lead to a rupture among nations and a resort to arms. The current situation was not a replay of July 1914, he determined, not yet anyway, but certainly there were worrisome signs. In the final half of August, he hustled between German cities—Munich, Hamburg, Berlin—seeing in each place ample evidence of the fearsome Nazi disinformation machine at work, stoking tensions with the Poles over Danzig and the corridor. In Berlin he rendezvoused briefly with Joe Junior, who was on his own inspection tour of the Reich. Joe was now less enamored of the Nazi German state than he had been on previous visits, even as he held staunchly to his father's worldview. "The anti-Polish campaign is beyond description," Joe wrote. "Every edition of the newspapers has a more gruesome tale to tell of Polish outrages against the Germans, of planes being attacked and of German soldiers tortured." The intent was obvious: when war came, "the Poles will be shown to be the aggressors, and it will be the duty of every German to stop them." Newsreels showed the same thing, he added, with even young children brought forth to testify to the terrible deeds of the dastardly Poles.[40]

War might be close after all, Jack now sensed, a notion given credence by the secret message Alexander Kirk of the U.S. embassy in Berlin asked him to bring back to his father in London: Germany, the message read, would likely attack Poland within a week.[41] But still Jack wondered: Would Hitler actually go through with it if it meant hostilities with Britain and France? This was indeed the question on all Germany watchers' minds. Already months before, in early April 1939, Hitler had authorized a secret military directive for the destruction of Poland anytime after September 1 (but before the fall rains began in mid-September). The German leader doubted Western resolve, and he was not deterred when, over the early summer, Paris and London leaders reaffirmed their commitment to the Poles and the Poles themselves refused to yield on Danzig and the corridor. Britain and France, he still believed, would in the end refuse to fight. On August 19, the very day Jack arrived in Berlin, the first German formations began moving toward the Polish frontier; within four days, they were in place. Other units followed, leading ultimately to a massive attacking force of 1.5 million men. Meanwhile, weapons and soldiers were smuggled into Danzig so that the city, already Nazi-dominated, could be taken immediately upon the beginning of operations.[42]

Hitler wanted war in the summer of 1939, but he hoped it would be a local affair, involving only Germany and Poland. The obstinacy of Chamberlain and Daladier, and of Polish foreign minister Józef Beck, the key player in Warsaw, surprised and annoyed him and complicated his plans. With his generals warning him that Poland should not be attacked unless Germany could be assured of Russia's neutrality, the Führer now launched one of the most astonishing about-face gambits in modern history (albeit one that took shape over several weeks), the news of which sent shockwaves around the world. In opposition to everything he had preached about the evils of Soviet Communism, he sent his obsequious foreign minister, Joachim von Ribbentrop, to Moscow on August 23 to negotiate a nonaggression pact with Joseph Stalin—who himself did a volte-face, having hammered for years on the absolute heinousness of fascism.[43] In the early hours of the twenty-fourth the deal was signed, with a secret protocol splitting Poland and northeastern Europe between them. "All the isms," a British midlevel official remarked, "are now wasms." Hitler, overjoyed at what he saw as a triumph of colossal consequence, expected to hear of the swift collapse of the French and British governments, and he felt more certain that the Western powers would not fight for Poland. "Our enemies," he had told his commanders the day before he dispatched Ribbentrop to Moscow, "are tiny little worms. I saw them at Munich. I'll cook them a stew they'll choke on."[44]

Britain and France had made their own approaches to Stalin in the weeks prior, hoping that an entente between the three powers would be sufficient to constrain Germany once and for all. Had the effort succeeded, it might well have had the desired effect. But the plan was never as close to realization as some later observers claimed. On the Western side, the effort was desultory and late in coming—Chamberlain in particular could not shake his visceral suspicion of Communists in general and Stalin in particular, and, like most British officials, he held a low opinion of Soviet military effectiveness—while for Stalin there was logic, however ultimately misplaced, in casting his lot with the Germans, especially in view of his bottomless mistrust of British and French intentions. A ruthless practitioner of realpolitik (even if forced to justify his decisions with reference to Marxist-Leninist ideology, which, lucky for him, was an infinitely malleable doctrine), Stalin played with a Western alliance mostly, it seems, in order to pressure Berlin into making a deal that would bring concessions to his side. Specifically, he sought and received territory in eastern Poland, Bessarabia, and the Baltic states. In addition, the deal bought him time to build up the Red Army, which had been crippled by his recent paranoia-induced purges of senior officers, and to consolidate his defenses against the attack from the west that he had always feared.[45]

In London and Paris, officials had to pick themselves up off the floor after learning of the Nazi-Soviet pact. Even now, they hoped against hope that some means could be found to avoid the catastrophe and that Hitler would agree to negotiate.[46] His willingness to meet on successive days with British ambassador Nevile Henderson, an arch-appeaser inclined to grasp at any straw, seemingly gave substance to this possibility. But not much substance. Neither Chamberlain nor Daladier was under any illusion about the fate that would soon befall Poland. When Joseph Kennedy encouraged Chamberlain to make more concessions to Berlin, the despondent prime minister shook his head. "I've done everything I can think of, Joe," he said, "but it looks as if all my work is of no avail."[47]

Kennedy, resigned to an imminent German attack, still hoped Britain would wriggle free of its commitment to the Poles. France would then assuredly follow suit, and a wider war would be averted. Certainly, the ambassador told American journalists on August 23, from a U.S. point of view one should hope for Chamberlain to abandon Poland and revert to the policy of appeasement. "I don't see what we've got to gain if Britain goes to war," he said. "I don't care if Germany carves up Poland with British support. I'm for appeasement one hundred percent, and if one thousand percent is more than one hundred percent, I'm for it one thousand percent." To which Ralph Barnes of the *New York Herald Tribune* responded, "Have you been telling this to Mr. Chamberlain?" Kennedy answered, "I've been telling him that every chance I had every day for more than a year."[48]

VI

War came the following week. In the predawn hours of Friday, September 1, waves of Stukas, Messerschmitts, and Heinkels began bombing targets deep within Poland, and German armored columns crossed the frontier in overwhelming strength from the north, west, and (through Slovakia) south. Even now Chamberlain dithered, announcing to the House of Commons (with Joe Kennedy in the visitors' box) that he would work with the French to get mediation through the good offices of Italy's Mussolini. The chamber responded with stunned silence, then fury. Facing a revolt also within the Cabinet over the absence of a declaration of war, the prime minister at last agreed to issue an ultimatum to Hitler to withdraw; when, on the late morning of September 3, the appointed hour passed without a withdrawal, Chamberlain told the British people in a mournful, eloquent radio broadcast from 10 Downing Street that "this country is at war with Germany." Even Chamberlain's detractors found it a moving, resolute declaration. All over the nation, people gathered anxiously around their radio sets to hear the announcement, then stood up when the national anthem was played at the end, whereupon in London the first prolonged air-raid alarm sounded, causing widespread chaos.[49]

In the House of Commons early that afternoon, with Jack, Kick, and Joe Junior present in the visitors' gallery along with their mother, Chamberlain spoke in sepulchral tones: "Everything I have worked for, everything that I have hoped for, everything that I have believed in during my public life, has crashed into ruins. There is only one thing left for me to do: that is devote what strength and power I have to forwarding the victory of the cause for which we have sacrificed so much."[50]

Mrs. Kennedy was deeply stirred, as her husband had been by the earlier radio address. After the speech, the ambassador called 10 Downing Street. "Neville, I have just listened to the broadcast. It was terrifically moving. . . . I feel deeply our failure to save a world war." Chamberlain thanked Kennedy for reaching out and for his unfaltering support. "We did the best we could have done but it looks as though we have failed. . . . Thanks, Joe, my best to you always and my deep gratitude for your constant help—Goodbye—Goodbye."[51]

In his diary that day, Joe stayed on the theme, writing that the broadcast was so touching it almost made him cry. "I had participated very closely in this struggle and I saw my hopes crash too." But the British leader could hold his head high: "It is a terrible thing to contemplate, but the war will prove to the world what a great service Chamberlain did to the world and especially for England." By rejecting war at the time of Munich, eleven months earlier, Joe wrote, Chamberlain had given British officialdom a precious year to rearm and to line up popular support.[52]

Jack, however, found greater power in another speech on that extraordinary September day. Winston Churchill, now joining the Cabinet as First Lord of the Admiralty, rose slowly from the backbenches after Chamberlain had spoken. His remarks ran a mere four minutes, but they left the young American—and many others in the hall—spellbound. No one should underestimate the size of the challenge ahead, Churchill declared gravely, or fault the prime minister for his sadness at the failure to avert war, but a generation of Britons stood ready to prove themselves equal to the task.

This is not a question of fighting for Danzig or fighting for Poland. We are fighting to save the whole world from the pestilence of Nazi tyranny and in defense of all that is most sacred to man. This is no war of domination or imperial aggrandizement or material gain; no war to shut any country out of its sunlight and means of progress.

It is a war, viewed in its inherent quality, to establish, on impregnable rocks, the rights of the individual, and it is a war to establish and revive the stature of man. . . . We are sure that these liberties will be in hands which will not abuse them, which will use them for no class or party interests, which will cherish and guard them, and we look forward to the day, surely and confidently we look forward to the day, when our liberties and rights will be restored to us, and when we shall be able to share them with the peoples to whom such blessings are unknown.[53]

The drama played out differently in Berlin. The world war that Hitler had insisted would not materialize suddenly seemed a reality. Early that morning of September 3, Hitler's chief interpreter, Paul Schmidt, had arrived at the Reich Chancellery with the text of the British ultimatum. Ushered into the presence of Hitler and Ribbentrop, Schmidt read it to them slowly, taking care to enunciate each word. "When I finished," he wrote in his memoirs, "there was complete silence. Hitler sat immobilized, gazing before him." Some moments passed, the quietude deafening, whereupon the Führer turned to Ribbentrop and said sharply, "What now?" Other subordinates, including press chief Otto Dietrich, likewise would recall Hitler's stunned reaction to the ultimatum. When propaganda minister Joseph Goebbels arrived at the chancellery later in the day, he found Hitler furious with the British yet determined to fight. There would be no thought of pulling troops back from Poland. That evening, after the French had followed Britain's lead and declared war, the German leader reiterated his belief that the threats by the two Western powers were empty; neither would wage a real military campaign.[54]

In Washington, the Roosevelt administration followed developments closely through near-constant communication with embassy staff in Berlin, Warsaw, Paris, and London. In the early morning of September 3, Washington time, soon after Britain's declaration of war, President Roosevelt took a call from Joe Kennedy, who had given in to hopelessness and said a new dark age had descended on Europe, which meant "it's the end of the world . . . the end of everything." The president replied with soothing words.[55] That night, FDR delivered a fireside chat in which he told the nation that while the United States would remain neutral in the new European struggle, he could not ask that every American remain neutral in judgment as well—a deliberate revision of Woodrow Wilson's plea in 1914 that Americans be impartial in both thought and deed.

In London that evening, nerves were on edge as residents expected German bombers to arrive in the skies at any moment. A nightly blackout had been imposed, and a haunting quiet fell over the city. Most residents stayed inside their homes, listening to the BBC on the radio behind blackout blinds. "It is an eerie experience walking through a darkened London," Kick Kennedy wrote of the blackout's effects. "You literally feel your way, and with groping finger make sudden contact with a lamppost against which leans a steel helmeted figure with his gas mask slung at his side. You cross the road in obedience to little green crosses winking in the murk above your head. You pause to watch the few cars, which with blackened lamps, move through the streets. . . . Gone are the gaily-lit hotels and nightclubs; now in their place are somber buildings surrounded by sandbags."[56]

At 2:30 A.M., an aide called Ambassador Kennedy with stunning news: The British liner SS *Athenia*, bound for Canada and carrying thirteen hundred passengers, including three hundred Americans, had been torpedoed by a German submarine, seventeen hours after Britain's declaration of war. The unarmed ship, ripped by explosions, was sinking somewhere west of the Hebrides. Jolted awake, Kennedy ordered that a list of the passengers be produced as quickly as possible. (Due to incomplete manifests, it would take weeks to get the final numbers and to determine that 112 passengers had perished, including twenty-eight Americans.) Before dawn, he walked down the hall and woke up Jack. In short order the youth hurried off to Scotland, accompanied by Eddie Moore. Many of the rescued passengers were being brought to Glasgow, and the ambassador wanted Jack to be present as his representative. With the regular embassy staff now overloaded with work, he had no one else to send.

The crowd that greeted Jack Kennedy at the Beresford Hotel demanded answers about what had occurred, as well as protection once they resumed their transatlantic voyage. "We want a convoy!" they hollered at him as soon as he arrived. "We refuse to go without a convoy!" Some shook their fists. According to the London *Evening News*, the young American showed a "boyish charm and natural kindliness," as well as the "wisdom and sympathy of a man twice his age," as he did his best to field questions and express understanding. Citing Roosevelt's claim that convoys were unnecessary because Germany would not attack an American vessel, Jack told the passengers they should not expect protection on their homeward journey, which prompted shouts of "What about the submarines? You can't trust the German Navy! You can't trust the German Government!" Jack held his ground and kept his composure as he strove to be heard above the din. "You will be safe on a ship flying the American flag under international law," he insisted. "A neutral ship is safe."* The most he could do, he went on, was to pass on their concerns to his father. This seemed to defuse the tension and calm the room. While in Glasgow, Jack also visited injured Americans in area hospitals, garnering respect for his calmly authoritative, courteous, and accessible demeanor. An "Ambassador of Mercy," one journalist dubbed him.[57]

He was touched by what he saw. "The natural shock of the people would make the trip to America alone unbearable . . . because of the feeling that they will have that the United States exposed them to this unnecessarily," he wrote to his father in arguing for a convoy to accompany whatever ship or ships brought the *Athenia* survivors back to U.S. shores.[58]

Once back in London, Jack was put in charge of the repatriation of the survivors. The work kept him in England longer than planned—the USS *Orizaba* left Glasgow on September 19, bound for New York, with some four hundred *Athenia* survivors on board—and he wrote to Harvard for permission to enroll for the fall semester late. The permission was granted. Jack expected to return to the university on September 29, but to his surprise he found a last-minute seat aboard a Pan American Dixie Clipper, the four-engine "flying boat" that had just commenced transatlantic passenger service that summer. He flew from Foynes, Ireland, on September 20, via Newfoundland, the aircraft swooping down, like an enormous metallic duck, at Port Washington, New York, the following day. According to *The Boston Globe,* Jack was "the general favorite with all on the *Dixie,* not because he was Ambassador Kennedy's son but because he was himself, bright and helpful and interesting."[59]

It had been an astonishing seven months overseas, more consequential than he ever could have anticipated, more eventful, surely, than the experience of any Harvard junior that year—or perhaps any year. He had received communion from the pope and taken tea with Princess Eliza-

---

* After the war it would be determined that the *Athenia* sinking was a mistake; an overeager German submarine commander had mistaken the civilian vessel for a Royal Navy auxiliary cruiser.

beth; had read high-level diplomatic dispatches in London and Paris; had been accosted by Nazi toughs in Munich; had flipped his car south of Paris and survived; had paid visits to Poland and Russia; had darted south to Turkey, North Africa, and the Middle East; had traveled behind German lines in occupied Czechoslovakia and crisscrossed Germany in the immediate lead-up to war, before carrying a top-secret message back to London; had been present in the House of Commons for the historic session on September 3; and, to top it off, had made his debut as a public figure in response to the sinking of an ocean liner on the first day of Britain's war.

It was the kind of exposure and training that no future president since John Quincy Adams had enjoyed at so young an age. And the experience left its mark, cultivating in him an intensified passion for foreign policy and world affairs that he never abandoned, and completing his transition to adulthood.[60]

Now he was back at Winthrop House, a college student once more, twenty-two years old and focused on the principal task ahead: taking all he had experienced and learned on his grand overseas adventure and turning it into a worthy senior thesis. No one yet knew it, but here, too, John Fitzgerald Kennedy, with a generous assist from his father, would do something extraordinary and put his name before the public once again.

NINE

A HISTORY OF THE PRESENT

The Harvard to which Jack Kennedy returned in September 1939, following his grand overseas adventure, seemed on first glance the same as it ever was. Newly arrived freshmen wandered about the Yard, feigning nonchalance and trying not to look lost, while returning students sat under the trees and on the steps of Widener Library in little knots or alone, smoking cigarettes. Others lounged down by the river with the Radcliffe girls, stretching out on its grassy banks as the crew teams glided by, their oars moving in metronomic rhythm.

Yet everyone knew that all was not the same. Germany had invaded Poland, and the British and French empires had responded by declaring war on the aggressor. It meant the end, effectively, of the international system established at the conclusion of the Great War, twenty years before, and the return to global conflict. The European order, and therefore the world order, had been torn apart in the span of a few days. If some of Jack's Harvard classmates failed to understand the full implications of Hitler's extraordinary gambit, all sensed that a historic moment had come. World politics had been rocked off course, its new destination unknown.

Down the road in New York, "in one of the dives on Fifty-second Street," W. H. Auden captured the moment in "September 1, 1939":

> *Waves of anger and fear*
> *Circulate over the bright*
> *And darkened lands of the earth,*
> *Obsessing our private lives;*
> *The unmentionable odour of death*
> *Offends the September night.*[1]

Jack, though he had witnessed the prewar drama up close, got no special recognition for the fact, either at the Spee Club or at Winthrop House, where he and Torby Macdonald had moved into a two-person suite. "Everyone here is very much excited about the war situation and have been busy telling exactly what the situation is," he deadpanned to his father in his first week back. "So I guess I shouldn't have gone over there, as I could have learned a lot more right here."[2]

The German blitzkrieg in Poland dominated the headlines as the semester began. The Poles battled bravely, surprising the Wehrmacht with the strength of their rearguard actions and with their dogged defense of Warsaw. The German High Command announced on September 15 that the Polish capital had fallen, but the news was premature: the surrounded city resisted tenaciously until September 27 and inflicted significant casualties on the Germans. But any hope of the Poles holding out for long was lost when the Russians invaded from the east on the seventeenth, as per the secret agreement with Berlin, and when the Western Allies made devastatingly clear that they would not honor their stated obligations to Poland's defense. (Polish leaders had gone to war in the expectation that if they held out for fifteen days, the French would launch a major attack on western Germany.) The last Polish unit capitulated on October 5, and on the same day Hitler entered Warsaw for his victory parade.

Harvard's president, James B. Conant, was vacationing in New Hampshire on September 1 when he learned that German tanks were rolling across the Polish frontier. For the past several years Conant had felt alienated from the powerful tide of American isolationism, and was increasingly convinced that Hitler wanted to do much more than revise the Versailles settlement—he sought to dominate all of Europe. The enlightened, culturally rich Germany that Conant had known as a young researcher and scientist had changed fundamentally as the Nazis crushed free expression and persecuted Jews. Yet he had moved cautiously, aware that, as Harvard's president, his every utterance could generate reaction. "Being the head of an institution with eight thousand young men under my direction who may get shot if we go into the war, while I shan't, I am a bit estopped from saying much," he wrote to Archibald MacLeish on September 7. "I don't like the moral dilemma I find myself in, but my personal emotions are a small matter in these times of world grief." But as the days passed and the Germans pressed the attack, Conant could stay silent no longer. "Every ounce of our sympathies," he told Harvard students from the pulpit in Memorial Church in late September, must be with those fighting the Nazis. The United States could not set itself apart; quite the contrary, on its response rested "not only the fate of humanity's experiment with free institutions, but the potency of man's belief in a life of reason—in short, what we now venture to designate as modern civilization."[3]

There were nods of approval in the pews, but also considerable skepticism. Many students were more inclined to follow Joseph P. Kennedy's line of argument than Conant's—to believe, in other words, that this was a European quarrel from which the United States should stand aloof, if not in thought then certainly in deed. In their eyes, America's intervention in World War I had not yielded the promised results—it hadn't made the world "safe for democracy," let alone "ended all wars"—and they were suspicious of being bamboozled into another bloody war by grizzled old men who could remain safely detached from the blood-red battlefields. A poll of eighteen hundred Harvard students a few weeks later found that 95 percent were "against immediate American entry" into the conflict, and 78 percent opposed intervention "even if England and France were defeated." A narrow majority favored "an immediate peace conference" with Nazi Germany.[4] The *Crimson* student newspaper, under Jack's classmate and fellow Spee member Blair Clark, followed this line, arguing vociferously against American intervention even as it predicted a German victory. ("We are frankly determined to have peace at any price. We intend to resist to the utmost any suggestions that American intervention is necessary to 'save civilization' or even to 'save democracy and freedom.'")[5]

Within the faculty, too, opinions ranged widely, though as a group they were more interventionist than were the students; many, including several of Jack's professors, saw things as Conant did and favored robust American aid to Britain and France. According to the *Crimson*, Professor Payson Wild denounced the Neutrality Acts as dangerously outmoded— only if European democracies were given the means to hold their own would America be able to stay out, in Wild's view. Arthur Holcombe, in a lecture to the Harvard Student Union, said it was foolish to believe the United States could remain neutral, and that Washington "would have to decide on which side to throw its influence." Jack's tutor Bruce Hopper, meanwhile, warned of the rise of an aggressively expansionist Japan in the Far East, as did Professor William Y. Elliott, who also cautioned that "a truce at present would consolidate the Italian and German position in Europe," which "would be disastrous for this country."[6]

Jack himself now joined the fray, penning an editorial for the *Crimson*, under the title "Peace in Our Time," that in large measure parroted his father's positions. The defeat of Poland, however regrettable, should be ignored, the piece read, and President Roosevelt should "exert every office he possesses to bring about . . . peace." France and Britain were both eager to end the fight, yet neither was in a position to make a direct overture to Berlin; only FDR stood well placed to do so. The alternative might well be disastrous, especially for Britain: "There is every possibility— almost a probability—of English defeat. At the best, Britain can expect destruction of all her industrial concentrations and the loss of the tremendous store of invested wealth. . . . At the worst she can expect extreme political and economic humiliation." The editorial did not deny that a peace deal would entail "considerable concessions to Hitlerdom"— control over Poland, a free economic hand in the rest of Eastern Europe, and a redistribution of colonies—but, Jack asked, what choice was there? Moreover, if, in exchange for these concessions, "Hitler could be made to disarm, the victory would be likewise great for the democracies. Hitlerism—gangsterism as a diplomatic weapon—would be gone, and Europe could once more breathe easy. The British and French Empires would be reasonably intact. And there would be peace for our time."[7]

It was a strikingly naive claim, especially coming from a young man who had just seen the European crisis up close, and who had a subtler grasp of world politics than Joe Senior did. He wrote as though Chamberlain's appeasement policy had not suffered a mortal blow, as though Hitler's actions had not obliterated the prospect that he could be persuaded

to disarm. The editorial dismissed would-be critics of the proposal as acting on sentiment instead of "solid reality," but the same charge could be
made against the author himself.

Just what possessed Jack to argue along these lines is not altogether
clear. Loyalty to his father was certainly a factor, and moreover he bought
into the current defeatism characterizing not merely the ambassador's
assessment but those of many other observers who saw Britain and
France facing long odds against the German war machine. (It's hard to
recall today how widespread this view was in 1939–40.) The United
States, Jack believed, should take major preparedness measures but
should avoid entangling itself militarily in the European struggle. Some
later authors also see in the editorial Jack's penchant for going against the
grain, for staking out an independent position, especially in pushing for
an American diplomatic intervention.[8] But this seems far-fetched in view
of the *Crimson*'s editorial position that fall, and the prevailing attitude
among Harvard students, both of which were broadly in line with Jack's
perspective; at most, it can be said that he stood in opposition to some of
his professors, and to President Conant.

Whatever the case, Jack could consider himself lucky that editorials in
the *Crimson* were unsigned. His first foray into published political com-
mentary was one he would come to regret making.

II

That would come later. At the time of publication, Jack was pleased with
his effort, and said so to his father.[9] Joe, in turn, felt paternal pride at seeing his second son writing for *The Harvard Crimson* and personal satisfaction that the line of argument so closely matched his own. It was a tonic
that, frankly, he needed, for the fall of 1939 was in other respects a miserable time for him. He toiled alone in London, having sent most of his family back to America at the outbreak of hostilities. (Rosemary stayed
behind at her Assumption Convent School, reestablished at Belmont
House, in Hertfordshire, thirty miles northwest of London, after the start
of the war.) The dinner invitations that had come thick and fast during his
and Rose's first year in England now were few and far between; many evenings he spent by himself. The solitude weighed on him, made him morose, rendered his charcoal worldview darker still.

"I haven't changed my opinion at all about this situation," he wrote his two eldest sons on October 13. "I think that it will be a catastrophe financially, economically, and socially for every nation in the world if the war continues and the longer it goes on, the more difficult it will be to make any decent rearrangement." To Arthur Krock he expressed even deeper distress: "One couldn't be more pessimistic than I am as to the future outlook for the world if this war continues any length of time."[10]

All around him Kennedy could see preparations for a war he hated: parks bristling with anti-aircraft guns and big black arrows pointing in the direction of air-raid shelters. His formerly close relationship with Neville Chamberlain's government was fast fraying, on account of the changed circumstances: Britain was at war and ruling out early negotiations with Hitler, while Kennedy remained steadfast that Germany would win and that America must not intervene. Britain's glory days had long since passed, he felt certain, and he told Roosevelt he saw "signs of decay, if not decadence, here, both in men and institutions. . . . Democracy as we now conceive it in the United States will not exist in France and England after the war, regardless of which side wins or loses." Consequently, "we [in America] should curb our sentiments and our sentimentality and look to our own vital interests."[11] Invariably, these assessments got back to 10 Downing Street and to the Foreign Office, which in September began keeping a "Kennedy dossier" on him.

The file, which remained classified for the next several decades, contains various explanations for the ambassador's gloom: his Irish American heritage, which made him delight in "seeing the lion's tail twisted"; his innately pessimistic worldview; his acceptance, thanks to the reports of Charles Lindbergh and Joe Junior, of the notion of German air superiority; and his laser-like focus on "the financial side of things," which rendered him unable, "poor man, [to] see the imponderabilia which, in a war like this, will be decisive." William Hillman, a U.S. journalist and friend of Kennedy's, told a Foreign Office contact that Kennedy was "a professing Catholic who loathed Hitler and Hitlerism almost, though perhaps not quite, as much as he loathed Bolshevism, but he was also a self-made man who had known poverty and who did not want to know it again." Hillman got the poverty bit wrong, but on the whole his assessment rang true. The prospect of "bankruptcy and defeat" had become obsessions in the ambassador's mind, he said, which had the effect of making him immune to reason.[12]

The Foreign Office, in a cable to Philip Kerr, Lord Lothian, the newly appointed British ambassador in Washington, summarized the emerging analysis:

> Kennedy has been adopting a most defeatist attitude in his talk with a number of private individuals. The general line which he takes in these conversations as reported to us is that Great Britain is certain to be defeated in the war, particularly on account of her financial weakness. . . . While it is very regrettable that Kennedy should be adopting this attitude, we do not propose, for the time being at any rate, to pursue the matter further. We have thought it well, however, to let you know about his indiscreet utterances in case it should later become necessary for us to ask you to drop a hint in the proper quarter, and because in the meantime you may perhaps hear echoes of his talk and be able to trace them to their proper source.[13]

England's monarch expressed his own frustration with Kennedy's narrowness of vision. "He looked at the war very much from the financial and material viewpoint," King George wrote in his diary after the two men met on September 9. "He wondered why we did not let Hitler have SE Europe, as it was no good to us from a monetary standpoint. He did not seem to realise that this country was part of Europe, that it was essential for us to act as policemen, & to uphold the rights of small nations & that the Balkan countries had a national spirit."[14]

In Washington, too, Kennedy found his influence, such as it was, further reduced. In September he urged Roosevelt to initiate negotiations involving the Allies and Nazi Germany ("It appears to me that this situation may resolve itself to a point where the President may play the role of savior of the world"), only to be rebuked in no uncertain terms by Secretary of State Cordell Hull: "This government, so long as present European conditions continue, sees no opportunity nor occasion for any peace move to be introduced by the President of the United States." Roosevelt privately called Kennedy's plea "the silliest message to me I have ever received."[15]

This was a curious claim, given that FDR himself had pondered a diplomatic intervention, but it spoke to the vast gulf now separating the two men. Kennedy's unrelieved bleakness and fears for the future exasperated the president. "Joe has been an appeaser and will always be an appeaser," he complained to Henry Morgenthau. In contrast to the ambassador's staunch opposition to any form of military intervention, Roosevelt was more and more of the opposing view, that only war could bring about the end of an intolerable and wicked regime. The United States might yet be able to avoid belligerent status, but the president felt certain that his country needed to provide abundant assistance to France and Britain. The American people, Roosevelt declared, could not "draw a line of defense around this country and live completely and solely to ourselves." It hadn't worked when Thomas Jefferson and Congress tried it with the 1807 embargo against Britain and France, Roosevelt said, and it wouldn't work now. America could not insulate itself from world war.[16]

FDR's problem was that a great many Americans shared Joe Kennedy's perspective: they *did* believe the nation could—and should—isolate itself from overseas conflict. The more informed among these observers in many cases seconded the ambassador's claim that Britain did not have a prayer of prevailing militarily. Germany was simply too strong, which meant that America needed to accommodate itself to the new reality. A *Time* cover article on the ambassador in September lauded him for his wary analysis of England's war and his insistence on coldly preserving U.S. freedom of action.

"From one point of view," the article enthused, "Joe Kennedy is a common denominator of the U. S. businessman—'safe,' 'middle-of-the-road,' a horse-trader at heart, with one sharp eye on the market and one fond eye on his children. But he is a super common denominator, uncommonly common-sensible, stiletto-shrewd, practical as only a former president of a small bank can be. As Ambassador Kennedy his attitude is the same as that of Businessman Kennedy: Where do we get off?"[17]

That month, Roosevelt called for revising the Neutrality Acts on the grounds that they were too inflexible. Specifically, he wanted authority to decide who the aggressors were in a war, and who the victims, and to withhold or provide aid accordingly, which in this case would allow the selling of arms to France and Britain if they carried them away in their own ships. But the isolationists rose up in force, determined to block him. Their stronghold was in the U.S. Senate, and especially in the delegations from the West and the Midwest. William Borah, Republican of Idaho, a stalwart of the opposition and a man widely admired for his oratorical skills, took to the airwaves to warn against any revision of the neutrality legislation, as did Burton K. Wheeler, Democrat of Montana, Hiram Johnson, Republican of California, and Gerald Nye, Republican of North Dakota. Charles Lindbergh did the same on all three national radio networks. Germany was no threat to American democracy, the aviator declared in his spindly, high-pitched voice, and moreover it was entitled to certain revisions of the Versailles Treaty. Sending arms and munitions to the Western powers, meanwhile, would not bring victory but only ensnare America in Europe's eternal feuding, and this *would* threaten the very survival of American democracy. Sounding exactly like Joe Kennedy, Lindbergh advised his huge radio audience to view the global crisis clinically, never allowing "our sentiment, our pity, our personal feelings of sympathy, to obscure the issue [or] to affect our children's lives. We must be as impersonal as a surgeon with his knife."[18]

Above all, Lindbergh added, Americans should be under no illusions about the cost of intervention. Merely providing munitions to the Allies would never be enough; U.S. ground forces would inevitably follow. "We are likely to lose a million men, possibly several million. . . . And our children will be fortunate if they see the end in their lives."[19]

In a subsequent radio address, Lindbergh made a Nazi-like appeal to racial solidarity. America's ties to Europe, he declared, were "a bond of race and not of political ideology." He explained: "It is the European race we must preserve; political progress will follow. Racial strength is vital; politics, a luxury. If the white race is ever seriously threatened, it may then be time for us to take part in its protection, to fight side by side with the English, French, and Germans, but not one against the other for our mutual destruction."[20]

Here the aviator went too far for many, and he encountered sharp criticism from elements in the press. Still, his identification with the isolationist campaign generated deep concern among White House analysts, who understood all too well the breadth of his appeal among grassroots voters. In response, the administration called on its own band of heavy hitters, among them Henry Stimson, secretary of state under Herbert Hoover, and Frank Knox, Alf Landon's running mate on the GOP ticket in the 1936 presidential election. Conant, too, contributed speeches to the effort, and the White House got backing as well from syndicated columnist Dorothy Thompson, whose column ran in more than 150 newspapers nationwide and who had a weekly radio program on NBC, and from William Allen White, the revered editor of *The Emporia* (Kansas) *Gazette,* whose homespun and no-nonsense analysis made him a prominent voice in the nation's heartland. Thompson in particular was relentless: she had observed Hitler's rise up close as a foreign correspondent in Germany and Austria early in the decade and had developed a deep loathing for the man and his regime. In column after column she railed against the Führer and against the fecklessness of the Western powers' response, and she often continued the diatribe at dinner parties and other social gatherings. "If I ever divorce Dorothy," her husband, the Nobel Prize–winning novelist Sinclair Lewis, quipped, "I'll name Adolf Hitler as co-respondent."[21]

The battle for the hearts and minds of the American people was on. For a time it seemed the isolationists had all the momentum—of eighteen hundred pieces of mail received by one Republican senator, only seventy-six were in favor of repealing the arms embargo contained in the Neutrality Acts. But White House officials saw reason for hope in other numbers. Although most Americans were insistent about the need to keep out of the war, a large majority (85 percent in one survey) hoped to see Britain and France win. Other surveys showed roughly even splits between those who wanted to give aid to the Allies, those who did not, and those who would approve the selling of arms to belligerents on cash-and-carry terms. This was the opening FDR needed, and he could argue as well that the new policy would create American jobs. In early November the White House got what it sought: a repeal of the arms embargo and a new law authorizing the sale of arms to belligerents on a cash-and-carry basis, meaning they would carry the goods from U.S. ports in their own ships.[22]

As if all this were not enough to distress Joe Kennedy, he found himself further eclipsed by the rise—in both London and Washington—of Winston Churchill, the First Lord of the Admiralty and a possible successor to Chamberlain as prime minister. Unbeknownst to Kennedy, FDR in September bypassed his ambassador and opened a secret direct channel of communication with Churchill, with the messages sent by diplomatic pouch but sealed so that no one could read them at the respective embassies.[23] Upon learning of the scheme three weeks later, Kennedy was furious: the clandestine correspondence, he wrote in his diary, was yet "another instance of Roosevelt's conniving mind which never indicates he knows how to handle any organization. It's a rotten way to treat his ambassador and I think shows him up to the other people. I am disgusted." It galled Kennedy that the president put any faith at all in Churchill, a man he considered grandstanding and slippery, and consumed by his desire to draw America into the war. "He is just an actor and a politician. He always impressed me that he'd blow up the American Embassy and say it was the Germans if it would get the U.S. in. Maybe I do him an injustice but I don't trust him."[24]

It annoyed Kennedy that Churchill never bothered to learn the little things about him. Whenever they met, the Briton would invariably offer him a drink, forgetting that Kennedy seldom touched alcohol. Meanwhile, Churchill himself refused to be put off by the ambassador's abstinence. When Kennedy on one occasion pointedly remarked that he had sworn off drinking and smoking for the duration of the war, Churchill muttered, "My God, you make me feel as if I should go around in sack cloth and ashes," and poured himself another brandy.[25]

Ever more marginalized, Kennedy turned to family for support. He treasured his communications with Joe Junior, now a student at Harvard Law School, who told him that "everyone at home is unanimous in wanting to stay out of the war," as well as with Jack, at Harvard College, and with Rose, back in Bronxville, who counseled him to mind his spiritual health. ("I'm praying that I shall see you soon. Do pray, and go to church, as it is very important in my life that you do just that.") On Sundays Rose lined up the children still living at home to speak to their father on the one weekly transatlantic call the security precautions allowed him. From daughter Kick he learned that she had been denied admission to Sarah Lawrence College and would attend Finch women's college, in Manhattan, and that her heart was still with Billy Cavendish, not with any of her innumerable American suitors. Of her readjustment to U.S. soil, Kick wrote her father, "That's the amazing thing when one's been away: one expected things to have changed & they haven't."[26]

Kennedy also arranged for regular visits to Rosemary, in Hertfordshire, by himself and—when work kept him away—by Mr. and Mrs. Moore.[27] She seemed to be thriving at her school, with its Montessori method of hands-on, individualized instruction. On her twenty-first birthday, in September, she remarked that "it is the most wonderfulest place I've been to." The school's staff, aware of her disabilities, assigned to her an extra aide, paid for by Joe, and reported to him and Rose that she seemed content, apart from periodic eruptions when she would lose her temper and lash out at everyone around her, including younger classmates. Joe, encouraged by what he heard, also provided a telephone for the school, as well as a fire-extinguishing system for use in the event of a bombing. The measures gave him peace of mind, and the school authorities expressed their fulsome gratitude. To provide Rosemary with a change of scenery, Joe would occasionally arrange for her to spend Saturday and Sunday at the embassy, accompanied by a caretaker.[28]

In wartime England, of all places, the Kennedys seemed to have found the right placement for their eldest daughter—a convent school in a lovely, bucolic setting whose devoted staff followed a method of instruction that suited her well. "It becomes definitely apparent now that this is the ideal life for Rose[mary]," Joe exulted in a letter to his wife on October 11. "She is happy, looks better than she ever did in her life, is not the slightest bit lonesome, and loves to get letters from the children telling her how lucky she is to be over here (tell them to keep writing that way)." It was even possible, the letter went on, taking a troubling turn, that Rosemary should remain in Hertfordshire "indefinitely, with all of us making our regular trips, as we will be doing, and seeing her then. I have given her a lot of time and thought and I'm convinced that's the answer. She must never be at home for her sake as well as everyone else's."[29]

Rosemary, for her part, clamored for her parents' love and support. "She thinks of you very specially and loves you *heaps*," the mother superior of the school reminded Rose in December. "[She] loves to hear from you, [and] to get your approval [and] her father's too." Nothing pleased Rosemary more, the staff noticed, than spending time with her father. "Many, many thanks for coming to see me on Friday," she wrote to him after one visit in early 1940. "You were a darling. I hope you liked everything here. . . . Mother says I am such a comfort to you. Never to leave you. Well Daddy, I feel honor because you chose me to stay."

She added a postscript: "I am so fond of you. And. Love you very much. Sorry, to think that I am fat you. think—"[30]

III

In Cambridge, Jack was beginning to second-guess his "Peace in Our Time" editorial. The national debate over the neutrality legislation influenced his thinking, as did his discussions with his fellow undergraduates in the classroom, as well as his one-on-one conversations with professors. (He took four courses, all in government: Elements of International Law, Modern Imperialism, Principles of Politics, and Comparative Politics.) Though he was not ready to renounce the editorial—not yet—and he remained partial to his father's overarching philosophy, Jack backed off his certitude and acknowledged the merits in the interventionist arguments by President Conant and others. He foreswore penning more *Crimson* pieces.[31]

It marked a reversion, in a way, to the old Jack, clinical and observant rather than mixing it up in the arena. The editorial was out of character for him, something to expect from his more strident and doctrinaire older brother. Looking back decades afterwards, Arthur Holcombe remarked of Jack that "the style of the man was formed while he was quite young. . . . He was never a crusader, as some men are. You can pick some crusaders out of a class, while they're still undergraduates; they have that commitment to act upon an idea, which to them is decisive of their behavior. That wasn't the challenge to which [Jack] responded." The issue was not lack of talent, the professor went on, for Jack had it in abundance; rather, it was a lack of direction, hardly unusual even among upperclassmen at Harvard. "Everybody knew that he was going to make a great success of whatever he turned his attention to," Holcombe said, no doubt with the benefit of hindsight.[32]

For now, however, Jack kept his focus on his courses, on laying the groundwork for his thesis, and on his pursuit of women—not necessarily in that order. Frances Ann Cannon, his infatuation of junior year, remained the chief object of his affections. To his sister Kick he had revealed that he intended to ask Cannon to marry him. "Jack is taking out Frances Ann this weekend so we can all hardly wait," Kick wrote to her father. How much his parents knew of his plan is not clear; in her memoirs, forty years later, Rose would say merely that Frances Ann was "an attractive girl in whom Jack seemed to be quite interested at that time and evidently she was interested in him, too. At least Kick seemed to be implying that some 'announcement' was in the offing." Jack's former roommate Charlie Houghton also had his eye on Miss Cannon, and he had the advantage of being a Protestant. In any event, neither suitor won his prize: when Jack and Charlie showed up together on the doorstep of Frances Ann's apartment one evening, she introduced them to her new fiancé, an aspiring writer named John Hersey. The two Harvard men beat a hasty retreat.[33]

The rejection stung Jack deeply. To friends he would claim it was he who broke off the relationship, but his closest confidants—Kick, Torby

Macdonald, Lem Billings—knew better.* As if to compensate, he resumed playing the field more energetically than ever, and with his usual knack, astounding his Winthrop House mates with the ease with which he seemed to score date after date with woman after woman. One frequent companion was Charlotte McDonnell, a friend of Kick's from her Catholic girls' school; on other occasions it would be models and actresses, few of whom would get a second call and none of whom he introduced to his family. "I went to N.Y. last weekend for Thanksgiving," he reported to Billings in late November, "—and had quite a time. Met that model Georgia Carrol[l] who is really something—and met some other good stuff."[34]

McDonnell was under no illusions about her prospects. "I went out with Jack lots of times," she remembered, "but he was never in love with me. He liked to think he was, when things were going bad and he didn't have anyone else, but he really wasn't. He'd come down and talk to his friends. He'd talk to Lem and he'd talk to Torby and he'd say, 'Hey, what would you think if I married Charlotte?' And they'd have a big pow-wow. But when it comes down to the nitty-gritty, did he ever ask me to marry him? No, he did not. . . . We just had a good time together."[35]

Just as Jack's general disregard for women's feelings stayed the same, his cavalier attitude toward material possessions also had not changed. Suits would be left behind on trips, driver's licenses would disappear, library books would go missing. When another in a long line of wristwatches somehow vanished, Paul Murphy, who oversaw Joe Senior's New York office and often paid the family's bills, intervened on Mrs. Kennedy's behalf:

> She is very much disturbed about the loss of your wristwatch as she feels that you have lost altogether too many watches. She wants you to know she has had her gold wristwatch since she was twenty-one. She would like to have you buy an inexpensive but reliable watch to replace the one you have lost. If you can keep the new watch for about five years, she will then buy you a better one with the money received from the insurance company. Your mother has talked with your father about the above suggestion and he has agreed to it. And

---

* Jack attended the Cannon-Hersey wedding, in North Carolina in April 1940, having swallowed the reluctance he expressed humorously to a friend: "I would like to go but don't want to look like the tall slim figure who goes out and shoots himself in the greenhouse halfway through the ceremony." (Treglown, *Mr. Straight Arrow*, 56.)

he has asked me to advise you that he does not want your mother annoyed with any arguments.[36]

In the classroom, Jack stayed on the upward trajectory he had started in his junior year. His travels overseas, often solo, had deepened both his knowledge and his engagement with global politics in all its dimensions, and he also brought to bear his broad understanding of contemporary international history, cultivated during a lifetime of serious reading. He had grown more mature, more focused, a point noted by his closest professorial contacts, Payson Wild and Bruce Hopper, who now directed him in what was assuredly the most intensive period of academic study he would ever undertake. Jack's notes from his classes in the fall of 1939 support this notion, as he delved deeply into the twentieth-century "isms"—communism, socialism, fascism, capitalism, nationalism, totalitarianism, imperialism, militarism.

Fascism, Jack recorded, was largely pragmatic in nature, "a system built up by trial & error, by experiment and practice. Whatever survives the test of experience is valid, the rest is discarded." Thus, both Mussolini in Italy and Hitler in Germany felt free to reverse themselves as situations warranted, whereas Stalin in Russia felt obliged to pay "at least lip service to the doctrines of Marx." Yet the similarities between Marxism (as practiced in the Soviet Union) and fascism were obvious, not least in their brutally antidemocratic nature and their de facto one-party rule. "The [Communist] may insist that he is truely Dem. in wishing the collective rule of the people to triumph but in practice his [state] is as totalitarian & intolerant to opposition as the Fascist [state]." In practice, Jack's notes read, "both the Soviet and Fascism system are coming closer and closer together upon the assault upon priv. capitalism. Both represent an attack on *individualism,* on the sense of personal dignity & freedom which is the heritage of the 19th century in the West. Both subordinate the individual to the collectivity."[37]

In a case study for Wild's international law class, Jack examined the rights and responsibilities of neutrals in wartime, through an analysis of four different scenarios. Drawing upon a range of published sources as well as a close reading of the Hague Convention of 1907, he offered nuanced and tightly argued analyses of each situation, in clear and succinct prose. With respect to neutral pilots guiding ships of belligerent nations through neutral waters, for example, he concluded that existing international law was not altogether clear but that the best interpretation nevertheless presented itself: "If they are employees of the state, it is a breach of state A's neutrality to allow its licensed pilots to pilot the vessels of state Y to a point ten miles beyond in the high seas unless there are conditions of distress. If they are merely private individuals licensed by the state, it is not a breach of state A's neutrality."[38]

Most interesting of all, in that it seemed to disavow entirely the thrust of his *Crimson* editorial and to anticipate arguments in his senior thesis, was a thirty-five-page investigation of British policy toward the League of Nations in the two decades that had passed since the organization's founding, in 1919. From the start, Jack asserted, collective security foundered on the unwillingness of the great powers to surrender national sovereignty to the decisions of the League. Even so, Britain "could have made herself the champion of small nations by standing for international law and a League policy" but refused to do so, on account of her fear of Soviet Communism and her lack of support from a standoffish United States. The Nazi threat, meanwhile, was consistently and grievously minimized as British policymakers somehow assumed that once Hitler's territorial grievances were addressed, his power would collapse or at least be contained. "They seem to entertain the notion that when there are four Caesars in power at the same time, not one of them will ultimately succeed in conquering the world," he wrote. "The danger lies in having one Caesar who stops only when defeated by a world coalition."

A throwaway aside in the paper's conclusion revealed a starkly different take on U.S. participation in the First World War than either his father's or his older brother's take—or, for that matter, those of most members of the class of 1940. "This is not the place to speak of America's entry into the World War except to remark that American participation did not fail to save democracy. Had she not joined, democratic England and France would be powerless and the United States would in no way claim isolation for herself today. There is reason to believe that continued American participation in international efforts for peace and the establishment of law and order would have borne much fruit."[39]

IV

By this point in the school year, with the days growing shorter and the gray clouds rolling low and moist above the buildings, the familiar image of Jack around the Yard was of him with a stack of books under his arm, collar turned up against the cold and wind, too hurried to stop and talk.[40] Much of the time, the books were not for his courses but for his senior thesis. Bruce Hopper had urged him to use the ringside experience he had gained during his European sojourn to good effect, and the English historian John Wheeler-Bennett, too, had nudged him in this direction, but the final choice for the topic—an in-depth examination of the origins of Britain's appeasement policy and the concomitant failure to rearm—was Jack's own.[41] It reflected his lifelong interest in British history and statecraft, and his deepening affinity for the country and its ways. Not least, it took advantage of his extraordinary personal circumstances: the American ambassador in London was his own father, whom he accompanied to various high-society functions and who introduced him to some of the British leaders he would now be writing about.

How was it, Jack wanted to know, that Britain found itself on the cusp of another destructive war so soon after escaping the most devastating conflagration in history?

He hit Widener hard in the late fall, reading parliamentary debates and newspaper reports on British attitudes—official and popular—in the 1930s, and checking out pertinent books as he found them.[42] A hypothesis took hold: Chamberlain's accommodation of Hitler was a logical outcome of Britain's lackluster rearmament efforts earlier in the thirties, and of the entrenched opposition among the public to another war. Jack consulted regularly with Hopper, meeting once a week in the tutor's handsome, oak-walled room, with its majestic fireplace and its framed Latin plaque, which read in translation, "It will give you pleasure to look back on the scenes of this suffering." In addition, Jack took other steps unavailable to his less privileged, less connected Harvard peers. In Palm Beach over the Christmas holidays, he sought insights from the British ambassador, Lord Lothian, who happened to be visiting the Kennedy home. Lothian pledged to help the thesis project in whatever way he could, and he encouraged the young man to pay a visit to the British embassy in Washington on his way back to Harvard, which Jack duly did.[43]

Still more helpful was James Seymour, the press attaché at the U.S. embassy in London, whom Jack recognized could be hugely beneficial to him in procuring source material. On January 11, 1940, Jack sent Seymour an urgent cable:

SEND IMMEDIATELY PAMPHLETS, ETC, CONSERVATIVE, LABOR, LIBERAL, PACIFIST ORGANIZATIONS FOR APPEASEMENT THESIS DISCUSSING FACTORS DISCUSSING PRO CON 1932 TO 1939 STOP SUGGEST LASKEY [sic] AS REFERENCE ALREADY HAVE TIMES, MANCHESTER GUARDIAN, HANSARD, THANKS, JACK KENNEDY.[44]

Seymour, a Harvard alumnus (class of 1917) who earned the French Croix de Guerre in World War I and later wrote scripts for Hollywood, set right to work by calling a range of organizations and securing their ready agreement to provide materials. He gathered these together in shipments to be sent to Jack, often by way of Paul Murphy. Speeches by Conservative, Labour, and Liberal party leaders; pamphlets from trade unions, pacifist organizations, isolationist movements, and appeasement groups; magazine articles of various kinds—mounds of items soon found their way to Jack in Cambridge, thanks to Seymour, who also took time to pen elegant personal notes to his young acquaintance. "We have had our share of cold and fog which has not improved our lovely black-out," he wrote on one occasion. "London is a different and almost incredibly beautiful place in these conditions. I get a rare kick out of walking the empty streets— moonlight especially makes it lovely. . . . The spirit of the people is marvelous—firm, serious and courageous, ready I feel to face any sacrifice or privation to achieve the one and only end they are willing to accept." Then the sign-off: "You probably know more about world affairs than I—but you may not know one thing, that your cheery presence is really greatly missed here. I mean it. Good luck to you—and here's hoping to hear from you before I see you. Ever, Jim."[45]

How much Ambassador Kennedy knew of his son's ideological shift over the late fall and winter of 1939–40 is not clear, and in a sense it doesn't really matter—neither he nor Bruce Hopper nor anyone else had significant influence on Jack's emerging interpretive stance. For that matter, it had never been Joe Kennedy's style to insist that his children adhere to his positions on policy issues. He could be domineering and overbearing in any number of ways, but not here, as he urged Joe Junior and Jack and their siblings to come to their own judgments on things. It was and would remain one of his most appealing personal qualities.

Of course, the flip side of that characteristic was that he himself could be remarkably resistant to outside persuasion. On December 8, 1939, shortly after returning to the United States for an extended restorative vacation—the stress in London had caused his stomach troubles to flare up, and he was down fifteen pounds—the ambassador spoke extemporaneously at Boston's Our Lady of the Assumption Church, where as a youngster he had been an altar boy. "As you love America," he exhorted the Irish American parishioners, many of whom felt scant love for England, "don't let anything that comes out of any country in the world make you believe you can make a situation one whit better by getting into war. There is no place in this fight for us. It is going to be bad enough as it is." Kennedy could see no reason for America to enter the struggle, and he warned against being seduced by a "sporting spirit," by an aversion to seeing "an unfair or immoral thing done." This was no time for such sentimentality.[46]

In Washington, the ambassador told a group of Army and Navy officers—in direct opposition to what Jim Seymour had suggested to Jack—that morale in France and England was low and going lower. Economic conditions in both countries were terrible, and people longed for peace. Nazi submarines were being launched faster than the Royal Navy could sink them. Could England hold out beyond another year? Kennedy doubted it. By the end of 1940, if not sooner, he told the officers, the people of England and France, and perhaps all of Europe, might well be ready to embrace Communism. At the White House, he struck similarly downbeat tones. "Joe is usually a bear," one nameless aide remarked, "but this time he is a whole den."[47]

Kennedy's problem was not so much what he said; it was how he said it. A great many people in that gloomy winter of 1939–40 shared his low confidence in the prospects for the Western democracies and his fervent belief that the United States should stand apart from the fighting. This was indeed still the majority view among Americans. For that matter, Kennedy's views were somewhat more nuanced than his words often suggested: he did not mind the November 1939 revision to the neutrality laws, for example, and he supported providing aid to Britain and France. But he lacked a certain filter, lacked a true sense of empathy, and seemed almost to take a kind of perverse satisfaction in his public prognostications of ruin. The concept of honor in international affairs, always mysterious to him, remained elusive and left him immune to the dazzling eloquence of a Winston Churchill or the impassioned advocacy of a Dorothy Thompson.

For British officials, the worry was not that his defeatism would infect their own people, but that it would undermine morale among neutral nations and in particular in the United States.[48] In January 1940, Robert Vansittart, the government's chief diplomatic adviser, scrawled a comment that reflected a broadly held view within British officialdom: "Mr. Kennedy is a very foul specimen of double crosser and defeatist. He thinks of nothing but his own pocket. I hope this war will at least see the elimination of his type." A few weeks later, while the ambassador was still in America, the British Ministry of Information intercepted a telegram destined for Jim Seymour at the U.S. embassy that read "Rush Pacifist Literature" and was signed, simply, "Kennedy." The ministry analysts, suspecting the worst, saw it as one more sign of Joe Kennedy's treacherous behavior. ("Becoming a Pacifist!" wrote one alarmed officer in the margin.) The cable, of course, was Jack's.[49]

That same month, rumors flew anew of a possible Kennedy dark-horse candidacy for the upcoming presidential election. Kennedy allowed the story to percolate for a few days—he may indeed have stoked it to begin with—before shutting it down after a conference with Roosevelt at the White House. Though he endorsed FDR for another term, he could be harshly critical when the mood struck him. On one occasion in February, for example, he joined a conversation in progress at the State Department between William Bullitt, the U.S. ambassador to France, and two reporters. Bullitt, never known for his discretion and now also a confirmed Kennedy foe, related the conversation to Harold Ickes (himself hardly the most discreet of men), who wrote in his diary:

He [Kennedy] cheerfully entered into the conversation and before long he was saying that Germany would win, that everything in France and England would go to hell, and that his one interest was in saving his money for his children. He began to criticize the president very sharply, whereupon Bill took issue with him. . . . Bill told him he was abysmally ignorant on foreign affairs and hadn't any basis for expressing an opinion. He emphasized that as long as Joe was a member of the Administration he ought to be loyal—or at least keep his mouth shut. They parted in anger.[50]

Kennedy had no desire to return to London to resume his duties, but return he did, arriving on February 28, 1940. His four-day ocean voyage, aboard the SS *Manhattan,* had been made more pleasant by the opportunity to spend each night in the company of Clare Boothe Luce, journalist and playwright and the wife of *Time* and *Life* media mogul Henry Luce. The Luces had been guests at the London embassy in the spring of 1938; sometime after that, Joe and Clare began secretly seeing each other when circumstances permitted, usually in London, occasionally in New York. ("Golly that was nice," she cabled him after a fall 1938 visit to England; in May 1939, another cable read, "Sailing *Normandie* Tuesday. Save me lunch and/or dinner. Chat. Alone. Love, Clare." He did better than that: he offered to meet the ship at Southampton and drive her to London.) Kennedy loved her good looks, her indefatigable energy and ambition, her keen intelligence; she relished the same things about him. Somehow in their pillow talk they looked past their sharply divergent views on world politics—Clare was an interventionist through and through.[51]

Nothing and no one could alter Kennedy's view. "I haven't changed one idea of mine in the past year," he told Arthur Krock. "I always believed that if England stayed out of war it would be better for the United States and for that reason I was a great believer in appeasement. I felt that if war came, that was the beginning of the end for everybody, provided it lasted for two or three years. I see no reason yet for changing my mind one bit."[52]

The war was entering its seventh month as Kennedy returned to his post, but so far little had occurred. In the opinion of *Life* magazine, it was "a queer sort of world war—unreal and unconvincing." Following Poland's surrender, in early October 1939, no real fighting between Germany and the Western powers had occurred. There were no German aerial raids over Paris or London, no Allied thrusts on the Ruhr. The Germans did launch a submarine campaign against Allied shipping, but only on a modest scale, as Hitler did not wish to agitate the Western powers, hoping for a peace that would leave him with a free hand in the east. The Phony War, it came to be called, or the Bore War, or Sitzkrieg (the sitting war), or, in France, La Drôle de Guerre.

British and French leaders breathed a sigh of relief, as did their populations. "The pause suits us well," Foreign Secretary Halifax remarked.[53] An air of complacency set in, born of the fact that the Allies had prevailed in 1918 and were, on paper, numerically superior. They could claim 3,500 tanks, for example, against Germany's 2,500. In theory, their strengths were complementary, with the Royal Navy ruling the seas and the French boasting huge and well-equipped land forces. The Maginot Line, the vast string of fortified positions along the Franco-German border designed to keep out the Wehrmacht, added a sense of security.

In the United States, President Roosevelt felt certain that the quietude of the Phony War would not last, and he warned Americans against being complacent. ("It is not good for the ultimate health of ostriches to bury their heads in the sand.")[54] But he didn't exactly practice what he preached. When the Soviet Union attacked Finland in November 1939, he issued a strongly worded condemnation but did nothing more, such as send assistance to the intrepid Finns. Over the winter he allowed America's defense buildup to lag and did little to mobilize support for the Allies. Roosevelt had expended great effort and political capital to win the battle of revising the neutrality laws in the fall, but it was as though he decided that was enough; he would go no further.[55] Even his plan to produce ten thousand aircraft per year was soon slashed by almost 70 percent. Congressional leaders, focused on the upcoming elections and seeing no real fighting in Europe, were in no mood to spend big on defense; FDR, his own standing on Capitol Hill still diminished, was reluctant to press them, even as he railed privately against the isolationists. His distrust of Joe Kennedy greater than ever, he remained determined to keep him in London, where he could do the least damage to the administration's political fortunes.

Kennedy felt further undermined when Roosevelt dispatched Undersecretary of State Sumner Welles on a fact-finding mission to Germany, Italy, France, and Britain in the late winter of 1940. Publicly, the urbane and stylish diplomat's only task was to listen and observe—"the visit is solely for the purpose of advising the President and the Secretary of State as to present conditions in Europe," Roosevelt told the press on February 9. Privately, however, the president authorized Welles to actively explore whether some means could be found to end the war before it escalated further. The chances were next to nil, Roosevelt believed, but it was worth one final shot. Kennedy, though he had agitated for months for a presidential peace initiative, was livid upon learning of the mission. "Now just where does that put me?" he thundered, just prior to his departure from the United States. "You would think I had just been pouring tea over there instead of working my head off. If they think they need a special ambassador over there to get all the British secrets I failed to get, they can count me out." But when Welles landed in London on March 10,

Kennedy dutifully accompanied him to meetings with the British leadership.[56]

Nothing came of the Welles effort. He returned to Washington at the end of March with a sense of foreboding. "The leaders he talked to," Secretary of State Cordell Hull recorded in his memoirs, "offered no real hope for peace."[57]

V

More and more that winter and spring, the Kennedy brothers at Harvard saw the European war in contrasting ways. Joe Junior kept on trumpeting an unvarnished isolationism, more stark even than his father's. Jack, on the other hand, came back to school after the Christmas break more convinced than ever that isolationism was untenable, its adherents guilty of underestimating the Nazi threat. "He was very much disturbed by Nazism," Payson Wild observed of Jack in this period. "He was somewhat embarrassed by his father's position, but he didn't get on any stands or pulpits to declare his difference of opinion. He was a very loyal son."[58]

One reason for his discretion may have been that he had a more pressing matter at hand: writing his thesis. The work was all-consuming that winter, and friends recalled the long hours he spent in the Spee Club library, toiling away, surrounded by stacks of books and documents, his Underwood typewriter in front of him, as the fireplace burned orange and red and the snow fell outside. "How's your book coming?" they would ask him—in jest, as no one really believed it would become a published work. He would respond with a disquisition on whatever section he was working on. "We used to tease him about it all the time," one of them remembered, "because it was sort of his King Charles head that he was carrying around all the time: his famous thesis. We got so sick of hearing about it that I think he finally shut up."[59]

The friends also marveled at the pristine typed drafts of chapters that seemed to show up magically at the Spee front door at all hours of the day. Fearing that he would miss his mid-March deadline for completing a full draft of the thesis, Jack hired secretarial help, in the form of typists and stenographers (he dictated parts of the draft), to expedite the work. This got him in trouble with the university administration, for it involved having women in men's rooms, a violation of school policy that he had previously bypassed when the circumstances differed.[60] He even took out an ad in the *Boston Herald*, then left for a wedding in Chicago and asked Torby Macdonald to make the arrangements in his absence. The ad specified that the candidate be "young," and the response created tumult at Winthrop House. "On the day I'd set for interviewing applicants," Macdonald observed, "I spent an uncomfortable half-hour in the office of one of the college administrators trying to explain the presence of 60 clamoring females outside our dormitory at 9:30 A.M."

"You were always a ladies' man, Torby," Jack offered, "but this time I think you carried things a bit too far."[61]

Hardly anyone before Jack had undertaken this kind of study, investigating the birth and development of appeasement in Great Britain. (A great many would follow him, however.) Asked by Jim Seymour to recommend to Jack some existing works to take into account, his putative teacher Harold Laski came up more or less empty. For most Britons, the events were too close, too painful to examine in the exacting way the young American set about doing—and largely by himself, notwithstanding the important help he received from Seymour, Hopper, and Wild, and from the army of stenographers and typists. Jack himself brought the strands of his story together, assembling into a coherent narrative the untold account of how British politicians, labor and religious leaders, students, and writers debated preparedness and international affairs during the 1930s. Subsequent claims that Jack could not have produced the finished entity, that he must have had professional help with the organization, writing, and analysis, do not hold up under scrutiny. This was his own work, right down to the poor spelling and errors of syntax. "I'll never forget," remembered Timothy "Ted" Reardon, Joe Junior's roommate, "when I was out of college I got a call from Jack and he was doing his thesis. . . . He called me and said, 'Ted, you're an English major, come on over, will ya, and look at my thesis.' So I went over and looked and made some grammatical changes—but I'll never forget saying, 'How the hell do you expect me to go over all this stuff? When are ya handing it in, tomorrow?' "[62]

Jack made his deadline, just barely, submitting the work, "Appeasement at Munich: The Inevitable Result of the Slowness of Conversion of the British Democracy from a Disarmament to a Rearmament Policy," with minutes to spare. It clocked in at 147 pages, plus six pages of annotated bibliography, and flowed from an overarching question: Why, at the time of Munich, was England "so poorly prepared for war"? To get the answer, Jack suggested, one must of course look to decisions by political leaders such as Stanley Baldwin and Neville Chamberlain, but also beyond them, since after all the leaders operated in a democratic system and, as such, had to contend with the whims of the electorate and the machinations of powerful and competing interests in society, many of which favored collective security but were unwilling to pay for it. Indeed, the thesis argued, these systemic factors were determinative. Chamberlain was hemmed in politically in 1937–38, constrained by public and elite opinion, and his efforts to accommodate Hitler made strategic sense, inasmuch as he needed to delay any possible war in order to give his country a chance to rearm.

> Now a shattering in the ideal that was the League and the dawning realization of Germany's great productive capacity had made the country ready for rearmament. But it was still a democracy which was leisurely and confidently turning to rearmaments, not a frightened and desperate nation. It was not a nation with a single purpose with all its energies directed in a single direction; this was not to come until after Munich. No, it was still a democracy and the fear for their national self-preservation had not become strong enough for them to give up their personal interests, for the greater purpose. In other words, every group wanted rearmament but no group felt that there was any need for it to sacrifice its privileged position. This feeling in 1936 was to have a fatal influence in 1938.[63]

Remembering his debate with his British pals two years before, Jack gave close attention to Stanley Baldwin's self-incriminating speech to Parliament in 1936. He quoted the most controversial part: "Suppose I had gone to the country [in 1933] and said that Germany was rearming and that we must rearm, does anybody think that this pacific democracy would have rallied to that cry at that moment? I cannot think of anything that would have made the loss of the election from my point of view more certain." In analyzing this segment, Jack wrote:

> I am neither trying to attack or to defend [Baldwin], but merely trying to get at what he really meant. . . . What I think he was trying to show—and he used the election [of 1933] as the best barometer of

a modern democratic state's popular will—was the impossibility of having gotten support for any rearmament in the country due to the overwhelmingly pacifist sentiment of the country during these years. And I think from my study he was right. I think his choice of words was extremely unfortunate and opened him to enormous criticism [for playing politics with foreign policy], but I think it is very important that we try and get at his real meaning. . . . I have gone into this at some lengths as it is a very crucial point in this thesis.[64]

Here Jack anticipated later struggles over how best to respond to totalitarian threats while upholding democratic governance and civil liberties. With clinical detachment he maintained that dictatorships by their nature have an easier time than democracies do in mobilizing resources—the latter, he argued, invariably must spend valuable time and energy attempting to reconcile competing priorities and competing interpretations of the national interest. Whereas citizens in totalitarian societies can be instructed on what to do, those in free societies must be won over, and that doesn't always happen quickly.

Thus the central problem: "In this calm acceptance of the theory that the democratic way is the best way, it seems to me, lies the danger. Why, exactly, is the democratic system the better? It may be answered that it is better because it allows for the full development of man as an individual. But it seems to be that this only indicates that democracy is a 'pleasanter' form of government—not that it is the best form of government for meeting the present world problem." If Americans wished for their democratic system to succeed, it would be imperative, Jack wrote, for them to "look at situations much more realistically" than they did currently. "We can't afford to misjudge situations as we misjudged Munich. We must use every effort to form accurate judgements—and even then our task is going to be a difficult one."[65]

To critics then and later, the analysis seemed at its core to be a defense of Joe Kennedy's pro-Chamberlain and pro-appeasement position. It was partly that, but Jack also had kind words to say for Chamberlain's foremost critic, Winston Churchill, praising him for invoking Britain's national purpose and resolve. In this way the thesis showed Jack's growing separation from his father's viewpoint. And the study had a broader ambition as well, addressing as it did a matter that commentators had been raising at least since Alexis de Tocqueville, a century before: Can popular rule readily lend itself to the making of effective foreign policy? And can democracy, geared for a time of peace, respond effectively in a time of war? Jack's answers: Yes and yes, but the task would not be easy. It required intelligent and committed leadership at the highest levels, able to articulate effectively to the public why fighting was necessary, and it required a capacity and willingness to plan for the long term. In the near run, totalitarianism had notable advantages.

To read the thesis today is to be struck above all by the impressive source base, by the acuity and authenticity of the analysis, and by the commitment to making historical judgments only on the basis of carefully examined evidence. One wishes for a more thorough proofreading, and there are occasional pedantic flourishes. The interpretation at times verges on the deterministic; elsewhere it's underdeveloped, giving the narrative a hodgepodge feel. The prose is passable at best. Perhaps out of deference to his father's and brother's isolationism, he is mostly opaque on the debate swirling around him, at Harvard and throughout the country, between interventionists and isolationists. But there's a confidence and vitality in the writing that is all the more notable coming from someone so young. Not least, the study shows the now familiar Jack Kennedy detachment—so much a feature of his letters and other writings during his overseas travels during the previous two and a half years—and commitment to an unsentimental realism in international affairs. Foreign threats cannot be dealt with by ignoring them or wishing them away, he writes; they must be confronted by clearheaded and informed calculation. In the same way, personalizing policy decisions is unproductive, as it diminishes the decision-maker's capacity to render dispassionate judgment. In later life, Jack Kennedy would not always adhere to these precepts of world affairs, but they would become touchstones for his responses to most foreign policy crises. In historian Nigel Hamilton's apt assessment of the thesis, "Nothing else Jack would write in his life would so speak the man."[66]

As an attempt at first-cut history, written without access to archival sources, the thesis still stands up quite well. Many later historians would echo the revisionist argument that appeasement made strategic sense in the domestic and international context of the time—that is, impersonal forces and structural constraints limited the options open to policymakers—and would echo Jack Kennedy's finding that a broad cross section of British society in the mid-1930s was deeply averse to doing anything that might threaten war. Memories of Passchendaele and the Somme were just too strong, and there was broad agreement as well that the Versailles Treaty had been unfair to Germany. (So numerous were the scholarly adherents to this view that they came to constitute a "revisionist school"; John F. Kennedy, though he is seldom acknowledged in the historiography, can legitimately be called a founding member.[67]) In his preface, Jack wisely noted that "many of the documents and reports are still secret; until they are released it is impossible to give the complete story." Even so, he had amassed a large body of material, published and unpublished, and made discerning and judicious use of it—and under great time pressure. Not every undergraduate thesis can truly be called an original contribution to knowledge, but Jack's fit the bill. His conclusion that Britain's existential crisis was primarily the result of societal forces—in particular, a fickle and war-averse public that made scapegoats of individual leaders—is, if somewhat overstated, a thoughtful and cogent one, even at eighty years' remove.

The contemporary assessments were mixed. "Jack rushed madly around the last week with his thesis and finally with the aid of five stenographers the last day got it in under the wire," Joe Junior wrote to his father. "I read it before he had finished it up and it seemed to represent a lot of work but did not prove anything. However he said he shaped it up the last few days and he seemed to have some good ideas so it ought to be very good."[68] The government department faculty committee evaluating the finished product faulted the spelling and grammar but complimented its author on his penetrating assessment of a complex and historically important issue. Professor Henry A. Yeomans recommended magna cum laude, while Professor Carl Friedrich, more critical of what he saw as the work's excessive length, inconclusive judgments, and careless writing, reduced the grade to cum laude plus. Arthur Krock read the thesis at the start of April and reported to Ambassador Kennedy that Jack had done "an excellent job, though I regret he has many doubts of the efficiency of democracy." In revised form, Krock added, the thesis could make for an interesting book. He even had a new title to suggest: *Why England Slept*, a brash play on *While England Slept*, the American title of Churchill's *Arms and the Covenant*, which Jack had read and discussed with his friends in the summer of 1938.[69]

VI

The ambassador was delighted to get this news. He had long wanted his sons to become published authors. It would add luster to their résumés and enhance their reputations, as he himself had found with his slim, ghostwritten campaign volume for FDR's reelection in 1936. "You would be surprised how a book that really makes the grade with high-class people stands you in good stead for years to come," he wrote to Jack.[70] Over the previous months Kennedy had worked tirelessly to push Joe Junior's writings on publishers, both in the United States and in Britain, suggesting that they bring out a book-length collection of Joe's travel letters. He even tapped his speechwriter Harvey Klemmer to help polish the material. Still, the editors politely declined. Though Joe Junior's serious demeanor gave the impression of gravitas, his ideas as expressed on the page were at times banal and sophomoric ("Does it ever occur to people that there are happy people in Italy and Germany?"), his prose earnest and wooden. Even magazine and newspaper editors rebuffed the father's entreaties on his oldest son's behalf (though Young Joe did get one short piece placed in *The Atlantic Monthly*[71]). Now, with Krock's enthusiasm for Jack's manuscript, the second son might get his name on a dust jacket first.

Krock's faith in the study's publication potential was genuine, but he also had an ulterior motive: he had long seen Joe Kennedy as a man of destiny, someone to whom he ought to hitch his wagon, someone who might succeed Franklin Roosevelt—a man Krock detested—as president of the United States. Well aware of the ambassador's ambitions for his sons, Krock wanted to please him by helping out. He also saw great potential commercial success in a memoir by Joe Kennedy focused on his ambassadorship—when he sent Jack's thesis to Gertrude Algase's literary agency in New York, he told Algase he had in mind a twofer: a book by the father as well as one by the son.[72]

The ambassador intended to give his son a thorough critique of the thesis well in advance of the revision, but real life intervened. On April 9 the Phony War came to an abrupt and violent end as the Nazis invaded Denmark and Norway, mostly in order to secure the route by which high-grade Swedish iron ore reached Germany. In the days prior, the Royal Navy had begun mining Norwegian waters in order to force freighters bound for Germany into the open sea, where they could be subject to the

British blockade. But the Allies were unprepared for the bold German pre-emptive stroke. Nine Wehrmacht divisions, backed by the Luftwaffe, knocked out the Danes in a single day and seized control of all the southern ports and airfields in Norway. There followed two weeks of skirmishing in central Norway between German and Allied forces, with the Germans prevailing and forcing a British and French withdrawal. By late spring the whole of Norway was under German control.

Churchill had been chiefly responsible for the planning and execution of the Norwegian operation, and Joe Kennedy expected him to suffer the consequences. "Mr. Churchill's sun has been caused to set very rapidly by the situation in Norway which some people are already characterizing as the second Gallipoli," Kennedy cabled to FDR and Cordell Hull in late April.[73] Such was the irony, however, that the Scandinavian disaster elevated Churchill's position at the expense of Neville Chamberlain. Many in Parliament blamed the prime minister for the outcome, and on May 7 thirty-three Conservatives voted against Chamberlain's government following a debate on the operation. One of them, Leo Amery, offered a stinging rebuke of Chamberlain that he ended by quoting Cromwell's dismissal of the Long Parliament, in 1653: "Depart, I say, and let us be done with you. In the name of God, go!" Shaken to the core, a downcast Chamberlain departed the chamber, shouts of "Go! Go! Go!" ringing in his ear.[74]

King George and many Tory grandees wanted Lord Halifax to take the helm. In their eyes he was the natural choice, whereas Churchill was an unscrupulous and volatile maverick with a checkered political past. But Halifax, who had a deeply imbued sense of public service, believed Churchill would make a stronger war leader and refused the appointment. Chamberlain, hoping to the end to survive in power, recognized the game was up when the Labour Party refused to back him—on May 10, he advised the king to send for the sixty-five-year-old Churchill. The king, after one more failed attempt to get Halifax to take the post, agreed.

"We have before us an ordeal of the most grievous kind," Churchill declared that day, in his first speech to the House of Commons as prime minister. "We have before us many, many long months of struggle and of suffering. You ask, what is our policy? I can say: It is to wage war, by sea, land and air, with all our might and with all the strength that God can give us; to wage war against a monstrous tyranny, never surpassed in the dark, lamentable catalogue of human crime. That is our policy. You ask, what is our aim? I can answer in one word: It is victory, victory at all costs, victory in spite of all terror, victory, however long and hard the road may be; for without victory, there is no survival."[75]

What a time to take power! Early on the day of Churchill's appointment, May 10, Germany launched a massive offensive in the west, with attacks on the Netherlands, Belgium, and Luxembourg. The British and French generals responded by moving their forces toward the Dyle River, in Belgium, expecting to receive the weight of the German thrust there. Instead, on the thirteenth, the first German units in Army Group A, under Gerd von Rundstedt, broke through the tightly forested and ill-defended Ardennes near Sedan, on the Meuse River, past the western terminus of the vaunted Maginot Line. A two-day battle ensued, whereupon the victorious Germans dashed into the open countryside and curved west. As historian A. J. P. Taylor would write, "When they ran out of petrol, they filled up at the local pump without paying. They occasionally stopped to milk a French cow." On May 20, the 2nd Panzer Division, under Heinz Guderian, covered sixty miles and reached the Channel coast near Abbeville. The lines of communication between the Allied front lines in Belgium and the rear areas had been completely cut.[76]

The world looked on in stunned disbelief. How could this have happened? The total strength of the German military, on the one hand, and the French, British, Belgian, and Dutch forces, on the other, were after all roughly comparable. The French had more wheeled vehicles and tanks, and arguably the edge in the quality of their tanks and artillery. Even in the air, France and its allies had a comparable number of bombers and fighters to the Germans. To top it all off, the signs were abundant in the lead-up to the attack that Hitler was massing troops for an assault through the Ardennes forest. Yet now, less than a week in, the battle had the makings of a rout. In tactics and leadership, the Germans had shown themselves superior. The French general staff didn't even fully grasp what was happening to them as radio communications broke down between General Maurice Gamelin, the overall commander, and his officers at the front.[77]

It got worse from there. In the north, masses of French and British troops were soon trapped in the coastal area of Calais and Dunkirk—300,000 men were pinned against the sea. They appeared to be doomed, until Hitler astonished his generals by ordering Guderian to halt (probably in a mistaken belief that Britain would wish to sue for peace). The British Expeditionary Force, and many French units, too, were able to escape from the Dunkirk beaches thanks to the heroic efforts of an armada of ships—some of them crewed by naval personnel, some manned by their civilian owners and crew—though despite later mythology, it was hardly an Allied victory.[78] In the east, the Wehrmacht captured the fortresses along the Maginot Line in short order; in the center, the Allies fell back in confusion. On June 17, with the French war effort collapsing wholesale, and with German armies south of Dijon and pressing down the coastline, Prime Minister Paul Reynaud—who had succeeded Daladier three months before—resigned. From there the end came quickly. On June 22, France capitulated at Compiègne, in the same railway car used for the signing of the armistice in November 1918. In the earlier war, Germany had sacrificed a million of its soldiers over four years in a vain effort to defeat France; this time it had succeeded in six short weeks, at the cost of a mere 27,000 German lives. A jubilant Hitler, visiting Paris for the first and only time in his life, posed like a tourist before the cameras next to the Eiffel Tower.

In London, Joseph Kennedy despaired at the developments. "The situation is terrible," he wrote to Rose on May 20. "I think the jig is up. The situation is more than critical. It means a terrible finish for the Allies." Disappointed to see Neville Chamberlain's government give way to one headed by Winston Churchill, the ambassador implored President Roosevelt to sue for peace on behalf of the Allies. "I saw Halifax last night," he cabled Cordell Hull on May 24. "The situation according to the people who know is very very grim. The mass of the people just never seem to realize that England can be beaten or that the worst can happen to them. . . . I do not underestimate the courage or guts of these people but . . . it is going to take more than guts to hold off the systematic air attacks of the Germans coupled with terrific air superiority in numbers. . . . [Halifax] is definitely of the opinion that if anybody is able to save a debacle on the part of the Allies if it arrives at that point it is the President. Halifax still believes that that influence is one that the Germans still fear."[79]

FDR refused the suggestion, but his ambassador had not exaggerated the sense of imminent doom on the part of Halifax and other senior British officials, and among London's upper classes in general. "A miracle may save us," Alexander Cadogan, the head of the Foreign Office, confided in his diary on May 21, "otherwise we're done." On May 25, the day after Kennedy sent his cable, the War Cabinet commenced an extraordinary three-day debate, unknown to anyone outside this tight circle, over whether to seek a negotiated settlement with Hitler, by way of Italian mediation. Halifax argued in favor: even as he conceded that the chances of gaining an agreement that preserved Britain's independence and freedom of maneuver were slim, every political alternative, he said, should be pursued. Churchill stood in firm opposition—"peace and security could never be achieved in a German-dominated Europe," he insisted. But the new prime minister had to move gingerly, his hold on power in these early weeks more tenuous than we tend to remember. He knew he could scarcely afford a Halifax resignation. Bit by bit, through cajolery and rhetorical flourish, Churchill won his colleagues over, and by May 28 there was agreement: Britain would fight on, alone if necessary.[80]

One can't help but wonder: What if Churchill had lost the debate? What if the War Cabinet had chosen differently in those indigo days of May 1940 and Britain had sued for peace? What would have been the effect on the war, on the course of the twentieth century, on America's standing in the world? And what would it have meant for Joe Kennedy and his family?

A few days later, Kennedy was ushered into a meeting with the prime minister, who told him that England stood next on Hitler's list and that therefore the United States must provide more aid. "The president can't do anything with Congress lined up against him," Kennedy replied, "and Congress won't act unless it feels that the American people are behind it." The argument had always worked with Chamberlain, but Churchill barreled ahead. "The American people will want to come in when they see well-known places in England bombed," he assured his guest. "After all, Hitler will not win this war until he conquers us, and he is not going to do that. We'll hold out until after your election and then I'll expect you to come in. I'll fight them from Canada. I'll never give up the fleet."[81]

VII

A third development on May 10, 1940, was of rather less consequence than the leadership change in Britain or Hitler's attack in the west, though in time it would prove highly significant in our story: young John F. Kennedy, having completed his last exams as a Harvard undergraduate, launched into the task of revising his senior thesis for publication. The new European situation compelled changes to the manuscript, he realized—Chamberlain's leadership had plainly been found wanting, and Jack understood it would be necessary to shift more of the responsibility for Britain's predicament to the decisions at 10 Downing Street and away from the broader electorate. His father reinforced this notion, informing his son that he had shown the thesis to several people and all of them converged on this point. "The basis of this criticism," the ambassador wrote, "is that the National Government was in absolute control from 1931 to 1935, and that it was returned to office in November 1935, with another huge majority. This mandate, it is contended, should have been used to make the country strong. If the country supported such a policy, well and good; if not, then the National leaders should have thrown caution out the window and attempted to arouse their countrymen to the dangers with which Britain obviously was confronted." In other words, the thesis had been too cynical in its acceptance of politicians doing whatever was necessary to get elected.[82]

To undertake the work, Jack ensconced himself in the library of Arthur Krock's home in Washington, D.C. "I can't say that I did much more than polish it and amend it here and there because it was very, very definitely his own product," Krock later said. This seems correct, for a close comparison of the two versions shows the core content and structure to be substantially the same. (Nor were all the alterations necessarily for the best—notwithstanding Krock's "polishing," some sections of the thesis follow a cleaner, clearer line.) In addition to assigning somewhat more blame to Baldwin and Chamberlain, Jack also scrapped his earlier conclusion, measured and academic in tone, for a sharper one geared specifically to an American reading audience. "We must always keep our armaments equal to our commitments," he wrote. "Munich should teach us that; we must realize that any bluff will be called. We cannot tell anyone to keep out of our hemisphere unless our armaments *and the people behind these armaments* are prepared to back up the command, even to the ultimate point of going to war."[83]

As if to underscore the point, Jack dashed off a letter to *The Harvard Crimson* protesting the paper's staunch opposition to American rearmament. It ran in the June 9 issue, mere days before its author's graduation:

In an editorial on Friday, May 31, attacking President Conant's speech you stated that "there is no surer way to war, and a terribly destructive one, than to arm as we are doing." This point of view seems to overlook the very valuable lesson of England's experience during the last decade. In no other country was this idea that armaments are the prime cause of war more firmly held. . . . Senator Borah expressed the equivalent American opinion, in voting against the naval appropriations bill of 1938 when he said, "one nation putting out a program, another putting out a program to meet the program and soon there is war."

If anyone should ask why Britain is so badly prepared for this war or why America's defenses were found to be in such shocking condition in the May investigations, this attitude toward armaments is a substantial answer. The failure to build up her armaments has not saved England from a war, and may cost her one. Are we in America to let that lesson go unlearned?[84]

Barely had the ink dried on Jack's letter when there came crushing news from New York: Harper & Brothers had decided to cancel an offer to publish the revised thesis, on the grounds that the study had been eclipsed by recent events. It would be "practically impossible," the editors said, "to get attention for any historical survey" of this kind, given the crisis situation in France. The decision put a damper on Jack's commencement ceremony, but he determined to enjoy the big day in any event, surrounded by his college pals and with grandfather Honey Fitz, mother Rose, sisters Rosemary (newly returned from England), Kick, and Eunice, and brothers Joe Junior and Bobby in attendance in Harvard Yard.*

"He was really very handsome in his cap and gown as he had a tan which made him look healthy," Rose reported to her husband, "and he has got a wonderful smile." Though Joe's ambassadorial duties kept him in London, he instructed Paul Murphy to send Jack a graduation gift in

---

* The commencement speeches showed the continuing campus divisions over the war. Class orator Tudor Gardiner ('40) called it "fantastic nonsense" to aid the Allies and said the United States should instead focus on "making this hemisphere impregnable." David Sigourney ('15), the class orator from twenty-five years before, spoke differently at a reunion event, extolling his class's service in the Great War: "We were not too proud to fight then and we are not too proud to fight now." His remarks were met with loud and sustained boos, mostly from members of recently graduated classes. Commencement speaker Cordell Hull, for his part, condemned isolationism as "dangerous folly" as an appreciative President Conant nodded in agreement. (Bethell, *Harvard Observed*, 132–33; Lee Starr ['40], interview with the author, May 2, 2017.)

the form of a $1,000 check, "with his deep appreciation and congratulation for the work you have done and with all his love." Jack wrote immediately to say thanks (the sum would allow him to "remain solvent for a bit more"), to inform his father that he intended to attend Yale Law School in the fall, and to say he was still working on finding a publisher for his thesis. "I have changed it considerably, it is now about 210 pages where formerly it was only 150, and I have tried to make it more readable."[85]

Freshly minted college graduate.

Nonetheless, another rejection soon followed, this one from Harcourt Brace. Publisher Alfred Harcourt, who like Harper saw only the original thesis, not the revised manuscript, conceded that "the boy has written a much better than average thesis," but he questioned whether the subject matter would resonate with American readers. His chief editor agreed: the European situation was simply moving too fast to proceed with publication. Sensing a pattern with the established presses, agent Gertrude Algase changed tack and tried upstart Wilfred Funk, who had recently created a small imprint bearing his own name. Algase sent Funk the revised version and got back word immediately: he would publish. The author was Joseph P. Kennedy's son, after all, and Algase had hinted that Henry Luce would read the manuscript and perhaps pen a foreword. Funk secured the book, paying its author an advance of $225 ($250 minus the 10 percent agent's commission).[86]

A shrewd decision it was. Advance sales exceeded expectations by a wide margin, and Wilfred Funk realized he would at least recoup his investment. Whether the early interest "is just a flurry because of the youngster's name and curiosity on the part of the book stores, we can't tell," Algase wrote candidly to Krock. "It probably is, and whether or not the book will renew its sale after the book shops have available copies I don't know." She added that the author himself left a winning impression: "Jack Kennedy is one of the nicest youngsters I've met, unaffected, cordial and hard-working in his own right. I'd like to watch him grow up and go places."[87]

Algase would get her chance to see him "go places," and could justifiably claim to have played a part in setting him on his way. For the book she helped shepherd into production would strike a chord among Americans and would signify for all to see that Jack Kennedy, age twenty-three and a freshly minted Harvard graduate, was his own man, not beholden to his father's isolationist views. Indeed, he was willing to rebuke in print the core tenets of appeasement.

It was a message whose time had come. In ways not yet fully clear as *Why England Slept* hit the shelves in the middle of 1940, the fall of France had changed the calculus for millions of Americans, even the man in the White House. Adolf Hitler suddenly seemed poised to conquer all of Europe, including Great Britain, and meanwhile the Japanese threat grew steadily in East and Southeast Asia. Preparedness took on a whole new meaning, a whole new level of importance—could it be that the slim new volume by the ambassador's handsome second son offered useful lessons?

TEN

INTERLUDES

The defeat of France in June 1940 had a transformative effect on American attitudes toward the European war, and toward national defense in general. The Nazi threat was now real, in a way it hadn't been before. Hitler's previous conquests had been regrettable but explicable, worrisome but involving comparatively small nations about which many Americans knew little. France was different. France was a storied world civilization, a center of art and literature and music, the home of high fashion and high cuisine. France was Paris, with its Arc de Triomphe and Eiffel Tower, its beautiful boulevards and charming sidewalk cafés, familiar even to Americans who had never been there. And France was a major world power, its empire second only to Britain's in size, its military the most powerful (by some measures) in the world. Yet it had just been vanquished—brutally, with fearsome totality, in six short weeks.

Jerome Kern and Oscar Hammerstein II spoke to the moment in song:

> *The last time I saw Paris*
> *Her heart was warm and gay*
> *No matter how they change her*
> *I'll remember her that way*

Overnight, the complacency that had characterized U.S. thinking during much of the Phony War gave way to acute apprehension, even panic. Not since the early years of the republic had overseas developments seemed so close to America's shores, so capable of threatening the nation's security. If the Nazi war machine could trounce the Low Countries and France with such clinical efficiency, wouldn't it sooner or later present a direct and existential threat to the United States?[1]

Even in the short term, numerous analysts warned, a Germany that toppled Great Britain and thereby gained control of the Atlantic sea lanes would post severe challenges to U.S. interests. "We have been deluding ourselves," the influential columnist Walter Lippmann wrote, "when we have looked upon a vast expanse of salt water as if it were a super Maginot Line. The ocean is a highway for those who control it. For that reason every war which involves the dominion of the seas is a world war in which America is inescapably involved."[2]

Franklin Roosevelt wholeheartedly agreed. As a former assistant secretary of the Navy who fancied himself an expert on sea power, the president shuddered at the thought that Hitler would soon conquer Britain and its formidable Royal Navy. British chances of survival, he mused privately in July, were one in three. FDR wanted very much to meet Prime Minister Winston Churchill's pleas for U.S. assistance with a tangible offer of support, but what could he do? America's defenses were grievously underdeveloped in all areas (in 1939 the U.S. Army, with 190,000 men, ranked seventeenth in the world in size, just behind Romania's), insufficient to guard the nation's geographic approaches, never mind help allies. Nor was Germany the only looming threat: in East Asia the Japanese were poised to expand their reach southward. At Roosevelt's insistence, the administration moved with rare certitude and dispatch to secure a massive arms buildup, gaining congressional support for a staggering $12 billion in new military spending. Over objections from the War Department, FDR also gained the release of significant quantities of arms and ammunition to be sold to private firms and then, through cash-and-carry, to Great Britain.[3]

Simultaneously, Roosevelt made one of the most critical decisions of his presidency: he would run for an unprecedented third term—out of duty, he insisted, not personal ambition. Aware that the move would be controversial in some quarters, he proceeded with care, working behind the scenes and quietly allowing political lieutenants to fashion a "spontaneous" show of support for him at the Democratic convention in Chicago. The tactic worked to perfection, and he coasted to the nomination. At the same time, Roosevelt shrewdly built bipartisan support for his leadership by appointing two prominent Republicans, former secretary of state Henry Stimson and 1936 vice presidential candidate and newspaper publisher Frank Knox, to head the War and Navy departments. In a speech at the University of Virginia on June 10, the president pledged to build up U.S. defenses and to provide those fighting the Axis powers with "the material resources of this nation," even as he continued to downplay the notion that the United States might become a belligerent. "We will not slow down or detour," he declared. "Signs and signals call for speed—full speed ahead."[4]

John Wheeler-Bennett, the British historian and propagandist who had assisted young John F. Kennedy on his thesis (enough so that he got a mention in the acknowledgments), was in the audience for the speech. He recalled the "shock of excitement which passed through me. . . . This was what we had been praying for—not only sympathy but pledges of support. If Britain could only hold on until these vast resources could be made available to her, we could yet survive and even win the war. It was the first gleam of hope." As Wheeler-Bennett understood, it would take time for the tangible support to materialize, but he saw the moment as crucial regardless. So did *Time*—with the president's address, the magazine declared, American neutrality was effectively over. "The U.S. has taken sides. . . . Ended is the utopian hope that [it] could remain an island of democracy in a totalitarian world."[5]

Not so fast, Roosevelt would have replied. Always fearful of isolationist strength—too much so, in the minds of some aides and more than a few historians—he was acutely averse to getting ahead of public opinion. And Americans, he knew, remained divided. If the fall of France propelled interventionist organizations such as William Allen White's Committee to Defend America by Aiding the Allies (which by August 1, three months after its founding, had nearly seven hundred chapters in forty-seven states), it also energized the opposition. In July, a group headed by Yale students and midwestern businessmen formed the America First Committee, which drew adherents from across the political spectrum and declared itself unalterably opposed to intervention—and to assistance to Great Britain, since this would ultimately lead to intervention. Membership would rise to 800,000 and would include figures such as Frank Lloyd

Wright, Walt Disney, Lillian Gish, Gerald Ford, and Chester Bowles. Not all America Firsters were isolationist in the strict sense; most supported foreign trade, for example, and many backed maintaining cultural links with other nations. Few were pacifists or conscientious objectors. What drove them, rather, was the conviction, voiced consistently by people such as Joseph P. Kennedy and Charles Lindbergh (neither a member of the group, though Lindbergh would in time join), that the United States should steer clear of the European power struggle and, more broadly, should retain its freedom of action and stay unencumbered by commitments to other countries.[6]

Joe Kennedy's conviction on this score had not lessened one bit as a result of the French collapse. His oldest son, too, thought it more important than ever that Washington remain aloof from the European maelstrom; to the extent that the administration involved itself, father and son maintained, it should be to try to encourage an accommodation of Hitler through diplomacy. Now entering his second year at Harvard Law School, Joe Junior became one of the leaders of the Harvard Committee Against Military Intervention, which saw as its purpose "making vocal the opinion of that overwhelming majority of Harvard students who want America to stay out of the wars in Europe and Asia." Soon Joe Junior found himself speaking before student and civic groups around Cambridge. He gave no quarter, insisting at every turn that the White House seemed poised to take the nation down the slippery road to war, and that the result would be calamitous. Far better, he argued, for the United States to steer clear of the fighting and seek trade deals with Nazi Germany.[7]

More than principle was at stake for Young Joe—the debates and the talks were also useful practice for him in his budding political career. He liked public speaking but had a tendency to become tense and trip over his words, so he enrolled in evening classes at Staley School of the Spoken Word. He also got involved in the state Democratic Party, even supporting James Farley as the party's candidate for president over FDR. As a delegate to the Democratic National Convention in Chicago, Joe Junior shook off the pleadings of party officials to switch his allegiance and, despite knowing Farley could not win, voted for him on the first ballot, one of seventy-two delegates to do so (against 946 who went with Roosevelt). When Roosevelt's men called Joe Senior in London and asked him to intervene with his son, the ambassador refused. "No, I wouldn't think of telling him what to do." Though Joe Junior never revealed the exact motivation for his vote, one factor was surely his desire to stick it to a president and an administration that, as he saw it, had humiliated and marginalized his father.[8]

Jack was home in Hyannis Port with friends when he learned of his brother's convention controversy. He immediately questioned Joe's action. Why stick it to a sitting president when it risked alienating powerful party members, whose support Joe would need when he himself ran for office—as everyone, not least Joe himself, knew he intended to do? And all for a Farley candidacy that never had a prayer to begin with? To Jack's pragmatic mind it seemed a foolish, unnecessary move, one that was also dubious on the merits—did it really make sense to change horses in midstream, to reject an experienced, popular chief executive at a time of acute international tension?[9]

II

History has little to say on how the hypercompetitive Joe Junior felt about another development that summer of 1940: his brother's sudden literary success. To his father he offered gracious words about Jack's book, but to a friend's father in California he was reportedly more measured, noting that Jack had benefited from professionals' help.[10] If indeed Joe struggled with being outshone in this way, one can see why. After all, it wasn't supposed to be like this. All his life he had been the golden child, the one who had barely emerged from the womb when his grandfather predicted he would grow up to be president. He had always been the more diligent student, the stronger athlete, whereas Jack had been content to coast along, to goof off—when, that is, he wasn't laid up in the infirmary. For years Joe had heard his father's voice in his ear, urging him to write a book. He had tried his damnedest to make it happen, even risking life and limb to file lengthy reports from the Spanish Civil War with the thought that these might then be gathered into a volume. No book resulted, yet now here was his brother, snapping up a contract for a senior thesis that he'd dashed off in a few months from the comfort and safety of Cambridge, then spent a few days revising for publication. Maybe Jack had the better and timelier topic, but the whole thing still seemed unfair.

Jack's book hit store shelves on July 24. The timing was sublime, coming one month after the fall of France, three weeks after the first German daytime aerial attacks against British land targets (the communities of Wick and Hull), and two weeks after the Luftwaffe started hitting convoy ships in the Channel. The American reading public suddenly clamored for information about the war and its origins, and *Why England Slept* was one of the first books to offer it. Shrewdly—and brazenly, given that he had been carrying on a long-term love affair with the man's wife—Joe Kennedy had asked Henry Luce to pen a brief foreword, and the famed publisher agreed. (First Arthur Krock of *The New York Times* had assisted with revisions and now the legendary head of Time Inc. contributed an introductory essay: Jack did not lack for high-powered help.)[11]

More and more, Henry Luce was emerging as a leading exponent of American internationalism. Isolationism, as he saw it, might have been an acceptable strategy when the nation was weak; now that it had become a full-fledged member of the great-power club—and seemed destined, by dint of geography and demography, to become the most powerful of all—such a stance would no longer do. Instead, he believed, leaders in Washington must grab the mantle of world leadership. They must defend U.S. territory, to be sure, but they must also defend and promote democratic values far beyond America's shores, indeed to all four corners of the globe. The nation's security depended on it.[12] A few months later, in early 1941, Luce would articulate his vision in what would become one of the most influential articles in the history of U.S. statecraft. "The American Century," it would be titled, and it would be a kind of blueprint of grand strategy for a succession of administrations, Democratic as well as Republican, John F. Kennedy's among them. Americans, Luce would write, must "accept wholeheartedly our duty and our opportunity as the most powerful and vital nation in the world and in consequence to exert upon the world the full impact of our influence, for such purposes as we see fit and by such means as we see fit." Even now, in the middle months of 1940, as he sat down with Jack's book, Luce was coming to this expansive assessment of the nation's role in the world. At the Republican National Convention in Philadelphia in late June, he helped engineer the stunning victory of Wendell Willkie, a corporate executive and an avowed internationalist, to be the party's standard-bearer in that fall's presidential election.[13]

"When the manuscript, or rather the proofs, arrived, I was very impressed by it," Luce remembered. "At this time, of course, it was after Munich and the hot war was on. England, as they said, stood alone and the popular tendency was to put all the blame on the so-called appeasers, namely, Mr. Chamberlain and the Tory appeasers, the Cliveden Set." *Why England Slept*, however, showed that blame had to be spread across nearly all levels of British society. "What impressed me was, first, that he had done such a careful job of actually reviewing the facts, the facts such as attitudes and voting records, with regard to the crisis in Europe. And I was impressed by his careful scholarship, research, and also by his sense of personal involvement, responsibility in the great crisis that was at that time in flames. And that's what made me very optimistic about the qualities of mind and of involvement in public affairs that was displayed in this book."[14]

In his foreword, Luce lauded the young author's penetrating analysis and his crucially important concluding message: that Americans must expend every effort to prepare for the likelihood of war. "I cannot recall a single man of my college generation who could have written such an adult book on such a vitally important subject during his Senior year at college," he enthused.[15] Though the essay excoriated the pro-appeasement position of observers such as his father, Jack responded with fulsome gratitude: "The foreword is wonderful, and makes the book far more timely. Especially is this true of the point about the similarity of Chamberlain's 'Peace in Our Time,' and our 'We Will Never Fight in Foreign Wars,' and the parallel effect that they have had on our war efforts. I missed this and it was very vital. Also, I am very glad that you gave the background regarding the American responsibility for the present situation, as it is really vitally necessary for any understanding of the problem."[16]

Luce's endorsement no doubt helped sales, although they would have been healthy regardless. Within two days, the first allotment of thirty-five hundred copies had been snapped up, and Wilfred Funk quickly arranged for a second, larger printing. By year's end Funk could claim sales in the United States and Britain totaling well into five figures—a remarkable result for what was after all a revised undergraduate thesis. The book made the *New York Times*'s "bestsellers of the week" list for Boston and was a *Washington Post* "Reader's Choice" selection.[17] The later claim that Joe Kennedy boosted sales by buying cartons of copies that he stored in his Cape Cod basement, though plausible enough in theory (it's the kind of thing one would expect from him), lacks evidence; even if true, it would not have made much of a difference to a book that rode a wave of highly favorable reviews, in *The New York Times*, the *San Francisco Chronicle*, *The Wall Street Journal*, the *New York Herald Tribune*, the *Minneapolis Tribune*, and *Time*, among other publications. A few discordant notes aside—some critics felt Jack was too easy on Baldwin and Chamberlain, and that he left fuzzy what exactly should be the lesson for Americans—the young author won praise for the power and nuance of his argument and the wealth of evidence he marshaled in support of it.

Some reviewers noted the titular allusion to Churchill's earlier collection of essays, *While England Slept*, but for the most part they missed the key philosophical difference between the two works: whereas Churchill stressed the role of individuals in shaping history, Kennedy was clinical, impersonal, placing heavy emphasis on structural determinants. ("Personalities," he lamented in his introduction, "have always been more interesting to us than facts."[18])

No less a figure than the president of the United States offered his congratulations. In a letter addressed to "My dear Jack," Franklin Roosevelt wrote that he found the book lucid and perceptive, "a great argument for acting and speaking from a position of strength at all times." Former teachers also reached out, including one from the early years. "I wish now to congratulate little 'Jackie' Kennedy of the Devotion School, Brookline," wrote Mrs. Roberts. "I must confess I am very proud of your success. You are indeed a splendid example of American youth, and your success so early, I am sure, warms your mother and daddy's heart with pride." The old Choate headmaster himself, George St. John, lauded Jack's book for its "restrained, scholarly, and convincing" nature. "That could have been said of the book if it had been written ten or twenty years later in light of History. Coming to the people of America now, it is the work of a patriot, a prophet, and a missionary."[19]

Inevitably, the favorable publicity and heavy sales figures rubbed some people the wrong way. One detects more than a little professional envy in the pompous response of famed British economist and professor Harold Laski, onetime teacher of Joe Junior and, briefly, Jack. It would have been easy "to repeat the eulogies Krock and Harry Luce have showered on your boy's work," Laski wrote Joe Kennedy, but "I choose the more difficult way of regretting deeply that you let him publish it." Labeling the work "very immature," Laski said it lacked any semblance of structure and dwelled "almost wholly on the surface of things."[20]

The sounder British judgment was that by the distinguished military historian and theorist B. H. Liddell Hart, who praised *Why England Slept* for the "outstanding way it combines insight with balanced judgment—in a way that nothing that has yet been written here [in Britain] approaches. It is all the more impressive by comparison with other recent books which I have read, by both English and American writers, who were apt to get led astray by superficial appearances, so that they too often miss the wood for the trees, even if they do not go astray down some by-path." Liddell Hart, whose own book *The Defence of Britain* had appeared the previous year and covered some of the same ground, did identify several errors of fact or interpretation Jack had committed, but his overall assessment was praiseful—and this from a scholar infinitely more expert on the topic than was Laski.[21]

The British reviewers were as a group highly complimentary, a fact that gave Jack special satisfaction—he was, after all, writing about their country. John Wheeler-Bennett (who, given his association with the book, should have turned down the assignment) was effusive, commending Jack in *The New York Sun* for writing not as "the ambassador's son" but "forming his opinions for himself, sifting his evidence and finally evolving a political and psychological analysis of rare penetration, with an immensely appealing quality of freshness and breadth of understanding." A tad overheated, maybe, but basically right. Another Englishman, Nigel Dennis, writing in *The New Republic*, was likewise impressed: "Mr. Kennedy's is probably the first book that tries to distribute the blame for Britain's inefficiency in diplomacy and military preparedness among the British people generally. This is a bold departure from the common rule, and the author believes that writers who refuse to take it are fooling their countrymen as well as themselves." Dennis acknowledged that "a more exact distribution of blame" must await a larger study, but he found it hard to deny either the book's general thesis or the import of the topic.[22]

And the contribution would endure. The British historian Hugh Brogan, writing near the end of the century, conceded some shortcomings—Jack drove home some assertions too repetitiously; the assessment of the Munich Crisis did not hold up all that well—but ringingly proclaimed that *Why England Slept* "will always have an honourable place in the small library which the controversy about British policy under Baldwin and Chamberlain has called into being." Like the other books on Brogan's select list—among them Churchill's *The Gathering Storm*—Kennedy's effort was not merely a contribution to historical understanding; it was also,

Brogan maintained, a political intervention, in the way it roused its American readers to the great and vital task before them: to confront the reality of the Nazi threat and prepare to meet it, with eyes wide open.[23]

Of course, it is in biographical terms that *Why England Slept* really matters to us. We care about it because of what it tells us about John F. Kennedy, age twenty-three and just out of college. And because the book is substantially the same as the thesis, we can again recall Nigel Hamilton's assessment of the latter: "Nothing else Jack would write in his life would so speak the man." Two things in particular stand out. First, the book marked a significant early step by Jack toward a public career. To read the book is to see that its young author was clearly fascinated by the problems of democratic leadership in foreign affairs, and the dilemmas that confront policymakers who seek to do what is required of them while not alienating their temperamental constituents. It's a theme Kennedy would return to in a later book, *Profiles in Courage,* and a conundrum he would confront to the end of his days. In 1940 he was not a candidate for political office, and the book could certainly have foreshadowed a career in, say, journalism, or academia, or the law. But no contemporaneous reader of the thesis or the book could doubt that here was a potential future politician—especially if that reader also happened to be aware of his lengthy earlier course paper on Congressman Bertrand Snell. Even less can a reader of a subsequent generation fail to see the author's future implicit in line after line—in the need for an energetic leadership that will awaken and educate the people (the 1960 campaign), for example, and in the importance of "keep[ing] our armaments equal to our commitments" (the Berlin Crisis). The theme of the 1961 inaugural seems, in Brogan's words, "to be foreshadowed in the observation about Britain in the 1930s, that 'there was a great lack of young progressive and able leaders. Those who should have been taking over were members of the war generation, so large a portion of whom rested in Flanders Fields.' "[24]

Second, the book represented for Jack Kennedy a political emancipation from his father. He remained the devoted son, and would stay under his father's influence in important respects (though not as much as many later authors and documentary filmmakers would have us believe), but he showed here a capacity for independent thought that is notable—and that the father, to his credit, did not discourage. As Stephen C. Schlesinger notes in the foreword to a recent reissue of the book, *Why England Slept* constituted "a studied rebuke to the whole idea of appeasement—and so, in part, to his own father's views." (That a young man who saw Hitler's Europe up close would abandon the pro-appeasement position isn't surprising; indeed, the oddity is that Joe Junior, who also traversed the Continent in the lead-up to war, stayed doggedly true to Joe Senior's outlook.) When, in August, a reporter from the *Boston Herald* had the temerity to ask Jack if he was a "mouthpiece" for his famous father, he offered a biting reply: "I haven't seen my father in six months, nor are we of the same opinion concerning certain British statesmen." Six months was about how much time had elapsed since he started serious work on the thesis that became the book. With his book, Jack had staked out his own independent position on the most pressing international issue of the day: how to respond to the menace of German power. And his audience was no longer just his father or his thesis committee, but readers everywhere.[25]

III

Solicitations of all kinds now flowed thick and fast into his mailbox. Some correspondents urged him to write a follow-up volume, others that he pen a series of magazine articles, still others that he take his show on the road with a major lecture tour. A New York University professor of history, Geoffrey Brown, offered his help in getting Jack connected to a big-name publisher. But Bruce Hopper, Jack's Harvard mentor, urged caution. "Because of your years, you will be the object of all kinds of offers," Hopper wrote him in late summer. "Beware them all."

> Of course, there are some of your readers who will assume that you got your material from your father. I know you got your material by yourself, and wrote your thesis by yourself. In the end it doesn't matter what anyone thinks. What does matter is that you protect yourself from the pressure to lend your name to this or that cause. The public is fickle, and, in the end, ungrateful. And the public ruins its idols, yes?
>
> I can't imagine you getting excited over public acclaim, so this word is really unnecessary. It is just that I know your mailbox must be full of laudatory reviews, letters of appreciation, and offers (maybe even from Hollywood!). Take them all in perspective, as reward for a job well done, and then try to forget them.[26]

Jack took Hopper's advice to heart, more or less. He flirted with writing a second book, this one focused on America's role in the collapse of peace between the wars, but soon shelved the idea. He rejected requests for shorter articles and turned down myriad speaking invitations, contenting himself with granting interviews, many conducted on the phone from the family home in Hyannis Port, in between touch football games and sailing outings. Charles "Chuck" Spalding, a tall and gangly new acquaintance who in time would become one of his closest friends, recalled, on his first visit to the home, seeing Jack seated in the living room, signing copies of the book, a stack of admiring letters strewn about—one of them, from the prime minister of some country or other, was on the floor under a damp bathing suit. (Like countless other visitors, Spalding marveled at the extraordinary energy in the home as family members buzzed all around, everyone "vitally involved" in everything. It was infectious. "Right then it seemed to me this was something special," Spalding remembered. "It is a very startling thing to run into. You can go your whole life without finding that kind of excitement.")[27]

Sooner or later, the interviewers got to the question of *What next?* Jack had a ready answer: he would enroll in Yale Law School. Some months before, he had asked Harvard to send his transcript to the admissions office in New Haven, and Yale responded promptly to say he was in.[28] But though he had made noises to Hopper and others about being interested in international law, the idea of pursuing a legal education was half-formed at best, more a postgraduate plan that sounded good and sensible than something he had thought through. To friends like Lem Billings, Jack seemed much more inclined—whether he fully admitted it to himself or not—to a career in journalism or academia or politics. For that matter, for Jack as for many college graduates that summer, the darkening world situation made all plans fluid. Was war in the offing? Would there be conscription, as the Washington bigwigs seemed to hint? (The answer would be yes: a congressional bill that September authorized the first peacetime draft.) In Billings's recollection, he and Jack Kennedy and their peers, regardless of their immediate employment status, were merely marking time, playing the waiting game.[29]

Health problems also reared up to complicate Jack's planning. In addition to experiencing the ill-diagnosed gastrointestinal issues of old, he suffered from back pain. The cause was uncertain, but he speculated it was his college football injury flaring up. He also appears to have had a malady that his doctors at the Lahey Clinic, in Boston, and the Mayo Clinic, in Minnesota (to which he returned for tests in early September), kept carefully hidden—namely, venereal disease. The urologist at Lahey, whose report said the infection occurred in the spring of 1940, effectively treated the gonorrhea but could do little with the accompanying symptoms. Jack soon complained to his older brother about the painful urination and repeated the doctors' grim word that the urethritis would be his occasional companion for the rest of his days. For the combination of ailments, the physicians at Lahey and Mayo recommended against the stress of full-time legal studies and in favor of quiet convalescence.[30]

And so, in the late summer of 1940, Jack scrapped his law school plans, at least for the time being, and set out for California.[31] He wanted to get his health in order in the sunshine, he told friends and family, and vowed to keep productive by auditing classes at Stanford University. Joe Junior's friend Tom Killefer had waxed lyrical about the country-club quality of Stanford, nestled among rolling hills thirty miles south of San Francisco, and had reminded Jack that, unlike most of the Ivy League, the school was coeducational, which meant the presence of some two thousand female students (who were forbidden from walking on the quad unless they wore silk stockings). Jack had all the information he needed and headed west. It was a lark more than anything else. He intended to study business but soon found that the topic bored him, and he drifted instead into classes on politics and international relations. Even more, he drifted into student hangouts on and around campus, often pulling up in his slick new Buick convertible coupe with red leather seats, purchased with earnings from *Why England Slept*.[32]

A minor celebrity on account of his book and being the son of Ambassador Kennedy, Jack made few male friends on the overwhelmingly Republican campus (it didn't help that he insisted on wearing an FDR button everywhere he went, or that he didn't smoke and seldom touched alcohol), but he was popular among the coeds, who were drawn by his casual appearance and tousled hair, and by—several later said—his undeniable magnetism and sex appeal. He fell especially hard for Harriet Price, a witty and strikingly beautiful member of the Pi Phi sorority who went by the nickname of Flip and was considered a campus queen. The two drove to Carmel and San Francisco together (taking breaks en route so that Jack could get out and stretch his sore back), attended Stanford football games, went to movies, and dined at L'Omelette and Dinah's Shack. What they did not do was have sex: Flip rebuffed his every attempt, insisting that she would not exchange her virginity for anything but marriage. "I was wildly in love with him," she recalled. "I think Jack was in love with me . . . but no, he wasn't ready for marriage."[33]

Ambassador Kennedy was a frequent topic of conversation. "He talked of his father's infidelities," Price remembered, and clearly "knew everything that was going on in the marriage. . . . I think his father had a tremendous influence, I don't think there's any question about that, but not all to the good! It seemed to me that his father's obvious rather low opinion of his wife and the way he treated her, that some of that rubbed off on Jack. He wasn't mean or anything about his mother, but I think that denigration, that came from the father, rubbed off on the son. And that's where all the womanizing and everything came from!"[34]

Price would have felt confirmed in her view if she'd seen some of the correspondence between father and son. The letters from this period (and later) make amply clear that the ambassador expected Joe and Jack to carry on sexually in the same way he did, and to view women as little more than objects to be conquered. "It strikes me that you and Joe must have done some great work over there when I wasn't looking," he says in one missive, a reference to a "beautiful blonde" from England who'd contacted him to express her gratitude for Jack's help in getting her a residence permit in the United States. Jack, for his part, after a trip to the American South earlier in 1940, reports to his father that "an awful lot of people were down—three girls to every man—so I did better than usual—the girls—having a bit of a battle at first but finished up the week in a blaze of glory."[35]

The West Coast interlude is notable for one additional reason. On October 29, three thousand miles away, a blindfolded secretary of war, Henry Stimson, facing a phalanx of news cameras, reached into a large glass bowl shortly after noon to select the first draft lottery slips. He handed each slip to President Roosevelt. The eighteenth one bore the serial number 2748. "The holder of 2748 for the Palo Alto area," reported *The Stanford Daily* on its first page, "is Jack Kennedy, son of Joseph P. Kennedy, U.S. ambassador to the Court of St. James's, and student at Stanford Business School. Young Kennedy is the author of a recent best-seller on the conditions of England before the outbreak of World War II."[36]

Jack Kennedy, too sick for law school, had been drafted.

To his embarrassment, the news spread far beyond the campus newspaper. Jack's close friend Rip Horton recalled being in a movie theater in New Jersey "just at the time the draft was being put into effect—drafting men into the Army. . . . [Jack's] picture was flashed on the screen and I remember getting quite a kick out of it, thinking of him being drafted into the service." There followed teasing cables and letters to Jack from various friends, all of whom could see the incongruities: not merely that their sickly friend faced a call-up, but that his father was a vociferous opponent of U.S. intervention in foreign wars.[37]

IV

Though Jack didn't mention it in his correspondence with friends, one other element factored into his thinking: the association of his surname with cowardice, courtesy of his father's ostensible routine in wartime London. In recent months, some British observers had accused the ambassador of lacking grace under fire because of his habit of retreating most every evening from the city to his sixty-room rented mansion in Windsor rather than face the German air raids in central London: the Blitz had begun on September 7 and would last until May 10, 1941. (By October the Luftwaffe had ceased daytime operations in favor of night attacks alone.)[38] "Jittery Joe," the critics called him, and soon the accusation made its way into the press. "I thought my daffodils were yellow until I met Joe Kennedy," one Foreign Office wit sneered, and even some Americans took notice: "Once the Blitz started," Kennedy's aide Harvey Klemmer recalled, "he went to the country almost every night. He kept saying he had nine kids to look after, this big family he was responsible for. He took off every night before it got dark."[39]

The "Jittery Joe" charge was largely bogus. By all accounts, Kennedy showed scant fear when the German bombs fell close to him, including at least once near his country home. Henry Luce remembered speaking with him on the transatlantic phone on one occasion when aerial attacks could be heard in the background; Kennedy spoke calmly and conveyed no special concern.[40] What really lay behind the cowardice claim, one suspects, was British annoyance at the ambassador's unyielding bearishness. He still believed—as did, it should be noted, a great many other informed observers on both sides of the Atlantic—that Britain faced ultimate, inevitable defeat against the Germans and should therefore seek to make peace with them.[41] He failed to realize that this defeatism, and in particular his willingness to express it so openly, only served to reduce his already plummeting influence with policymakers. Winston Churchill didn't trust him, and neither did the Foreign Office. His own government in Washington kept him out of all high-stakes bilateral negotiations, including the destroyers-for-bases agreement, sealed in early September, in which fifty aging U.S. destroyers were transferred to the Royal Navy in exchange for access to air and naval bases in British colonies. The isolation left Kennedy angry and humiliated in equal measure.*

"The people here keep saying their chin is up and that they can't be beaten," he vented in a letter to Jack in September, "but the people who have had any experience with these bombings don't like it at all. . . . The only thing I am afraid of is that I won't be able to live long enough to tell all that I see and feel about this crisis. When I hear these mental midgets (USA) talking about my desire for appeasement and being critical of it, my blood fairly boils. What is this war going to prove? And what is it going to do to civilization? The answer to the first question is nothing; and to the second I shudder even to think about it."[42]

Having long since grasped that he remained in London only because Franklin Roosevelt wanted to keep him from inserting himself into the hotly contested presidential campaign back home (FDR and Willkie were neck and neck in the polls), Kennedy in October took the risky step of demanding to be recalled. If the State Department did not do so, he added, aide Eddie Moore would release to the press a document containing a full and frank expression of Kennedy's views. The ensuing hoopla, the ambassador implied, could be enough to swing the election to Willkie. It was naked blackmail, and it worked: Kennedy was summoned to Washington in late October, with instructions to make no public comment of any kind until he had met with the president. Before departure he called on the king and queen and visited Neville Chamberlain, dying of throat cancer, who whispered to him, "This is goodbye. We will never see each other again."[43]

---

* Joe Kennedy's personal frustration in the fall of 1940 did not keep him from plugging *Why England Slept* whenever possible, including in the highest places. "Her Majesty the Queen yesterday spoke to me about my son Jack's book. Inasmuch as Her Majesty expressed interest, I am sending this copy of the English edition for her." (JPK to A. Harding, October 21, 1940, box 4A, JFK Personal Papers.)

No love lost: Joe Kennedy and Winston Churchill outside
10 Downing Street, in the final days of Kennedy's ambassadorship.

Thus came to an end, for all practical purposes, the great adventure
known as "Joseph P. Kennedy, Ambassador." He was, it must be said, miscast for the role, as some had suspected from the start. He lacked the successful diplomat's skill at discretion, lacked a sense of history, lacked a
subtle understanding of people and their motivations, lacked a feel for
the abstractions of world politics. Cynical and pessimistic by nature, he
tended to view political matters, including foreign affairs, mostly accord-

ing to what they meant for him personally and for his family; if the same could be said for many people in this world, with Kennedy it was more extreme, more unfiltered, and left him without a broad sense of responsibility to a shared cause. Though no champion of Nazi Germany, he tolerated Hitler far longer than did most other appeasers, including Chamberlain— through the invasion of Poland, through the fall of France, through even the Blitz and the end of his ambassadorship. Some part of him even lamented the stoic fortitude of his British hosts, since the longer they endured, the greater the likelihood of a U.S. military intervention.[44]

For all that, Kennedy's tenure in London was not without successes. He won deserved praise, for example, for reorganizing embassy operations to make them more efficient and productive. He was affable, vigorous, and hardworking, and his early dispatches to Washington showed that he could be an insightful observer of the British political scene. (Even seasoned State Department experts appreciated his missives, which drew on his close contacts with Chamberlain and Halifax in particular.) In bilateral trade talks he was in his element, and he proved adept at negotiating trade issues with skill and finesse. If Europe had remained in a state of peace during his ambassadorship, Kennedy might have departed triumphantly, his political future still rosy at age fifty-two; instead he left under the darkest of clouds, his prospects for high elected office shattered forever.[45]

His sons, though, were a different story. They still had the future open to them, even if their father's troubles added a layer of uncertainty. Franklin Roosevelt shrewdly played to this notion at a White House dinner on the evening of October 27, nine days before the election. Since Kennedy's return earlier that day, the speculation had been intense: would he endorse Wendell Willkie, come out for the president, or stay quietly neutral? Henry and Clare Boothe Luce and top GOP leaders urged him to declare for the internationalist Republican; Rose Kennedy argued with equal fervor that he would be condemned as an ingrate if he turned against the president now. Joe suspected she was right, and moreover he saw Willkie as barely distinguishable from Roosevelt on the pressing issues of world affairs. (To frustrated isolationists, the two candidates were the "Willkievelt twins," whose repeated proclamations that they would keep America's boys out of foreign wars were not to be trusted.) That evening, with Mrs. Kennedy and several others present, Roosevelt mixed charm and not-so-veiled threats. "I stand in awe of your relationship with

your children," he said, after nodding in sympathetic support as Kennedy
went through his list of grievances. "For a busy man as you are, it's a rare
achievement. And I for one will do all I can to help you if your boys should
ever run for political office." According to FDR's son James, the president
then pivoted, warning that if Kennedy endorsed Willkie, he would become an outcast, his sons' prospective political careers scuttled before
they could even begin. Two days later, in an evening address on CBS
Radio, Kennedy endorsed Roosevelt for another term. One week after
that, Roosevelt won a decisive victory, though with lower margins than in
1932 or 1936.[46]

The story of Joseph Kennedy as diplomat still had one more sorry
chapter. Three days after the election, he sat for a ninety-minute interview in Boston with Louis Lyons of *The Boston Globe* and two reporters
from the *St. Louis Post-Dispatch*. Accustomed to the British system, where
journalists typically took care to shape an interviewee's remarks to fit
within the strict borders of acceptable discourse, and assuming—he subsequently said—that his most provocative comments were off the record,
Joe launched in. "Democracy is all finished in England," he declared, and
"it may be here," too. If the United States entered the war, "everything we
hold dear would be gone." Warming up, he said he supported FDR because he was the only man who could control the "have-nots" who
"haven't any stake of ownership." He tossed in inappropriate remarks
about the queen (she had "more brains than the Cabinet" and would be
the one to salvage a deal with Hitler in the end) and reminded the reporters that Charles Lindbergh's views had a lot to commend them. To the
question of whether America would refuse to trade with the Nazis if Hitler won the war, Kennedy shot back, "That's nonsensical."[47]

The story ran in the *Globe* on November 10, 1940, right beside the
announcement of Neville Chamberlain's death. The uproar was instan-
taneous, in Europe as well as in the United States. Only the Berlin *Börsen-
Zeitung* editorialized in support. Kennedy pressured the *Globe*'s executives
to repudiate Lyons's story, but the damage was done.[48] Kennedy officially
resigned his post and retreated to Palm Beach, as convinced as ever of the
correctness of his geopolitical views and resentful of the ostracism he had
suffered. As he often did when feeling aggrieved, he pointed the finger at
American Jews for what he saw as their outsize power in Washington and
their nefarious schemes to get America into the war. He longed for some
means of hitting back at his critics, and asked Jack to outline an article for

him; the resulting pair of documents, belatedly and rapidly produced, one of them nine pages in length, are remarkable for what they show of Jack's sharpening political skills and his changing relationship with his father—it was now a more complex and dynamic bond than the one Joe had with Joe Junior. Jack was his own man in a way his brother would never be.[49]

Jack urged his father to avoid going nasty—the high road was the only road worth traveling in this instance, not least because journalists had endless opportunities to strike back. This meant being calm and judicious and avoiding any hint of defensiveness. "I don't mean you should change your ideas or be all things to all men, but I do mean that you should express your views in such a way that it will be difficult to indict you as an appeaser unless they indict themselves as war mongers." Here Jack hit upon one of his main themes: the "appeaser" label was an albatross from which his father needed to free himself. And he needed also to disabuse critics of the notion that he saw little to worry about in Hitler and the other dictators of the world:

> I would think that your best angle would be that of course you do not believe this, you with your background cannot stand the idea personally of dictatorships—you hate them—you have achieved the abundant life under a democratic capitalist system—you wish to preserve it. But you believe that you can preserve it by keeping out of Europe's wars etc. It's not that you hate dictatorships less [than the interventionists do]—but that you love America more. . . . The point that I am trying to get at is that it is *important that you stress how much you dislike the idea of dealing with dictatorships,* how you wouldn't trust their word a minute—how you have no confidence in them.[50]

The accompanying draft article, sketched out by the son on the father's behalf, flowed from these judgments. "On November 6, the day after the election, I resigned from a post that I have held for nearly three years," Jack began, before laying out the older man's explanation for his belief in appeasement and his grim analysis of the geopolitical situation: "My views are not pleasant. I am gloomy and I have been gloomy since September, 1938. It may be unpleasant for Americans to hear my views but let me note that Winston Churchill was considered distinctly unpleasant to have around during the years from 1935 to 1939. It was felt he was a gloom monger," Jack wrote, neatly attempting to tie his father to the Briton's coattails. And so on the piece went, for several pages and in clear and economical prose, stressing Joe Kennedy's faith in open diplomacy and his determination to do his level best to aid President Roosevelt in keeping the United States out of the war.[51]

A striking feature of the cover memo is the almost complete lack of deference. Twenty-three-year-old Jack is writing as an equal, as though addressing a colleague or friend trapped in a fraught situation. Upon mailing the items, he evidently felt the urge to say more, and so, on board a United Airlines flight from San Francisco to Los Angeles, he penned a nine-page "supplementary note," this one hammering a simple point: the United States had no choice but to come to Britain's aid. The isolationists in America had done grievous damage, Jack argued, for they failed to see that "if England is forced to give in by summer [1941] due to our failure to give her adequate supplies, *we* will have *failed* to meet *our* emergency, as England did before us. As England failed from September 1938 to September 1939 to take advantage of her year of respite due to her feeling that there would be no war in 1939, we will have failed just as greatly." The simple reality, he went on, was that a British defeat would leave the United States "alone in a strained and hostile world," spending huge amounts on defense and leaving voters to wonder "why we were so stupid as to not have given Britain all possible aid."

Having thus admonished his father, Jack added a plea: "Of course, I do not mean you should advocate war, but you might explain with some vigour your ideas on how vital it is for us to supply England. You might work in how hard it is for a democracy to get things done unless it is scared and how difficult it is to get scared when there is no immediate menace—We should see that our immediate menace is not invasion, but that England may fall—through lack of our support." History would not look kindly upon an America that followed Chamberlain's lead, and in the future, "as we look back, we may be shocked at our present lack of vigour." Jack loyally acknowledged that the picture of his father in the popular imagination was wrong—the older man did not oppose all assistance to Britain. But he warned that perception was reality: in the common view "you are [an] appeaser + against aid—This you have to nip."[52]

Soon thereafter, following some hobnobbing in Hollywood (at one party he chatted up Clark Gable and Spencer Tracy, and he roomed for a

A young author in Hollywood signs his book for actor Spencer Tracy.

few days with aspiring actor Robert Stack) and an academic conference in Riverside at which he served as rapporteur, Jack Kennedy left California behind.* He missed his East Coast social life, missed his family. For a time

---

* Stack would later win fame as FBI agent Eliot Ness in the ABC television crime drama *The Untouchables*, during the time Jack Kennedy was president. Of Jack's way with the opposite sex, Stack would remark in his memoirs, "I've known many of the great Hollywood stars, and only a few of them seemed to hold the attention for women that Jack Kennedy did, even before he entered the political arena. He'd just look at them and they'd tumble." (Stack, *Straight Shooting,* 72–73.)

he exchanged love letters with Harriet Price; as the weeks passed the letters grew more infrequent, then they ceased altogether. In one of her last notes, Harriet referred to Jack's fatalistic view of life when she informed him that she'd almost been killed in a car accident—she was thrown out of the car yet somehow emerged unscathed. "But as you say, 'That's the way it goes.' "[53]

V

Dr. Sara Jordan of the Lahey Clinic, in Boston, took one look at Jack Kennedy and was aghast. It was the morning of December 9, 1940, and he had arrived in her office for an examination. The sojourn in the California sunshine, she could see, far from restoring the young man to robust good health, seemed to have had the opposite effect, as he now weighed less than before he went. He looked emaciated and drawn. Jordan insisted that Jack return to Boston after Christmas for further tests at New England Baptist Hospital and urged him to avoid any further full-time studies until fall 1941. He did as instructed, spending part of January 1941 in confinement in the hospital. From his bed there he penned a short article—his first publication since his book appeared—for the *New York Journal-American,* under the headline "Irish Bases Are Vital to Britain."

Much to Jack's satisfaction, his father had taken the advice in his December letters to heart, at least partially. When, in December, the Roosevelt administration called on Congress to pass a "Lend-Lease" bill—the United States would lend or lease military goods to the British, much as one lends a garden hose to a neighbor to fight a fire, out of compassion as well as enlightened self-interest—Joe Kennedy expressed opposition. It would be a giant step toward war, he declared. Some in the administration worried that Kennedy might go further, deploying his bottomless resources to try to thwart the plan. As the days passed, however, he shifted ground until, in a highly anticipated address on NBC Radio on January 18, he dropped his opposition. On the twenty-first, one day after Franklin Roosevelt's third inauguration, Kennedy crushed the hopes of Capitol Hill isolationists by offering not a peep of dissent to Lend-Lease when he appeared before a congressional committee considering the bill.[54]

Admittedly, more than Jack's advocacy was at work. For one thing, the elder Kennedy hoped against hope to be appointed to another high-level post in the administration, and thought it prudent to go along with the president's wishes. For another, now that he was back on American soil, he better understood that his isolationist cause was faltering. The weight of public opinion strongly backed Lend-Lease, backed aid for Britain. Against his predictions, the British were holding on, but they were desperate for more help, and Kennedy could see that most Americans wanted to give it. They were buying the administration's arguments, he perceived, and he saw as well the growing influence of radio correspondents such as Edward R. Murrow, whose rich, low-key, nicotine-scorched reports from wartime London kept Americans spellbound. ("This . . . is London," he would begin each broadcast, a distinctive hesitation suggested by his old high school teacher.) Murrow was resolutely pro-British, and there is no doubt his broadcasts bolstered the interventionist side in the U.S. debate by stressing Winston Churchill's greatness and England's bravery. More than that, though, correspondents like Murrow, speaking through the blaring of sirens, the whine of aircraft, and the roar of bomb bursts, brought the war home to Americans in a uniquely powerful way, one that made them feel closely connected to sufferers an ocean away. As the writer Archibald MacLeish said of Murrow's reports, "Without rhetoric, without dramatics, without more emotion than needed be, you destroyed the superstition of distance and of time."[55]

Joe Junior, meanwhile, argued the isolationist position more strongly than ever. Intensely stubborn by nature, he could also be tone-deaf in framing his arguments, and combative to the point of recklessness. Through the winter of 1941 he railed against the Lend-Lease measure, and he didn't let up even after Congress approved the bill by comfortable margins, in early March, thereby granting the executive branch extraordinary new powers. (The president alone would decide what to lend and to whom.) In a Ford Hall Forum in Boston on January 6, Joe insisted that the United States could not afford to bolster a doomed Britain and should instead prepare to implement a bartering system with Germany. Better to accede to Nazi domination of Europe, he went on, than to leap into a war that would strain the American economy beyond the breaking point and let loose the forces of radicalism. Late that month, Joe told another Boston audience that America should even resist sending food convoys if doing so risked pulling the nation into the war. He stuck to that position in the weeks thereafter.[56]

Jack thought his pugnacious brother foolhardy to speak so dogmatically on the issue, not to mention wrong on the merits. But Joe was also his sibling, so there could be no question of denouncing him. Jack contented himself during these weeks with quietly endorsing the administration's policy and thinking about what he should do next. Planning too far ahead was pointless, he believed, as war clouds threatened both in the west and in the east. In March, he again asked Harvard to send his transcript to Yale Law School, but he seemed no more committed to the prospect of legal studies than he had been the year before, and apparently did not submit a new application. His health stabilized, he indulged his interest in travel, visiting first Bermuda and then South America, where his mother and Eunice were already touring. Jack flew from Miami to join them in Rio de Janeiro, then moved on without them to Argentina. The pro-Nazi mood in Buenos Aires stunned him, as did the palpable undercurrent of anti-Americanism. From there it was on to Uruguay and Chile by plane, then, on June 10, by cruise ship from Valparaíso back to the States, with stops in Peru, Ecuador, and Colombia, followed by passage through the Panama Canal.[57]

Throughout the trip there had been ominous signs that world tensions were ratcheting up still further. In the Far East, the Japanese were pushing deeper into China and strengthening their hold on Southeast Asia. In the Atlantic, meanwhile, British shipping losses to the German U-boats rose to perilous heights that spring, prompting pleas from Churchill and top White House aides for U.S. convoys. In a major speech on May 27, FDR did not call for convoys—he feared moving too far ahead of public opinion—but he left little doubt that he thought developments in the Atlantic could bring the United States into the war at almost any moment. Announcing an unlimited state of emergency, the president warned of Hitler's global ambitions and pointed to the threats to island outposts such as Iceland, Greenland, and the Azores, from which the Nazis could launch aerial attacks on North and South America. Behind the scenes, U.S. negotiators worked to bring Iceland under American protection, and in June Roosevelt extended the U.S. defense perimeter well out into the North Atlantic.[58]

Then, on June 22, Hitler launched his boldest move of the war. Tossing out his August 1939 pact with Stalin, he ordered a massive assault on the Soviet Union, involving 3.2 million men, 3,600 tanks, and 600,000 motorized vehicles along a front that stretched for two thousand miles. Supporting aircraft numbered 2,500, and there was a throwback to the battles of old: 625,000 horses used for transport.[59] It was the largest land operation in history. For the Western Allies the invasion, code-named Operation Barbarossa, had one salutary effect in the short term: it eased the pressure on Great Britain. It also served to draw London and Washington officials closer together and to bring the United States nearer to active participation in the Battle of the Atlantic. Roosevelt, convinced that Soviet survival was crucial to Nazi Germany's defeat, pledged to provide Lend-Lease assistance to Stalin's government, despite deep aversion among many in Washington to helping the Kremlin leader—who had systematically and ruthlessly purged dissidents, signed a pact with Hitler, and brutalized eastern Poland.

It was a stunning development, changing the whole complexion of the war. Earth-shattering events had passed in a blur. Jack, still on his cruise ship en route home, was pondering the implications when there arrived news of a more personal nature: his brother had volunteered for military service! It seemed unthinkable: through April and into May, Joe Junior had continued his strident anti-war and anti-administration rhetoric, insisting in an address at Temple Ohabei Shalom, in Brookline, on April 29 that it would be "perfectly feasible for the United States to exist as a nation, regardless of who wins the war."[60] American escorts for ships carrying Lend-Lease aid would be a terrible mistake, he had added, as it would inevitably lead to the sending of men. Yet mere weeks later, this co-founder of the Harvard Committee Against Military Intervention, this frequent admirer of Hitler's Germany, this fervent proponent of America First principles, opted to forgo the final year of law school and sign up for the Naval Aviation Cadet Program of the U.S. Navy Reserve.

Joe Senior was dumbfounded. His firstborn not only had volunteered but had chosen the most dangerous branch of service, naval aviation. The Ambassador (as he was now often called, even as a private citizen) offered to pull strings and get Joe assigned to a desk job in the Office of Naval Intelligence, in Washington, but his son refused. For months it had infuriated him that people were questioning the Kennedys' courage, were leveling snide accusations against his father. How dare they? What did they know about bravery? He would prove them wrong by becoming a Navy flier. Joe Senior, knowing better than to stand in his proud son's way, gave his blessing. "My father, especially, approves of what I'm doing," Joe told the press, in a revealing exaggeration. "He thinks I'm doing what I should be doing, and he's glad for it." In late June, Young Joe was inducted, along with FDR's youngest child, John, and several other would-be aviators from Harvard. They became seamen second class, at a pay rate of $21 per month. Joe's physical examination at Chelsea Naval Hospital, in Boston, showed him to be in sterling physical shape—he stood five feet eleven and weighed a robust 175 pounds, and without a single blemish on his health record.[61]

Jack knew what he must do: he had to follow suit. He promptly volunteered for the Army Officer Candidate School, but failed the physical on account of his bad back. He then tried the Navy, with the same result. He vowed to press on, and in Hyannis Port that summer he embarked on an exercise regimen to strengthen his back, in anticipation of his next attempt to enlist. How effective the workouts were, he couldn't tell, but he felt good overall, free to enjoy his favorite place and time: the Cape in the summer. An early highlight was the Fourth of July weekend—always a time of special celebration in the Kennedy household, with a festively decorated porch and a long wooden table piled high with summer delicacies. The scene was frenetic as always, and filled with laughter. Jack and his siblings loved it, but on this holiday their father found himself worrying that his worst fears were coming true: a war he detested was drawing ever closer to America, and one son had already enlisted, with a second determined to join him. Fifteen-year-old Bobby was not too far behind, and Kick and Eunice were musing aloud about joining the Red Cross or even the Women's Army Corps. If U.S. intervention came, Joe wondered, would there ever be another family gathering like this one?

There were more fun times in that sun-drenched Hyannis summer—the touch football games on the sloping lawn, the board games, the movie nights, the outings to Rexall's for ice cream. Joe Junior was around a lot, commuting on weekends from his training base at Squantum, near Boston. Visitors came and went. Torby Macdonald showed up, which was unexceptional except that his letters to Jack, always playfully sarcastic, had of late taken on darker tones, the sarcasm more biting, more caustic, as though he resented Jack's successes. The two also disagreed politically, with Torby espousing pro-appeasement and indeed even pro-German views.[62] Lem Billings came, too, of course, as did John Hersey. Chuck Spalding, ever observant, marveled anew at the spectacle he had first encountered the summer before, one he found at once unique and quintessentially American. "It was a scene of endless competition, people drawing each other out and pushing each other to greater lengths. It was as simple as this: the Kennedys had a feeling of being heightened and it rubbed off on the people who came in contact with them. They were a unit."[63]

That they were—an extraordinary constellation of eleven handsome and energetic people, close-knit and loving, protective of one another, living under one roof in the three-gabled house overlooking Nantucket Sound. But not for much longer. The patriarch was right to feel a sense of foreboding: that summer of 1941 would be the last time his family was all together.

ELEVEN

IN LOVE AND WAR

t is a marked feature of John F. Kennedy's early adult years that at certain key junctures, family connections got him to places he otherwise
would never have reached. Such was the case in October 1941, when he
became an officer in the Navy Reserve and was assigned to the Office of
Naval Intelligence in Washington, D.C., the same posting Joe Junior had
turned down the previous spring. In August, Joseph P. Kennedy had approached Captain Alan Kirk, who had been naval attaché in London during Kennedy's ambassadorship and who now headed the office, about
getting his second son into the Navy despite his dodgy health record. "I
am having Jack see a medical friend of yours in Boston tomorrow for
physical examination and then I hope he'll become associated with you in
Naval Intelligence," Kennedy wrote.[1] Kirk was happy to help. In London
he had headed the inquiry into the *Athenia* sinking in 1939, and in that
capacity had gotten to know Jack. The young man's mind and affability
had impressed him, and he welcomed the idea of bringing Jack into naval
intelligence, where physical robustness counted for little and brainpower
counted for a lot.

And so it was that a few weeks later, the board of medical examiners
declared Jack "physically qualified for appointment" as an officer in the

Navy Reserve. The exam had been, at best, perfunctory, and the report miraculously omitted mention of his long hospital stays and recurring illnesses. The ONI expressed its delight at bringing on this "exceptionally brilliant student" who "has unusual qualities and a definite future in whatever he undertakes," and assigned him to the Foreign Intelligence Branch in its Washington office. As an ensign, Jack outranked his older brother, a seaman second class. In theory, at least, Joe Junior would have to address him as "Sir."[2]

It was another blow to the previously undefeated contender for family honors. Joe was shattered. He'd put in the grueling work to get his wings while Jack sauntered along, his usual casual self, yet in an instant Jack had been elevated above him. A family friend found Joe genuinely worried for his brother's ailing back and—for a baser reason—irritated with his father for helping Jack get into uniform. He knew, moreover, that by long-held custom, naval precedence, unlike the army's, was assigned for life and dependent on date of commissioning; it marched on, forevermore, independent of merit. Jack had passed him and he would never catch up, no matter how hard he tried.[3]

Jack's work turned out to be more tedious than advertised. He did not have top-secret clearance, so mostly he spent his days compiling intelligence digests based on reports from overseas stations. Six days a week he toiled, from 9:00 A.M. to 5:00 P.M., editing and condensing, out of a dingy room with metal desks. A glamour position it was not. But at least he was in Washington, the nerve center of American statecraft, where tensions ran high and critical policy choices loomed. And at least he could spend time with Kick, who, after two years in college, had taken a job as a reporter with the staunchly isolationist *Washington Times-Herald*. Rosemary was also there—having been moved back to the States the previous year, she now lived under nuns' care at St. Gertrude's convent. Even Lem Billings resided nearby, in Baltimore, where he worked in advertising and sales at Coca-Cola.

As always, Jack delighted in Kick's company, and she in his. They shared a similar sensibility and self-deprecating sense of humor, a similar love of gossip, and—following their father's ambassadorship in London—a similar affinity for upper-class English society. Even casual friends could see the special chemistry that existed between them, one that neither had with any of the other seven siblings. They finished each other's sentences and seemingly could read each other's minds. They even looked alike, with the same mop of thick hair, the same blue eyes. Upon arrival in the city, Jack had rented an apartment on Twenty-first Street, a few blocks from Kick, and she soon introduced him to her social circle. One figure stood out: Inga Arvad, an effervescent Dane who spoke four languages and wrote a breezy profiles column for the *Times-Herald.* Four years older than Jack and on her second marriage, she bowled him over from the first meeting.[4]

She was, everyone agreed, stunningly gorgeous, blond and blue-eyed, with high cheekbones and a flawless complexion, a woman who turned heads wherever she went. A slight gap between her two front teeth somehow only added to her mystique. But what really set Inga apart and drove an endless parade of suitors to distraction was her sensuality. It owed something to her looks, of course, but more to the ease and grace with which she carried herself as a former ballet dancer, to her warm and ready laugh and quick wit, to her elegance and warmth and the timbre of her voice.

Arthur Krock, who had helped get Inga the *Times-Herald* job when she was still a student at the Columbia Graduate School of Journalism, was "stupefied" by her classic beauty, while to John B. White, a reporter at the paper, she was "totally woman." Frank Waldrop, the paper's editor, said no photo "ever did her justice," and journalist Muriel Lewis, following an interview with Arvad a few years before, wrote that no words could adequately describe her—"they would ring flat as the laudations of a cinema star in a magazine."[5] Jack Kennedy wholly agreed, but he also appreciated something else: Arvad's obvious smarts. He saw her as an intellectual equal, with her linguistic prowess and her sharp mind.* She had seen as much of the world as he had, if not more. She was confident and straightforward without being the slightest bit conceited. And she had an absurdist sense of humor that he relished.

The appeal was mutual. Kick had waxed lyrical about Jack in advance of his arrival (unlike the rest of the family, she thought Jack, not Joe Junior, was the Kennedy destined for greatness), and Inga found that her

---

* Inga's fluency in so many tongues was a source of eternal fascination and admiration for the two Kennedy siblings, both of whom had a tin ear for languages. Kick, though she had spent the better part of a year in France, always struggled with the language. And on a visit to Italy, after getting separated from her friends on a packed sightseeing bus and being pinched by a male passenger, she was heard to shriek, "Stoppa the bus! Stoppa the bus!" (McTaggart, *Kathleen Kennedy,* 62.)

Inga Arvad in 1931, as the newly
crowned Miss Denmark.

friend "hadn't exaggerated. He had the charm that makes birds come out
of the trees." To White she confided, "Jack's an interesting man because
he's so single-minded and easy to deal with. He knows what he wants.
He's not confused about motives and those things. I find that refreshing."
In a profile she wrote of Jack that ran in the November 27 issue of the
Times-Herald, Arvad remarked on his selfless curiosity and called him "the
best listener between Haparanda and Yokohama. Elder men like to hear
his views which are sound and astonishingly objective for so young a
man." She marveled at his ability to write a bestselling book at so tender
an age ("here is really a boy with a future") and at his skill at "walking
into the hearts of people." By the end of that month he had walked into
hers, and they were lovers.[6]

It mattered to Jack that Kick had played the role of matchmaker. Her
opinion of the girls he dated had always been important to him, even in

his teenage years. He trusted her judgment. Not infrequently, he turned to her for advice on matters of love, and to more than a few dates over the years he had emphasized how important it was that they make "a good impression on Kick." Inga had clearly passed the bar, with room to spare. She and Kick hit it off from the start, and Kick was eager to connect her with Jack, despite the fact that Inga was married. (Almost certainly, she did not expect the affair to last. And, like her mother, Kick believed there were different rules for men and women; for herself she ruled out sex outside marriage, but she did not expect her father or brothers to do the same. When told in 1939 about a husband's unfaithful ways, she replied, "That's what all men do. You know that women can never trust them."[7])

To his parents, Jack said nothing about the nascent romance—for obvious reasons. In his letters to his mother during this period, he maintained a lighthearted tone that in a later generation could be called condescendingly sexist but was also affectionate and witty, and that suggested he had little on his mind but family and work. "I enjoy your round robin letters," he wrote to Rose in November, echoing John Keats in his final flourish:

> I'm saving them to publish—and that style of yours will net us millions. With all this talk about inflation and where is our money going—when I think of your potential earning power—with you dictating and Mrs. Walker beating it out on that machine—it's enough to make a man get down on his knees and thank God for the Dorchester High Latin School which gave you that very sound grammatical basis which shines through every slightly mixed metaphor and each somewhat split infinitive. . . .
>
> My health is excellent. I look like hell, but my stomach is a thing of beauty—as are you, Ma,—and you, unlike my stomach—will be a joy forever.[8]

Jack also got to know Kick and Inga's boss, the flamboyant *Times-Herald* publisher, Eleanor "Cissy" Patterson, who was impressed that he could come out with a high-profile book right out of college and invited him to a dinner at her mansion in Dupont Circle on November 10. Also in attendance that night were Undersecretary of the Navy James Forrestal, journalist Herbert B. Swope, financier Bernard Baruch, and isolationist senator Burton K. Wheeler. Jack was entranced by the discussion, which featured a spirited debate over intervention between Forrestal (for) and Wheeler (against), and afterwards he wrote up a summary for himself of what had occurred. Wheeler, Jack jotted, insisted that "there was not a real emergency here now—no one could possibly invade this country," and therefore America should stand apart. "He admitted he was a cold-blooded Yankee and said while he was sorry for the Poles and the Czechs he believed that their misery should serve as a warning, not as an incentive for duplicating it." Jack saw the power in this perspective, and acknowledged to the group that he had once shared it, but he now found himself agreeing with Forrestal's twin claims: that America was already at war in all but name, and that it was better to take on the Germans now, while the United States still had allies, than to wait for those allies to fall and have to fight Hitler alone. When Forrestal insisted that the United States must become "the dominant power of the 20th century," Jack voiced full agreement.

He had become, if he wasn't before, a full-fledged interventionist. To himself he remarked dryly that he hoped he wouldn't need these dinner notes for a follow-up volume on "Why America Slept."[9]

The first week of December 1941 began uneventfully: Jack hosted his father for lunch at his apartment and received a shipment of furniture from the family residence in Bronxville, which had just been sold. (Thenceforth the Kennedys would alternate between the homes in Hyannis Port and Palm Beach, fifteen hundred miles apart.) That Wednesday, December 3, he wrote to Lem Billings to urge him to come to Washington for the weekend, and to bring his tuxedo, as "we might go to Chevy Chase." Lem, as always, was happy to oblige. On Sunday, December 7, the young men had just finished a rousing game of touch football with strangers near the Washington Monument when the news came in: Pearl Harbor was under attack.

II

It was ironic, in a way, that war came to America by way of Asia and the Pacific, not Europe and the Atlantic. Though armies had been fighting in the Far East since Japan attacked China in 1937, developments there never loomed as large in the American consciousness as those in Europe. (The ties with Europe were closer, and the threat there seemed bigger.)

When Franklin Roosevelt and Winston Churchill met on a British battleship at Argentia Bay, off the coast of Newfoundland, in August 1941, the Nazi threat dominated much of the discussion, with Japan getting less attention. The two leaders also issued the Atlantic Charter, a universalistic set of war aims espousing collective security, self-determination, disarmament, economic cooperation, and freedom of the seas. According to Churchill's recollection, the president assured him off the record that, although he could not ask Congress to declare war against Nazi Germany, "he would wage war" and "become more and more provocative."[10]

Soon after their meeting, American and German ships clashed in the North Atlantic. On September 4, a few weeks before Jack Kennedy began his job with the Office of Naval Intelligence, a German submarine fired torpedoes at the U.S. destroyer *Greer*, narrowly missing the target. Roosevelt declared in response that henceforth the U.S. Navy would have the authority to fire first when under threat, and he added that American warships would commence convoying British merchant vessels. It marked the start of an undeclared naval war with Germany. In early October, a German submarine torpedoed the U.S. destroyer *Kearny* off the coast of Iceland, and later that month the destroyer *Reuben James* went down after a torpedo attack, claiming more than one hundred American lives. Congress promptly scrapped the cash-and-carry policy and altered the Neutrality Acts to allow transport of munitions to Great Britain on armed U.S. merchant ships.

The isolationists were a dwindling band, both on Capitol Hill and in the country at large—in one fall poll, only 20 percent of respondents would admit to being isolationist, while 75 percent regarded "defeating Nazism" as "the biggest job facing the country." But FDR continued to fear their power, and they knew how to make themselves heard. On September 11, Charles Lindbergh, in a speech in Des Moines, Iowa, carried to a nationwide radio audience, asserted that three groups were pushing the United States into war: the New Dealers, the British government, and the Jews. "Instead of agitating for war, the Jewish groups in this country should be opposing it in every possible way, for they will be among the first to feel its consequences," Lindbergh declared, his familiar high-pitched voice growing ever more fervent. "Their greatest danger to this country lies in their ownership and influence in our motion pictures, our press, our radio, and our government." Wendell Willkie, who remained the titular head of the GOP a year after his election loss, called it "the most un-American talk made in my lifetime by any person of national reputation."[11]

Tensions in Asia rose alarmingly that fall, notwithstanding Roosevelt's desire to avoid war with Japan in order to concentrate on the German threat. The previous year, in September 1940, after Germany, Italy, and Japan signed the Tripartite Pact (and thus became the Axis powers), FDR had slapped an embargo on shipments of scrap metal and aviation fuel to Japan. When Japanese troops occupied French Indochina in July 1941, the administration froze Japanese financial assets in the United States, expanded the embargo, and stopped the export of all oil to Japan. The implications were huge for a country that consumed roughly twelve thousand tons of petroleum each day, most of it imported from America. Prime Minister Fumimaro Konoe, a moderate, proposed a summit meeting with Roosevelt and offered to withdraw Japanese forces from Indochina as soon as Japan's struggle with China was resolved. Roosevelt balked, persuaded by his aides to insist on Japanese disengagement from China as a precondition for any summit. The proposal collapsed, and Konoe was ousted in favor of Hideki Tojo, the militaristic army minister. In November, Tojo offered to disengage from Indochina immediately, and from China right after the establishment of peace, in return for a million tons of aviation gasoline. Secretary of State Cordell Hull turned down the offer and reiterated the U.S. insistence on Japanese withdrawal from China and Southeast Asia. An intercepted message that U.S. analysts decoded on December 3 instructed the Japanese embassy in Washington to burn codes and destroy cipher machines—a clear indication that war was coming.[12]

But where might it come? Neither Jack Kennedy nor his superiors in naval intelligence, nor any other American officials, were aware of what Japanese commanders were secretly planning: a daring raid on Hawaii, with the aim of knocking out the U.S. Pacific Fleet and thereby buying time to complete Japan's southward expansion. An armada of sixty ships, with a core of six carriers bearing 360 aircraft, crossed three thousand miles of ocean, each ship maintaining total radio silence to avoid detection. In the early morning of December 7, some 230 miles northwest of Honolulu, the carriers unleashed their planes. Shortly before 8:00 A.M., they swept down on the unsuspecting naval base and nearby airfields at Pearl Harbor, dropping torpedoes and bombs and strafing buildings. An hour later came a second wave of planes. Twenty U.S. ships were crippled or destroyed, along with three hundred airplanes; 2,403 Americans died, and 1,143 were wounded. By chance, three aircraft carriers at sea escaped the disaster.

Critics would subsequently accuse Roosevelt of purposely leaving the Pearl Harbor fleet exposed to assault so that the United States could enter World War II through the "back door" of Asia.[13] The charge was spurious. Although American cryptanalysts had broken the Japanese diplomatic code, the intercepted messages never revealed detailed naval or military plans and never mentioned Pearl Harbor specifically. A late message sent from Washington to Pacific posts warning of imminent war had been too casually transmitted by a routine method and had arrived in Hawaii too late. Base commanders also believed Hawaii too far from Japan to be a target for all-out attack; they expected an attack on Thailand, British Malaya, or the Philippines. The Pearl Harbor disaster stemmed from errors and inadequate information (or, more to the point, a surfeit of information, pointing in myriad directions), not from conspiracy.

The attack brought to an end the long and bitter debate over America's involvement in the war. The core isolationist argument—that the United States could remain aloof from the fighting, secure within its own sphere—had been shredded. Its chief adherents now put forth a new message, one of solidarity and determination, and of obeisance to presidential authority. "We have been stepping closer to war for many months," Charles Lindbergh declared. "Now it has come and we must meet it as united Americans, regardless of our attitude in the past." Robert McCormick, the staunchly isolationist publisher, spoke similarly in a front-page editorial in the *Chicago Tribune:* "All of us, from this day forth, have only one task. That is to strike with all our might to protect and preserve the American freedom that we all hold dear." Joseph Kennedy, mere hours after the attack, cabled Roosevelt: "Name the Battle Post, I'm Yours to Command."[14]

It wasn't going to happen. Kennedy had burned too many bridges, had bad-mouthed the administration once too often. "The truth of the matter is that Joe is and always has been a temperamental Irish boy," FDR wrote to his son-in-law John Boettiger a few weeks later, "terrifically spoiled at an early age by huge financial success, thoroughly patriotic, thoroughly selfish and thoroughly obsessed with the idea that he must leave each of his nine children with a million dollars (he has told me that often). He has a positive horror of any change in the present methods of life in America. To him the future of a small capitalistic class is safer under a Hitler than under a Churchill. This is subconscious on his part and he does not admit it. . . . Sometimes I think I am 200 years older than he is." The president tossed in that personally he was "very fond of Joe," but the upshot was clear: no job offer would be forthcoming, either then or later.[15]

In the late morning of December 8, Roosevelt entered the House chamber to thunderous applause. Gripping the lectern, a sea of microphones arrayed in front of him, he delivered an address that, to an extent no one could yet know, transformed the world. "Yesterday," he began, "December 7, 1941—a date which will live in infamy—the United States of America was suddenly and deliberately attacked by naval and air forces of the Empire of Japan." He went on to ask Congress for a declaration of war against Japan, noting that the Japanese had also attacked Malaya, Hong Kong, the Philippines, Guam, Wake Island, and Midway, and he expressed the prevailing sentiment when he vowed that Americans would never forget "the character of the onslaught against us." Then a promise: "No matter how long it may take us to overcome this premeditated invasion, the American people, in their righteous might, will win through to absolute victory." Though only twenty-five sentences long, the speech took ten minutes to deliver, so frequent and lengthy were the interruptions for applause.[16]

The Senate voted unanimously in favor of war, while in the House only Jeannette Rankin of Montana, a pacifist and the first woman elected to Congress, voted against (as she had the last time around, in 1917). Britain declared war on Japan, but the Soviet Union did not. Three days later, Germany and Italy, honoring the Tripartite Pact, declared war on the United States. "Hitler's fate was sealed," Winston Churchill, who grasped America's immense productive potential in wartime better than most, later wrote. "Mussolini's fate was sealed. As for the Japanese, they would be ground to powder. . . . I went to bed and slept the sleep of the saved and thankful." Charles de Gaulle, leader of the Free French government in exile, felt the same: "Of course, there will be military operations, battles, conflicts, but the war is finished since the outcome is known from now on," he remarked. "In this industrial war, nothing will be able to resist American power."[17]

In time, Churchill's and de Gaulle's optimism would be rewarded, but at this moment, in the second week of December 1941, when the future had yet to come, the outlook was ominous. Much of the U.S. Navy had been decimated, and the Army was as yet a mass of civilians without adequate equipment, training, or experienced officers. (The administration's survey of war preparedness, named the "Victory Plan" and completed earlier in 1941, estimated that the nation could not be ready to fight before June 1943.) Industrial production, though theoretically just as awesome as de Gaulle surmised, still had to be converted from peacetime production. In Asia, Japan's potential expansion in the short term seemed limitless—might it seize India, Australia, and Hawaii in addition to all of Southeast Asia?—while in Europe, Hitler's forces controlled Western Europe and had reached the outskirts of Moscow. (Forward units were close enough to see the Kremlin's golden domes.) They looked invincible, having already laid deadly siege to Leningrad (St. Petersburg) and cut deeply into Ukraine, taking Kiev in September. More than a million Soviet soldiers had already perished in the fighting; another three million were captive. Who dared predict that the Red Army would withstand German power through another year, or another six months? Who dared deny that Hitler might put a stranglehold on the Mediterranean and impose his total will on the Middle East and North Africa, where his units were on the march and where British diplomats in Cairo were burning their papers? Anything seemed possible.

Still, Germany's declaration of war solved a big problem for Roosevelt: it got the United States formally into the campaign against Nazi tyranny. And although historians forever after would puzzle over Hitler's war declaration—the terms of the Tripartite Pact did not actually oblige him to join Japan's struggle—in his eyes he was merely formalizing a state of affairs that had existed for months with the undeclared war in the Atlantic. The Führer also harbored a deep personal animus against Roosevelt (in his war declaration speech he said the "mentally disturbed" FDR was kept in power only by the sinister "power" of "the eternal Jew"), and he had long been preoccupied with what he saw as the colossal threat posed by American-led global capitalism. If major conflict with the United States was inevitable, and Hitler did not doubt it, why not claim the prestige of instigating it immediately, thereby assisting the Japanese by forcing on the Americans a two-front war? Only in hindsight is his poor timing fully evident. The declaration of war against Washington came within a week of his offensive against Moscow stalling as Stalin's troops took German prisoners for the first time.[18]

III

Following the president's speech and the congressional vote, the federal government shifted immediately into wartime gear. The Office of Naval Intelligence was no exception. The old closing time of 5:00 P.M. was scrapped in favor of a round-the-clock schedule, and Jack Kennedy got the late shift. "This will gripe your arse but I can't come to the wedding," he informed Lem on December 9, in reference to another pal's imminent nuptials. "I'm on a new schedule—from 10:00 at night to 7 in the morning—it's a 7 day a week schedule. . . . Please convey my thanks and regrets to Pete's bride who was very kind to have us." Then a P.S.: "Isn't this a dull letter—but I'm not sleeping much nights."[19]

The new work hours left little time for socializing, or for Inga Arvad, who, for that matter, had a new preoccupation of her own. A few days after Pearl Harbor, Page Huidekoper, a *Times-Herald* reporter (and former press assistant in Joe Kennedy's London embassy), learned that a colleague had supposedly discovered a photograph of a smiling Inga sitting in Adolf Hitler's box at the 1936 Berlin Olympics. Might this mean she was a spy for the Germans? Huidekoper wasn't sure, but she passed the information on to Kick Kennedy and editor Frank Waldrop. He determined that he and Huidekoper should accompany Arvad to the FBI's Washington office to try to clear her name.[20] Arvad agreed. The agent who met with them sent a memorandum to director J. Edgar Hoover:

> On the afternoon of December 12, 1941, Mr. Frank Waldrop, editor of the Washington *Times Herald,* called at this office with Miss. P. Huidekoper, a reporter of that paper, and Inga Arvad, columnist for the *Times Herald.* . . . Briefly, Miss Huidekoper several days ago stated to Miss Kathleen Kennedy, a reporter on the *Times Herald* and the daughter of former Ambassador Kennedy, that she would not be surprised if Inga Arvad was a spy for some foreign power. She remarked to Miss Kennedy that one of her friends had been going through some old Berlin newspapers and had noted a picture of Inga Arvad taken with Hitler at the Olympic games in Berlin. . . .

Miss Kennedy, a very close friend of Inga Arvad, told her of Miss Huidekoper's statement.[21]

The agent no doubt already knew the basics of Arvad's glamorous and cosmopolitan story. Born in Copenhagen in 1913, she spent much of her youth in South Africa and England, as well as in Germany and France. Crowned a beauty queen in Denmark at age sixteen, she competed in Paris for the Miss Europe title the next year, and soon after that eloped with an Egyptian diplomat, divorcing him at age nineteen. In 1935, at age twenty-one, she met Hungarian American movie director turned explorer Paul Fejos, who was almost twice her age and whom she would later marry. That year she also signed on with the Danish newspaper *Berlingske Tidende*, and in that capacity she visited Germany on numerous occasions. An enterprising reporter, Arvad secured an interview with Hermann Göring and attended his wedding, where she met Hitler (who reportedly referred to her as "the perfect example of Nordic beauty"). She subsequently interviewed the German leader twice and also talked with Nazi propaganda chief Joseph Goebbels.

To the FBI agent, Inga denied being any kind of spy for anyone, and insisted that her interviews with German leaders were entirely nonpolitical. Hers was the "human interest" beat—what they thought of marriage, what they ate for breakfast, and so on. She insisted she had little but contempt for the Germans for what they had done to Europe and to the world.[22]

Unbeknownst to Inga, the FBI had already begun investigating her months earlier, in the spring, upon learning of her "friendship" with Hitler and of the suspicion among several of her fellow students at Columbia that she harbored pro-German and anti-Semitic sentiments. (There is little explicit evidence to substantiate the latter suggestion, but her newspaper articles, all written several years before, had been sympathetic to German life and to the Germans she profiled, many of them Nazis. "One likes him immediately," she had written of Hitler in *Berlingske Tidende* on November 1, 1935, after their first interview. "He seems lonely. The eyes, which are tender hearted, look directly at you. They radiate power."[23]) Agents also looked into her and her husband's friendship with Swedish businessman Axel Wenner-Gren, one of the wealthiest men in the world—his net worth was estimated at $1 billion—who had made his fortune by popularizing the home vacuum cleaner and then become an arms contractor, and who was thought to be on friendly terms with Göring and other German leaders. Wenner-Gren's yacht, the *Southern Cross*, was the largest private luxury vessel in the world and carried a crew of 315, in addition to being outfitted with machine guns, rifles, and sophisticated radio equipment. U.S. naval intelligence suspected that the yacht was being used to refuel German submarines, and in December 1941 the Roosevelt administration formally blacklisted Wenner-Gren.

If Arvad thought her appearance at the FBI office cleared things up, she was mistaken. Through the early months of 1942, the Bureau kept her under surveillance, tapped her phone, and intercepted her mail. Even Franklin Roosevelt briefly got into the act: "In view of the connection of Inga Arvad . . . with the Wenner-Gren Expeditions' leader, and in view of certain other circumstances which have been brought to my attention, I think it would be just as well to have her specially watched," the president wrote Hoover.[24]

At this point one might have expected Jack Kennedy to leave Inga Arvad alone, at least until she cleared her name. Prudence dictated as much in a time of war. But the two lovers carried on as before, perhaps unaware of the FBI's surveillance of her apartment on the fifth floor at 1600 Sixteenth Street. Or perhaps they simply doubted—accurately, as it turned out—the Bureau's competence in acting on whatever it uncovered. Agent C. A. Hardison, setting up watch on the flat, duly noted the arrival of Inga's husband, Paul Fejos, and his departure, but seemed to have no clue about the identity of the mysterious lover who then entered the residence and stayed the night—a young man who, according to "Informant A," wore "a gray overcoat with raglan sleeves and gray tweed trousers. He does not wear a hat and has blonde curly hair which is always tousled."[25]

Jack's affectionate cable of New Year's Day 1942, successfully intercepted, likewise left Hardison stumped as to its source:

THEY ARE NOT KEEPING THEM FLYING SO I WON'T BE THERE UNTIL 11:30 BY TRAIN. I WOULD ADVISE YOUR GOING TO BED, BUT IF YOU COME, BUY A THERMOS AND MAKE ME SOME SOUP. WHO WOULD TAKE CARE OF ME IF YOU DIDN'T? LOVE, JACK.[26]

There matters might have rested were it not for the sleuthing efforts of gossip journalist Walter Winchell, whose column appeared in more than two thousand newspapers nationwide. Relying in part on his sources within the FBI, Winchell reported in the *New York Daily Mirror* on January 12, 1942: "One of Ex-Ambassador Kennedy's eligible sons is the target of a Washington gal columnist's affections. So much so she has consulted a barrister about divorcing her exploring groom. Pa Kennedy no like." Coincidentally or not, within twenty-four hours Jack received orders transferring him from Washington to a desk job in Charleston, South Carolina, and "Pa Kennedy" soon appeared in Frank Waldrop's office to press him for details about Arvad and her past.[27] Joe had always nodded and winked at his older boys' skirt-chasing ways, had even egged them on—they were, after all, following in his footsteps. But as Jack and Inga grew serious, he sensed trouble. Inga was four years older than Jack, she was on marriage number two, and she was suspected of being a German spy—a problematic trifecta, to say the least. Even worse, Arvad seemed intent on divorcing Fejos (from whom she had been estranged for some time) so she could be with Jack. A marriage between them would scuttle any hopes Jack might have for elected office and might also damage the political aspirations of Joe Junior, who would be tainted by association. The elder Kennedy, more and more frustrated by Roosevelt's steadfast refusal to grant him a wartime posting and sensing that henceforth he would have to channel his ambitions through his sons, made clear to Jack that the relationship should end.[28]

Jack resisted, showing again his growing independence from the old man. Instead he arranged for "Inga Binga," as he liked to call her, to come to Charleston in late January and again in early February, surely aware that the authorities would find out what he was up to. (As indeed they did: the FBI bugged the pair's hotel room and overheard a little gossip, a lot of sex, and no discussion of state secrets.) He couldn't get enough of her, loved just listening to her speak, loved how—like many otherwise fluent Scandinavian English speakers—she sometimes mixed up her *v* sounds and her *w* sounds, so that *vegetable* became *wegetable* and *shovel* became *showel*. More than that, Jack cherished Inga's warm, womanly affection; never before had he experienced anything remotely like it.[29] He felt free around her in a way he felt around few others, free to confide his fears and hopes and dreams. (Including political ones: the letters and intercepted conversations reveal that high elected office was already on his mind.) She, for her part, was completely taken by his boyish energy, his looks, and his curiosity about the world.

"Go up the steps of fame," she exhorted him in a letter on January 26. "But—pause now and then to make sure that you are accompanied by happiness. Stop and ask yourself, 'Does it sing inside me today.' . . . Look around and don't take another step till you are certain life is as you will and want it." Elsewhere, she bemoaned his reluctance to reveal his innermost feelings: "Maybe your gravest mistake, handsome, is that you admire brains more than heart, but then that is necessary to arrive." And she was motherly, concerned about his bad back: "It is because you are dearer to me than anybody else that I want to be with you when you are sick. Maybe it is my maternal instinct."[30]

"To you I need not pretend," Jack told her. "You know me too well." She agreed: "I do, not because I have put you on a pedestal—you don't belong there, nobody does—but because I know where you are weak, and that is what I like." But she saw greatness in his future: "I can't wait to see you on top of the world. That is a very good reason why war should stop, so that it may give you a chance to show the world and yourself that here is a man of the future. . . . Should I die before you reach to the top step of the golden ladder, then Jack dear—if there is life after death, as you believe in—be I in heaven or hell, that is the moment when I shall stretch out a hand and try to keep you balancing on that—the most precarious of all steps."[31]

When she was not with Kennedy in Charleston, Inga was restless, counting the hours until she could see him again. When her husband asked her if she was in love with Jack, she admitted she was. She spent much of her free time with Kick and Kick's friends, who now included Torbert Macdonald, newly arrived in Washington and looking for a job, his marriage plans having fallen through. Torby continued to be anti-war and anti-Roosevelt, and to express mild resentment about Jack's successes. He felt some relief when Jack got banished to South Carolina, as it showed "I am not the only confusion maker in the country." On meeting Inga, Torby found she only wanted to talk about the love of her life, and, he wrote to Jack, "[I] controlled my nausea long enough to do a good journeyman job—she is either crazy about you or is fooling a lot of people."[32]

Later, Torby visited Jack in Charleston. Upon his return to Washington, he called Inga on the evening of February 3. The conversation was picked up by the FBI.

"Big Jack is very good and looking well," Torby said, and living in a house "right up the street from the Fort Sumter Hotel. It's a brick house on Murray Boulevard about ten [buildings] up from Sumter."

"Does he like it?"

"He is not crazy about the people whose house it is but I guess he likes it. He misses you, Inga." Together the two friends had attended the President's Ball on Friday evening, and "I discovered a new Kennedy," Torby went on. "It seems to me that he has a sort of different attitude towards girls now."

"Oh you're just kidding," she answered, though grateful for the compliment. "You're just the sweetest thing in the world."

"Does he say anything about going to sea?" she asked later in the call. "I can feel it in my bones that he is going to sea."

"If he does it will surprise him," Torby replied.[33]

Late that same night, Jack phoned Inga.

"Why don't you come here?" he said.

"I may," she replied teasingly.

"Don't say you may. I know I shouldn't ask you to come here twice in a row but I'll be up there as soon as I get permission."

"Isn't that sweet. I'll come maybe."

"I hate for you to come all this way just to see me."

"Darling, I would go around the world three times just to see you."

On they prattled, until Inga suddenly revealed what she had learned through her husband's "spies": that Jack had assured his father that he would never marry her and didn't care about her all that much. Taken aback, Jack did not deny the claim but asked what else Fejos had said.

"Why, he said I could do what I wanted. He said he was sad to see me doing things like this. I'll tell you about it and I swear that he is not bothering us and that you needn't be afraid of him. He's not going to sue you though he is aware what he could do by suing you."

"He would be a big guy if he doesn't sue me."

"He's a gentlemen," Inga stressed. "I don't care what happens, he wouldn't do things like that. He's perfectly all right."

"I didn't intend to make you mad," Jack said.

"I'm not mad. Do you want me to come this weekend very much?"

"I would like for you to."

"I'll think it over and let you know. So long, my love."

"So long."[34]

Inga did come for the weekend, and agents followed the pair's every move: "At 5:35 P.M. [on February 6], John Kennedy arrived at the Fort Sumter Hotel, driving a 1940 black Buick convertible Coupe, 1941 Florida license #6D4951, and went up to Mrs. Fejos' room. He stayed there with her until 8:40 P.M., at which time subject and Kennedy went to the mezzanine floor of the Fort Sumter Hotel for dinner. No contacts were made by the party while at dinner. At 10:03 P.M., the subject and Kennedy took a walk down Murray Boulevard framing the harbor, and returned to her room by 10:35 P.M. without making any contacts. At 1:10 A.M. the subject and Kennedy were in bed and apparently asleep."[35]

Though Hoover's agents didn't pick up on it, an air of uncertainty permeated the visit, less on account of Fejos than of Joe Kennedy, who had kept on pressuring his son to end the affair. The lovers' feelings for each other had not dissipated, but each wondered if the end was nigh. Adding to the stress was their growing certainty that they were under at least partial surveillance when they were together. In late February, following another weekend rendezvous in Charleston, Jack asked for, and received, special permission to fly briefly to Washington. There he and Inga met and talked and agreed to separate. (Unbeknownst to Jack, she had resumed contact with a Danish ex-boyfriend, Nils Blok, and, according to the FBI, spent a night with him.)[36]

In the days thereafter Jack was tormented, second-guessing his action. He called her.

"Surprised to hear from me?"

"A little, maybe."

"It's about time."

"Kathleen says every day that you will call me."

"I've been in bed with a bad back. . . . Why didn't you come [to Charleston]?"

"What a question. Don't you remember that we talked it over on Sunday?"

"I know it."

"Oh, you don't think it's going to stay?"

"Life's too short."

"Oh Kennedy!" Inga exclaimed. Was Jack going back on their agreement to split up?

"No," he replied, "not till next time I see you. I'm not too good, am I?"

"Did you think I was coming to Charleston?" she asked a little later.

"I had big hopes."

They moved to other topics, turning finally to Inga's planned divorce.

"I know that I will never go back to him."

"I just wanted to be sure that this is what you want to do. From what you have said, I didn't have anything to do with you getting the divorce."

"You pushed the last stone under my foot but that doesn't hold you responsible for anything. Meeting you two and a half months ago was the chief thing that made up my mind. As far as I'm concerned, you don't exist anymore. That's how I felt an hour ago. I still love you as much as always and always will. But you don't figure in my plans whatsoever."

"O.K."

"You know what I mean."

"Yes."

"I'm still going to [divorce him]."

"O.K."

"Drop me a line."

"I will and I'll call you next week."[37]

IV

Jack Kennedy's desk job in Charleston proved no more stimulating than the one he'd had in Washington. "Jack finds his present post rather irksome," his mother said in a round-robin letter to her children in February, "as he does not seem to have enough to do and I think will be glad to transfer." Billings would later recall that his friend found the work "a waste of time. He was very frustrated and unhappy."[38]

News from home may have added to his disaffection, though to what degree we cannot know. A few months before, in November 1941, Joe Kennedy had made a decision that would haunt him to the end of his days, and shadow his wife and children to the end of theirs. Eldest daughter Rosemary, now twenty-three, was increasingly frustrated and aggressive, feeling marooned at St. Gertrude's as she fell further and further behind her hard-driving siblings. "In the year or so following her return from England," Rose Kennedy wrote in her memoirs, "disquieting symptoms began to develop. Not only was there noticeable retrogression in the mental skills she had worked so hard to attain, but her customary good nature gave increasingly to tension and irritability. She was upset easily and unpredictable. Some of these upsets became tantrums, or rages, during which she broke things or hit out at people. Since she was quite strong, her blows were hard. Also there were convulsive episodes." At St. Gertrude's that fall there occurred troubling episodes in which Rosemary wandered out of the urban school after midnight on her own. Nuns would fan out to find her and bring her back and put her to bed, but all worried about what would happen the next time if a male stranger happened upon her and got ideas.[39]

Distraught at these developments, her parents suspected that, as Rose put it much later, "there were other factors at work besides retardation. A neurological disturbance or disease of some sort seemingly had overtaken her, and it was becoming progressively worse." Joe, always impressed by innovations in healthcare, consulted with prominent practitioners, among them Dr. Walter Freeman, the chair of the department of neurology at the George Washington University Medical School and a leading figure in the new field of psychosurgery. Following in the path of Portuguese psychiatrist Egas Moniz, who in 1935 performed the first lobotomy for relief of complex mental disorders (and in 1949 won a Nobel Prize for his work), Freeman helped pioneer the practice in the United States, performing hundreds of lobotomies with his associate, the surgeon James Watts. A charismatic and articulate self-promoter, Freeman was the subject of fawning profiles in the press—one early story, in *The New York Times* on June 7, 1937, gushed about his "new surgical technique, known as 'psycho-surgery,' which, it is claimed, cuts away sick parts of the human personality, and transforms wild animals into gentle creatures in the course of a few hours." By 1941 Freeman had convinced many experts that the lobotomy procedure was relatively harmless, with only minor side effects, and highly beneficial in many cases.[40]

The favorable coverage continued. "Few surgical events can top the dramatic simplicity of a typical frontal lobotomy as performed in an up to date hospital," enthused Marguerite Clark in *The American Mercury* in 1941. Top scientists in the field had determined that the frontal lobes were responsible for the frustration, depression, and worry experienced by some people, and further that "these unfortunates may, in some cases, be brought back to useful life by the surgical removal of the frontal lobes of the brain." An article in the May 1941 issue of *The Saturday Evening Post* that Joe and Rose may well have read highlighted the work of Freeman and Watts and praised the "sensational procedure" for transforming patients who were "problems to their families and nuisances to them-selves . . . into useful members of society," even as it also noted that some neurologists denounced the operation. It's less likely Joe and Rose read another, more specialized article, this one in the August 1941 issue of *The Journal of the American Medical Association,* that warned against the use of lobotomies until more research could be done.[41]

The nature of the communication between Kennedy and Freeman is unknown—Joe never wrote or talked about what was said, and no other records have come to light. But one can guess that Freeman impressed upon him the progressive nature of the procedure, the positive results he had seen in cases like Rosemary's, and the likelihood that the operation would alleviate the young Kennedy's depression and control her tan-trums and emerging sexual drive, thus permitting her to remain with the family for the remainder of her life. Perhaps he also articulated to Joe the astonishing thesis of the book he and Watts had just completed and were about to publish: "In the past, it's been considered that if a person does not think clearly and correctly, it is because he doesn't have 'brains enough.' It is our intention to show that under certain circumstances, an individual can think more clearly and more productively with less brain in actual operation." The results, they claimed, backed them up: 63 per-cent of their patients had improved, 23 percent had not changed, and 14 percent were in poorer condition.[42]

Kennedy evidently liked what he heard, or at least thought the risk worth taking—in his mind, it seems, the procedure was a kind of silver bullet that could simultaneously help his daughter and spare his family the embarrassments that could result from her violent outbursts and noc-turnal wanderings. And so, on a cold day in mid- or late November 1941, Rosemary was transported to the hospital and the operation was per-formed: Watts drilled two holes into her skull, inserted a surgical instru-ment, and cut the tissue connecting the frontal lobes to the rest of her brain.[43]

"The doctors told my father it was a good idea," Eunice later told an interviewer.[44]

The results were disastrous. Rosemary came out far worse than she had been before. Though in time she recovered some of her motor skills, she lost much of her memory and her speech, and her cognitive disabili-ties went from mild to severe. The surgery had destroyed a vital part of her brain, obliterating years of emotional and intellectual development and leaving her completely unable to care for herself. Thenceforth she walked with her foot turned in awkwardly, and her vocabulary would be limited to a few words. Not all of these results were known right away, but certainly the hospital staff understood immediately that things had gone horribly awry. The attending nurse was so distraught by the outcome that she left the profession, never to return.[45]

How soon Jack and his siblings came to understand the extent of the calamity that had befallen their sister is not clear. The Kennedys were a family that fetishized the appearance of unbounded success, and they were fiercely protective of one another; they could be masters of opacity and denial when the situation called for it. They had years of practice in concealing the nature of Rosemary's condition; this now continued. Soon after the operation, she was moved to Craig House, in Beacon, New York, an exclusive facility where the wealthy hid away their disabled or mentally ill family members. Joe determined that only he should have contact with the Craig House staff, and only he should visit Rosemary. Such was his authority that the rest of the family complied, even if, as Doris Kearns Goodwin suggests, "her sudden disappearance must have been met by dozens of questions that were never fully answered, surrounding the incident with an aura of forbidden mystery. . . . [Why] after all these years, did she have to be institutionalized now? And why couldn't any of the family see her? And most ominously, why wouldn't anyone really talk about what was happening?" Or, as family biographer Laurence Leamer hauntingly puts it, "In this family where all the important events of the day were discussed over the dinner table, surely it was time to confront Joe with what he had done, to have it out, to discuss, to cry, to ask God's mercy and forgiveness, and then go on. But it did not happen."[46]

Instead, a kind of erasure occurred, made possible by Joe's iron grip on the flow of information. Jean and Teddy, ages thirteen and nine, accepted their father's explanation that Rosemary had gone to teach at a school for disabled kids in the Midwest and that the doctors felt it best that she not visit her family. Eunice, her closest sibling (they had played tennis and swum as kids, hiked the Swiss Alps together, toured Notre-Dame in Paris), later said she did not know where Rosemary was for at least ten years after November 1941. Patricia and Bobby likewise seemed to be in the dark. The older trio of Joe Junior, Jack, and Kick surely knew more (Kick had helped investigate the psychosurgical options beforehand), though perhaps not much more, as their father withheld a lot of details prior to the operation and forbade visits to Rosemary afterwards. In the months to come he continued to conceal the truth—in letters to Jack in 1942 and 1943 he reported that Rosemary was "swimming every day," "looking good," "getting along quite happily," and "feeling better." In early 1944 he wrote to Joe Junior and Kick along the same circumspect lines, in almost identical language.[47]

Rose, for her part, went silent on the matter, at least as far as the family record is concerned. In an upbeat round-robin letter to her other children in December 1941, mere weeks after the operation, she chronicled the various activities of the rest of the brood but did not mention Rosemary, which was unusual. The silence continued in 1942 and 1943 and 1944—in her many group letters from these years, which averaged one or two per month, one finds not a single mention of her eldest daughter.[48]

Had Rose agreed to her daughter's operation in advance? The record is murky. In her memoirs she suggested she had, but there is fragmentary evidence that she expressed opposition to her husband beforehand and urged him not to proceed. In an interview late in life, conducted long after she wrote her memoirs, she claimed she had learned about the operation and its devastating consequences only when she visited Rosemary (in Jefferson, Wisconsin, where she had been moved in 1949) sometime after Joe suffered a stroke in 1961. Now ninety, she recalled that the operation "erased all those years of effort I had put into her. All along I had continued to believe that she could have lived her life as a Kennedy girl, just a little slower. But then it was all gone in a matter of minutes." Yet even then Rose could swiftly pivot, rationalizing that the nuns in Jefferson were "marvelous" and that "at least there was always the knowledge that she was well cared for."[49]

V

A few hours away from his sister yet somehow worlds apart, Jack passed his spare time in Charleston writing notes and letters to family and friends on the war situation, wondering if and when he would get to enter the fray. At times he turned more philosophical, as when he mused to sister Kick on the meaning of the fall of Singapore, Britain's supposedly impregnable base in Southeast Asia. "After reading the papers, I would strongly advise against any voyages to England to marry any Englishman," he wrote, referring to Kick's great love Billy Cavendish. "For I have come to the reluctant conclusion that it has come time to write the obituary of the British Empire. Like all good things, it had to come to an end sometime, and it was good while it lasted. You may not agree with this, but I imagine that the day before Rome fell, not many people would have believed that it could *ever* fall. And yet, Rome was ready for its fall years before it finally fell, though people, looking only at it through the rosy tinted glasses of its previous history, couldn't and wouldn't see it." France, too, he went on, had become a second-rate power long before her crushing defeat in 1940, and Britain was on the "toboggan" of irreversible decline.[50]

He received a boost from a letter his father had received from former paramour Clare Boothe Luce, which Joe then forwarded to Jack. Luce, who had met with Jack some weeks before, worried that the elder Kennedy's gloomy worldview was rubbing off on his children, especially his "darlyn" second son. Jack, she wrote, "has everything a boy needs to be a great success in the world, and one of the things that gives me comfort is the thought that no set of circumstances can lick a boy like Jack . . . and surely there are a lot of Jacks left in America, so we *will* be saved." At the same time, however, "he is vaguely unhappy about your pessimism. It alarms him ('so unlike Dad') and dispirits him, and I do think that you . . . and I have no right to add the burden of doubt to the other burdens that he, and a million like him, must carry from here on out." Luce went on to summarize the geopolitical situation and to call on Americans to grab hold of the challenge before them, and to fight to the utmost.[51]

Her analysis even made its way into a draft article (never published) that Jack pecked out on his typewriter in mid-February. Emphasizing the grave situation confronting the United States, he exhorted his compatriots to fight, for this war was "a serious and long business" that could not be run as a political battle. If Japanese forces prevailed against Singapore and the Dutch East Indies, "the Indian Ocean would become a Jap lake, and the Japanese position would approach invincibility." And if, in the meantime, the Germans pushed through to the Persian Gulf via Turkey, "the first phase of the war would be ended in defeat. The situation facing the Allies then would be a question of gloomy alternatives. Churchill would be thrown out of office on the recoil of these double defeats and undoubtedly appeasement forces would be busy in Britain. The tremendous strength of the German-Japanese position would make Britain feel that providing she could be given suitable guarantees in regard to the empire, peace would be preferable."

Thus, the stakes could hardly be higher, but Jack warned that the American people "might not be willing to make [the necessary] sacrifices for victory. The fundamental isolationism of [the] American character, the feeling of invulnerability bred in their bones by centuries of security behind the broad expanse of the Atlantic and the Pacific Oceans; this feeling, strengthened by the presence of a large army and navy, and air force, might cause it to prefer peace, however fitful." It was a concise summary of his father's philosophy, but Jack said it must be resisted, even if the outcome was gravely in doubt. He concluded, "We are embarked on a war that will bring either certain defeat or such blood, such sweat, and such tears that no one in America from the White House to the man in the street has ever imagined."[52]

Much to his consternation, Jack's back problems grew more severe that spring of 1942, prompting a Navy doctor at the South Carolina base to declare him unfit for duty. The pain was not constant but would come and go, though with sufficient frequency that in May he received authorization to travel to the naval hospital in Chelsea, Massachusetts, for further evaluation and treatment. While there, he also met with specialists at Boston's Lahey Clinic. Surgery was discussed, but everyone understood that it could bring an end to Jack's military career. Besides, the Navy doctors were not convinced an operation was necessary. They found no ruptured disk and surmised that tight muscles in the legs and "abnormal posture consequent thereto" were responsible for the pain. Instead of going under the knife, Jack would be prescribed a regimen of exercise and massage.[53]

Ironically, many people in this period remarked on his robust physical appearance. "You can't believe how well he looks," Rose Kennedy wrote to Joe Junior. "You can really see that his face has filled out. Instead of being lean, it has now become fat." Quite possibly, this was on account of the steroid therapy Jack appears to have begun some time before, in order to deal with his ulcerative colitis. Still in an experimental stage, with little understanding of proper dosage or possible side effects, corticosteroids may have worked as desired on the colitis, but at the possible price of back and adrenal problems. In 1947, Jack would be officially diagnosed with Addison's disease, an illness of the adrenal glands characterized by a lack of the hormones necessary to regulate blood, potassium, and sugar; it's possible that his use of the steroids contributed to the disease.[54]

On June 24, en route back to South Carolina from Boston, he made a late-night stop in Washington, D.C., in hopes of seeing Inga. He called her shortly after 1:00 A.M. and asked if he could come over. She refused but, according to the FBI, was affectionate in words and tone. She also declined to see him off at the airport later in the day, but promised to stay in touch. Jack's feelings for her had not diminished, and he called Kick frequently to muse aloud over what might have been. Yet his well-honed ability to compartmentalize had not disappeared, for to others in the family he showed his usual devil-may-care self. His clever wit, as well as his contemplative side, came out in a letter to his mother, one whose playful opening sentence suggests he did not yet know the full seriousness of Rosemary's condition:

> Thank you for your latest chapter of the "9 little Kennedys and how they grew" by Rose of Old Boston. Never in history have so many owed so much to such a one—or is that quite correct? If you would look into that little book of yours under Churchill, Winston—I imagine you can check it.
>
> They want me to conduct a Bible class here every other Sunday for about ½ hour with the sailors. Would you say that is un-Catholic? I have a feeling that dogma might say it was—but don't good works come under our obligations to the Catholic church? We're not a completely ritualistic, formalistic, hierarchical structure in which the Word, the truth, must only come down from the very top— a structure that allows for no individual interpretation—or are we?[55]

The letter was one sign among several that Jack had begun asking probing questions about his religious faith and his church. According to John B. White of the *Times-Herald*, Kick Kennedy confided to him in early May that Jack had experienced a crisis of faith and seemed on the verge of renouncing Catholicism. Perhaps his awareness—however incomplete—of Rosemary's situation disillusioned him, and perhaps his subsequent breakup with Inga, in which Catholic dogma certainly played a role (she was married, and a Protestant), also contributed. Or perhaps his questioning mostly reflected something more ordinary: a grown person's effort to make sense of the teachings inculcated in him as a child. Most people of faith will go through such phases from time to time—belief and doubt, after all, go together in intelligent minds. Whatever the case, Jack did not abandon his Christian faith or his Catholicism that spring—he continued to attend Mass faithfully, and even in the White House he got on his knees to pray before bed—but he would continue throughout his life to question aspects of organized religion. The black-and-white world of his mother he could never quite recognize; he saw too many shades of gray.[56]

One day around this time, passing a church, he said to Chuck Spalding, "How do you come out on all this?" Spalding, who had been raised a Catholic, responded that he'd never taken the time to figure it all out; if he did, he guessed he would conclude by saying, "I don't know." Jack replied that he would say the same thing.[57]

Jack's serious side also came out in a stirring speech he delivered in Charleston during an induction ceremony for new recruits, timed to coincide with a July 4 Independence Day celebration. (Why he was tapped to give it is not clear.) "For What We Fight," he titled the address, and he began by praising the Founding Fathers and the Declaration of Independence. "Some may argue that the ideals for which we fight now, those embodied in the Atlantic Charter and the Four Freedoms, are . . . impossible to achieve," Jack allowed, pointing to a world aflame with war and misery. But he insisted on the need to hold to these ideals, come what may. "A world which casts away all morality and principle—all hopeless idealism, if you will—is not a world worth living in. It is only by striving upward that we move forward."

Already now, he went on, Americans should think about the attitudes they would adopt after the guns fell silent: "Weary of war, we may fall ready victims to post-war cynicism and disillusionment, as we did at the end of the last war." It would be a dreadful mistake, for victory would be no less consequential for being incomplete. "Even if we may not win all for which we strive—even if we win only a small part—that small part will mean progress forward and that indeed makes our cause a worthy one." Then a ringing finale: Americans must strive, like their forebears, to reach for that goal, to "renew that heritage" and maintain that idealism, even in the face of great odds. "The sacrifice is not too great," the young ensign declared. "As young men, it is, after all, for our own future that we fight. And so with a firm confidence and belief in that future, let us go forward to victory."[58]

Brothers in the service: Lieutenant Junior Grade Jack and
Ensign Joe Junior, late 1942.

Would he himself get to contribute to that good fight? It seemed doubtful, given his infirmities, but through the spring he persistently lobbied for combat service. In late July 1942, there finally came welcome news: he was being transferred to midshipmen's school at Northwestern University, in suburban Chicago. On the way there, he stopped once more in Washington and called Inga. She again refused to sleep with him but agreed to meet the next day. His physical condition shocked her. In a phone call to a friend monitored by the FBI, she said, "He is going on active sea duty. Only you know, his back—he looks like a limping monkey from behind. He can't walk at all. That's ridiculous, sending him off to sea duty."[59]

One wonders about the mood overall of the young men who reported on that first day of midshipmen's training. The war news had been mostly grim since Pearl Harbor. In the months after the attack, the area of Japanese conquest spread like spilled ink on a map—Hong Kong and British Malaya fell in December 1941, followed by Singapore in February, then Burma and the Dutch East Indies (Indonesia), then the Philippines. The U.S. bases at Guam and Wake Island also succumbed.[60] Meanwhile, China grew weaker and India appeared threatened, as did Australia. In the Atlantic, German submarines were sinking ships faster than the Allies could replace them (in the first months after America's entry into the war, the U-boats sank 216 vessels, some so close to U.S. shores that people could see the glow of burning hulls), while on land the German forces resumed their advances in Russia and the British defense of Egypt faltered. By the spring of 1942, the Axis powers controlled more than a third of the world's population and mineral resources. It seemed only a matter of time before the Wehrmacht would be at the gates of India, to be met there by ally Japan, advancing from the east. In June, Jack and his mates in Charleston cheered the epic U.S. naval victory against Japan in the Battle of Midway, but the decisive nature of that encounter would become clear only in time.[61]

Despite the Japanese advances in the Pacific, Roosevelt's war strategy was "Europe First," a commitment he affirmed in a conference with Winston Churchill in Washington a few weeks after Pearl Harbor. In the president's view and those of his chief advisers, Germany represented a greater danger to the United States than did Japan. If Hitler conquered Stalin's Soviet Union, they felt certain, he would pose an acute existential threat to U.S. security. American planners also worried that the USSR, suffering almost unimaginable losses in the face of the Wehrmacht's ferocious power, might pursue a separate peace with Nazi Germany and consequently shred the Allied coalition. Washington must therefore work first with Britain and the Soviet Union to defeat the Germans, then confront an isolated Japan.

But there would still be plenty to do in the Far East in the short term, and it was the likely destination for Ensign Kennedy, given the heavy naval effort there—provided he could get through his training program. He pronounced himself less than impressed by the curriculum and the facilities. "This goddamn place is worse than Choate," he informed Lem Billings, "and Lt. J. makes Jack Maher look like a good guy—well maybe not a good guy, but a better guy. But as F.D.R. always says, this thing is bigger than you or I—it's global—so I'll string along." Jack added that he wanted to command one of the motor torpedo boats, or PTs (for "patrol torpedo"), as they were popularly known. "The requirements are very strict physically—you have to be young, healthy and unmarried—and as I am young and unmarried, I'm trying to get in. If I last we get command of a torpedo boat—and are sent abroad—where I don't know."[62]

Jack's desire for a PT command likely owed something to the remarkable publicity a handful of torpedo boats in the Philippines had received in the United States after the Japanese invasion. The papers were full of tales of the heroic deeds of these small craft and their skippers, in particular Lieutenant Commander John Bulkeley, who had won a Congressional Medal of Honor for extracting General Douglas MacArthur from the fighting on the Bataan Peninsula, in the Philippines, in March and transporting him back through five hundred miles of Japanese-dominated waters to safety. Bulkeley, a self-aggrandizing but extremely skillful promoter of the PTs, had exaggerated mightily in selling their importance to FDR and the American public. Jack bought into the hoopla. His natural skepticism made him dubious that the lightly armed vessels were inflicting as much damage on the Japanese as Bulkeley claimed, but there was an undeniable swashbuckling quality to the PT missions that appealed to him. The boats had glamour, pure and simple. And if commanding a torpedo boat got him away from the tedium of office work or—he imagined—toiling as a subordinate on a destroyer or aircraft carrier, so much the better.

And there was, one imagines, one additional reason for his attraction: on a summer day the previous year, Jack had sailed his beloved sloop *Victura* from Hyannis Port across Nantucket Sound and into Edgartown, on Martha's Vineyard. When he entered the harbor, he spied a sleek new type of vessel he had not seen before: a PT boat the Navy had brought from Newport and put on display. Mesmerized by her trim lines and powerful aura, Jack had the urge in that instant to hop on board, take the wheel, and open the throttles wide. Now perhaps he could get his opportunity.[63]

Then again, the chances of Jack Kennedy becoming a PT commander should have been vanishingly small, even leaving aside his bad back. The competition was fierce, with more than a thousand applicants for fifty slots. Yet Jack was tapped, thanks in large measure to an assist from his father, who invited Bulkeley to a leisurely lunch at the Plaza Hotel, in New York, and asked him if he had the power to get Jack into a torpedo boat.

Bulkeley said he did, and promised to interview Jack when he returned to Northwestern. Joe expressed his thanks, adding that he hoped his son would be sent someplace that wasn't "too deadly." Jack performed well in the ensuing interview, impressing Bulkeley and Lieutenant Commander John Harllee with his obvious intelligence and leadership qualities, and with the fact that he had grown up around boats and was an expert sailor who had won a regatta for Harvard. Questions regarding his physical health did not come up.[64]

To Harllee's mind there was nothing wrong with Joe Kennedy lobbying on his son's behalf: "There's a lot of people in America who use political influence to keep *out* of combat," he told a later interviewer, "but Jack Kennedy used it to get *into* combat!"[65]

VI

On October 1, 1942, Jack Kennedy commenced an eight-week PT officer training course on Narragansett Bay in Melville, Rhode Island. He was now a lieutenant, junior grade, which meant he again outranked his brother Joe, who had been promoted to ensign. And he was suffering. "Jack came home," Joe Senior wrote to Joe Junior after Jack had spent some days in Hyannis Port on his way to his new assignment, "and between you and me is having terrific trouble with his back. . . . I don't see how he can last a week in that tough grind of torpedo boats, and what he wants to do . . . is to be operated on and then have me fix it so he can get

Jack's Navy ID card.

back in that service when he gets better." If this was indeed Jack's objective, he didn't follow through: he began his Melville training on schedule a few days later. His only concession to his aches and pains was a piece of plywood he procured at a local lumberyard to put under his mattress.[66]

"He was in pain," a roommate remembered, "he was in a lot of pain, he slept on that damn plywood board all the time and I don't remember when he wasn't in pain." But Jack relished the training, most of it in Elco motor torpedo boats of the PT 103 class. Low and squat and measuring eighty feet in length, with a twenty-foot, eight-inch beam, the vessels had wooden hulls and were powered by three twelve-cylinder Packard engines, each with 1,350 horsepower, allowing a speed of forty-three knots. Each carried four twenty-one-inch torpedoes and four .50-caliber machine guns on two twin turrets, as well as depth charges, rocket launchers, and mine racks. A normal complement was two to three officers and nine men. Jack, comfortable on the sea from his many years of sailing off the Cape, loved handling the boats, and he loved their speed. Most of all, he cherished the freedom they brought. "This job on these boats is really the great spot of the Navy," he crowed to Lem, "you are your own boss and it's like sailing around in the old days."[67]

Even the evident inadequacies in the training—the men received little instruction on the handling and use of torpedoes and virtually no nighttime training, though it was well known that the PT boats were too vulnerable to enemy aircraft to operate except under cover of darkness—didn't deter him, and he impressed his mates with his seafaring skills and intelligence as well as his self-deprecating wit and lack of pretension. He was "receptive to everybody," recalled Sim Efland, a roommate, and in no way "a stuck-up individual" with a superior attitude. "When I think of my association with Jack: he associated with people no matter who—and that was unusual. Here I was, a southerner, and all these other people from Harvard, Yale, and these other places would give me hell. Say, 'We can't understand what you're talking about, you don't talk like we do, you talk too slow,' or something. Now Jack didn't do that. He respected people. He was also a good analyst, I felt. . . . I had a lot of respect for him."[68]

Another roommate, Fred Rosen, likewise held Jack in high regard, notwithstanding one rocky episode in their Quonset hut. As Rosen recalled in an interview many years afterwards, Jack one evening observed casually that Jews were all "going into the Quartermaster Corps" in order to avoid combat. Rosen, who was Jewish, bristled. "They must be good at trigonometry, Jack," he shot back. "Why?" "Because the navy's navigators are drawn from the Quartermaster Corps." An extended exchange followed, in which Rosen persuaded Jack to recant his anti-Semitic assertion. To Rosen, Jack's casual, unthinking prejudice likely owed much to his father's pontifications around the family dining table over the years, and he admired Jack all the more for his willingness to admit his error.[69]

At the end of the eight weeks, in late November, John Harllee, the senior instructor, graded Jack superior in boat handling, good in engineering, and "very willing and conscientious." So impressed was Harllee that he selected Jack to be a PT instructor, which meant he would remain stateside for a minimum of six additional months instead of getting a combat assignment. (It's possible there was more involved in the decision than Jack's stellar performance: his father had made clear to Bulkeley and perhaps to Harllee his anxiety about seeing his sons in combat.) Far from being flattered or relieved at the news, Jack reacted angrily, insisting that he be sent overseas to one of the war zones. (He was being "shafted," he said to his Navy pals, who promptly gave him the nickname "Shafty.") Harllee refused to bend. "I told him that we needed people of his ability for instructors. I absolutely insisted that he remain, which made him extremely unhappy."[70]

Jack did not give up. With the help of his grandfather Honey Fitz, he arranged a one-on-one meeting with Massachusetts senator David I. Walsh, the chairman of the Senate Naval Affairs Committee. Walsh liked what he saw—"Frankly, I have not met a young man of his age in a long time who has impressed me so favorably," he wrote to Honey Fitz. "He has a fine personality, energetic and outstanding qualities of leadership, and with all a becoming modesty"—and urged the Navy Department to transfer Jack to a combat zone.[71] The appeal evidently had an effect, for in January 1943 the young officer was detached from his Melville duties and ordered to take four boats to Jacksonville, Florida, and await further instructions on his next assignment. En route to Florida, one of the boats ran aground and Jack dove into the freezing water to clear a towrope that had become tangled in a propeller. He became ill and was laid up in Morehead City, North Carolina, with a temperature of 103, but soon recovered and rejoined his flotilla in Jacksonville. Expecting a combat assignment ("Am on my way to war," he wrote to brother Bobby, who was in his final year of prep school), Jack learned, to his annoyance, that he was being sent not to a war theater but to patrol duty at the Panama Canal. He again turned to Senator Walsh, who again wrote on his behalf.[72]

How to explain this unrelenting determination to see military action? More than a few fellow draftees, after all, whatever their subsequent claims to the contrary, were quite content to wear the uniform in safer locales, far from enemy concentrations—locales like, well, Panama. Was it because he felt invincible, as young men often do? This seems unlikely, given his checkered health history and that, even this early in the war, he was writing sober letters about college chums who had been killed or were missing in action. Did he want a war record on which he could later run for political office? Again, maybe, though it seems far-fetched to believe that this calculation drove him, even if one folds in a perceived need to overcome any lingering "Kennedys are cowards" whispers arising from his father's actions in London during the Blitz. No, the real answer seems more basic: Jack's long immersion in world politics, through reading and writing and travel, together with the inspirational exhortations of people like James Forrestal, John Bulkeley, and Clare Boothe Luce, had convinced him that this was a crusade against totalitarianism, in which the future of Western civilization was at stake and in which all must do their part. Thus he applauded Lem Billings (who had been rejected by the Army and the Navy because of his poor eyesight) for getting himself close to combat as an ambulance driver in North Africa, and Rip Horton for contemplating switching from the Quartermaster Corps to a paratrooper role. And thus he cheered brother Joe's efforts to become a Navy flier.[73]

Senator Walsh's intervention did the trick. On March 6, 1943, Lieutenant John Fitzgerald Kennedy boarded the troop carrier *Rochambeau* on pier 34 in San Francisco, bound first for San Diego for a troop pickup and then for the New Hebrides, eleven hundred miles northeast of Australia. He was on his way to the war.

TWELVE

OVERBOARD

t was like a scene out of an old Hollywood blockbuster. On March 28, 1943, after a desultory voyage of eighteen days, the *Rochambeau* neared her destination, Espiritu Santo, a Navy staging base in the New Hebrides (now Vanuatu), south of the Solomon Islands. Jack Kennedy and a fellow officer, James Reed, an Amherst College grad from Pittsfield, Massachusetts, were at the rail, taking it in. "I must say, as I look back on it, it was one of the most dramatic moments I have ever seen in my life," Reed remembered. "As we came in from the ocean into Espiritu Santo, there was a river a few hundred yards wide." The sheer tropical beauty of the tableau before them—lush green rainforests sloping down to powdery white beaches and turquoise water—stunned the two young Americans, as it had a lieutenant commander by the name of James A. Michener, whose *Tales of the South Pacific* would appear in a few short years and draw its inspiration from this very place. Quietly the *Rochambeau* entered the river, the wreckage of a sunken transport ship silently slipping by. Then, a little farther in, American "fighter planes came down and flew over us," after which came a final bend into the harbor and the magnificent sight of a large fleet—some twenty destroyers and four cruisers—riding at anchor around the aircraft carrier *Saratoga*. "Jack and I were standing looking at this thing, and I remember him saying, 'What a sight!' I mean, it really made the hair stand up on the back of your neck. It was so exciting."[1]

Just like that, they had arrived at the war. For Lieutenant John F. Kennedy, the next few months in the South Pacific would be the decisive phase of his life, would shape him like no other event. For the first time ever, he was truly on his own, ten thousand miles from his family, from his father. Here his family's fortune and his Ivy League degree would count for little. The same was true of the political and academic debates that had so consumed him during the past several years—about isolationism versus interventionism, about appeasement and its effects, about military preparedness and the fickleness of public opinion. Two months shy of his twenty-sixth birthday, Jack Kennedy was entering a new arena, the kind that had made the heroes he'd read about as a young boy.

It is perhaps meaningful that on the way across the Pacific he read John Buchan's memoir *Pilgrim's Way,* which would become one of his favorite books and which he would go back to again and again in the years to come. (He promised Reed he would send him a copy at war's end, and fulfilled his pledge.) Little remembered today, the book, a sterling example of English prose, is among other things a paean to an age when panache and daring were treasured, when the great and honorable in literature and politics and statecraft were deemed worthy of emulation. In particular, Buchan's depiction of Raymond Asquith, a young Briton whose glittering promise (his father was prime minister) was cut short by his death in the Battle of the Somme in 1916, stirred something in the combat-bound American: "There are some men whose brilliance in boyhood and early manhood dazzles their contemporaries and becomes a legend. It is not that they are precocious, for precocity rarely charms, but that for every sphere of life they have the proper complement of gifts, and finish each stage so that it remains behind them like a satisfying work of art."[2]

"He disliked emotion," Buchan added of Asquith, "not because he felt lightly but because he felt deeply." Two decades later, Ted Sorensen would use this phrase to describe John F. Kennedy.[3]

Jack's mates on the *Rochambeau* remembered him as soft-spoken and friendly. Reed spoke of a "certain aura of shyness," which "in itself was rather engaging" and which Reed emphasized was a "pure" reaction on his own part—that is, he was attracted to Jack's personality with no prior knowledge of who he was, for his new friend had introduced himself merely as "Jack." Edgar Stephens, an ensign from Missouri, remembered sitting next to Jack at the mess table. "He impressed me then as a real quiet, very nice person . . . the type of person who knew how to state a point concisely, and a man who, having chosen a position, would stand by it." When, during the first evening at sea, a spirited debate broke out about Neville Chamberlain and appeasement, Jack held firm to his long-established position but showed respect for others' views and made no attempt to bulldoze them by bringing up his book. "He always made the listener feel that he, the listener, knew a great deal more about the subject than he really did," Reed later said of the shipboard discussions. "One of his great traits."[4]

As often happens with young officers headed to a war zone with time on their hands, conversation ranged to the broad trends in the war and the strategic choices of top leaders. The previous months had seen positive developments for the Allies in both theaters. The Germans had gained against the Russians in their summer 1942 offensive against oil fields in the Caucasus, but in November the Red Army, under Generals Georgy Zhukov and Aleksandr Vasilevsky, counterattacked, surrounding the million-strong German Sixth Army at Stalingrad, on the Volga River. Fighting block by block in the deadly cold, racking up huge losses, the Russians took the city in early 1943 in what would later (but only later) be deemed a major turning point on the Eastern Front. Three hundred thousand Germans were captured, including twenty-five generals. Though the Kremlin didn't trumpet the fact, Lend-Lease aid from the United States was highly beneficial to the Soviet effort. In North Africa, meanwhile, a joint Anglo-American force drove the Germans out of Morocco, Tunisia, Algeria, and Libya, and the British and Australians scored an epic victory against General Erwin Rommel's Afrika Korps at El Alamein.[5]

In the Pacific, American success at the Battle of Midway, in June 1942, made possible landings at Guadalcanal and nearby islands in the Solomons. Furious fighting ensued amid swamps, heat, driving rain, disease, snakes, and crocodiles—not to mention screaming cockatoos—as well as an acute shortage of rations. Some eight thousand Americans died in six months of fighting, while the Japanese lost more than thirty thousand men. At sea, the Solomons campaign claimed some fifty major U.S. and Japanese warships, and many lives on both sides—when the cruiser USS *Juneau* blew up in mid-November, Mr. and Mrs. Sullivan of Waterloo,

Iowa, lost five sons. Uncertainties abounded. U.S. pilots taking off could never be sure that when they returned from their mission there would be an intact flight deck to land on; at one point the Americans had only a battleship and a damaged carrier to keep open the supply lines to the besieged Marines on Guadalcanal.[6] Little by little, however, as 1942 turned into 1943, U.S. forces gained the upper hand, on land and on sea, and the battered Japanese withdrew from Guadalcanal.

The sheer productive muscle of the United States was making itself felt—in both theaters of the war. Here in the Pacific, it announced itself through the gradual arrival of a new fleet of Essex-class aircraft carriers, starting with the *Essex*, which was commissioned in December 1942 and arrived in Pearl Harbor a few months later. The *Yorktown* and the *Intrepid* soon followed (the former renamed for the *Yorktown* lost during the Battle of Midway the previous year), and others were on the way, creating the largest carrier force in history. With a top speed of thirty-three knots, the vessels were speedier than their predecessors; they were also longer and broader, and could hold some ninety aircraft each, considerably more than their Japanese counterparts. Also coming online were several light fleet carriers (CLVs)—starting with the *Independence*, a converted cruiser, in January 1943—each capable of carrying forty-five planes.[7]

To the officers aboard the *Rochambeau*, the implications of this astonishing carrier output were at best dimly perceived. They did, however, have opinions about General Douglas MacArthur's decision to pursue an "island-hopping" campaign toward Tokyo—in essence, bypassing heavily fortified Japanese positions in favor of islands that were less well defended but still strategically significant. Some, including Lieutenant Kennedy, thought it a dubious strategy, wasteful of men and resources. But they were in no position to argue. When Franklin Roosevelt and Winston Churchill met at Casablanca in January 1943 to plot objectives for the year, they agreed among other things on a U.S.-led two-pronged westward advance through the Pacific, aimed at capturing mighty Rabaul, the heavily fortified Japanese forward base on the island of New Britain, some six hundred miles off the northeastern tip of Australia. Forces in the South Pacific under Admiral William F. Halsey would advance northward through the Solomons to Bougainville while MacArthur's Southwest Pacific units would move up the northeast coast of New Guinea, cross the Dampier and Vitiaz straits, land on New Britain, and seize control of Rabaul and its five airfields. Lack of resources soon compelled a modification, and the Joint Chiefs of Staff directed MacArthur to seek to advance only as far as Cape Gloucester, at the far end of New Britain from Rabaul, while Halsey moved up as far as southern Bougainville.[8]

The exotic names spoke to the strange and forbidding world the men were entering. Locales in the European theater might be remembered from schoolbooks, but who had heard of Leorava or Kolombangara? Where on earth was Vella Lavella? And how was one to distinguish between New Britain, New Caledonia, New Ireland, New Guinea, and the New Hebrides? Samuel Hynes, who fought on Okinawa, would write of the islands in the Pacific theater as remote, mysterious places, seemingly untethered from the continents. It was a corner of the world where people spoke in unfamiliar tongues, where there were no towns, no bars, nowhere to go, where history seemed hidden and where there were no monuments of the past, at least ones that Westerners could recognize.[9]

II

A few days after arriving in Espiritu Santo, Jack Kennedy boarded a transport vessel, LST 449, bound for Tulagi, a tiny island off Guadalcanal where his PT squadron would be based and where Halsey had ordered the erection of a giant billboard on a hillside, visible far and wide: "KILL JAPS. KILL JAPS. KILL MORE JAPS. You will help to kill the yellow bastards if you do your job well."[10]

As the ship approached the northern coast of Guadalcanal, she suddenly came under attack. The Japanese had chosen this day, April 7, to launch a major aerial assault on U.S. shipping in the area, using 177 aircraft from bases in New Georgia and Bougainville. Jack, who was in his bunk reading when the action commenced soon after 3:00 P.M., scrambled onto the deck just in time to see nine enemy planes bearing down on the 449 and the nearby destroyer *Aaron Ward*. U.S. Grumman Wildcats were racing from Henderson Field, on Guadalcanal, to engage the Japanese aircraft but had not yet arrived. A five-hundred-pound bomb splashed into the water, knocking the boat into a twenty-degree list to starboard and lifting the stern out of the water. Another bomb hit fifty feet off the port bow, and yet another just off the bridge on the starboard side. Miraculously, the 449 avoided a direct hit—she was loaded with fuel and ammunition and, if struck, might have gone up in a giant fireball—but the

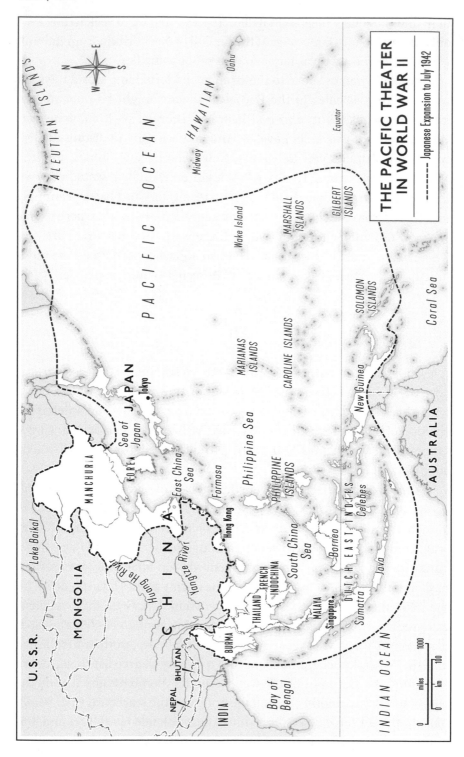

THE PACIFIC THEATER
IN WORLD WAR II

------- Japanese Expansion to July 1942

Aaron Ward was not so lucky. "They dropped all around us—and sank a destroyer next to us, but we were OK," Jack wrote coolly to Lem Billings.[11]

But the drama was not quite over, as the 449 soon came upon a downed Japanese pilot bobbing in the water some twenty yards away. To Kennedy he looked impossibly youthful, with his close-cropped, jet-black hair. "He suddenly threw aside the life belt he was wearing, pulled a pistol, and started firing," Jack wrote afterwards in a letter to his parents. "We let go with everything but he didn't seem to get hit until finally an old soldier aimed with his rifle and took the top of his head off. He leaped forward and sank out of sight. That I understand is the usual story with the officers. With the men, however, there would seem to be no such desire for the glorious death."[12]

This unvarnished realism would be a theme in Jack's letters home in the weeks to come, both before and after he assumed command of his boat—PT 109—on April 25. He'd gotten an early lesson in the perils of combat and the die-hard commitment of the enemy, and it gave him pause. His training, he realized, had not prepared him for the arena he had now entered, as he relayed in an early letter to Torby Macdonald. To Inga Arvad he wrote that a visit to the "very simple grave" of George Mead, a friend from Cape Cod whom Inga had met and who had been killed in the fighting for Guadalcanal, was "about the saddest experience I've ever had, and enough to make you cry." When he learned from home that "all the nuns and priests along the Atlantic coast" were "putting in a lot of praying time" on his behalf, Jack was comforted but said he hoped "it won't be taken as a sign of lack of confidence in you all or the Church if I continue to duck."[13]

All the signs pointed to a long and brutal struggle, he surmised, though one that his side, with its technological superiority and immense productive capacity, would probably ultimately win. "Our stuff is better," he wrote in an early letter. "Our pilots and planes are—everything considered—way ahead of theirs—and our resources are inexhaustible—though this island to island stuff isn't the answer. If [the U.S. commanders] hold to that motto out here 'The Golden Gate by 48' won't even come true."[14]

It struck Kennedy that few of the men he met who had been in the war zone for any length of time expressed any longing for combat—they just wanted to get home alive. ("It's one of those interesting things about the war," he told Inga, "that everyone in the States . . . want[s] to be out here killing Japs, while everyone out here wants to be back. It seems to me that someone with enterprise could work out some sort of exchange, but as I hear you saying, I asked for it, honey, and I'm getting it.") Nor did anyone have many good words for the high command. When told by his parents of MacArthur's popularity in the United States, Jack answered, "Here he has none—is, in fact, very, very unpopular. His nickname is 'Doug-Out-Doug,' " for his alleged refusal to use Army forces to relieve the Marines at the time of the first invasion of Guadalcanal, and for not coming out of his "dugout" in Australia. "No one out here has the slightest interest in politics—they just want to get home—morning—noon—and night. . . . I didn't mean to use 'They'—I meant 'WE.' " It all meant, he added, that Joe Junior, who had received his wings the previous year but was still stateside, should be in no hurry to get out to the South Pacific. "I know it's futile to say so, but if I were he I would take as much time about [it] as I could."[15]

The local commanders seemed scarcely better than the top brass. "Just had an inspection by an Admiral," he informed Inga in one witty passage. "He must have weighed over three hundred, and came bursting through our hut like a bull coming out of chute three." At the machine shop, the admiral seemed confused about its purpose.

> After it was gently but firmly explained to him that machinery was kept in the machine shop, and he had written that down on the special pad he carried for such special bits of information which can only be found "if you get right up to the front and see for yourself" he harrumphed again, looked at a map, wanted to know what we had *there*—there being a small bay some distance away. When we said nothing, he burst out with, "well, by God, what we need is to build a dock." Well, someone said it was almost lunch and it couldn't be built before lunch. . . . After a moment of serious consideration and a hurried consultation with a staff of engineers he agreed and toddled off to stoke his furnace at the luncheon table. . . . That, Binga, is total war at its totalest.[16]

Jack's concerns with his situation may have owed something to his dawning realization that the PT boats, however glamorous in the popular imagination, were of questionable military utility. Fast, nimble, and versatile, their prows riding high in the water, the boats could make hit-and-run attacks in narrow waters or close to land, and they were excellent for rescuing downed fliers and trapped Marines. But their torpedoes, designed in the 1920s, were outmoded and had to be launched through tubes that often caught fire. The torpedoes were also slow, traveling at a speed of only twenty-eight knots, insufficient to catch the faster-moving Japanese vessels. To compound the problem, the guns were inadequate and the radios frequently conked out. Worst of all, with their thin mahogany shells (two layers of one-inch planking) and heavy fuel loads, the PTs were, to say the least, combustible, prone to turning into floating infernos when hit. Both in Melville and on Tulagi, Kennedy was drilled on the importance of avoiding detection by enemy aircraft and ships, which meant, above all, operating under the cloak of darkness and moving stealthily. It took guts to make your close approach in this way—the enemy could obliterate you in an instant if his lookouts ever saw you.[17]

"The glamour of the PT's just isn't except to the outsider," he wrote his sister Kick after reading a John Hersey *Life* magazine feature on the boats. "It's just a matter of night after night patrols at low speed in rough water—two hours on- -then sacking out and going on again for another

Lieutenant Kennedy on board PT 109, July 1943.

two hours." Even so, Jack continued, the position was "a hell of a lot better" than any other in the Navy. "As a matter of fact this job is somewhat like sailing, in that we spend most of our time trying to get the boat running faster."[18]

James Michener offered a more unvarnished assessment in *Tales of the South Pacific*: "I have become damned sick and tired of the eyewash written about PT boats. I'm not going to add to that foolish legend. . . . They shook the stomachs out of many men who rode them, made physical wrecks of others for other reasons. They had no defensive armor. In many instances they were suicide boats. In others they were like human torpedoes. . . . Even for strong tough guys from Montana it was rugged living."[19]

PT 109 had already seen considerable action by the time Kennedy assumed command. Produced by the Electric Launch Company (Elco) and plunked into the oily waters off Bayonne, New Jersey, the previous June, the boat had performed well in early testing runs and by September 1942 was en route to the South Pacific, where she soon saw heavy action north of Guadalcanal around the turn of the year. By April 1943 she was grimy and battle-scarred, infested with rats and roaches, and in need of an engine overhaul and a general sprucing up; mechanics at the Sasape port, on Tulagi, worked on the engines while Jack and his crew performed the cosmetic work of cleaning and painting. They were a varied lot, all but one chosen by Jack (Ensign Leonard "Lennie" Thom, the executive officer, a barrel-chested bear of a man who had played tackle at Ohio State, had only recently come on board under the previous commander and so stayed put), and they appreciated that he got right down to work with them, scraping and painting the bottom of the boat. Jack had learned that a good PT crew stuck together, enlisted men and officers alike.[20]

Action was sparse in the early weeks—a lull had set in after the Allied victory at Guadalcanal—which gave Jack time to arrange for flowers to be sent to his mother for Mother's Day and to write letters home, all of them thoughtful, some of them vivid and evocative.[21] "On good nights it's beautiful," he wrote his parents in mid-May. "The water is amazingly phosphorescent—flying fishes which shine like lights are zooming around and you usually get two or three porpoises who lodge right under the bow and no matter how fast the boat keep just about six inches ahead of the boat. It's been good training. I have an entirely new crew and when the showdown comes I'd like to be confident they know the difference between firing a gun and winding their watch."[22]

On land, the conditions were rougher, with heavy rains every day that caused his blue uniform to grow a quarter-inch-thick "green-mold," and primitive living quarters featuring huts with no walls in which the rats and roaches roamed at will. Yet Jack kept his sense of esprit de corps and his quick humor, a fact much appreciated by his crew and, no doubt, by his family. To Kick he remarked wistfully that his vision of "lying on a cool Pacific island with a warm Pacific maiden hunting bananas for me is definitely a bubble that has burst." Even swimming was a no-no: "There's some sort of fungus in the water that grows out of your ears—which will be all I need. With pimples on my back, hair on my chest and fungus in my ears I ought to be a natural for the old sailors home in Chelsea, Mass."[23] Then again, he was an officer, which, he deadpanned to his parents, brought certain perks: "They have just opened up an Officer's Club which consists of a tent. The liquor served is an alcoholic concoction which is drawn out of the torpedo tubes, known as torp juice. Every night at about 7:30 the tent bulges, about five men come crashing out, blow their lunch and stagger off to bed. This torp juice, which is the most expendable item on the island, makes the prohibition stuff look like Haig and Haig but probably won't do any one any permanent harm as long as their eyes hold out."[24]

Kennedy himself seldom touched alcohol, and he was not much for card playing, preferring instead to sit around and talk or write letters or read. (Among his companions: Tolstoy's *War and Peace*.) With someone else, such seemingly "refined" preferences might have caused grousing among the men, but by all accounts—contemporaneous as well as retrospective—Kennedy was liked and respected for his sunny demeanor and his wit as well as his calm self-possession and unflappability. Lennie Thom, who, in addition to being Jack's executive officer, roomed with him, wrote his fiancée that he liked Jack from the moment they met. A second roommate, Johnny Iles, felt the same, while a third appreciated that the young Kennedy wore his celebrity status lightly and did not act like the Ivy League son of an ambassador. "He just seemed like the ordinary young fellow—just like Lennie and Johnny." Radioman John Maguire, for his part, recalled, "I knew just three things about him. The kid himself was a millionaire. His father was an ambassador. And once, when a ship's carpenter bawled the hell out of him for accidentally splashing some water on him, the lieutenant just stood there in his skinny green shorts and said, 'Excuse me,' and let it go at that. The carpenter did a lot of gulping later when he found out the kid was PT 109's skipper."[25]

The squadron commander, too, evidently liked what he saw. He gave Jack a perfect 4.0 in "ship-handling" and a 3.9 for his ability to command.[26]

III

That ability to command would soon be tested. In June 1943, preparations began at the key staging bases in the South Pacific—at Guadalcanal and Tulagi and farther south at Nouméa, in New Caledonia—for a major Allied offensive designed to capture the New Georgia islands (where the Japanese had an important airfield at Munda Point) and then oust the Japanese from New Guinea. Suddenly the PT night patrols took on new significance, as the boats were to disrupt Japanese supply vessels, most of them destroyers escorting reinforcements through the New Georgia Sound, the sea lane running through the middle of the Solomon archipelago, which U.S. commanders referred to as "the Slot." The supply ships they called the "Tokyo Express."[27]

The PT 109 crew off Guadalcanal, July 1943. Back row, from left: Allan Webb, Leon Drawdy, Edgar Mauer, Edmund Drewitch, John Maguire, and Jack Kennedy. Front row, from left: Charles Harris, Maurice Kowal, Andrew Kirksey, and Lennie Thom.

PT 109 was dispatched to the Russell Islands, southeast of New Georgia, and then, in July, to the epicenter of the war zone, west of New Georgia near Lumberi Island, in the mid-Solomons. Japanese aircraft struck frequently, seeking to destroy bases and ships and to regain the air superiority over the area that they had lost in recent months. On the night of August 1, Lieutenant Kennedy's boat was one of fifteen PTs sent from Rendova Harbor into Blackett Strait, in four groups, in order to try to intercept a Rabaul-based Japanese transport convoy streaming southward to Vila, on the southern tip of Kolombangara, laden with supplies as well as nine hundred soldiers. One of the Japanese ships, the two-thousand-ton destroyer *Amagiri*, carried thirteen officers and 245 men under Lieutenant Commander Kohei Hanami, a compact, muscular thirty-four-year-old graduate of Etajima, the Japanese naval academy. Hanami's superior, Captain Katsumori Yamashiro, commander of the 11th Destroyer Flotilla, was also aboard the *Amagiri* that night.

The fifteen PT boats were quite a sight—and sound—rumbling to life in the harbor, each with three engines of twelve cylinders each. Five hundred and forty cylinders drummed in unison. The sun had dipped below Lumberi Island, and the sleek boats looked menacing in the twilight, their guns pointed to the sky. Engines growling, the boats mustered by division, and Kennedy maneuvered through traffic to fall in behind PT 159, PT 157, and PT 162 in Lieutenant Henry J. Brantingham's Division B. This division had the farthest to go, having been assigned the station on the Kolombangara coast off Vanga Vanga, about forty miles away, so it moved out first, followed by the other three groups. Off the starboard side, barely visible in the fading light, the crews could just make out the low-slung coastal hills of New Georgia. Behind them, cloaked in a thin cloud, was the top of Rendova Peak, rising 3,400 feet.*[28]

One wonders if Kennedy, as he steered his boat into the night, reflected

---

* Jack's crew aboard PT 109 that night consisted of: Executive Officer Leonard "Lennie" Thom, Sandusky, Ohio; Ensign George "Barney" Ross, Highland Park, Illinois; Seaman First Class Raymond Albert, Akron, Ohio; Gunner's Mate Second Class Charles A. "Bucky" Harris, Watertown, Massachusetts; Motor Machinist's Mate William Johnston, Dorchester, Massachusetts; Torpedoman Andrew Jackson Kirksey, Reynolds, Georgia; Radioman John E. Maguire, Dobbs Ferry, New York; Motor Machinist's Mate Harold W. Marney, Springfield, Massachusetts; Seaman First Class Edgar E. Mauer, St. Louis, Missouri; Motor Machinist's Mate Patrick ("Pappy" or "Pop") McMahon, Wyanet, Illinois; Torpedoman Second Class Raymond Starkey, Garden Grove, California; and Motor Machinist's Mate Gerard E. Zinser, Belleville, Illinois.

on a comment he'd made in a letter to his family mere days before: "I myself am completely and thoroughly convinced that nothing is going to happen to me. I think this is probably the way everyone feels—someone else, yes—themselves no. Feeling that way makes me anxious to see as much of it as possible and then to get out of here and back home. The more you see [the war], the quicker you get out—or so they tell us."[29]

By 9:30 P.M. the PT boats had reached their respective patrolling stations without incident. It was a moonless, starless night, so dark that it was hard to tell where the water ended and the sky began. At around midnight the Japanese destroyers passed through the strait, and some minor skirmishing occurred involving a few PTs, whereupon the destroyers continued on their way. Poor communication among the PTs meant that several of the boats without radar, including Kennedy's 109, did not know what had occurred. The 159 and the 157, having fired their torpedoes, left the scene, leaving Kennedy's boat as well as Lieutenant John Lowrey's 162 behind. The two skippers stayed put, patrolling at idling speed and straining their eyes in the darkness looking for ships they didn't know had already passed through. To conserve fuel and reduce the size of their wake so it wouldn't be spotted by enemy boats or aircraft, Kennedy and Lowrey throttled down, operating on only one of three engines. A third boat, the 169, under the command of Lieutenant Phil Potter, emerged out of the blackness to join them. He, too, throttled down. The three boats now formed a picket line as they continued their slow patrol. Unbeknownst to them, the Japanese convoy had already discharged their cargoes and were now on the way back up the strait.[30]

At 2:27 A.M., a silhouette suddenly appeared out of the darkness off Kennedy's starboard bow, some two to three hundred yards away. *Must be another PT boat that will soon veer off,* the men thought. So did the crews on the 162 and the 169, who spotted the vessel at about the same time. But it kept coming, and suddenly everyone on the 109 understood what was happening: a Japanese destroyer was bearing down on them, like some charging skyscraper. Kennedy turned the wheel, but it was too late—with only his center engine in gear, he had no hope of maneuvering out of harm's way, or of firing his torpedoes. Maguire grabbed his Miraculous Medal and had just begun to say, "Mary, conceived without sin, pray for us," when the *Amagiri* sliced into the starboard bow of the 109 at a twenty-degree angle, shearing off a portion of the boat, then moved on into the night.[31]

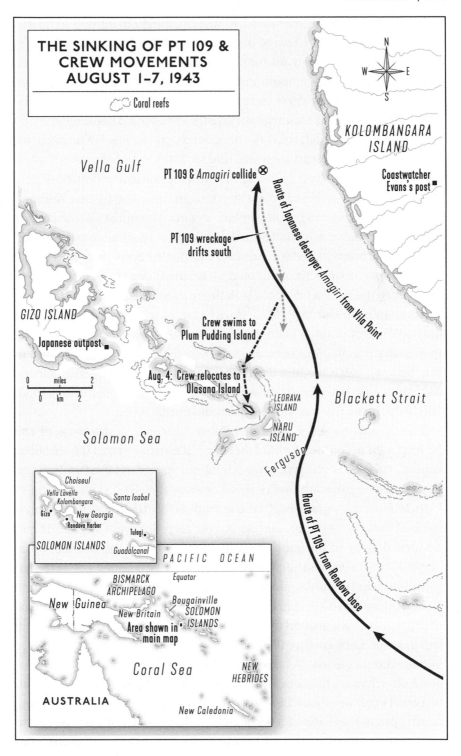

**THE SINKING OF PT 109 &
CREW MOVEMENTS
AUGUST 1–7, 1943**

Coral reefs

Vella Gulf

PT 109 & *Amagiri* collide ⊗

PT 109 wreckage
drifts south

*KOLOMBANGARA
ISLAND*

Coastwatcher
Evans's post ▪

Route of Japanese destroyer Amagiri from Vila Point

GIZO ISLAND

Japanese outpost ▪

0   miles   2
0   km   2

Crew swims to
Plum Pudding Island

Aug. 4: Crew relocates to
Olasana Island

*LEORAVA
ISLAND*

Blackett Strait

*NARU
ISLAND*

Solomon Sea

Ferguson

Route of PT 109 from Rendova base

Choiseul

Vella Lavella
Kolombangara

Santa Isabel

Gizo •
New Georgia
Rendova Harbor

Tulagi •

SOLOMON ISLANDS

Guadalcanal

PACIFIC OCEAN

*BISMARCK
ARCHIPELAGO*

Equator

New Guinea

New Britain

Bougainville
SOLOMON
ISLANDS

Area shown in ▪
main map

Coral Sea

*NEW
HEBRIDES*

AUSTRALIA

New Caledonia

"This is how it feels to be killed," Kennedy thought to himself as he was thrown onto the deck.[32] Two of his men—Machinist's Mate Harold Marney, who was in the forward turret, and Torpedoman Andrew Kirksey, who had had strong premonitions of death in the days prior—perished more or less instantly; their bodies were never found. But Jack and ten others on the boat miraculously survived, most of them floating amid the debris and burning fuel, some of them barely conscious. Fortunately for them, the *Amagiri*'s churning wake had sucked most of the flames away from the wreckage, even as it cast the entire scene in a phantasmagoric light. Half of the wrecked boat stayed afloat, and one by one the men made their way over to it and climbed aboard. Machinist's Mate Patrick McMahon, however, who had been belowdecks at the time of the collision and then had been carried some distance under the destroyer's propellers, was too burned to make it on his own, so Kennedy dove back in and towed him back to the boat, a laborious task that took the better part of an hour. He also hauled in Gunner's Mate Bucky Harris, who'd badly hurt his leg and could barely swim. ("For a man from Boston, you're certainly putting up a great exhibition out here, Harris," Kennedy said. Harris told him to go to hell.) Maguire, meanwhile, rescued Machinist's Mate Gerard Zinser, and Lennie Thom hauled in William Johnston, another machinist's mate who had inhaled gasoline fumes and could hardly move.[33]

The cacophony subsided and stillness returned. With eleven of the thirteen men accounted for and on board, the men of the 109 set about waiting. They knew the wreckage would not stay afloat forever. Initially, they expected either an enemy vessel or the other PTs to happen upon them, but no boats appeared. In the seconds before the collision, Lowrey's 162 had tried to attack the *Amagiri*, but the torpedoes didn't fire and Lowrey turned away to the southwest. Immediately after the ramming, the 169 fired two torpedoes that missed their target, whereupon Potter moved out of the vicinity. The two skippers would later say they thought the crew of the 109 had been killed in the collision or the flames, so there would be no point in sticking around in these dangerous waters, with more enemy destroyers perhaps coming through.

Some hours passed. "As dawn came up," one crewman recalled, "we found ourselves on the boat with the boat under water all the way up to the bow. There was about 15 feet of the boat, which was 80 feet long, still sticking out of the water at a 45 degree angle, right side up."[34] They were deep in hostile territory, with Kolombangara to the east, Vella Lavella to the northwest, and the Gizo anchorage to the west-southwest. All were enemy-held, and the airstrip on Gizo was close enough that Kennedy and his men could see Japanese Zekes and Zeros taking off and landing.

As the morning progressed, the PT took on more water and began to turn her keel; soon she would disappear altogether in the dark blue waters. Jack asked the men for their suggestions on what to do—"There's nothing in the book about a situation like this," he said—and they made clear that the decision was his. He determined that they would swim to a coral island that could just be made out on the horizon some miles away, east of Gizo. He guessed that the island was too small to be enemy-held, but he could not be sure. Nor could he know if sharks were lurking nearby. They would have to chance it. Kennedy ordered the most severely hurt crew members and the poorest swimmers to hold on to a two-by-eight-foot plank (which had been part of the 37-millimeter gun mount) from which they would paddle along while he towed the ailing McMahon, holding the strap of the engineer's life jacket in his teeth.[35]

"Will we ever get out of this?" someone asked.

"It can be done," Kennedy replied. "We'll do it."[36]

Thus began an epic swim across Blackett Strait—in broad daylight, with the enemy close at hand. Four hours it would last. Jack would do the breaststroke for ten or fifteen minutes, rest a little while, then resume swimming, all the while reassuring McMahon and the other men that they were getting closer to their destination. Near sundown they finally made it, reaching the sandy beach of their precious refuge, Plum Pudding Island (known to locals as Kasolo), which turned out to be not much bigger than a football field and was partly covered in brush. There were coconuts in a handful of trees, but none within reach. A quick scan confirmed Jack's hunch: no Japanese in sight. Utterly exhausted, he lay panting, his feet in the water and his head in the sand. His back throbbed. When at last he stood up, he vomited, on account of all the salt water he had swallowed. Gradually, he and McMahon made their way up the beach and collapsed under a bush as the others neared the island on their plank.[37]

Back at Tulagi and Rendova, meanwhile, word had spread rapidly about the ramming of the 109. The boat had exploded and been totally consumed by fire, reports indicated, and all men aboard were assumed dead. Preparations were made for a memorial service. Paul "Red" Fay, a spry and convivial PT officer who had met Jack briefly at Melville and later became a good friend—and would serve as undersecretary of the Navy in the Kennedy administration—despaired at the news, especially as his close pal George "Barney" Ross was on board. Fay wrote his sister, "George Ross lost his life for a cause he believed in stronger than any one of us, because he was an idealist in the purest sense. Jack Kennedy, the Ambassador's son, was on the same boat and also lost his life. The man that said the cream of a nation is lost in war can never be accused of making an overstatement of a very cruel fact."[38]

On his tiny island, Kennedy now had to calculate the odds of being rescued by Allied forces versus being found by the enemy. A Japanese barge floated by close to the shoreline; the men hid as best they could and breathed a sigh of relief when the vessel continued gently on its way. Next time they might not be so lucky. Time was also a factor, with McMahon in bad shape and several of the others, notably William Johnston, also suffering. With friendly boats unlikely to come into this part of Blackett Strait, Kennedy determined that, come evening, he would swim alone into Ferguson Passage, one of the approaches into the strait, in the hope of signaling a PT boat out on patrol. His usual approach in his young life—letting events come to him, being the detached if often perspicacious observer—would not suffice here, he realized. He had to seize control, had to bend destiny to his will. It was a brave idea, and a long shot. Even if an Allied skipper somehow spotted the lone light flashing in the darkness, would he really take his craft over to investigate? And if he did, who's to say he or an overeager crew member wouldn't shoot first and ask questions later? Kennedy acknowledged the odds against him, but he had no better idea, and doing nothing was tantamount to suicide. The men agreed, or at least offered no resistance.[39]

As darkness fell, Kennedy stripped down to his underwear, grabbed the battle lantern, and went on his way. To protect his feet from the coral, he wore shoes. On a lanyard around his neck hung his .38 revolver.

The eeriness of that night would stay with him always. Exotic creatures flitted about near him in the water, and he worried about the presence of sharks and barracuda. Much of the time, not a sound could be heard other than his own breathing and swim strokes. He was alone in the world. For a time he could rest, standing in waist-deep water on the barrier reef. As the hours went by, Kennedy realized there would be no rescue that night—by the flares in the far distance he could see that the PTs were patrolling elsewhere. He turned to swim back to his men, making steady progress until suddenly the current began taking him sideways. He fought it as best he could, swimming harder and ditching his shoes, but fatigue overtook him and he surrendered to the tide, to the immensity, to the blackness. He drifted, clutching his lantern, not sure whether he would live or die, until in the predawn hours he found himself near the tiny islet of Leorava. He straggled onto the beach, his feet bleeding from the coral, his back aching, and promptly fell asleep. Upon waking shortly after dawn, he swam the half mile back to Plum Pudding Island, collapsing in exhaustion as soon as he laid eyes on Lennie Thom and Barney Ross.[40]

That evening Ross took his turn swimming out into the strait; again, no friendly boat appeared. Hunger was now a major concern, and thirst even more so, so Jack decided the group would take to the water again, bound for Olasana Island, a slightly larger atoll to the south. The journey, on the morning of August 4, took close to three hours against a strong current, Jack again towing McMahon by a strap between his teeth, and it proved a wise move: Olasana had coconuts, in the trees and on the ground, that provided crucial sustenance. But rescue seemed as far away as ever, so on the following day Kennedy and Ross set out once more, swimming to a still larger island, Naru (also known as Cross Island), directly on Ferguson Passage. Here they happened upon a damaged one-man canoe as well as small bags of Japanese candy and crackers and a drum of potable rainwater. They also spotted, some distance away, what appeared to be two native islanders in a canoe. Kennedy and Ross waved at them to stop, but the men, afraid that they were Japanese, paddled frantically away.[41]

When Kennedy returned to Olasana late that night (Ross had stayed behind on Naru), he was astonished to see the same two locals there, communing with the men of PT 109. Their names were Biuku Gasa and Eroni Kumana, and they were teenage scouts working for the Allies. A new excitement gripped the Americans: could this be the break they needed? Kennedy persuaded Biuku to paddle him back to Naru for another attempt at flagging down a friendly boat in Ferguson Passage. The effort failed, but, at Biuku's suggestion, Jack scrawled a now famous message on the husk of a coconut: NAURO ISL COMMANDER NATIVE KNOWS POSIT HE CAN PILOT 11 ALIVE NEED SMALL BOAT KENNEDY. Biuku and Eroni took the coconut, along with a handwritten note by Thom, and made for the Rendova base, some thirty-eight miles away, through dangerous waters. En route, the two men stopped off at a nearby island to inform a fellow scout of the news; he in turn informed an Australian coastwatcher (an intelligence operative who observed enemy ship and troop movements, and also helped rescue stranded Allied personnel), Lieutenant A. Reginald Evans, who promptly dispatched seven of his scouts to Olasana in a large canoe laden with food, drink, and cigarettes.[42]

The scouts carried a message for Kennedy: "I strongly advise that you come with these natives to me. Meanwhile, I shall be in radio communication with your authorities at Rendova and we can finalize plans to collect the balance of your party."[43] The following day, Saturday, August 7, the islanders brought Jack, who was hidden under ferns in the boat, to the Australian's camp. From there, things moved rapidly. The brass at Rendova, fearing it could be a trap to lure American forces into an ambush, allotted only one boat to the rescue attempt, William "Bud" Liebenow's PT 157, which got to the scene without incident.

"Where the hell you been?" Kennedy shouted when the boat picked him up en route to Olasana, shortly after 11 P.M.

"We got some food for you," Liebenow called back.

"No, thanks," Kennedy answered. "I just had a coconut."[44]

Soon all eleven men were aboard PT 157 and on their way to Rendova for medical attention, arriving there at 5:30 A.M. on August 8. Their ordeal was over, seven days after it began.

IV

In due course, many questions would be raised about what happened to PT 109 on that moonless night of August 1–2, and why. Some questioned why John F. Kennedy's boss, Lieutenant Commander Thomas G. Warfield, did not make a more determined effort to locate and rescue survivors after learning of the disaster. He could have done more, certainly, but given that he was assured by Potter and Lowrey that Kennedy's boat had gone up in a ball of flames, with "nothing left," one can see why he didn't. U.S. planes did search the area on August 3, but not until dusk, by which point Kennedy and his men were hiding in the bushes on the island. But why didn't Potter and Lowrey come to the rescue immediately after the fiery crash? The two commanders were clearly unnerved by the sight of the Japanese destroyer slicing through the 109, and they worried that other enemy vessels were nearby. If an understandable reaction, it was also a problematic one. Potter insisted in the face of questions that he spent thirty or more minutes crisscrossing the crash site looking for survivors but did not find any. Several of his crew members disavowed the claim, saying no serious effort at rescue was made.[45]

Kennedy's own actions have been subjected to endless scrutiny over the years. To many journalists and historians he was a hero, particularly for his decisions and his leadership after the ramming. To these analysts his exploits showed his poise, tenacity, bravery, resourcefulness, and imperturbability under intense pressure. Critics, however, have wondered how a commander of a PT boat—a vessel whose great asset was its speed and agility—would ever allow himself to be rammed. In particular, they questioned why Kennedy was sitting in the middle of the strait with only one of his three engines in gear. It may have reduced the amount of churning that could be spotted by enemy boats and planes, but it also made it impossible for him to make a quick escape. Kennedy himself acknowledged afterwards that when he saw the destroyer, he had pushed the throttle forward, stalling his engines. He had neglected to open his flaps first.[46]

Overall, though, the principal failure that night lay not with the skipper of PT 109, his crew, or the other PT commanders but with the broader tactics and circumstances beyond their control. Only four of the fifteen torpedo boats in the operation had radar (Kennedy's was not among them), a handicap under any circumstances but especially on a jet-black night. Was it really reasonable to expect the other eleven commanders, instructed to stay off their radios for the most part, to either follow the lead PTs or spot enemy vessels on their own, using nothing but their eyes to guide them? As it was, the radar-equipped boats in the squadron, having fired their torpedoes, hurried back to base, leaving the other boats to fend for themselves. "Abandoned by their leaders and enjoined to radio silence, the remaining PT boats had no real chance, in pitch dark, of ambushing the Japanese destroyers," one of the skippers said later.[47] For his part, the division leader, Brantingham, had done little before the mission to explain tactics and procedures to the other three commanders in his group, a problem made worse by the fact that the radios on the boats periodically lost their frequencies. As for Kennedy's decision to operate with only the center engine engaged, that was good and sensible PT doctrine for night patrol—Lowrey and Potter were doing the same at the time of the collision. They knew what Kennedy knew: that a phosphorescent wake was a golden invitation to Japanese aircraft to attack.

The ramming of PT 109 was more a freak accident than anything else. From the moment the *Amagiri* loomed up out of the dark night, Kennedy had perhaps ten seconds to get clear before being hit—a tall order for anyone in his position. Nor did his Japanese counterpart have appreciably more time; Hanami spotted the American boat at about the same time Jack spotted his. There is some question as to whether Hanami tried to avoid ramming the 109 or did so on purpose. He would subsequently say he did it intentionally, the better to protect his own vessel, but Captain Yamashiro, his superior, insisted that he had ordered Hanami to avoid a collision—he worried that the PT would explode on impact and thereby damage or sink the destroyer—but that there was no time to act on the command.[48]

Critics would also fault Kennedy's decision to swim alone into Ferguson Passage, calling it reckless and futile. Perhaps it was, but the solo effort nonetheless speaks to Kennedy's courage, stamina, and refusal to be defeated. He was a strong swimmer, having competed in meets since boyhood and suited up for Harvard. It's surely meaningful that his attempt, unsuccessful though it was, earned him the undying respect and devotion of his crew. None of them had a word of criticism about how their commander acted after the collision, either then or later.[49]

Squadron commander Al Cluster, writing home to his parents, said Kennedy was "one of the finest officers I have. He did commendable work in getting his crew out O.K. and we're all very proud of him. Somehow, when we heard of his boat going down, I could not believe that he was lost. He's just that type of fellow. You know that he can take care of himself and you can always depend on him." Of Kennedy's family and fame, Cluster went on, they "never enter into any of our thoughts here. I've only known him about six months but I am proud to serve with him in my outfit. Whatever he does, he earns solely by his capabilities and not by the prestige of his name. People like that make me realize what an American is, something you find nowhere else in this world—men and women achieving ends in spite of their background. In fact, I'd say it would be just as hard for a boy like Jack to make good as it is for a kid from the slums. Both have disadvantages to overcome. No one out here has done a better job than Jack."[50]

Ultimately, Jack Kennedy deserves no accolades for losing the first boat he commanded in the war, but he does merit praise for his resourceful and, yes, heroic actions on behalf of his crew, and in particular Pat McMahon. The initial swim from the wreckage, in which Kennedy pulled the severely burned engineer along for close to four hours, was by any measure an extraordinary feat, as McMahon's recollection makes clear: "I knew he was in no great shape himself; he had been bounced down bad by the ramming. And he never looked more than 140 pounds to me, even on a good day, and today was no good day. But he was swimming for both of us now and not counting the cost. He'd pull and rest, pull and rest, and say, 'How are you, Mac?' to keep my spirits up."[51]

Author Garry Wills, hardly uncritical in his assessment of John F. Kennedy's life and career, notes the Kennedys' later willingness to embellish the PT 109 story to suit Jack's political purposes, yet also concludes, "The heroism was real. Kennedy saved the life of Patrick McMahon. He undertook the most dangerous assignments in looking for rescuers. His physical courage can never be questioned."[52]

The military evidently felt the same way. Some months after the incident, Kennedy would be awarded the Navy and Marine Corps Medal, the Navy's highest award for gallantry, for his actions. He also received a Purple Heart.[53]

V

In Hyannis Port, Joseph P. Kennedy had received confidential word soon after the initial disaster in Blackett Strait that Jack was missing. Precisely who told him is not known, but likely it was a contact in the Navy Department. Kennedy opted not to tell Rose, instead spending agonizing days wondering alone what had happened and fearing the worst. He had wanted desperately to keep his sons out of the war, but when they made clear their determination to serve and to see action, he had supported them to the hilt and, in Jack's case, had even pulled strings to get him his PT assignment. Now the nightmare seemed to be coming true.

It says something about Joe Kennedy's stoicism—and perhaps the nature of his marriage—that he would keep such devastating information from his wife. Rose, it seems, first learned of the rescue on August 19. "*The Globe* called me up about 8:20 in the morning," she wrote her children in a round-robin letter, "when I was in your father's room waiting to hear the morning radio news. Of course, I was very much surprised and excited and I told them I would contact your father, who had gone over to the farm for his early morning ride. . . . Dad knew he was missing for two weeks, although he gave no sign—for which I am very thankful—as I know we should all have been terribly worried. He just complained about his arthritis and I said it was funny he was nervous now, little knowing what he had to be nervous about."[54]

Her husband was driving back from his horseback ride that morning of the nineteenth when he, too, heard the happy news on the car radio. He was so overcome with joy, he later told his son Teddy and his nephew Joey Gargan, that he momentarily lost control of the car and drove into a field.[55]

A day or two later, there arrived at the Cape a letter that Joe and Rose read and reread, and then read again. "Dear Folks, This is just a short note to tell you that I am alive—and not kicking—in spite of any reports that you may happen to hear. It was believed otherwise for a few days—so reports or rumors may have gotten back to you. Fortunately they misjudged the durability of a Kennedy—am back at the base now—and am OK. As soon as possible I shall try to give you the whole story. Much love to you all Jack."[56]

The news of Lieutenant Kennedy's exploits hit the front pages on August 19, after clearing censors. By chance, two leading war correspondents, Frank Hewlett of United Press and Leif Erickson of the Associated Press, were at the Rendova base on the day of the rescue and hopped aboard the PT boat for the pickup. They promptly filed accounts that made headlines across the country. KENNEDY'S SON SAVES 10 IN PACIFIC; KENNEDY'S SON IS HERO IN THE PACIFIC, read one of them. *The New York Times*, in a story datelined "Aug 8 (delayed)," reported on page 1, KENNEDY'S SON IS HERO IN PACIFIC AS DESTROYER SPLITS HIS BOAT. "Former Ambassador and Mrs. Kennedy today shouted in joy when informed of the exploit of their son," read a separate *Times* story by Arthur Krock, but also "expressed deep sorrow for the two crewmen who lost their lives." Congratulatory telegrams and letters flowed into the family home from near and far, and Joe set about trying to answer each one.* "I've been a little lax in writing you recently," he wrote one London friend, "but Jack's

---

* Jack, too, received congratulatory letters, including one from his Choate headmaster, George St. John. "God bless you," the older man wrote, "I have just been reading the account of your rescue—and of the resourcefulness you used in making the rescue possible. I wish I could be with you and the other Choate men these days. To be in the sixties . . . is almost a humiliation." Jack replied with warm assurance: "What you and others are doing at Choate and schools like it constitutes an essential ingredient to any worth while peace—which is what we are all hoping and working for." (George St. John to JFK, August 23, 1943, box 4b, JFK Personal Papers.)

exploits in the South Pacific have kept me pretty well tied up. It is the consensus of the newspaper men here that there hasn't been a better story
since the war started than the one of young Jack. He really came through
with flying colors."[57]

Joe and Rose implored their son to ask to be sent home. He had more
than fulfilled his obligations, they believed, and moreover they worried
about his health. Jack refused. He spent a week in the hospital in Tulagi,
looking more emaciated than ever and brooding about the lack of rescue
attempts following the ramming and about the loss of two of his men. To
his squadron commander, Cluster, Jack poured out his frustration that
neither Potter nor Lowrey had come to his boat's aid, even though they
clearly knew something bad had happened. But his frustration only
strengthened his desire to return to duty, and he felt as well a deeper connection to his men. "On the bright side of an otherwise completely black
time," he wrote his parents, "was the way everyone stood up to it.

"Previous to that I had been somewhat cynical about the American as
a fighting man. I had seen too much bellyaching and laying off. But with
the chips down, that all faded away. I can now believe—which I never
would have before—the stories of Bataan and Wake. For an American it's
got to be awfully easy or awfully tough. When it's in the middle, then
there's trouble. It was a terrible thing though, losing those two men. One
[Andrew Kirksey] had ridden with me for as long as I had been out
here. . . . He had a wife and three kids. The other fellow [Harold Marney]
had just come on board. He was only a kid himself. It certainly brought
home how real the war is—and when I read the papers from home, how
superficial is most of the talking and thinking about it."[58]

But his overarching view of the war had not changed. Upon learning
that his seventeen-year-old brother Bobby was clamoring to get into a PT
boat, Jack insisted that he was "too young to be out here," and that "the
fun goes out of the war in a fairly short time and I don't think that Bobby
is ready yet to come out."[59] In September, he assumed command of a new
boat, the former PT 59, which had been retrofitted—the torpedoes were
removed and replaced with guns—to become Gunboat No. 1, making
Jack the first gunboat commander in the Pacific. Later that month he remarked to Inga Arvad on how slowly the fighting was progressing.

This war here is a dirty business. It's very easy to talk about the war
and beating the Japs if it takes years and a million men, but anyone

who talks like that should consider well his words. We get so used to talking about billions of dollars and millions of soldiers that thousands of casualties sounds like drops in the bucket. But if those thousands want to live as much as the ten that I saw, the people deciding the whys and wherefores had better make mighty sure that all this effort is headed for some definite goal and that when we reach that goal we may say it was worth it. . . .

I received a letter from the wife of my engineer, who was so badly burnt that his face and hands and arms were just flesh and he was that way for six days. He couldn't swim and I was able to help him and his wife thanked me, and in her letter she said, "I suppose to you it was just part of your job, but Mr. McMahon was part of my life and if he had died I don't think I would have wanted to go on living."

At the end he turned personal, and showed his depth: "I used to have the feeling that no matter what happened I'd get through. . . . It's a funny thing that as long as you have that feeling you seem to get through. I've lost that feeling lately, but as a matter of fact, I don't feel badly about it. If anything happens to me, I have this knowledge that if I lived to be a hundred, I could only have improved the quantity of my life, not the quality. This sounds gloomy as hell, [but] you are the only person I'd say it to anyway. As a matter of fact knowing you has been the brightest point in an extremely bright twenty-six years."[60]

He still had feelings for Inga, strong feelings, even though the relationship was over. He loved everything about her—her looks, her sexiness, her sophistication, her sense of humor, her warmth. She had awakened something in him he didn't know he had, had believed in him, had encouraged him to reach for the stars and to cultivate his interests in a potential political career. Even before meeting her, he had begun to move out of his older brother's shadow, but there's little doubt that her bullish and indefatigable advocacy was further incentive for him to see himself as coequal—at least—with Joe. Now, with his wartime exploits capturing headlines at home, some part of him understood the process was complete.

Joe Junior sensed it, too. Testy and irritable that summer of 1943, he agitated to get into combat, and seemed to his fellow fliers to have a giant chip on his shoulder. In July he seized on the chance to volunteer for a highly dangerous mission patrolling the English Channel in order to hunt down German U-boats near where they lived, in the Bay of Biscay and along the French coast south of Brest. As he waited for the order to ship out, Joe learned to fly the new B-24 Liberator and soon found himself flying them across the country, from the factory in San Diego to Norfolk, Virginia. On one of the San Diego stops a family friend showed him a letter indicating that Jack was missing in action. "I read this about three hours before I saw the papers [indicating the rescue]," Joe wrote to his family, "and got quite a fright." But it seems he did not call his parents at the time, because some days later his father wrote to say he and Rose "were considerably upset that during those few days after the news of Jack's rescue we had no word from you. I thought that you would very likely call up to see whether we had any news as to how Jack was."[61]

Young Joe's reply bespoke his frustration about having a younger brother who had allowed his boat to be lost to the enemy and yet somehow still came out looking every bit the conqueror. "With the great quantity of reading material coming in on the actions of the Kennedys in the various parts of the world, and the countless number of paper clippings about our young hero, the battler of the wars of Banana River, San Juan, Virginia Beach, New Orleans, San Antonio, and San Diego, will now step to the microphone and give out a few words of his own activities," the letter began. Only once did it mention his brother's name.[62]

Granted a few days' leave at the start of September, Joe returned to Cape Cod in time for his father's fifty-fifth birthday celebration. During a festive dinner, Judge John J. Burns, a longtime acquaintance of Joe Senior's, rose to offer a toast "to Ambassador Joe Kennedy, father of our hero, our *own* hero, Lieutenant John F. Kennedy of the United States Navy." That was it. No mention of the older son, who was seated right next to his father and who in a few days would be heading to England to go against the thrust of the ferocious Nazi war machine. As the judge sat down, Joe Junior lifted his glass and smiled stiffly. But another guest, Boston police commissioner Joe Timilty, said that that night he could hear Young Joe sobbing in the bed next to his and muttering, "By God, I'll show them."[63]

Decades later, his mother would acknowledge the import of the PT 109 episode: "In their long brotherly, friendly rivalry, I expect this was the first time Jack had won such an 'advantage' by such a clear margin. And

I daresay it cheered Jack and must have rankled Joe Jr."[64] This seems half-right: yes, Jack had indeed gained the "advantage" over his brother, but it rings false to suggest that the fraternal competition was a zero-sum game that still mattered equally to both of them. The drive to be supreme among the nine Kennedy children had always been an all-out obsession for Joe more than for Jack. And especially in recent years, as Jack scored impressive accomplishments of his own, he had become less mired in the rivalry than his brother was.

VI

On October 8, 1943, Jack received promotion to full lieutenant, and on the sixteenth his Gunboat No. 1, along with the rest of the squadron, moved to Lambu Lambu, the new forward base on the island of Vella Lavella, west of New Georgia. There followed numerous missions through the end of October and into November, many of them aimed at intercepting Japanese barges at the western and southern approaches to Choiseul Bay. On November 2, Jack rescued wounded Marines trapped on Choiseul Island, then endured seeing several of the men suffer on board his boat, including one who died in his own bunk. On the night of November 5–6, with his friend Byron "Whizzer" White on board, No. 1 opened fire and destroyed three Japanese barges at Moli Island.[65]

Jack volunteered for many of these missions, and seemed unfazed by risk. "He had guts," said one crewman. "No matter how dangerous the mission was, he'd always volunteer." At one point, senior commanders wanted to send a boat through Blackett Strait to draw enemy shell fire so that American aircraft could identify the guns. Jack offered to do it. "He said he'd go if they could find somebody else to go with him," the crewman remembered. Since no one else came forward, the mission was scrapped. But through his leadership and calm friendliness in these autumn weeks, Jack won respect and affection. "He was a good officer in that he knew how to handle men," related Chief Petty Officer Glen Christiansen.[66]

His health, however, was spiraling downward. His back troubles and stomach pains intensified in the weeks after the PT 109 ordeal, and his weight, already worryingly low, dropped still further. He suffered headaches and fever. The precise cause was not clear, but the long hours and lack of sleep didn't help. On November 18, a doctor at the base in Lambu Lambu ordered Jack to shore and he returned to Tulagi. Additional tests there, including X-rays, identified an "early duodenal ulcer" and the presence of malaria.[67] Barred from further duty, he bided his time in Tulagi, penning letters and waiting for his orders home. To brother Bobby, who had joined the Navy Reserve while in his final months at Milton Academy, he wrote:

> The folks sent me a clipping of you taking the oath. The sight of you up there, just as a boy, was really moving, particularly as a close examination showed that you had my checked London coat on. I'd like to know what the hell I'm doing out here, while you go stroking around in my drape coat, but I suppose that what we are out here for—or so they tell us—is so that our sisters and younger brothers will be safe and secure. Frankly, I don't see it quite that way—at least if you're going to be safe and secure, that's fine with me, but not in my coat, brother, not in my coat. In that picture you look as if you are going to step outside the room, grab your gun, and knock off several of the house-boys before lunch.[68]

Four pals in Tulagi, autumn 1943. From left: George "Barney" Ross,
Kennedy, Paul "Red" Fay, and James Reed.

Jack spent abundant time with Red Fay, who tried every method to get Jack interested in playing cards. Results were poor. Instead Fay and a few others would descend on Jack's tent, where he would lead informal group discussions on the topics of the day—on wartime strategy, politics, military leadership, education, and, inevitably, girls. Ideas interested him, the others could see—he kept a loose-leaf notebook to record thoughts—and he was stimulated by debate. "There was no question in my mind or the minds of Barney Ross, Jim Reed, and Byron White that Jack Kennedy was an exceptional man," Fay, an admitted devotee, later said. Making book on who among them could become president of the United States, Fay and Ross set Jack's odds at ten thousand to one ("because he was still out in the war zone, his health was poor, he was young and unforeseen circumstances could make it impossible for him to reach the White House"), and their own odds at between one million and two million to one. "Jack Kennedy's greatness was so apparent to me," Fay added, "that I did something unusual for a man. I saved every letter or note that he ever sent to me, beginning during the war years."[69]

The orders home came through on December 14, 1943. By then the great campaign of which he had been a part was well on the way to success, with Allied forces mopping up the central Solomons to claim Vella Lavella and Bougainville and put themselves in a position to cut off and neutralize Rabaul, key to the entire Japanese position in the South Pacific. By the end of the month they would capture Cape Gloucester, at the western end of New Britain. And days after that, a major air offensive would render Rabaul more or less useless to enemy aircraft and ships, leaving its 100,000-strong garrison bereft and strategically irrelevant.[70]

Jack was granted thirty days' leave starting upon arrival in the United States, and he would then report to Melville for his next assignment. He left Tulagi on the twenty-first, bound first for Espiritu Santo and then—aboard the USS *Breton*—San Francisco. He arrived on U.S. soil on January 7 and the following day headed south to Los Angeles, where he met with Inga Arvad, who had relocated there some months prior to write a gossip column called "Hollywood Today" for a national newspaper syndicate. (The FBI, having found no evidence she was engaged in espionage activities, had ceased its surveillance of her.)

Any hopes Jack had of rekindling the romance were immediately dashed. Life had moved on, and so had Inga. In her son's recollection, "she'd been through the thing about the old man's violent objections and just didn't want to go through it again." She loved Jack, and when she saw his cadaverously thin frame in her doorway she felt a rush of maternal compassion; some part of her thought she would never feel the same way about any man ever again. But she knew that sooner or later Jack, if he had designs on a political career, would again conclude—as he had almost two years before—that he could not marry her. What's more, Inga found she liked her new life as a Hollywood columnist and had no desire to give it up. To punctuate the new reality, she even introduced Jack to her new beau, William Cahan, a naval doctor. Jack got the message. At Inga's apartment, he chatted amicably with Cahan about Harvard, football, and show business, but after a while it became clear that one of them would have to leave. Exit Jack.[71]

But Inga had one parting gift for her love, in the form of a high-profile newspaper article that did much to cement the legend of Jack's heroics in the Solomons. Based on an interview they conducted during his visit, the article—a puff piece that would be ethically problematic today—appeared in dozens of papers, including on page 1 of *The Boston Globe* on January 11, 1944, under the heading JFK TELLS STORY OF PT EPIC: KENNEDY LAUDS MEN, DISDAINS HERO STUFF. "This is the story of the 13 American men on PT Boat 109 who got closer than any others to a Japanese destroyer and of the 11 men who lived to tell about it," Inga began. She heaped praise on the skipper for swimming "long hours through shark-infested waters to rescue his men" and quoted his description of the moment of impact on the night of August 2: "I can best compare it to the onrushing trains in the old-time movies. They seemed to come right over you. Well, the feeling was the same, only the destroyer did not come over us, it went right through us."

Inga emphasized Jack's reluctance to talk about himself and his preference for heaping praise on his crew. But there was also acclaim for him. Inga wrote of meeting Patrick McMahon's wife, a resident of Los Angeles who "with tears in her eyes and a shaky voice . . . said, 'When my husband wrote home, he told me that Lieutenant Kennedy was wonderful, that he saved the lives of all the men and everybody at the base admired him greatly.' "[72]

Jack, however, rejected the hero label that Inga tried to pin on him. "None of that hero stuff about me," the article quoted him as saying. "The real heroes are not the men who return, but those who stay out there, like plenty of them do—two of my men included."[73]

On the evening of January 10, just a few hours before the story ran, Jack Kennedy boarded an airplane in L.A., bound for points east. He was only on a thirty-day leave, but in his mind he had already made his determination: if he never saw another day of combat in his life, it would be too soon.

THIRTEEN

LOST PRINCE

n late November 1943, as John F. Kennedy was preparing to depart the Solomons and return to the United States for his thirty-day leave, the "Big Three" of Roosevelt, Stalin, and Churchill held their first-ever joint meeting, in the Iranian capital, Tehran. In strategic and political terms it would prove to be the most important of all the wartime conferences, with monumental implications for not only the rest of the war but the postwar era as well—and for Kennedy's career. Quite apart from the fact that the three leaders represented, in Churchill's formulation, the greatest concentration of power the world had ever seen, this was also the first—and last—time they had a chance to thrash out the core objectives of the Grand Alliance before the decisive military campaigns were joined. Though the Yalta Conference of February 1945 is often viewed as the great policy-making conclave of the war, Yalta mostly filled in the outline sketched out at Tehran.[1]

The cacophonous city was a curious mix of old and new, its boulevards crowded with late-model American cars and horse-drawn droshkies, its architecture blending Mongol and modern. Sidewalks remained unpaved, which gave the city a dusty air; next to luxurious residential neighborhoods stood poor, grimy ones. In anticipation of the conference, many areas of the city had been cordoned off, with only official traffic permitted. Security measures were unprecedented, with Soviet, American, and British soldiers patrolling the streets, and aircraft flying constant vigil overhead.[2]

From the start of the proceedings Stalin, bedecked in a mustard-colored, tightly buttoned military uniform, projected confidence and energy, and no wonder: his power had risen significantly during 1943 as his forces gained the upper hand on the Eastern Front, this time without the aid of winter weather. In July, the Red Army, under General Zhukov, beat back Germany's summer offensive against the Kursk salient in history's greatest tank battle, despite Hitler's throwing thousands of tanks and planes into the fray. Bit by bit through the year, territory seized by the Germans fell back into Soviet hands, even though Stalin's troops were up against 80 percent of the Nazi striking force and even though the second front that the Kremlin leader had been promised by Roosevelt had yet to materialize. At the battlefield level, the Germans were still formidable—the Russians were losing five or six men for every German soldier—but they simply couldn't match the endless Soviet reinforcements. At the same time, Stalin knew he had been liberally supplied with Lend-Lease aid, and during one evening meal he offered a revealing toast: "To American production, without which this war would have been lost."[3]

Churchill, too, understood that the United States was the Allied paymaster, and moreover that he was now clearly the junior member of the triumvirate. Over the previous year, global leadership had passed to Washington, which meant that American generals would be commanding the combined Allied forces in the great battles to come. Churchill accordingly stayed mum when Roosevelt refused to caucus privately with him prior to the formal sessions, out of concern that Stalin might think they were scheming against the Kremlin. He smiled gamely when the American teased him in Stalin's presence and made cutting remarks about the nefarious effects of British and French colonialism. And he acquiesced when Roosevelt turned him down for lunch in order to meet with Stalin and his foreign minister, Vyacheslav Molotov. "Stalin hates the guts of all your top people," FDR told Churchill. "He thinks he likes me better and I hope he will continue to do so."[4] When the prime minister made noises about focusing Anglo-American military efforts in 1944 on the Balkans and the Mediterranean, he was shot down: Stalin and Roosevelt would permit no narrowing of the parameters for the long-planned cross-Channel invasion, code-named Operation Overlord, which the three leaders tentatively scheduled for May 1944. Certain that the Soviet Union would be preeminent in Eastern Europe after the war, Roosevelt hinted to Stalin that he would not challenge Kremlin domination of Poland and the Baltic states, so long as Stalin made token concessions to limit objections in the West. (Here can be found seeds of the Cold War yet to come.)

In exchange, FDR got what he most wanted at Tehran: a pledge from Stalin that once Germany was beaten, the USSR would enter the war against Japan. Stalin also agreed to match the Overlord invasion with a grand offensive of his own, from the east, though he offered few details, and neither FDR nor Churchill pressed him for any. The three men agreed in principle to Roosevelt's notion of a postwar system in which four policemen—the United States, Britain, the Soviet Union, and China—would deal with conflicts as they arose (the embryo of the United Nations). France, they concurred, would occupy a much-reduced place on the global stage. And they determined that Germany should be dismembered after its defeat, a plan pushed hard by Stalin, who also wanted to extract heavy reparations. Details, again, were to be tackled later.

Though Roosevelt could later claim, legitimately, that he had made no formal commitments at Tehran, he certainly made tacit agreements, from which could be seen Europe's future. As Charles Bohlen, a member of the American delegation, summarized the outcome in a memorandum: "Germany is to be broken up and kept broken up. The states of eastern, southeastern, and central Europe will not be permitted to group themselves into any federations or associations. France . . . will not be permitted to maintain any appreciable military establishment. Poland and Italy will remain approximately their present territorial size, but it is doubtful if either will be permitted to maintain any appreciable armed force. The result will be that the Soviet Union would be the only important military and political force on the continent of Europe."[5]

All that still lay ahead. In assessing the war and its outcome, we should avoid the trap of hindsight bias, or what the philosopher Henri Bergson called "the illusion of retrospective determinism"—the belief that whatever occurred in history was bound to occur.[6] At the end of 1943, nothing was as yet decided. True, the situation for the Allies had improved dramatically over the preceding months, with the clearing of North Africa in May, Italy's surrender in September, and the Soviet successes in the east.

But uncertainties remained. The Red Army was still confined to Soviet territory; it had yet to break into Eastern Europe, much less into Germany itself. The timing and outcome of the cross-Channel invasion was anyone's guess. And in the Far East, the Japanese were on the defensive but had long since established their unshakable fighting spirit. The Pacific war might go on for years more—Jack Kennedy, from his perch in the Solomons, had anticipated as much—which is why Roosevelt came to the Iranian capital with the overriding goal of getting the Russians into that theater.

Yet it remains the case that a pronounced optimism permeated the Tehran discussions. No one present—not the leaders, not their chief advisers, not the staff assistants—would have traded places with the enemy, in any of the war's theaters. And as Stalin's toast suggested, an enormously important reason for the rosy outlook was that America's immense productive capacity was now making itself felt. Churchill got the point—recall his relief upon learning of the Pearl Harbor attack two years before. There would be tough fighting to come, but victory would result. "All the rest," he had then written, "was merely the proper application of overwhelming force."[7]

The numbers are startling. Beginning in 1942, huge numbers of American factories, many of them in California (which saw its population increase by 14 percent in 1942), turned to manufacturing for the war. Often they operated around the clock, every day of the week. Auto plants made bombers; typewriter companies turned out rifles; dress factories sewed military uniforms. Rock-Ola, a Chicago manufacturer of jukeboxes, made M1 carbines, while Frigidaire, in Ohio, switched from refrigerators to airplane propellers and Browning M2 machine guns. By 1943, 41 percent of the gross national product went to war production; the arms bill for that year was a colossal $52.4 billion, including $25 billion combined on ships and aircraft and $5.9 billion on vehicles. By early 1944 the United States was producing 40 percent of the world's weaponry. Over the course of the conflict, U.S. factories turned out roughly 300,000 airplanes, 102,000 armored vehicles, 77,000 ships, twenty million small arms, six million tons of bombs, and forty billion rounds of small-arms ammunition.[*8]

---

* To put these numbers in some perspective, consider that when the Germans launched their blitzkrieg against the Low Countries and France in May 1940, they utilized 3,034 aircraft, 2,580 tanks, 10,000 artillery pieces, and 4,000 trucks.

At Ford's bomber-producing Willow Run plant, in Michigan, which featured assembly lines almost a mile long, workers by early 1944 were turning out 650 B-24 Liberators per month, or one every eighty minutes. Pilots and crews slept on cots at the plant, waiting to fly the bombers away as soon as they were built. On the West Coast, Henry Kaiser used mass-production techniques to cut construction time for Liberty ships—the huge 440-foot cargo vessels that transported the tanks, trucks, and guns overseas—from 355 to 56 days. (In one publicity stunt, Kaiser's Richmond shipyard, near San Francisco, constructed a Liberty ship in four days, fifteen hours, and twenty-six minutes.) In Long Beach, California, the giant Douglas Aircraft plant would churn out some 31,000 aircraft over the course of the war. Chrysler, meanwhile, manufactured thousands of tanks for the Army, and refined its technique sufficiently to build one Swedish Bofors anti-aircraft gun in ten hours; it had taken 450 hours to make one by hand in Sweden. In Connecticut, Igor Sikorsky opened the world's first helicopter assembly line, while, in Maine, the Bath Iron Works launched a destroyer every seventeen days.[9]

The other combatant nations could only marvel at the output. In the all-important year of 1943, the United States built three and a half times as many aircraft as Nazi Germany and well over five times as many as Japan. In the Battle of the Atlantic, U-boats sank 105 Allied ships in the month of March 1943, but U.S. shipyards were by then producing 140 cargo ships per month, which allowed supplies to keep flowing. German U-boat losses, meanwhile, were mounting, and new ones couldn't come off the line fast enough to replace them.

The American advantage went beyond industrial capacity and output. In terms of the various basic products critical to war fighting—coal, steel, petroleum, cotton (for explosives), and copper, for example—the United States was the best placed of all the combatants, and by a vast margin. With respect to petroleum, the most vital refined product of them all, the numbers are eye-popping: German crude oil production (including imports) in 1943 had edged up to nine million metric tons; the American total was 200 million metric tons. And the Japanese petroleum disadvantage was even greater—long before U.S. submarines had annihilated Japan's oil tanker fleet, its navy and air force were already severely hamstrung by inadequate fuel supplies.[10]

II

Jack Kennedy, like most junior officers in America's war, could see this transformational change in his nation's global position. In Red Fay's recollection, the issue was a frequent topic of conversation in the bull sessions held in Jack's Tulagi tent in late 1943. "We felt the United States was now numero uno," Fay said, "that we had taken that role, and the United States was leader of the free world—that the British and the French and the Allies really weren't going to make it without us." Isolationism, the young men knew, was dead back home, with only a small handful of senators still calling forlornly for America to go it alone. On the question "Should the Senate resolve its willingness to join in establishing international authority to preserve peace?" the tally was 85 yes, 5 no, 6 absent. The vote on a similar resolution in the House of Representatives was equally lopsided.[11]

And there would be no going back, Kennedy and his mates sensed. Already a quarter century earlier, Woodrow Wilson had deduced that the United States, secure in its domains, faced a world of qualitatively different threats, on account of the emerging technologies of mass destruction and the insatiable ambitions of great powers in Asia and Europe. Already then, Wilson had determined that Americans could not afford to remain insular, could not depend solely on their own military and the two oceans to protect them; they needed to actively engage with the rest of the world in an arduous but vital long-term project aimed at winning universal respect for the ideals of liberty and the rule of law. Wilson's vision, which combined idealism and realism in a uniquely potent way, went unrealized through the 1920s and '30s; now, however, in the midst of another world war, Franklin Roosevelt and his lieutenants were determined to create a new, Wilsonian world order—one led by the United States and serving U.S. interests but also benefiting other nations—based on free trade, stable currency exchange rates, and multilateralism.[12]

As the year turned, though, Kennedy's principal focus was not on the grand political questions of war and peace, nor on the steady march of history, but on something more immediate: taking full advantage of his monthlong leave back home. With Inga Arvad summarily rejecting his attempt at rekindling their romance during his brief stopover in Los Angeles, he headed for the family home in Palm Beach, stopping en route at the Mayo Clinic, in Minnesota, to have his health evaluated. On the plane he penned a brief note of condolence to Clare Boothe Luce, whose daughter had just been killed in an auto accident. "I can't tell you how shocked I was to hear about Ann," he wrote. "I thought I had become hardened to losing people I like, but when I heard the news today, I couldn't have been sadder. She was a wonderful girl—so completely unspoiled, and thoughtful—and so very fond of you—I can't believe it."[13]

In Florida, his mother registered, with uncharacteristic abandon, her joy at having him back. She wrote in her diary, "He is really at home—the boy for whom you prayed so hard—at the mention of whose name your eyes would become dimmed—the youngster who you would think dead some nights & you would wake up with sorrow clutching at your heart. What a sense of gratitude to God to have spared him. What joy to see him—to feel his coat & to press his arms (*& know he's here*) to look at his bronze tired face which is thin and drawn."[14]

Jack went clubbing the first night with his good friend Chuck Spalding. From the start, something felt off. He'd been to war, had seen death and dying up close, and the sight of young people in a bar living it up as though nothing had changed was too jarring. "It was a great shock," Spalding said, "having got back from this thing he'd been through, and going to this place where he used to dance all the time, and seeing everybody and trying to fit in. The difference between the tensions of being at war and the pleasures of Palm Beach. It was kind of a tough night, even for him—and he could usually make those kinds of transfers easily."[15]

Others, too, noticed that Jack had been changed by his firsthand experience with war. The stabbing memories of violence and death had left their mark. Inga Arvad could see it—both in his letters from the war zone and in person when he stopped by in Los Angeles—as could Spalding and (in letters) Lem Billings. To his mother he seemed tightly wound, like a highly geared racehorse. Al Cluster, Jack's squadron commander in the Solomons, detected a newfound seriousness in him, and a cynicism that many of Cluster's men developed as they saw the disconnect between the supposed glamour of PT operations and the dirty, mundane reality, as well as the often nonsensical decisions by woolly-headed superior officers.[16] Jack had become jaded, in other words, even as he remained a patriot, even as he held firm to the conviction that the Axis powers must be defeated and the United States must assume the responsibilities of world leadership.

"Munda or many of these spots are just God damned hot stinking corners of small islands in a group of islands in a part of the ocean we all hope never to see again," he had remarked bitterly to Inga in a letter not long before leaving the Solomons. "We are at a great disadvantage. The Russians could see their country invaded, the Chinese the same. The British were bombed. But we are fighting on some islands belonging to the Lever Company, a British concern making soap. I suppose if we were stockholders we would perhaps be doing better, but to see that by dying at Munda you are helping to insure peace in our time takes a larger imagination than most men possess." A letter to his parents from around the same time maintained the antiheroic mood: "When I read that we will fight Japs for years if necessary and will sacrifice hundreds of thousands if we must—I always check from where's he's talking—it's seldom from out here."[17]

He emerged from his war experience hardened, wiser, more mature, and with self-confidence from having performed his duties and earned the esteem of his men. Thrown together with individuals from vastly different backgrounds and economic circumstances, he developed a greater appreciation for the diversity of the American national experience. He was glad he had served. But perhaps in part because, at twenty-six, he was older than a lot of servicemen, he didn't find the war as thrilling on a personal level as some did. He didn't share the perspective, for example, of newspaperman Ben Bradlee, who served on a destroyer in the Pacific and would in time become a close friend, and who wrote of his own service, "I just plain loved it. Loved the excitement, even loved being a little bit scared." Kennedy's view was closer to that of Norwegian resistance fighter Knut Lier-Hansen: "Though wars can bring adventures which stir the heart, the true nature of war is composed of innumerable personal tragedies, of grief, waste and sacrifice, wholly evil and not redeemed by glory."[18]

After a couple of weeks of rest and relaxation in Florida, Jack flew to New York on February 5. He secured a date with Florence "Flo" Pritchett, a bright and peppy ex-model who was the fashion editor of the *New York Journal-American* and who had recently divorced her wealthy Catholic husband. The two went out with writer John Hersey and his wife (and former Jack Kennedy girlfriend), Frances Ann Cannon, seeing a play and then repairing to the Café Society nightclub, where they had the good fortune—as it turned out—to bump into William Shawn from *The New Yorker*. Inevitably, Jack's PT 109 episode came up, and Hersey asked if he could write about it, in an article he'd try to place in *Life* magazine. Jack was reluctant but eventually agreed, though he insisted that Hersey first interview those crew members who were now back on U.S. soil. Hersey assented and was soon on the road to the PT base at Melville, Rhode Island, to speak at length with four of the men, first individually, then collectively.[19]

From New York, Jack went on to Boston for his grandfather Honey Fitz's eighty-first birthday party, a luncheon with three hundred guests at the Parker House Hotel. Delayed in arriving on account of a snowstorm, Jack entered the hall to a rapturous welcome. Honey Fitz was thrilled, and *The Boston Globe* ran a photograph of the ex-mayor and his grandson the following day, February 12. That evening, Jack was the featured speaker at a Lincoln's Birthday War Bond rally presided over by Governor Leverett Saltonstall and Mayor Maurice J. Tobin. More than nine hundred people heard him expound on the sobering theme that the Pacific war seemed likely to last a long time. "The boys [would] like to know they won't have to pay for the war they have to fight," he declared, and the message evidently hit home—the rally raised a remarkable half million dollars in war bond purchases.[20]

With Jack's thirty-day leave about to expire, he now asked to delay reporting for duty until March 1, in order to undergo medical tests at New England Baptist Hospital. At issue were his continuing stomach troubles and back pain. X-rays were taken and the surgeons made a determination: if Jack wanted to walk properly again, he should undergo the surgery that had been recommended a year earlier while he was stationed in South Carolina.

While weighing whether to go under the knife, he sat for a long interview with Hersey. They talked in Jack's small and nondescript hospital room, with him propped up on the bed. From press accounts and the interviews in Rhode Island, Hersey had pieced together the basic chronology of the harrowing episode in the Blackett Strait, which he now took Jack through, step by step. Gradually, a fuller picture emerged. At one point Jack drew a map of the area in Ferguson Passage where he got off the reef and was in the water throughout the night, carried off by the current. Mesmerized by the image of that night and its dreamlike quality, Hersey asked for details; Jack did his best to provide them. For hours they talked as the afternoon disappeared and twilight bathed the room. Hersey came away impressed. "He had a kind of diffidence about himself that seemed to be genuine," he later said. "So in a joking way he wondered how he looked to [the crew]. They were wildly devoted to him, all of them. Absolutely clear devotion to him by the crew. No reservation about it. They really did like him."[21]

Jack opted to hold off on the surgery and managed instead to be reassigned to the Submarine Chaser Training Center, in Miami, near the family home. The relocation allowed him to spend some time with little brother Teddy, now twelve. One night, he took the young boy to another nearby naval base and, under the cover of darkness, smuggled him onto a PT boat. He also introduced Teddy to some of his favorite writings, including Stephen Vincent Benét's epic poem "John Brown's Body," which the two took turns reading aloud. Teddy, reveling in his brother's presence, listened with rapt attention as Jack talked about the key developments in the Civil War. "Never be without a book in your hand," Jack told him.[22]

The work requirements in Miami were not exactly arduous. "In regard to conditions here," he wrote Hersey, who was now at work drafting the article, "may I say that I am playing it slow and deep—with no strain or pain. Once you get your feet up on the desk in the morning the heavy work of the day is done."[23] In fact, though, the strain and pain soon returned, more intense than before. By May he realized he could put the surgery off no longer and, having secured permission from the Navy, entered Chelsea Naval Hospital on June 11. The following day, in a simple service at the hospital, Jack received the Navy and Marine Corps Medal for "extremely heroic conduct as Commanding Officer of Motor Torpedo Boat 109 following the collision and sinking of that vessel in the Pacific War Area on August 1–2, 1943." On June 22 Jack was transferred to New England Baptist, and a team of surgeons performed the serious operation the following day. They found not a ruptured or herniated

Captain Frederick Conklin congratulates Kennedy on the awarding of the Navy and Marine Corps Medal, Chelsea Naval Hospital, Chelsea, Massachusetts, June 11, 1944.

disk, as anticipated, but, perhaps more alarmingly, "abnormally soft" cartilage, which they removed. They also reported "fibrocartilage with degeneration."[24]

III

From his hospital bed before and after the surgery, Kennedy kept up with war developments and family affairs. He worried about Joe Junior, who for the previous ten months had been stationed in England with the Fleet Airwing Seven squadron, the first American unit attached to the RAF Coastal Command. In that capacity, Joe flew radar-equipped B-24 Liberators on round-the-clock antisubmarine missions over the Channel and the North Sea. It was dangerous work, and Jack found ominous the growing number of airmen on Joe's unit who were being shot down. "Heard from Joe a while back—they have had heavy casualties in his squadron—I hope to hell he gets through O.K.," he wrote to Lem Billings. The riskiness convinced him that Bobby should not follow in Joe's path. "I really think that Bobby shouldn't go into aviation," he wrote. "I don't see where it is any more fun than P.T.'s or D.D.'s [destroyers], or any other small ship—especially as Bobby has spent so much of his life on small boats. I'm going to write him to that effect + I wish you would advise the same thing. It would be just his luck to get hit when old worn out bastards like you + me get through this with nothing more than a completely shattered constitution."[25]

On his furloughs, Joe Junior often visited his sister Kathleen, who had given up her newspaper job in Washington and moved to London to work for the American Red Cross. With her older brothers involved in the fighting, Kick wanted to be part of the action, to be, her mother recalled, "involved in the war and to make her own contribution that would be constructive."[26] She also wanted to be near her first love, Billy Cavendish, the tall and elfin-faced heir to the Duke of Devonshire. Cavendish, having been defeated in a bid to win election to Parliament for West Derbyshire, had become an officer in the Coldstream Guards, a venerable regiment of the army, and was in uniform.

Kick wrote openly to her siblings of the romance. "I'm sure I would make a most efficient Duchess of Devonshire in the postwar world," she told Jack, "and as I'd have a castle in Ireland, one in Scotland, one in

Yorkshire, and one in Sussex I could keep my old nautical brothers in their old age. . . . I can't really understand why I like Englishmen so much, as they treat one in quite an offhand manner and aren't as nice to women as are Americans, but I suppose it's just that sort of treatment that women really like. That's your technique, isn't it?"[27]

Yet she knew that the relationship was a star-crossed affair. Billy knew it, too. The Cavendishes, one of England's oldest and most prominent families, with an impeccable lineage dating back to the seventeenth century, were devoutly and militantly Protestant—the first duke, William, fought the Catholic king James II in a bloody rebellion—while the Kennedys were no less staunchly Catholic. Kick could not be married in the Church of England, as that would mean excommunication, while for Billy conversion to Catholicism was a nonstarter, as it would constitute a betrayal of three centuries of family history. Still, their love persevered. Ultimately, tormented by guilt and uncertainty, and urged on by the steadfast support of Joe Junior, Kick agreed to a civil ceremony, which, though not a legitimate marriage in the eyes of the Catholic Church, was also not grounds for excommunication. On May 6, 1944, she became the Marchioness of Hartington in a brief service in London. Billy's parents were present, while the Kennedys were represented by Joe Junior. Kick's father, though disappointed by his daughter's decision, never thought of forbidding the marriage, and cabled her that "with your faith in God you can't make a mistake. Remember you are still and always will be tops with me." Rose, disconsolate and bereft at having "lost" a daughter, sent no message.[28]

Joe Junior tried to reassure his mother, cabling on the wedding day, EVERYTHING WONDERFUL DON'T WORRY. SHE IS VERY HAPPY WISH YOU COULD HAVE BEEN HERE. LOVE, JOE. But Rose was unmoved, for reasons her husband laid out in a letter to his eldest son, after restating that he personally was not that bothered by the marriage. "But of course with Mother, it's different. Mother just feels that [Kathleen] couldn't be happy outside of the Church, but I think the thing that gave her the greatest concern is the fact that she thought she was setting a very grave example to other Catholic girls who might properly say . . . 'If Kathleen Kennedy did it why can't I?' and I think that is the thing that upset her most, along with the fact that she felt she had given her life to bringing up her children as good Catholics and that her job was not very well done."[29]

"Never did anyone have such a pillar of strength as I had in Joe [Ju-

Happy newlyweds: Billy and Kick tie the knot, with the
groom's mother and the bride's brother in the
background, London, May 6, 1944.

nior] in those difficult days before my marriage," Kick wrote afterwards.
"From the beginning, he gave me wise, helpful advice. When he felt that I
had made up my mind, he stood by me always. He constantly reassured
me and gave me renewed confidence in my own decision. Moral courage
he had in abundance and once he felt that a step was right for me, he
never faltered, although he might be held largely responsible for my decision."[30]

As for Jack, he was happy for his sister, and not much impressed with
his mother's objections. "Your plaintive howl at not being let in on Kathleen's nuptials reached me this morning," he wrote to Lem Billings. "You

might as well take it in stride and as sister Eunice from the depth of her Catholic wrath so truly said, 'It's a horrible thing—but it will be nice visiting her after the war, so we might as well face it.' At family dinners at the Cape, when you don't pass Hartington the muffins, we'll know how you feel."[31]

The newlyweds had only a month together before Billy joined his Coldstream Guards regiment for the long-awaited Allied invasion of Normandy, initiated on June 6 under the command of General Dwight D. Eisenhower. Kick soon made preparations to return to the United States to ride out the rest of the war with her family. There would be tensions with her mother, she knew, but she delighted at the prospect of seeing her siblings, not least Jack, whom she knew to be in sorry shape. His surgery, it turned out, had failed—he experienced acute back spasms when he tried to get up and about, the pain also shooting down one leg; he suffered severe abdominal pain; he lost weight. ("The doc should have read one more book before picking up the saw," Jack remarked.)[32] Upon transfer back to Chelsea Naval Hospital, where he would remain until August, physicians predicted it would be at least six months before he could return to active duty.

On the flip side, Jack could take satisfaction in the appearance of John Hersey's long article on PT 109. *Life* had rejected the piece—the editors had already published one Hersey article on the PT boats and moreover did not want to give so much space to a feature story that would limit their ability to cover fast-breaking military developments—but Hersey remembered that *The New Yorker*'s William Shawn had indicated interest in the story during their chance encounter at Café Society; he now pitched the article to him. Shawn and editor in chief Harold Ross responded quickly: they would publish.[33] Jack had been shown an early draft and liked what he saw ("Even I was wondering how it would all end!"), though he offered two suggestions: that crew members Lennie Thom and Barney Ross be given more recognition; and that Hersey omit allusions to an unnamed crew member (in actuality Raymond Albert) who'd lost his nerve during the ordeal and had subsequently been killed in the war. "I feel . . . that our group was too small, that his fate is so well-known both to the men and in the boats and to his family and friends that the finger would be put too definitely on his memory—and after all he *was* in my crew." Hersey agreed and omitted the mention.[34]

The article appeared on June 17, under the title "Survival." That was indeed its principal theme: Hersey, writing in the vivid and evocative yet spare style for which he would become known—two years later, the same magazine would devote an entire issue to his gripping 31,000-word account of the Hiroshima bombing—sought to explore the nature of human endurance in conditions of extreme adversity.

"At about ten o'clock the hulk heaved a moist sigh and turned turtle," Hersey wrote of the morning after the ramming, shortly before the epic four-hour swim. "McMahon and Johnston had to hang on as best they could. It was clear that the remains of the 109 would soon sink. When the sun had passed the meridian, Kennedy said, 'We will swim to that small island,' pointing to one of a group three miles to the southeast. 'We have less chance of making it than some of these other islands here, but there'll be less chance of Japs, too.' "[35]

But this theme of unyielding determination wasn't what Joseph P. Kennedy was primarily interested in. Rather, he hoped to use the publication to exploit what he saw as his son's unvarnished heroism, the better to advance Jack's career and to reverse his own lingering reputation for cowardice. In this regard Kennedy was disappointed that *Life*, with its large circulation, had taken a pass, and he moved energetically to persuade *The New Yorker*'s Ross to allow a condensed version of the article to run in the massively popular *Reader's Digest*. Ross, who hated the rival magazine, said no, but Kennedy persisted, convincing *Digest* publisher Paul Palmer to drop his customary stipulation that his magazine have the right to reprint the condensed version in perpetuity. Palmer agreed to purchase a single, one-time publication right. With the new terms, Ross relented. Hersey, for his part, agreed to donate his *New Yorker* author's fee to Kloye Ann Kirksey, the widow of one of the two men who died on the boat.[36]

It's hard to overestimate the long-term benefits of this masterstroke of public relations on Joe Kennedy's part. Expert marketer that he was, he understood what few others did, namely, the crucial importance that the timely advertising of Jack's performance could have going forward.[37] In the years to come, Joe would ignore the contract and reprint the abridged version, without permission, in mass quantities to be distributed during Jack's campaigns. The tale of wartime heroism played extremely well before these audiences—and, crucially, could be used to explain, and lionize, his various infirmities. Yes, voters would learn, the candidate suffered from ailments, but they could be attributed to the PT 109 ordeal or to the malaria he contracted while in the service. (Sometimes, for variation, the maladies were blamed on "old football injuries.")

In the early months after publication, however, Jack himself was more hesitant. He wrote to Lem Billings, "What I said to you about the break I got when Hersey did the article is true I guess [but] it was such an accident that it rather makes me wonder if most success is merely a great deal of fortuitous accidents. I imagine I would agree with you that it was lucky the whole thing happened if the two fellows had not been killed which rather spoils the whole thing for me."[38]

IV

Try as he might, Joseph Kennedy could not control the speed and direction of events that fateful summer of 1944. He had stood by powerless as his daughter Kathleen married out of her faith. His son Bobby was now an ROTC cadet, likely to be in harm's way before too much longer. Jack's surgery had gone awry, and he seemed destined for a long and difficult recovery at best. (He remained laid up in the naval hospital but was allowed to spend weekends in Hyannis Port.) And Joe Junior, though nearing the end of his second tour of duty and entitled to return home, continued to fly risky antisubmarine missions over the English Channel and the North Sea.

What fueled the eldest son's dogged pursuit of dangerous gambits is not altogether clear, but certainly it had something to do with a desire to outdo Jack. Or at least keep pace with him—according to Angela Laycock, the wife of the commanding officer of the British Commandos, Joe confided to her one evening that "he was sure it was his brother Jack who would ultimately be President." Laycock got the strong sense that "Joe was in awe of Jack's intelligence and believed that his own was no match for it."[39] On August 10, Joe wrote Jack to say he had read Hersey's article and was "much impressed with your intestinal fortitude." But he couldn't resist asking, "Where the hell were you when the destroyer hove into sight, and what exactly were your moves, and where the hell was your radar?" (Jack's boat, it will be recalled, was not radar-equipped.) In other words: *Some hero you are, allowing your boat to be sunk.* Always conscious of who got which awards, Joe congratulated his brother on the Navy and

Marine Corps Medal, then added, "To get anything out of the Navy is deserving of a campaign medal in itself. It looks like I shall return home with the European campaign medal if I'm lucky."[40]

It was not to be. On the afternoon of August 13, a warm and pleasant Sunday, the Kennedys gathered for a picnic-style lunch in the sunroom of the Hyannis Port home. Jack was there on weekend leave from the Chelsea hospital, as were the other children, save Kick (due to arrive from London soon) and Rosemary (institutionalized in Wisconsin). After the meal, Joe Kennedy went upstairs for an afternoon nap. At about 2:00 P.M., as Bing Crosby's chart-topping "I'll Be Seeing You" was playing on the phonograph, a dark car pulled up in front of the house. Two priests stepped out. Rose, thinking it could be a routine visit regarding church matters or the solicitation of funds for a charity (such visits were not uncommon at the home), invited the men to join the family in the living room while her husband completed his nap. No, one of the priests replied, the matter could not wait. Her son, he informed her, was missing in action "and presumed lost." Rose raced upstairs and woke her husband. She was barely coherent, and Joe leaped out of bed and hurried downstairs, his wife close behind. "We sat with the priests in a smaller room off the living room," she later wrote, "and from what they told us we realized there could be no hope, and that our son was dead."[41]

The children were still in the sunroom. They sensed that something bad had occurred. Their father appeared, his face ashen, and told them the news. He said he wanted them to be brave, to remember their brother but also that life is for the living, and to be "particularly good to your mother." Then he went upstairs to his bedroom and locked the door.[42]

Joe Junior had told his parents about a new, final mission he was undertaking before returning home to America, but he had lied about its nature. To them he had said it was "far more interesting than patrolling over the bay," but also that they shouldn't worry, as "there is practically no danger."[43] In actuality, he had volunteered for an operation that was dangerous almost to the point of suicidal. Code-named Project Anvil, the mission was a response to the terrifying new German weapon, the V-1 rocket, a kind of early cruise missile that had been pummeling London since soon after D-Day. In France, the Nazi command bunkered their rocket bases in sites that had proved seemingly impervious to Allied bombers. The U.S. Navy stripped down some of the Liberators that Joe had been flying so that they could be packed with explosives. Two pilots would take

Joe Junior at the Fersfield RAF base, England, in August 1944, not long before his death.

each plane up to two thousand feet, set it on its course, then parachute to safety. Two B-17s following behind would then guide the "flying bomb" by radio control to its target in coastal France.[44]

Later, after the fighting had ceased, some would say Joe's mission was nothing but foolish bravado, a senseless attempt to match Jack's exploits in the Pacific and a desperate plea for fatherly approval. Perhaps, but what, then, of the other fliers who volunteered for Project Anvil? Did the same demons drive them? Would they have been held to the same unsparing scrutiny for their decision to step forward? Joe's fellow officers at his base noted his gambler's nature, his unrestrained eagerness to sign on to anything and everything, but they also respected him for his sense of commitment, his piloting skills, his bravery. They liked that he didn't wear his virtue on his sleeve and that he refrained from indulging in the name-dropping that his family name and history afforded him. Nor did he pontificate about his postwar plans, being content merely to say that politics was likely in his future, partly on account of his father's wishes, and to leave it at that.[45]

Still, one wonders about his brusque dismissal of warning signs in the days before his mission. The entire Anvil project seemed half-baked at best, with test flights that went awry and logistical and tactical uncertainties. Twice a fellow pilot cautioned Joe that the electronic circuitry was not functioning as it should, that the arming panel and so-called safety pin could blow up the aircraft. Joe waved him off both times, forgoing the sensible option of asking his commanding officer that the mission be put off until the plane was fully examined. On the morning of August 12, with the operation definitely on for that evening, he left a message at Kick's flat, asking her to inform his current girlfriend, Pat Wilson, that he'd be a day late joining her in Yorkshire. "I'm about to go into my final act," he said. "If I don't come back, tell my dad—despite our differences [over Kick's wedding, presumably]—that I love him very much."[46] No mention of Mom; just Dad.

Late that afternoon, Joe and his copilot, Wilford J. Willy, a thirty-five-year-old Navy regular and father of three from Fort Worth, Texas, slid behind the controls of the stripped-down Liberator, which was loaded with 23,562 pounds of explosives. They took off without a hitch from Fersfield Aerodrome. Elliott Roosevelt, the president's son, flew behind them in a special Mosquito photoreconnaissance plane to take pictures of the mission and thereby memorialize it. (Which suggests another possible motivation for the mission: that Joe wanted to remove once and for all any lingering suspicion that the Kennedys were "yellow."[47]) Some twenty minutes in, Joe switched over to remote guidance, and he and Willy prepared to bail. Suddenly, with Roosevelt snapping photos from behind, Joe Junior's plane exploded in a giant yellow circle of flame. Pieces of wreckage were scattered over a mile-wide area in coastal Suffolk, and more than fifty homes were damaged. So immense was the blast that not a trace of either pilot was ever found.

In due course it would be determined that Kennedy and Willy's act of ultimate self-sacrifice had been completely unnecessary. The specific target of their mission was Mimoyecques, a fortress in the Pas-de-Calais region where an underground military complex was being built to house Germany's latest "V" weapon, the V-3 cannon, which would be aimed at London, one hundred miles away. Unbeknownst to Allied planners, work on the site had been suspended because of the disruptions caused by conventional British and U.S. bombers. Even had the work been completed, there would have been no V-3s to install, the weapon having proved to be thoroughly defective in trials. In a final irony, less than three weeks after Joe's fateful flight, the empty site at Mimoyecques would be overrun by Canadian troops.[48]

V

In Ted Kennedy's recollection of that awful Sunday on the Cape, Jack turned to him after the priests had left and said, " 'Joe wouldn't want us to sit here crying. He would want us to go sailing. Let's go sailing.' . . . And that's what we did. We went sailing." Afterwards, Jack wandered the beach alone before returning to his hospital bed in Boston. He had time now to think about his brother's death and the strangeness of it all: Joe, with his robust good health, was gone, while he, laid up in a sick bed, got to live. Jack commented in writing a few months afterwards that "the best ones seem to go first," and that there was "a completeness to Joe's life, and that is the completeness of perfection." Jack was proud of his actions in Blackett Strait one year before, but he knew there was a sharp distinction between his experience and the top-secret mission that led to his brother's death. It surprised him not at all when Joe was posthumously awarded the Navy Cross "for extraordinary heroism and courage."[49]

His father's demeanor in the weeks following the tragedy only confirmed the sense that the best one had gone first. Joe Senior was bereft, his grief all-consuming. He withdrew inside himself, spending hours alone listening to classical musical and avoiding social interactions. Young Joe, his firstborn and namesake, had been the embodiment of his dreams and ambitions, of his determination to take the Kennedys to the pinnacle of American public life. He was the crown prince, and now he was dead. "It was as though Joe Kennedy had mounted," one observer later said, "with painstaking attention to the smallest detail, a drama intended to be long and triumphant, only to see the curtain rung down with cruel finality after the prologue." To a friend Kennedy confessed, "You know how much I had tied my whole life up to his and what great things I saw in the future for him. Now it's all over."[50]

An enveloping sense of guilt may have deepened the sorrow. Arthur Krock, who knew his man well, later confided that the fatherly despair at the death was among the most severe "that I've ever seen registered on a human being." He speculated that there was a specific reason for Joe Kennedy's extreme reaction: "Joe Jr. when he volunteered on this final mission which was beyond his duty, beyond everything, was seeking to prove by its very danger that the Kennedys were not yellow. That's what killed that boy. That's why he died. And his father realized it. He never admitted it, but he realized it."[51]

For Rose, the early weeks after the tragedy were the darkest time she had ever known. Joe had always been her great joy, ever since he smiled up at her from his crib in the little house in Brookline three decades before. She couldn't sleep at night as she pictured the terror he must have experienced in his final moments of life. She kept seeing him as a young boy, "running into my arms and snuggling into my lap," and thought about the steady presence he had always been in the Kennedy household, as a kind of surrogate parent and consummate role model for his siblings. Then, as letters poured in from near and far, Rose's anguish began, ever so slowly, to lift as she willed herself to acknowledge that Joe's death was part of God's mysterious plan, a plan she did not have to understand in order to accept it.[52]

On August 16, Jack was on hand at Boston's Logan Airport as Kathleen arrived from England. She collapsed into his arms, weeping. From there the two siblings went to little St. Francis Xavier Church, in Hyannis Port, for some quiet time together. According to her biographer, Kick was shocked by Jack's appearance: "He couldn't have weighed more than a hundred and twenty-five pounds. His cheek and jaw bones jutted out prominently, and his skin had a terrible yellow cast to it."[53] But she relished being with him, and he with her, and they saw each other frequently in the weeks that followed. Then, only a month later, on September 19, another stunning blow: news arrived that Kick's husband, Billy Cavendish, had been killed in action in Belgium nine days earlier, shot through the heart by a German sniper. "So ends the story of Billy and Kick," she wrote in her diary as she prepared to return to England for the memorial service. "Yesterday the final word came. I can't believe that the one thing that I felt might happen should have happened. Billy is dead—killed in action in France Sept 10th. Life is so cruel."[54]

Jack, reflecting on Joe's and Billy's deaths while laid up in the hospital that fall, filled a notebook with fragments about them—a letter from Kick about her husband's passing, condolence notes from Billy's fellow Coldstream officers, a *Washington Post* editorial about Joe as well as his posthumous citation. Jack's thoughts went back to two accounts he had read of Raymond Asquith's death in 1916, one in Buchan's *Pilgrim's Way*, the other in Churchill's *Great Contemporaries*. He inserted both in the notebook:

Buchan: "He loved his youth, and his youth has become eternal. Debonair and brilliant and brave, he is now part of the immortal England which knows not age or weariness or defeat."

Churchill: "The War which found the measure of many men never got to the bottom of him, and, when the Grenadiers strode into the crash and thunder of the Somme, he went to his fate, cool, poised, resolute, matter-of-fact, debonair."[55]

An idea took root in Jack's mind: he would honor his brother by putting together a memorial book, made up of recollections and reminiscences from family and friends. He would serve as editor and pen the introduction. The undertaking became bigger than he anticipated—"The book on Joe is going slower than I had hoped," he wrote Lem Billings in early 1945, "but it should be out in another month or so and I think will be pretty good"—but he took it seriously, spending long hours, in sister Eunice's recollection, making calls and writing letters and gathering the collected pieces that made up the finished work, a slim but moving book titled *As We Remember Joe*. Three hundred and sixty copies were printed and privately distributed, mostly to friends and relatives and service colleagues.[56]

"The book, I am afraid—may make you sad," he wrote his parents upon publication. "I hope that the sadness will be mitigated by the realization—clearly brought out in the book—of what an extraordinarily full and varied life Joe had." (Mr. Kennedy was not willing to take the chance; for the rest of his days he could never bring himself to read more than a few pages of the volume.[57]) In his introduction, Jack wrote of his brother's early acquisition of a "sense of responsibility towards his brothers and sisters, and I do not think that he ever forgot it. Towards me who was nearly his own age, this responsibility consisted in setting a standard that was uniformly high." Touching ever so lightly on Joe's shortcomings—his short fuse, his unwillingness to suffer fools—Jack said he would be forever grateful for the way his brother always led by example, and he left no doubt that the ill-fated mission on August 12, 1944, cut short a life destined for greatness: "His worldly success was so assured and inevitable that his death seems to have cut into the natural order of things."[58]

More than a few commentators would later say the same thing: that Joe was the Kennedy child marked for political stardom. These observers in effect embrace the narrative constructed with painstaking care by Mr. and Mrs. Kennedy, which put their eldest son above the others in the brood, not merely in God-given talent and worldly accomplishments but in future potential. The reality was different, as Joe Junior himself seemed to grasp near the end. Alongside his leading-man looks, his work ethic, his loyalty, his physical courage, and his ebullience stood other qualities. He was hot-tempered and domineering, and often socially aggressive. Relentlessly argumentative, he struggled to dial this tendency back in debates, his need to win all-consuming. His humor tilted to the belittling, sarcastic variety, and his writing lacked subtlety and grace.

Above all, Joe's policy misjudgments, not a few of which flowed from his unshakable determination to do his father's bidding, would have posed obstacles to any future hope of political prominence in the Democratic Party—here one thinks, for example, of the admiration for Hitler's Germany, expressed at various points through the 1930s; the stubborn vote against FDR's nomination at the 1940 party convention; the hard Lindbergh-like anti-interventionism, more extreme even than his father's and held long past the time most of the country had moved away from it; and the founding role in the Harvard Committee Against Military Intervention. The pro-Franco sentiments in Joe's senior thesis and in his post-graduation reports from Spain likewise would have elicited uncomfortable questions, particularly as the fascistic policies of Franco's regime became more widely known. (All copies of the thesis seem to have vanished in the years following his graduation, suggesting the family perceived the problem.[59])

Nor should we necessarily accept the corollary judgment, even more widely held, that John F. Kennedy chose politics for a career only because of his brother's passing and because his father commanded him. Jack had ample time to ponder his options that fall and winter of 1944–45, and there can be no doubt that Joe's death factored into his thinking. It's even possible to endorse historian Herbert Parmet's subsequent assertion that Jack's political career began with "an explosion high over the English coast." His father certainly wanted it to be so, and he began nudging Jack hard in that direction in Palm Beach as early as Christmas 1944. ("I can feel Pappy's eyes on the back of my neck," Jack confided to Red Fay that holiday season.[60])

But Jack had his own reasons for selecting his path. His youth had been imbued by the political legend of his grandfather John F. Fitzgerald, and he had been reared in a household that revered public service and preached the obligation to do something worthwhile with one's life. More than that, he had long been fascinated by politics, and his flirtation with law school was at least in part an expression of that interest. Professors and fellow students at Harvard who knew both brothers believed Jack had the greater interest in, and knowledge of, contemporary politics and political history.[61] Already with Inga Arvad in early 1942, he had mused at length about running for office—the two of them even joked about the highest office in the land—and his subsequent war experience deepened his understanding of world affairs and of what made people tick. At the nightly bull sessions he conducted in the South Pacific, politics was a frequent topic of discussion. And in the late winter of 1944, several months before Joe's death, Jack met with veteran Boston political operative Joe Kane to discuss potential political opportunities he might seek.[62] Jack also had more publicized achievements than did his brother, meaning that in popular terms he, rather than Joe, had the advantage (as Joe himself sensed). The most that can be said is that his brother's passing opened up an arena Jack might well have entered at some point anyway, not in order to take Joe's place but in order to express his own ideals and aspirations. In the recollection of Theodore Sorensen, later a top aide, "His entry [into politics] was neither involuntary nor illogical."[63]

In any event, nothing had been decided that December. Jack had not been released from the Navy, and his precarious health did not allow for firm planning. He also was not yet willing to commit himself to politics as a profession. He had other options. He liked writing, and moreover it was the only occupation for which he had some training and credentials. Plus his success with *Why England Slept* convinced him he could be good at it. To Chuck Spalding and others, he said he might make writing his career, perhaps as a journalist. Academia also held appeal for him, but not the years of additional study it would require. Business enticed him not at all.

VI

But first things first: he needed to get his health in order before committing to any particular path. In December 1944 he appeared before the Retirement Board in Washington, D.C., where it was determined that he would be transferred to the retired list at the rank of lieutenant, "by reason of physical disability," bringing an end to John F. Kennedy's military career. (His official release would be March 1, 1945.) In January 1945 he went to Arizona to try to recover his health in the warm sunshine, renting a room at the Castle Hot Springs Hotel, in the Bradshaw Mountains. On February 20 he reported to Billings that recovery was slow, and that he would return yet again to the Mayo Clinic if he did not feel improvements soon. Still, he was well enough to pay a visit to Phoenix: "Their [sic] was some pumping which interested me, and I did take [actress] Veronica Lake for a ride in my car. . . . I don't mean by all this that I pumped her or that if you should ever see her you should get a big hello. You would get the usual blank stare you get under similar circumstances."[64]

In his cottage he also pecked out a draft article, "Let's Try an Experiment in Peace," which focused on rearmament and the prospects for postwar stability. Whereas previously Jack had championed military preparedness to counter the threat of German and Japanese aggression, he now warned that a postwar arms race could threaten great-power peace and undermine American democracy. ("Democracy sleeps fitfully in an armed camp.") Instead, U.S. leaders should pursue the kind of "intelligent and imaginative statesmanship" required to prevent a renewed arms scramble after the Axis powers were defeated, lest a rival power—here he anticipated it would be the Soviet Union—should try to match America's might, and lest weaker nations "bind together for security against us." *Reader's Digest* took a pass on the article, as did *The Atlantic Monthly*, its editor lamenting that Jack had tried to cover too much ground in too little space, "with the result that your argument does not clinch the reader as it ought." It was a fair critique; the draft lacked spark, and Jack did not offer a particularly novel argument in the context of early 1945, when innumerable other observers were likewise preaching the importance of disarmament, arms limitation, and vigorous diplomatic engagement. Still, the piece provides insight into its author's evolving views on the efficacy of military power, and on his concern—well founded, it would turn out—that postwar strife among world powers could put serious strains on American democratic institutions.[65]

Most notable of all was this farsighted passage: "Science will always overtake caution with new terrors against which defense cannot be anticipated. It is not an exaggeration to expect that missiles will be developed to a point where theoretically any spot on the globe can send to any community in the world, with pinpoint accuracy, a silent but frightful message of death and destruction."[66]

Foreign affairs remained, as always, Jack's principal policy interest, but he sought in Arizona to round himself out by learning a bit more about domestic issues. He befriended a wealthy Chicagoan named Pat Lannan who was likewise in the desert to gain back his health. Lannan impressed on Jack his belief that organized labor would be extremely influential in American politics going forward, and he urged him to learn all he could about the subject. Jack promptly got his father to ship a crate of books on labor unions and labor law, and he dove into them as soon as they arrived. Lannan recalled that Jack, with whom he shared a cottage, "sat up until one or two in the morning reading those books until he finished the whole crate."[67] The episode spoke to Jack's curiosity and drive, and was a further clue that he saw elected office in his future.

Lannan, however, didn't necessarily see presidential material in his new friend. "Certainly when I met Jack in 1945," he later said, "never in my wildest imagination was there an idea that he would become a future president of the United States!" Rather, Jack struck him as a "thoroughly amusing guy," but normal and pragmatic, not on the fast track to high office. What did come through, however, was Jack's devil-may-care bravado, back problems notwithstanding, especially when the two went riding in the hills. "It was a wonderful place to ride horses, and we did that every day. He was a wild rider. He would charge his horse down a mountainside. He loved speed. He was a very daring fellow, but not that good a horseman. He was always taking chances. He always wanted a race—he was very competitive, but in a nice way."[68]

As the two young men whiled away their days in the Arizona sunshine, they could sense that big changes were in the offing. War, it seemed, would soon give way to postwar, and to uncertainty over what that would mean for America, for the world, and for their own futures.

FOURTEEN

"POLITICAL TO HIS FINGERTIPS"

n April 1945 Jack Kennedy was still in the West recuperating when shocking news arrived from across the country: President Franklin D. Roosevelt had suffered a massive cerebral hemorrhage at his retreat in Warm Springs, Georgia, and died. He was ten weeks beyond his sixty-third birthday.

For several years Roosevelt had suffered from hypertension, but it had been mostly ignored—his blood pressure, measured at 188/105 on February 27, 1941, was seldom checked again until 1944. That spring, the president was diagnosed with acute bronchitis, hypertension, breathlessness, cardiac failure of the left ventricle, and long-term heart disease, all showing themselves in a gray pallor and listlessness. His appearance worried friends and associates, including his running mate in the presidential election that November, Senator Harry S. Truman of Missouri. (FDR, determined to see the war through to the end, had decided much more quickly than in 1940 that he would seek another term.) Voters were mostly unaware of his condition, however, and gave him a fourth election win, albeit with a smaller popular-vote margin than in the past.[1]

By then, victory in both theaters looked increasingly likely. Though the D-Day invasion, in June 1944, could have ended in catastrophe—

Nazi forces put up fierce resistance—the Normandy beachhead became the center of a huge buildup; by late July close to a million and a half troops had been transported across the English Channel and were beginning to break out of the coastal perimeter. By the end of August the Allies had liberated France and Belgium. (On the twenty-fifth, Free French leader Charles de Gaulle made his triumphal march down the Champs-Élysées.) In September, they reached the Rhine as the Wehrmacht conducted a fighting retreat. Canadian forces cleared the Scheldt estuary, and General George Patton's U.S. Third Army captured Strasbourg and Metz.

It had the makings of a rout, until Hitler launched a ferocious counterattack in December in the Ardennes, scene of the Panzers' triumph in 1940. After weeks of heavy fighting in what came to be called the Battle of the Bulge—because it created a bulge sixty miles deep and forty miles wide in Allied lines—U.S. forces gained control in late January 1945, but not before incurring 100,000 casualties, including nineteen thousand killed. By that point, strategic bombing had drastically debilitated Germany's war-production capacity and devastated its economy. Meanwhile, battle-hardened Soviet troops marched through snow-covered Poland and East Prussia and cut a path to Berlin. (They entered the death camp at Auschwitz, in southern Poland, on January 27, liberating more than seven thousand surviving prisoners, most of them ill and dying.) In the south, the Red Army took Budapest and pressed up the Danube valley toward Vienna, and American forces crossed the Rhine and took the heavily industrial Ruhr valley. In the Pacific, Admiral Chester Nimitz's amphibious campaign, in which Jack Kennedy had played a part, was readying for assaults on Iwo Jima and Okinawa, stepping-stones to the Japanese home islands, while in the Philippines, MacArthur's units were bearing down on Manila.[2]

As the vise closed on Nazi Germany, with the Western Allies coming in from the west and the Red Army standing on the Oder River, within walking distance of Berlin, Roosevelt, Stalin, and Churchill convened again to discuss the peace, this time at Yalta, the Black Sea resort town on the Crimean peninsula, in early February. In ten days of back-and-forth bargaining, the leaders agreed that Germany would pay reparations but not the full cost of the struggle, and that some eastern German territory would be transferred to Poland (in compensation for the Soviets' taking a comparable amount of eastern Poland), with the remainder of Germany divided into four occupation zones—one each to be administered by the

United States, the Soviet Union, Great Britain, and France. Berlin, within the Soviet zone, would itself be divided among the four victors. Roosevelt, weak and ailing, lobbied hard for the establishment of the United Nations and prevailed, though with the proviso that the major powers—the United States, the Soviet Union, Britain, France, and China—would be permanent members of a Security Council and would have veto power over any resolution of the body. Stalin, for his part, appeared to get his way on Eastern Europe, insisting that the Soviet Union must have non-hostile governments on its western borders, lest the region again be a launching pad for an invasion of the USSR. Roosevelt and Churchill were hardly in a position to argue. In exchange for an American vow to back Soviet claims on territory given up to Japan in the Russo-Japanese War of 1904–05, and to grant Moscow concessions in northeast China, Stalin agreed to sign a treaty of friendship with Chiang Kai-shek, America's ally in China, rather than with the Communist Mao Zedong, and to declare war on Japan within three months of Hitler's defeat.[3]

For the remainder of the century and beyond, critics on the right would refer to Yalta as a sellout, an abandonment of Eastern Europe's people by a dying U.S. leader who ended his presidency preferring cosmetic cooperation and easy deals to conflict with a Kremlin antagonist clearly bent on aggression and expansion.[4] (In the early years after the war, Jack Kennedy himself would occasionally level this charge.) A simpler and better explanation for Roosevelt's behavior holds that the military realities at the time of Yalta gave him few cards to play. Soviet troops occupied Eastern European nations they had liberated, including Poland, where Moscow had installed a pro-Soviet regime despite a British-supported Polish government-in-exile in London. With the Soviet Union having suffered twenty to twenty-five million killed in the war, and with Red Army troops already in place, FDR and Churchill had limited negotiating power over Eastern Europe.[5]

II

After the three leaders left the Crimea, the onslaught continued as the Allies enveloped the Ruhr and captured more than 300,000 German prisoners, then seized Mannheim and Frankfurt. The end was near. In early April, Paris once again became the City of Light as the blackout was lifted.

Vast sections of major German cities—Berlin, Dresden, Hamburg, Essen, Nuremberg, Düsseldorf, and Frankfurt—had been reduced to rubble. On April 11, the U.S. Ninth Army reached the Elbe and was a mere fifty-seven miles from Berlin.

The following day, FDR died. His performance as president and commander in chief had its critics, then and later, but of his immense and lasting influence there can be no doubt. His New Deal fundamentally changed major facets of American life: labor relations, welfare, economic security, conservation, banking, infrastructure, and agriculture, to name but a few. Under Roosevelt, the federal government entered irreversibly into the economic life of the nation—even "small government" conservatives of later decades, while inveighing rhetorically against the welfare state, had no choice but to accept its parameters. In foreign policy, too, Roosevelt claimed enhanced presidential authority, especially after Congress passed Lend-Lease, in early 1941. Here he oscillated between an idealism verging on utopianism and a hardheaded pragmatism, between espousing a capacious global vision and contenting himself with narrow, piecemeal, short-term aims, taking care always to preserve his power in a world of shifting allegiances and constant intrigue. (Here indeed lay part of his strength: it was never easy to know which Roosevelt one was dealing with.) "The Juggler," historian Warren Kimball called him, and the name fits. And certainly, Roosevelt's role in the Allied war effort was colossal—more than anyone, he was the architect of the core strategic decisions that had, by the time of his death, brought victory within sight. To the American men and women engaged in the vast struggle, he was a brilliant commander in chief, superbly adept at articulating the ideals of freedom for which they and their nation were fighting.[6]

Small wonder that historian William E. Leuchtenburg titled his synthesis of the later twentieth-century presidencies, including John F. Kennedy's, *In the Shadow of FDR*.[7]

FDR's singular service to humankind, said Isaiah Berlin, who had served in the British embassies in Washington and Moscow during the war, was in showing that "it is possible to be politically effective and yet benevolent and human"; that the promotion of liberty and social justice need not mean the demise of effective government; and that "individual liberty—a loose texture of society"—could be reconciled with an "indispensable minimum" of organization and authority.[8]

Skeptics would note that Roosevelt could be temperamental and spiteful, and that he did not always exhibit grace under pressure. They would say he made contradictory promises, cynically and unabashedly, to groups and individuals and foreign governments. They would point to the black marks on his record—the forced internment during the war of 100,000 Japanese Americans, notably, and the inaction in the face of the Holocaust. (To critics he should have done more to disrupt the death camps; they were unmoved by his claim that the best way to rescue European Jewry was to win the war as fast as possible.[9]) To this one could add his undue caution, right up to the Pearl Harbor attack, in confronting isolationist strength in Congress.

Yet it remains that as the news of his death hit, that spring day in 1945, many Americans were left bereft, uncomprehending. It seemed impossible. Those in their teens and twenties had never really known another president—Jack Kennedy was fifteen when FDR first took the oath of office, sister Eunice was eleven, and brother Bobby was seven—and even older Americans, including many who opposed him, found it hard to imagine life without the thirty-second president. He had led the country through the depth of the Depression and the challenges of a two-front war. Even in the darkest days of 1942, when it seemed the Axis steamroller might be unstoppable, he had maintained his firm belief that victory would come in the end—made possible by America's industrial and manpower might. Anne O'Hare McCormick, writing in *The New York Times* soon after his passing, said Roosevelt had "occupied a role so fused with his own personality after twelve years that people in other countries spoke of him simply as 'The President,' as if he were President of the World. He did not stoop and he did not climb. He was one of those completely poised persons who felt no need to play up or play down anybody. In his death this is the element of his greatness that comes out most clearly." For GOP senator Robert A. Taft, the message was simple: "He dies a hero of the war, for he literally worked himself to death in the service of the American people."[10]

And there was something else, something of particular interest to our story: Roosevelt's extraordinary capacity to connect with voters, partly through his dauntless optimism and charismatic appeal and partly because of his expert exploitation of the newest technological innovation of the era, radio. His mastery of the medium proved a remarkable political asset. In particular, radio allowed him to make emotional connections with the electorate in a way previous U.S. politicians—remote figures, for the most part, visible only in grainy photographs on the front page of newspapers—had not. In this way Roosevelt was the first media president, the originator of what came to be called media politics, which a quarter century later, under John F. Kennedy, would produce a television presidency.[11]

Not all Americans grieved the great man's passing. Joseph P. Kennedy, though he offered a tribute in the press, told daughter Kick that Roosevelt's death was "a great thing for the country." Still smarting over being bypassed for a cabinet position after resigning from the ambassadorship, Kennedy also in effect blamed FDR for causing Joe Junior's death. By pushing Britain toward war, and in particular by pushing Neville Chamberlain to guarantee Polish sovereignty in the spring of 1939, Kennedy told former president Herbert Hoover, Roosevelt had steered Britain and ultimately the United States into an unnecessary conflagration. It was a dubious interpretation of events, especially coming from an up-close observer, but the Ambassador was adamant. According to Hoover's notes, "Kennedy said that if it had not been for Roosevelt the British would not have made this, the most gigantic blunder in history." Hitler, left to his own devices, would have turned his attention to the east, and Western Europe would have been spared. Roosevelt's subsequent embrace, at Casablanca in 1943, of the doctrine of "unconditional surrender" was another foolhardy move, in Kennedy's judgment: it foreclosed the possibility of a negotiated peace that might have shortened the war.[12]

Nor, in the Ambassador's myopic view, had Roosevelt laid the basis for a sound postwar order. Where others saw the emergence of a new, U.S.-led framework for world politics, Kennedy saw just waste and anarchy. "It's a horrible thing to contemplate," he wrote to Kick, "with the death of all these boys and with the world economically and socially in chaos, that we haven't anything to look forward to in the line of peace for the world as the pay-off for everyone's sacrifices."[13]

Absent was any acknowledgment of what the Allied liberation of Nazi concentration camps that spring had shown: the profound malevolence of a system of systematic terror, torture, and killing, one with a genocidal component at its core. The appalling film footage from Bergen-Belsen and Buchenwald shocked even the most hardened of observers, as much for the neglect it showed as for the cruelty, with huge numbers of unburied dead who were the victims of starvation and unchecked disease. Suddenly, it seemed Winston Churchill had spoken the most basic of truths when he had told his compatriots, in the gloomy days of June 1940, "If we fail, then the whole world, including the United States, including all that we have known and cared for, will sink into the abyss of a new Dark Age made more sinister, and perhaps more protracted, by the lights of perverted science."[14] This dimension of the war as a moral struggle that saved liberal civilization never fully registered with Joe Kennedy.

Yet for all his ongoing bitterness, Kennedy knew he had to follow the line he had long preached to his brood: that life is for the living. Resigned to the reality that his own career in public life was in all likelihood over, he fastened his attention ever more firmly on his children. That meant, above all, Jack. It would be Jack, the father hoped, who would restore the Kennedy name to prominence, Jack who would live out the life plan Joe had imagined for Joe Junior. In April, accordingly, the Ambassador got the Hearst-owned *Chicago Herald-American* to hire Jack to cover the upcoming United Nations conference in San Francisco for the paper as well as for Hearst's *New York Journal-American*. Jack jumped at the opportunity—the work would test his suitability for a journalistic career, and might also be a useful prelude to running for office. His beau ideal Churchill, after all, had at one point been a young correspondent in the Sudan and in the Second Boer War, before standing for Parliament.

III

By this time Jack had completed his period of rest and recovery in Arizona's Bradshaw Mountains and had also paid a visit to Hollywood, in the company of Pat Lannan and Chuck Spalding. There they roomed at the fashionable Beverly Hills Hotel and sampled the nightlife, hobnobbing with film celebrities such as Gary Cooper, Walter Huston, Olivia de Havilland, and the ice skater Sonja Henie. Jack had a blast, even if Cooper's lack of depth and conversational skill during dinner stunned him— "That's about a three-word dinner we had," Jack remarked to Spalding, who had penned a bestselling book, *Love at First Flight*, that Cooper was interested in adapting for the screen. "Nobody said anything, and if we did, Gary said zero!" An afternoon at de Havilland's home ended in comical fashion as Jack, his eyes fixed firmly on the movie star, turned the wrong doorknob and opened a tightly packed hall closet, sending tennis rackets, balls, and shoes crashing down on him.[15]

The trio also met with Inga Arvad, and Spalding could immediately see why Jack had fallen for her, quite apart from her looks—she was warm and witty and enchantingly cosmopolitan. But the relationship was by now purely platonic, whatever faint hopes Jack may have had for more. (Some weeks earlier, he had told Billings that he planned to visit Southern California and "tangle tonsils with Inga Binga.") Inga's relationship with William Cahan held steady, and she liked her West Coast life. She feared (wrongly) that she was still under FBI surveillance, moreover, and had no interest in restarting the difficulties she and Jack had experienced in 1942, particularly given his possible pursuit of a political career.[16]

On April 25, 1945, after a brief stop at the Mayo Clinic for medical tests, Jack headed back west to cover the founding conference of the United Nations, in San Francisco, the greatest gathering of world statesmen since the Versailles Conference of 1919.[17] Though the suggestion would subsequently be made that Hearst executives were doing the Kennedys a favor by employing him, it was really shrewd self-interest that drove them—for a modest fee of $750, they got sixteen informative and lucid articles from a war hero who had written a respected book on international affairs and had important family connections to senior U.S. and British officials. He might have still been shy of twenty-eight, but he had credibility.[18]

The young correspondent's first story, filed on April 28, reflected his realist outlook, as he cautioned readers that the conference had been given too much of a buildup, with exaggerated hopes for what it could accomplish in a world still driven by core national interests. "There is an impression that this is the conference to end wars and introduce peace on earth and good-will toward nations—excluding of course, Germany and Japan. Well it's not going to do that." The leading powers would wish to preserve considerable latitude for themselves—one of them, the Soviet Union, seemed intent on raising a ruckus at the meeting and getting its way on several important issues. Jack then noted that the average GI on San Francisco's streets had little inkling of the purpose of the conference. He quoted a decorated Marine: "I don't know much about what's going on—but if they just fix it so that we don't have to fight anymore—they can count me in." Jack added, "Me, too, Sarge."[19]

A marked feature of the conference and a constant theme in Kennedy's dispatches was the growing friction between the Soviet Union and the Western Allies. The schism had been evident for months. Already the previous year, the Soviet leadership had distanced itself from the new World Bank and the International Monetary Fund (IMF), created at the Bretton Woods Conference, in New Hampshire, in July 1944 in order to stabilize finance and trade. The former was designed to provide developing nations with needed capital, the latter to monitor exchange rates and lend reserve currencies to nations with trade deficits. Stalin and his lieutenants held, correctly, that the United States dominated both institutions, and they anticipated that Washington would use them to promote private investment and open international commerce, which to Moscow smacked of capitalist exploitation. More to the point in Stalin's eyes, it bespoke America's hegemonic ambition, as did the fact that the conferees at Bretton Woods agreed to make the U.S. dollar the standard currency of world trade, replacing Britain's pound sterling.[20]

"Winston Churchill once said that Russian policy was an enigma wrapped in a mystery," Jack reported on April 30. "I'd like to report to Mr. Churchill that the Russians haven't changed." A quarter century of mutual distrust between Russia and the rest of the world could not be overcome easily or quickly, he went on, and history would place a heavy burden on all negotiations. And on May 2: "This conference from a distance may have appeared so far like an international football game with [Soviet foreign minister Vyacheslav] Molotov carrying the ball while [the Western representatives] tried to tackle him all over the field."[21]

To a degree, Kennedy suggested, the Soviets' go-it-alone style in the proceedings was understandable, rooted as it was in genuine security concerns, and an absolute conviction that Mother Russia, having endured colossal hardship over the previous four years, must never be invaded again. The Red Army, moreover, had borne the brunt of the fighting against the German war machine, suffering huge casualties, while the Americans and the British dithered over launching the second front; why should the West be trusted now?[22] Yet Kennedy cautioned American and British leaders against simply acquiescing to Moscow's demands, and he anticipated the Cold War that was to come. "There is growing discouragement among people concerning our chances of winning any lasting peace from this war," he wrote in the third week of the conference. "There is talk of fighting the Russians in the next ten or fifteen years. We have indeed gone a long way since those hopeful days early in the war when we talked of union now and one world." The following day he was gloomier still, predicting that, in the absence of a meaningful settlement, Soviet-

American relations would rapidly worsen. The political battle would go on in Europe and spread to Asia at the conclusion of the war with Japan.[23]

On May 7, the day of Germany's surrender and a week after Hitler and his bride of thirty-six hours committed suicide in their Berlin bunker as the Soviets closed in, Jack articulated the American servicemen's assessment of the conference. "It is natural that they should be most concerned for its result, because any man who has risked his life for his country and seen his friends killed around him must inevitably wonder why this has happened to him and most important, what good will it all do," he wrote. "In their concern, and as a result of their interest, and because they wish above all else to spare their children and their brothers from going through the same hard times, it is perhaps natural that they should be disappointed with what they have seen in San Francisco. I suppose that this is inevitable. Youth is a time for direct action and simplification. To come from battlefields where sacrifice is the order of the day—to come from there to here—it is not surprising that they should question the worth of their sacrifice and feel somewhat betrayed."[24]

A private letter to a wartime friend expanded the point, and spoke powerfully to Jack Kennedy's overall worldview in that spring of 1945:

It would have been very easy to write a letter to you that was angry. When I think of how much this war has cost us, of the deaths of Cy and Peter and Orv and Gil and Demi and Joe and Billy and all those thousands and millions who have died with them—when I think of all those gallant acts that I have seen or anyone has seen who has been to war—it would be a very easy thing for me to feel disappointed and somewhat betrayed. . . .

You have seen the battlefields where sacrifice was the order of the day and to compare that sacrifice to the timidity and selfishness of the nations gathered at San Francisco must inevitably be disillusioning. . . .

Things cannot be forced from the top. The international relinquishing of sovereignty would have to spring from the people—it would have to be so strong that the elected delegates would be turned out of office if they failed to do it. . . . We must face the truth that the people have not been horrified by war to a sufficient extent to force them to go to any extent rather than have another war. . . . War will exist until that distant day when the conscientious objector enjoys the same reputation and prestige that the warrior does today.[25]

At the midpoint of the conference, Jack gloomily predicted that "the world organization that will come out of San Francisco will be the product of the same passions and selfishness that produced the Treaty of Versailles." The larger countries in particular were not about to cede their sovereignty to any supranational organization. And later, on May 23, he criticized the veto power being granted to the five major powers on the Security Council: "Thus, any of the Big Five can effectively veto assistance for an attacked nation. With this grave weakness in the new world organization, it is little wonder that the smaller countries have attempted to make treaties with the neighbors for protection against aggressors."[26]

He jotted in his notebook, with respect to the UN:

Danger of too great a build-up.
Mustn't expect too much.
A truly just solution will leave every nation somewhat disappointed.
There is no cure all.[27]

The young reporter worked diligently by day, but, true to form, he shifted gears in the evenings, taking full advantage of the social opportunities at the conference. On at least one occasion, the fun interfered with the job. Arthur Krock described the scene one evening at the Palace Hotel, with Jack propped up on his bed in his tuxedo, ready for the evening's festivities, "a highball in one hand and the telephone receiver in the other. To the operator he said, 'I want to speak to the Managing Editor of the *Chicago Herald American*.' (After a long pause) 'Not in? Well, put someone on to take a message.' (Another pause) 'Good. Will you see that the boss gets this message as soon as you can reach him? Thank you. Here's the message: Kennedy will not be filing tonight.' "[28]

IV

Jack had secured a room at the hotel for Chuck Spalding and his wife, Betty, and saw them most every day. The Spaldings noted his bad back and overall lack of robustness, and his need to spend many mornings resting. "We used to go in and talk to him in the morning before he got out of bed," Betty recalled. "He was his usual wry kind of humorous self, but not full of energy, not jumping around." Jack also reconnected with another old acquaintance, Mary Meyer, née Pinchot (her father, Amos Pinchot, was a Progressive Era ally of Theodore Roosevelt), whom he had dated on occasion when he was at Harvard and she was a free-spirited Vassar student of extraordinary beauty. Immediately before the conference she had married Cord Meyer Jr., an intense, brainy veteran of the Pacific war who was in San Francisco as an aide to Commander Harold Stassen, former "boy governor" of Minnesota and now a member of the U.S. delegation. Cord Meyer and Jack sparred early and often at the conference, perhaps on account of their differing temperaments and world outlooks, or perhaps because Jack showed excessive interest in Meyer's wife. (And indeed, Mary would in time come back into Jack's life, shortly before his premature death—and her own.)[29]

Anita Marcus, later to become Red Fay's wife, remembered meeting Jack at an evening party at the Presidio. "I went to the powder room. All the girls there were talking about Jack Kennedy." When Marcus came out and sat down at a table, Jack joined her and introduced himself. She was bowled over. "I think the main thing was that when he talked to you, he looked you straight in the eye and his attention never wandered. He was interested in finding out what I was doing there—why I was there. It was a drawing-me-out thing. It was undivided attention. I was the most envied girl in the room. He had a way with women. There was no question about it."[30]

In late May, with the conference still going (on June 26, fifty nations would sign the UN charter at the San Francisco Opera House), Jack Kennedy returned to the East Coast, spending a few days in New York and Boston and celebrating his birthday. He then continued eastward to England, in order to cover the British elections for Hearst. It was his first European visit since 1939, when he was in Germany immediately before the Polish invasion and then in the House of Commons when a grim-faced Chamberlain announced that Britain was at war. Now the struggle in Europe was over, and Europe's leaders faced the task of responding to their restive populations.[31] While still in San Francisco, Jack had speculated presciently that Winston Churchill and his Conservatives were vulnerable, even in the afterglow of victory, as many Britons struggled with privation—food rationing, fuel and housing shortages, and bombed-out public buildings. Few American observers then shared this view, and most in Britain likewise predicted a Tory win, but as the election neared it seemed increasingly likely that the great man would be removed.[32] Jack followed him on the campaign trail, as full of admiration as ever, and told his readers that the Conservatives might eke out a narrow win. Still, "Churchill is fighting a tide that is surging through Europe, washing away monarchies and conservative governments everywhere, and that tide flows powerfully in England. England is moving towards some form of socialism—if not in this election, then surely at the next."[33] It would be this one: in July voters rejected Churchill and gave Labour, under Clement Attlee, a sweeping victory.

Kennedy had seen it coming, but even so, he was stunned. He'd always understood, in a way his father never did, that Churchill, whatever his flaws, whatever his strategic and tactical errors, was the wartime leader Britain needed, the one who'd assumed power in the darkest of hours in May 1940, and, through his extraordinary speechmaking, had brought out in his people qualities they had forgotten they possessed: resilience, steadfastness, unflappable determination. Thenceforth, observers every-where understood, only defeat following a direct invasion would take Britain out of the struggle. In the grueling years thereafter, Churchill made his share of miscalculations and saw his influence within the Grand Alliance eclipsed by Roosevelt and Stalin, but he hung tight, firm in purpose and unhesitating in action, his fearless tenacity ultimately vindicated. Yet now he was ousted, just like that.

Pat Lannan, who had secured his own reporting gig and was with Jack in London, marveled at the number of Brits who now flocked to see his friend, often for late-afternoon drinks and political talk in the suite at the Grosvenor House Hotel that the two Americans shared. David Ormsby-Gore came, as did William Douglas-Home and Hugh Fraser, whom Jack had met through Kick. "Oftentimes in this little sitting room which wasn't very large there could have been seven or eight of us at one time, and they would all have been his friends," Lannan remembered. "I think Jack was very seriously excited about the election, about what was going to happen to Europe, what sort of Europe was going to emerge from the war." Fraser agreed. It impressed him that Jack drove for much of the night in sister Kick's cramped Austin to accompany him as he campaigned (success-fully) as the Tory candidate in Stone, 130 miles northwest of London.[34]

Jack also covered the campaign of Alastair Forbes, a distant cousin of Franklin Roosevelt who was running (unsuccessfully) as the Liberal candidate in Hendon, north London. Kick had introduced the two men, and they hit it off immediately.[35] Like Fraser, Forbes was struck by Kennedy's interest in coming to routine campaign appearances and listening to the speeches, absorbing how it was done in Britain, taking mental notes, asking the right questions. He seemed to Forbes to be the most intellectual member of the Kennedy family, even if not an *intellectual* per se—that is, someone interested in ideas for ideas' sake. "He had a fantastically good instinct," Forbes recalled, "once his attention was aroused in a problem, for getting the gist of it and coming to a mature judgment about it." But there was also in Jack a detachment of a type Forbes saw as well in Churchill, one he suspected grew out of both men's privileged backgrounds: "Money was the great insulator. If you don't sort of make your bed and get your own breakfast and have a certain amount of conversation with people who are doing all sorts of ordinary, simple jobs, it does rob you of a great deal of empathy. I mean, whole areas in which empathy should naturally play a part are closed to you."[36]

The economist Barbara Ward, another friend of Kick's, recalled meeting Jack on that same visit and finding him insatiably fascinated by the electoral process, down to the narrow particulars. "You could see already that this young lieutenant was political to his fingertips. So my chief memory is of a very young man, still hardly with the eggshell off his back, he seemed so young, but with an extraordinarily, I would say, well-informed interest in the political situation he was seeing."[37]

This passion for politics comes through clearly in Jack's articles and in his trip diary, as does his capacity for independent thought and tendency to seek out the pragmatic middle ground. He could see that the Conservative Party was, in the eyes of a great many voters, hidebound and reactionary, the defender of the rich and privileged, and that it needed to broaden its appeal in order to have any hope of winning future elections. The kind of conservatism that existed for an "unproductive few, quaffing port and oppressing the peasantry," was "out," he told Ormsby-Gore.[38] Yet Kennedy also saw little to admire in Labour's habit of promising everything to everyone, assuring farmers, shopkeepers, small business owners, and workers that glorious days were ahead. Holding actual power "may be Labour's great crisis," he predicted in an article on July 10. Of Harold

Laski, his old teacher and now Labour's chairman, he had little good to say: "He spoke with great venom and bitterness," Jack recorded in his diary after attending an election rally featuring the famed economist. "Odd that this strain runs through these radicals of the Left. It's that spirit which builds dictatorships, as has been shown in Russia. . . . I think unquestionably, from my talk with Laski that he and others like him smart not so much from the economic inequality but from the social."[39]

And this, from another diary entry: "Socialism is inefficient. I will never believe differently. But you can feed people in a socialistic state, and that may be what will ensure its eventual success."[40]

A post-election diary entry on July 27 revealed Jack's penchant for quantifying what he saw:

It is important in assaying this election to decide how much of the victory was due to a "time for change" vote which would have voted against any government in power, whether Right or Left, and how much was due to real Socialist strength. My own opinion is that it was about 40 per cent due to dissatisfaction with conditions over which the government had no great control but from which they must bear responsibility—20 per cent due to a belief in Socialism as the only solution to the multifarious problems England must face— and the remaining 40 per cent due to a class feeling—i.e., that it was time "the working man" had a chance.[41]

He could also show a lighter touch. On meeting Billy Cavendish's father, the Duke of Devonshire, at Compton Place in Eastbourne, accompanied by Kick, Jack observed in the diary that he "is an eighteenth-century story book Duke in the beliefs—if not in the appearance. He believes in the Divine Right of Dukes, and in fairness, he is fully conscious of his obligations—most of which consist of furnishing the people of England with a statesman of mediocre ability but outstanding integrity."[42]

From England Kennedy proceeded to pay his first visit to Ireland, whence his immigrant forefathers had come, penning a thoughtful article on the nation's political situation, including vis-à-vis the Commonwealth.[43] In his diary, meanwhile, he revealed little sentimental attachment but showed his reporter's instincts, remarking that the people "are cheerful and there is none of the chronic fatigue that sharpens tempers in London. Food is plentiful, what rationing there is is applied with Irish tolerance and good humor, there are none of the queues of London."

> In Dublin there are few cars, petrol is difficult to get, but the people walk or ride their bicycles. The streets are scrupulously clean and the famous doors of Dublin are freshly painted and the brass is shining.
>
> But the appearances are superficial. Ireland which has escaped the devastation and the bombing of Europe has had its casualties. More than 250,000 of its population crossed to England to serve in the armed forces or in the factories. How many of these went direct into the armed forces has not been disclosed, but the fact that residents of Southern Ireland received seven Victoria Cross[es] while people in the North received none has caused some satisfaction among the people in the South.[44]

He then pressed on to the Continent, at the invitation of Navy secretary James Forrestal, a former New York banker who knew Joseph Kennedy well. Short and trim and intensely driven, with a penchant for intellectual sparring, Forrestal had risen from humble roots in upstate New York to make a fortune on Wall Street, then had used his connections to gain a high position in Washington, first as special assistant to FDR, then as undersecretary of the Navy, then, starting in May 1944, as secretary.[45] Long impressed by Jack, he hoped to recruit the younger Kennedy to a position in the Navy Department, and imagined that some travel together to the Berlin suburb of Potsdam (where an Allied leaders' conference was under way) and through war-torn Germany might strengthen the bond between them and seal the deal. They met in Paris in late July and flew from there to the German capital, the utter destructiveness of the war easy to see from the air.

It looked still worse from the ground. Hotel Excelsior, Jack's home on his previous visit to Berlin, in the days just before the outbreak of war in 1939, was literally a shell of its former grand self, on account of the bombing damage. But elsewhere, too, the devastation seemed complete.

"Unter der Linden [a major thoroughfare] and the streets are relatively clear, but there is not a single building which is not gutted," he scribbled in the diary. "On some of the streets the stench—sweet and sickish—is overwhelming. The people all have completely colorless faces—a yellow tinge with pale tan lips. They are all carrying bundles. Where they are going, no one seems to know. I wonder whether they do. They sleep in cellars. The women will do anything for food. One or two of the women wore lipstick, but most seem to be trying to make themselves as unobtrusive as possible to escape the notice of the Russians"—who, he noted in another entry, routinely engaged in gang rape. With respect to Hitler, the room where he "was supposed to have met his death showed scorched walls and traces of fire. There is no complete evidence, however, that the body that was found was Hitler's body. The Russians doubt that he is dead."[46]

Forrestal and Kennedy drove the short distance to Potsdam, "through miles of Russian soldiers. They were stationed on both sides of the road at about 40 yard intervals—green-hatted and green-epauleted—Stalin's personal and picked guard. They looked rugged and tough, unsmiling but with perfect discipline."[47] The following day, July 30, the two embarked on a three-day tour of war-ravaged German ports and cities, among them Bremen, Bremerhaven, and Frankfurt. They flew to Salzburg and visited the Führer's bombed-out mountain chalet at Berchtesgaden and his mountaintop aerie, the Eagle's Nest.

About the future, the diary was at times prescient. "One opinion here is that the Russians are never going to pull out of their zone of occupation but plan to make their part of Germany a Soviet Socialist Republic. . . . If we [Americans] don't withdraw and allow [the Germans] to administer their own affairs, we will be confronted with an extremely difficult administrative problem. Yet, if we pull out, we may leave a political vacuum that the Russians will be only too glad to fill." Regarding the United Nations, Kennedy anticipated the common later view that, with "its elaborate mechanics," the organization would prove ineffectual in resolving the great issues of war and peace, especially given that the larger countries would refuse to entrust it with sufficient decision-making power.[48]

At other times the diarist's anticipatory powers fell short. He missed how strong a leader France's Charles de Gaulle would prove to be, and was plainly wrong—if understandably, at the time—in thinking a divided Berlin would be a "ruined and unproductive city." His prediction about Hitler's posthumous reputation, jotted after seeing Berchtesgaden and the Eagle's Nest, was perplexing: "After visiting these two places, you can easily understand how that within a few years Hitler will emerge from the hatred that surrounds him now as one of the most significant figures who ever lived."[49] (The argument seemed to be that if a leader were evaluated merely by how much he or she transformed the world, whether for good or ill, Hitler must be judged a colossal figure in history. But the phrasing was, to say the least, insensitive to the murderous ravages of the Third Reich.)

As with his six-month overseas sojourn in 1939, Jack Kennedy's 1945 visit to Germany offered the young man some uncanny brushes with history as he suddenly found himself—thanks to his family connections—visiting the inner sanctums of Nazi power and rubbing elbows at Potsdam with top U.S. officials. (He and Forrestal even got to inspect the interior of Hitler's bombed-out office in the Reich Chancellery.) Though not permitted into the Potsdam sessions, he met or saw up close the new president, Harry Truman, supreme Allied commander and future president Dwight D. Eisenhower, Army chief of staff General George C. Marshall, and a slew of senior State Department figures: Secretary of State James Byrnes as well as W. Averell Harriman, Charles Bohlen, John McCloy, Robert Murphy, and William Clayton, among others.

It was heady stuff for a twenty-eight-year-old, and the experience showed that he belonged, or was on his way to belonging, and that in due course he, too, might take his place on the international stage. Even now, Kennedy could legitimately claim to be as well versed on the issues as were many of the journalists who crowded into Potsdam, and arguably more informed than Truman, who had been in office only three months and before that had been kept out of almost all war-related planning during his brief time as vice president. Roosevelt had barely known Truman and—shockingly—had not even informed him of the atomic bomb project that was nearing completion in the New Mexico desert. (Stalin, on the other hand, through spies, knew a great deal about the Manhattan Project.*) To Secretary of State Byrnes and Secretary of War Henry Stimson, the two key cabinet members on foreign policy, the new president was a

---

* Almost certainly, Kennedy did not at this point know any specifics of the Manhattan Project, but his diary entry for July 10, continuing a theme he articulated in his unpublished article from Arizona early in the year, suggests he may have had an inkling something big was under way: "The clash [between Russia and the West] may be indefinitely postponed by the eventual discovery of a weapon so horrible that it will truthfully mean the abolishment of all the nations employing it. Thus Science, which has contributed so much to the horrors of war, will be the means of bringing it to an end."

figure of mystery; they didn't know him more than to say hello. Though Truman prided himself on being a well-read student of history, he had no background in foreign policy, and little international experience—this was his first visit to Europe since being an artilleryman in France in World War I.[50]

No one knew it, but present in Potsdam at the same time that summer was not only the thirty-third president of the United States, but the thirty-fourth and the thirty-fifth as well. About number 33 Jack has little to say in his diary, noting merely and without context or elaboration that "Truman is deader than Kelsey's nuts." (He would later come to see Truman as a courageous and decent man.) But number 34 is another matter. "Eisenhower talked with Forrestal for a few minutes," reads an entry from August 1, "and it was obvious why he is an outstanding figure. He has an easy personality, immense self-assurance, and gave an excellent presentation of the situation in Germany." An earlier entry, from June 30, remarks on Eisenhower's hold over the British people: "He was heard to say after the Eighth [Army] had marched past, 'To think that I, a boy from Abilene, Kansas, am the Commander of troops like those!' He never lost that humble way and therefore easily won the hearts of those with whom he worked."[51]

On at least one occasion in Germany, Jack got to meet the man, if only in passing. The scene was Frankfurt, and the witness was Seymour St. John, who in two years would take over from his father as headmaster at Choate. When Forrestal's plane arrived on the tarmac, St. John, then a Navy lieutenant assisting with the logistics of the visit, recalled, "the plane doors opened, and out came Forrestal. Then, to my amazement, Jack Kennedy. Ike was meeting Forrestal, so Jack met Ike." A surviving photograph shows Eisenhower greeting Forrestal on the tarmac, with Kennedy and St. John in the background.[52]

Truman was less patient with Stalin at this Big Three conference than Franklin Roosevelt had been at the previous ones, in part because he had learned, as the conference opened, that a test in New Mexico of the new atomic weapon had been successful, and in part because Japan now seemed an utterly spent force. At home, its cities were gutted by massive U.S. aerial attacks (with the loss of several hundred thousand Japanese lives), and its sea power, on which protection from invasion had rested, had been destroyed. The United States no longer needed the Soviet Union's help in fighting the Pacific war. Even so, Potsdam was important in setting the details of the postwar occupation and treaty arrangements, in a sense finalizing the basic agreements reached at Tehran and Yalta. Stalin also gained a more formal acceptance by the Americans and the British of the Soviet sphere of influence in Eastern Europe. The specifics concerning the occupation of Germany—and, within it, Berlin—were hashed out, and Stalin (anxious to get his share of the spoils in the east) reaffirmed his vow to join the war against Japan as soon as possible.[53]

Of the broader geopolitical reality there could be no dispute: this was now effectively a two-power world, whatever the fictions expressed in the makeup of the UN Security Council. Britain was drastically weakened and badly overstretched; France, struggling to emerge from the living death of Nazi occupation, was prostrate. Germany had been demolished. Japan, on the brink of defeat, faced the humiliation of occupation, while China, which had yet to emerge as the world power its population suggested it should be, was rent by divisions so deep it would soon spiral back into civil war. Only the United States and the Soviet Union were emerging stronger from the long and bitter struggle.

Yet they were not coequal, and the differences in their wartime experiences were profound. The Soviets had turned back the mighty Nazi war machine and secured the strategic power position in Eastern and Central Europe. Their battle-tested Red Army was by far the largest in the world. But the successes on the Eastern Front had come at unimaginable cost: in addition to twenty-five million dead—in a prewar population of 170 million, one out of seven people—the USSR had suffered the destruction of seventeen hundred cities and towns, seventy thousand villages and hamlets, six million buildings, forty thousand miles of railroad, and ninety thousand bridges. The Germans ransacked the countryside and stole and slaughtered seventeen million heads of cattle, twenty million hogs, and seven million horses. U.S. losses, meanwhile, at the start of the Potsdam Conference stood at roughly 400,000 men. In three and a half years of fighting, its homeland had never been seriously threatened; its citizens' standard of living had actually grown. Overseas, the tentacles of American economic and military power now reached almost every corner of the globe, as exemplified by the creation of a gargantuan network of U.S. military installations and bases—in South America, throughout the Pacific, across the Middle East, in South Asia, even in Africa. By the middle of 1945, American bases were being built at the mind-boggling rate of more than one hundred per month; by year's end, the total would be more than two thousand bases and thirty thousand military installations.[54]

It all made a deep impression on the young lieutenant turned reporter, as Ted Sorensen, an admitted partisan, would later write of Kennedy's 1945 experiences in San Francisco and Europe: "All this had sharpened his interest in public affairs and public service. . . . Jack Kennedy knew he wanted to be a participant, not an observer. He was, in many ways, an old-fashioned patriot—not in the narrow nationalistic sense but in his deep devotion to the national interest. He had compared firsthand the political and economic systems of many countries on several continents and he greatly preferred our own. He shared [John] Buchan's belief that 'democracy was primarily an attitude of mind, a spiritual testament' and that 'politics is still the greatest and most honorable adventure.' "[55]

This seems right. The journalistic stint in the spring and summer of 1945, however much pushed by the father, honed Kennedy's already established interest in the pressing issues of international and domestic affairs, and sharpened his sense that politics might be a more stimulating career choice than either journalism or academia, the other options he was considering. He'd rather be in the inner sanctuary of power, in other words, than writing about it in the pressroom or in the ivory tower.

A letter to his former Choate teacher Harold Tinker early in the year hinted at his thinking. His experience in the South Pacific, he wrote, had made him disillusioned by the savagery of war. "I should really like—as my life's goal—in some way and at some point to do something to help prevent another."[56]

As Jack's political persona began to take shape, his fallen brother's life was commemorated. On July 26, a new 2,200-ton Gearing-class destroyer, the USS *Joseph P. Kennedy, Jr.*, was launched from the Bethlehem Steel Corporation's Fore River Shipyard, in Quincy, Massachusetts—the same shipyard where Joe Senior had worked during World War I. The invitation list to the launch included countless political power players and media luminaries, and Jack's friends, too, were out in force—Torby Macdonald, Lem Billings, Charlie Houghton, John Hersey and Frances Ann Cannon, Chuck Spalding, Red Fay, and Charlotte McDonnell Harris. Representing the family were Joe, Rose, Eunice, Pat, Bobby, Jean, and Teddy, as well as grandparents Honey Fitz and Mary. Young Jean, as the designated sponsor, swung the bottle of champagne to christen the vessel.

Jack's return to America in early August coincided with the dawn of the atomic era and the end of World War II—on August 6 and 9, the United States dropped A-bombs on Hiroshima and Nagasaki, respectively, and on the eighth the Soviet Union declared war on Japan. On August 14, the government in Tokyo, under Emperor Hirohito, surrendered. An era had ended and a new one begun—for Jack Kennedy and for the world.

He had anticipated this moment. Already at the start of 1945, in his unpublished "Let's Try an Experiment in Peace" article, he'd speculated that science would soon create weapons capable of delivering unimaginable destruction over vast distances. Later, he reiterated the point in his diary. Now, with two Japanese cities instantaneously laid to waste, Jack grasped the bomb's transformative effect, understood how the splitting of the atom had split the century, creating a *before* and an *after*. In a little-noticed speech to the United War Fund on October 8, he mused aloud on the topic, articulating sentiments he would refine and espouse to the end of his days. "We have gone a long way from those trying days of '42, '43, and '44 when victory lay in the balance," he told his modest-size audience. "Now the guns have cooled, the men are returning home, the catastrophic days of war are over, the grueling days of peace are ahead—one chapter has ended, another has begun." Atomic weapons would be central to this new era, he went on, and the Western democracies, with their righteous reluctance to wage war, could be at a colossal disadvantage in a military conflict that could be over in an hour.

Yet all was not lost. Perhaps the very destructiveness of the new weapon would compel nations to preserve the peace. "In the past years, we have heard much about the horrors of war, but we have always felt that war was preferable to certain alternatives. There are certain things for which we have always fought. War has never been the ultimate evil. Now, however, that may be changed." Consequently, humanity "may be forced to make the sacrifices that will insure peace. We can only pray that man's political skill can keep abreast of his scientific skill; if not, we may yet live to see Armageddon."[57]

Would he himself contribute to that urgent work, and if so, how? A new international order was coming into being, one with his own country in a position of supreme power, in a kind of Pax Americana; perhaps he could find a place in the arena. Within a few weeks of his return from Europe, Jack heard from Forrestal. "Do you want to do any work here?"

the Navy secretary wrote from Washington. "If so, why don't you come down and see what there is at hand?"[58] Jack, thankful for the offer, had other ideas. Opportunities loomed for him to experience that "greatest and most honorable adventure," and he dared not miss them.

Politics, that is to say, beckoned.

PART
III

―――

POLITICS

FIFTEEN

THE CANDIDATE

I t looked like a giant half shell tucked up against the coastline. Misshapen by gerrymandering and stretching out in various directions, the Eleventh Congressional District took in East Boston and the North and West End as well as the northern tip of Brighton, then crossed the Charles River into Cambridge and a large chunk of Somerville. Charlestown, with its wooden "three-deckers" and its heavy concentration of Irish, was also within its confines. Predominantly working class and overwhelmingly Democratic and Roman Catholic, the district was among the poorest in the state, but it also included the middle-class Ward Twenty-two, in Brighton, and the elegant, tree-lined streets of West Cambridge, home to Harvard and Radcliffe professors, old Brahmin families, and business executives commuting to the city. Historic events in the nation's early years unfolded here—in the North End stood the Old North Church, made famous by Paul Revere on the evening of April 18, 1775, when he made his midnight ride, while Charlestown was the setting for the Battle of Bunker Hill, two months later. Two weeks after that, on July 3, 1775, George Washington took command of the Continental Army on the north end of Cambridge Common.

The Kennedys had deep roots in the Eleventh. P. J. Kennedy, Jack's grandfather, owned saloons in East Boston and represented the area in the state legislature; his son Joseph Patrick was born, came of age, and attended Harvard here, as did his sons after him. Jack's maternal grandfather, John "Honey Fitz" Fitzgerald, hailed from the North End, in due course became its political overlord, and saw his daughter Rose born here. At the turn of the century, Fitzgerald represented this district (then the Ninth) in the U.S. House of Representatives. And the eastern edge of the district's Ward Twenty-two in Brighton was only seven or eight blocks from Jack's birthplace on Beals Street, in neighboring Brookline.

In 1945 the seat was held by James Michael Curley, a legendary, roguish figure in Boston and archnemesis of Honey Fitz. (It was Curley who in 1913 floated the rumor about Honey Fitz's dalliance with cigarette girl "Toodles" Ryan and thereby forced him to withdraw from the mayor's race.) The epitome of the crooked urban pol, Curley, now seventy years old, had fallen on hard times after a fraud conviction in 1937, only to bounce back and win election to Congress five years later, taking the seat from Thomas H. Eliot, a New Dealer who had helped write the Social Security Act. Soon, however, Curley found that he hated life as an obscure lawmaker in Washington; he longed to be back in the hubbub of the Boston mayoralty. In November 1945 he got his chance, and voters returned him to his former throne in city hall. What few appreciated at the time—including, it seems, Jack Kennedy—was that Joe Kennedy may have helped Curley pay off a considerable debt burden arising from his legal problems in exchange for his leaving his congressional seat to run for mayor, thereby creating a convenient opening for an enterprising new candidate.[1]

Whatever Joe's role in the affair, a vacancy in the Eleventh District now opened up, to be filled in the fall 1946 midterm election. It was perfect timing for Jack, yet he hesitated. Always his own most exacting critic, he questioned whether voters in the district, accustomed to the ebullient, glad-handing breed of politician, would take to a wealthy, reserved young newcomer who had no political experience—and who, moreover, could be seen as a carpetbagger, having never lived in the district except during his time in college.[2] In addition, the false (or at least fleeting) camaraderie required in this kind of politicking, perfected by that champion backslapper Honey Fitz, was alien to his nature. And what about his world of prep schools, Harvard, international travel, and debutante parties—might it not seem off-putting to the working-class residents he'd be wooing, many of them living in squalid conditions in crowded tenements? Nor did the district have cohesion in political terms; instead, it consisted of warring Irish and Italian factions, which meant that the Democratic primary in June 1946—the real election, since the victor would certainly crush whoever the Republicans put up in the fall campaign—would be a wild and unpredictable free-for-all in which any number of things could happen.

Even Joe Kennedy began to doubt that his emaciated, still-ailing son could prevail in such a tough race, even with the matchless family resources. When Maurice Tobin, the state's tall and wavy-haired governor (he was the son of an Irish-born carpenter), hinted that he might wish to have Jack on his ticket in 1946 as the candidate for lieutenant governor, Joe expressed interest, especially after Tobin assured him that Jack would face no competition for the slot in the Democratic primary. Indeed, this particular post had long intrigued the Ambassador—in earlier years, while scheming about Joe Junior's postwar entry into politics, he had put the lieutenant governorship high on the list of possibilities. It would be an ideal perch from which Jack could begin molding a statewide political machine and then, a few years down the road, launch a bid for the governorship. Jack, however, never warmed to the idea. Neither local nor state politics much interested him, for one thing. For another, he worried that the ticket might go down to crushing defeat in what was shaping up to be a year for Republican gains nationally, as Harry Truman and the Democrats struggled to respond to the demands of peacetime. Honey Fitz, for his part, pushed hard for the congressional race, for sentimental reasons.

By the end of 1945, Jack's mind was made up: he would seek the House seat. In view of the common claim that his father called the shots in this period, it's important to note that the decision was Jack's alone—Joe Kennedy continued well into the new year to prefer the lieutenant governor's race, but his son held firm. The journalist Charles Bartlett, a Navy veteran who met Jack in a Palm Beach nightclub soon after the Christmas holiday and would in time become a friend (and matchmaker), detected no hesitation on the young man's part, though he did see a good dose of self-deprecating humor: "Some of the Palm Beach figures would come by and pat him on the back and say, 'Jack, I'm so glad you're running for Congress.' I remember his saying, 'In only a year or so they'll be saying I'm the worst son of a bitch that ever lived.' "[3]

And there were skeptics. After chatting with one knowledgeable acquaintance, Dan O'Brien, about his chances, Jack jotted down the key points in his diary: "Says I'll be murdered—No personal experience—A personal district—Says I don't know 300 people personally. . . . O'Brien says the attack on me will be—1. Inexperience 2. . . . father's reputation. He is the first man to bet me that *I can't win!* An honest Irishman but a mistaken one."

The candidate also scribbled some axioms he thought pertained to his endeavor. Among them:

> In politics you don't have friends—you have confederates.
> One day they feed you honey—the next you will find fish caught in your throat.
> You can buy brains but you can't pay—loyalty.
> The best politician is the man who does not think too much of the political consequences of his every act.[4]

II

To establish his legitimacy in the district and the state, Jack moved into a nondescript, sparsely furnished two-room suite at the Bellevue Hotel, on Beacon Hill, where his grandfather Honey Fitz, now eighty-two and as garrulous as ever, lived. A stone's throw from the State House, the suite became the hub of the still nascent, still undeclared campaign, the place where the initial strategy and tactics were hashed out. Local campaign offices then sprouted up in various parts of the district, with a headquarters in a dingy suite on the second floor at 18 Tremont Street, in Boston. Rival candidates had yet to get started, or even in some cases to decide if they were running, and thus was established a phenomenon that would be a chief characteristic of all of John F. Kennedy's political campaigns: he started earlier and worked harder than his competition. Months before his official entry into the race, on April 22, he was diligently stumping, spending money, and lining up his campaign team.

And it was a good thing he got going early, for his inexperience was glaringly obvious. He could be reasonably effective in speeches when he expounded on international affairs—an early lecture at an American Legion post, on the topic of postwar Europe, won accolades and more than a hundred requests for copies—but whenever he ventured into the stuff of municipal or state politics, he lacked confidence.[5] His delivery turned

Jack files his first nomination papers with Election Commissioner
Joseph Langone at Boston City Hall, April 23, 1946.

wooden and stiff, and he spoke too fast, eyes glued to his text, in a high-pitched voice that seldom modulated. He lacked the seasoned politician's ability to riff extemporaneously; instead, whenever he ad-libbed he fumbled for words, which only made him more diffident. Afterwards, he would be glum about his performance, and he and his father would go over the speech from start to finish in order to determine what needed to be done. "I can still see the two of them sitting together," sister Eunice later said, "analyzing the entire speech and talking about the pace of delivery to see where it worked and where it had gone wrong."[6]

Nor did Jack cut an imposing figure at these events. He was frail, almost skeletal, which made him look, in the words of one Rotarian, like "a little boy dressed up in his father's clothes." His skin had a yellow hue on account of ongoing periodic bouts of malaria. Especially early on, his demeanor betrayed shyness and embarrassment, and an instinct for privacy, and he showed scant interest in kissing babies or swapping stories with strangers in bars. "He wasn't a mingler," one campaign aide remembered. "He didn't mingle in the crowd and go up to people and say, 'I'm Jack Kennedy.' "[7]

But he also had a number of things going for him, starting with his family name. Joe Kennedy's reputation might have plummeted outside of Massachusetts, but Boston voters still viewed him as the patriarch of a legendary family, a family they wanted to rub elbows with. He was an exceptionally wealthy patriarch, moreover, who made clear he would spend whatever Jack needed to prevail. Together father and son soon assembled a crack campaign team that included Joe's cousin Joe Kane—they always addressed each other as "Cousin Joe"—a brusque, cynical, bald-headed veteran political operative and raconteur who operated out of a diner near city hall and who said politics hadn't changed since the time of Julius Caesar; adman John Dowd, brought in to do advertising and public relations work; Joe Timilty, an ex–police commissioner now serving as an all-purpose Joe Kennedy aide; and Billy Sutton and Patsy Mulkern, both of whom were recommended by Honey Fitz and who, like Timilty, performed a variety of roles. Mark Dalton, a brainy law school graduate and former newspaperman who had served with distinction in naval intelligence during the war, assumed a key managerial role, and Dave Powers, a streetwise and affable young politico with a photographic memory and a deep understanding of Irish Boston, signed on as a top aide. Inevitably, the ever loyal Eddie Moore came out of retirement to run errands and disperse funds. Even some of Jack's friends—Lem Billings, Torby Macdonald, and Red Fay—joined up to help out as their schedules permitted. (Fay flew all the way from California to do so. He stayed for two months, until a stern letter from his father ordered him back to his job in the family construction firm.)[8]

Mulkern, a foulmouthed political junkie who didn't drink yet always managed to look sauced, anticipated a difficult road ahead. "The first day I met Kennedy he had sneakers on. I said, 'For the love of Christ, take the sneakers off, Jack. You think you're going to play golf?' It was tough to sell the guy. We had a hell of a job with him. We took him to taverns, hotel lobbies, club rooms, street corners. Young Kennedy, young Kennedy, we kept saying. But they didn't want him in the district. The Curley mob wouldn't go for him right away. They called him the Miami candidate. 'Take that guy and run him down in Miami . . . [or] Palm Beach . . . give him an address over in New York.' We had a helluva fight."[9]

Before long, however, the millionaire's kid from Harvard proved himself to be an effective campaigner in the hardscrabble wards of the district. His very reticence and amateurishness worked with voters who found his sincerity and informality and seeming shyness a refreshing contrast with the cynical, voluble Irish office seekers of yesteryear. (He relished hearing stories about these larger-than-life figures and their baroque style of politics, but he didn't want to be like them.) Jack didn't condescend to these residents, didn't take them for granted, didn't resort to the forced familiarity of the how's-your-mother-give-her-my-love variety. And he scored points by keeping his speeches short and leaving time for questions. "As you observed him in the course of his actions, you saw that he had a very good handshake, he knew how to smile at people, he remembered people's names," said Tony Galluccio, a Harvard friend who worked on the campaign. "Everybody that you introduced him to liked him as a person, liked him as an individual." A local journalist who covered the campaign agreed: "To meet him was to vote for him, I think it's that simple. If you start to look for complicated reasons [for his success], you won't find any."[10]

"There was a basic dignity in Jack Kennedy," Dave Powers remarked, "a pride in his bearing that appealed to every Irishman who was beginning to feel a little embarrassed by the sentimental, corny style of the typical Irish politician. As the Irish themselves were becoming more middle-class, they wanted a leader to reflect their upward mobility." Powers would until his dying day be an unstintingly loyal Jack Kennedy partisan, a keeper of the JFK flame, and his recollections must be considered in that light, but in this assessment he was far from alone. Given his candidate's likability, Powers saw his main job as a simple one: "My goal then was to have Jack Kennedy meet as many people as he possibly could."[11]

"People were subconsciously looking for a new type of a candidate," Galluccio echoed, "and Jack fitted into this. He had the naive appearance, he had the shock of hair that fell over his forehead. He was a multimillionaire who was very humble. As people would say, this fellow is not the kind of a fellow who would steal. This I think was the very beginning of this political revolution in Massachusetts. Jack Kennedy fitted into this pattern. The rest he did with money, with his ability to make friends, with his tremendous capacity for work. He didn't have to earn a living, but he did utilize his time every minute of the day going where you wanted him to, getting out and meeting people."[12]

The last point is key: Kennedy was tireless, driving himself forward, never resting for long. More than anything, this work ethic—common to many successful first-time candidates—is what campaign aides and other observers remembered of those critical weeks in the late winter and spring of 1946. War had been a toughening experience, and he showed it on the trail. From early morning until late at night he would chug along, day after day, using every ounce of the characteristic Kennedy energy, never mind his various ailments. Often he would get no more than four or five hours of sleep. "We had him out to the Catholic Order of Foresters Communion Breakfast one morning," an aide said. "He walked in and he was limping. I knew his back was bothering him and we had to walk up three flights of stairs, and he had about six other places he had to go that day. When we came downstairs, I said, 'You don't feel good?' And he said, 'I feel great.' . . . That's the way he was; he would come out and he would go, go, go. I don't know when he stopped." The aide recalled instances when Jack would be in his suite in the Bellevue, shaving with his coat on while someone downstairs waited to drive him to his next event. "And it would go on and on and on."[13]

Often his only real meal of the day would be breakfast, and it was almost always the same: two four-and-a-half-minute boiled eggs, four strips of broiled bacon, toast, coffee, and orange juice. On a rare evening off, he liked to go to the movies. Upon entering the theater he would hunt for a seat behind an empty one—so that he could prop up his knees and thereby relieve the pain in his back. His favorites that year included *The Lost Weekend* and *The Bells of St. Mary's.*[14]

Behind the scenes, the candidate also proved his worth. In the late evenings he would go down to the Ritz-Carlton and have a bowl of tomato bisque. Campaign aide Peter Cloherty would meet him there with a folder of letters that had been typed earlier that evening or afternoon. "He was very meticulous about every single letter," Cloherty remembered. "It wasn't just a question of signing them. If the letter was addressed to 'Dear Mr. Stewart' and it should have been 'Dear John,' he would change it, possibly have that one retyped, or add a personal footnote to it in his own hand. Then we'd bring them back up in the morning and put them in the mail."[15]

George Taylor, Jack's African American valet from Winthrop House days, marveled at the determination and the attention to detail. Since Jack's graduation, the two men had kept in touch, Jack penning occasional letters to George from one of his naval postings. Now Taylor was back in his employ, as valet and chauffeur. The two enjoyed a casual, teasing relationship, smoking cigars together and chatting about their mutual interest in women. Occasionally, too, Taylor would be a political sounding board—after a campaign speech Kennedy would ask Taylor to offer his frank critique, which Taylor duly did. He also introduced Jack to leaders in Cambridge's black community. And always, when motoring from one event to another, the candidate would urge his driver to step on it: "He'd say to me sometimes, 'George, you're driving too slow. Push over and let me take the wheel.' And when he took the wheel, he was a fast driver."[16]

The hard-charging approach resulted in part from a realization on the part of Jack and his aides that orthodox campaigning alone would not do the job. People who showed up at rallies were already committed to you, and handshaking on street corners, though not without worth, wouldn't bring many new voters into the fold. Radio time and newspaper ads had their place, but their effectiveness was diluted by the fact that these media covered all of metropolitan Boston.[17] So how to reach uncommitted or apathetic voters? The only way was to go where they lived—literally. For Jack Kennedy this meant trekking through neighborhoods, scaling the stairs of three-decker upon three-decker, and knocking on door after door, sore back be damned. (Often he wore a brace.) And it meant organizing house parties in all corners of the district, with refreshments and flowers provided by the campaign. With careful logistical planning, Jack's team found that he could take in six or more of these parties in a single evening; at each one, aides would take attendees' names and add them to a mailing list. On some evenings, sisters Eunice and Pat would join in.* The candidate was, moreover, in his element in these more intimate settings, winningly shy at the outset but then flashing his high-voltage smile and his self-effacing humor as he laid out, as succinctly and clearly as he could, why he sought their votes. And he took the high road, refraining as a matter of course from discrediting or disparaging the other candidates.

One group of voters responded especially well to this approach, the campaign quickly realized: women. Joe DeGuglielmo, a councilman in Cambridge, saw a clear pattern in the house parties there.

---

* Campaign aide Bill Kelly recalled the pattern for East Boston: "We'd set up six to nine parties—or more—for a single evening, with anywhere from twenty-five to seventy-five people at each. Jack, Pat, and Eunice would set out for party number one. They'd drop Pat or Eunice at number one. Then Jack would go on to number two and drop another sister. Then Jack would go alone to number three. The sisters would circulate, shake hands, and talk. Then we'd backtrack to number one, pick up the sister, and take her (and Jack) to number four and drop her and so on and on, carrying this on for hours." (William F. Kelly oral history, JFK Library.)

Somehow or the other the minute he came into a room where there was one or more women, the females that were in the room forgot everything else. It didn't make any difference what emergency there was. They gravitated towards him. And that would happen many times. . . . The minute the women would see him they'd drop everything, and I know I've gone into those same homes in the past and since and, heck, I can go in and they'll keep on doing what they were doing. It doesn't make a particle of difference. But when he came in, at that time, there was some sort of—I don't know what you'd call it—some sort of electricity or something, some indefinable electricity in the air that would make the women stop and come to him. And they didn't want him to go.[18]

Powers saw the phenomenon, too, soon after he answered a knock on the door of his third-floor apartment in the Bunker Hill section of gritty Charlestown and found the young Kennedy standing there in the dimly lit hallway, out of breath and smiling. Though ostensibly committed to another as-yet-undeclared candidate in the race, Powers agreed to Kennedy's plea to join him for an evening event with Gold Star Mothers (mothers who had lost a son in the war) at the local American Legion hall. As Kennedy concluded his prepared remarks, which ran ten minutes in length, he paused, then said softly, "I think I know how all you mothers feel because my mother is a Gold Star Mother, too." In that instant, Powers remembered, the candidate established a kind of "magical link" with everyone in the room, made himself real, showed that he understood their grief. "Suddenly, swarms of women hurried up to the platform, crowding around him and wishing him luck. And I could hear them saying to each other, 'Isn't he a wonderful boy, he reminds me so much of my own John' or 'my Bob.' It took a half hour for him to get away." To Powers, a political junkie who'd been going to rallies since he was ten, "this reaction was unlike any I had ever seen. It wasn't so much what he said but the way he reached into the emotions of everyone there." He joined the campaign that evening.[19]

The anecdote speaks to another element in Jack Kennedy's favor: his record of service in the war. Veterans, who numbered some sixteen million by conflict's end (fewer than half saw combat), were a formidable political force in America in 1945–46. Their sheer number was one factor, but so was the fact that they came from every corner of the union and from all walks of life—from the most humble to the loftiest. Hollywood stars like Jimmy Stewart, Clark Gable, and Tyrone Power had donned uniforms, as had several hundred major league baseball players, including Ted Williams, Hank Greenberg, Bob Feller, and Joe DiMaggio. All four of Franklin and Eleanor Roosevelt's sons served. At the unit level, the experience of having so many men from different backgrounds thrown together generated tensions (African Americans and Japanese Americans served in separate units, while Chinese Americans, Native Americans, and Hispanics served in "white" units), but it also brought cohesion and, to a degree at least, a blurring of the lines between classes, a diminution of prejudice and provincialism. In time, that cohesion would dissipate, but in 1946 it remained potent, as reflected in the success of veterans all across the country who sought political office that fall.

Kennedy, moreover, had a particularly powerful personal story to tell. At stop after stop, he introduced himself to voters as a combat veteran returning to help lead the country for which he had fought. ("The New Generation Offers a Leader," read the campaign slogan, coined by Joe Kane, who adapted it from Henry Luce's foreword to *Why England Slept:* "If John Kennedy is characteristic of the younger generation, and I believe he is, many of us would be happy to have the destinies of the Republic turned over to his generation at once.") He regularly referred to his older brother's service and selfless courage, and organized a new Veterans of Foreign Wars post named for him. He sought invitations to speak at events honoring veterans.

About his own specific experiences in the South Pacific he was reluctant to say much. Then and later, he played down his PT 109 heroism with his famous quip "I had no choice. They sank my boat." To an aide he remarked early in the campaign that he had no taste for "trying to parlay a lost PT boat and a bad back into political advantage." But gradually Kennedy came to see that his story, already familiar to some voters, was too good not to use, and he crafted a concise and powerful speech that described the sinking of the 109, minimizing his own role in the rescue effort and lauding the perseverance of his men. At his father's insistence, some 100,000 reprints of the condensed version of John Hersey's "Survival" article (the one that appeared in *Reader's Digest*) were distributed, at a cost of $1,319 (for the printing and the envelopes), plus postage, arriving in mailboxes mere days before the vote. Volunteers were recruited to address the envelopes and do the mailing. The effort paid off. One opposing candidate's wife reportedly was so moved by the article that she said she might have to vote for Kennedy.[20]

III

For all the positive attributes Jack Kennedy brought to the table, he still faced the tall task of prevailing against a deep field of rivals on the Democratic side. All told, ten candidates made the ballot, including one woman. Several of them were better known in the district and more experienced in local politics than Kennedy. The most formidable of them was Mike Neville, of vote-rich Cambridge, the son of a blacksmith from Cork and an affable, experienced attorney. Neville had worked for the phone company and gone to law school at night, then had climbed the political pole to state legislator and mayor; he had the backing of Governor Tobin as well as many of the older lawmakers in Cambridge and Somerville. John F. Cotter, of Charlestown, also caused worry on the Kennedy side—as administrative assistant to two former congressmen, Jim Curley and John P. Higgins, Cotter had built close connections to numerous wards in the district, and he knew how to campaign.

Leaving nothing to chance, Jack's team worked to spread his support across as much of the district as possible, the better to minimize the damage done by favorite-son candidates like Neville and Cotter. And they were not above bare-knuckle shenanigans: when a respected Boston city councilman named Joseph Russo declared his candidacy and looked likely to win broad support in the Italian North End and among Italian Americans elsewhere, Joe Kane scrounged up *another* Joseph Russo and got him on the ballot, in order to divide the councilman's tally.[21]

Throughout, Joseph Kennedy made heavy use of his checkbook, though just how heavy remains unclear. He himself quipped that "with what I'm spending I could elect my chauffeur," and many subsequent accounts give the impression of virtually unlimited outlays of money, much of it handed out in cash by Eddie Moore. But Mark Dalton, a key member of the campaign team, maintained otherwise: "The way congressional campaigns go, I would say it was not an extraordinarily expensive campaign. I would say certainly it was well financed and it was. We had many, many billboards, and we had the advertising material which was presented all through the community. There certainly was no shortage of funds, but on the other hand, I say this with all sincerity, it was not an exorbitant campaign." Though the figures $300,000 and $250,000 were thrown around, another campaign insider estimated the amount spent to be in the neighborhood of $50,000. Whatever the ultimate sum, the Kennedys certainly outspent the competition, which led to no little grousing among other candidates, all of whom got precisely what Joe Kane meant when he said it takes three things to win an election: money, money, and money.[22]

In the final weeks before the vote, the Kennedy family came out in force. Eunice, Pat, and Jean walked up and down streets, knocking on doors and holding out their brother's campaign brochure, often to the startled delight of the person inside. Young Teddy, age fourteen, sometimes accompanied them and also served as general errand boy. Bobby, now twenty and out of the Navy, was assigned the job of running a cam-

The candidate at dinner with family and friends. Seated, from left:
Francis X. Morrissey, Josie Fitzgerald, Eunice, Jack, Honey Fitz Fitzgerald, and
Joseph F. Timilty. Lem Billings is standing behind Josie. Kenny O'Donnell—
later to become a close aide—and Helen Sullivan (the future
Mrs. O'Donnell) are standing behind Jack and Honey Fitz.

paign office deep in enemy territory, in East Cambridge, with the hope that he could trim the anticipated vote against Jack from five-to-one to four-to-one. Working three mostly Italian wards, and doing much of it on foot, Bobby shook hands and handed out literature, from early morning until late at night, occasionally pausing to eat spaghetti with a receptive family. Rose Kennedy, too, became a dedicated and effective campaigner, especially with women in the district—as a Gold Star Mother, she could speak mom to mom about her treasured Jack. She was, moreover, comfortable in this environment, having grown up accompanying her father, Honey Fitz, on the hustings. She not only knew how the game was played but enjoyed playing it.

Most of all, of course, it was the candidate's father who made his presence felt, in ways large and small. Though officially Mark Dalton had the title of campaign manager, everyone knew (not least Dalton) that the job really belonged to Joe Kennedy. No decision of consequence was made without his involvement. He and his son would strategize continually, in person and on the phone, and he insisted on being in the know on every aspect of the campaign. "Mr. Kennedy called me many, many times, to know exactly what was happening," Dalton said afterwards. "As a matter of fact that was one of my problems. He'd keep you on the phone for an hour and a half, two hours."[23] A master of media manipulation and PR, Joe spent hours on the phone with reporters and editors, seeking information, trading confidences, and cajoling them into publishing puff pieces on Jack, ones that invariably played up his war record in the Pacific. He oversaw a professional advertising campaign that ensured ads went up in just the right places—the campaign had a virtual monopoly on subway space, and on window stickers ("Kennedy for Congress") for cars and homes—and was the force behind the mass mailing of Hersey's PT 109 article.

To some observers, then and later, the old man was more than a de facto campaign manager; he was a puppet master, a Svengali who had decided before war's end what he wanted—to get his oldest surviving son into political office—and then set about making it happen. He called all the shots, according to this view, and made every strategic decision of consequence. It's not really true. Jack Kennedy, as we've seen, had his own attraction to politics as a career, had made his own decision to run in the Eleventh, and he was at all times central in his own campaign. When the two men disagreed on strategy or tactics, Jack's view prevailed. (He admired his father's business accomplishments no end, but doubted his political discernment.)[24] Still more untenable is the opposite argument, made by some Jack loyalists, that the father's role in 1946 was incidental.[25] Joe's bottomless finances and forceful personality ensured that he would loom large, as did his son's deep devotion to him. He was a legendary figure in Massachusetts, one who was not shy about using his varied connections on his son's behalf. He hadn't built his empire by leaving things to chance, and he was not about to change his modus operandi now.

The elder Kennedy made only one public appearance with his son, but an extraordinary one it was. Having noted Jack's appeal to female voters, the campaign conceived an event that would become a staple of his future races: a tea reception for women voters that allowed them to meet the candidate and members of his family. Eunice served as coordinator, supervising a team of twenty-five volunteer secretaries to hand-address thousands of engraved invitations requesting the pleasure of the recipient's company at a formal reception at the Commander Hotel in Cambridge, just off Harvard Square. Seasoned pros scoffed at the notion—who had ever heard of voters getting dressed up just to meet a political candidate?—and the Kennedys themselves were unsure how it would go. But on an unseasonably hot Sunday evening in mid-June, some fifteen hundred mostly female voters showed up at the hotel, many in rented ball gowns. The queue snaked around the block. At the head of the receiving line stood Joe and Rose, he in white tie and tails, she in a stylish new dress from Paris.[26]

To Mike Neville's campaign manager, the Commander Hotel event was the clincher, not only because of the large turnout but because of the media coverage it received. Photos and stories filled the local press, and one reporter called it "a demonstration unparalleled in the history of Congressional fights in this district."[27] How many votes it actually gained Kennedy is unknowable, but in the primary election, three days later, he coasted to victory, taking 22,183 votes to Neville's 11,341, John Cotter's 6,671, and (the original) Joe Russo's 5,661. (The "Kennedy Russo" managed to siphon off 799.) In a ten-candidate race, his share of the vote, at 41 percent, was impressive, as was the fact that he almost bested Neville in Cambridge. Turnout fell below expectations, however, in part because of a steady rainfall; only 30 percent of eligible voters cast ballots. In the evening, Jack took in a movie—the Marx Brothers' *A Night in Casablanca*—while the returns were coming in, then he visited each campaign office before returning to headquarters well after midnight to celebrate in the low-key style that would become his custom. Honey Fitz, however, did not hold back: the octogenarian danced a jig on a table and belted out his theme song, "Sweet Adeline."[28]

"Of course I am a happy man tonight," Honey Fitz declared. "John F. Kennedy has brains, industry, and above all, character. He will make a great representative of the 11th Congressional District."[29]

Joseph Kennedy, on the other hand, was strangely subdued. "I couldn't understand it," Dalton recalled. "He wasn't going around saying, 'Thank you, thank you, thank you for what you've done for my son.' He wasn't doing that at all."[30] Perhaps the patriarch was holding his enthusiasm in check pending the outcome of the general election, in November. Or perhaps he was haunted by what might have been. Joe Junior, after all, was the son he had envisioned in this role, the one carrying the Kennedy name to new and glorious political heights—not the frail and reticent second son. Perhaps it was both. And perhaps there was also this: to Joe Kennedy, a congressional seat was but a first step for Jack, and therefore not something to get too excited about.

The Boston Traveler, in accounting for the victory, downplayed the importance of Joe's money: "If any of the other candidates had spent twice as much as the Kennedy campaign cost, Kennedy would still have won. . . . Kennedy as a candidate had attributes which his opponents did not have and could not buy—a well-known name and family background and connections. He also had personality and a superior war record." No less important, the paper went on, Kennedy had an asset that should have been "of the utmost concern to the older politicians": a political machine that was "built overnight" and "based on voters under the age of 35," many of them veterans full of enthusiasm and idealism. "Most of the workers who crowded into his seven headquarters nightly for two months, addressing envelopes and making telephone calls, also were youthful. They may have been amateurs, but they did the tiresome tasks which bring in votes, and they were worth more than all the ward 'pols' in the district combined."[31]

Congratulatory notes flowed in from all over. Jack's sister Kathleen, who had just purchased a house in London (long enamored of England, she had decided to make her home there), wrote "just to tell you how terrifically pleased I am for you. Everyone says you were so good in the election and the outcome must have been a great source of satisfaction. It's nice to know you are as appreciated in the 11th Congressional District as you are among your brothers and sisters. Gee, aren't you lucky?" Then she added, "The folks here think you are madly pro-British so don't start destroying that illusion until I get my house fixed. The painters might just not like your attitude!"[32]

IV

With the hard-fought primary behind him, Jack Kennedy could look forward to a much easier contest in the general election. His party could not say the same, even though in theory 1946 should have been a good year for Democrats. World War II had ended in complete victory the year before, after all, and despite fears of a postwar recession or depression, the economy adjusted quite well, fueled by consumer spending. (Americans had taken home steady paychecks during the war but had had little to spend them on; now they were ready to buy.) Farm income rose to an all-time high. Unemployment stood at a mere 3 percent and, after a decade and a half of privation—the Depression followed by wartime rationing and shortages—consumer goods were again available, including new ones such as washing machines and televisions. Thanks to the Servicemen's Readjustment Act of 1944, better known as the GI Bill of Rights, veterans could get home mortgages, embark on college educations, and set up small businesses. In comparative terms, meanwhile, the United States was ever more of a colossus: by war's end, the nation had three-fourths of the world's invested capital, and two-thirds of all gold reserves.

The transformation was stunning. In 1939, America's gross national product—the total value of the services and goods produced by the nation's residents—had been $91 billion. In 1945 it was $215 billion, a leap unlike any seen in the history of the world. At the start of the twentieth century, the United States had nearly a quarter of the world's economy; by the end of World War II it had almost half. This, too, was unprecedented in human history.[33]

Yet the party of Harry Truman was in trouble as the fall campaign began. Though the reconversion to a peacetime economy had been relatively smooth, acute shortages remained, and the demand drove prices up. A dearth of flour, for example, created long lines in Chicago and other cities, while pent-up demand for beef drove the price up by 70 percent.

Truman, struggling with the mountainous task of easing shortages while holding prices down, in mid-1946 imposed a price ceiling on meat. American cattlemen responded by keeping their animals from the market, causing butchers to go out of business and leading to "meat riots" in cities throughout the land. Car buyers likewise found themselves frustrated by the lack of supply, as did couples on the hunt for a washing machine. Women struggled to find nylons.[34]

Nor did the president prove adept at handling the labor unrest that erupted immediately after the end of the war, when management proved slow to respond to grievances and inflation ate away at workers' real income. In late 1945, 200,000 General Motors workers walked off the job, and they did not return for 113 days. They were followed in early 1946 by meat-packers and steelworkers, then electrical workers and coal miners. All told, nearly five million workers walked off the job in 1946, resulting in 116 million man-days of labor being lost—three times the total of any previous year. Neither management nor government officials seemed to know how to deal with the problem, and a frustrated public gradually lost patience with the strikers and the Truman administration. When Truman wielded the power of the federal government to shut down a railroad workers' strike, he alienated the important labor wing of his party.[35]

Many of Jack Kennedy's fellow veterans, too, voiced frustration with their lot, notwithstanding the GI Bill's provisions. For the most part their homecomings from the war had been joyful affairs, but when the celebrations died down, many realized that life had moved on for the people around them. The world they'd known had grown unfamiliar. And it all seemed deeply unfair: while they had answered the call and been yanked away for years, risking their lives and in some cases suffering grievous injuries, others had avoided service, stayed home, and prospered. Some veterans, including thousands who had married quickly before enlisting or while home on leave, never adjusted to matrimony, with the result that the divorce rate in 1945 shot up to double that of the prewar era, to thirty-one divorces for every hundred marriages—or more than half a million total. (In subsequent years the rate trickled down to prewar levels.)[36] In 1946, moviegoers flocked to the ironically titled motion picture *The Best Years of Our Lives*, which took home nine Academy Awards for its powerful depiction of three veterans grappling with the difficulties of readjusting to life back home. The film was the highest-grossing picture of its time, and a close second in viewership to *Gone with the Wind*.

Candidate Kennedy addressed the readjustment problems experienced by some returning men. "Home was built up out of all proportion to reality when they were away," he remarked on the stump. "This built-up conception served them well when the going was tough. It was the same as heaven—and made it easier for them to live amid suffering and boredom and desolation. But reality is a little different. There are no high salaries for inexperienced veterans. . . . Homes are hard to find—jobs are frequently monotonous. Some men even feel a faint nostalgia for army life," for the comradeship, for the feeling of mutual interdependence. And, he went on, there was nobility in this longing, for after all, "we are dependent on other people nearly every minute of our lives—for our food, for help when we are sick. Even when we drive a car we are depending on the skill and judgment of the other people on the road. In a larger sense, each one of us is dependent on all the people of this country—on their obedience to our laws, for their rejection of the siren calls of ambitious demagogues. In fact, if we only realized it, we are in time of peace as interdependent as soldiers were in the time of war. I think it is high time that we recognize this truth. If we did, how much easier would be our time ahead!"[37]

There was hope and power in this message, and it worked well for Kennedy in the Massachusetts Eleventh. Nationally, however, Republicans schemed to make the November election a referendum on Truman. Working with a top advertising firm, party leaders came up with a simple and powerful slogan: "Had Enough?" They used every opportunity to push the pun "To err is Truman." More important, the GOP recruited a strong slate of congressional candidates—especially in those races that were legitimately winnable. The Massachusetts Eleventh was not one of these, so the party put up a sacrificial lamb, Somerville's Lester W. Bowen. The outcome was all but preordained, which gave Kennedy the opportunity to focus in much of his speechmaking on his preferred turf: foreign policy and national security.

Here the picture had changed dramatically in the year since World War II's end. Already at the Potsdam Conference, before the fighting in the Pacific even ended, American officials had grasped that Soviet leaders were determined to dominate the areas then under Red Army control. U.S. planners determined they would not try to thwart these Soviet designs, but would resist any effort by Stalin and his lieutenants to move farther west, to those parts of Europe that the Allied powers occupied.

Likewise, the Soviets would not be allowed to interfere in Japan, or be permitted to take over Iran, where their troops had lingered in the north. After Stalin, in February 1946, delivered a speech that depicted a world threatened by rapacious capitalist expansion, the U.S. chargé d'affaires in Moscow, George F. Kennan, sent a bleak "long telegram" to Washington that said Kremlin fanaticism made diplomatic engagement impossible. His report strengthened the sense among American policymakers that only firmness could yield results with Moscow. The following month, Winston Churchill delivered an electrifying speech in Fulton, Missouri. With Truman at his side, the former British prime minister proclaimed that an "iron curtain" had descended upon Europe, splitting East from West.*[38]

With the Grand Alliance a rapidly fading memory, the Soviets and the Americans feuded across the board. When the United States gave a hefty reconstruction loan to Britain but withheld one from the Soviet Union, Stalin's government admonished Washington for using its currency to control other countries. The two powers also squabbled over Iran, where the United States had helped secure the pro-West shah's ascension to the throne and where the Soviets sponsored separatist groups and sought to gain access to oil reserves. Deeply split on the terms of German unification, the former allies developed their zones independently.

Not every American analyst backed the administration's harsh anti-Soviet position. Secretary of Commerce Henry A. Wallace, who had been FDR's vice president before Truman, charged that Truman's hard-line posture was wrongly exchanging military and economic pressure for diplomacy. In a speech at Madison Square Garden in September 1946, Wallace called for conciliation vis-à-vis Moscow and warned that "getting tough never brought anything real and lasting—whether for schoolyard bullies or businessmen or world powers. The tougher we get, the tougher

---

* Before venturing to Missouri for his speech, Churchill visited Florida to receive an honorary degree from the University of Miami. While there he bumped into Joe Kennedy at the Hialeah Park racetrack, a few miles outside town. An awkward encounter ensued, according to Kennedy's notes of the conversation. "You had a terrible time during the war," Churchill said. "Your losses were very great. I felt so sad for you and hope you received my messages." Kennedy replied that he had received them and was grateful. "The world seems to be in frightful condition," Churchill added. "Yes," Kennedy replied. "After all, what did we accomplish by this war?" "Well," the prime minister said sharply, "at least we have our lives." "Not all of us," Kennedy answered. (Joseph P. Kennedy, memo of conversation, January 31, 1946, printed in Smith, *Hostage to Fortune*, 622–23.)

the Russians will get." Truman soon dismissed Wallace from the cabinet, berating him privately as "a real Commy and a dangerous man" and bragging that he had now "run the crackpots out of the Democratic Party."[39]

Jack Kennedy, for his part, applauded the tough Truman-Churchill line. In a radio speech in Boston, he castigated Wallace for being naive and called for a firm U.S. policy vis-à-vis the Soviet Union. True, he said, people like Wallace maintained that "the Russian experiment is a good one, since the Russians are achieving economic security at a not too great cost in loss of personal freedom," but these observers were wrong. "The truth is that the Russian people have neither economic security nor personal freedom," Kennedy went on; they lacked the right to strike and were subject to arbitrary arrest and punishment, including being sent to Siberian labor camps. Kremlin leaders, meanwhile, had gobbled up the Baltic states, eastern Poland, and the Kuril Islands (seized from Japan immediately before the end of the Pacific War) and were looking to expand their reach, including into Greece, Turkey, and Iran. Washington therefore had no option but to adopt Secretary of State James Byrnes's preferred policy: "get tough with Russia." Anticipating what would soon come to be called the Cold War, Jack concluded, "The years ahead will be difficult and strained, the sacrifices great, but it is only by supporting with all our hearts the course we believe to be right, can we prove that that course is not only right but that it has strength and vigor."[40]

The candidate and his political team must have liked what he said: the radio talk was converted into a speech he gave several times in the closing days of the fall campaign.

On occasion Kennedy turned more philosophical, as when he delivered the annual Boston Independence Day oration at historic Faneuil Hall, where Revolutionary Era colonists had met to plot and protest. Half a century before, Honey Fitz had been the featured speaker at the event, in this same locale, and Jack now took his turn, on the topic of "Some Elements of the American Character." Pointing to the vital role played by religious and idealistic conviction in the nation's history, including in the eradication of slavery and in the recent victory over Nazi Germany and imperial Japan, he warned his audience that moral conviction alone was never enough; a healthy dose of pragmatic realism would be required as well. Thus, in World War I, "the idealism with which we had entered the battle made the subsequent disillusionment all the more bitter and revealed a dangerous facet to this element of the American character, for this bitterness, a direct result of our inflated hopes, brought a radical change in our foreign policy and a resulting withdrawal from Europe. We failed to make the adjustment between what we had hoped to win and what we actually could win. Our idealism was too strong. We would not compromise."

He concluded with a ringing affirmation of his core philosophy:

Conceived in Grecian thought, strengthened by Christian morality, and stamped indelibly into American political philosophy, the right of the individual against the State is the keystone of our Constitution. Each man is free. He is free in thought. He is free in expression. He is free in worship. To us, who have been reared in the American tradition, these rights have become part of our very being. They have become so much a part of our being that most of us are prone to feel that they are rights universally recognized and universally exercised. But the sad fact is that this is not true. They were dearly won for us only a few short centuries ago and they were dearly preserved for us in the days just past. And there are large sections of the world today where these rights are denied as a matter of philosophy and as a matter of government.[41]

In several speeches, he quoted a line from Rousseau that he'd jotted down in a loose-leaf notebook the previous year: "As soon as any man says of the affairs of state, 'What does it matter to me?' the state may be given up as lost." He used the line before an audience of young Democrats in Pennsylvania, for example, and again before students and faculty at his alma mater Choate, which was celebrating its fiftieth anniversary and had invited him to be the featured speaker. Kennedy told both groups to resist becoming cynical about politics and politicians, for the survival of American democracy ultimately depended on civic duty, on having an engaged and informed citizenry that embraced the call to public service. This claim would be central to his historic inaugural address of 1961; it's remarkable to see it articulated already here, at the very outset of his political career, in speeches he wrote to a significant extent by himself. To the audience at Choate he added a corollary, one that would likewise become a bedrock principle in the years to come: namely, that effective politics must involve mutual give-and-take by people acting in good faith. "In

America, politics are regarded with great contempt; and politicians them-selves are looked down upon because of their free and easy compromises. It is well for us to understand that politicians are dealing with human be-ings, with all their varied ambitions, desires, and backgrounds; and many of these compromises cannot be avoided."[42]

V

The nitty-gritty politicking did not cease with the victory in the primary, but it was cut back dramatically, victory in November being more or less a foregone conclusion. The campaign offices in the district stayed open but with reduced hours, and most of the volunteers went back to their former lives.

Never one to stint on R&R, Jack took advantage of the summer lull to spend time in Hyannis Port and New York City, and to make another so-journ out west to Hollywood. On the set of the film *Dragonwyck*, he met screen star Gene Tierney, riding high from her Oscar-nominated role in *Leave Her to Heaven* (1945) and her title role in *Laura* (1944). Tierney fell hard for the congressional candidate, who was three years her senior. She recalled how, on the set, "I turned and found myself staring into the most perfect blue eyes I had ever seen on a man. . . . He smiled at me. My reac-tion was right out of the ladies' romance novel. Literally, my heart skipped. . . . A coy thought flashed through my mind: I was glad I had worn a lavender gown for my scene that day. Lavender was my best color." The young Kennedy was thin, she went on, and "had the kind of banter-ing, unforced Irish charm that women so often find fatal. He asked ques-tions about my work, the kind that revealed how well he already knew the subject."[43]

Jack also proved a sympathetic listener as Tierney described the trauma of institutionalizing her mentally disabled daughter, Daria. "He told me about his sister Rosemary, who had been born retarded, and how his family had loved and protected her. The subject was awkward for him. The Kennedys did not survive by dwelling on their imperfections. 'Gene,' he said, after a silence had passed between us, 'in any large family you can always find something wrong with somebody.' "[44]

So enamored did Tierney become of Jack that she supposedly spurned the advances of Hollywood leading man Tyrone Power. But though she saw Jack in Hollywood and later in New York and on the Cape ("Jack met me at the station, wearing patched blue jeans. I thought he looked like Tom Sawyer"), the affair did not last. Jack was not about to commit to any divorcée or Hollywood starlet, not with his political career just getting launched.[45] That summer the gossip pages in L.A. also linked him with Peggy Cummins, an aspiring Irish actress, but, according to Chuck Spalding's wife, Betty, "it wasn't a serious thing. She was just a girl to date." And he lost interest, Spalding added, when Cummins ("a nice girl") refused to go to bed with him.[46]

Betty Spalding found it interesting that Jack, though "amusing and bright and fascinating to listen to" and "marvelous company," was no chivalrous gentleman, in the sense of opening doors for women or standing up when an older woman entered a room. "He was nice to people, but heedless of people, heedless about his clothes, and heedless about money. He never had any money with him." Gene Tierney also remarked on this capricious aspect of Jack's character: "I am not sure I can explain the nature of Jack's charm, but he took life as it came. He never worried about making an impression. He made you feel very secure. . . . He was good with people in a way that went beyond politics, thoughtful in more than a material way. Gifts and flowers were not his style. He gave you his time, his interest."[47]

Yet the time and interest could be ephemeral, with male as well as female friends. Before embarking for California, Kennedy had promised Red Fay that he would make a stop in Woodside, near San Francisco, to see him and meet his parents and friends. He almost reneged on the vow, then showed up late and made a poor impression on all concerned, bailing early on a party in his honor in order to go to a movie with another friend and showing scant interest in ingratiating himself with his hosts. Characteristically short on cash, he borrowed $20 from Fay and paid him back only months later, and after Fay had written him twice about it. The nonchalance left Fay feeling bitter, especially after he had traveled all the way to Boston to help out in Jack's primary campaign. To Fay it was a disconcerting sign that his friend might be undergoing a change as he donned his political mantle, and not for the better—a congressman to be, he suddenly seemed less dedicated to maintaining the attachments of old.*[48]

---

* Fay's bitterness did not last, it seems. In an effort to make amends, Jack sent him a multivolume biography of Benjamin Franklin, and Fay responded with an affectionate handwritten letter. (Paul "Red" Fay to JFK, December 13, 1946, box 4A, JFK Personal Papers.)

Jack's friend Henry James, whom he had known during his Stanford interlude, six years before, likewise detected a troubling change in him around this same time. "I didn't see the whole evolution of the process," James told a later interviewer, "but I did see certain signs, which made it very clear to me that I was losing him as a person and that perhaps the only way I could ever see him again was as a former friend, unimportant probably, for I wasn't going to be his toady like Lem Billings—I put more value on myself than that. . . . I envied people like Billings for their continuing close relationship to Jack, but I didn't respect them for it."[49]

VI

The November election went more or less as expected, in the Massachusetts Eleventh as well as nationally. Jack Kennedy sauntered to victory in his race, winning 69,093 votes to Bowen's 26,007. But he was a rare bright spot for his party that autumn. In Massachusetts the Democrats lost a U.S. Senate seat—Henry Cabot Lodge Jr. trounced the old stalwart incumbent David I. Walsh, who had helped smooth Jack's passage to combat service in 1943—as well as the governorship. Nationally, they were brutalized, relinquishing control of both houses of Congress for the first time since 1932 as the GOP gained twelve seats in the Senate and a whopping fifty-five in the House. In California's Twelfth District, an ambitious Republican Navy veteran named Richard M. Nixon rode the anti-incumbent wave to victory, falsely accusing his Democratic opponent, Representative Jerry Voorhis, of being a Communist, or at least of working with a political action committee that was infiltrated by Communists. In Wisconsin, another Republican, ex-Marine Joseph R. McCarthy, won election to the U.S. Senate, partly by playing the anti-Communist card and partly by misrepresenting his military service. (He exaggerated the number of combat missions he had flown in the Pacific.) Overall, some forty veterans won election to the House, and eight more in the Senate.

For John F. Kennedy, age twenty-nine, an extraordinary moment had come. He was a United States congressman–elect. He had overcome his precarious health and political inexperience, as well as his father's humiliating exit from public life, to win a seat in the Eightieth Congress. If his success stemmed in part from his family name and family wealth, it also had deeper roots. Say what one will about Joseph P. Kennedy, it's not every multi-millionaire father who takes such broad interest in his children, who believes in them so fervently, and who, together with his wife, instills in them, from a young age, a firm commitment to public service. Joe Kennedy did. From his mother, meanwhile, Jack inherited a lasting interest in history and in books, and an abiding curiosity about the world.

Yet Jack's victory was also very much his own. His war story from the Pacific resonated with voters, as did his quiet charm and dignified affability on the campaign trail. As aide after aide quickly saw, voters just liked him, plain and simple. He also campaigned hard, taking nothing for granted, and motivated people to want to work for him. In substantive terms, he had fashioned, through his writing and his speechmaking, a political philosophy that transcended the narrow, selfish vision of his father and elder brother, in the form of a pluralist, liberal internationalism—idealistic yet infused with pragmatic realism—that would in time resonate with a broad cross section of Americans. Already in his senior thesis in 1940, Jack Kennedy had depicted a more messy and congested world than did either his father or his older brother, and in the event-packed half dozen years that followed, he'd honed and expanded that worldview. All the while, he conveyed a dedication to ideals larger than self.

Thus was established the prototype for all future Jack Kennedy campaigns: a disciplined and efficient organization, energetic family support, a campaign war chest bulging with resources, and, most important of all, a talented, winsome, hardworking candidate, highly adept at using others to the extent they were helpful to him.

"You have my best wishes for success in the tough job with which you have been entrusted," journalist Herbert Bayard Swope wrote to Kennedy the day after his victory. "My crystal ball reveals you as the center of a fascinating drama—one that carries you far and high. I hope I am a true prophet."[50]

And so Swope was. In November 1946, it may be said, came the end of the remarkable early life of John Fitzgerald Kennedy. His even more extraordinary public life was about to begin.

SIXTEEN

THE GENTLEMAN FROM BOSTON

O n January 3, 1947, John F. Kennedy was sworn in as a member of the U.S. House of Representatives, representing the Eleventh District of Massachusetts. With his boyish smile and big shock of hair, he looked even younger than his almost thirty years, and more than a few old hands on Capitol Hill mistook him for a college student on hiatus from his studies and working as an aide. Even those who knew him to be a congressman took scant notice—the Kennedy name that meant so much in his home state here signified little, for the capital was filled with scions of the rich and prominent.

If Kennedy was bothered by the lack of attention, he didn't show it. "Well, how do you like that?" he declared with mock indignation as he burst into his office one morning. "Some people got into the elevator and asked me for the fourth floor!" He maintained his sloppy sartorial style, frequently showing up to work in wrinkled khakis and a rumpled seer-sucker blazer, his tie askew. Sometimes a shirttail would hang out. To the exasperation of his valet, George Thomas, a stocky, baby-faced black man who'd been recommended to him by Arthur Krock (and who should not be confused with George Taylor, his previous valet), Jack would often don whatever piece of clothing was within reach, including suits that the fastidious Thomas had set aside to be laundered.[1]

It was a heady time to be in the nation's capital. The Washington in which Kennedy had lived five years before, at the time of the Pearl Harbor attack, was a sleepy, parochial place; the city to which he now returned was the capital of the free world. For his residence the young lawmaker selected a gracious three-story townhouse in Georgetown, at 1528 Thirty-first Street, that had formerly been the home of a Polish military attaché. It had a small garden and patio in the rear. Rent was $300 a month. There Jack lived with his sister Eunice, who, through her father's connections, had secured a job as special assistant to the Justice Department's juvenile delinquency committee. They shared the place with aide Billy Sutton and the doting housekeeper and cook Margaret Ambrose, and Thomas was ever present, too, driving Jack to work and bringing home-cooked meals to his office.

Visitors to the townhouse were constant, and the feel was hectic, casual, collegiate. Joseph Alsop, the journalist, is said to have looked behind

The youthful freshman lawmaker in his office, early 1947.

some books on the mantelshelf and found the remnants of a half-eaten hamburger. Billy Sutton likened the atmosphere to a "Hollywood hotel," with people coming and going. "The Ambassador, Rose, Lem Billings, Torby, anybody who came to Washington. You never knew who the hell was going to be there but you got used to it." Fellow lawmakers soon began dropping by as well, including Florida congressman George A. Smathers and Representative Henry M. "Scoop" Jackson of Washington State. Senator Joe McCarthy, a fellow Catholic and bachelor, also came for dinner more than once. R. Sargent Shriver, a handsome Yale graduate and Navy veteran who had been a student at Canterbury School with Jack and was now working for Joseph Kennedy, was a fixture at these evening salons, in good part because he had fallen hard for Eunice and was wooing her.[2]

Most of all, a steady stream of young women darkened the doorway of the home, there to see Jack. His Choate friend Rip Horton recalled the scene: "I went to his house in Georgetown for dinner. A lovely-looking blonde from West Palm Beach joined us to go to a movie. After the movie we went back to the house, and I remember Jack saying something like, 'Well, I want to shake this one. She has ideas.' Shortly thereafter another girl walked in. . . . I went to bed figuring this was the girl for the night. The next morning a completely different girl came wandering down for breakfast. They were a dime a dozen."[3]

And a varied mix they were: in addition to secretaries and stewardesses, in this period he still saw actress Gene Tierney and sultry, dark-haired fashion editor Flo Pritchett, whom he had first dated in early 1944, as well as Kay Stammers, a glamorous English tennis player who had reached number two in the world in singles and won the Wimbledon women's doubles trophy. Famous for wearing her tennis skirts and shorts a full four inches above the knee, Stammers later said Jack was "spoilt by women. I think he could snap his fingers and they'd come running. And of course he was terribly attractive and rich and unmarried—a terrific catch, really. . . . I thought he was divine." Journalist Nancy Dickerson, who also dated Jack, put it similarly: "He was young, rich, handsome, sexy, and that's plenty for starters. But the big thing about him was that he was overpowering—you couldn't help but be swept over by him."[4]

The women Kennedy dated had several things in common: they were pretty, bright, and amusing. The sense of humor was key—one guesses he got a kick out of Pritchett's racy letter to him dated June 5, 1947: "Instead of making history with the Knights of Columbus, why not make something of your nights. The summer will be long and hot. So [I] think you should adjourn occasionally and help make [June] hotter. . . . I hope you will be up this way again, and that when you do, we can play."[5] Importantly, too, they were "safe" girls he would face no pressure to marry.[6] Pritchett, for example, was divorced, while Tierney was in the process of parting with her husband, the designer Oleg Cassini; as a Catholic, Jack could never marry a divorcée and hope to sustain his political career. He seemingly had learned from his father's near-disastrous affair with Gloria Swanson two decades prior—ever after, Old Joe had kept his affairs fleeting and numerous. His son did the same.

Not infrequently, father and son played the same field—or, more accurately, the father played the son's field. Washington socialite and longtime Kennedy family friend Kay Halle remembered an evening at a posh restaurant in the capital when a waiter brought her a note saying friends at another table wanted her to join them. It was Joe, Jack, and Bobby. "When I joined them the gist of the conversation from the boys was the fact that their father was going to be in Washington for a few days and needed female companionship. They wondered whom I could suggest, and they were absolutely serious."[7]

Mary Pitcairn, a friend of Eunice's who dated Jack Kennedy on occasion, offered more disturbing detail:

> Mr. Kennedy always called up the girls Jack was taking out and asked them to dinner. He came down and took me to the Carleton Hotel—then the fanciest dining room in Washington. He was charming. He wanted to know his children's friends. He was *very* curious about my personal life. He really wanted to know. He asked a lot of personal questions—*extraordinarily* personal questions. . . .
>
> He did something that I heard he did to everyone. After dinner he would take you home and kiss you goodnight as though you were a young so-and-so. One night I was visiting Eunice at the Cape and he came into my bedroom to kiss me goodnight! I was in my nightgown, ready for bed. Eunice was in her bedroom. We had an adjoining bath. The doors were open. He said, "I've come to say goodnight," and kissed me. Really kissed me. It was so silly. I remember thinking, "How embarrassing for Eunice!" But beyond that, nothing. Absolutely nothing.
>
> I think all this confused Jack. He was a sensitive man and I think

it confused him. What kind of object is a woman? To be treated as his father treated them? And his father's behavior that way was blatant. There was always a young, blonde, beautiful secretary around. I think it was very confusing to Jack.[8]

How Eunice felt about the fraternity-like atmosphere in the Georgetown house is not clear. She adored her brother; in her eyes he could do no wrong. Though she always indignantly dismissed the stories of their father's extramarital flings—they were unfounded rumors, Eunice insisted, spread by people who mistook innocent flirting for immoral behavior—she saw little of concern in Jack's dalliances. He was single, after all; this was how unmarried men behaved.

For that matter, Eunice was too busy pursuing her career to pay much mind to the comings and goings on Thirty-first Street. Tall and thin, with reddish-brown hair and high cheekbones, the fifth child of Joe and Rose had from a young age stood out for her deep religious conviction, fierce intelligence, and almost superhuman willpower. Like Jack, she had suffered chronic health maladies throughout her life, including back problems and stomach ailments that left her perpetually underweight (the family nickname for her was "Puny Eunie"), and, like him, she had willed herself through the pain, ignoring doctors' pleas to slow down, put on weight, and get adequate rest. Instead she pressed on, racking up sporting trophies left and right (she was a superior athlete) and exuding seriousness of purpose. "Eunice was born mature," her mother later said, "and because she was so close to Rosemary a special social responsibility developed within her, which later showed up when she went to Harlem to do social work."[9]

"Of all the kids in the family, Eunice was far and away the strongest-minded," George Smathers would observe in 1976. "Sort of the leader of the clan. Very tough when she wanted to be." He added that the twenty-five-year-old Eunice would have loved to be the Kennedy to run in the Eleventh District in 1946: "If she'd been a little older, and if it had been today, when a lot of women are running for office, I suspect the history of the Kennedy clan would have been quite different." Mary Pitcairn said: "She was highly nervous, highly geared, and worshiped Jack. I always thought she should have been a boy." In the Georgetown salons, when the men adjourned for political talk and cigars after the meal, Eunice often went with them, lighting her own stogie, rather than join the women in the drawing room. She shared with her brother a keen political sense, which is one reason they got on so well. Both of them had a singular ability to size up a political situation almost instantly.[10]

In Washington she threw herself into her work on behalf of troubled youth, even bringing boys and girls home to Georgetown for dinner on occasion. She organized a celebrity golf tournament to raise money for projects helping local youth offenders, and encouraged a national organization of sportswriters and broadcasters to have its members write about the matter and coach troubled youths in sports they themselves played. She even took to the road, speaking in various locales around the country on the plight of children languishing in juvenile detention centers such as the DC Receiving Home in Washington. Shriver assisted her in these efforts, having been dispatched to Washington from Chicago by Joe Kennedy to serve as her all-purpose aide. (Thus the peculiar characteristics of Shriver's position: working for Eunice, and courting her, while being paid by her father.)[11]

Shriver, naturally, saw a lot of the townhouse, and therefore of Jack. He found he liked the congressman, liked his intelligence and charm and self-possession, and enjoyed spending time with him. Shriver also relished attending the dinners over which Jack presided, since they afforded a chance to meet politicians from various parts of the country.

On one occasion, Shriver remembered:

> I ended up alone at a table with this freshman Republican from California I'd never met before. It was the oddest experience: I felt like I couldn't get a handle on this guy. I couldn't pin down what his opinions on anything were. He bobbed and weaved, like a cowardly boxer. Half the time, it seemed he was barely paying attention to me. He'd be looking over my shoulder at the other tables, as though he were trying to eavesdrop, trying to figure out what the other congressmen were saying. It's rare that someone makes as strong an impression on you as this guy did on me. But I came away thinking that he was smart, crafty, and a scheming conniver, more interested in establishing his position with Jack and other luminaries than in anything I was saying.[12]

So went Sargent Shriver's first encounter with Richard Nixon.

II

Jack Kennedy, it's fair to say, was less interested in his work than his sister was in hers. And, true to form, when he was unengaged, he didn't apply himself. "He wasn't totally engrossed in what he was doing," Eunice acknowledged. "He sort of drifted along. He wasn't making any effort to be Speaker of the House. He did an ordinary probably performance."[13]

Jack would not have claimed otherwise. Strange as it seemed, entering Congress was a letdown for him. The previous years had been exhilarating ones, befitting the son of Ambassador Kennedy, and had culminated in a thrilling campaign victory before adoring crowds in Boston. Now Jack saw what countless freshman House members had discovered before him: that he was but one of 435 lawmakers, and a junior one at that. What's more, his Democrats had taken a drubbing in the election, and were suddenly the minority party in both houses, with an unpopular leader in the White House. The Massachusetts delegation in the House had fifteen members (ten Republicans, five Democrats), including Speaker Joseph Martin and Minority Whip John McCormack. It would be a long time, Jack could see, before he could gain real authority on key committees, let alone match the clout of the senior members of his party. His only role was one he did not relish: acting as the voice for the humdrum local needs of voters in the Eleventh District.

Whether he lost any sleep over his lowly status is questionable. He always understood that the House of Representatives provided scant opportunity for the kind of national leadership he craved, and he appears to have seen his post mostly as a launching pad for greater things. "I think from the time he was elected to Congress, he had no thought but to go to the Senate as fast as he could," Arthur Krock remarked. "He wanted scope, which a freshman in the House cannot have, and very few actually of the seniors; so I think the House was just a way-station." Of a fellow member of the Massachusetts delegation Kennedy revealingly remarked, "I never felt he did much in the Congress, but I never held that against him because I don't think I did much. I mean you can't do much as a Congressman."[14] Content to leave the running of his Washington office to aides Billy Sutton and Timothy "Ted" Reardon and secretary Mary Davis, Kennedy flew back to Boston as often as possible, taking an apartment directly across from the State House, at 122 Bowdoin Street, that would remain his main address for the remainder of his days (including on his driver's license when he was president). Or he escaped to Palm Beach for a long weekend, or to New York City to meet a paramour.

The frequent absences left his poor staff scrambling to stay on top of the work that came into the office, much of it in the form of requests from people in his district. Lucky for him, they were up to the task. Davis in particular was known for her superhuman efficiency and all-around ability. A Washington native and a product of its parochial schools, she had worked for three congressmen prior to joining Kennedy's staff, earning raves from each. According to Sutton, she could answer the phone, type a letter, and eat a candy bar all at once. "She was the complete political machine, knew everybody, how to get anything done." Even so, Davis recalled working until seven or eight at night, taking work home, and coming in on weekends. And she despaired at Kennedy's habit of leaving his possessions all over the place. "He was constantly replacing or trying to retrieve his coats," she said. "He'd leave them, or his camera or radio, on a plane or on a pushcart someplace. He very rarely carried a briefcase in those days. Thank God! That would have been lost too." But Davis also saw another side to her boss: "One thing that really surprised me were his formal speeches. He wrote his own. He appeared to be such a disinterested guy, couldn't care less but then he'd say, 'Mary, come on in.' Then he would start dictating off the top of his head. The flow of language, his command of English was extraordinary. It would come out beautifully— exactly what he wanted to say. And I'd think, 'This, coming from *you?*' I surprised myself, but I came to the conclusion that he was brilliant—the brightest person I've ever known."[15]

Congressman Kennedy was given two committee assignments: the Committee on Education and Labor and the lowly Committee on the District of Columbia. He focused a lot of his early attention on housing, especially for veterans. Since the end of the war, the armed services had demobilized rapidly, and the nation faced an acute residential shortage. Millions of people were forced to live in cramped quarters—attics, basements, even boxcars and chicken coops. Soon after taking office, Jack spoke fervently on the issue before the National Public Housing Conference, in Chicago. "Veterans need homes and they need them quickly," he declared. "Any veteran who watched the American supplies pouring ashore on the Normandy beaches; who saw the Pacific Islands cleared and our air landing strips rolled out in four or five days; who saw the endless waste of war and the seemingly never ending productivity that replaced that waste; is it any wonder that the veteran cannot understand why he is not housed?"[16] When the House GOP leadership blocked a bipartisan Senate bill to create 1.25 million new urban housing units per year for the next ten years, Jack went to the House floor and accused Republicans of being beholden to lobbyists. "I was sent to this Congress by the people of my district," he proclaimed, "to help solve the most pressing problem facing this country—the housing crisis. I am going to have to go back to my district on Saturday, a district that probably sent more boys per family into this last war than any in the country, and when they ask me if I was able to get them any homes, I will have to answer, 'Not a one—not a single one.' "[17]

On this and most other domestic legislation, Jack generally aligned with the Truman administration and liberal northern Democrats. He opposed a tax bill for favoring the rich over everyone else and a lowering of the appropriation for school lunches. He also voted against a weakening of rent control and tax relief for the oil industry. He backed more robust social security, stepped up minimum wage provisions, and offered support for expanded immigration and housing programs. In his committee votes, he aligned closely with the wishes of organized labor—according to the *CIO News* rating system, Jack voted "wrong" only twice during his time in the House.[18]

Yet he also showed an occasional willingness to cut an independent path. When, in 1947, Mayor James Curley was convicted of mail fraud and sent to Danbury penitentiary (the judge ignored Curley's plea that he was suffering from nine separate maladies and likely did not have long to live), party leaders in Boston and Washington urged President Truman to pardon him, using a petition drawn up by House Majority Leader John McCormack and signed by Republican as well as Democratic representatives. But Kennedy refused to sign, even though Curley was immensely popular among Boston voters and even though it could be said that Jack owed Curley for having retired from the House and left his seat open. To Kennedy's mind, signing the petition would show him to be just another hypocritical pol, no better than the man he had replaced, and he waved aside aides' fears that by failing to sign he risked alienating party leaders as well as the voters of his district. (Later in the year, Truman did commute Curley's sentence, and the mayor's mystery ailments suddenly disappeared.)[19]

On other issues, too, Kennedy showed a marked disdain for dogmatism, whether from the left or the right. On labor legislation he took relatively nuanced positions, showing a greater openness to reforms than most Democrats while at the same time rejecting Republican claims of what constituted appropriate changes to labor law. A champion of New Deal policies, he privately worried about the expansion of government power that many of the programs necessitated. The guest list for his salons in Georgetown typically had as many Republican as Democratic names on it, and in his speeches he sometimes expounded on the importance in democratic politics of a spirit of compromise, of bargaining in good faith. He grew close to several conservative Democrats and often expressed admiration for Senator Robert A. Taft, the austere Republican from Ohio, whom he considered honorable and trenchant.[20]

Kennedy also got on well with Richard Nixon. Both served on the Education and Labor Committee and, given their freshman status in different parties, were seated at opposite ends of the table. "We were like a pair of unmatched bookends," Nixon recalled. The thirty-four-year-old Californian admired Kennedy's languid grace and ease of manner, and envied him his Harvard degree, while Jack found Nixon knowledgeable and respectful. ("Listen to this fellow," Jack said to an aide early on. "He's going places.")[21] In certain core respects their views also aligned—both sought to keep organized labor in check (Nixon went further, seeking to drive it back); both thought that Communism should not be allowed to drive union activity.

One evening in April 1947, as part of the committee's road show, the two young lawmakers found themselves debating the proposed Taft-Hartley Act (which restricted the power and activities of labor) in the small steel town of McKeesport, Pennsylvania, near Pittsburgh. Nixon, a champion undergrad debater at Whittier College, expressed full support for worker rights but warned the audience that big labor was growing "by leaps and bounds" and threatening economic growth. He listed the strikes that had roiled the nation since the war ended. Some hisses could be heard from the largely pro-labor crowd. Jack was more conciliatory, warmer, smoother in his delivery. He mostly ignored Nixon as he struck a moderate line, commending American workers while cautioning against policies that could lead to a "war" between management and labor.[22]

Someone could write a novel about what happened next (and indeed someone has). At midnight, after munching hamburgers and chatting about baseball in a local diner, the two congressmen boarded the Capitol Limited together for the long train ride back to Washington.[23] They drew straws for the lower berth; Nixon won. They then stayed up for hours, talking mostly about foreign policy, each man's preferred topic, and in particular the rising tensions with the Soviet Union. In the fullness of time, each would revise his opinion of the other, in a downward way, but on this night, with the train chugging through the quiet countryside, Nixon and Kennedy felt a mutual kinship. They had some things in common, they realized, beyond being Navy veterans who were new to Congress: both had lost a golden-child older brother, and both labored under heavy parental expectations. Moreover, Nixon later said, "We shared one quality which distinguished us from most of our fellow congressmen. Neither of us was a backslapper, and we were uncomfortable with boisterous displays of superficial camaraderie. He was shy, and that sometimes made him appear aloof. But it was a shyness born of an instinct that guarded privacy and concealed emotions. I understood these qualities because I shared them."[24]

Some who observed Jack in this period took a less benign view, finding him too casual by half, and too aloof. "He never seemed to get into the

House freshmen participate in a radio broadcast in 1947.
Kennedy is second from right in the rear; Richard Nixon is at the far right.

midstream of any tremendous political thought, or political action," remarked William O. Douglas, Supreme Court justice and Kennedy family friend. "He didn't seem to be caught up in anything, and was sort of drifting." And though in time he would develop a thicker skin than most politicians, in this period he brooded over slights, as longtime political ally Thomas "Tip" O'Neill noted. "If a group of politicians were talking and somebody said something mean about Jack and it got back to him, he'd be over to see me. 'Why doesn't so-and-so like me?' he'd ask. Why can't he and I sit down and straighten this thing out? . . . He hadn't grown up in the school of hard knocks. Politically, he had lived an easy life and was used to people loving him."[25]

And for the most part people did love him. Press treatment by the Boston dailies was generally favorable, and not infrequently laudatory, as reporters championed his support for veterans and his outspoken views on labor issues dear to the people of his district. Criticism of his decision on the Curley petition was muted and fleeting. One detects the hand of Joseph P. Kennedy in at least some of this coverage—the Ambassador had not ceased his relentless behind-the-scenes PR efforts to promote his son—but there was also a broadly felt sense that Representative Kennedy looked out for his constituents' interests and, in general, acquitted himself well. Nor was it just Boston journalists who took this view. As Congress went into recess that first summer, national columnist Drew Pearson offered his take on the Eightieth Congress. The most promising thing about it, he told his readers, was the presence of several talented new lawmakers. John F. Kennedy was at the top of his list.[26]

III

It did not escape the attention of observers such as Pearson that Jack Kennedy was particularly comfortable in one policy area of growing salience: foreign affairs. Despite his tender age, he had abundant international experience to his credit, and a well-received book on foreign policy. He'd also won widespread acclaim for his service in the war and had covered the San Francisco Conference and the British election of 1945 as a journalist. It all gave Kennedy enhanced authority when he ventured into matters pertaining to overseas crises.

He had ample opportunities to do so, for in 1947 the East-West conflict was growing more serious by the week. Early in the year, the British government requested U.S. help in Greece to defend its conservative client government in a civil war against leftists. Truman responded in March by asking Congress, in a speech before the House, to allocate $400 million in aid to Greece and Turkey. Lawmakers were skeptical, the president knew, so he talked up the danger, lacing his speech with alarmist language intended to stake out America's role in stopping relentless Communist expansion in the postwar world. "If Greece should fall under the control of an armed minority," he gravely proclaimed, in an early version of the domino theory, "the effect upon its neighbor, Turkey, would be immediate and serious. Confusion and disorder might well spread throughout the entire Middle East." Such an outcome simply had to be prevented, he added, in articulating what became known as the Truman Doctrine: "I believe that it must be the policy of the United States to support free peoples who are resisting attempted subjugation by armed minorities or by outside pressures."[27]

Critics questioned the logic. They noted that the Soviet Union was barely involved in the Greek civil war, that many Communists in Greece were hardly enamored of Stalin, and that the resistance movement had many non-Communist members. Nor did the Kremlin appear to have designs on Turkey. Others argued that all assistance should be channeled through the United Nations. Still others, including Joseph P. Kennedy, maintained that Communism would fail on its own, and that the United States should leave the Greeks and the Turks to their own devices. In late April, the elder Kennedy told a columnist that he was ready "to admit from now on that the term 'isolationist' described my sentiments perfectly. We never gave 'isolationism' a chance. . . . I'm proud I warned against participation in a war which could only leave the world in a worse condition than before." Three weeks later, he told *The New York Times* that, on economic grounds alone, it was folly to spend millions on Greece and Turkey: "Personally, as I have said before, I believe our efforts to stem communism in Europe with dollars will eventually prove an overwhelming tax on our resources that will seriously affect the economic well-being of our country."[28]

Jack rejected his father's argument outright, and he showed scarcely more patience with the other opponents of Truman's plan, such as columnist Walter Lippmann, who reminded his readers that the Soviets had genuine security fears and were motivated mostly by a defensive desire to prevent the reestablishment of German power. Though Jack, in his jour-nalistic writings in 1945, had argued along similar lines, he now stressed Moscow's offensive designs, and he rejected the calls by Lippmann and others for diplomatic overtures to the Kremlin. At the University of North Carolina in late March, Jack said the president was right to warn against allowing any one power to dominate either Europe or Asia. What had U.S. interventions in both of the world wars been about, after all, except deny-ing such continental domination to hostile entities? That determination must not now slacken, the young lawmaker went on, and he expressed confidence that most Americans would staunchly oppose "the suffering people of Europe and Asia succumbing to the false, soporific ideology of Red totalitarianism." The next month, Jack told reporters that if Greece and Turkey succumbed, "the road to the Near East is open. We have no alternative but to support the President's policy."[29]

It's a fascinating thing that father and son would take such starkly op-posing positions on the most pressing foreign policy issue of the day and, more, that the Ambassador would be so intent on proclaiming his own view loudly and for all to hear. In any event, Jack's perspective carried the day, even if many legislators—in both parties—were more ambivalent than he was about the issues at stake: both houses approved by comfort-able margins Truman's proposal for aid to Greece and Turkey. When Sec-retary of State George C. Marshall, in a commencement speech at Harvard in June 1947, announced that the United States would finance a colossal European recovery program (subsequently known as the Mar-shall Plan), the Kennedys were again on opposite sides, with Joe firmly against and Jack strongly in favor.[30] And they disagreed on the National Security Act of July of that year, which created the Office of the Secretary of Defense (which became the Department of Defense two years later), to oversee all branches of the armed services; the National Security Council (NSC), to advise the president; and the Central Intelligence Agency (CIA), to conduct spy operations and information gathering overseas. Taken to-gether, the components of the National Security Act gave the president enhanced powers with which to conduct foreign and defense policy, a condition that Jack accepted as necessary in the circumstances, with the Soviet threat looming large. His father did not.

There was a legitimate question here, both at the time and among his-torians afterwards, about whether the Cold War might have been averted before it really began, through imaginative diplomacy on areas of potential East-West agreement.[31] But to freshman congressman John F. Kennedy the answer was clear: no such opportunity existed. He was, it may fairly be said, an original Cold Warrior.

No doubt Joe Kennedy had his son in mind when he wrote to a friend, a few months later, "I look to see Communism spread all over the world, and, the horrible part of it is, I don't think we can do anything about it. However, there are a great many people in this country, based on their own judgment or some form of idealism which they possess, that believe we should continue to help Europe. I would be perfectly willing to gamble five billion dollars for one year's trial because, if we stop giving money now and Communism spreads, there will always be a great number of people in this country who will think the world could have been saved if we sent money abroad."[32]

Even within the realm of domestic politics, Jack often made anti-Communism his leitmotif. When Russ Nixon, a representative of the United Electrical, Radio, and Machine Workers of America, appeared before the Education and Labor Committee, Kennedy waited patiently while his colleagues tried in vain to tear the man down over the extent of Communist influence within America's unions. The intellectually agile Nixon, who held a Ph.D. in economics and had taught Kennedy at Harvard before joining the labor movement (Jack received a B-minus in the class), got the better of each exchange. Then it was Kennedy's turn. Calmly and methodically and at a brisk pace, he pressed Nixon on the work of the UE, then asked him whether he thought Communism constituted a threat to the American political and economic system. No, Nixon replied, "I think what is a threat is our failure to meet some of the basic economic problems of the people in a democratic way, and also what is a threat is our failure year after year to expand the basic civil rights of our people" and thus address "the problems of the Negro people."

"Mr. Nixon," Kennedy replied, "I agree with a great deal that you have said." But, he continued, wasn't it a fact that Communists were central in the union's leadership? He quoted a doctrine stressing the need to "resort to all sorts of artifices, evasion, subterfuges, only so as to get into the trade unions and remain in them and to carry on Communist work in them, at all costs."

"I did not teach you that at Harvard, did I?" Nixon replied.

"No, you did not. I am reading from Lenin, in which is described the procedure which should be adopted to get into trade unions and how they conduct themselves once they are in."

Kennedy's performance won plaudits from reporters. Though not a lawyer like most of his colleagues, he pierced Russ Nixon's dominance and put him on the defensive through crisp questioning that was free of sophistry or platitudes. "A freshman House member with the coral dust of Pacific Islands still clinging to his heels stole the show from older colleagues yesterday," the United Press's George Reedy reported in a radio broadcast. As a bonus for Jack, Nixon acknowledged after the session that his former pupil was one of the committee's few pro-labor members.[33]

On the last day of August, with Congress in recess, Kennedy crossed the Atlantic in order to monitor the progress of the Marshall Plan aid and look into Communist infiltration of labor unions. Or at least that was the official explanation—he also wanted to spend time with sister Kick and reunite with his British pals. Kick, he saw immediately, was flourishing, hobnobbing with the upper-class set, hosting tea parties, and haunting the bars and dining rooms of the House of Commons. Might she have elective politics in her future? Quite possibly. A generation before, Nancy Astor had blazed the path, as an American-born woman who became a member of Parliament. Some speculated that Kick, with her quick wit, phenomenal social intelligence, and expansive contacts among high-placed Tories and Liberals, would follow suit.

Soon after his arrival, Jack joined Kick for a party she hosted at the Duke of Devonshire's Lismore Castle, in southern Ireland, attended by, among others, Anthony Eden, once and future British foreign secretary and future prime minister. (Eden, separated from his wife and smitten with Kick, though she was barely half his age, would write to Kick a few weeks later while traveling in the Middle East: "I love your letters, especially when you write as you talk, for then I can imagine that you are here. How I wish that you were here. . . . But if one has not the delight of your company it is a joy to imagine it.") The party was a rousing success, and Kick reported to her father that Jack had gotten along famously with Eden.[34]

Some days later, Jack, accompanied by Kick's friend Pamela Churchill, the beautiful and vivacious ex-wife of Winston Churchill's son Randolph, drove in Kathleen's new American station wagon to New Ross to find their family ancestors. The four-hour trip took them through the rolling green countryside across the bottom tip of County Kilkenny into County Wexford. Predictably, locals were bemused when Jack introduced himself and said he was looking for his forebears. "Auch now, and which Kennedys will it be that you'll be wanting? David Kennedys? Jim Kennedys?" Finally, they were directed to a little white house on the edge of town with a thatched roof and chickens, goats, and pigs wandering in and out the front door. Mr. and Mrs. Kennedy were friendly but wary. The conversation over tea was pleasant and dignified but yielded no proof of a direct link. Churchill was bored, but Jack, a romantic underneath his cool exterior, loved every minute.* "I spent about an hour there surrounded by chickens, pigs, etc., and left in a flow of nostalgia and sentiment," he recalled later. It was an alien place to him, but also familiar, magical. He vowed to one day return.[35]

Kick had little interest in her brother's genealogical expedition, but she relished spending the better part of a month with him at Lismore. Their mutual affection was as evident as ever—Pamela Churchill and others could see it right away. Kick now revealed to him that she had fallen hard for Peter Fitzwilliam, a fabulously wealthy aristocrat who had been decorated for bravery in the war and who happened to be married. (He had ownership of the Fitzwilliam family seat, Wentworth Woodhouse, a 365-room palace in Yorkshire measuring some 250,000 square feet and said to be the largest private home in the United Kingdom.) Charismatic and charming, Fitzwilliam was also a notorious philanderer—a bit like Kick's father, some said. She told Jack that in Peter she had found her Rhett Butler, a man's man who could make her laugh and sweep her along with him. Yes, he was married, and yes, he was Protestant, but she didn't care. All that mattered was that he planned to divorce his wife and marry Kick. Jack delighted in his sister's radiant happiness, perhaps even envied it, and readily agreed to her plea that he say nothing to their parents for now—could there be any doubt about how Rose in particular would respond to the news?[36]

Jack's health, meanwhile, took a nosedive during the trip. Kick insisted he see a local doctor; he said he would but did not follow through. In late

---

* When Jack asked his hosts what he could do for them to express his thanks, they politely waved him off. Sensing they had something in mind, he asked again; they broke down and asked if he would drive their children around the village in the station wagon. Soon there was the sight of Congressman Kennedy driving slowly up and down the streets, in a new American vehicle, with half a dozen or more Irish Kennedy kids crammed in the back.

September, having arrived in London, he felt worse; he now couldn't get out of his bed at Claridge's hotel. His blood pressure plummeted. When Kay Stammers came to see him, he tried to stand up but couldn't do it. He called Pamela Churchill, who in turn dialed a doctor friend, Dr. Daniel Davis, who promptly had Jack admitted to the London Clinic. Davis diagnosed Addison's disease, an illness marked by the failure of the adrenal glands that caused extreme weakness, low blood pressure, weight loss, circulatory problems, and a brownish skin cast. When first discovered by physician Thomas Addison, in the mid-1850s, the disease was considered fatal, for it gradually killed the body's ability to fight off infection. Novelist Jane Austen had succumbed to it at age forty-one. With the development of adrenal hormone therapy in the 1930s, however, the death rate plunged dramatically. Still, Davis was gloomy after diagnosing Kennedy, telling Pamela, "That American friend of yours, he hasn't got a year to live."[37]

The Boston papers, upon learning of the congressman's travails, accepted the explanation issued by the congressman's office, which attributed his hospitalization to a recurrence of the malaria he had contracted during the war. *The New York Times* and *Time* followed suit. Behind the scenes, Joe and Rose were beside themselves with worry, and Joe confided to Arthur Krock that he feared Jack was near death. A Kennedy family nurse—Anne McGillicuddy, who had cared for Jack at the Chelsea Naval Hospital in 1944 and whom he had also dated—was flown to London in October with instructions to bring him back to America. On October 13, still in his pajamas, he was carried aboard the *Queen Elizabeth* at Southampton. He spent the five-day voyage in the sick bay, cared for by Anne and chatting up the economist Barbara Ward, whom he had first met in London two years before. Jack was "flat on his back, yellow as a pot of honey, cheerful as all get-out, and again asking questions," Ward remembered. "This time it was about the development of the Labour government, about social change in Britain, the medical health scheme [the planned National Health Service]. It was just the same extraordinary intellectual vividness, though coupled in this case with a fever that had him absolutely strapped on his back."[38]

He got worse. When the ship reached U.S. shores, his condition was so grave that a priest gave him last rites. Death grazed him. On the evening of October 18 he was carried ashore on a stretcher (through a lower-level hatch on the ship, to avoid detection) to a waiting ambulance, which took him to LaGuardia Airport and a chartered DC-3 to Boston.

There followed weeks of treatment at the Lahey Clinic, during which he was a no-show in the House of Representatives. His attendance record would be among the worst in the Eightieth Congress. Thanks to his superb staff, however, he kept on top of numerous duties sufficiently well. His standing with his constituents might have even risen, as people took pity on him for his "malaria struggle." On February 1, 1948, *The Boston Post*, perhaps with an assist from the Ambassador's public relations team, exulted that Congressman Kennedy was fully on the mend, his political future rosy: "He has overcome the malaria he brought back from the South Pacific with him and he is in better physical condition now than at any time since his discharge from the Navy. In fact, according to his supporters, his health is almost as robust as his political courage."[39]

IV

It was a brutal Boston winter, with snowstorm after snowstorm, but by the end of February 1948, all the Kennedys—save Rosemary, who was still institutionalized at her facility in Wisconsin—were lapping up the sun at the family home in Palm Beach. Even Kick was there, having arrived from England for a two-month stay. Jack had kept his promise not to tell their parents about Peter Fitzwilliam, but Kick knew she could not hide the truth much longer. Still, she vacillated, sure of the reaction she'd

The Palm Beach home on North Ocean Boulevard.

get. Only on April 22, shortly before her return to England, did she find the courage to tell them of Fitzwilliam and her plan to marry him. Rose responded by vowing to disown her daughter if she married a divorced man. Joe said nothing, suggesting he agreed with his wife.[40]

Or perhaps not. Perhaps, Kick hoped, her father's silence meant she could yet bring him around. She was a favorite of his, and she'd often been able to get her way with him in the past. Upon her return to London she convinced Joe, who was visiting Paris, to at least meet Fitzwilliam. The couple planned a brief two-day holiday in Cannes before joining Mr. Kennedy for lunch in the French capital on Saturday, May 15. On May 13, their chartered plane landed at Le Bourget airfield, outside Paris, to refuel. They met friends for a meal and returned midafternoon to reports of inclement weather in the Rhône valley, to the south. Pilot Peter Townshend recommended that they wait out the storm, but Fitzwilliam insisted on flying right away, even after being told that all commercial flights had been grounded.

Flying at ten thousand feet, they entered the storm just north of the Ardèche Mountains. Townshend and his copilot tried desperately to steady the aircraft as violent crosscurrents tossed it from side to side. Visibility was zero. They lost radio contact, and the instruments spun uselessly. The pilots didn't know if they were descending or climbing. Suddenly the plane emerged from a cloud and they saw a mountain ridge straight ahead. Townshend yanked the controls to avoid a crash, but it was too late. For several seconds all four people aboard would have realized they were going to crash.[41]

It was Eunice who answered when the phone rang at midnight in Georgetown. A *Washington Post* reporter introduced himself and said a report indicated that a Lady Hartington had been killed along with three others in a plane crash in France; might this be her sister? Eunice replied that she was not sure, as there was also a second Lady Hartington—Kick's ex-sister-in-law Debo. To which the reporter offered a crushing detail: a passport found at the crash site, on a mountainside near the tiny village of Privas, showed the victim's Christian name to be Kathleen. While Eunice spoke on the phone, Jack was on the couch, listening to a recording of *Finian's Rainbow*, a musical that had opened on Broadway the previous year. Billy Sutton was there, too. Jack got on the phone and asked the reporter to read the dispatch to him, then hung up and immediately dialed his aide Ted Reardon and instructed him to check the story out; Reardon called back soon thereafter and confirmed the worst. As Jack put down the receiver, "How Are Things in Glocca Morra?" was playing on the stereo. "She has a sweet voice," he murmured of the vocalist Ella Logan. Then he turned away and wept.[42]

The following day, Reardon made arrangements for the two Kennedy siblings to fly to Hyannis Port. Once there, Jack hunkered in a back room, refusing to see anyone and having his meals delivered to him. He was disconsolate, unable to make sense of what had happened. Joe's death had been awful, but at least it happened in wartime; he had given his life for his country, as had countless others. Kick's was different. She had died on account of love, and the stifled romantic in Jack had always admired her refusal to repress her affections. More than that, she was his soulmate, the one he could confide in about anything, the one who completed his sentences, his thoughts, the one to whom he didn't have to explain his feelings, his moods, for she intuited them. She had always believed in him, had always championed his prospects, even more than she had Joe Junior's, had always prized him for who he was. And now she was gone.

With Kick to be buried in England, Jack sent word that he would come over for the May 20 service, arranged by Kick's former in-laws, the Devonshires. He arrived in New York City on the eighteenth, with plans to fly across the Atlantic that evening. In his distressed state he had neglected to bring his passport. Hasty arrangements were made to try to secure an emergency replacement that would be rushed to him at the airport. His staff determined it could be done, if barely. Jack, however, suddenly called a halt, as though he could not bear the thought of attending his sister's funeral. He instead returned to Washington. Among the Kennedys, only a grief-stricken father would be present for the requiem Mass. He cut a solitary figure, in light of his ignominious tenure as ambassador. "He stood there alone," Alastair Forbes said, "unloved and despised."[43]

For weeks Jack had insomnia, telling Lem Billings that when he drifted off he would be jolted awake "by the image of Kathleen sitting up with him late at night talking about their parents and dates. He would try to close his eyes again, but he couldn't shake the image." During congressional hearings, his mind would drift to all the things he and Kick had done together and all the friends they had shared, in England as well as at home. To make matters worse, Billings added, "there was no one in the family with whom he could share this loss." He didn't feel close enough to any of them. So he kept quiet, saying little that has been recorded, though years later he remarked to campaign biographer James MacGregor Burns that both Kick and Joe had perished just when "everything was moving in their direction." That made losing them doubly hard to take. "If something happens to you or somebody in your family who is miserable anyway, whose health is bad, or who has a chronic disease or something, that's one thing. But for someone who is living at their peak, then to get cut off—that's the shock."[44]

Kick's death, coming so soon after his own severe health scare in London, made him acutely aware of his own mortality. Suddenly only he remained of the supposed golden trio of Kennedy children, and they had effectively also lost Rosemary, who was closest to him in age. Could he be far behind, especially considering his alarming recent diagnosis? He thought not, and told acquaintances flatly that he did not expect to live past forty-five. He began to obsess over the mind's workings in the moments before death—would one think about all the joyous things that had occurred, or would one feel regrets about choices made, things not experienced? On a fishing trip with George Smathers he mused out loud on the topic, then leaned over to Smathers and said, "The point is that you've got to live every day like it's your last day. That's what I'm doing."[45]

Although this fixation on mortality and his own premature death might have made Kennedy self-pitying and sullen, he was nothing of the kind. If anything, associates noted, his belief that his days were numbered, and that he had to live each one to the fullest, made him more convivial and expressive. Like Raymond Asquith and the other gallant World War I figures he so admired, he made a point of smiling at fate. In Chuck Spalding's recollection, "There was something about time—special for him, obviously, because he always heard the footsteps, but also special for you when you were with him. So whenever he was in a situation, he tried to burn bright; he tried to wring as much out of things as he could. After a while he didn't have to try. He had something nobody else did. It was just a heightened sense of being; there's no other way to describe it."[46]

V

Jack's knowledge that only he remained of the charmed Kennedy trio, combined with his sense that his own days might be numbered, lent urgency to his political ambitions. If he had always considered the House of

Representatives as but a stepping-stone to bigger and better things, this conviction grew stronger in the wake of the Addison's diagnosis and Kick's death. He became more restless on the job and ramped up his speaking schedule around Massachusetts, eagerly accepting invitations from any organization that would have him—in places like Worcester, Springfield, Chicopee, Fall River, and Holyoke. Aides later spoke nostalgically of dingy, poorly lit hotels, of wolfing down hamburgers and milkshakes on the go, of seeing the congressman shaving in the men's room of a bowling alley between events. The pattern, Dave Powers recalled, was usually the same: "Jack would try to get up here every Friday, Saturday, and Sunday to speak. Frank Morrissey or Bob Morey and I would go around with him. I remember he'd fly up on Friday. Then on Sunday he'd take a train, The Federal, a sleeper that left South Station at eleven at night. He'd get a bedroom. When the train got to Washington, it just sat in the station and they'd let the passengers sleep in until nine or ten o'clock. Then he'd get up and go back to work on the Hill."[47]

The Boston press took notice of his frequent trips home, speculating about a possible Kennedy run for the Senate that fall against the craggy-faced, blue-blooded Republican incumbent Leverett Saltonstall, a descendant of Puritans and tenth-generation Harvard man. The notion had appeal, but Jack's team worried it was too soon, opening him up to charges that he lacked sufficient experience, that he was driven by self-serving ambition rather than a commitment to public service. Saltonstall, moreover, would be no pushover, especially in a presidential election year in which the Democrat in the White House looked extremely vulnerable and the Republicans looked poised to add to their majorities in Congress. Jack also liked and admired Saltonstall personally and didn't relish taking him on.

Another option was to challenge Governor Robert F. Bradford, who was up for reelection in 1948 and rumored to be in ill health. (It would be revealed that he had Parkinson's.) Billy Sutton, for one, thought this race winnable for Jack, and that it would give him four years to build a statewide political machine before challenging Henry Cabot Lodge for the state's other U.S. Senate seat in 1952.[48] But this option, too, had drawbacks, not least that Jack would face serious rivals in the primary election, including potentially Maurice Tobin or Paul A. Dever, both popular vote-getters with political machines of their own. The Kennedy team opted to take a wait-and-see attitude while planning in the meantime to keep Jack where he was, in the House of Representatives. In 1948 he faced no op-

position in either the primary or the general election, so victory was assured.

As always, Kennedy made sure to keep abreast of issues that were
resonating most strongly among Massachusetts voters: veterans' housing, labor rights, education, rent control, taxes, and healthcare. He also
made a determined move in a new policy direction: civil rights. This effort
was, to a degree, unexpected—though in personal terms Kennedy was
largely free of racial prejudice, he'd shown little interest in the plight of
African Americans. Except for the family's chauffeurs, domestics, and va-
lets, he hadn't interacted much with blacks in Bronxville or Hyannis Port
or Palm Beach, nor did he encounter many of them during his student
days at Choate or Harvard. Apart from his naval stint in Charleston,
South Carolina, in early 1942, he had spent little time in the Deep South.
And though his wartime experience in the Pacific exposed him for the first
time to Americans from many walks of life, few of them were African
American. Racial segregation was enforced in the military, nearly as
strictly as in the Jim Crow South. Black sailors serving alongside Kennedy
in the South Pacific were usually mess attendants or cooks. There were no
black crewmen on the PT boats.[49]

Still, many black Bostonians were struck, upon meeting the congressman, by his courtesy and his easy informality. "Northern pols were normally stand-offish," said Harold Vaughan, a Boston lawyer who got to
know Jack in 1948. "But Kennedy would just walk into a beauty salon in
a black neighborhood, go right up to the woman below the hairdryer and
say: 'Hi, I'm Jack Kennedy.'" That same year, when a memorial was un-
veiled in Cambridge honoring two African American war heroes, Kennedy delivered a moving speech at the dedication ceremony. In
Washington, he fought for new civil rights legislation. Notably, he lent
firm support to bills calling for the abolition of the poll tax and a ban on
lynching, and he publicly lauded the efforts of Franklin Roosevelt's wartime Fair Employment Practices Committee, which had worked to prevent
discrimination against African Americans in defense and government
jobs. In 1948, Kennedy backed efforts to strengthen the Civil Rights Division of the Department of Justice, and opposed funding for the Registered
College Plan, which financed segregated educational institutions.[50]

On the District of Columbia Committee, meanwhile, Kennedy advocated for the city's black residents, who, almost a century after the Civil

War, lived each day with the burden of segregation. In many Washington restaurants, African Americans were denied service altogether, or restricted to the counter (where they often had to stand). If they boarded a southbound train at Union Station, they had to sit in "colored only" cars. As elsewhere in the country, movie theaters in the city excluded African Americans altogether or confined them to seats in the balcony. Swimming pools were segregated, and most downtown hotels would not rent rooms to blacks. Even on Capitol Hill, unwritten rules kept black employees from the pool, from the barbershop, and from various cafeterias and restaurants.[51]

To Kennedy and other advocates of change, Washington's racial problems owed much to the fact that the city had no mayor or local council but was run by three commissioners, who in turn took orders from two congressional committees—one in the House (on which Kennedy served) and one in the Senate. Segregationists dominated the House committee in particular, but Kennedy was undaunted. He championed home rule for the city, arguing that its residents, a majority of whom were black, deserved a voice in their own affairs. The effort came to naught, but Kennedy won praise from liberal colleagues and black leaders for his work.[52]

He also came up short in a campaign to block a new 3 percent city sales tax, which he maintained would unfairly target African Americans. In a House speech on June 8, 1948, Kennedy used charts and diagrams to assert that the new tax "would put the main burden on the people who cannot afford to pay it." When the issue reemerged the following year, with the tax now in place, Kennedy again argued in opposition, noting that the tax placed "the major burden on the people in the lowest income groups." If the District needed more revenue, the affluent should carry the burden, he said. Ultimately, the House voted 177 to 176 to retain the tax, but Kennedy's advocacy did not go unnoticed. "The congressman who did the most to save the District from the burden of a sales tax is a tousle-haired bachelor named 'Jack,'" read an admiring profile in *The Washington Daily News*. "He looks like the Saturday Evening Post's idea of the All-American Boy, and his vote-getting appeal to New England's womenfolk must be terrific. He is also something of a political curiosity . . . born with a silver soup ladle in his mouth, but with the welfare of the humble in his heart."[53]

VI

All the while, Kennedy maintained his passionate interest in foreign policy and international affairs. In late June 1948, five weeks after Kick's funeral, he traveled to Europe, ostensibly on behalf of the House Education and Labor Committee to gather information on labor issues. His travel companion was his Harvard roommate Torbert Macdonald, who now worked for the National Labor Relations Board. For months, Cold War tensions had been ratcheting up, especially over the status of Germany. Earlier in June, U.S., British, and French officials resolved to merge their German zones, including their three sectors of Berlin, in order to better integrate West Germany into the Western European economy. On June 24, the same day Jack and Torby departed by sea for England, Stalin, fearing a resurgent Germany joined to the American Cold War camp, severed Western road and rail access to the jointly occupied city of Berlin, located well inside the Soviet zone. He hoped that West Berliners, starved of resources, would be compelled by economic necessity to reject their alliance with the United States and throw their lot in with East Germany and the USSR. It was a bold move, and it put the Western powers in the position of either giving in or attempting to overcome the blockade—a step that could lead to a war in which they would be drastically outmanned.

Harry Truman, after consulting with his advisers and with the British government, responded with a bold action of his own: he ordered a massive airlift of food, fuel, and other supplies to West Berlin, in order to forestall an economic collapse that would have driven residents into the arms of the Soviets. Stalin now faced the choice of shooting down the supply planes, an act that would surely trigger U.S. retaliation, or letting the airlift continue and hoping it would be insufficient. He opted for the latter course, but the situation remained tense as Kennedy arrived in London on June 29 and then proceeded from there to Paris.

He was determined to see the Berlin situation up close. He had no official reason for going, but then again, that had been equally true when he visited in the summer of 1939, on the eve of war, and when he returned in 1945, just as the struggle was ending. Whereas a decade before Jack had used his father's connections to gain entrée to places where history was being made, this time he used his status as a U.S. congressman to arrange meetings with General Lucius Clay, who led the American occupying command in the city, and General Curtis LeMay, commander of the U.S. Air Forces in Europe and the head of operations for the airlift.[54] Kennedy voiced full support for Truman's airlift decision and his overall firmness in the showdown with the Soviets. Truman's resolute action on Berlin stood in sharp contrast to Chamberlain's appeasement at Munich in 1938, Jack believed, and it pleased him to see Winston Churchill—out of power for three years but slowly edging his way back to the center of things—make the same argument. It further pleased him that the first volume of Churchill's grand narrative history of the Second World War, covering the origins of the struggle and published to great fanfare that summer, interpreted the development of British appeasement in the 1930s in ways broadly consistent with his own take in *Why England Slept*.[55]

Churchill remained a giant figure for him, a kind of intellectual and political lodestar on account of his historical sensibility and his authorial and oratorical acclaim, and he thrilled at the thought that the great man might yet return to power. Jack followed with keen interest the Conservative Party's annual conference in Wales in October 1948, devouring newspaper reports and taking mental and written notes. Churchill's speech to the gathering, a stem-winder heavy on fulminations against the menacing Soviet threat, resonated with him. "We support the foreign policy of His Majesty's Government in taking a firm stand against the encroachments and aggressions of Soviet Russia, and in not being bullied, bulldozed, or blackmailed out of Berlin, whatever the consequences may be," Churchill thundered. "Nothing stands between Europe today and complete subjugation to Communist tyranny but the atomic bomb in American possession." He closed with a passage from Luke 23:31, in which Christ, shortly before his crucifixion, asks metaphorically, "If they do this when the wood is green, what will they do when it is dry?" Jack underlined the passage and would later use it in his own speeches.[56]

Ultimately, Truman would see his decision on the airlift vindicated. An unusually mild winter and a remarkably efficient aerial operation delivered a total of 2.3 million tons of food, medicine, and fuel. On a single day, April 16, 1949, some fourteen hundred aircraft brought in close to thirteen thousand tons within twenty-four hours—an average of one plane touching down every minute. Stalin, increasingly frustrated, dangled better rations before any West Berliner who registered with Communist authorities, but only a small minority took him up on it. In May 1949, he in effect gave up, lifting the blockade and authorizing negotiations with the Western governments about formalizing the status of Berlin.[57]

The successful airlift helped to salvage Truman's political career: he surprised experts in November 1948 by narrowly beating Republican Thomas E. Dewey in the presidential election. Safely returned to office, Truman took the momentous step of formalizing what was already in essence a military alliance between the United States, Canada, and the countries of Western Europe. In April 1949, the North Atlantic Treaty Organization (NATO) came into being, as twelve nations signed a mutual defense pact. An attack on any one of them would be viewed as an attack on all, the members agreed. Skeptics on Capitol Hill, led by the GOP's Robert Taft, charged that NATO would only heighten the risk of general war, while others wondered if the alliance met a military threat that didn't exist. U.S. officials conceded that a Soviet armed attack on Western Europe was unlikely, but they maintained that, should the Kremlin ever make threatening moves westward, NATO would constitute a "tripwire," bringing the full weight of American power to bear on the USSR. The Truman team also hoped that NATO would keep Western Europeans from shifting toward Communism or neutralism in the Cold War. On July 21, the Senate ratified the treaty by a vote of 82 to 13.[58]

By then, Jack Kennedy was well into his second term in Congress. At age thirty-two, he continued to give the sense of a man in a hurry, looking for the next thing, hungry to make more of an impact. "We're just worms," he said of being a congressman. "Nobody pays much attention to us nationally."[59] His attendance record on the Hill improved, but only marginally, and he darted off from the capital most weekends, often to New York City and the Waldorf or the St. Regis and usually in the company of one woman or another. Yet Kennedy managed to keep his name before Massachusetts voters with well-timed policy pronouncements and legislative interventions. In 1949 the House at last approved a major housing bill of the type he had sought since he arrived on Capitol Hill; he declared it a triumph, even as he lamented that the delay had caused needless suffering, especially among veterans. He also exploited his experience in foreign affairs and military policy to get himself invited as an expert witness to Senate hearings on the defense structures of European allies. Recognizing that staunch anti-Communism was a surefire winner in U.S. political discourse in 1949, he talked up the threat, warning against domestic subversion and Soviet overseas adventurism.

More and more, Kennedy criticized the Truman administration for what he saw as its insufficiently vigilant foreign policy. When, in September 1949, the White House announced that a specially equipped U.S. weather plane had detected radioactivity in Soviet airspace above Siberia—a clear sign that the USSR had tested its own atomic bomb, thereby ending America's monopoly—Jack criticized the president for implementing inadequate civil defense measures. On China he was even tougher, joining with the "China lobby" (the group of journalists, business leaders, and right-wing lawmakers who had become arch defenders of Chiang Kai-shek) to attack the White House for "allowing" Communist forces under Mao Zedong to make advance after advance against Chiang's Nationalists in that nation's long-running civil war. On January 25, 1949, after news arrived that the Nationalists had begun withdrawing from Beijing, Jack said on the floor of the House that "the responsibility for the failure of our foreign policy in the Far East rests squarely with the White House and the Department of State."[60]

Five days later he returned to the theme in a speech in Salem, Massachusetts:

Our relationship with China since the end of the Second World War has been a tragic one, and it is of the utmost importance that we search out and spotlight those who bear the responsibility for our present predicament. . . . Our policy in China has reaped the whirlwind. The continued insistence that aid would not be forthcoming unless a coalition government with the Communists was formed was a crippling blow to the national government. So concerned were our diplomats and their advisors . . . with the imperfections of the diplomatic system in China after 20 years of war, and the tales of corruption in high places, they lost sight of the tremendous stake in a non-Communist China. This is the tragic story of China whose freedom we once sought to preserve.[61]

When Mao completed his victory that autumn, compelling Chiang's government to flee in humiliating fashion to the offshore island of Taiwan (then known as Formosa), Kennedy again pinned responsibility for the disaster on U.S. policy, even as he acknowledged Chiang's weaknesses and missteps.

The "twin shocks" of 1949—the Soviet A-bomb and Mao's victory in

China—would continue to reverberate in world politics and U.S. domestic politics for years to come. Jack Kennedy anticipated as much, and although he worried about the implications for American security, he also saw advantages for himself. This was his turf, where he could stand out among his congressional peers, where he could make his mark, if not right away, then in due course, when he had a bigger platform. His fellow House freshmen in the Eightieth Congress, Richard Nixon and George Smathers, could contest (and win) Senate races already in 1950, but for Kennedy that opportunity was not available. He had to wait, confident in the expectation that his patience would be rewarded. In the meantime, he would bide his time and continue to do the work expected of him on behalf of the Eleventh District in Massachusetts.

Here he drew encouragement from the fact that his physical condition had improved markedly that fall of 1949, due chiefly to the finding that cortisone could dramatically improve the lives of Addison's sufferers, whose adrenal glands do not produce enough of the hormones cortisol and aldosterone. Though it is likely Kennedy had begun taking corticosteroids periodically a number of years before, only now was the drug synthesized and declared to be broadly effective for people with Addison's. The announcement, by researchers at the Mayo Clinic, set off a mad rush for cortisone, and the Kennedys scrambled to store away supplies of it in safe-deposit boxes around the country so that Jack would never go without.[62] The drug boosted patients' energy, muscular strength, and endurance, doctors found, and enhanced their overall sense of well-being. The mere fact of having a diagnosis also helped Jack, as he now had an explanation for at least some of the mystery illnesses he had suffered over the years—Addison's sufferers, he learned, were particularly vulnerable to infection.

As a new year and a new decade dawned, his family and friends and associates could see it: John F. Kennedy was back, and ready to begin anew.

SEVENTEEN

RED SCARE

ust as John F. Kennedy's political rise coincided with the start of the Cold War, so it tracked with the beginning of an anti-Communist crusade inside America's borders, a crusade that contained a healthy dose of partisan politics—and that had no real analogue in any other Western nation.[1] Opposing the Soviet Union overseas and leftists at home became a way of corralling votes and building electoral strength, or of avoiding being labeled a Red sympathizer. As a result, the range of acceptable political discourse narrowed. By the late 1940s, the chance for in-depth discussion and criticism of policy toward the Communist world vanished as those on the left and center-left who might have articulated a different vision lost political and cultural license.[2]

Jack Kennedy's political career cannot be understood apart from a close consideration of this "Cold War at home"; as such, it bears reflecting on how the situation came to be.

Already in the 1946 midterm campaign, the Republican Party had accused Harry Truman and the Democrats of weakness in the face of Communist expansionism. "The choice which confronts Americans this year is between Communism and Republicanism," said Tennessee congressman B. Carroll Reece (who doubled as the chairman of the Republican National Committee) shortly before voting day. James Kem, a Senate hopeful from Missouri, called Truman "soft on communism." Even Senator Robert Taft, notwithstanding his reputation for rectitude, often used the words "Communist," "left-winger," and "New Dealer" synonymously and charged that Democrats were "appeasing the Russians abroad and fostering Communism at home."[3] Truman and his aides, stung by their party's losses in the election, got the message. The following spring, soon after the president announced the Truman Doctrine, his administration established the Federal Employee Loyalty Program, which authorized government officials to screen more than two million federal employees for any intimation of political subversion. Hundreds lost their jobs, and thousands more resigned rather than subject themselves to investigation. In the vast majority of instances there was no evidence of disloyalty.

Journalist David Halberstam's summary is apt: "Rather than combating the irrationality of the charges of softness on Communism and subversion, the Truman Administration, sure that it was the lesser of two evils, moved to expropriate the issue, as in a more subtle way it was already doing in foreign affairs. So the issue was legitimized; rather than being the property of the far right, which the centrist Republicans tolerated for obvious political benefits, it had even been picked up by the incumbent Democratic party."[4]

But it was the Republicans who proved most willing to wield the anti-Communist club, and as a result became the more skillful at it. The party was badly split, with an internationalist wing, reflecting the views of Wall Street and East Coast elites, and an isolationist one, rooted in the small towns and cities of the Midwest. The internationalists looked eastward, across the Atlantic, and had supported U.S. entry into the European war as necessary and just. More often than not, these Republicans endorsed the broad outlines of Franklin D. Roosevelt's wartime internationalism, and in 1940 and 1944 they endorsed GOP candidates for president who often sounded much like the president himself. And they backed with conviction the new U.S.-led postwar international order.

The other wing took a very different view: it held to the isolationist fears of being sucked into overseas squabbles, especially those involving the nefarious Europeans, and raged against FDR's "socialistic" New Deal programs at home. To the extent that its adherents looked outward, it was to the west, to Asia; their ocean of choice was the Pacific. Even after the war, this isolationist wing of the party retained broad support—in numerical terms it may have been larger than the internationalist wing—but it lost out to the eastern elite in the selection of the party's standard-bearer in the 1940, 1944, and 1948 elections (Wendell Willkie, Thomas Dewey, and then Dewey again). To many heartland Republicans, Willkie and Dewey were pusillanimous copycat candidates scarcely distinguishable from their Democratic opponents, first Roosevelt and then Truman.[5]

Still, even the Republican right was stunned by Dewey's loss to the supposedly hapless Truman in 1948—as was everyone in the party, and pretty much everyone outside it as well. The Democrats had been in power for sixteen years, and surely their time was up. Evidently it wasn't. The Republicans overestimated the degree of unhappiness in the country and underestimated Harry Truman, who may have lacked Roosevelt's charisma and patrician self-assurance but had virtues of his own: he was plainspoken, unpretentious, and decisive, and was deemed by ordinary Americans to be one of them. A high school graduate moving among the better educated, he was well read on U.S. and world history and on the shifting demands of his office. More than that, Truman was politically canny, shrewdly isolating both Henry Wallace's left-wing campaign and Strom Thurmond's Dixiecrats. The result: four consecutive GOP presidential losses became five. Roosevelt was gone, but somehow Republicans had lost yet again, conquered by the little Kansas City haberdasher, who carried twenty-eight states and 303 electoral votes to Dewey's 189. The Democrats even picked up nine seats in the Senate.

The full effect of the defeat on the morale of the Republican Party is hard to fully recapture in hindsight. Even at the time, many observers failed to see it, not least celebratory Democrats. To many within the GOP, it seemed an open question whether they would ever win the presidency again. They seemed destined to be a permanent minority party—unless, that is, they could hit upon an issue on which to rebuild momentum. They found it in subversion. Loyalty and anti-Communism would be the watchwords, to be used to attack Democrats at every opportunity. There would be no holding back. After years in which Democrats had castigated Republican domestic priorities as cold and cruel, as benefiting the rich at the expense of everyone else, now the favor would be returned, with interest.[6]

The party profited enormously in this effort from the twin shocks of 1949—the Soviet detonation of an atomic device and the victory by Mao Zedong's Communists in the Chinese Civil War. Only Americans could have caused these developments, Republican leaders charged. Soviet spies, working alongside American accomplices, must have stolen U.S. secrets and thereby drastically sped up the Kremlin's atomic program, and the Truman administration must have "lost China" by allowing America's longtime Nationalist ally Chiang Kai-shek to be vanquished. Robert Taft spoke of officials in the State Department "liquidating" the Nationalists, and charged that State "was guided by a left-wing group who have obviously wanted to get rid of Chiang and were willing at least to turn China over to the Communists for that purpose."[7]

To the administration and its defenders, the charges were absurd. At the end of World War II, they pointed out, Chiang had overwhelming military superiority vis-à-vis his Communist foes, who were ill-equipped and undertrained. By early 1949, however, his army had withered after defeats and desertions, and he had been compelled to take refuge on the island of Taiwan. To blame his defeat on U.S. inaction made no sense whatsoever. "[The Chinese people] had not overthrown the government," Secretary of State Dean Acheson declared. "There was nothing to overthrow. They had simply ignored it."[8] As for the GOP's broader "soft on Communism" charge, that struck Acheson as senseless, given how many Republicans had voted against foreign aid bills and clamored for reducing U.S. standing-troop levels (by May 1949, the Army consisted of only 630,000 men), not to mention how many of them showed zero interest in committing American military power to check Communist expansion abroad.

Even so, the White House took every chance to trumpet its anti-Soviet vigilance. Rejecting calls by the likes of George Kennan and Walter Lippmann for high-level diplomacy, Truman in early 1950 gave the approval to begin work on a hydrogen bomb, the "Super," and ordered his senior foreign policy aides to undertake a thorough review of policy. Kennan, about to leave his post as head of the Policy Planning Staff in the State Department, lamented the militarization of the Cold War; his successor, Paul Nitze, felt no such concern. Nitze would be the primary author of a National Security Council report, NSC-68, that predicted continued global tension with Soviet-directed Communism, in the context of "a shrinking world of polarized power."[9]

The Republican attacks kept coming, and Acheson was a frequent target. With his impeccable establishment credentials—Groton, Yale, Harvard Law, Covington & Burling—and his haughty demeanor, he represented for the Republican right a much more enticing target than the midwestern, small-town, unassuming Truman.[10] Acheson made things worse for himself in 1949 when he seemed to emphasize his friendship with accused spy Alger Hiss. (In fact, the two men were not close friends.) Himself an elegant, self-possessed, Ivy League–educated symbol of the establishment, Hiss had been a member of the U.S. delegation at Yalta in 1945 and later that year helped organize the UN's San Francisco Conference (at which John Kennedy was a reporter). After the war he became president of the Carnegie Endowment for International Peace.

In 1948, a *Time* editor named Whittaker Chambers asserted that during the 1930s he and Hiss had been fellow members of the Communist Party and that Hiss (at that time working in the Agriculture Department) had passed secret government documents to him to give to the Soviets. Hiss vehemently denied it, but the young Republican congressman Richard Nixon doggedly pressed the case as a member of the House Un-American Activities Committee. Nixon's efforts were going nowhere until microfilmed documents hidden in a hollowed-out pumpkin on Chambers's farm swung the momentum against Hiss. After an initial trial ended in a hung jury, a second one convicted him, in January 1950, of two counts of perjury: for denying that he had ever given Chambers any documents and for insisting he had not seen Chambers after the start of 1937. (The statute of limitations for charges of espionage had lapsed.)* The case, pitting the slender, patrician Hiss, impeccable in dress and comportment, against the disheveled, portly Chambers, generated headlines for months, and Nixon emerged as a hero on the right. He declared that a "conspiracy" existed to prevent Americans from "knowing the facts."[11]

All eyes now turned to Acheson, the nation's top diplomat. "I do not intend to turn my back on Alger Hiss," he grandly told reporters after the verdict was announced. Republicans seized the opening. Senator Joseph McCarthy of Wisconsin called a halt to a Senate hearing to report the "fantastic statement the Secretary of State has made in the last four minutes." McCarthy wondered aloud if this meant that Acheson would not turn his back on other Communist sympathizers in Washington as well. Richard Nixon, meanwhile, called Acheson's remarks "disgusting," and subsequently referred to him as the "Red Dean of the Cowardly College of

---

* Hiss was sentenced to five years in prison, of which he served three. To his dying day, in 1996, he maintained his innocence. Almost certainly he was guilty as charged, though the documents passed were of modest importance.

Containment." When, a few days later, British scientist Klaus Fuchs was arrested on atomic espionage charges, it fed Republican claims of a conspiracy that needed to be exposed.[12]

Nor was it just about Communism. Conservatives saw in the Hiss verdict a validation of what they had long been saying about elitist, overeducated, big-government-loving eastern sophisticates. "For eighteen years," Senator Karl Mundt, Republican of South Dakota, thundered, the nation had "been run by New Dealers, Fair Dealers, Misdealers, and Hiss dealers, who have shuttled back and forth between Freedom and Red Fascism like a pendulum on a cuckoo clock."[13]

II

The Hiss verdict came on January 21, 1950. Truman announced his hydrogen bomb decision on January 31. The Fuchs arrest occurred on February 3. And on February 9, Joe McCarthy gave a speech that hit like a thunderclap and cemented his place in U.S. history textbooks forevermore. In a speech in Wheeling, West Virginia, before the Ohio County Women's Republican Club, McCarthy declared, "While I cannot take the time to name all the men in the State Department who have been named as members of the Communist Party and members of a spy ring, I have here in my hand a list of 205—a list of names that were made known to the Secretary of State as being members of the Communist Party and who nevertheless are still working and shaping the policy of the State Department." He had no evidence, either then or in the days that followed, when in his speeches the number dropped to fifty-seven, then rose to eighty-one, then became "a lot." McCarthy in fact had no list, and almost certainly had no proof that *anyone* in the State Department actually belonged to the Communist Party.[14]

It's not even clear that McCarthy had any real interest in either espionage or Communism. "Joe couldn't find a Communist in Red Square—he didn't know Karl Marx from Groucho Marx," journalist George Reedy, who was later an aide to Lyndon Johnson, memorably remarked. Facing lagging popularity at home in Wisconsin and the prospect of a tough reelection battle two years away, McCarthy needed an issue with which to revive his political fortunes.[15] He felt sure he'd found it. He was at bottom a salesman, an actor, someone for whom accuracy mattered far less than attention, and he had a talent for imagining subversion and conspiracy and for humiliating the scared and vulnerable. A lazy man unwilling to do the work required to back up his claims, he relied on allusion and inference. But he was also shrewd: he understood the resentments and fears that existed just below the surface in many people—resentment of the elites, fears of the other—and indeed felt them himself.[16] Like all demagogues, he knew that people sought simple answers for why the world seemed not to be going their way, knew that he could captivate them by appealing to emotion rather than intellect. And he understood that merely by making bombastic claims he sent the message that there must be some truth to the claim that the government was teeming with traitors secretly taking orders from the Kremlin.[17]

McCarthy's timing was right, moreover, for the national fever that had been building for years rose sharply with the twin shocks and the espionage cases. And indeed, McCarthy's Wheeling remarks and those that immediately followed (in Denver, Salt Lake City, and Reno) gained him the headlines he craved—reporters knew both that he was a shameless fabulist and that sensational stories sell papers. (The wilder the charge, the bigger the headline.) Rarely did journalists press him to back up his claims with evidence. He moved copy; that was all that mattered.[18]

Still, the reporters who covered him could see what he was doing, could see that he always kept his claims deliberately vague, that he cared only about gaining publicity, which meant issuing a steady stream of new claims, new accusations. When caught in a lie, he never apologized or recanted; he attacked his accuser or simply moved on to another target. "Talking to Joe was like putting your hands in a bowl of mush," said Reedy, who found the experience of covering McCarthy for the United Press so loathsome that he quit journalism.[19] Insecure and eager to please, and saddled with a serious drinking problem (he liked nothing more than to pal around with reporters in bars in the evenings), McCarthy was perfectly willing to give the pressmen around him a story when they needed one, if necessary by conjuring up some new charges. If the reporters wanted to know what the party leadership was contemplating on this or that issue, McCarthy happily called up Senator Taft's office and asked him questions while the journalists listened in silently on an open receiver.[20]

"McCarthyism" was the name later given to the senator's antics, a term signifying a ruthless search for Communists, publicly and with little or no evidence, and in a manner that savaged the reputations of its targets. So ubiquitous did McCarthy become that it was easy to forget that the phenomenon had existed before him—since 1946–47 in its new incarnation, and in a different, lesser form since an initial "Red Scare" immediately after World War I. But undeniably, the Wisconsin senator gave this second Red Scare added fuel.

McCarthy's position was further strengthened by the sudden outbreak of war on the Korean Peninsula in late June 1950. Colonized by Japan in 1910, Korea had been divided in two by the Soviet Union and the United States after Japan's defeat in 1945, with the Soviets in control of the land north of the thirty-eighth parallel and the Americans in charge in the south. The division was supposed to be temporary, but as Cold War tensions deepened, the split persisted. Both the North's Communist leader, Kim Il Sung, and the South's president, the U.S.-backed Syngman Rhee, sought to take control of a reunified Korea. Kim struck first; on June 25, after securing the reluctant approval of Stalin and Mao, he sent his troops across the parallel into the South. In short order they captured the southern capital of Seoul and appeared well positioned to march all the way down the peninsula and hand Kim control over the entire country.[21]

The invasion caught Washington by surprise, but Truman responded rapidly. He deployed U.S. forces to South Korea to repel the invasion, and got the United Nations Security Council to pass a resolution condemning the North's attack and summoning member states to send their own troops. (The Soviet representative was unable to veto the resolution because the Soviets were boycotting the UN in protest of its refusal to grant membership to the People's Republic of China.) In this way the defense of South Korea became a UN operation, albeit one led and dominated by the United States. Truman called the military effort a "police action," which allowed him to avoid going to Congress for a declaration of war. Following a brilliant amphibious landing at Inchon, on the west coast of Korea, more than a hundred miles behind North Korean lines, UN forces under General Douglas MacArthur reversed the tide of battle in the late summer and proceeded to march north, beyond the original demarcation line. In so doing, MacArthur went beyond the UN directive, which authorized only the defense of South Korea, but Truman gave his commander the go-ahead; the president sensed an opportunity to score a complete victory and rebut GOP charges that he had "lost China" the previous year. Onward MacArthur's units drove, toward the Yalu River and the Chinese frontier, until Chinese troops suddenly attacked in massive force in November, driving UN and South Korean forces southward once again. Gradually, a stalemate set in near the original demarcation line at the thirty-eighth parallel.

As the fighting in Korea ramped up, so did McCarthy's rhetorical blasts. With U.S. troops being shot at by North Korean and Chinese Communists, few observers in or out of government were brave enough to condemn him. Few registered any objection when he attributed the loss of China and the failure to win a swift victory in Korea to the "pretty boys" and "homos" in the State Department, "with their silver spoons in their mouths." Many GOP lawmakers indeed welcomed his crusade, even if they privately thought it extreme, because he targeted almost solely Democrats and liberals and because they could see that his portrayal of these individuals as privileged and soft elites hit home with a lot of voters in Middle America. That year McCarthy received hundreds of invitations to speak on behalf of Republican candidates, more than all of his Senate colleagues combined.[22]

The rare colleague who tried to take him on did so at personal peril. Senator Margaret Chase Smith, a freshman Republican from Maine and a moderate, learned this firsthand in early June 1950 when she condemned McCarthy's methods in a speech titled "The Declaration of Conscience." The American people "are sick and tired of being afraid to speak their minds lest they be politically smeared as 'Communists' or 'Fascists' by their opponents," Smith proclaimed. "Freedom of speech is not what it used to be in America."[23] McCarthy hit back hard, mocking her and the Senate co-sponsors of her declaration as "Snow White and the Six Dwarves." Millard Tydings, the conservative Maryland Democrat who had publicly opposed McCarthy after his subcommittee found that McCarthy's first charges against the State Department were bogus, got labeled an "egg-sucking liberal" and a "Commiecrat." Soon all the co-sponsors except Wayne Morse, an iconoclastic Republican from Oregon (he would later become an independent, and still later a Democrat), drifted away from Smith, and she herself eventually beat a quiet retreat. Tydings lost his bid for reelection that fall, after McCarthy loyalists smeared him by distributing a composite image depicting him as an ally of Earl Browder, leader of the American Communist Party.[24]

John F. Kennedy was not one of the six dwarves. Quite the contrary, in 1950 he offered his own criticisms of Truman's and Acheson's handling of the Chinese Civil War, and his own gripes that the administration had been insufficiently vigilant in combating espionage. He thought Hiss guilty as charged and believed that Truman's fiscal prudence undermined military preparedness. Kennedy also voiced reservations about Truman's decision to commit combat units to Korea—he feared that U.S troops were being spread too thin, threatening the nation's ability to thwart Communist expansion in other, more vital areas, especially in Europe, where, he pointed out, the Red Army had eighty divisions to NATO's twelve. When American forces suffered a string of early defeats in Korea, Kennedy saw it as proof of "the inadequate state of our defense preparations," and he advocated raising taxes to pay for the war and the broader military buildup. That fall, in a seminar at the Harvard Graduate School of Public Administration (later to be renamed the John F. Kennedy School of Government), he offered candid observations about U.S. foreign policy and the men behind it. He was critical of the leadership of Dean Acheson, he told the students, and said President Truman had been mistaken in vetoing the McCarran Act, which mandated the registration of Communists and Communist-front organizations and provided for their internment in the event of a national emergency. (Congress overrode the veto almost immediately.)[25]

More than that, Kennedy knew Joe McCarthy and got on well with him. He was a fellow Irish Catholic who, like Jack, had served in the South Pacific during the war (they may have first met in the Solomons) and who had come around for dinners at the Georgetown home in 1947, when both men were new on Capitol Hill.* Jack got a kick out of McCarthy's affability and energy on these evenings, and Eunice, too, welcomed his presence. McCarthy's penchant for profanity didn't bother Jack; he himself could curse like the sailor he had once been. In due course McCarthy would squire both Eunice and on occasion her sister Patricia to evening events in Washington and Boston, and would visit the Kennedys in Hyannis Port. He attended Robert Kennedy's wedding to Ethel Skakel in Greenwich, Connecticut, in June 1950. At Eunice's birthday party on the Cape

---

* Never shy about talking up his war record, McCarthy claimed to have been known in the South Pacific as "Tail-Gunner Joe." In 1951 he secured a Distinguished Flying Cross for supposedly flying close to thirty combat missions and being wounded. Contrary to later claims, he did see some action, but he spent the war mostly as a deskbound intelligence officer debriefing pilots after their missions. He was never wounded in action; most likely, he hurt his foot falling down the stairs at a party.

the following month, the Kennedy siblings "gave [McCarthy] the boat treatment, i.e. throwing him out of the boat, and then Eunice, in her usual girlish glee pushed him under," Rose reported in a letter to the newlyweds. "To everyone's concern and astonishment, the senator came up with a ghastly look on his face, puffing and paddling. The wonder of it all was that he did not drown on the spot because, you see, coming from Wisconsin, he had never learned to swim." On another Hyannis Port visit, McCarthy played shortstop for Team Kennedy in a softball game on the family lawn against a squad of neighbors, promptly committed four errors, and was retired to the porch. (Jack, too, ended up on the porch early in the game, his back problem flaring up.)[26]

Joseph P. Kennedy in particular took a shine to McCarthy, admiring the very things others found so unpleasant: the brashness, the no-holds-barred attacks on the political establishment, the contempt for genteel manners and diplomacy. He himself could be said to possess these attributes, albeit to a milder degree. The Ambassador also relished McCarthy's rowdy amiability whenever they were together, and he shared his disdain for left-wingers and his love of gossip. "In case there's any question in your mind," Kennedy told an interviewer years later, in 1961, "I liked Joe McCarthy. I always liked him. I would see him when I went down to Washington, and when he was visiting Palm Beach he'd come around to my house for a drink. I invited him to Cape Cod." On occasion the Ambassador even called McCarthy to offer advice on political tactics and strategy. At no point, it seems, did he indicate concern for the victims of the senator's attacks.[27]

McCarthyite tactics were everywhere in the midterm elections in 1950. In Florida, George Smathers defeated his mentor, Senator Claude Pepper, in an ugly, bruising, red-baiting primary before coasting to victory in the general election. "Joe [Stalin] likes him and he likes Joe," Smathers said of Pepper. In the Senate race in California, Richard Nixon, who had studied Smathers's tactics, hammered his opponent, Helen Gahagan Douglas, as a fellow traveler who was hopelessly leftist. (She was "pink right down to her underwear," he said, sexism as much a part of his tactics as red-baiting.) Nixon won handily. In Illinois, Republican Everett Dirksen beat Democratic incumbent senator Scott Lucas, vowing to clean house on Communists and their supporters. And in New York, in a losing race for the Senate, John Foster Dulles said of his opponent, Herbert

Lehman, "I know he is no Communist, but I also know that the Communists are in his corner and that he and not I will get the 500,000 Communist votes that last year went to Henry Wallace in this state."[28]

III

Jack Kennedy studied the national election results closely that fall as he cruised to another victory in the Eleventh District.[29] More and more, speculation in the state turned to his plans for 1952, and in particular whether he would seek statewide office. His own thoughts had long since gone in that direction—three terms in the House would be quite enough, thank you—and he seemed to draw additional inspiration from the public response to two tragedies in the state in 1950. On February 11, Mary Curley, the daughter of ex-mayor James Michael Curley—who had already lost his wife and five of his nine children—collapsed and died of a cerebral hemorrhage while speaking on the telephone. That evening, in the same room and at the same phone, her brother Leo collapsed and succumbed in the same way. The double calamity brought a huge outpouring of people to the mayor's home to pay their respects—some fifty thousand, according to press accounts, forming long lines in the freezing temperatures. One of them was Congressman John F. Kennedy, who, according to aide Dave Powers, was deeply moved by the experience, and by the sight of the ashen-faced Curley shaking hands with people and thanking them as they filed past the biers.[30]

Then, on October 2, John "Honey Fitz" Fitzgerald died in Boston, at age eighty-seven. He had been ailing for months with a chronic circulatory problem, but his passing was nonetheless a blow to Jack. The two had always been close, ever since little Jack first accompanied his grandfather on his political rounds or to Fenway Park for a Red Sox game. They shared an amiable temperament, a quick wit, a romantic sense of history, a relish for politics, and a superhuman capacity for hard work. Jack indeed resembled his maternal grandfather in personality more than he did either of his parents, even as he became a different kind of politician—reticent, patrician, and urbane, words no one ever used to describe Honey Fitz. Rose, in Paris on vacation when her father died, did not make it back in time for the funeral, at which thirty-five hundred mourners jammed the Cathedral of the Holy Cross. Jack represented the family, along with

Eunice, Pat, Jean, and Teddy.[31] President Truman sent his sympathies, and the pallbearers included both of the state's senators, Henry Cabot Lodge Jr. and Leverett Saltonstall; two future U.S. Speakers of the House, John McCormack and Tip O'Neill (then Speaker of the state legislature); and Mayor Curley. As Honey Fitz was carried to his final rest, from the cathedral to St. Joseph Cemetery, in West Roxbury, thousands gathered along the streets, some singing "Sweet Adeline" as the procession passed.

"All his life he had loved his city of Boston," Jack later said of his grandfather, "and now Boston was returning that love." From all walks of life they came, "the great, the near great, and the humble." This outpouring of affection, first for Curley in his personal loss and then for Honey Fitz, left a deep impression on him, made him more inclined to seek higher office. In Lem Billings's recollection, "There was something in the pageantry and the richness of those two occasions that really got to Jack. It made him realize the extraordinary impact a politician can have on the emotions of ordinary people, an impact often forgotten in the corridors of Capitol Hill."[32] Moreover, the immediacy of the public's generosity in the face of back-to-back tragedies—their coming together as a community—inclined him to leave the House (which felt removed, desiccated) and seek an office that would serve a broader population than the precincts of his congressional district.

The path to a statewide run was not yet clear, however, as Jack waited for incumbent governor Paul Dever to make up his mind. If Dever opted to take on the widely respected Lodge in the Senate race, Jack would likely seek the governorship; if he didn't, Jack would be free to challenge Lodge. The latter was his preference from the start—running the State House, he said, meant little more than "deciding on sewer contracts," and offered scant chance to expound on the pressing issues in world affairs.[33] There was always the option of going full tilt for the Senate and, if necessary, taking on Dever in the primary, but such a strategy carried immense risks, especially given Dever's proven skills as a vote-getter and the inherent advantages he would bring to the primary race as a sitting governor.[34]

So the Kennedy team watched and waited, in the meantime exposing Jack to as many voters as possible across the state through an ambitious speaking schedule and manifold media appearances. The pattern he had tried out intermittently in previous months, that of spending Thursday through Sunday at home in Massachusetts, appearing before any audience that would have him—Moose clubs, Elks, Shriners, Kiwanis,

Rotarians, VFWs, volunteer fire departments, church groups—became regularized; over the course of 1951, he spoke in nearly seventy communities, both large and small, often covering five or six hundred miles in a weekend. Typically in these addresses, he would touch on the pressing policy issues of the moment, but he also ranged broadly, urging his audience to be informed, to register to vote, to consider entering public service.

That summer, meanwhile, two aides, Joe DeGuglielmo and Tony Galluccio, made a multi-week canvassing trip through the state to test Kennedy's favorability for both potential races. "At my suggestion Tony and I adopted a procedure that we would divide when we'd get into a town and we'd go get a shave whether we needed it or not, we'd go get a haircut, go in a restaurant, talk to waitresses and the rest," DeGuglielmo recalled. "And what we were trying to do was evaluate the various strengths of Kennedy, Lodge, and Dever. And when we came back after two weeks, then we took a trip down around the New Bedford–Fall River area and then we took other trips around Lawrence and Lowell. And after we got through, Tony and I evolved the theory that Dever could not be reelected and Jack Kennedy would be a lead pipe cinch to knock him off as governor, that probably he could defeat Lodge, but it would be a much closer fight than the other fight."[35]

Galluccio also did a lot of solo work, crisscrossing the state over a period of a year, ultimately visiting each one of its 351 cities and towns, avoiding politicians and seeking out respected local citizens—shopkeepers, teachers, lawyers, dentists—to gauge their views on a potential Kennedy candidacy. If they showed interest, Galluccio would ask if they could see themselves working for a potential campaign. Many said yes, some said maybe. He would take down names and addresses and ask if they could recommend anyone else he should contact.

Joseph Kennedy, relentless as always in promoting his son's interests, worked to build up a statewide organization—needed for either race—and to buttonhole reporters to give Jack favorable newspaper coverage. Joe even reduced his involvement in his myriad business interests in order to involve himself more fully in the fledgling campaign. (After the war he'd moved aggressively into real estate and acquired several oil and gas ventures.) When private polls he commissioned and paid for showed that Jack had a legitimate if long-shot chance of defeating Lodge, father and son were strengthened in the conviction that this was the race they should seek. (The same polls showed that Saltonstall, not up for reelection until 1954, would be harder to beat.)

They were a curious pair, the two Kennedys: so close, so loving, so mutually respectful, yet so far apart in their views of human motivation and purpose, of diplomacy and statecraft, of America's role in the world. With his son eyeing a run for statewide office, one might have thought Joe Kennedy would seek to avoid public controversy, but one would be wrong. In December 1950 he took on a starring role in an emerging "great debate" (in *Life* magazine's words) that threatened to draw in Jack. Invited to give a speech before the University of Virginia Law School's Student Legal Forum (whose president was none other than Robert F. Kennedy), Joe rejected the anodyne draft prepared by an aide—on lawyers and public service—to offer instead a robust articulation of his starkly isolationist foreign policy views. Communism was "neither monolithic nor eternal," he told his audience, and would ultimately fail on its own, without external pressure. Thus Washington leaders could and should withdraw from all commitments abroad and instead focus their energies on strengthening the American economy. What exactly, after all, had the billions and billions spent overseas accomplished? Precious little. Truman's policies indeed were "suicidal" and morally wrong. It followed, Kennedy said, that the United States should stop fighting in Korea—where the Chinese troops had recently entered the fray en masse—and withdraw from there and from the rest of Asia, then do the same thing in Europe. "What business is it of ours to support French colonial policies in Indo-China or to achieve Mr. Syngman Rhee's concepts of democracy in Korea? . . . We can do well to mind our business and interfere only where somebody threatens our business and our homes."[36]

The Ambassador ensured that he got wide press coverage by sending out advance copies of the speech to friends in the business world. The Hearst papers were enthusiastic, publishing long excerpts and glowing editorials. Arthur Krock, as always, lathered on the praise and noted that "a bipartisan group" was coming around to Kennedy's position. Even the venerable Walter Lippmann, in a column titled "The Isolationist Tide," which decried Kennedy's hardcore Fortress America stance, acknowledged that it might resonate with a public increasingly wary of Harry Truman's globalism. When former president Herbert Hoover echoed many of Joe's themes in a nationally broadcast address a few days later, analysts began speaking of a "Hoover-Kennedy" position on world affairs. Supporters cheered, but criticism also followed, the two men being derided as reactionaries and appeasers, as naive dupes, as Kremlin sympathizers. *The New York Times* seemed to relish pointing out in an editorial that the official Soviet Communist Party newspaper, *Pravda*, had published the full text of both speeches.[37]

Joe Kennedy's position was in fact a reasoned one, and he held it consistently. He viewed Communism in the forties as he had viewed Nazism in the thirties—as a wrongheaded system but not one that fundamentally threatened U.S. security. Such were America's geographic and demographic advantages that it did not need to project its power globally in some kind of crusade for democratic capitalism. No urgency required it, and moreover any such crusade risked bankrupting the Treasury and spawning endless charges of imperialistic meddling. "Russia does not want a major war now or in the near future," he wrote as early as March 1946, expressing a view that more than a few historians of the period would come to share. Stalin was a realist, flexible and cautious, and he would always subordinate Soviet Communist ambitions to Russian national ambitions, which were regional rather than global. Kennedy's more thoughtful critics, among them his son, conceded him these points, even if they disagreed with them. Where they objected sharply was to his claim that the United States had no meaningful stake in preserving a balance of power in Europe or, later, East Asia. For them, Jefferson's declaration from 1814 still held: "It cannot be to our interest that all Europe should be reduced to a single monarchy"; it would be preferable to wage war than to "see the whole force of Europe wielded by a single hand."[38]

IV

When the "great debate" about foreign policy spilled into Congress in January 1951, Jack was happy to skip town for an extended European tour, again with Torby Macdonald along for the ride. Such was the luxury of being wealthy and occupying a safe House seat: one could zoom off for weeks without worry about the monetary or political costs involved. Always keen to spend time in the Old World, Jack also saw in the trip (which consumed a month and took him and Torby to England, France, West

Germany, Yugoslavia, Italy, and Spain) an opportunity to bolster his foreign policy credentials in advance of a potential Senate run the following year. With luck, he could avoid embarrassing questions from journalists about the growing chasm between his father's worldview and his own.

He kept a diary on the trip, which ran to 158 pages and which has been preserved for posterity. To read it today is to see, in addition to the characteristic sloppy handwriting and questionable spelling, that its author had a keen journalistic eye, and moreover that he carried on much like a diplomatic correspondent: that is, he liked to spend his days meeting with governmental leaders, U.S. and foreign diplomats, and journalists, and cared far less for communing with ordinary men and women. If he paid much attention to his physical surroundings, he didn't think it important to make note of it, but he had considerable powers of observation when he decided to use them:

> Yugoslavia—Belgrade—Stones cold and damp—no heating— windows bleach clothes of poor quality—the streets full of crowds— partly due to the fact that there are such few stores. The crowds seem young and energetic many soldiers among them. Tito guards with . . . machine guns over their shoulders—all with red stars on their vests. Though they look strong, they are not healthy—the disease rate particularly tuberculosis is the highest rate of any country in Europe.

While in Belgrade, Jack had an hourlong session with Marshal Josip Broz Tito at the Yugoslav leader's luxurious villa on the outskirts of town. Tito had broken with Stalin two and a half years before and proclaimed an independent Communist state. The Truman administration, hopeful that his action could serve as a model to others within the Soviet orbit, sent him economic and military assistance. Tito, affable and charming and chain-smoking through the entire conversation, advised Jack to ignore rumors that several Warsaw Pact nations—Hungary, Bulgaria, and Romania—intended in the spring to attack Yugoslavia on Stalin's orders. Nor, he went on, did it seem remotely plausible that Stalin planned an onslaught on Western Europe; the Kremlin leader was having enough trouble holding what he already had. "My people are confident of the future," Jack recorded his host as saying. "But I am not a prophet and we are preparing for any eventuality." Tito added that the Americans were playing Moscow's game, getting bogged down in an unwinnable war on the Korean Peninsula.[39]

To Jack's suggestion that the 1938 Munich Conference and the political misjudgments that led up to it had caused grievous and lasting damage to the world, Tito was dismissive. If anyone blundered in 1938, he charged, dubiously, it was the Czechs. They were well armed and had strong defenses, and should have stood their ground. They lost their nerve, failed to think clearly, and thereby allowed Hitler to seize his opening. Yugoslavia would not make the same error; it would take on the Red Army if necessary. Jack was impressed by his host's passion and obvious intelligence, but he held firm to his long-held view: Munich was the disastrous by-product of appeasement, the failure not of the Czechs but of Britain and France.[40]

Here and elsewhere in the diary, Jack was content mostly to record what others said rather than offer his own analysis. Still, it is clear on the pages that, as on his previous European sojourns, his interactions with people in other countries deepened his appreciation for the complexities of the modern age, and for the hard choices that leaders everywhere had to confront. The easy left-right verities that worked so well in American political discourse didn't cut it so easily overseas, he realized anew. Thus, while the Italians should rightly have to contribute to their own defense, "the Italian economy is so precarious—so poor—with the necessity of paying for food 6% of which they must export, that they hate to give up economic recovery for rearmament." The French, for their part, felt overwhelmed, beleaguered by the "overpowering" strength of Soviet power, causing Jack to "doubt if the French who are expected to provide the mass of land troops for the defense of Europe can do so." From David Bruce, the charming and sagacious U.S. ambassador in Paris, Jack heard that NATO was Europe's best hope.[41]

From Belgrade it was on to Rome, where Jack and Torby had a private audience with Pope Pius XII. They genuflected before him and kissed his hand, and the pope reminisced nostalgically about his past meetings with the Kennedy family. He gave the young men rosaries and Catholic medals and pronounced a blessing upon each of them. Thence to Spain, where Jack came away impressed by the staunch anti-Communism of the military officials he met. Their armaments were obsolete, however, and Jack found himself in full agreement with one of David Bruce's claims to him in Paris: that Spain needed American military assistance and should be offered NATO membership.

On his return to America, Jack offered a nuanced assessment of the trip, first in a nationwide radio address carried on 540 stations of the Mutual Broadcasting Company on the evening of February 6, then in testimony before the Senate Foreign Relations and Armed Services committees. The radio talk, a kind of public tutorial of the type American politicians no longer give, ran twenty-five hundred words in length and concerned "Issues in the Defense of Western Europe." Utilizing parts of his diary, Jack offered a general survey of the countries he'd visited and made no effort to talk down to his audience: "The tax structure [in France], where only fifteen percent of the tax receipts come from direct taxation with the balance derived from hidden taxes, seems to slant away from bringing home to the public the burdens that a defense effort must entail. Wages are low and prices high and no adequate price control exists. A prevalent criticism of France's government is that it is unable to get through to working people whereas the Communists succeed in doing so."

Would America's transatlantic partners make the commitments necessary to stand up to Soviet pressure? Kennedy left the answer disconcertingly open: "The firmness and quality of Europe's will to resist is not an easy subject of analysis. Besides the war-weariness of her peoples, there are the conflicting political ambitions of her nations. There is the precariousness of her hard-won economic recovery that could be overthrown by the heavy drain of rearmament, while waiting for just such an opportunity are the millions of disloyal Communists within her own borders."[42]

Yet this was no time for undue alarmism, Jack cautioned when he appeared before the Senate Foreign Relations Committee on February 22. (Presiding during the session and calling Jack to the stand was his potential election foe Henry Cabot Lodge.) His conversations with European leaders as well as U.S. representatives had convinced him, he told the lawmakers, that the Soviets were not about to invade Western Europe. Why should they, "when the best that they could get would be a stalemate during which they would be subjected to atomic bombing?" And even if they could somehow succeed with such an invasion, how would they cope with ruling over the conquered peoples? Even feeding them would be an immense challenge. Jack saw no reason why the Soviets would take such a huge gamble when they didn't need to—"especially when things are going well in the Far East. In addition, Stalin is an old man, and old men are traditionally cautious." The congressman had no objection to adding four new U.S. divisions to the two already in Europe, but he stressed that the Europeans had to step up and contribute more to their defense.

Inevitably, the senators asked Kennedy to account for his father's Virginia speech, in which the older man had urged withdrawal from Europe. He calmly replied that he and his father viewed the situation differently: whereas Ambassador Kennedy, like many other Americans, saw the creation of a viable European defense posture as a nearly hopeless endeavor, he himself felt certain that losing the "productive facilities" of Western Europe would be potentially catastrophic for U.S. security, which meant "we should do our utmost to save it. . . . That is my position," he said firmly. "I think you should ask my father directly as to his position."[43]

It was the perfect ending to Jack Kennedy's European expedition of 1951. He had indulged his love of visiting the Continent, whose culture and politics and history had so defined his early adulthood years. He had met interesting and important people in six countries and deepened his understanding of the issues facing the Western alliance at this fulcrum of the century. He had returned to an attentive and appreciative American audience and received a respectful hearing in the Senate, whose halls he hoped soon to walk himself. And he had demonstrated that he was no puppet of his controversial father. Small wonder that *Boston's Political Times* ran a flattering front-page article headlined "Kennedy Acquiring Title, 'America's Younger Statesman.' "[44]

Encouraged by the burst of attention provided by the trip, Jack laid the groundwork for another overseas journey, this time starting in the Middle East and winding up in the Far East, to take place in the late summer or autumn. In his Senate testimony he had noted the growing danger of Soviet expansion in Asia, and he elaborated the point in remarks at a meeting of the Massachusetts Taxpayers Foundation in Boston in April. He also sensed growing agitation throughout the colonial world, telling the Boston audience that "nationalistic passions" were stirring against the European imperial powers, with major implications for American security. Military techniques would not be enough to keep the Communists from taking control in these areas, Jack continued, which meant it would be vital for Washington and the West to stand for something that these oppressed peoples would find appealing. If Communism prevailed in Asia, it would be because the democracies failed to offer a compelling alternative. Yet U.S. policy seemed to consist mostly of rushing to support anyone and everyone who professed to be anti-Communist. "That puts us in partnership with the corrupt and reactionary groups whose policies breed the discontent on which Soviet Communism feeds and prospers—groups which might have long ago collapsed if it had not been for our assistance. In short, we even support and sustain corruption and tyranny to maintain a status-quo wherever we find existing regimes anti-communistic."[45]

V

The fall trip would be a monster, covering twenty-five thousand miles over six-plus weeks, with stops in France, Israel, Iran, Pakistan, India, Singapore, Thailand, Indonesia, French Indochina, Malaya, Burma, Korea, and Japan. With his various aches and ailments, the congressman could have been forgiven for keeping the itinerary crisp and clean, flying into one capital city, having a meeting or two and a photo op, and then zipping off to the next country. That's usually how it went on lawmakers' "fact-finding" junkets, after all. But that wasn't Jack Kennedy's way, never had been. He wanted to see things for himself, get a feel for the place, talk with more people (if mostly of the well-placed variety). This required more time—and more planning. For weeks the congressman's staff was kept busy arranging logistics, making reservations, scheduling meetings.

It would prove to be a highly consequential trip, and not only for substantive policy reasons but for personal ones as well. Accompanying Jack this time around were brother Bobby, age twenty-five, and sister Patricia, twenty-seven. For the two brothers in particular, the experience was a revelation. They had never spent this kind of extended time together, at least when they were old enough for it to be meaningful—the eight-and-a-half-year age difference was too great. Jack wondered how it would go, musing to Lem Billings about whether Bobby would be "a pain in the ass." Bobby, for his part, had no such worries. Jack's wit, his intelligence, his grace, his courage in war—Bobby revered it all. And now he would get to be side by side with him as they traversed much of the globe.[46]

In personality, Bobby was intense and combative, more akin to the departed Joe Junior than to Jack, though also more straitlaced than either.[47] Always close to his mother, he shared her religiosity, but it was his father's love and approval he especially craved. Following Milton Academy and a stint in the Navy Reserve (1944–46), Bobby scraped by at Harvard, graduating in the class of 1948, then set his sights on law school. His grades were too low for Harvard or Yale, his and his father's preferred choices, but the University of Virginia took him, albeit with a warning that he would need to step up his academic game.[48] While in Charlottesville, Bobby earned a reputation for rudeness and pugnacity, and he had few friends.[49] But he showed promise in the classroom (if also a tendency toward absolutist, black-and-white judgments) and graduated in the middle of his class, in the spring of 1951, while serving in his final year as the president of the Student Legal Forum. By then he was married, to the former Ethel Skakel, an athletic, spirited, and devoutly Catholic extrovert who had volunteered on Jack's 1946 campaign and was a close friend of sister Jean's. Jack served as best man at the wedding, and younger brother Teddy was an usher.

In addition to inviting his father to speak to the forum, Bobby also brought in other luminaries, among them Supreme Court Justice William O. Douglas and former Harvard Law School dean James M. Landis, both Joe Kennedy cronies. Then, in the spring of 1951, shortly before graduation, Bobby welcomed Joe McCarthy, whose visit was notable less for his lecture than for the dinner afterwards, at Bobby and Ethel's home. As the evening progressed, the senator consumed more and more alcohol and became less and less coherent, until embarrassed attendees began to slip out. At one point McCarthy groped a female guest. Bobby eventually had to help him into bed, but the incident did not sour him on the lawmaker. "I liked him almost immediately," Bobby later said.[50]

At the start of October 1951 the siblings set off, with a brief initial stop in Paris, where Jack met with General Eisenhower at Supreme Headquarters Allied Powers Europe on October 3. Once again keeping a detailed travel diary, he jotted down the legendary commander's take on the postwar situation:

> Eisenhower looking very fit. . . . Attacked those who [disavowed criticism of the] settlements made during the war. Said he was merely fighting a war. Had very little to do with them. States that he asked Truman at Potsdam not to beg Russians to come into war. . . . He mentioned that only one conversation he had had of importance at Potsdam and Truman mentioned there about supporting him for Pres in 1945 and had done so several times since. . . . Said

$64 question was whether Kremlin leaders were fanatics—doctrinaires—or just ruthless men—determined to hold on to power—If first, chances of peace are much less than 2nd. . . . He talked well—with a lot of God damns—completely different type than MacArthur, seems somewhat verbose as does Mac. Does not believe Russ[ia] can be frightened into aggressive war by the limited forces we are building up.[51]

In Israel, Jack was the same detached yet empathetic observer he had been on his visit in 1939. He was impressed by David Ben-Gurion's leadership of the three-year-old nation, but also expressed understanding of the plight suffered by Arab refugees whom Israel refused to take back.

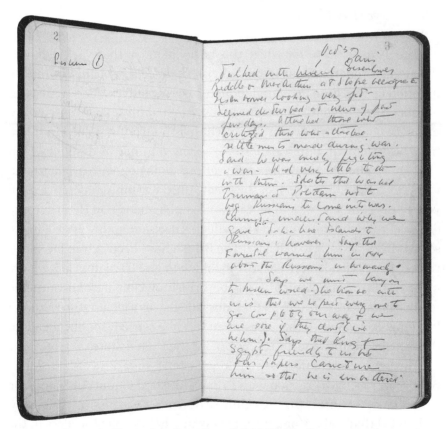

A page in Kennedy's diary from fall 1951. The first part reads:
"Oct. 3—Paris—I talked with General Eisenhower Biddle and MacArthur at SHAPE Headquarters. Eisenhower looking very fit—seemed disturbed at news of last few days."

Back in his hotel after the dinner, Jack—who had a love of poetry that he kept mostly hidden, perhaps for fear that it seemed unmanly—jotted down four lines from a poem by Shelley penned in 1819, after the Peterloo Massacre in Manchester that year, in which government forces fired on a gathering of unarmed protesters seeking Parliament reforms. The poem, harshly critical of government ministers Sidmouth and Castlereagh, has been called an early statement of the principle of nonviolent resistance, and one wonders why Jack excerpted it. Whatever his reason, one reads the lines today with foreboding:

> *I met Murder on the way—*
> *He had a mask like Castlereagh—*
> *Very smooth he look'd, yet grim;*
> *Seven bloodhounds followed him.*[52]

The Israel stay established the basic pattern that Jack followed throughout the trip: he would meet with high leaders of the country in question as well as top U.S. and foreign representatives, then some journalists or intellectuals. Sometimes Bobby joined him, and, more rarely, also Pat; often he went solo.[53] And whereas a different politician might have been content with a handshake, a few minutes of desultory chit-chat, and a photograph, Jack sought serious dialogues with his interlocutors. Thus, in Tehran, scene of the great Allied wartime conference eight years before, he met at length with U.S. ambassador Loy Henderson to discuss President Mohammad Mossadegh's decision, only days before, to seize British-controlled oil fields. "The British have been extremely short-sighted here," Henderson told him, in failing to give Iranians a large share of the spoils. "Almost stupid." Yet the British officials Jack encountered seemed unfazed, assuring him that Mossadegh was a clown who wouldn't last long. Jack doubted this assessment, and he sensed trouble ahead for the British in Iran—and, by extension, for the United States.

The tensions were no less great in Pakistan—four days after Jack and Bobby held a lengthy session with Prime Minister Liaquat Ali Khan, one of the nation's founders, he was gunned down by an assassin. In his diary, Jack noted that "assassinations have taken a heavy toll of leaders in the Middle and Far East," and then listed some of the killings of the previous four years. The Khan murder reinforced the congressman's sense of the precariousness of political power in newly emerging nations, and his belief that Asia would become an increasingly vital concern for U.S. foreign policy. Khan had stressed the importance of Kashmir, which both Pakistan and India claimed as theirs, and gave his guest no sense that the issue could be resolved peacefully anytime soon.

Next it was on to India, where Jawaharlal Nehru offered no more assurances on Kashmir and proved an indifferent yet inspiring host. Over a lunch at the presidential palace, attended also by Nehru's daughter Indira Gandhi, he mostly ignored Jack and Bobby and focused his charm on Pat, but after the meal he and Jack met for an extended discussion. Suave and self-assured, the British-educated Nehru, who would soon turn sixty-two, eschewed specifics in favor of the big picture (he breezily professed to have no clue when Jack asked him how many divisions the Indian army could field), and he defended forcefully his nation's neutrality in the Cold War. Aware that the Kennedy trio would soon be visiting Indochina, Nehru called the French war against Ho Chi Minh's nationalist forces there an example of doomed colonialism. Communism, he stressed to Jack during a dinner conversation, offered the masses "something to die for," whereas the West promised only the status quo. War of the type the French were attempting against Ho would never stop Communism; it would only strengthen it, "for the devastation of war breeds only more poverty and more want."

Jack found power in this argument; indeed, he had argued similarly in his speech to the taxpayers' group in Boston in April. And he could see the force of the Indian leader's personality. Normally scornful of people who didn't know their topics down to the specific details, Jack in this case gave the older man a pass, so taken was he with Nehru's quiet eloquence. "He is interested only in subtler and higher questions," Jack jotted approvingly in the diary. "Generally agreed Nehru is everything in India—the works. Tremendously popular with the masses."[54]

In Thailand, the Kennedys toured the sites, including the Grand Palace and its Temple of the Emerald Buddha, and Jack got an audience with the prime minister. From there the Americans pressed on to Indonesia and Singapore and then Malaya and French Indochina. The Malaya stop was brief but gave the Kennedys a snapshot of the country's protracted guerrilla struggle against British rule: on October 6, just days prior to their arrival, revolutionary forces had ambushed and assassinated the British high commissioner, Sir Henry Gurney. Tensions, already on the rise that fall, ratcheted up further, and British officials insisted on giving

Jack heavy police protection as he traveled without his siblings to see a mining operation just a few miles outside Kuala Lumpur.[55]

But it was the ten days in Indochina that would be the most momentous stop of all during John F. Kennedy's globe-trotting adventures of 1951. ("The most interesting place by far," he wrote his father.[56]) Even before the aircraft touched down at Saigon's Tan Son Nhat airport on a sunny day in mid-October, Jack felt a special sense of anticipation, for he knew that the war had become a major skirmish in the broader East-West struggle, transformed from its initial status as a straightforward Franco-Vietnamese affair into something broader, something that took it into the epicenter of Asian Cold War politics. Over the previous year and a half, Washington had steadily stepped up U.S. aid to France and its Indochinese allies, while on the other side Mao Zedong's Communist Chinese government provided growing (if still comparatively modest) assistance to the Ho Chi Minh–led Viet Minh. As such, Jack understood, the Indochina war could have major ramifications for American foreign relations and, by extension, for his own political future.*[57]

At the airport, the Kennedys were greeted by Bao Dai, the former emperor of Annam (central Vietnam), whom the French had ensconced as a token head of state. Jack noted that he seemed "in [S. J.] Perelman's words—'fried in Crisco.'" Then, on the drive into the heart of Saigon, they were startled to hear small-arms fire nearby. "Another attack by the Viet Minh," the driver calmly explained. It was proof positive that the siblings were now in the midst of a shooting war, and that the appealing bustle of this "Paris of the Orient" was a thin veneer over deep insecurity and tension. The heavy police presence gave it away, as did the anti-grenade netting over the terraces of many restaurants. The heavy fighting might have been in the north, in Tonkin, where the Viet Minh were concentrating their forces, but Saigon lay in the heart of a contested area.[58]

That evening the three Kennedys whiled away the hours on the rooftop bar of the Majestic Hotel. Occasionally they caught glimpses of artillery fire in the night sky as the French took aim at Viet Minh mortar sites

---

* Given the Indochina struggle's growing importance in world politics, and given what was to come for America in Vietnam, it's stunning that Kennedy was either the first or among the first congressmen to pay a visit to the country. Meanwhile, a head count that same year showed that 189 House members had visited Italy since the end of World War II.

across the Saigon River. "Cannot go outside the city because of guerrillas," Bobby wrote in his diary. "Could hear shooting as the evening wore on."[59]

The next afternoon, keen to gain a deeper understanding of developments, Jack headed off alone to the apartment of Associated Press bureau chief Seymour Topping. The two talked for hours, and Topping laid out why the war was going badly for the French and likely wouldn't get better: Ho Chi Minh's support was too broad and too deep, plus he had the backing of Mao's China, immediately to the north. Jack was struck by what he heard, and he got a similar downbeat assessment from Edmund Gullion, the young counselor at the U.S. legation, who told him American officials in Saigon were split in their views on French prospects in the war.[60] In the days to come, Jack asked tough questions during briefings with the U.S. minister, Donald Heath, and the charismatic French military commander and high commissioner, General Jean de Lattre de Tassigny. De Lattre, who impressed Jack with his dynamism and self-assurance, insisted that France and its allies would see the challenge through and would prevail, but Jack was dubious. His doubts didn't fade when de Lattre, after complaining to Heath about the congressman's frank and questioning atti-

General de Lattre, second from right, with U.S. general J. Lawton Collins in Hanoi, October 23, 1951. Congressman Kennedy is visible in profile at right in the rear.

tude, hosted the Kennedy siblings for a fancy dinner and arranged for them to travel north to see the fortifications guarding the Red River Delta approaches to Hanoi.[61]

"We flew over the paddies of the Delta where the French and the guerrillas were locked in a deadly struggle, and through which the Chinese must come if they seize Southeast Asia," Jack related in a speech a few weeks later, when back on U.S. soil. "Marshal de Lattre pointed from the window of the plane with the cane he had carried since his only son's death in the fighting of last summer. 'As long as the Delta can be held,' he said, 'Indo China can be held, but if the Delta is lost, Indo China and all of Southeast Asia will be lost with all of its resources and all of its manpower.'" All well and good, Jack thought, but how could such an outcome be prevented? The key to victory, he told his audience, "is to get the Asians themselves to assume the burden of the struggle. As long as it's a conflict between native communists and western imperialists, success will be impossible. This then must be the pattern for all of our future actions in the Far East. The support of the legitimate aspirations of the people of this area against all who seek to dominate them—from whatever quarter they may come."[62]

In a diary entry from Vietnam, he spoke in similar terms: "We are more and more becoming colonialists in the minds of the people. Because everyone believes that we control the U.N. [and] because our wealth is supposedly inexhaustible, we will be damned if we don't do what they [the emerging nations] want." U.S. officials, he said, must avoid the path trodden by the declining European empires and instead demonstrate that the enemy is not just Communism but "poverty and want," "sickness and disease," and "injustice and inequality," all of which were a feature of life for millions of Asians and Arabs.

Bobby saw things in much the same way. "It is generally agreed," he wrote his father from Saigon, "that if a plebiscite were held now throughout the former Indochina the Communist leader Ho Chi Minh would receive at least 70% of the vote. Because of the great U.S. war aid to the French we are being closely identified with the French the result being that we have also become quite unpopular. Our mistake has been not to insist on definite political reforms by the French toward the natives as prerequisites to any aid. As it stands now we are becoming more & more involved in the war to a point where we can't back out. . . . It doesn't seem to be a picture with a very bright future."[63]

VI

Jack's fears that Bobby would be a "pain in the ass" travel companion proved wholly unfounded. From day one to the end, he found he valued his little brother's insights, his energy, his good cheer. They grew closer, bonded in a way they had never done before. Pat could see the change in their relationship, as could other family members after they returned home. They themselves sensed it. When Jack fell deathly ill in Tokyo— most likely from a flare-up of his Addison's disease—and was rushed by military aircraft to a U.S. Navy hospital on Okinawa, Bobby never left his side.[64] As Jack's temperature soared past 106 degrees and the hospital staff feared they would lose him, his brother's steadfastness calmed everyone's nerves, including the patient's.

Earlier in the trip, Jack had jotted down some lines from Andrew Marvell's poem "To His Coy Mistress," which now seemed addressed specifically to him:

> But at my back I always hear
> Time's winged chariot hurrying near.

Later, Bobby related of the Okinawa scare that "everybody there just expected he'd die."[65] But he didn't. Within a few days Jack regained his strength and the crisis passed, whereupon the trio continued on to Korea, where the war was stalemated around the thirty-eighth parallel, with no end in sight. The sheer difficulty of the rugged terrain surprised the brothers and helped them better understand why the fighting had proved so challenging for American troops. Jack further concluded that inadequate airpower had been instrumental: if MacArthur had been given a sufficient number of planes, he never would have been subjected to the massive counterattack the Chinese had launched against his units the previous fall.

Upon returning to the United States, Jack wasted few opportunities to talk up the expedition and to stress that Americans ignored world developments at their peril. Foreign policy mattered enormously, he told several audiences, indeed overshadowed all else. But the choices for statesmen were not easy, for the world was a complex place. Communism might mean one thing in country A and something else in country B and yet another thing in country C; U.S. policy had to respond accordingly.

"I cannot say that I have returned pleased by our achievements through these critical post-war years," he told a nationwide radio audience over the Mutual Broadcasting Network in mid-November. "Certainly, I do not and one cannot blame America and her policies for all that has happened, for no matter what America might have done, nothing could have avoided nor will avoid the inevitable birth-pangs of Asia's rising nationalism. But mindful of this turmoil I should have hoped that with our traditional concern for the independence of other peoples, our generosity, our desire to relieve poverty and inequality, we would—whatever else happened—have made friends throughout this world. It is tragic that not only have we made no new friends, but we have lost old ones." More than anything, the experience of seeing the Middle East, Southeast Asia, and the Far East up close demonstrated for him that the Communist threat "cannot be met effectively by merely the force of arms. It is the peoples themselves that must be led to reject it, and it is to those peoples that our policies must be directed."[66]

With respect to Indochina, Jack declared before the Boston Chamber of Commerce a few days later that France was "desperately trying to hang on to a rich portion of its former empire against a communist-dominated nationalist uprising."

> The so-called loyal native government is such only in name. It is a puppet government, manned frequently by puppeteers once subservient to the Japanese, now subservient to the French. A free election there, in the opinion of all the neutral observers I talked with, would go in favor of Ho and his Communists as against the French. . . . We have now allied ourselves with the French in this struggle, allied ourselves against the Communists but also against the rising tide of nationalism. We have become the West, the proponents of empire—carriers of what we had traditionally disdained—the white man's burden.[67]

On NBC's nationally televised *Meet the Press* on December 2—a show on which no junior congressman had ever appeared—Jack stayed on the theme, telling the journalist panel that in Asia and the Middle East, the United States had "fallen heir to much of the hatred [the European imperial powers had] incurred by their policies," and that it could never succeed if it sought merely to impose its will on other countries.[68] To panelist

May Craig's suggestion that U.S. troops in Korea were not being permitted to fight to win, Jack gently pushed back; military victory might not be possible, he told her, and thus the administration was doing the right thing in pursuing a negotiated settlement. ("Yes, I do believe that we ought to take agreement where we can get it.") And to *Newsweek*'s Ernest Lindley he said that in Indochina no success would be possible until the "natives" were promised the right of self-determination and the right to govern themselves— and by a specific date. "Otherwise this guerrilla war is just going to spread and grow and we're going to finally get driven out of Southeast Asia."[69]

Kennedy before the Boston Chamber of Commerce after his return from Asia, November 1951.

Here we find the second reason why Jack Kennedy's Asian tour of 1951 matters in historical terms (the first being that it caused him and Bobby to grow much closer): it altered his outlook on U.S. diplomacy in what would come to be called the Third World. Already in previous months he had moved away from the simplistic idea that the spread of Communism in Asia occurred only or mostly because of State Department bungling; the expedition reinforced this shift. More important, the trip convinced him that America must align itself with the newly emerging nations, that colonialism was a spent force, and that Communism could never be vanquished exclusively or even principally by military means. One had to meet colonized and recently independent peoples where they lived, had to speak to their needs, their aspirations. Did U.S. officials understand these essential truths? Jack was skeptical. Many of "our representatives abroad seem to be a breed of their own," he told reporters in November, "moving mainly in their own limited circles not knowing too much of the people to whom they are accredited, unconscious of the fact that their role is not tennis and cocktails, but the interpretation to a foreign country of the meaning of American life and the interpretations to us of that country's aspirations and aims."[70]

In Robert Kennedy's later assessment, the trip left "a very major impression" on his brother, for it showed "these countries from the Mediterranean to the South China sea all . . . searching for a future; what their relationship was going to be to the United States; what we were going to do in our relationship to them; the importance of the right kind of representation; the importance of associating ourselves with the people rather than just the governments, which might be transitional, transitory; the mistakes of the war in Indochina; the mistake of the French policy; the failure of the United States to back the people."[71]

Jack's problem, one he would wrestle with throughout the rest of the decade, was how to align this more subtle interpretation of Communism and Cold War dynamics with the increasingly Manichaean political debate at home in the United States. As an ambitious politician angling for higher office, he understood that many voters liked simple explanations and quick fixes, and moreover that Republicans in the forthcoming 1952 election would seek to discredit the Democrats at every turn, hammering hard on the theme that Truman's party was weak-kneed and irresolute on combating Communist agitation at home and abroad.

He knew, moreover, that Joe McCarthy continued to ride high. Back in April, after Truman fired Douglas MacArthur for publicly airing his disagreements with the White House over the conduct of the Korean War, the Wisconsin senator condemned the action and called for the president's impeachment. Two months after that, on the Senate floor, McCarthy had gone after none other than General George C. Marshall, who had been Army chief of staff during World War II and then had led the State and Defense departments. He was a national symbol, an icon, a man seemingly beyond reproach, yet McCarthy charged him with "a conspiracy so immense and an infamy so black as to dwarf any previous such venture in the history of man; a conspiracy so black that, when it is finally exposed, its principals shall be forever deserving of the maledictions of all honest men." Specifically, McCarthy proclaimed, Marshall had willfully allowed China to be lost and had squandered American prestige and power. Democrats were outraged and called on GOP leaders to condemn the speech, but McCarthy's colleagues mostly stayed silent, while the right-wing press heaped praise on his assessment. That fall, while the

Kennedy siblings journeyed through Asia, the Wisconsin man again claimed that the State Department harbored Communists.[72]

McCarthy made the cover of *Time* that October—the surest sign he had arrived. Editor in chief Henry Luce, a staunch Republican and member of the China lobby, bowed to no one in the depth of his anti-Communist fervor, but he had little regard for the kind of simplistic populism McCarthy represented and, moreover, found him coarse and crude. To Luce, the senator's exaggerations and grandstanding threatened to discredit more authentic anti-Communist efforts. And he had an inkling that McCarthy's popularity had peaked. So on this occasion *Time* did what the Luce publications had thus far generally refrained from doing: it hit McCarthy hard, accusing him of peddling in innuendo, of answering legitimate questions with savage attacks, of having little curiosity and little regard for common decency. "Joe, like all effective demagogues, found an area of emotion and exploited it. No regard for fair play, no scruple for exact truth hampers Joe's political course. If his accusations destroy reputations, if they subvert the principle that a man is innocent until proved guilty, he is oblivious. Joe, immersed in the joy of battle, does not even seem to realize the gravity of his own charges." Yet " 'McCarthyism' is now part of the language," the article acknowledged, and anyone choosing to take on McCarthy faced an immense challenge: "His burly figure casts its shadow over the coming presidential campaign. Thousands turn out to hear his speeches. Millions regard him as 'a splendid American' (a fellow Senator recently called him that)."[73]

McCarthy, as always, hit back hard, blasting *Time* for "desperate lying" and sending letters to advertisers urging them to stop giving business to *Time* and its sister publications *Life* and *Fortune*. At Time Inc., executives worried that Luce, usually so astute in judging the public mood, had miscalculated—McCarthy, they believed, was not losing public support but gaining it. Luce backed off. His magazines returned to a safer position, occasionally chiding the senator, sometimes praising him, and generally holding to the line that he was a necessary counterweight to the Truman administration's timidity on Communism.[74]

Such was the tricky path Jack Kennedy would have to navigate should he seek statewide office the following autumn; he knew it, his aides and confidants knew it. McCarthy remained deeply popular among Catholics in Massachusetts, and he was, moreover, a friend of the family. He still enjoyed support among Republican leaders who, however objectionable they found him personally, believed he was winning votes for the party. (Robert Taft came to McCarthy's defense when Harry Truman described him as "a Kremlin asset.")[75] Truman's popularity, meanwhile, was low and going lower—in 1951 it never rose above 32 percent. Jack accordingly walked a middle path, boosting his anti-Communist credentials by voicing policy differences with the White House on specific matters, including China policy and military preparedness, while also noting near the end of the year that accusations of Communists in the Foreign Service were "irrational."[76]

It was a savvy strategy in the circumstances, but would it be enough in a tough battle to unseat the formidable Henry Cabot Lodge? For that matter, would Jack even get the opportunity to wage that fight? As the year turned, Paul Dever had yet to decide if he would seek another term in the governor's mansion or take on Lodge for the Senate seat. Until he did, John F. Kennedy and his team could do nothing but continue their behind-the-scenes preparations. And wait.

EIGHTEEN

TWO BRAHMINS

Paul Dever didn't even really want to run—for either office. He was tired, plain and simple. Tired of ruling the State House, tired of politics, tired of the endless demands, the internal party squabbles, the machinations that were always part and parcel of Massachusetts state politics. Heavyset and with an ailing heart, he also worried about his health. He knew, moreover, that either race would be tough—against Republican challenger Christian Herter to hold the governorship, or against Henry Cabot Lodge Jr. for the U.S. Senate. For all that, Governor Dever knew deep down that he couldn't back away. Too many people depended on him and were counting on him to stay in the arena. He was a public servant, and a public servant he should remain.[1]

But which office should he seek? He preferred going to Washington, truth be told, and felt certain he had the know-how and the temperament to be an effective senator, responsive to the needs of his state and his nation. But that looked to be the tougher of the two contests. Quietly, Dever commissioned a poll of western Massachusetts—a double poll: Dever versus Lodge and John F. Kennedy versus Lodge—and it showed that Lodge would likely beat Dever, while Lodge and Kennedy were dead even, fifty-fifty. Lodge, moreover, was a proven statewide vote-getter, having beaten

James Michael Curley by 142,000 votes in 1936 and then demolished David I. Walsh in 1946 by a whopping 346,000 votes.

On April 6, 1952, Palm Sunday, after weeks of agonized indecision, Dever made his choice. "Jack, I'm a candidate for reelection," he said simply, in a brief one-on-one meeting at the Ritz-Carlton near the Boston Public Garden. "That's fine," Kennedy replied. "I'm a candidate for the Senate." He had gotten the race he wanted.[2]

It was also the race his father wanted. Once his son had defeated Lodge, Joseph P. Kennedy liked to say, a puckish smile lighting his face, he would have beaten the best—why try for anything less? It would be no harder to win the presidency, he then would add dramatically, than to beat Lodge in Massachusetts. To Joe it seemed clear that Jack's push to gain statewide name recognition over the previous three years was paying dividends, with internal polling showing him running even with Lodge or slightly ahead. More important, Massachusetts was at root a Democratic state, one that had not voted for a Republican candidate for president since Calvin Coolidge, who was one of its own; if Jack secured his party's voters and held his own among independents, he would win. "It's ridiculous in this Democratic state that has been able to elect Curleys and Hurleys and even Dever that we should have Republican senators for almost twenty years," the elder Kennedy wrote a friend. "Lodge is very weak with the Republicans, themselves, and he had always been elected because he was able to get the Democratic vote. Nobody has ever fought him . . . who was competent to take him on, but Jack can easily do that."[3]

Kennedy took further encouragement from his son's visible maturation as a politician. If Jack's health could hold, the Ambassador believed, there was no limit to what he could do and where he could go. His command of policy, his international experience, his winning personality, his telegenic looks—all of it came together in a formidable package. And there was something else, too, the Ambassador could see: his son's general comfort in the glare of publicity, including in the new medium of television, which seemed destined to fundamentally change the practice of American politics. Here Jack's smooth and engaging performance on *Meet the Press* in December, soon after his return from the Far East, had been a revelation, even to many who knew him to be an up-and-comer among Democrats. John F. Royal, NBC's head of programming, was bowled over, telling Joe Kennedy immediately afterwards that Jack's showing reminded him of the song in the musical comedy *Babes in Arms* in which the children shout, "They say we're babes in arms, but we are babes in armor." "Jack certainly didn't look away from the camera or the television audience. In his few appearances on television he has caught on to all the tricks, and he was very warm and confident. He will be a hell-cat with both young and old." The elder Kennedy agreed. To Lawrence Spivak, the co-producer of the show and a frequent panelist, he wrote some weeks afterwards, "*Meet the Press* established Jack once and for all as a major personality, so there you are!"[4]

Immediately after the April 6 meeting with Dever, the Kennedys checked with Archbishop Richard Cushing to be sure it would be appropriate for Jack to declare his candidacy during Holy Week. Cushing assured them it would be, and the campaign released an official statement that evening.[5] "Other states have vigorous leaders in the United States Senate," it read, "to defend the interests and the principles of their citizens—men who had definite goals based on constructive principles and who move toward these goals unswervingly. Massachusetts has need for such leadership." The next day, every morning paper had the announcement: *Kennedy Opposes Lodge for Senate.*[6]

No reader that morning could doubt the scale of the challenge Jack Kennedy had set for himself, especially in what looked to be a Republican year nationally. Harry Truman's approval ratings were low and going lower, and both he and his party were burdened with a stalemated war in Korea; the levelheaded president, casting an eye on the treacherous political landscape in front of him, prudently decided not to seek reelection. In Lodge, moreover, Jack faced an incumbent respected far and wide for his probity and independence, a member of the Senate Foreign Relations Committee who spoke fluent French, stood six foot three, and bore one of the most iconic political names in America. His grandfather, the first Henry Cabot Lodge, had held sway in Massachusetts for two decades (he defeated Honey Fitz by a scant 33,000 votes in the Senate race of 1916) and had led the fight against Woodrow Wilson's effort to get the United States into the League of Nations. Further back were other Lodges and Cabots who had built the wealth and the reputation on which the present Senator Lodge rested so squarely. (George Cabot, his great-great-great-grandfather, had attended Harvard and served as a U.S. senator in the Second Congress, from 1791 to 1796.) Prone at times to a quick irascibility that detractors chalked up to haughtiness, Lodge was a blue blood through and through, the paragon of the patrician New Englander. A

Brahmin's Brahmin, people called him. With his dignified bearing, handsome features, and impeccable manners, he was every movie casting agent's idea of a Yankee establishment political figure, yet one who had shown an impressive ability in previous elections to win support among a broad cross section of voters.[7]

Here it helped that Lodge's war record was so exemplary. Initially opposed to U.S. intervention, he changed his mind with the Pearl Harbor attack. In 1942, while a senator, he joined the U.S. Army and fought courageously in North Africa. When President Roosevelt decreed that members of Congress serving in the armed forces must choose one path or the other, Lodge left the military, but only briefly: upon winning reelection in 1942, he gave up his seat and returned to combat duty, as a commissioned major with the American Sixth Army Group. "He was utterly without fear," remembered one fellow officer, and he won accolades for his actions in battle. Notably, he single-handedly captured a four-man Wehrmacht patrol, a feat that gained him the French Croix de Guerre and Légion d'Honneur. Later he served as a translator and liaison officer to General Jean de Lattre de Tassigny, the prickly French commander John Kennedy would subsequently meet in Indochina. Massachusetts voters, including Irish Catholics, paid due attention, and Lodge returned from the fighting more popular than ever.[8]

Small wonder that several of Jack Kennedy's Capitol Hill colleagues had advised him against taking Lodge on. At a luncheon in the Cambridge home of Arthur M. Schlesinger Jr. and his wife, Marion, in early 1952, Senator Paul H. Douglas of Illinois told Jack that Lodge would likely be unbeatable, especially if the Republicans nominated Dwight Eisenhower for president. Why not accumulate seniority in the House instead, or perhaps pursue the governorship? Kennedy listened politely but said little. He had heard the same message from Senator George Smathers of Florida, who had come into the House with him in 1947 and won a Senate seat in 1950, and was perhaps his closet friend in Washington. Smathers considered Jack a young man of immense political gifts, but, like Douglas, he urged him to stay in the House and bide his time, on the grounds that an unsuccessful Senate race could be political suicide. And odds were this one would be unsuccessful, Smathers said, in view of the nation's Truman fatigue and Lodge's absolute annihilation of David Walsh—supposedly unbeatable, and an Irish Catholic to boot—the last time around.[9]

The senators' arguments failed to carry the day. Within the Kennedy family, all the doubts were waved off. Instead, sister Eunice later said, there would be "only a mighty roar every time Jack came home. . . . 'Jack run for the Senate. You'll knock Lodge's block off!' "[10]

To add to the intrigue, the two candidates were in core respects remarkably similar. Both were tall, lean, and handsome. Both were graduates of Harvard who served with distinction in World War II. Both flirted with journalism before choosing a political career. Both had isolationist forebears but were themselves internationalists who supported foreign aid, and on domestic issues both men gravitated toward the political center. Both came across as thoughtful and sensible and gentlemanly; both were composed under pressure. Of the two, Lodge seemed the more polished and suave, and the better public speaker, while Kennedy looked more boyish and untested, but these differences were minor. Even the patrician label seemed interchangeable between the two men, at least to a degree: "Jack is the first Irish Brahmin," Dever said.[11]

Or, in James MacGregor Burns's formulation, "Rarely in American politics have hunter and quarry so resembled each other."[12]

II

The Kennedy campaign was poised for a fast start. Already in 1951, when Jack knew he would wage a statewide campaign but not yet which one, he hung on the wall in his Bowdoin Street apartment a map of Massachusetts. He and Dave Powers put pins on the communities, large and small, that he had visited, then plotted how to cover the blank areas. "He used to say, 'Gosh, we don't have anything up there,' " Powers remembered, "and he'd point up to the Western part of the state around Springfield, Chicopee, and Holyoke, and I said, 'well, we'll work on it.' " Calls would be made, and soon Congressman Kennedy would have pro bono speaking engagements in these locales. By the end of 1951 "we had every one of the [state's] 39 cities covered" with pins, Powers said; by April 1952, when he announced, even the smaller towns in the western parts of the state had been pinned.[13] Everywhere Jack went, moreover, aides would jot down the names and addresses of notable people he met. The information would be transferred onto three-by-five-inch index cards and added to an existing file of names from the House campaigns. The result: even before the campaign launched, Jack Kennedy had a contact in virtually every community in the state.

To manage the campaign, Jack turned to attorney Mark Dalton, who had been with him since the first campaign in 1946. Powers, too, was a holdover, as were a trio of local operatives: Frank Morrissey, Joe DeGuglielmo, and Tony Galluccio. But the other principals were new, starting with the acerbic, sharp-featured Kenny O'Donnell, who was Robert Kennedy's friend from Harvard (where he had captained the football team) and who had flown thirty missions over Germany as a bombardier during the war, once crash-landing between enemy and Allied lines; early in the year, Bobby had convinced him to quit his position with a paper firm to join the nascent campaign. Larry O'Brien, a burly and genial political junkie from Springfield who worked in advertising and public relations, signed on as well—Jack Kennedy, he told friends, was a new type of Irish politician, respectable and courteous—and in short order proved his worth with voter registration and precinct organization. Together with Powers, the two men formed the core of what would become known as the Irish Mafia, or the Irish Brotherhood—a small group of loyal, extremely capable aides so in sync that they could communicate with mere snippets of words and subtle alterations in facial expression.[14] In addition, Joe Kennedy tapped his own people, notably James Landis, a veteran New Dealer and longtime Kennedy family friend who had been dean of Harvard Law School and could serve as a liaison of sorts to the Cambridge intellectuals; John Harriman, a financial writer at the *Boston Globe*, who came on board to write speeches; J. Lynn Johnston, an attorney who had helped run the Ambassador's Merchandise Mart, in Chicago, then the world's largest building; and Sargent Shriver, who still sought Eunice's hand in marriage and who took a leave from his job with Kennedy Enterprises in Chicago to join the campaign. Headquarters were set up at 44 Kilby Street, in the heart of Boston's financial district.

Joe Kennedy was omnipresent, if not quite the omnipotent force some historians would later suggest. He took an apartment at 84 Beacon Street, near Jack's place on Bowdoin Street, so he could be close to the action.[15] He called in old political debts, involved himself in tactical and strategic decisions, especially concerning advertising layouts, and kept his checkbook permanently open. According to terrified junior aides, he even told people where to sit in meetings. The candidate, feeling the need to assert his authority, announced in one early meeting that he was delegating to his father the task of forking out all the money ("We concede you that role," he grandly announced, to chuckles around the room), while he preserved for himself primary responsibility for the core decisions regarding campaign strategy, messaging, and speechwriting.[16]

That the two Kennedys often agreed on these big-ticket items should not obscure the reality, which had already emerged well before 1952: John F. Kennedy, keen student of government and history, was always his own political boss. He trusted his own political judgments over those of his father, who was a whiz at making money but lacked a feel for what made people tick. The two of them saw the world and America's role in it differently, saw U.S. democracy differently. Whenever, in an election campaign, these views clashed, Jack's prevailed.

"The Ambassador worked around the clock," one campaign speechwriter later remarked. "He was always consulting people, getting reports, looking into problems. Should Jack go on TV with this issue? What kind of ad should he run on something else? He'd call in experts, get opinions, have ideas worked up. He'd do all this from an office in his apartment on Beacon Street. But Jack would make the final decisions."[17]

For all the advance work, however—the years of speeches around the state, many of them in tiny hamlets before tiny audiences; the internal polling; the cultivation of favorable press coverage; the assembling of a team—the campaign stumbled out of the gate. Mark Dalton, smart, friendly, and mild-mannered, with a tendency toward nervousness, was miscast in his role as manager of a large and complex statewide campaign, and moreover he had not been given clear marching orders on how to build his apparatus. Though Jack professed surprise and irritation at the lack of progress on the organizational front, he was being disingenuous—in O'Donnell's later recollection, the candidate knew perfectly well that no organizing had been done because he had given no one authority to do it.[18] Frequently in Washington to attend to his congressional duties, he left the initiative to his father, who tore into the hapless Dalton at every opportunity.

"We were headed for disaster," O'Donnell remembered. "The only time the campaign got any direction was when John Kennedy . . . was able to get up to Massachusetts to overrule his father. . . . The Congressman and I had a big argument one day, and I told him that the campaign could only be handled by somebody who could talk up to his father; nobody had the courage to, and I certainly didn't have the qualifications, and it just wasn't going to work unless Bobby came up." Jack reluctantly agreed, and asked O'Donnell to reach out to Bobby, who, upon graduation from law school, had taken a job with the Justice Department. O'Donnell did as instructed, over dinner and in follow-up phone calls, but Bobby demurred. He had a new job, a child at home, and another on the way, and moreover he knew little about electoral campaigning. Nor did he possess his brother's intrinsic interest in politics. "I'll just screw it up," he told O'Donnell. They hung up. The more Bobby pondered it, though, the more he saw he had no choice—loyalty to family came first. He called O'Donnell a few days later. "I'm coming up. I've thought it all over, and I suppose I'll have to do it."[19]

He was all of twenty-six years old when he arrived in Boston to seize control of the foundering operation. Tanned and wiry, with a toothy smile and a mop of unruly hair, he set the tone from the start, arriving at Kilby Street by eight thirty each morning and toiling until midnight, day after day after day. Often he was the person to unlock the door in the morning and lock it again at night. And he was not above taking on mundane tasks, such as licking envelopes and knocking on doors. One day, he determined there should be an enormous "Kennedy for Senate" poster on the side of a building adjacent to the heavily traveled bridge between Charlestown and the North End of Boston. "Drive me over there," he instructed Dave Powers. "I'll put up the sign myself." To reach the height where he wanted the sign hung, Bobby had to balance himself on the top rung of the long ladder. "While I was holding the ladder," Powers recalled, "I was wondering how I could explain it to the Ambassador and Jack when Bobby fell and broke his neck. I said to myself, if I had his money I would be sitting at home in a rocking chair instead of being up there on the top of that ladder."[20]

Low-level aides learned that they had to keep busy at all times, lest Bobby thrust a pencil in their hand and tell them to get to work; soon they were referring to the pre-Bobby period as "before the revolution" and to the new reality as "after the revolution."[21] Those workers who expected him to be but a mouthpiece for the Ambassador were stunned to see that, on the contrary, the young man could and did stand up to his father, thus proving O'Donnell's hunch to be right. Soon the old man moved back into the shadows, where everyone preferred him to be—still involved, still opinionated, still the overseer, but from behind the scenes. His cadre of old-time hangers-on, men like Frank Morrissey, a loyal aide who had expected to play a central campaign role, were assigned lesser tasks.

One for all: the candidate at his campaign headquarters with, from left, siblings Eunice, Pat, Bobby, and Jean.

In one sense, ironically, Bobby *was* an extension of his father, for in short order he took on all the attributes ever given to the old man, which is to say he was deemed ruthless, caustic, relentless, defiant, and ferocious. ("I don't care if anybody around here likes me, as long as they like Jack," he would say.) Veterans of the state political establishment were appalled by his lack of tact and respect, by his insistence that he was running an organization whose allegiance was to Jack Kennedy, not to the Democratic Party and not to Governor Dever and his team. More than once, these encounters ended on the verge of fisticuffs. But even the naysayers had to concede that Bobby got things done; he was effective in his role. Or at least behind closed doors—whenever he had to make even brief public remarks on his brother's behalf, he suffered stage fright and turned timid, if sometimes in an endearing sort of way. "My brother Jack couldn't be here," he murmured at one early event. "My mother couldn't be here. My sister Eunice couldn't be here. My sister Pat couldn't be here. My sister Jean couldn't be here. But if my brother Jack were here, he'd tell you Lodge has a very bad voting record. Thank you."[22]

Together with Larry O'Brien, Bobby devised an organizational structure in which campaign "secretaries" around the state would function as shadow units to the regular Democratic Party machinery, in a kind of supra-party system. For this role the campaign sought people who had little or no prior involvement in campaigns, who were either nonpolitical or apolitical and had no allegiances to the state party. Tony Galluccio's ready-made list of such folks, compiled during his excursions over the previous year, now came in wonderfully handy.[23] Ultimately, 286 of these "Kennedy Secretaries" would toil on the candidate's behalf, backed by an army of more than twenty thousand volunteers. (Thus was followed O'Brien's First Law of Politics: the more campaigners, the better.) The offers to help were indeed so constant as to be burdensome, which may help account for a pair of ingenious decisions by Dave Powers. First, although Jack Kennedy did not face a contested primary, he was obligated to secure at least twenty-five hundred signatures on his nomination papers. The thought occurred to Powers: Why stop at that number? Why not blow past it and get as many names as possible by the deadline? The candidate agreed, and over several weeks workers duly collected more than a hundred times the required number of signatories—262,324—which they submitted on ten thousand sheets.[24]

Second, Powers, reflecting back on a fellow who told him he had signed nomination papers for twenty-five years and never received a thanks, hit upon the idea of having volunteers type up thank-you letters to every one of the quarter-million-plus signatories. The recipients would be touched by the gesture, Powers reasoned, and the volunteers—the overwhelming majority of them female—would be kept busy. "These girls would come pouring in on their lunch hour and want to do something and every day we had to have a project," Powers recalled. "And in the evening they'd come in after work and stay something like 5 to 7 and 6 to 8 and want to type. We'd have as many as 200 girls in there." To save on postage and use up more volunteer hours, the thank-you letters were in most cases hand-delivered, often by crews of female students from colleges such as Smith and Wellesley—which only strengthened the impression on the recipient.[25]

Other volunteers, numbering in the several hundreds, were put to work making evening telephone calls. The callers each got a list of names and numbers of Democrats and independents in a given neighborhood and a prepared message to recite, plus a list containing John F. Kennedy's stances on key policy issues. If they received a question they couldn't answer, they were to make a note that someone from the Kilby Street headquarters should call the person back with the missing information. In the lead-up to Election Day, the volunteers would again call the same people they'd contacted before, urging them to vote and asking if they needed a ride to the polls.

The close attention to detail became a hallmark of the campaign. At Joe Kennedy's direction, carefully produced ads were placed in newspapers around the state on pages and at times likely to garner the highest readership. A glossy eight-page tabloid extolling Jack's heroics in the South Pacific went out to households across the state, along with the *Reader's Digest* reprint of John Hersey's PT 109 story in *The New Yorker.* (Some 1.2 million of the tabloids were ultimately printed.) For French-speaking communities in the hills of Worcester County the campaign made a recording narrated in French by the candidate's mother, and there were efforts targeted at specific ethnic groups in and around Boston. There were even campaign committees for specific professions—there were Doctors for Kennedy, Dentists for Kennedy, Teachers for Kennedy. Seasoned politicos were impressed, however grudgingly, by what they saw. When Boston mayor John B. Hynes appeared with Jack at a rally in Copley Square in June, he was surprised to see not one but two teleprompters set up and ready to go. He wondered why—until one broke down and campaign aides switched smoothly to the second. Hynes understood he was in the presence of perfectionists.[26]

The campaign also made a determined effort to woo the state's African American voters, who numbered between fifty thousand and seventy thousand and lived mostly in the Roxbury and Dorchester areas of Boston. Mailings went out to them citing Kennedy's long-standing support for civil rights, and black journalists were kept abreast of the candidate's votes and speeches on the issue. (In January 1952, in a speech on the House floor, Kennedy called for President Truman to launch an immediate federal investigation into the Miami murder of NAACP official Harry T. Moore and his wife, Harriet, who had been killed on Christmas night by a bomb planted by segregationists. Kennedy kept on drawing attention to the case in the months thereafter, receiving favorable notice in the black press.) In addition, staffers laid plans to have Kennedy spend significant time come August and September speaking in Boston's six predominantly black wards. Sensing Lodge's vulnerability on the topic—in 1946, the senator had won only one of these wards—the campaign hit the Republican hard, warning African American voters that he could not be trusted to champion black advancement.[27]

A fascinating document uncovered by journalist Nick Bryant offers insights into Kennedy's thinking on race in this period. In handwritten notes for a campaign speech he may or may not have delivered, the candidate issued a strong declarative opening: "There is nothing worse in life than racial bigotry." He then crossed out "bigotry" and replaced it with "prejudice," and inserted the discarded word into the next sentence: "There is nothing lower than bigotry." From there Kennedy linked the cause of civil rights with the battle against Communism: "Those who view fellow Americans—regardless of race, color, or national origin—as anything other than fellow Americans are fostering the very climate in which the seeds of Communism flourish." Lest his listeners miss the point, the next sentence underscored it: "A strong civil rights program—one that guarantees every American a fairly-earned share of those opportunities to better oneself and his family which only our country can offer—is vital to the continued strength and progress of the United States." There followed an examination of Lodge's weak civil rights record as compared with his own, followed by a brief peroration: "I want to go to the Senate to continue my fight for Civil Rights legislation."[28]

At no point in the draft did Kennedy touch on the daily indignities suffered by blacks, or offer specific ideas for ending entrenched segregation practices in the South—a sign, perhaps, of his limited imagination on the topic of race (neither here nor elsewhere in the Senate campaign did he appear to show deep interest in the political sources of black discontent) or perhaps simply a reflection of his belief that, since he was campaigning in Massachusetts, not Mississippi, he need not dwell on southern practices. Whatever the case, he was content here to merely call for the "good treatment" of all Americans—in schools, in courts, and in the armed services.[29]

III

In May and June it was still too soon for campaign rallies, but not for more specialized events. Remembering the great success of the women's tea reception at Cambridge's Commander Hotel in the closing days of the 1946 primary campaign, the Kennedy team planned a series of similar "teas" throughout the state, to be held in hotel ballrooms or high school gymnasiums, usually on Sundays. "Reception in honor of Mrs. Joseph P. Kennedy and her son, Congressman John F. Kennedy, Sunday afternoon," the gilt-edged invitations, on sleek white cards, would read; encased in expensive, hand-addressed vellum envelopes, they would be put in boxes and driven to the town in question so they would bear a local postmark. Attendees would get to hear a few words from the candidate and his mother—and sometimes also from one or more of his sisters—and there would be a receiving line. Tea and cake or cookies would be served; often an orchestra would play. As with the 1946 event, the response was overwhelming. The first tea, at the Bancroft Hotel, in Worcester, on May 18, drew five thousand women; the second, in Springfield the following week, was almost as large. In Fall River, Dave Powers stood at the door with a clicker, counting the women as they entered; when he got to two thousand, he quit.[30]

Jack inserted himself into the early planning for the teas. In late April he asked Pauline "Polly" Fitzgerald, a second cousin by marriage, to meet him at his apartment to discuss how best to proceed. "I'd like to have a tea in Worcester to kind of open my campaign," he told her, and "I'd like to have you set this up for me." Fitzgerald said yes on the spot. Jack told her he thought there should be invitations, worded in such a way that nobody would feel excluded. Fitzgerald agreed, and the two determined that the bottom right corner of the card should read, "Guests invited," meaning the recipient could bring along others. "So it would have a sort of dual purpose," Fitzgerald later said, "in that a person who got it would feel that she was very lucky and it was personal, and yet people who didn't get it would know that they could be invited."[31]

"In the first place," the congressman said in his brief remarks in Worcester, "for some strange reason, there are more women than men in Massachusetts, and they live longer. Secondly, my grandfather, the late John F. Fitzgerald, ran for the United States Senate thirty-six years ago against my opponent's grandfather, Henry Cabot Lodge, and he lost by only 30,000 votes in an election where women were not allowed to vote. I hope that by impressing the female electorate that I can more than take up the slack."[32]

Thrilled by the turnout in Worcester, Jack found Fitzgerald in a corridor of the hotel after the event. He had been shaking hands for hours and was exhausted, yet elated. This woman clearly knew what she was doing. "Now, come in to see me and let's talk about doing more teas," he told her. Soon Fitzgerald found herself appointed chief planner for the receptions, which would total three dozen throughout the state and be attended by more than seventy thousand women. The work was arduous for her and all involved, she later said, but wholly worth it, "because there was just something about him that communicated so to people. And as the women went through that line, he had an indefinable something that made every woman there feel that he needed her to work for him. It's nothing that could be put on."[33]

It was about sex appeal, no question, as it had been in the earlier campaigns—the smile, the tousled hair, the good looks and graceful bearing, the bachelor status. But there was more to it. John F. Kennedy's public persona just drew people in. It had been evident in the house parties and halting early campaign speeches in 1946, and it was evident now, six years later. His opponent would subsequently acknowledge as much, telling an interviewer that Jack Kennedy "had a tremendous and well-deserved popularity and he was an extraordinarily likable man. In fact, I liked him. So often in a campaign, you look for a man's faults and then campaign on them. Well, in this case you didn't do that." A former mayor of Pittsfield, reflecting back a few years later, said something similar: "There's something about Jack—and I don't know quite what it is—that makes people want to believe in him. Conservatives and liberals both tell you that he's with them, because they want to believe that he is, and they want to be with him. They want to identify their views with him."[34]

Of the Cambridge tea party, again held at the Commander Hotel, one reporter remarked:

> For approximately two hours, an unbroken line of women filed slowly across the stage, shaking hands with each of the Kennedys, mumbling confused introductions and pleasantries, and pushed on through a side door into the lobby still packed with those waiting their turn to go through the receiving line. Along one side of the spacious room were long tables with harassed waitresses—pouring tea and coffee and serving cookies. (Total consumption was reported later at 8,600 cups.) . . . An air of pleasant, chattering amiability in spite of a few splattered dresses and two faintings. When the handshaking in the ballroom was finally completed around 10:30 [P.M.], the Kennedys, looking wilted but determined, came in for tea themselves.[35]

In addition to the large-scale tea receptions, smaller house parties like this one were a core part of the campaign. Mother Rose is on the right with a pearl necklace. Sister Patricia is in a white dress on the left.

The reporter picked up on one of the defining features of the receptions: they were family affairs, and winningly so. Rose Kennedy in particular, modish and youthful at age sixty, won universal accolades for her role as hostess. Campaign aides would prepare written remarks for her, but they needn't have bothered: invariably she followed her own script, usually without notes, describing her experiences raising nine children (often she brought a prop, in the form of the index card file she had used to keep track of illnesses and vaccinations and dental work) and dropping in artful and humorous references to her father, Honey Fitz. Though in one-on-one conversation Rose Kennedy could be frosty and remote, before a crowd she had an unerring social instinct, what Kenny O'Donnell called "a perfect knack for saying the right thing at the right time and always striking the right note." She charmed Italians in the North End with a few words of Italian and told them about growing up in the neighborhood. In Dorchester she reminisced lightly about her experiences at Dorchester High School. She even adapted her wardrobe to the individual locales, jettisoning her preferred high-priced Parisian offerings for plainer, if still elegant, styles when she ventured to the less prosperous areas. On more than one occasion she changed outfits in the car on the way from one event to another.[36]

Her daughters, meanwhile, with the exception of Rosemary, were seemingly everywhere, going door to door, speaking to women's clubs around the state, showing a short film of Jack's career, hosting house parties in and around Boston, and appearing at the teas.* Jean also doubled as office manager at the Kilby Street headquarters. Bobby's wife, Ethel, also got into the act, even giving a campaign speech in Fall River on the *same night* she gave birth to Joseph P. Kennedy II. "I'm just crazy about Jack," she enthused, "and I'm only an in-law."[37]

IV

The great secret of the 1952 campaign, though common knowledge to those around the candidate, was that he was often in acute back pain. In a May appearance at a fire station in Springfield, he gamely agreed to slide down a fire pole for the cameras, from the third floor to the first. When he hit bottom he winced in agony. The succeeding days brought scant relief, and he was forced to use crutches to get around. Aides, worried it would become a campaign issue, explained away Jack's absences from headquarters by pointing to a recurrence of an old war injury—a transparent effort to evoke sympathy for the military hero. They insisted the issue would soon pass and that his overall health was excellent. In truth, candidate Kennedy was in near-constant pain that summer and fall, finding relief only when he soaked in the bathtub at the end of a long day—or, when the schedule permitted, between events in midafternoon. The painkillers helped, but not enough. Before he entered an auditorium for a speech, Powers or another aide would usually take his crutches and discreetly hide them away so no one in the audience could see them. Jack would stride in, lean and sinewy, the seeming epitome of youthful good health. He would give his short speech and then stand for hour upon excruciating hour in the receiving line, never giving anything away but leaning subtly against a piano or a wall when possible. Only when no such aid was available and the pain got too great would the crutches come back out.[38]

---

* When asked about Rosemary, the campaign said she was a "schoolteacher in Wisconsin." Also absent was Teddy, now twenty, who had cheated on an exam in his freshman year at Harvard and been expelled. He enrolled in the Army and spent most of his brother's 1952 race stationed in Europe. In the fall of 1953 he applied successfully for readmission to Harvard.

He drove himself forward, relentlessly. He smelled victory, could almost taste it, but feared that any letdown could spell doom for his campaign—and thus for his political career. For six months he traversed the state, from Cape Cod to the Berkshires, hitting the larger cities eight or nine times and the small towns at least once, shaking hands and giving speeches, time after time, usually eating a cheeseburger on the fly. "Now we were starting literally—this is not exaggerated—at five or five-thirty in the morning," recalled Frank Morrissey, whose task was to get the candidate up in the morning and put him to bed at night. "We were speaking at a very tight split-second schedule, going across this whole commonwealth, and we'd go until one or two until we put him to bed." When the candidate proved hard to wake up, Morrissey resorted to a trick in which he picked up the phone and pretended to make a call. "I'd say, 'Joe, I'm sorry we have to cancel this first one . . . ' And I'd no sooner get the word 'cancel' out, than Jack would let out a yell, get up, and away we'd start. We'd do that repeatedly."[39] It didn't make Morrissey's task easier that Kennedy much preferred to sleep each night at home on Bowdoin Street, where he had a mattress he knew, with a board under it, rather than get a hotel room locally; this meant longer days and more time on the road.

Sometimes the candidate and his aides would repair to Schrafft's, in Charlestown, for late-night strategy sessions over milkshakes until the place closed, then move on to his apartment for still more scheming. Alcohol seldom factored in. A running gag in the campaign was that Kennedy, at the end of a bruising day, would exclaim, "Boy, do I need a drink," his aides would eagerly agree, and he would take them to a drugstore for a chocolate shake.[40]

All the while, the team tried, with modest success, to manufacture campaign issues. One argument, laid out by Jim Landis and others, blamed the two Republican senators—Lodge and Leverett Saltonstall—for the state's industrial decline and unemployment, an awkward assertion given Paul Dever's simultaneous campaign boast that the economy was humming under his leadership. Another attacked Lodge for supposedly being inattentive to his Senate duties. An internal campaign document titled "Lodge's Dodges" vilified the senator for supposed policy reversals, and during the summer months the campaign hit him from both the left and the right: from the left for opposing key aspects of the Truman administration's Fair Deal legislation, including with respect to housing and labor; from the right for being *too* supportive of Truman on foreign policy, too reticent in opposing Communism. Lodge was accused of favoring the withdrawal of U.S. forces from Korea, and more generally of being timidly bipartisan, while by contrast Jack Kennedy had the courage to oppose numerous parts of the administration's foreign policy. In this regard, a campaign document declared, Congressman Kennedy "has been much closer to the position of [Ohio Republican Robert] Taft than has Lodge."[41]

The reference to Senator Taft was a shrewd suggestion by Joseph Kennedy, who saw a chance to pick up support for Jack among Massachusetts conservatives dismayed by what was happening within the GOP: the growing support for General Dwight D. Eisenhower in his battle with Taft for the party's presidential nomination. By all rights the nomination should have belonged to Taft, a widely respected and highly intelligent lawmaker—he had graduated first in his class at Yale and then again at Harvard Law— who had waited twelve years for this moment and had been deeply loyal to his party throughout. (He was proud of his "Mr. Republican" nickname.)[42] The eastern establishment wing of the party might have snagged the previous three nominations, but Taft felt certain that he was closer to the hearts of most rank-and-file party members than was Tom Dewey, twice the candidate and twice the loser. Perhaps he was, but he hadn't counted on an Eisenhower candidacy. Into the fall of 1951, as both parties courted him, the five-star general stayed publicly coy about his plans, in part because he was uncertain about running. His competitive instincts, which ran deep behind his sunny disposition, inclined him toward jumping in. But he had already held a more important job—overseeing the invasion of Europe in 1944—and he did not relish subjecting himself to a potentially sordid and dehumanizing nomination battle.[43]

Gradually, however, Eisenhower edged toward seeking the Republican nomination, urged on by the eastern wing of the party and impelled by his own concern that a President Taft would take the country in a sharply isolationist direction, perhaps even pull the United States out of the Western alliance.* In January 1952 he allowed his name to be entered in the New Hampshire primary; in April he asked to be relieved of his duty in

---

* Democratic Party hopes that Eisenhower might agree to be their standard-bearer were in vain: he was a Republican through and through, always more comfortable consorting with powerful businessmen than with their liberal opponents. He voted for FDR only once, in 1944, and only because the war was on. In 1948 he backed Dewey over Truman.

Paris as commander of NATO so he could come home to contest the GOP nomination; the request was granted. Though in hindsight it is tempting to see the outcome of the ensuing battle as foreordained, with the renowned general and his military bearing and high-wattage smile cruising to victory over the stiff and colorless Taft, in fact their fight was a rancorous, closely contested affair—heading into the party convention, in Chicago that July, Taft indeed had a clear lead in delegate support. But Eisenhower's forces were better organized and better on the convention floor, and he prevailed. Taft and many of his backers left Chicago deeply embittered.[44]

Eisenhower's decisive first-ballot win obscured a deep split within the party. To secure his victory, he had accepted a party platform that contained isolationist elements and at the same time condemned Truman's containment policy and called for the "liberation" of Eastern European nations. It denounced the 1945 Yalta agreement and accused the Democrats of harboring traitors in the government. As a further sop to conservatives, Eisenhower accepted the selection of Richard M. Nixon as his running mate.[45] The California man soon made good on his selection, going after the "spineless" Truman and his party with gusto. Of the Democratic presidential nominee, the urbane and articulate Illinois governor Adlai Stevenson, Nixon said he was an "appeaser," with a "Ph.D. from Dean Acheson's Cowardly College of Communist Containment."[46]

None of this would have mattered much to the Senate race in Massachusetts had not Henry Cabot Lodge been one of the principal figures behind Eisenhower's candidacy. As much as anyone, it was Lodge who had leaned on the general to leave his Paris post to return to America to contest the nomination; in January 1952 it was Lodge who entered the general's name in the New Hampshire candidacy. In subsequent months he became Ike's de facto campaign manager and a principal strategist in the convention struggle in Chicago.[47] As a result, Lodge was distracted throughout the summer, paying little attention to his own campaign and seldom setting foot in Massachusetts. To make matters worse, his actions on Eisenhower's behalf alienated Taft-supporting conservatives in the state, some of whom vowed to sit out the Senate race and others of whom went a step further, pledging their support to John Kennedy. Basil Brewer, Taft's manager in Massachusetts and the publisher of the New Bedford *Standard-Times*, which had a wide readership in the southeastern part of the state, flipped his paper from acclaim of Lodge to condemnation, calling him a "Truman socialistic New Dealer." After a meeting with Joe Kennedy, Brewer endorsed Jack's candidacy.[48]

V

Only at the start of September, after a leisurely Caribbean vacation and with the election but two months away, did Lodge turn his full attention to his own campaign. By then Kennedy had been going full bore for more than four months and had made important inroads with key constituencies around the state, including labor and women. (On August 22 the Massachusetts Federation of Labor endorsed Kennedy at its annual meeting.)[49] To aides Lodge expressed confidence that he would ultimately prevail, but it was a sign of his anxiety that he challenged his opponent to a series of debates—"anywhere and any place of his own choosing."[50] The Kennedy camp agreed to two, the first of which took place on September 16, before an overflow crowd at South Junior High School, in Waltham. Both men were respectful and substantive; both were content to shadowbox and say nice things about each other. But the challenger won plaudits for his calm, direct, and poised demeanor, and for his frank acknowledgment of Democratic mistakes over the past twenty years. At the same time, he stressed, his party's policies should be judged against the complexity of the challenges involved with the Depression, the Nazi threat and World War II, and the reconversion to peacetime. "It is against this panorama that our actions must be judged—and not merely through the trick binoculars of hindsight, which makes all things easy, all men wise. To claim our successes were bipartisan, our failures Democratic, is good politics perhaps, but not good sense." Jack reminded his audience that his party had been crucial in furthering the rights of labor, in stopping the exploitation of children and women, and in enacting a minimum wage law.[51]

Reporter Mary McGrory, covering the debate for *The Washington Star,* judged Kennedy the clear winner. "He was totally self-possessed, had all the facts at his command, and charmed everybody." Jack himself, self-critical as always, felt he had only mustered a draw, but he conceded aides' claims that a tie was as good as a win, given Lodge's experience, stature, and popularity. Lodge didn't disagree; he knew he had failed to knock his younger, greener opponent down a peg or two. The response of one Waltham resident who was in the audience played more to Kennedy's advantage than to Lodge's: "I liked 'em both."[52]

The Waltham debate was carried only on radio, but, in a sign of the changing times, the scene for the second encounter shifted to a television studio in New York City. Hundreds of thousands tuned in to the broadcast, which was simulcast by a Boston station, and once again the challenger held his own on substance while seeming the more comfortable of the two men in the new medium.[53] Joe Kennedy was thrilled. He had raised his children to be at ease in front of a camera, and his belief in the transcendent importance of the small, grainy black-and-white screens for the future of U.S. politics had only deepened over the summer. The Ambassador strategized constantly about how his son should be used on television, how he should be dressed, how he should speak, where he should fix his gaze. Jack needed no persuasion, and he worked diligently to hone his skills, even participating in a CBS "television school" in July. His early performances were mixed—he tended to lapse into a monotone when reading from a script—but he improved with practice. Talented at repartee and skillful in debate, he did better in unscripted settings in which he shared the stage and could let his natural charm come through.

In October the campaign aired two installments of a special thirty-minute TV program on Boston's WNAC-TV, *Coffee with the Kennedys*, hosted by Rose and featuring appearances by the candidate and his sisters. Seated on a plain living room couch, the matriarch welcomed viewers and talked about her family, explaining why she believed her son's qualities made him ideally suited to represent Massachusetts in the U.S. Senate. She spoke of his childhood accomplishments, his early interest in politics and history, and the invaluable experience he gained from his extensive travels across Europe while his father served as ambassador to Britain. Then the program shifted to the congressman's campaign headquarters and shots of two or three of the Kennedy sisters at work. Viewers were invited to call in toll-free with questions for the candidate, and the show finished with Jack fielding the queries and asking those with cars to volunteer to drive fellow voters to the polls on Election Day. Not content to simply air the programs, the campaign organized five thousand viewing parties across the state, with each host—almost invariably a woman—encouraged to invite ten to fifteen friends over to watch the shows.[54]

Sensing trouble, Lodge redoubled his efforts in the final weeks, working sixteen-hour days and hitting every corner of the state, only to find that wherever he went, Jack Kennedy had been there before him, greeting workers at the factory gate, chatting with patrons at the diner, lining up volunteers.[55] A later estimate suggested that Kennedy shook five hands for every one that Lodge shook. The incumbent nonetheless took encouragement from his own touring—from the mood at his events and from the size of the crowds. And, in truth, many voters liked both candidates, who seemed so alike in so many ways, including in their political centrism. "People, even Democrats, would say to you, 'Gosh, isn't it too bad he's running against Lodge, because we need both of them,'" Dave Powers remembered. "Lodge had the same kind of reputation, he was the same type of man as Jack Kennedy. He was a Republican Jack Kennedy. Some people called Jack Kennedy a Democratic Henry Cabot Lodge. People in Massachusetts felt we need them both and it was a shame that one of them had to fall by the wayside."[56] Even seasoned journalists saw little daylight between the two men on core issues, especially in foreign policy, and there was no mistaking the broad similarity in their campaigning styles: a focus on the issues and on being quietly approachable, an avoidance of gutter politics or personal invective.

The candidates even shared a common problem: how to handle Joseph McCarthy. The firebrand senator remained a formidable if controversial figure in American politics as he cruised toward reelection in Wisconsin. Over the previous two years he had perfected what one reporter would call his "unique distortion technique": stating as facts a set of fictitious claims, then doubling down on these "facts" when challenged.[57] McCarthyite tactics were again commonplace that fall, with Republican candidates using the slogan K1C2—Korea, Communism, and Corruption—to pummel Democrats. Nixon took a leading role in the assault, and even Eisenhower dabbled in red-baiting. At the urging of aides, who feared offending McCarthy on his home turf, Eisenhower removed from a speech in Milwaukee a tribute to his mentor General George Marshall's "profoundest patriotism" in "the service of America." (McCarthy, it will be recalled, had accused Marshall of treason in a lengthy Senate speech the previous summer.) But Ike kept in the Milwaukee address passages that might well have come from the senator's own mouth. Two decades of laxity about Communism reaching high levels in Washington, he exclaimed, had meant "contamination in some degree of virtually every department, every agency, every bureau, every section of our government. It meant a government by men whose very brains were confused by the opiate of this deceit," causing the loss of China and the "surrender of whole nations" in Eastern Europe. At home, meanwhile, acceptance of Communism had allowed policy decisions to be made by "men who sneered and scoffed" at the threat, allowing "its most ugly triumph—treason itself."[58]

Lodge, for his part, disliked McCarthy personally and loathed his demagogic tactics, but he knew full well that McCarthy had broad support among Massachusetts's three-quarters of a million Irish Catholics, many of whom loved his brash style and brazen tactics. So, like Eisenhower, the senator moved carefully, avoiding overt criticism while keeping McCarthy at arm's distance. When McCarthy offered to come to the Bay State to help the campaign in the interests of party unity, Lodge was inclined to accept, until he heard the condition: he himself must publicly ask McCarthy to come. "I cracked that one," McCarthy crowed to conservative backer William F. Buckley Jr. "I told [the Lodge campaign] I'd go up to Boston to speak if Cabot publicly asked me. And he'll never do that—he'd lose the Harvard vote."[59]

But what if Lodge changed his mind? What if he determined that the Harvard vote mattered far less to him than the Irish vote? That was the Kennedy team's consuming fear. For that matter, Jack faced his own delicate dilemma on the issue, even though McCarthy was from the opposing party and had virtually no history with Massachusetts. He was a friend of the family, for one thing; he got on well with Joe Kennedy in particular. For another, there were too many votes to be lost in going after him, especially in "Southie" (South Boston) but also in other urban areas of the state. Yet embracing the Wisconsin senator risked losing the support of liberals, intellectuals, and labor leaders. When Adlai Stevenson, soon to arrive for a campaign swing through Massachusetts, asked Sargent Shriver how he could best help Kennedy's cause, Shriver requested three things: that Stevenson tell voters of Jack's support for the liberal aspects of Truman's Fair Deal; that he emphasize Jack's willingness to stake out principled and courageous policy positions, including on behalf of the black residents of Washington, D.C.; and that he refrain from attacking Joe McCarthy. The stronger Jack appeared on Communism and subversion, Shriver said, the better his chances of peeling away support from Republicans upset with Lodge for undermining Robert Taft's candidacy. And besides, McCarthy was very popular in the state, including among

Kennedy with Adlai Stevenson in the final days of the campaign.
Seated behind them is Governor Dever.

Democrats. "Up here this anticommunist business is a good thing to emphasize," Shriver remarked.[60]

Jack didn't share his father's enthusiasm for McCarthy, but he saw only pitfalls in publicly opposing him. In February 1952, well before he knew which statewide office he'd be seeking that autumn, Jack had attended a reunion of the Spee Club at Harvard. When a speaker congratulated the university for not producing either an Alger Hiss (though he was in fact a graduate of the law school) or a Joe McCarthy, Jack reportedly objected that only Hiss, a convicted traitor, deserved such opprobrium. Yet it's clear that Jack's views were changing that winter. His Far Eastern trip of the previous fall had made him skeptical of claims that Communist gains overseas somehow derived from the duplicity or incompetence of Americans; his subsequent interactions with his state's influential academic community deepened these doubts while simultaneously impressing on him how widespread was the disdain on the campuses for what was coming to be called McCarthyism. Privately, Jack told friends that McCarthy was "just another shanty Irish" who would contaminate any politician who drew close to him. He resolved to keep his distance.[61]

The standoffish approach did not endear Kennedy to the state's Jewish voters, deeply distrustful of McCarthy and already wary of Jack because of his father's presumed anti-Semitism. (In July 1949, *The Jewish Weekly*

Times, responding to the State Department's release of papers delineating Ambassador Kennedy's meetings with his Nazi German counterpart in London, Herbert Von Dirksen, in 1938, had placed the correspondence under the headline "German Documents Allege Kennedy Held Anti-Semitic Views.") Jewish leaders implored Jack to denounce the Wisconsin senator, but he refused to budge. "I told you before, I am opposed to McCarthy," he told Phil Fine, his chief liaison with the Jewish community. "I don't like the way he does business, but I'm running for office here, and while I may be able to get x number of votes because I say I'm opposed to him, I am going to lose . . . two times x by saying that I am opposed. I am telling you, and you have to have faith in me, that at the proper time I'll do the proper thing."[62] A series of meetings with community leaders followed, as well as campaign events in Jewish neighborhoods, and there emerged a "Friends Committee" to back Jack's candidacy. At one dinner, sponsored by the committee and held at the Boston Club, Jack told the heavily Jewish audience of three hundred of his 1951 visit to Israel and his meeting with Ben-Gurion, and of his pro-Israel voting record in the House. Sensing lingering doubts in the room, he asked, "What more do you want? Remember, *I'm* running for the Senate, not my father." It was the firm declaration his audience had been waiting for, and the room erupted in applause.[63]

Right up until Election Day, the Kennedy camp fretted that Lodge would get his miracle: he and McCarthy would magically surface together at a triumphant rally, arms raised in tandem, generating headlines and causing significant Irish Catholic defections from their man to the incumbent. Anecdotal evidence suggests that Joe Kennedy may have taken matters into his own hands, either by calling McCarthy personally and asking him not to campaign for Lodge or by having columnist Westbrook Pegler phone on his behalf. Joe may also have sent several thousand dollars to the Wisconsin senator, who had recently undergone a pricey medical operation and was supposedly almost broke. (Jack Kennedy later denied that his father sought assistance from McCarthy.)[64] This intervention, if indeed it occurred, doesn't appear to have been decisive, at least judging by the later testimony of Lodge, who insisted it was he and not Joe Kennedy who was most responsible for keeping McCarthy out of the state. Lodge told McCarthy biographer David Oshinsky that at the eleventh hour he had in fact asked him "whether he would come into Massachusetts and campaign against Kennedy *without* mentioning me in any way. He told me that he couldn't do this. He would endorse me but he would say nothing against the son of Joe Kennedy. I told McCarthy 'thanks but no thanks.' So he never did come into Massachusetts."*65

Lodge made this last-ditch appeal to McCarthy because of what the internal polling told him in the dying days of the campaign: he was behind. Eisenhower had opened a big lead over Stevenson among Massachusetts voters, and Christian Herter was closing fast on Paul Dever in the governor's race, but he himself lagged behind his challenger. Every indicator said so. With the McCarthy option gone, he had to hope for two things: that some undecideds would "come home" to the incumbent and that he might yet ride Eisenhower's coattails. The game was not lost. But he knew he had to keep up the pressure, and to focus his campaigning on Boston, where, if he could cut substantially into Kennedy's all-but-certain plurality, he could give himself a chance, since the rest of the state should go Republican, if narrowly. (Three-quarters of the state's 4.6 million inhabitants lived within a forty-mile radius of the city.)66 After Kennedy jabbed him for his voting record in Congress—an audacious claim, given the congressman's own absenteeism—Lodge said he and Kennedy were "away from Washington in 1952, but with different purposes. One difference is that I was away working to put Eisenhower in the White House, whereas he was away campaigning for himself in Massachusetts." The senator was puzzled, he remarked some days later, by the challenger's slogan that he would do "More for Massachusetts": "I wonder if he means he will do many of the things he should have done and failed to do in Congress." Kennedy "had a magnificent opportunity to aid our state and failed miserably," sitting "sheeplike" as he waited "for the Administration to tell him when and how to vote during the past six years, while I sponsored 91 legislative proposals—32 of which became law."67

This line of attack seemed to resonate with voters, much to Team Kennedy's chagrin. It raised the alarming prospect that Lodge was finding his footing for the sprint run. No less concerning was the growing evidence of trouble in Stevenson's presidential campaign—if he got blown out nationally, he might take Jack down with him.

---

* The campaign had even drafted a speech for the Wisconsin man to deliver, stressing Lodge's anti-Communist credentials. "Lodge has never sought publicity for himself," read one passage, "but I want you people of Massachusetts to know whenever anything came up having to do with the communist menace, he was one man we could turn to with complete confidence who would not only say he was opposed to communism but would actually take off his coat and go to work." (Reel 18, Henry Cabot Lodge Papers II.)

Stevenson had looked formidable early on, in the immediate aftermath of the party convention, impressing political insiders and ordinary voters with his probity, eloquence, and wit. (At one rally, a supporter hollered, "Governor Stevenson, you have the vote of all the thinking people," to which he answered, "That's not enough, madam. I need a majority.") Balding and bug-eyed, he projected a warm, civilized, professorial air, and combined high-mindedness and self-deprecation in a powerfully appealing way. But he also possessed a lofty disdain for politics that, though initially part of his appeal, created problems as the campaign progressed. Glad-handing seemed to Stevenson crass and undignified—after one long day on the trail he complained to a friend, "Perhaps the saddest part of all this is that a candidate must reach into a sea of hands, grasp one, not knowing whose it is, and say, 'I'm glad to meet you,' realizing that he hasn't and probably never will meet that man."[68] Even with a stable of formidable speechwriters such as Archibald MacLeish, John Hersey, Bernard DeVoto, and Arthur Schlesinger Jr., Stevenson thought nothing of personally reworking each text, agonizing over passages, keeping audiences waiting, even letting them disperse, until he felt ready. He could be querulous and indecisive and was disdainful of political advertising and of the new technologies—he hated television and shunned teleprompters. Worse, although Stevenson's cultivated approach worked wonders with liberals and others who thrilled to his elegant, epigrammatic phrase-making and his idealized picture of an America characterized by virtue and reason, he struggled to reach a sufficiently broad constellation of voters. By the end of October, only die-hard supporters gave their man a fighting chance of victory against the war hero turned politician.

Though neither man knew it in the fall of 1952, Jack Kennedy and Adlai Stevenson, fellow Choate graduates (Stevenson was Class of 1918), would become central characters in each other's political careers for the rest of their days.

VI

With Kennedy and Lodge trading blows in a final grassroots blitz—they visited residential neighborhoods and local shopping centers, even rang doorbells, in a desperate effort to gain the edge—the conservative *Boston Post*, which everyone believed would back the GOP candidates for statewide office, stunned the chattering classes by endorsing Jack Kennedy and Paul Dever in a front-page editorial. Publisher John Fox, a flamboyant self-made millionaire who had bought the struggling paper the year before and taken it in a sharp rightward direction editorially, cited Jack's firm anti-Communism as a principal reason for the endorsement, but he was also annoyed by Lodge's failure to reach out to him, and by the refusal of either Robert Taft or Joe McCarthy to publicly support the senator. After drafting the endorsement, Fox tried without success to reach Jack Kennedy. He got ahold of the candidate's father and they met for a drink on the eve of publication. Joe was overcome with joy upon hearing the news, Fox recalled, and asked if there was anything he could do in return. Fox explained the *Post*'s financial woes and—it emerged years afterwards—received a half-million-dollar loan from the Kennedy patriarch right then and there. In later years, both men vigorously denied the suggestion of a quid pro quo. It was a purely commercial transaction, Joe Kennedy insisted, repaid with interest in sixty days.[69]

Then, suddenly, a Lodge lifeline: Eisenhower's headquarters announced that the general would wind up his national campaign in Massachusetts, with a glittering all-star extravaganza at the Boston Garden on election eve. The news caused acute distress among Kennedy staffers—a rousing rally featuring the GOP standard-bearer would surely swing many undecided voters over to Lodge's side, especially as Eisenhower seemed set to sweep the state in the presidential vote. Lodge was thrilled, but the event, though a raucous and energizing affair, did not go quite as he'd hoped. Slated to introduce Eisenhower, he spent hours polishing his remarks, but so rapturous and lengthy was the ovation for the supreme Allied commander when he arrived onstage that it forced cancellation of Lodge's introduction for fear of running overtime with the networks. Lodge was left to smile stoically on the stage and to ponder what might have been. "We couldn't understand what happened to you, that you didn't introduce the General at the most important time," one dejected Lodge backer told him afterwards.[70]

On Election Day, November 4, Kennedy projected quiet confidence, even joking with his friend Torby Macdonald about which job the defeated Lodge might be offered in Eisenhower's administration. Inside, though, his stomach churned—his mother wrote in her memoirs that one of the few times she could recall seeing her son "really nervous was on election night '52." He kept pacing from room to room, kept taking his jacket on and off, she recalled. Still, the candidate told aides that they had run the best race they could and were in a strong position to take down the supposedly invincible Lodge. "I can't think of anything we could have done that we haven't," he said.[71]

With nothing left to do but wait and hope, the aides wondered among themselves about the unknowns. How much of a difference had Eisenhower's grand Garden party the previous night made? Would the dramatic *Boston Post* announcement shift a lot of votes their way, or were people's minds already made up? How much would the spadework done on Jack's behalf in the rural areas of the state matter? Would he rack up a big enough plurality in metropolitan Boston to overcome Lodge's margins elsewhere? Would Dever's evident weakening since the summer be a drag on Jack's candidacy?

The early Boston returns that evening looked good for the challenger, but when reports came in showing Eisenhower running up high margins in Lynn and Brockton, the Kennedy team grew apprehensive. "Whatever initial optimism had existed disappeared immediately," Kenny O'Donnell recalled.[72] By 11:00 P.M. it was clear that Eisenhower would sweep the state by at least 200,000 votes, a figure that placed the entire Democratic ticket in jeopardy. Jack, getting pessimistic reports in his Bowdoin Street apartment from his father and his father's cronies, called Bobby. It looked worryingly close, Bobby agreed, but he urged his brother to focus on the campaign's own chief internal metric: Jack's vote totals as compared with Truman's in 1948. Here the numbers remained promising, Bobby said—they showed Jack running even or ahead of where Truman was then, including in the rural areas, whereas both Dever and Stevenson ran behind the president's 1948 numbers. Still, Bobby conceded, the outlook was uncertain. Around midnight, *Boston Globe* reporter John Barry appeared on television to announce that, on the basis of current projections, it was "definite" that Dever had been defeated for governor and Kennedy had also lost.[73]

The candidate grabbed his coat and walked the short distance to headquarters. He wanted to see the internal data for himself. "There we stood," O'Donnell recalled of the moment when Kennedy strode in, "resplendent in our shirts: smelly, sweaty, ties pulled down or off, sleeves rolled up; the air replete with stale coffee, even staler donuts; cigarette and cigar smoke." Jack, surveying the scene, deadpanned, "If this is what victory looks like, I'd hate to see defeat." He sat down on a metal chair and began to run the numbers, silently and determinedly. His brother, he soon could see, hadn't been lying: they might yet pull this off.[74]

At three o'clock in the morning, Dever's campaign called to say that on the basis of their computations, both men had lost. The Kennedy team replied that *their* calculations showed Jack winning narrowly. But it was the most disheartening moment of the evening, O'Donnell remembered, "because Dever was not the type of fellow that threw things off lightheartedly."[75] To compound the worry, media reports were agreeing with the governor, though in circumspect language that left wiggle room. Little by little, Bobby remembered, campaign staff began shuffling out of headquarters; by 4:00 A.M. only a handful remained. Then, when the Worcester returns came in, showing Jack with a small but clear win there (by five thousand votes), shouts of jubilation rang out, for it meant Lodge was running out of places to turn the tide. Not many votes remained to be counted. Staffers began trickling back in, their mood expectant. As dawn approached, the Kennedy forces no longer had a doubt: their man had prevailed.[76]

Lodge, however, seemed in no hurry to concede, which caused renewed consternation: Did he know something they didn't know? Did he have some additional returns up his sleeve? Was there a mistake in the count?

At seven thirty, some Kennedy staffers stationed at the windows at Kilby Street spotted the tall, straight-backed patrician exiting his nearby headquarters. "Everyone be polite to him," Jack Kennedy instructed. "Give him a hand when he comes in." The Republican never arrived; he got into a waiting limousine and sped right past the Kennedy command post. Jack fumed in disgust at the perceived slight ("Son of a bitch," he muttered, "can you believe it?"), but only momentarily. Lodge's concession arrived via telegram at 7:34, removing all doubt. Victory had come. John F. Kennedy had won a seat in the United States Senate.[77]

The final tally told the tale: Kennedy 1,211,984 (51.35 percent), Lodge, 1,141,247 (48.35 percent). Seventy-one thousand votes separated them, about the same number that attended the Kennedy teas. The challenger also racked up large majorities in Boston's black wards. In the governor's race, Dever lost narrowly to Herter, while in the presidential contest Eisenhower thumped Stevenson both nationally and in Massachusetts. (Ominously for Democrats, Eisenhower won three southern states that Republicans had claimed only once since Reconstruction: Texas, Florida, and Virginia.) The GOP also took control of both houses of Congress. On a grim night for Democrats nationally, one that brought their party's twenty-year reign to a crashing end, Jack Kennedy stood out as a beacon of light.[78]

How had he done it? In such a close race, any number of things could be called decisive—Lodge's late start; the Taft forces' lack of assistance to him; the Ambassador's money; the teas; the *Coffee with the Kennedys* programs; the Kennedy "ground game" (to use the later phrase) utilizing thousands of volunteers—but surely it mattered greatly that the candidate waged a determined "pre-campaign campaign," working over a period of years to build up his name recognition throughout the state and visiting every one of its 351 towns (as well as 175 of its factories and firms). According to Kenny O'Donnell, the small communities were indeed *the* key, as Kennedy consistently ran four or five or six percentage points ahead of Stevenson and Dever there. "And the margin of victory really came right there. The little communities where we had spent all this time, and all this work and met personally all these people, was paying off right at this moment. He was resisting the Eisenhower tide throughout the rest of the Commonwealth." Even in the senator's own stomping grounds, Essex County, Kennedy fought him to a draw.[79]

Then there was Robert Kennedy, who came on board at a critical moment and proved his worth in spades. The brothers were different men— different in age, in disposition, in outlook. Jack was more secure, more independent; Bobby was tougher, more committed to the family. Jack saw the gray areas of life, partly on account of his experience in war; Bobby thought in absolutes, in the dualism of light and dark. Jack was smoother, calmer, more given to understatement; Bobby, more intense and aggressive—he had the louder bark of the two. Jack had gotten on better with their father, Bobby with their mother, and the result was, as so often, contradictory. "Bobby was more like his father," said Justice William O. Douglas, who interacted a good deal with the brothers in this period, "and Jack was more like his mother. . . . Bobby was more direct, dynamic, energizing; Jack was more thoughtful, more scholarly, more reflective." Yet the bond between them, fully evident on their grand overseas journey the previous year, was unmistakable, and in the campaign they were beautifully in sync, as friends and campaign workers perceived from day one.

Jack understood the vital importance of having a political partner on whom he could count completely, 100 percent of the time, for loyalty, hard work, and results; he got one in his brother.[80]

"The Kennedy campaign in 1952 was the most nearly perfect political campaign I've ever seen," recalled Larry O'Brien, who saw more than a few. "It was a model campaign because it had to be. Jack Kennedy was the only man in Massachusetts who had the remotest chance of beating Henry Cabot Lodge that year and Kennedy couldn't have won without an exceptional political effort."[81] It wasn't just about the effort, of course, as O'Brien well knew—the candidate mattered, too. People who heard Kennedy speak, who took in the debates or the *Coffee with the Kennedys* specials, who knew of his wartime service and his famous family, were drawn to him; that's clear from countless testimonials at the time and later, and from the crush of volunteers who descended on Kilby Street every day, asking how they could help. As reporter Paul Healy pointed out in *The Saturday Evening Post* a few months after the election, Lodge was skillful and respected, with an "impeccable Massachusetts name and an excellent combat war record," but Kennedy had these things plus an additional quality: "He made people want to do something for him." On the campaign trail, every woman wanted "either to mother him or marry him," Healy wrote. One Boston woman, who was deemed illogical for voting for both Eisenhower and Kennedy, replied, "Ah, now, how could I vote against that nice lad?" A Republican observer grumbled, "What is there about Kennedy that makes every Catholic girl in Boston between eighteen and twenty-eight think it's a holy crusade to get him elected?"[82]

Healy hinted at something else that may have played to Kennedy's advantage: his natural diffidence, which saved him from appearing glib and which was deceptive, in that it hid his shrewdness and his limitless drive. Or, as O'Brien put it, "He could not be called a natural politician. He was too reserved, too private a person by nature. But he knew what he wanted and he would force himself to do whatever was necessary to achieve it."[83]

There was yet one more thing that made the Lodge-Kennedy election of 1952 extraordinary, at the time and in hindsight: the degree to which the Kennedy campaign exemplified a new kind of personalized politics, carefully crafted to enhance the candidate's image, relying on massive and varied uses of media, including television, and eschewing close collaboration with other campaigns (as Paul Dever learned to his frustration). Sophisticated advertising, targeting particular audiences at particular times, was a prime feature, as was internal polling conducted by professionals. If the Kennedys were not the first to utilize these elements, they strategized about them and honed them in ways few had done before. Which took resources. Though historians often exaggerate the role of money in the 1952 Massachusetts race—total expenditures were probably no greater than those of many other Senate contests around the country that year, in part because the Democratic campaign relied so heavily on volunteer labor and had relatively few paid positions—there's no doubt that the Kennedy team exploited the Ambassador's riches to undertake these pioneering efforts, and over many more months than was the norm at the time. (In 1952 political veterans scoffed at the Kennedys for opening a campaign headquarters so early, six months before the election; nobody ever sneered at such a move again.)[84]

The Sunday following the election, Kennedy appeared on *Meet the Press*, roughly a year after his much heralded debut on the show. Host Lawrence Spivak commended him on his "sensational victory," which seemed especially astonishing in view of Eisenhower's landslide presidential win. Spivak said the win had brought his guest to "national attention as the most important Democratic figure in New England," and he asked him how he'd pulled it off. "I worked a lot harder in Massachusetts than did Senator Lodge," Kennedy replied. "He was working for General Eisenhower and I think that he felt that would take care of his Massachusetts position."[85]

He basked in his win, as well he might. He was on his way back to Capitol Hill, but in a new role, a bigger role. Great things were in store, he sensed, and maybe not just professionally: in the hurly-burly of the campaign he had begun dating a woman he first met at a dinner party the year before, and he was sufficiently smitten to ask aide Dave Powers if he thought a twelve-year age gap between a man and a woman was too much. On the contrary, Powers had replied, his own fiancée was twelve years *his* junior. Powers, knowing his man, suspected Jack Kennedy had the answer to his question before he posed it.[86]

JACKIE

er name was Jacqueline Lee Bouvier. He first met her in the spring of 1951, at a dinner party in Georgetown. She was a freshly minted college graduate just shy of her twenty-second birthday, he a third-term congressman who would soon turn thirty-four. Charles Bartlett, their host for the evening along with his wife, Martha, had tried to introduce them even before that, at his brother's Long Island wedding in 1948; that effort had failed, as Kennedy left the reception early.[1] This time the encounter came off. Details of the dinner are lost to history, but at the end of the evening, as they stood by Jackie's car, the congressman asked shyly, "Shall we go somewhere for a drink?" Before she could answer, they both spotted, lurking in the back seat of the automobile, a handsome young Wall Street broker named John Husted, whom Jackie had been dating. Evidently he had come to surprise her and drive her home. Jack immediately withdrew, and that seemed the end of that.[2]

The Bartletts, however, were nothing if not persistent. (They were "shameless in their matchmaking," Jackie would recall.) Later that year, at Christmas, they concocted another meeting, this time in Palm Beach, where the Bartletts were visiting the Kennedys and where Jackie and her mother and stepfather were vacationing; if a rendezvous occurred, it was fleeting. Then, in the spring of 1952, upon learning that Jackie had broken off an engagement to Husted, they again invited her and Jack to a dinner party in their home, to take place on the evening of May 8. It would be the key date in their relationship. Jackie would subsequently say that she sensed immediately that Jack "would have a profound, perhaps disturbing" influence on her life. She also got the strong impression that "here was a man who did not want to marry." Jackie told a friend she was frightened, envisioning heartbreak for herself, but swiftly determined that such a heartbreak would be worth it. Kennedy's recollection was plainer: "I leaned across the asparagus and asked for a date."[3]

Kennedy family lore has it that Jack was enamored from the start. "My brother really was smitten with her right from the very beginning when he first met her at dinner," youngest sibling Ted remarked. "Members of the family knew right away that she was very special to him, and saw the developing of their relationship. I remember her coming up to Cape Cod at that time and involving herself in the life of the family. He was fascinated by her intelligence; they read together, painted together, enjoyed good conversation together and walks together." Lem Billings, who over the years had probably met more of Jack's girlfriends than anyone and who became a kind of connoisseur of the relationship, said he "knew right away that Jackie was different from the other girls Jack had been dating. She was more intelligent, more literary, more substantial."[4]

Still, the two saw little of each other in the early going, on account of his all-consuming Senate race. She paid a visit or two to Hyannis Port and tagged along on a couple of his campaign events (in Fall River and Quincy), and they caught an occasional movie on his brief trips to Washington for legislative business. That was it for the six months or so after the May 8 Bartlett dinner, though they compensated with phone calls—aides recalled seeing the candidate, after a long day on the hustings, disappear into a phone booth to dial her number. "He'd call me from some oyster bar up there, with a great clinking of coins, to ask me out to the movies the following Wednesday in Washington," Jackie said. Though she preferred French films, she catered to his preferences. "He loved Westerns and Civil War pictures. He was not the flowers-and-candy type, so every now and then he gave me a book—*The Raven*, which is the life of Sam Houston, and also *Pilgrim's Way*, by John Buchan." She reciprocated with books on French history or poetry.[5]

With Jack's election victory in early November, the pair rapidly made up for lost time, enough so that by mid-December the society columns could report that "rich dunkers who drop in for a dip at Joseph P. Kennedy's Palm Beach swimming pool will be surprised if they don't see Jacqueline Bouvier's shapely form at poolside this winter." There was speculation that a wedding of the dashing senator-elect and the luminous Miss Bouvier could well be in the offing.[6]

One wonders if Joseph Kennedy—never shy about using his extensive press contacts to spread advantageous news—was behind these stories, which appeared suspiciously fast after the election. The Ambassador had long believed his son's political future depended on his settling down and getting married. To remain single beyond one's mid-thirties was to invite questions about one's seriousness and maturity, and about one's sexuality. Given Jack's established reputation as a ladies' man, it's hard to imag-

Jack and Jackie in Washington, D.C., during their courtship.
Ethel Kennedy, Bobby's wife, is in front.

ine anyone believing he stayed unattached because he was homosexual, but Joe didn't want to take any chances. More to the point, in his mind—and, it seems, his son's as well—American voters expected their prominent politicians to have wives, to show a personal commitment to the nuclear family, to uphold, or at least appear to uphold, the traditional values of Middle America. On the stump in 1952, Jack murmured to aides that if he won the race he would seek to get married in relatively short order. Jackie Bouvier, beautiful and genteel and educated, and Catholic to boot, met the criteria. Plus Joe Kennedy approved of her.

II

Yet for all the political calculation that may have lurked in Jack's mind, the evidence is powerful that he was genuinely taken with Jackie, if not quite as head-over-heels besotted as he had been with Inga Arvad a decade before. "I've never met anyone like her," he told Dave Powers early on. "She's different from any girl I know."[7] Not exuberant and noisy, like his sisters, or overtly sexy, like many of his girlfriends, Jackie was coolly reserved in a way he loved. She didn't take herself too seriously yet was intelligent and tough, and she carried herself with assurance and elegance and refinement. She was gorgeous, too, in an enchantingly exotic way, with wide-set eyes and full lips, and she had an innate sense of style that he appreciated all the more for not having it himself (though it was probably no coincidence that, as his aides noticed, he began in the weeks after meeting Jackie to pay more attention to his appearance and his attire, to the cut of his suits and the fit of his shirts). Her sense of humor was similar to his, he thought, and she had a sense of irony that he found especially delightful. Plus she shared his love of gossip and his attraction to the Old World—her place was France, his Britain.[8] Never good with foreign languages himself, it awed him that she spoke superb French and excellent Spanish, and could get by in German, too. To top it off, she shared his interest in books. "Jack appreciated her," Chuck Spalding later said. "He really brightened when she appeared. You could see it in his eyes. He'd follow her around the room watching to see what she'd do next. Jackie interested him, which wasn't true of many women."[9]

For her part, Jackie loved Jack's looks and, even more, his quick wit and keen intelligence, his sense of the absurd, his appreciation for history and the written word. It impressed her that someone so young could write a well-received book about the road to war in Europe, and her opinion rose further after Jack presented her with an inscribed copy of *Why England Slept*—she gobbled it up right away, then read it again. His emotional reserve, which might have turned off another woman, seems for Jackie to have been a source of comfort. She herself could be remote, and she might have been, as one biographer has suggested, "put off rather than swept away by an ardent, articulate lover who offered too much too enthusiastically and therefore deserved or demanded the same in return."[10] Though she didn't share Jack's interest in politics, she appreciated his willingness to poke fun at the hypocrisies and pretensions that were so much a part of his chosen profession, his skill at deflating the pomposities of the moment.

His innate curiosity captivated her. "The luckiest thing I used to think about him," she remarked later, "was whatever you were interested in, Jack got interested in. . . . When I was reading all this eighteenth century, he'd snatch a book from me and read and know all of Louis XV's mistresses before I would." People fascinated him, and he had an appreciation for excellence in human endeavor—for virtuosity in performance, whatever the field—that Jackie admired and shared. At dinner parties, she said, Jack asked lots of questions, unlike the other politicians present, who would generally talk only about themselves.[11]

Then again, it's possible Jackie never would have given her suitor a second look if it hadn't been for another element in the equation: his wealth. Even though she had grown up in relative privilege in New York—in a Park Avenue duplex and an East Hampton summer home—money was often tight in the Bouvier household. Even after her mother's second marriage dramatically improved her financial position, Jackie was acutely conscious of the fact that she had no wealth of her own. Her mother reinforced this feeling. "He doesn't have *real* money," Janet Bouvier would sniff about this or that potential beau for Jackie, including John Husted. She could not say the same thing about Jack Kennedy. "Jack was exciting, there was that raw sexuality of his," said reporter Nancy Dickerson, who dated him on occasion. "But you've got to remember that at the time nobody was thinking of him as presidential material. As handsome and attractive as he was, there were plenty of other attractive, powerful men in Washington. There just weren't any with as much money as Jack."[12]

Of course, with Jack came not only his money but also his close-knit and ebullient family. Jackie formed an early bond with the Ambassador—in time he would become her favorite in the family other than Jack—and maintained a polite but wary relationship with Rose, but she struggled to connect with the younger Kennedy women, including Robert's wife, Ethel, who, with her rambunctious competitiveness, struck many as being "more Kennedy than the Kennedys." Their boisterousness was of a type Jackie had never encountered before, and it didn't help that they poked fun at her wispy, baby-doll voice and her demure and refined manners, or that they chuckled at her bringing pâté, quiche, and wine to an afternoon sail while they took peanut butter sandwiches. They called her "the deb," as in *debutante,* and mimicked her behind her back, determined to poke fun at what they saw as her superior attitude; she reciprocated by referring to them as "the rah-rah girls." Though physically stronger and more coordinated than is often suggested, Jackie puzzled over the intense family focus on sporting events (in the huddle of a touch football game on the family lawn, she said to one of Jack's aides, "Just tell me one thing: when I get the ball, which way do I run?"), and she gave her sister Lee a stinging account of the Kennedys' proclivity for games in which they "fell all over each other like gorillas."* Even at mealtimes, she noticed, the Kennedys seemed to be competing over who would say the most and talk the loudest. Jack, in a classic understatement, said his girl-friend was "sensitive by contrast to my sisters who are direct and energetic."[13]

During the cacophonous family dinners, Jackie usually kept quiet. "A penny for your thoughts," Jack once asked her, and the room fell silent with anticipation. "If I told them to you, they wouldn't be mine, would they, Jack?"[14]

"Jackie was certainly very bored by politics and very bored by the very aggressive camaraderie of the Kennedy family, [which was] absolutely foreign to her nature," said Alastair Forbes later. "Fortunately, I think, she also spotted that it was really foreign to Jack's nature. He was loyal to his

---

* A visitor to Hyannis Port spoke of participating in fourteen athletic events in one day, including sailing, waterskiing (twice), touch football (twice), tennis (twice), trampoline jumping, swimming, jogging on the beach, and baseball. He also mentioned eating a sandwich with sand in it. His efforts, he added, put him "something like only three events behind Ethel." (Martin, *Hero for Our Time,* 76.)

family . . . but he was of them and *not* of them." He was more sensitive than they were, Jackie determined, and less extroverted.[15]

Mutual acquaintances spotted another thing they had in common: they were competitive, including with each other. Early in the relationship, they often played Monopoly or Chinese checkers or word games such as Categories, at which Jack often excelled. It burned him and intrigued him when she held her own and sometimes bested him in these contests. (In Scrabble, she proved almost unbeatable.) "From the beginning there was a playful element between them," Lem Billings recalled. "Jackie gave him a good match: that's one of the things Jack liked. But there was a serious element too. Who was going to win?"[16]

"He saw her as a kindred spirit," Billings went on. "I think he understood that the two of them were alike. They had both taken circumstances that weren't the best in the world when they were younger and learned how to make themselves up as they went along."[17] Their pasts, that is to say, affected them in complex ways. Jackie didn't have Jack's health problems growing up, but she and her younger sister, Lee, endured a trying childhood in a dysfunctional family environment. Their parents, John Vernou Bouvier III, a flamboyant New York Stock Exchange member who claimed to trace his lineage to French soldiers who fought in the American Revolutionary War, and Janet Bouvier (née Lee), the daughter of a self-made millionaire, engaged in frequent alcohol-fueled fights over his serial womanizing and chronic financial failings. Then each would badmouth the other in front of the girls. We can only speculate about the effect of this behavior on the daughters; to a degree, at least, Jackie seems to have responded by retreating from the world and from other people. She found escape and refuge in books and horses, competing from an early age in equestrian competitions and even winning two events in the junior ranks at the equestrian national championships at Madison Square Garden.

Jack Bouvier, whose French immigrant ancestors in Philadelphia had experienced anti-Catholic prejudice not unlike that endured by County Wexford's Patrick Kennedy, was as charismatic as he was erratic. With the dark good looks and pencil-style mustache of Clark Gable, he was vain and self-absorbed. He exercised in the gym regularly and used a sunlamp to stay tan, and didn't mind at all when he acquired nicknames that bespoke his playboy ways—the Black Orchid, the Black Sheik, and, most commonly, Black Jack. By all accounts he was terrific company, a raconteur and bon vivant whose lecherous ways had compensating qualities, at least in the eyes of some women. "Bouvier was unusual among the philanderers of his day," one of his paramours said. "Women were not just collectibles for him. He actually liked their company, liked the feminine perspective and the social quality of women's lives." Both of his daughters felt closer to him than to their mother, even after Jack and Janet divorced and she married Hugh D. "Hughdie" Auchincloss, a kindly, serene Episcopalian and Standard Oil heir from Virginia. Janet, a social striver of the first order, had a fierce temper; she often took out her frustrations on her daughters, in particular Jackie, faulting her looks and clothing choices. Even Jackie's studiousness and love of books came in for rebuke— like many women of her class and period, Janet lived by the philosophy that men frowned on women who had their own intellectual interests and professional goals; accordingly, her daughters should cultivate the skills required to make men feel comfortable and important, and direct their own ambitions toward being effective homemakers.[18]

"All the fighting had an impact on both girls, of course," said Truman Capote, who got to know both Bouvier sisters and became especially close with Lee. "It made them both terribly cautious, a little afraid of people and relationships in general. . . . Even at that age, I think [Jackie] could appreciate that her mother was this sort of hideous control freak, a cold fish with social ambitions, and her father was a naughty, naughty boy who kept getting caught with his hand in the cookie jar. Of course, both girls loved him more. Who wouldn't, given the choice?"[19]

According to biographer Barbara Leaming, Jackie internalized many of her mother's harshest judgments about her—she was too tall, at five foot seven, too dark, too flat-chested, too boyish in figure. "In view of what Janet insisted was her utter lack of

Young Jacqueline with her parents at the Southampton Riding and Hunt Club's sixth annual Horse Show, August 1934.

physical allure, she cultivated seductive mannerisms such as a whispery, baby voice. . . . She trained herself to behave in an extremely flirtatious manner and presented herself as a fragile airhead, the antithesis of the strong, clever, curious young woman she really was."[20]

At fifteen, Jackie was enrolled at Miss Porter's School, in Farmington, Connecticut, one of the most respected finishing schools in New England, which still operated by its founding philosophy of a century before, that the core purpose of a young woman's education was to make her a more pleasing companion to her husband. Jackie chafed against this culture— in the school's yearbook she listed her ambition in life as "Not to be a housewife"—but only to a degree: she did not appear to question, either then or in the years that followed, the notion that it should be a chief goal in life to "marry well," or the corollary idea that a woman should live life through her man and make his successes her own.[21] A strong student, Jackie maintained an A-minus average and also involved herself in the drama and riding clubs and helped edit the school newspaper. But she also treasured solitude: when the other girls socialized after evening study hall, her roommate remembered, "Jackie seldom joined in, happily staying in her room, reading, writing poetry or drawing . . . by nature she was a loner."[22]

From Miss Porter's she moved on to Vassar College, in Poughkeepsie, New York, but not before being presented to society in Newport, Rhode Island, where the Auchinclosses maintained an estate. ("Queen Deb of the Year," wrote one New York society columnist, "is Jacqueline Bouvier, a regal brunette who has classic features and the daintiness of a Dresden porcelain. She has poise, is soft-spoken and intelligent, everything the leading debutante should be.")[23] At Vassar, Jackie, part of an entering class of approximately two hundred women, took courses in literature and history and joined the college newspaper staff, the drama group (as a costume designer), and the art club. Well liked by the other students, she could also be secretive, projecting a sense of apartness, even aloofness. "You never knew what she was thinking or what she was really feeling," one classmate said.[24]

The sense of mystery may have added to her allure among college men, who came calling with regularity. "Young men were constantly trying every kind of trick to make her go out with them," said Letitia Baldrige, who had been a year ahead of Jackie at Miss Porter's and would continue to know her in the decades to come (including as White House social secretary). "Her classic good looks were complemented by her sense of style, which had been apparent from her early teens." She would put on a simple skirt and shirt, add just the right belt, and, with her perfect posture and bearing, come off exquisite, Baldrige marveled. "Nothing ever looked wrong on her." But though Jackie accepted a number of dates—she went to football games and dances at Princeton, Yale, and Harvard, among other places—she avoided committing herself. When returning from a date with a young man in a taxi, she would tell the driver, "Hold your meter." Crestfallen escorts realized they would not get beyond the front door.[25]

Jackie didn't take to Vassar—she thought it hidebound and provincial—but she loved her junior year in France, in 1949–50, most of which she spent in Paris, studying French history and art history at the Sorbonne. All the instruction was in French. It thrilled her, she reflected afterwards, that here she didn't have to cloak her smarts or the fact that she had genuine intellectual interests, but she also led a full social life, venturing out on an almost nightly basis from her rented room on avenue Mozart, in the fashionable if slightly stuffy sixteenth arrondissement, sipping coffee or wine at the Ritz Bar or Café de Flore or La Coupole and hitting the nightspots on both banks of the Seine until all hours. She frequented the museums and galleries, the opera and the ballet. Her French, middling at the outset, became fluent. She also went on dates, seeing a French diplomat's son as well as an aspiring young writer named Ormonde de Kay and, some accounts say, losing her virginity in an elevator to a dashing young American writer, John P. Marquand Jr., son of the novelist. (The elevator to his apartment supposedly "stalled" between floors, a trick Marquand had used with women before her.)[26]

Jackie did not return to Vassar for senior year. She sought a more urban environment and transferred to George Washington University, from which she graduated in 1951 with a degree in French literature. She then explored, intriguingly, a job with the CIA, but either she did not pursue it or she was not granted an interview. Instead, she entered and won *Vogue* magazine's Prix de Paris contest for excellence in design and editorial ability, besting twelve hundred other entrants for the grand prize and the chance to live and work for the magazine in Paris.*[27] She turned down

---

* Her application essay showed her talent for writing and her self-deprecating sense of humor—and her mother's stifling influence: "I am tall, 5' 7" with brown hair, a square face, and eyes so unfortunately far apart that it takes three weeks to have a pair of glasses made

the award—her mother and stepfather felt she had already spent too much time abroad, and she herself worried that if she went she might never come back—and instead took a position with the *Washington Times-Herald* (where Inga Arvad had also worked) as the "Inquiring Camera Girl" who asked people lighthearted questions and took their photograph. ("Winston Churchill once observed that marriages have a better chance of survival when the spouses don't breakfast together. Do you agree?" "Should men wear wedding rings?" "If you had a date with Marilyn Monroe, what would you talk about?" "Would you like your son to grow up to be president?") Her weekly starting salary was $42.50; within a few months the figure rose to $56.75. On one occasion, she made the newly elected senator from Massachusetts her subject, snapping his photo and posting his answer to a question concerning the role of pages (assistants) in the work of the Senate.[28]

III

And so it was that John F. Kennedy appeared at Dwight Eisenhower's inaugural ball, on January 20, 1953, with Jacqueline Bouvier on his arm. It was a heady time to be in the nation's capital, and the new senator relished every minute. From the start, he found the clubby, collegial atmosphere of the Senate preferable to the rowdier, more plebeian spirit of the House of Representatives. The emphasis in the upper chamber on decorum, on tradition, on gentility appealed to his temperament and his historical sensibility. Here had walked the legislative giants he'd read about since boyhood—Clay, Webster, La Follette, and all the rest. Here had been hammered out many of the key policy decisions in the nation's history, especially during the long era when Congress held greater sway over policy than did the executive branch. That era of congressional supremacy had long since waned, yet even now Kennedy could expect to have much

---

with a bridge wide enough to fit over my nose. I do not have a sensational figure but can look slim if I pick the right clothes. I flatter myself on being able at times to walk out of the house looking like the poor man's Paris copy, but often my mother will run up and inform me that my left stocking seam is crooked or the right-hand top coat button is about to fall off. This, I realize, is the Unforgivable Sin." In a supplemental essay discussing three people she wished she had known, she chose Baudelaire, Oscar Wilde, and Ballets Russes founder Serge Diaghilev. (Prix de Paris application materials, box 1, JKO personal papers.)

more visibility as a senator than he ever could have hoped to achieve in the House, especially in the realm of foreign affairs.[29] If sporadically in the past he had been able to rub elbows with the highest-placed people in government, in the judiciary, and in the press, now he would be doing so on a regular basis, no longer as the Ambassador's son who had used his family's riches to acquire a House seat but as his own man—the intrepid wonder candidate who had stood against the Republican wave of 1952 and taken down the mighty Henry Cabot Lodge Jr.

His star, to be sure, had dimmed somewhat in the weeks since his monster win. He was still seen as a standout in an otherwise lackluster roster of new Democrats on the Hill, but the contemporaneous record shows few predictions of greatness either from within the party establishment or from the national press. Observers of an intellectual stripe questioned Kennedy's liberal credentials and his silence on McCarthyism, while others wondered about his Catholicism and how much it could shackle his ambitions. Skeptics in the mainstream press asked about the extent of his father's influence, mused about the role that his family wealth had played in his victory, and wondered what it said about him that he seemingly relied so heavily on female voters drawn by his youthful look and radiant smile.[30]

On his first day in the Senate, as he took his seat in the last row of the Democratic phalanx, Kennedy could see to his right the articulate and fiery Hubert H. Humphrey of Minnesota, now starting his fifth year in office, and, directly in front, the widely respected liberal Paul H. Douglas of Illinois, also beginning his fifth year. Not far away was yet another member of that class of 1948, the hulking and fleshy-faced new minority leader, Lyndon B. Johnson of Texas, and two courtly southerners, Richard Russell of Georgia, first elected in 1932, and J. William Fulbright, from the class of 1944. And in the distance, over the heads of the Democratic caucus, Jack could spot the dark jowls of his fellow House freshman from 1947, Richard M. Nixon, who, as the new vice president, served in the role of president of the Senate. As he gazed around the room, Jack knew he was a peon next to these men, a minnow among whales. He knew that the Senate's hierarchical structure, based on seniority and committee chairmanships and reputation, sharply limited his capacity for influence in the early going and perhaps beyond. But no matter: he was here, in the chamber, with a seat of his own.[31]

Some Kennedy associates who hoped to move up with him were disappointed. They learned what others before them had come to know: that with the Kennedys, loyalty went only so far. Tony Galluccio, a friend from Harvard days who had trekked all over Massachusetts for a year and a half on Jack's behalf, doing yeoman's work to help set up the statewide campaign apparatus and enduring endless bus rides and lousy restaurant meals in the process, expected now to have the chance to serve in the Washington office; it seemed a just reward for all he had done in the campaign. Weeks went by with no word. Finally Jack called him, but not with the hoped-for news. "I've got no money," the senator told him.[32]

Kennedy's secretary, Mary Davis, who'd been with him since he arrived in Congress six years before and regularly worked seven days a week, including from home on Sundays, found him unexpectedly resistant when she asked for a pay increase commensurate with a shift to a larger office in which she would have increased responsibilities. Currently, she reminded him, she was being paid $4,000 a year, and a freshman congressman from New York was offering her $6,000; would he match it? No, Kennedy replied, he would only go to $4,800. Nor would he agree to pay the new team of junior secretaries Davis had recruited to assist her in the office more than $60 a week.

She couldn't believe her ears. "Sixty dollars a week! You've got to be joking. Nobody I've lined up would be willing to accept a job at that salary. I have to have competent, capable staff who can back me up. If I don't, I won't have a life to call my own."

"Mary, you can get candy dippers in Charlestown for fifty dollars a week."

"Yes, and you'd have candy dippers on your senatorial staff who wouldn't know beans. If that's what you want, I'm not taking charge of it."

Back and forth they went, neither willing to budge. Davis thought it only right that she and the rest of the staff be paid the going rate for Senate office employees; Kennedy, having been urged by his father to keep a tight lid on office expenditures, disagreed. For him, as for the Ambassador, staffers were ultimately employees who could be replaced. Those who pressed to be compensated according to market rates were insufficiently loyal and should go. Mary Davis went.[33]

One of the hopefuls for a position in the office that January was a twenty-four-year-old attorney from Nebraska named Theodore Sorensen. Tall and intense, with a square face and horn-rimmed glasses, Sorensen hailed from a progressive, politically active family in Lincoln—his Danish American father, a close ally of U.S. Senator George Norris, had served two terms as a crusading state attorney general and made an unsuccessful bid for governor; his mother, a descendant of Russian Jews, was a suffragist deeply involved with progressive causes and the League of Women Voters. Young Ted, who was named for Theodore Roosevelt and shared a birthday with Harry Truman, starred on his high school debate team, made Phi Beta Kappa at the University of Nebraska, and then graduated first in his class from the university's law school, where he also edited the law review. Having come, as a friend commented, "campaigning from the womb," he worked in local Democratic campaigns and was active in the civil rights movement, even helping to found a chapter of the Congress of Racial Equality (CORE) in Nebraska. He also got married, to a woman named Camilla Palmer, who in short order bore him the first of three sons. But America's political mecca beckoned, and Sorensen soon relocated his young family to Washington and set about making his mark. Initially a lawyer with the Federal Security Agency, he gravitated to Capitol Hill and took a job as counsel to a minor congressional committee. From there he followed the 1952 election with rapt attention. The Democrats' poor showing dismayed him, but he was intrigued and impressed by the young victor in Massachusetts, and as the year turned he made his approach.

Kennedy liked what he saw in the application, especially a letter of reference that praised Sorensen's "ability to write in clear and understandable language," and also referred to him as a "sincere liberal, but not one that always carries a chip on his shoulder." A strong liberal voice from the nation's heartland could be useful to have around, Kennedy surmised, as he worked to establish a more national profile. There followed two interviews, the first a five-minute encounter outside the senator's office during which Kennedy would offer the job, of which Sorensen would write, "In that brief exchange, I was struck by this unpretentious, even ordinary man with his extraordinary background, a wealthy family, a Harvard education, and a heroic war record. He did not try to impress me with his importance; he just seemed like a good guy."[34]

But Sorensen had a nagging question, one he felt compelled to raise in the second meeting: Why had the senator to this point in his career been so elliptical about McCarthy and McCarthyism? If Jack was taken aback by the forthright query, he didn't show it, calmly responding that while he didn't accept Joe McCarthy's tactics or find merit in all of his charges, he was in a tough spot, in view of McCarthy's close ties with the Kennedy family and the widespread support he enjoyed among Irish Catholic voters in Massachusetts. Good enough, Sorensen decided. He also had an offer to join the staff of Senator Henry "Scoop" Jackson of Washington, but he knew what he would do: he would hitch his wagon to the young Democratic star from New England.[35]

The result would be one of the most extraordinary partnerships in modern American political history. From the start, the two men simply clicked. Kennedy liked Sorensen's cerebral approach; even more, he liked the pragmatic streak that ran through his liberalism. The young aide's definition of himself as someone moved less by sentimental than intellectual persuasion could have come from the senator himself; ditto Sorensen's corollary assertion that "the liberal who is rationally committed is more reliable than the liberal who is emotionally committed." A tireless worker willing to put aside everything to advance Kennedy's career (including the needs of his wife and children), Sorensen became a kind of alter ego to the senator, soon superseding in influence Ted Reardon, who had been tapped to run the Senate office just as he had the House operation.[36] He was that rarest of creatures: an aide who could work on the nitty-gritty of policy and also articulate the details in speeches and articles—the latter all under the senator's name alone—with simple fluency and grace. Soon it became hard to determine who had produced what, though one can think of them as the composer (Kennedy) and the lyricist (Sorensen). They were the Rodgers and Hart of politics. At twenty-four, and without the world exposure of his boss, Sorensen had neither the political experience nor the life experience to conceive the broad themes of speeches and articles—especially when they concerned foreign policy—but he was a quick study and a brilliant mimic, uncannily adept at finding just the historical allusion Kennedy wanted to express, the almost Churchillian cadences and spare language that embodied the senator's view of exemplary political rhetoric.[37]

It wasn't mimicry alone, though. From the moment Sorensen arrived, Jack Kennedy's speeches took on a new flavor, combining greater range and power and concision. They became more lyrical, more memorable, less burdened with data and detail. The two men quickly settled on a basic pattern, in which the senator laid out—often by dictating to a secretary—what he wanted to get across in a speech (or an article) and Sorensen produced a draft that Kennedy would then edit. Sorensen would polish some more and Kennedy would tweak yet again, often right up until he stepped behind the lectern. Frequently he would make further changes on the fly, during the actual address. (He would, in time, become an expert improviser, able to speak in full paragraphs even when departing from his text.) Long fascinated with the art of rhetoric and the secrets of superior orators, Kennedy would listen to recordings of Churchill and study the speeches of Lincoln, then talk with Sorensen about what he'd learned. He read and recommended to others a book Sorensen gave him, *A Treasury of the World's Great Speeches*. Often Sorensen would plant himself in the front row during a Kennedy address, making notes on the delivery and the audience reaction, seeing what worked and what didn't, then offer his suggestions for improvement. Kennedy never seemed put off by even tough appraisals, Sorensen noticed; he later wrote of the senator's "calm acceptance of criticism."[38]

For all the close collaboration between the two men, theirs was a purely working relationship. They didn't socialize; they never became pals as such. Sorensen learned immediately that here, as elsewhere, his boss was a champion compartmentalizer. Always deeply loyal in his friendships—from Choate, Harvard, the Navy—Kennedy saw his staff as employees. Reardon, who had been with Kennedy long enough to know how he worked, summed up the dynamic: "Jack had the ability to have guys around him whom, personally, he didn't give a damn about as a buddy . . . but he was able to get what he needed from them." Sorensen was okay with this arrangement—or at least claimed he was. "The times we were together socially over the eleven years we worked together were few enough that I can remember each one," he wrote near the end of his life. But "I never wanted to be JFK's drinking buddy; I wanted to be his trusted advisor. I felt lucky to have that role." Not for several years did Sorensen feel comfortable enough to address him as "Jack" instead of "Senator."[39]

Ruthless though he could be in "getting what he needed" from his staff, the senator also had a more forgiving side. As his personal secretary he brought on forty-year-old Evelyn Lincoln, another Nebraskan. "Mrs. Lincoln," as Jack always addressed her, was the daughter of a two-term Democratic member of the U.S. House of Representatives. Like Sorensen, she had ventured east to Washington, earning her degree at GWU and marrying Harold "Abe" Lincoln, a political scientist. Seeing in Kennedy a star in the making, she volunteered in his congressional office in 1952 (while also holding down a full-time clerical position in the office of a Georgia representative); then, after his Senate win, he hired her.

The learning curve, she soon learned, was steep. She struggled to decipher Kennedy's "dreadful handwriting" and to cope with his restlessness and carelessness. He couldn't sit still while dictating but would pace back and forth or swing a golf club or wander from one room to another, without ever slowing down his torrent of words. Clothing articles and briefcases would be left in hotel rooms and train stations; Lincoln, like Mary Davis before her, would call around until the wayward item was found. The senator would jot down telephone numbers on tiny scraps of paper, then not be able to find the right one when he emptied his pockets on his desk and scratched around in the pile. He would call out, " 'Mrs. Lincoln, what's Tom's number?' More often than not, I didn't even know who Tom was, much less where I might find his number."[40]

Lincoln impressed Jack with her devotion, patience, and capacity for hard work, but he questioned whether she had the capacity to manage the important phone calls and correspondence flooding the office. He talked to Sorensen about firing her, but each day Lincoln kept showing up at her desk, and she would continue to do so for the next decade, including in the White House. Her fidelity never wavered. Kennedy took notice and became devoted to her. He later told Sorensen, "If I had said just now, 'Mrs. Lincoln, I have cut off Jackie's head, would you please send over a box?' she still would have replied, 'That's wonderful. I'll send it right away. Did you get your nap?' "[41]

IV

The question for the new senator was how he might make his mark. As a member of the traditionally inactive freshman class, he had few outlets for influence, and it didn't help that he was left off the five most prestigious committees—Foreign Relations, Armed Services, Appropriations, Judiciary, and Finance. Instead he had to make do with two others: Labor and Public Welfare as well as Government Operations (the latter now under the chairmanship of one Joseph R. McCarthy). In both entities, Kennedy would be on the lowest rung of the ladder, as the junior member of the minority party. He resolved that his first effort would be directed at formulating an economic program for Massachusetts and the broader New England region, which made sense, given that the question of who could do more for Massachusetts had been a prime point of contention between him and Lodge. Sorensen, who knew little about the subject, flew to Boston to confer with a coterie of experts, among them Seymour Harris, a Harvard economist, and Jim Landis, the lean and laconic former Harvard Law School dean who now worked full-time for Joe Kennedy and who had contributed position papers to the Senate campaign.

There soon emerged an ambitious set of more than three dozen proposals for regional economic expansion, which Jack Kennedy laid out in three carefully crafted and extremely dry speeches—each lasting more than two hours—in the spring of 1953, under the collective title "The Economic Problems of New England: A Program for Congressional Action." He painted a picture of a region rich in history and accomplishment, now facing challenges on various fronts, not least from industries moving to southern states in search of cheaper, nonunion labor. (In the past seven years in Massachusetts alone, he noted, seventy textile mills had either closed or moved south, with the attendant loss of 28,000 jobs.) Its fisheries and forests, meanwhile, were being depleted. Kennedy called for a concerted effort to diversify and expand commercial activity throughout New England and to prevent further business relocations through tax incentives; expanded opportunities for job retraining; a higher minimum wage (from seventy-five cents to one dollar per hour); and better housing programs for the middle class. The federal government's role in the revitalization of the region was limited but crucial—Washington, he said, had to ensure "the preservation of fair competition in an expanding economy."[42]

Sorensen proved his extraordinary worth in these Senate speeches, and also in drafting, under Kennedy's name, several articles in leading publications—which got the senator's name before a broad reading audience. Thus, "What's the Matter with New England?" appeared in *The New York Times Magazine*, and "New England and the South" followed in *The Atlantic Monthly*. The latter piece denied any desire on the senator's part to initiate a regional economic war but insisted on the need for policies promoting the "stability and integrity of our entire national economy." Competition among parts of the United States should occur in the context of a "fair struggle based on natural advantages and natural resources, not exploiting conditions and circumstances that tend to depress rather than elevate the economic welfare of the nation."[43]

In foreign policy, Kennedy's junior status gave him fewer opportunities to enter the conversation, even though the first seven months of 1953 witnessed major developments overseas. First, in March, came shocking news out of Moscow: Joseph Stalin had died. His passing brought claims from various quarters—including Britain, where Winston Churchill had returned to power—that the opportunity existed for a less confrontational relationship with the new Kremlin leadership, whatever its makeup. Dwight Eisenhower and his secretary of state, the dour and seasoned John Foster Dulles, were unmoved. They saw little to be gained, in either international or domestic political terms, from seeking a grand Cold War compromise with the Soviets. At a meeting of Western leaders late in the year, Eisenhower generated nervous smiles from the Europeans with his coarse description of the new, post-Stalin Soviet Union: Russia, he declared, was "a woman of the streets, and whether her dress was new, or just the old one patched, it was certainly the same whore underneath."[44]

At the same time, Eisenhower and Dulles understood that "liberating" Communist-held lands was a tough assignment now that the division of Europe seemed a largely settled affair. Campaign-trail calls for an outright Cold War victory would have to be scaled back. But the two men agreed that a new policy—or at least a new name—would be needed to replace Truman's "Containment," which was identified in their minds and the minds of voters with Truman's ineffectual China policy and with the stalemated struggle in Korea. They called their strategy the New Look, and it emphasized airpower and nuclear weaponry over large-scale conventional forces, in part because of Eisenhower's desire to trim the federal budget ("more bang for the buck," as the saying went). Spurred by the successful test of the world's first hydrogen bomb, in November 1952, Ike oversaw a massive stockpiling of nuclear weapons—from twelve hundred at the start of his presidency to 22,229 at the end.[45]

Stalin's death had another important effect in world affairs: it breathed life into the stalled Korean War negotiations, leading to an armistice agreement in July 1953. The border between North and South was established near the thirty-eighth parallel, the prewar boundary, and a demilitarized zone was created between the two halves. Three years of bloody fighting came to an end. American casualties totaled 54,246 dead and 103,284 wounded. Close to five million Asians perished in the war—two million North Korean civilians and half a million soldiers; one million South Korean civilians and 100,000 soldiers; and at least one million Chinese troops—making it one of the bloodiest wars of the century.[46]

Domestically in the United States, Korea had large-scale consequences. The failure to win a swift victory and the public's impatience with a stalemated struggle undoubtedly helped Eisenhower and hurt Stevenson in the 1952 campaign. The war also enhanced presidential power vis-à-vis Congress as lawmakers repeatedly deferred to the White House. (Truman never asked Congress for a declaration of war, believing that, as commander in chief, he had broad authority to commit troops wherever he wished. His successors would follow this precedent.)[47] In addition, the war, which began in the throes of the "Who lost China?" controversy, inflamed American party politics. Republican legislators, including the party leadership, accused Truman and his aides of being "soft on communism" in failing first to head off the struggle and then to go full bore to win it; their rhetorical assault strengthened the Truman team's determination to take an unyielding position in the talks.

The impact on foreign policy was greater still. The Sino-American hostility fueled by the fighting ensured that there would be no rapprochement between Beijing and Washington, and that South Korea and Taiwan would become recipients of large-scale U.S. assistance. The alliance with Japan strengthened, and Washington signed a mutual defense deal with Australia and New Zealand. The U.S. Army, which grew from a postwar low of 591,000 troops to more than 1.5 million troops, dispatched four divisions to Europe, and the Truman administration launched plans to rearm West Germany. Finally, the Korean War convinced the president to do what he had refused to do before the outbreak of hostilities: approve a vast increase in military spending. Indeed, the military budget shot up from $14 billion in 1949 to $52.8 billion in 1953; it went down after the Korean armistice, but never to its prewar levels; it stayed between $42 billion and $49 billion per year through the 1950s.[48] Soviet leaders vowed to match this military buildup, and the result was a major arms race between the two nations. By the time John F. Kennedy entered the Senate, therefore, American foreign policy had been globalized and militarized in a way scarcely imaginable half a dozen years before, when he took his seat in the House.

Kennedy had no qualms with Eisenhower's resolute Cold War policy. He had long since grasped what every savvy, enterprising politician in midcentury America understood: that staunch anti-Communism was the only viable posture in domestic political terms. Preaching the need for accommodation with Moscow or Beijing might make intellectual sense, might be shrewd geopolitics, but it posed grave risks for one's career— why take the chance? Much better to vow eternal vigilance, to condemn any hint of compromise.[49] What's more, Kennedy genuinely believed in the existence of a Soviet threat, even after Stalin's death; he needed no convincing that the Western powers must remain united and resolute, with Washington in the lead role. "We are in truth the last hope on earth," he told the Boston College Varsity Club. "If we do not stand firm in the midst of the conflicting tides of neutralism, resignation, isolation, and indifference, then all will be lost." Yet Kennedy was no fire-breathing Cold Warrior—in the sense of seeing the struggle against the Soviets as primarily a military one—and he continued in 1953 to question, as he had over the previous two years, America's approach to the burgeoning anti-colonial struggles in Asia and Africa. Already now, in the early 1950s, he intuited the central importance of what would later be called "soft power"—the ability to attract and persuade, without force or coercion.[50]

The war in Indochina, which had made such an impression on him during his visit there in 1951, was of special interest. Kennedy followed press accounts of the fighting closely, and consulted occasionally with people such as Edmund Gullion, the former U.S. consular officer in Saigon whose dismal analysis had resonated with him during the visit. He even had Jackie translate some French-language reports for him.[51] Since his visit, the war had continued to go badly for the French, even as the United States steadily raised the level of its material support, with bombers, cargo planes, tanks, naval craft, trucks, automatic weapons, small arms and ammunition, radios, and hospital and engineering equipment, as well as financial aid, which flowed heavily. (Graham Greene, who wintered in Saigon in the early 1950s and could see the growing U.S. presence with his own eyes, opens his classic novel *The Quiet American*, set in Indochina in 1952, with the narrator, Fowler, seeing "the lamps burning where they had disembarked the new American planes.") By early 1953, with popular disenchantment rising at home, leaders in Paris began quietly considering a negotiated settlement to the war, only to be told by the Americans, in so many words: *You must stay in.*[52]

Kennedy saw little or no chance that the war effort as currently constituted would succeed, a view encouraged by Gullion. Outside of the main cities, Ho Chi Minh's forces were gaining in strength; even in the urban areas, support for the French and their Vietnamese allies was soft. Unless and until the French turned over real power—financial, military, political—to the Vietnamese, there could be no lasting victory. Even that might not be enough, Kennedy conceded, but it represented an essential first step. In April he asked Priscilla Johnson (later Priscilla Johnson McMillan), a research assistant, to look into French spending in Indochina (he suspected, correctly, it turned out, that it was directed overwhelmingly to the military campaign) and to examine whether the French were any closer to giving over meaningful governmental control to the non-Communist Vietnamese. (They were not, Johnson determined.) Armed with her report, the senator, in early May, privately told John Foster Dulles that the United States should take a firm line with the French, insisting that the further granting of U.S. aid be dependent on changes that would give "the native populations . . . the feeling that they have not been given the shadow of independence but its substance."[53]

There was power in this argument, as Dulles knew. That spring, the administration leaned hard on the French to press the war effort *and* promise "full independence" to the "Associated States" of Vietnam, Cambodia, and Laos, only to encounter the inevitable French response: Why should France continue to fight a bloody military struggle if the ultimate result would be the abandonment of French interests in Southeast Asia? The Americans had no good answer to this question, either then or in the year that followed, and therefore backed off, accepting vague French assurances that independence would come only at some unspecified point in the future. The logical conclusion might be that no satisfactory military solution therefore existed and that Washington should instead urge a negotiated settlement on whatever terms possible, but Jack Kennedy did not go there, at least not yet. In the spring of 1953, when the anti-Communist Vietnamese nationalist Ngo Dinh Diem visited Washington, Kennedy met with him and came away impressed—maybe, just maybe, Diem could be the figure around whom a democratic nation could be built. Through the summer and into fall, the senator continued to advocate coupling American assistance with French efforts at genuine democratic reforms, but he stopped short of urging a firm ultimatum: no aid without concrete evidence of real reform. He suggested instead that U.S.

assistance "be administered in such a way as to encourage through all available means the freedom and independence desired by the peoples of the Associated States."[54]

The irony was hard to miss: although the United States had placed its credibility behind the French war effort, providing an ever-growing amount of military assistance, victory for colonial forces seemed further away than ever. Therefore, the senator stressed, all future American assistance should be tied to granting independence and thereby generating support among the Indochinese people, who presently were deeply apathetic vis-à-vis the war effort—and for good reason. Without broad popular support, no effort at defeating Ho's revolution could ever have a chance of succeeding.[55]

V

The courtship of Jack and Jackie, meanwhile, continued apace, and early that same summer of 1953 he proposed. Details are murky, but it seems he popped the question over the transatlantic telephone, while Jackie was in England covering the coronation of Queen Elizabeth II and after he had received permission from Jack Bouvier. (Earlier he had sent her a telegram: ARTICLES EXCELLENT, BUT YOU ARE MISSED. LOVE, JACK.) She coyly replied that she would give him her answer soon. Upon her return, Jack met her plane and presented her with a 2.88-carat diamond engagement ring, set with a 2.84-carat emerald, from Van Cleef & Arpels. She said yes, but there are hints that she had hesitated, at least briefly. After the initial phone call, it seems she darted off to Paris from London to see John Marquand and to renew their dalliance for a few days. She wondered whether she could ever truly fit in with the Kennedy family, wondered what life as a politician's wife would be like, with the exhausting campaigns, the intrusive press attention, the endless stream of dinners not with artists or writers or musicians or other interesting people but with politicians and their spouses.[56]

No doubt, too, she wondered about her man's reputation as a womanizer. Already the previous year, soon after they began dating, she'd speculated in a letter, "He's like my father in a way—loves the chase and is bored with the conquest—and once married needs proof he's still attractive, so flirts with other women and resents you. I saw how that nearly killed

Mummy."[57] Then, in January 1953, Lem Billings had taken her aside one evening to tell her what it seems she already knew. "I told her that night that I thought she ought to realize that Jack was thirty-five years old," Lem later said, "had been around an awful lot all his life, had known many, many girls—this sounds like an awfully disloyal friend saying these things—that she was going to have to be very understanding at the beginning, that he had really never settled down with one girl before, and that a man of thirty-five is very difficult to live with. She was very understanding about it and accepted everything I said." (One wonders: did the still-closeted Billings, who treasured his friendship with Jack above all else, who had been in love with him twenty years before and perhaps still was, see her as a rival for Jack's time and affection?)[58]

Chuck Spalding went further. As he saw it, Jackie was not merely understanding about Jack's ways; his peccadilloes "made her *more* interested in him," made him more captivating, more like her father. "Dangerous men excited her. There was that element of danger in Jack Kennedy, without doubt." In another interview, Spalding said Jackie "wasn't sexually attracted to men unless they were dangerous like old Black Jack. It was one of those terribly obvious Freudian situations. We all talked about it—even Jack, who didn't particularly go for Freud but said that Jackie had a 'father crush.' What was surprising was that Jackie, who was so intelligent in other things, didn't seem to have a clue about this one."[59] For her, a recent biographer echoes, those attributes that some women would regard as deal breakers only made Jack more appealing: "She thought him excitingly unconventional and unpredictable, full of angles and surprises, in the way that her father had been. And if, like Black Jack Bouvier, Jack Kennedy was also a little dangerous, so much the better; at least he was not bland and boring like the fellow she had almost married." Moreover, after enduring years of criticism from her mother about every aspect of her appearance, it was to Jackie only a plus that she was now being wooed by one of America's most eligible bachelors, a reputed playboy who had been linked to screen stars, heiresses, and a host of other desirable women.[60]

If this seems overstated—is it really plausible that Jackie welcomed her suitor's rakish ways?—it may at least be said that she accepted what lay in store. The chronic womanizing of the father she adored had conditioned her expectations of men, had led her to believe they were congenitally inclined to infidelity. They weren't being consciously cruel in this cheating, to her mind; it was merely one of the fixed laws of nature. When, during her London visit, a male acquaintance cautioned her to beware of Jack Kennedy's roving eye, she shrugged him off. "All men are like that," she told him. "Just look at my father." Or, she might have added, just look at Jack's father, hardly a shining example of virtue. In her essay for the *Vogue* Prix de Paris competition, Jackie had quoted Oscar Wilde: "The only difference between a saint and a sinner is that every saint has a past and every sinner has a future."[61] Perhaps, too, some part of her thought she could change Jack, or that the mere fact of being betrothed would change him. Whatever the case, she expressed delight at her engagement, soon telling friends and relatives she couldn't wait to wed her man.[62]

An early call was to her father's sister. "Aunt Maudie, I just want you to know that I'm engaged to Jack Kennedy," Jackie said. "But you can't tell anyone for a while because it wouldn't be fair to the *Saturday Evening Post*." A puzzled Aunt Maudie asked why. "The *Post* is coming out tomorrow with an article on Jack," she explained, "and the title is on the cover. It's 'Jack Kennedy—the Senate's Gay Young Bachelor.'" Jack had known for weeks of the impending publication, but he was unhappy when he saw the piece, by Paul F. Healy, with its description of a swashbuckling lawmaker with a "bumper crop of lightly combed brown hair that shoots over his right eyebrow and always makes him look as though he just stepped out of the shower," and who liked nothing more than to dash around Washington in "his long convertible, hatless and with the car's top down," a glamorous woman by his side. This was not exactly the statesmanlike image Jack wanted to convey, and it troubled him that Healy gave scant indication that his subject had another side—serious-minded, reflective, knowledgeable about policy matters, especially relating to international affairs. The article irritated Jack, and confirmed in him the wisdom of getting married without delay.[63]

Jackie, notwithstanding her guarded relations with her mother-in-law-to-be, penned a touching letter to Rose in her distinctive, stylish handwriting. "It seems to me that very few people have been able to create what you have—a family built on love and loyalty and gaiety. If I can even come close to that with Jack I will be very happy. If you ever see me going wrong I hope you will tell me—because I know you would never find fault unless fault was there."[64]

The engagement was announced on June 24, 1953, and trumpeted in

The young couple being interviewed by mass-circulation *Life* magazine in Hyannis Port at the time of their June 1953 engagement. The accompanying article, which included a major photo spread, appeared in July under the title "*Life* Goes Courting with a U.S. Senator."

newspapers all across the country. SENATOR LOSES BACHELORHOOD TO CAMERA GAL, read the headline in the *New York Daily News*. "Come September, the Senate's gay young bachelor will be no more," began the accompanying article. "Hopeful debutantes from Washington to Boston, from Palm Beach to Hollywood, can begin unpacking their hope chests." EXIT PRINCE CHARMING, echoed the *Boston Herald*. "Yesterday was a difficult time for American women . . ." *The New York Times* published photos of the couple to accompany its story, while in *Time*'s formulation, Senator Kennedy had become "engaged to sultry Socialite Jacqueline Bouvier, 23, onetime *Washington Times-Herald* Inquiring Photographer."[65] Engagement parties followed in Hyannis Port and at Hammersmith Farm, the Auchinclosses' magnificent waterfront estate in Newport, with its vast gardens designed by Frederick Law Olmsted and a main house boasting a dozen full baths and an equal number of fireplaces.* The wedding, to take place in Newport, was set for September 12.

Jack remarked perceptively to his friend Red Fay that he was both "too young and too old" to marry. He was too young because he did not yet feel ready to fully quit his bachelor ways. He was too old in that, at thirty-six, he was stuck in his ways, a creature of habit whose practices could not be fully altered merely because of a ceremony in a chapel. He knew, moreover, as he acknowledged to Fay, the degree to which his electoral successes depended on his appeal to women. "This means the end of a promising political career as it has been based up to now almost entirely on the old sex appeal."[66]

Throughout the courtship, he kept on seeing other women. Often Evelyn Lincoln assisted with the arrangements. "He was a playboy, all right," she remembered. "I never saw anything like it. Women were calling all the time, day and night. I more or less organized the ones he wanted to deal with. I'd call them up, tell them where they were to meet him for dinner, that sort of thing." But Jack never asked her to call Jackie. "When he didn't ask me to call her, I knew she had to be someone special."[67]

When Jack and Torbert Macdonald headed to the French Riviera for a brief jaunt a few weeks before the wedding, his father—of all people—worried that Jack might get "restless" about his marriage and thereby land himself in trouble. "I am hoping that he will . . . be especially mindful of whom he sees," Joe Kennedy wrote to Macdonald, who was married and had his own reasons to tread carefully. "Certainly one can't take anything for granted since he became a United States Senator. That is a price he should be willing to pay and gladly."[68] Whether Macdonald passed on the message is not known, but the two men clearly partied hard on their rented yacht and on shore. In Cap d'Antibes one day, Jack ran into a British friend who introduced him to a pair of Swedish women in their early

---

* The Hyannis Port party was the more rambunctious of the two. Among the activities was a scavenger hunt in which first prize went to whoever brought back the largest object. Patricia Kennedy went into Hyannis, hot-wired a bus, and drove it home. (Perret, *Jack*, 192.)

twenties. They double-dated that evening, Jack being paired with Gunilla von Post, a strikingly pretty, petite blonde from a moneyed family, who bore more than a passing resemblance to his former Nordic love Inga Arvad. They danced and talked, learning about each other's families, whereupon Jack offered to drive von Post to Cap-Eden-Roc, where he had spent memorable time in his youth. In her own telling, there they sat together until deep into the night, looking out into the Mediterranean as a warm breeze blew. At one point they kissed and "my breath was taken away," she said later. And it was easy to talk with him: "When he asked questions, he really seemed interested in the answers."[69]

"I'm going back to the United States next week to get married," Gunilla recalled Jack suddenly saying. In her memory, he then told her that if he had met her even a week earlier, he would have "canceled the whole thing." If indeed he said this, it seems impossible to believe he truly meant it, given what scrapping the wedding could have meant for his life and career. But perhaps he was swept up in the moment, entranced by the woman next to him and acutely conscious that his bachelor days, his days of freedom in the pursuit of pleasure, were coming to an end. When he dropped her off, he asked if he could come in for a nightcap. She refused ("No, my dear Jack, I only want to wish you good luck, and that everything works out for you"), and he drove off.[70]

VI

In Janet Bouvier's mind, her daughter's wedding should be a sophisticated, sedate affair, away from the flash of cameras. The groom's father had other ideas. This would be the social event of the season, Joseph Kennedy insisted, and his word went, for he was paying for the affair, not Hughdie Auchincloss and not Black Jack Bouvier. He wanted to extract maximum publicity out of the celebration, make it something like the big Hollywood productions he used to finance. As such, the guest list for the ceremony, set for St. Mary's Church, a brownstone Gothic Revival structure dating to 1849, would include close to six hundred people (the chapel would seat no more); for the reception at Hammersmith Farm, it would top twelve hundred. Joe Kennedy, who flew to Newport on July 12 to finalize the arrangements with Janet, ordered six hundred bottles of champagne and a four-foot-high, five-tiered wedding cake, and had his press operation arrange for extensive coverage in major papers, including *The New York Times* and *The Washington Post*.

The patriarch clearly remained a dominant presence in his children's lives, even as they moved deep into adulthood. Just as Joe dictated major elements of the Newport extravaganza, leaving the bride and groom—and the bride's parents—on the sidelines, so had he done with daughter Eunice's wedding to Sargent Shriver, earlier in the year. (It took a decade of wooing, but Shriver at last won his bride.) Here, too, the Ambassador went all out, arranging for the ceremony to take place in St. Patrick's Cathedral in Manhattan, with Francis Cardinal Spellman officiating, and for the reception for seventeen hundred guests to follow in the Grand Ballroom of the Waldorf Astoria. "I found a man who is as much like my father as possible," Eunice revealingly told the wedding guests. Fittingly, the *Boston Globe* photograph of the event was not of the newlyweds but of the bride and her father.[71]

The Kennedy-Bouvier festivities in Newport began a few days before the wedding, with a cocktail party in honor of the bridal couple, followed the next evening by a black-tie bachelor party for eighteen given by Hughdie Auchincloss at the Clambake Club. All of Jack's close pals attended—many would be ushers at the wedding, including Lem Billings, Torby Macdonald, Chuck Spalding, Charlie Bartlett, George Smathers, Ben Smith, and James Reed—and Red Fay was master of ceremonies. Robert Kennedy, the best man, diligently sweated out a memorized toast to the groom, whereupon Jack rose from his seat and offered a toast to his bride. Then he instructed, "Into the fireplace! We will not drink from these glasses again." All the men tossed the expensive crystal glasses into the fire, in the manner of the Russian Imperial Guard. Auchincloss, looking suddenly pensive, summoned the waiter to replace the glasses. Jack rose again. "Maybe this isn't the accepted custom," he declared, "but I want to again express my love for this girl I'm going to marry. A toast to the bride." Everyone joined in the toast again, and once more the crystal stemware flew into the fireplace. Hughdie had had enough: for the next round the waiter brought ordinary drinking glasses.[72]

Spalding remembered of that evening:

> Jack was enjoying himself, and yet I had the strange feeling that Jack was watching everything with an extra eye, as if the eye was outside of himself, in a corner of the room, surveying the scene with a kind

of detachment. It was a very eerie thing to see this, and feel it, but there it was. I remember I cut myself and Jack was immediately at my side, looking at the cut, suggesting I should go to the hospital. It was one of his qualities that bound people to him. Concerned. Sensitive. But the point is, he could be part of what was going on, and yet that extra eye saw me. I know it sounds strange. But I felt he always had an extra eye.[73]

The wedding day dawned clear and breezy. Like her mother, Jackie had wanted a different kind of wedding, smaller and more cozy, with attendees who knew the bridal couple and cared about them. What she got was something else: many hundreds of guests, most of whom she had never laid eyes on before, as well as hordes of reporters and photographers recording her every move. When she arrived at the church for the eleven o'clock ceremony, a crowd of three thousand onlookers broke through police lines and for a moment seemed set on smothering her. She kept her composure, smiling bashfully in her cream taffeta gown, with tight-fitting bodice and bouffant skirt. Then more disappointment: her father was too hungover from drinking by himself the night before to give her away. (Janet Bouvier Auchincloss had forbidden him from attending the pre-wedding dinner.) Her stepfather did the honors instead, while Black Jack slipped into the chapel at the last minute and sat inconspicuously near the back. When Jack and Bobby walked down the aisle and took their places near the altar, they looked, one observer said, "too tanned and handsome to be believed."[74] Archbishop Richard Cushing, a close friend of the Kennedys, performed the ceremony, celebrating the nuptial Mass and reading a special blessing from Pope Pius XII. To the accompaniment of "Panis Angelicus" and "Ave Maria," the couple knelt at the flower-bedecked altar and recited their vows.

As Senator and Mrs. Kennedy stepped out of the church, the crowd surged forward again, the groom, according to *The New York Times,* smiling broadly "and the bride appearing a little startled."[75] Cars backed up for more than half a mile for the reception at Hammersmith Farm, and the couple spent more than two hours in the receiving line shaking hands. A buffet was served in the house and on the lawns outside overlooking Narragansett Bay, and the bride and groom distributed slices of the wedding cake as white-jacketed waiters fanned out with trays of champagne and an orchestra played. Among the guests were film star Marion Davies,

Mr. and Mrs. Kennedy with members of their wedding party. To the left of the groom are, from left, George Smathers, Lem Billings, Torby Macdonald, and Chuck Spalding. In front of Macdonald is Jackie's sister Lee, and in the very front is Ethel Kennedy. On the top right is Red Fay.

singer Morton Downey, several U.S. senators and congressmen and state legislators (including Jack's successor from the Eleventh District, Tip O'Neill), and a phalanx of industrialists and business-tycoon acquaintances of Joe Kennedy's. Hughdie and Janet's friends were fewer in number and more Waspy—more Republican—and they kept mostly to themselves during the reception, speculating sotto voce about what tragic fate might have befallen Jack Bouvier to keep him from giving his daughter away. Throughout the exhausting affair, bride and groom posed gamely for the photographers, Jackie balking only once, when she was asked to stand with her husband clinking champagne glasses. "Too corny," she declared.[76]

When evening came and the last of the guests departed, Joe Kennedy had every reason to be pleased: this was indeed a spectacular social celebration, certain to get attention from coast to coast in the coming days, with photos of the couple in newspapers large and small. Even the normally staid *New York Times* got carried away, gushing in a front-page story that the event "far surpassed the Astor-French wedding of 1934 in public interest."[77]

The newlyweds, for their part, were happy to be on their way, first to New York for a night at the Waldorf Astoria, then on to Acapulco and a pink stucco villa above the Pacific that Jackie had found enchanting on a previous visit with her mother and Hughdie.[78] One of her first acts there was to pen an affectionate letter of forgiveness to her father, while Jack, for his part, wired his parents: "At last I know the true meaning of rapture. Jackie is enshrined forever in my heart. Thanks Mom and Dad for making me worthy of her."[79] After a few days the couple flew to California, where they spent time at San Ysidro Ranch near Santa Barbara before continuing north to the Monterey Peninsula and then to San Francisco and the home of Red Fay and his wife, Anita. ("God, she's a fantastic-looking woman," Red had told Jack upon meeting the soft-spoken Jackie at Ham-

The couple share a moment at the wedding reception with
Bobby, Pat, Eunice, Teddy, and Jean.

mersmith Farm before the wedding, "but if you ever get a little hard of hearing you're going to have a little trouble picking up all the transmissions.") On the final day in California, Jack joined Red for a 49ers football game and left Jackie behind with Anita, who showed her some of the Bay Area sights. "I'm sure this didn't seem a particularly unusual arrangement to Jack," Red wrote, acknowledging Jackie's resentment. "The pressures of public life—not to mention those of an old shipmate and his wife—too often intruded on the kind of honeymoon any young bride anticipates."[80]

The pressures did not end with their return to the East Coast. Having not lived together before the wedding, they were unprepared for the intricacies of married life. Each emotionally reticent, each self-centered, they struggled to open themselves up to each other. Then there was Jack's busy work schedule, which left Jackie alone a great deal of the time, including on weekends. Even when he was around, she subsequently said, her husband seemed so preoccupied she "might as well be in Alaska." Jack, looking to his parents' example, didn't fully realize how these absences—literal and figurative—harmed the relationship. It didn't help that they resided initially not in their own home—a small, narrow rented nineteenth-century house at 3321 Dent Place, in Georgetown, that was not ready for occupancy—but in Hyannis Port, where Jackie put up with the compulsive athleticism of the Kennedys and chafed at the strict rules about punctuality at mealtimes, but where she also found a measure of calmness on the windswept Cape Cod seashore. She painted watercolors, several of which Joe Kennedy insisted on hanging on the walls of the house—one showed a crowd of young Kennedys on the beach, along with the caption "You can't take it with you. Dad's got it all."[81] She and her father-in-law found themselves kindred spirits, and spent hours talking. She liked him, trusted him; he felt the same about her.

She also penned a poem—an ode to her husband in the manner of Benét's "John Brown's Body"—the last part of which reads:

> *But now he was there with the wind and the sea*
> *And all the things he was going to be.*
> *He would build empires*
> *And he would have sons*
> *Others would fall*
> *Where the current runs*

He would find love
He would never find peace
For he must go seeking
The Golden Fleece

All of the things he was going to be
All of the things in the wind and the sea.[82]

Jack was so thrilled with the poem that he wanted to have it published, but Jackie refused. It was as private as a love letter, she told him, and must not be made public. He agreed, though not fully—he couldn't resist sharing it with family members and one or two friends. He also read her Alan Seeger's "I Have a Rendezvous with Death," which she later recited with pleasure, including Jack's favorite lines:

It may be he shall take my hand
And lead me into his dark land
And close my eyes and quench my breath . . .

But I've a rendezvous with Death
At midnight in some flaming town,
When Spring trips north again this year,
And I to my pledged word am true,
I shall not fail that rendezvous.

That first fall, Jackie also wrote and illustrated a book for her eight-year-old half sister. *A Book for Janet: In Case You Are Ever Thinking of Getting Married This Is a Story to Tell You What It's Like.* It began with a drawing depicting Jackie seeing her husband off to work, and went on to describe their life together. One drawing showed the dome of the Capitol at night, wholly dark except for one single lit window. "If he isn't home and that single light is on," the caption read, at least "you know the country is safe." The elder Janet Auchincloss, so often stingy with her praise where Jackie was concerned, called *A Book for Janet* "deeply touching in a beautiful way."[83]

Though at Miss Porter's School Jackie's ambition had been "not to be a housewife," in essence that's now what she became. "I brought a certain amount of order to his life," she later said about the first months of marriage. "We had good food in our house—not merely the bare staples that he used to have. He no longer went out in the morning with one brown shoe and one black shoe on. His clothes got pressed and he got to the airport without a mad rush because I packed for him."[84] She signed up for cooking classes, joined a bridge club, even tried to learn to play golf in order to get to spend more time with her husband. (After one interminable afternoon together on the links, he gently suggested she stick to horseback riding.)

Jackie got a sure sense of her role when the young couple was featured on *Person to Person,* Edward Murrow's popular half-hour TV program on CBS, in October. While the chain-smoking host introduced the senator as one who, at age thirty-six, had already accomplished everything most American boys dreamed of doing, Jackie sat demurely by Jack's side on the couch in his former "bachelor establishment" on Bowdoin Street in Boston, her elegant print dress harmonizing with his conservative business suit. The few questions Murrow directed her way she answered softly and quickly, highlighting her pride at what her husband had accomplished. Jack, prompted by Murrow, rose and displayed for the camera his wartime mementos—a model of PT 109, the famous coconut on which he had carved his rescue plea, and a photo of the destroyer named for Joe Junior. He then described the circumstances of his brother's heroic death, whereupon Murrow tossed him softball questions on public policy and on his recommendations for "inspirational reading." (Jack, clearly primed, reached for a nearby book and read to the camera an excerpt from a moving letter the poet Alan Seeger had written to his mother shortly before his death in World War I.)[85]

"The main thing for me was to do whatever my husband wanted," Jackie later said. "He couldn't—and wouldn't—be married to a woman who tried to share the spotlight with him. I thought the best thing I could do was be a distraction. Jack lived and breathed politics all day long. If he came home to more table thumping, how could he ever relax?" To a reporter she insisted, with just a little too much emphasis—and no mention of the fact that she had household help from the start—that "housekeeping is a joy to me. When it all runs smoothly, when the food is good and the flowers look fresh, I have much satisfaction. I like cooking, but I'm not very good at it. I care terribly about food, but I'm not much of a cook."[86]

As for Jack, the difference between a chic home and an unstylish one was mostly lost on him, as was the contrast between a bespoke suit and an off-the-rack model. He had little appreciation of good food or good wine, being perfectly content with a steak or a cheeseburger and some ice cream. Until, that is, his wife entered the picture. "She wouldn't go along with the Kennedy atmosphere," recalled Jack's British friend David Ormsby-Gore, who also became close to Jackie. "She had certain standards of her own which she insisted on in her house. They were standards about the manners [of] children, about having good food, about having beautiful furniture, the house well done up." Jack, impatient at first, adjusted, even came to share her sensibility, at least to a degree. Ormsby-Gore again: "I remember him saying when Jackie had gone off and bought some French eighteenth-century chairs or something, 'I don't know why, what's the point of spending all this money—I mean, a chair is a chair and it's a perfectly good chair I'm sitting in—what's the point of all this fancy stuff.' Well that was his first reaction but gradually he came to appreciate good taste in these other matters and really cared about it by the end."[87] Jackie broadened his taste in art and improved his manners. With her gentle guidance, Jack even turned himself into a minor fashion plate, with a preference for the single-breasted, two-button suit, often pinstriped and always perfectly pressed. For the first time, he learned which tie should go with which shirt and how the wrong shoes could kill a stylish ensemble.

He became so clothes conscious that he once told Chuck Spalding, "Your suit doesn't make a statement." When he realized what he'd said, they both broke out in laughter.[88]

In more substantive ways, too, Jackie soon proved her importance, even as she wondered if she'd ever be able to keep up with her husband intellectually. ("He has this curious, inquiring mind that is always at work; if I were drawing him, I would draw a tiny body and an enormous head."[89]) She continued to translate for him from the French, including reports on the Indochina War and the writings of Talleyrand, Voltaire, and de Gaulle, bon mots from which Jack would then sprinkle into his speeches. And she helped transform him into a better public speaker, coaxing him to abandon his high, nasal twang in favor of deeper, more sonorous tones. (A vocal coach had given Jack the same advice, and for a time he spent some minutes each morning barking like a dog to deepen his voice.) With Ted Sorensen's help, Jackie also got him to slow his delivery—his colleagues sometimes found his rapid-fire utterances hard to follow—and to modulate his pitch and use his hands to punctuate key points, to be less fidgety onstage. The changes were not evident overnight, but gradually, as Kennedy worked on his technique and as he and Sorensen fine-tuned their collaborative speechwriting efforts, he became notably more effective at the lectern—a self-composed, authentic communicator who employed the rhythms and language of powerful rhetoric.[90]

In January 1954, as he and his young wife settled into their Georgetown home, John F. Kennedy had reason to feel good about things. He had found his footing in the Senate, earning the respect of more senior colleagues, who appreciated his quiet manner, his studiousness, and his composed, good-humored, reasoned approach to policy issues. He had happened upon a once-in-a-generation political aide in Ted Sorensen, and enjoyed broad support in his home state. He had landed a bride in the beautiful, witty, sophisticated Jacqueline Bouvier, whose European sensibility he admired and shared. Their wedding had won wide coverage from coast to coast. If the patterns and demands of married life were proving a challenge in these early months, for him and for her, he felt lucky to have her, felt certain that she represented for him a political asset. Yet, as the year turned, all was not well. Jack Kennedy didn't know it, but his annus mirabilis of 1953 would be succeeded by something very different.

DARK DAYS

t should have come as no real surprise that 1954 would turn into John
F. Kennedy's nightmare year. After all, neither of the two problems that
erupted in full force that year was new to him. The first, indeed, had
been with him since birth, in the form of a congenital spinal problem
possibly made worse by injuries suffered in the South Pacific during the
war. He had been in acute pain at various times during 1953, even entering George Washington University Hospital for a few days in mid-July for
what were officially deemed "malaria" complications. At his wedding, in
September, friends worried that he might not be able to kneel at the
altar—or get back up if he did. But he pulled it off with aplomb, and managed during the subsequent honeymoon to hobble along next to his bride
reasonably well. (His ailment did not stop him from taking part, on the
eve of the wedding, in a touch football game in Newport that left him with
scratches on his face, the result of a tumble into a briar patch after a pass
play.) Though his bouts with pain were becoming more frequent, it seemed
reasonable to expect that he would go on as before, relying on crutches
when it got bad and making do the rest of the time.

His second problem was of more recent origin, though hardly brand-
new: the human juggernaut called Joe McCarthy. For four years, ever

since the Wisconsin demagogue burst onto the scene with his notorious speech in Wheeling, West Virginia, Kennedy's strategy had been to sidestep the issue, to keep private his misgivings about McCarthy's charges and tactics and to say as little as possible publicly. McCarthy was a family friend, much cherished and admired by Joseph Kennedy in particular, and had attended Eunice's wedding to Sargent Shriver in May 1953. That year, at the urging of the Ambassador, McCarthy had hired Robert Kennedy to serve as assistant counsel for his Permanent Subcommittee on Investigations; although Bobby lasted only seven months in the position, he remained devotedly loyal to McCarthy, as did his wife, Ethel.[1] Four Kennedys attended McCarthy's own wedding, to Jean Kerr, in September 1953: Joe, Bobby, Pat, and Jean.[2]

Beyond the family ties, Jack understood all too well that McCarthy maintained broad and deep support among the huge bloc of Irish Catholics in Massachusetts. Yet he had no desire, on intellectual grounds, to back him—McCarthy was, to his mind, a cynical and dishonest bully who scoffed at the legislative procedures and senatorial good manners he himself prized. What's more, he knew that retaining strong Democratic credentials required that he keep his distance, especially if he hoped at some point to win his party's nomination for higher office. Nor could he hope to retain support among the Harvard and MIT intellectuals, whose respect he coveted, if he was perceived as cozying up to McCarthy.

And so he played for time—on both issues—and instead focused his efforts early in 1954 on staking out a more national profile. In January he shocked his Bay State constituents by announcing his support for the St. Lawrence Seaway, a proposed river transit system through eastern Canada, connecting the Atlantic Ocean with the Great Lakes, that had been urged by president after president, by Canadian authorities, and by engineering and transportation experts, all of whom argued its value to the national economy in general and the Midwest in particular. In opposition stood an alliance of regional New England interests, and especially the Port of Boston, which felt imperiled by the low shipping rates that the seaway would permit. Their combined efforts had been enough to kill the project. As Kennedy himself pointed out, in twenty years of deliberations on the issue, not one Massachusetts senator or representative had ever voted for it.

Until now. When he rose on the floor of the Senate to speak on the seaway bill, Kennedy admitted that he had agonized over which way to go. There were compelling arguments on both sides, he told his colleagues, but the best one was in favor of the bill. Drawing on research done for him by Ted Sorensen, he declared that the seaway would not do the harm asserted, would serve the national interest, and would in all likelihood be built by the Canadians regardless of what the United States decided. Mindful of the hostile reaction that awaited him from Boston's longshoremen, Kennedy insisted that the city's port would suffer only minimally from the seaway and in the long run would indeed gain from its benefits to the larger economy. "I am unable to accept such a narrow view of my function as United States senator," he said to hometown critics of his stance. The defection of a senator from a key anti-seaway state made a difference in the debate, and the bill at last passed. President Eisenhower signed the legislation in May. *The Boston Post* accused Kennedy of "ruining New England," and even friendly editorial pages said he was committing political suicide. A friend on the Boston City Council advised him against walking in the upcoming St. Patrick's Day parade, lest he suffer catcalls or worse. He ignored the warning and marched—and encountered only limited griping. He took it as an important lesson: one could go against the easy vote, the vote favored by one's political base, and do the right thing, without suffering grievous damage as a result. Others agreed. "If I ever saw a person make a decision in conscience and on the merits," said Joe Healey, one of his father's attorneys, "it was the St. Lawrence Seaway decision made by Jack Kennedy."[3]

An idea took hold in his mind. There might be an article worth writing, he told Sorensen, about senators in American history who had bucked popular opinion and risked their careers for the sake of principle. In Herbert Agar's *The Price of Union* and Samuel Flagg Bemis's *John Quincy Adams and the Foundations of American Foreign Policy*, he had come upon stories of the attacks Adams endured almost a century and a half earlier after likewise voting against the Bay State's narrow economic interests when he backed President Jefferson's embargo on Great Britain in 1807. Why not write a series of compelling portraits of Adams and a few others who had shown similar political courage and lived to tell about it? Kennedy asked Sorensen to do some digging and pull some materials together.[4]

Tip O'Neill, who now held Kennedy's old seat in the House, saw a larger purpose in the seaway vote. "I knew Jack was serious about running for president back in 1954, when he mentioned that he intended to vote for the St. Lawrence Seaway Project," O'Neill remembered. "The whole Northeast delegation was opposed to that bill, because once you opened the Seaway, you killed the port of Boston, which was the closest port to Europe. The Boston papers were against it, and so were the merchant marines and the longshoremen. But Jack wanted to show that he wasn't parochial, and that he had a truly national perspective. Although he acknowledged that the Seaway would hurt Boston, he supported it because the project would benefit the country as a whole."[5]

II

On Indochina, too, Kennedy struck an independent line. As 1954 began, the outlook was grimmer than ever for French Union forces, but Paris leaders were staying in the fight. They felt the need to justify the deaths they had incurred (a sunk-cost dynamic the Americans would themselves encounter in Vietnam a dozen years later), and moreover their U.S. patrons, who were paying an ever greater share of the war-related costs, would countenance no thought of withdrawal. To Dwight Eisenhower and his secretary of state, John Foster Dulles, Indochina was a key theater in the broader Cold War struggle, which meant France had to remain in the fight. At every opportunity, they told their Paris counterparts that seven years of war had not been in vain, that the anti–Ho Chi Minh cause was both just and essential, and that negotiations should be avoided until the military picture had improved and France and the West could dictate the terms.[6]

"If Indochina goes," Eisenhower warned in a Seattle speech in August 1953, in an early articulation of the domino theory, "several things happen right away. The Malayan peninsula, with its valuable tin and tungsten, would become indefensible, and India would be outflanked. Indonesia, with all its riches, would likely be lost too. . . . So you see, somewhere along the line, this must be blocked. It must be blocked now. That is what the French are doing." A few days later, the president told two British officials over lunch that Indochina was more crucial strategically than Korea. It was the neck of the bottle, and it was essential to keep the cork in, which meant Congress needed to support an "all-out" effort in Vietnam for a year or eighteen months, even if it required the allocation of large additional sums. Vice President Richard Nixon spoke in similar terms, as did Secretary Dulles, with the latter telling Congress that defeat in Indochina could trigger a "chain reaction throughout the Far East and Southeast Asia."[7]

Senator Kennedy was not immune to this kind of thinking. In late January 1954, he used the occasion of a speech before the Cathedral Club of Brooklyn to warn that Ho Chi Minh's long-standing campaign against French colonialism had given him broad support among the Vietnamese people. Almost certainly, he would win a free election. Yet the loss of Indochina, Kennedy went on, whether by military or electoral defeat, would constitute a serious blow to Western security—"undoubtedly within a short time, Burma, Thailand, Malaya, and Indonesia and other new independent states might fall under the control of the Communist bloc in a series of chain reactions." Most alarmingly, the administration, with its emphasis on military means and the threat of atomic retaliation, seemed to have no plan for preventing this outcome: "Of what value would atomic retaliation be in opposing a Communist advance which rested not upon military invasion but upon local insurrection and political deterioration?"[8]

In March 1954, as it began to appear that France might soon lose the war, Admiral Arthur Radford, chairman of the Joint Chiefs of Staff, warned that such a result would inevitably cause the loss of the rest of Southeast Asia.[9] Eisenhower, in a National Security Council meeting on April 6, endorsed this view, mixing his metaphors with aplomb. "Indochina was the first in a row of dominoes," according to the notes of the meeting. "If it fell its neighbors would shortly thereafter fall with it, and where did the process end? If he was correct, said the president, it would end with the United States directly behind the 8-ball."[10] The next day, Eisenhower formally introduced his theory at a press conference: "Finally, you have broader considerations that might follow what you would call the 'falling domino' principle. You have a row of dominoes set up, you knock over the first one, and what will happen to the last one is the certainty that it will go over very quickly. So you could have a beginning of a disintegration that would have the most profound influences."[11]

It was a curious theory, really. In no previous case had the fall of a country to Communism triggered the rapid collapse of a whole string of other countries. Even in a weaker form, envisioning only a short row of dominoes, the theory seemingly bore little relation to reality. China, the most populous nation in the world, had gone Communist in 1949, but that event had not caused dominoes to fall (though many worried about what might have ensued in Korea had the U.S.-led forces not intervened). Yet the falling-domino notion would take hold of the American imagination for the rest of the decade and beyond, animating much of the public discourse about Vietnam and what needed to happen there.

Eisenhower's immediate concern was a big battle under way at Dien Bien Phu, a remote outpost in northwestern Vietnam near the Laotian border. Contrary to expectations, Viet Minh commander Vo Nguyen Giap got his China-supplied heavy artillery up the hills and thereby trapped the French garrison on the valley floor. By the end of March the Viet Minh forces had destroyed the garrison's airstrip and were closing in on the main base. Recognizing the symbolic importance of the battle—which had become a media sensation around the world—the White House considered direct U.S. military intervention, in the form of air strikes, to try to save the French position, under an operation code-named Vulture. (Some American analysts even contemplated the use of tactical nuclear weapons.[12]) Congress would be leery of any unilateral U.S. effort, administration officials knew, especially on the heels of a frustrating and bloody war in Korea, and thus Dulles introduced the concept of United Action, whereby a coalition of non-Communist nations would pledge collectively to defend Indochina and the rest of Southeast Asia against outside aggression.

Jack Kennedy was skeptical. In a powerful Senate speech on April 6, he blasted the administration for its lack of candor on the conflict. The time had come, he said, "for the American people to be told the truth about Indochina." United Action had logic behind it, the senator went on, and he personally was prepared to back a limited multilateral military effort to prevent an all-out Viet Minh win, but he feared where such a policy would lead the nation: "To pour money, matériel, and men into the jungles of Indochina without at least a remote prospect of victory would be dangerously futile and destructive." More to the point, would the United States ever be able to make much difference in that part of the world? "No amount of American military assistance can conquer an enemy which is everywhere and at the same time nowhere, 'an enemy of the people' which has the sympathy and covert support of the people." Any satisfactory outcome, he stressed, depended on France according the Associated States full and complete independence; without it, adequate indigenous support would remain forever elusive. It followed that, absent such a

French move, the United States should under no circumstances send its men and machines "into that hopeless internecine struggle." Kennedy concluded by quoting Thomas Jefferson on the vital importance of enlightening the public rather than hiding the truth.[13]

His grudging and qualified support for United Action was shared by many colleagues in both parties, as was his conviction that securing greater indigenous support was a prerequisite for success. Some lawmakers went further, wondering if any U.S. military intervention could be kept limited. "Once you commit the flag," Senator Richard Russell asserted, in words that would take on a haunting prescience a decade later, "you've committed the country. There's no turning back. If you involve the American air force, why, you've involved the nation." And if you involved the nation, ground forces would soon follow. Russell said he was "weary" of "seeing American soldiers being used as gladiators to be thrown into every arena around the world."[14] Kennedy agreed, and he reiterated his skepticism that the military measures, if undertaken, would yield significant results. Turning the discussion to the practical implications of United Action, Mike Mansfield, Democrat from Montana, asked Kennedy what he believed John Foster Dulles had in mind when he'd announced the concept in an address before the Overseas Press Club in New York the previous week.

"There is every indication," Kennedy replied, "that what he meant was that the United States will take the ultimate step."

"And that is what?"

"It is war."[15]

Kennedy maintained this cautionary line in speech after speech that spring. At a Cook County Democratic Party dinner in Chicago, for example, he stressed that the United States "cannot save those who will not be saved," and that Asian nations must do their part in regional and continental defense. "Indo-China should teach us," he went on, "that in the long run our cause will be stronger if it is clearly just, if we remain true to our traditional policies of helping all oppressed people, even though it may require unpleasant pressures in our relations with colonial powers and friends." In Los Angeles, he declared that the American people were being deceived about the true situation on the ground, while in Princeton, New Jersey, he bemoaned the seeming American inability to perceive the actual nature and significance of the Vietnamese independence movement. In a television interview, he in effect called Indochina a lost cause and warned that U.S. intervention with combat forces would fail, because Mao's Chinese Communists would only widen the struggle.[16]

Ultimately, Congress refused to give its support for military action in Indochina unless Great Britain also joined the effort. Dwight Eisenhower, who was more militant on Vietnam in 1954 than sympathetic historians and biographers generally acknowledge—much more serious about intervening militarily, at least with aerial bombing—now undertook an intense and concerted administration effort to persuade British leaders to get on board, but it was to no avail: Prime Minister Winston Churchill and Foreign Secretary Anthony Eden were dubious that any multilateral military intervention had much hope of salvaging the French position, and they worried that it might precipitate a disastrous war with China, if not with the Soviet Union, too. Eisenhower refused to go in alone, and no U.S. military intervention occurred that spring.[17]

Instead, following France's defeat and the (ostensibly temporary) division of Vietnam at the seventeenth parallel, Eisenhower committed the United States to building up and sustaining a non-Communist regime in the South, under Ngo Dinh Diem. It was, time would reveal, a hugely fateful decision, not merely for his presidency but for the three that came after.

III

Kennedy's comments on Indochina that spring, even more than his bold vote on the St. Lawrence Seaway, touched informed observers and ordinary voters like nothing he had said before. Letters flooded his Senate office, the overwhelming majority of them lauding him for his skeptical stance regarding military intervention and for, as one constituent put it, "remember[ing] there are Asians in Asia to be considered."[18] Editorials from coast to coast noted his admonitory words and anointed him an emerging leader in his party in the complex arena of foreign policy. "Keep your eye on young Democratic Senator John Kennedy," declared a columnist in the *Brooklyn Eagle*. "He's been getting a buildup for a nationwide campaign such as a Vice Presidential candidate." Hanson W. Baldwin, the respected military correspondent of *The New York Times*, said Kennedy's assessment of the war situation in Indochina was more accurate than that offered by the White House; Walter Lippmann did the same in his syndicated column.[19]

Others remarked that his growing visibility meant he would be utilized heavily as a Democratic warhorse for the coming midterm elections. And indeed, in the spring and early summer he crossed the country to champion party candidates for the House and Senate—he gave dinner speeches in Boise, in Chicago, in Pasadena, in Hartford, and elsewhere, delighting the attendees with his zingers aimed at the GOP in general and the Eisenhower White House in particular. In Malden, Massachusetts, in mid-May, a few weeks after attending his sister Pat's New York wedding to the British actor Peter Lawford, he spoke on behalf of none other than Torby Macdonald, running for Congress as a Democrat in the heavily Republican Eighth District. (Macdonald would win the election and go on to have a long and estimable House career, serving for more than two decades.)

The heavy travel schedule wreaked havoc on his fragile body and did nothing for his young marriage. Newspaper and magazine editors, eager to cover the handsome couple, ran feature stories depicting a model marriage, in which husband and wife worked, studied, and socialized together. The reality was different. Jack's dalliances with women continued. Jackie, like her mother-in-law early in *her* marriage, found herself alone for long stretches, and with few ways to nourish her interests in the arts. At Jack's suggestion, she took an American history class at Georgetown's School of Foreign Service (the only part of the university that admitted women) with Professor Jules Davids, earning B's on her papers and an 89 on her final exam. When Jack signed up for a speed-reading class in Baltimore, with brother Bobby and Lem Billings, in order to keep up with the mass of Senate work, she found one for herself to take locally. (Both of them became amazingly fast readers, and with their superb recall scored high on retention. Jack, in particular, would regularly astonish associates with his ability to quickly absorb the contents of books and memos and then recapitulate entire sections with ease.) But they bickered over what he considered her profligate spending habits, and she chafed at his long hours and at the frequent work-related phone calls when he was home. "It was like being married to a whirlwind," she later told a reporter. "Politics was sort of my enemy as far as seeing Jack was concerned."[20]

She did what she could to create a home life, even enlisting Jack's secretary, Evelyn Lincoln, to plead with him to knock off work early enough

Jackie, seeking to brush up on her American history,
heads off to class at Georgetown.

to be home in time for supper. For a time it worked, but soon he was back
to his old ways, toiling until eight o'clock or later, night after night. To
make sure he ate a proper lunch each day, Jackie brought him a home-
cooked meal or had his driver deliver it in covered china dishes. She took
a French cooking class, though cooking was never her strength. She
gathered their wedding photos into a pair of very attractive albums. Jack
was touched by her efforts, but apparently not touched enough to change
his habits. Tensions remained. Though in time he would come to appreciate her sense of separation from politics and public life and from the cus-
toms and mores of Washington, here in the early going he found it
discomfiting and unnatural, so different from the attitude of his sisters,
who lived and breathed politics.

Jackie, for her part, struggled with what she termed his "violent"
independence—that is, his love of hanging out with his male friends and

his promiscuity. To friends she continued to rationalize his unfaithfulness, insisting that all men cheat on their wives, that her father had done so, as had his father before him. She loved being married, she said.[21] But the cheating hurt all the same, especially coming so soon after their wedding. (Her earlier illusion that his womanizing was part of his appeal seems to have disappeared as soon as they took their vows.) And if most of the time he tried to follow his father's example and be discreet in his liaisons, she sensed what was going on. On at least one occasion, he was—also like his father—anything but discreet, as Jackie found herself humiliatingly stranded at a party after he suddenly disappeared with a beautiful woman who caught his eye.[22]

Her instinct was to blame herself. All her life, her mother had faulted her appearance, her clothing choices, her physique, suggesting that no man worthy of the name would be satisfied with her; maybe this just proved that Mother always knew best. Jackie responded by changing her appearance—cutting her hair short, Audrey Hepburn style, and sprucing up her wardrobe with the latest Paris offerings, all in an effort to make herself more alluring to her husband. He liked the new look, but the infidelity continued. At no point in this early period, it seems, did Jackie consider that it might be something within Jack, something *not* shared by all men everywhere, that caused him to behave as he did.[23]

Adding to Jackie's frustration was her inability to follow the expected pattern of a Kennedy wife and bear a child in the first year of marriage. The reason for the difficulties are not clear, but they may have had something to do with the venereal disease Jack had contracted as a senior at Harvard in 1940. In the years thereafter, he complained periodically of a burning sensation upon urination and of what one medical report, in 1952, called "varying degrees of urinary distress." If, as a result of her husband's gonorrhea, Jackie contracted chlamydia, that could help explain her childbearing problems. (In 1954 the couple did in fact succeed in conceiving, but Jackie soon miscarried.) Her biographer Sarah Bradford is surely right to speculate that Jack likely told Jackie nothing about his venereal condition, and, moreover, that "if she had succeeded in bearing a child that first year, or even the next, it would have saved her from some of the heartbreak and marital difficulty she experienced over the next few years."[24]

Some part of Kennedy pined for his former unattached life. When circumstances permitted, he mingled with New York's social set, hitting nightspots such as the Stork Club and El Morocco and the parties of the well-to-do, often in the company of an elegant woman. According to Gunilla von Post, the young Swedish woman he'd met in the South of France on his pre-wedding jaunt the previous summer, he wrote her on his Senate stationery in early March 1954, indicating that he planned to return to the French Riviera in September and would love to see her there. He then tried to reach her by phone in Stockholm, without leaving his number. In the summer he called again, asking to see her in France in early September. No rendezvous occurred, as the senator indicated in a cable from Hyannis Port: "Trip postponed."[25]

In truth, matters political as well as physical demanded that he remain stateside that summer. It was clear by the late spring that the Senate was headed for a showdown over McCarthy and his methods, and that Jack Kennedy's political future hinged in part on his handling of the issue. The Wisconsin senator had begun to overreach in the middle months of 1953, his sloppy habits and impulsive style finally catching up with him. But he remained a formidable force—as late as January 1954, half of the American electorate held a favorable opinion of him (as against 29 percent who viewed him unfavorably). In heavily Irish Catholic Massachusetts his support ran higher still, as the mail flowing into Senator Kennedy's office showed. But the letters also revealed deep rifts among his constituents, with some condemning McCarthy's fact-free demagoguery and others pledging undying support for him. Kennedy walked the narrow middle path in his responses. "I appreciate knowing of your support for Senator McCarthy," he wrote a woman from Fitchburg. "I have always believed that we must be alert to the menace of Communism within our country as well as its advances on the international front. In so doing, however, we must be careful we maintain our traditional concern that in punishing the guilty we protect the innocent."[26]

He could take such a compromise position in letters to constituents, but how would he vote on the Senate floor? He was too rational and moderate to remain indifferent to McCarthyite extremism, and in 1953 he joined with Democratic liberals in supporting the confirmation of his former Harvard president, James B. Conant, as high commissioner to West Germany, rejecting the claim of McCarthy and his supporters that Conant held views contrary to "the prevailing philosophy of the American people."[27] Kennedy also defied McCarthy in backing Charles "Chip" Bohlen to be ambassador to the Soviet Union, and in voting against the appointment of McCarthy's friend Robert Lee to the Federal Communications Commission (on the grounds that Lee was not qualified). When Jack joined a Senate Democratic effort to bar political speeches by McCarthy crony Scott McLeod—then security chief at the State Department—the rabidly McCarthyite *Boston Post* accused him in an editorial of sabotaging McLeod's laudable campaign to get "communist coddlers" out of Foggy Bottom. "Senator Kennedy hasn't discovered that cleaning communists out of government is not a party matter," the paper proclaimed. "If he wants to maintain his political viability he ought to consult a few solid and loyal Democrats in Massachusetts who are every bit as determined to clean communism out of government as is Senator McCarthy." If Jack took notice of the editorial, he hid it well: a short time later he led the fight in the Government Operations Committee, which McCarthy chaired, against another McCarthy friend, Owen Brewster, to be chief counsel of the committee.[28]

Still, Kennedy moved carefully, unwilling to denounce McCarthy directly, even after a great many Americans had determined that the Wisconsin senator should be condemned in every way possible, his name having become more and more symbolic of a mood of intimidation against civil servants, teachers, writers, and others deemed to hold unorthodox views. Kennedy's reticence was not unusual—his fellow Bay State senator, Leverett Saltonstall, for one, had even less to say on the matter, despite his lack of family ties to McCarthy. (Saltonstall was up for reelection and did not wish to offend Irish Catholic voters sympathetic to McCarthy; he kept silent through the first half of 1954, as did his Democratic opponent, Foster Furcolo.) Many other legislators, including virtually all Senate Democrats, were similarly tight-lipped, lest their constituents take umbrage. Even Dwight Eisenhower, though privately disdainful of McCarthy and his antics, acted cautiously and spoke elliptically, bemoaning the effects of McCarthyism without criticizing the senator by name.[29]

But a reckoning was coming in the Senate, as a result of McCarthy's disastrous decision to turn his crusade to the alleged presence of Communists in the U.S. Army. The origins of this gambit were complex, but when, in March 1954, the Army accused McCarthy and his chief aide, Roy Cohn, of seeking preferential treatment for G. David Schine, a member of the senator's staff who had been drafted, McCarthy countered that Army leaders were merely attempting to derail his investigation of Communistic influences in that branch of the service and that Schine was being held hostage to stop the investigation altogether. For the proud general in the White House, this attack on the Army was too much; his administration now launched a behind-the-scenes campaign to isolate McCarthy.[30] The Senate, for its part, established a committee to weigh the charges, and Minority Leader Lyndon B. Johnson, sensing an opportunity to deliver a crushing blow to McCarthy's popular appeal, arranged for the subsequent hearings to be televised.

It was a watershed moment. Though the nation's airwaves were not as saturated with the Army-McCarthy hearings as broadcast lore would have it (only the fledgling American Broadcasting Corporation and the soon-to-die DuMont network provided gavel-to-gavel coverage of all 180 hours), millions of Americans got to see McCarthy's rude and bullying conduct and to examine for themselves his wild charges against Army personnel. To many he came across as a ruthless charlatan, and his polling numbers, already sagging in the prior months, declined still more. Television, which had carried Joe McCarthy to the top, now brought him down. The nation's five million television sets in 1950, when he first made his mark, had mushroomed to thirty million by 1954.

Not everyone abandoned him. His core supporters, constituting about a third of the populace, doubled down and hung tight with him through the end of the hearings and afterwards. Many Irish Americans, among them Joe and Bobby Kennedy, were particularly stubborn—in their eyes he was one of them, a steadfast, courageous battler against the patronizing elites.[31]

Thus the quiet grumblings of concern by some lawmakers when Senator Ralph Flanders, a spirited Yankee Republican from Vermont, introduced a motion to curb McCarthy by stripping him of his committee chairmanships. Such an action lacked precedent and had little support, so in late July Flanders proposed instead that the upper chamber censure McCarthy for behavior unbecoming of a senator. McCarthy was a child, Flanders said, a kind of overgrown Dennis the Menace, for he displayed the "colossal innocence" of children "who blunder . . . into the most appalling situations as they ramble through the world of adults." Many on Capitol Hill nodded in quiet agreement. But with the fall campaign about to begin in earnest, those legislators up for reelection were reluctant to alienate McCarthy's die-hard backers, and journalists could see why: "If Senator Saltonstall were to make his position on McCarthy clear now," opined the Southbridge *Evening News* in early October, "he might well be committing political suicide." While Kennedy watched Minority Leader Lyndon Johnson for a signal as to which way the party would go, Saltonstall watched Kennedy.[32]

Kennedy opted in favor of the censure resolution, but on narrow grounds. In a carefully written speech he planned to give in support of the action, he said the issue involved "neither the motives nor the sincerity of the Junior Senator from Wisconsin," and he cautioned against overriding "our basic concepts of due process by censuring an individual without reference to any single act deserving of censure." Long-ago misdeeds were not grounds for censure, he went on, since neither Flanders nor most others had publicly objected at the time; instead, the task would be to identify specific censurable practices that had occurred since the start of McCarthy's current term, that is, since January 1953. For Kennedy the outstanding case was the Army-McCarthy hearings, which, he argued, showed in graphic detail how the Wisconsin senator had besmirched the honor and dignity of the Senate—whether personally or by approving the insulting language and threats of retaliation used against the Army by Roy Cohn.

On the evening of July 31, 1954, Ted Sorensen stood at the back of a packed Senate chamber holding a stack of copies of his boss's speech, ready for distribution. But there would be no Kennedy speech given or released that night. GOP majority leader William Knowland of California, adamantly opposed to the resolution, moved for the establishment of a select committee to consider the issue, effectively delaying any kind of vote until after the election. The sense of relief from all corners of the room was palpable. Although a bloc of twelve liberals opposed the postponement, among them Hubert Humphrey of Minnesota and Paul Douglas of Illinois, both of whom faced reelection contests in the fall, sixty-nine others, including Kennedy and Saltonstall, voted in favor of Knowland's motion.

IV

When the Senate showdown over McCarthy finally came, in December, Jack Kennedy would not be in the mix. Throughout the 1954 session of Congress he was in agonizing pain, and by early summer he could move around only with the use of crutches. X-rays showed that his fifth lumbar vertebra had collapsed, probably on account of the corticosteroids he was taking for his Addison's disease. He asked to get a new office closer to the Senate chamber, to spare himself the lengthy walk on hard marble floors, but the seniority system thwarted the plan. Often he resorted to simply remaining in the chamber between quorum calls rather than return to his office. A short stay in the Bethesda Naval Hospital in July brought scant relief, and as soon as the Senate recessed he went to Hyannis Port for rest. His condition did not improve. Doctors in New York suggested the possibility of spinal fusion surgery, but Sara Jordan, Jack's longtime physician at Boston's Lahey Clinic, advised against going ahead—the procedure could easily kill him, she said on the porch in Hyannis Port that summer, because his Addison's disease and his treatments for it greatly increased the chance of a fatal infection. (Steroids are immunosuppressives that can make infection more likely and more serious.) Her Lahey colleagues agreed, but the senator was undaunted.[33]

"Jack was determined to have the operation," Rose Kennedy said later. "He told his father that even if the risks were fifty-fifty, he would rather be dead than spend the rest of his life hobbling on crutches and paralyzed by pain." The Ambassador, having already in essence lost one child—Rosemary—to an operation that went horribly awry, pleaded with his son not to do it. "Joe first tried to convince Jack that even confined to a wheelchair he could lead a full and rich life," Rose recalled. "After all, he argued, one need only look at the incredible life FDR had managed to lead despite his physical incapacity."[34]

"Don't worry, Dad," Jack assured him. "I'll make it through."[35]

Before Kennedy could enter New York's Hospital for Special Surgery (at the time still known colloquially by its former name, the Hospital for the Ruptured and Crippled), however, he had one more distasteful task to complete in that generally distasteful political year of 1954. With the Senate race in Massachusetts heating up by the day, he felt pressure to come out strongly for Foster Furcolo, his fellow Democrat. But he was torn. He liked "Salty" Saltonstall personally, worked well with him, and shared his pragmatic sensibility; in fact, he felt less kindly toward Furcolo, an ambitious Springfield-based attorney who served as state treasurer and had offered Jack only tepid support in his 1952 race against Henry Cabot Lodge. Intelligent and bookish, Furcolo was a sometime playwright who had graduated from Yale College and Yale Law School, but Jack, seeing in him a rival for statewide power and perhaps national influence, dismissed him as an empty suit.[36]

Their simmering feud boiled over in early October 1954, just before Kennedy went in for his surgery. With Jack having agreed to endorse the entire Democratic ticket, including Furcolo and gubernatorial candidate Robert Murphy, on a television program in Boston, he flew up from the Cape, arriving at the studio in pain and with a fever. Furcolo showed up almost an hour late, right before the show was to start, and complained that the draft of Kennedy's endorsement that he'd read was weak. Jack, already irritated by Furcolo's tardiness, shot back, "Foster, you have a hell of a nerve coming in here and asking for these last-minute changes." He icily added that he had not forgotten Furcolo's standoffish posture in the Senate race in 1952. For a moment it seemed the telecast might not happen, but order was restored and it went off smoothly, even though Jack omitted any direct mention of Furcolo or criticism of Saltonstall. The press spoke of an open breach between the two Democrats, and even close Kennedy aides acknowledged that he had allowed his personal feelings to affect his political judgment. Kenny O'Donnell would call the shunning of Furcolo, who went on to lose the election, "the only wrong political move Jack Kennedy ever made."[37]

On October 10, Jack entered the hospital. The day before, over lunch at the Ritz-Carlton in Boston with once and future aide Larry O'Brien, he cheerfully declared, "This is it, Larry. This is the one that cures you or kills you." The team of surgeons, writing the following year in the *Archives of Surgery*, described their patient as "a thirty-seven-year-old man" with Addison's disease, whose condition presented unique complications:

> Orthopedic consultation suggested that he might be helped by a lumbosacral fusion together with a sacroiliac fusion. Because of the severe degree of trauma involved in these operations and because of the patient's adrenocortical insufficiency due to Addison's disease, it was deemed dangerous to proceed with these operations. However, since this man would become incapacitated without surgical intervention, it was decided, reluctantly, to perform the operations by doing two different procedures at different times if necessary and by having a team versed in endocrinology and surgical physiology help in the management of this patient before, during, and after the operation.[38]

This would be an experimental surgery, the team knew, with a low chance of success. (In time, they would also determine that it had been unwarranted, in view of the likely effects and risks involved.) Three times they postponed the operation. Finally, on October 21, they went ahead, led by Dr. Philip D. Wilson, who used screws to bolt a metal plate into bone in order to stabilize the lumbar spine. In Hyannis Port, Joe Kennedy was beside himself with worry, unable to sleep at all that night. As Rose recalled, "His mind kept wandering back to the last letter he received from Joe Junior, the letter written right before his death, assuring his father that there was no danger involved and that he would be sure to return. The memory was so painful that Joe actually cried out in the darkness with a sound so loud that I was awakened from sleep."[39]

Joe was right to fret. Three days after the surgery, his son developed an infection that failed to respond to antibiotics. Jack's temperature rose alarmingly and he slipped into a coma. His family was summoned at midnight to come to the hospital immediately, and a priest arrived to administer the last rites of the Church—the second time this had happened to him. Jackie Kennedy, chain-smoking throughout, clung to her father-in-law for support and, for the first time in her life, she said afterwards, "really prayed." The next day, the Ambassador wept before journalist Arthur Krock. "He told me he thought Jack was dying and he wept sitting in the chair opposite me in the office."[40] On Capitol Hill, rumors were floated that the end was nigh, and Evelyn Lincoln received word that her boss might have mere hours to live.

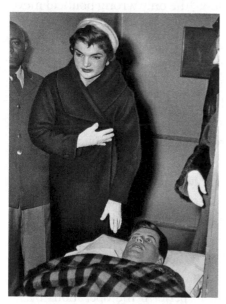

Having cheated death once again, the senator leaves the hospital with Jackie by his side, on December 22, 1954, in order to begin recuperation in Palm Beach.

And then, suddenly, just as he had done so many times before, Jack rallied, staving off the seemingly inevitable rendezvous with death. He remained critically ill, with an eight-inch wound from the incision that would not heal, but he was out of immediate danger. Expressions of relief and support flowed in—Pope Pius XII sent "a pledge of Heavenly assistance" for a full recovery, and President Eisenhower, visiting Boston, told the National Council of Catholic Women that he hoped and prayed Senator Kennedy would be "shortly restored to full health."[41] For several weeks Jack lay on his back in his darkened room, more or less immobile, until the doctors decided he might recover more quickly in Florida. Shortly before Christmas he was flown to the family's home in Palm Beach.

By then, the Senate had at long last held its vote on censuring McCarthy. The verdict went against him, 67 to 22, with only half the Republicans, and not a single Democrat, staying with him.[42] Almost certainly, Kennedy would have voted for censure if present, on the same circumscribed grounds that he had planned to do so in the summer. He disliked the senator's antics and crudeness, and had shown no hesitation in defying him over the appointments of Conant, Bohlen, and Lee. (More basically, with every voting Democrat opting in favor of censure, is it even remotely plausible to imagine Kennedy casting the lone vote against?) Yet it also must be said that Kennedy could have participated in the vote had he wanted to. Upon entering the hospital, he did not give his legislative assistant, Ted Sorensen, guidance on how to proceed in his absence. Sorensen took no action. He feared the wrath of the senator's father and brother if he declared Kennedy in support of censure, and also, as he later said, he "suspected—correctly—that there was no point in my trying to reach him on an issue he wanted to duck."[43]

Kennedy's failure to vote on the final censure resolution would cause him no end of grief in the years to come, especially at the hands of liberal Democrats, who deemed his moral position wobbly at best. His principal legalistic defense—that the Senate was acting like a jury, and no juror absent from the trial should have his predetermined opinion recorded—cut no ice with these critics. McCarthy was not in fact on trial, they rightly pointed out, and moreover his conduct over the past four years was a matter of common public knowledge. To them, it was obvious that Kennedy had acted on the basis of his family's ties to McCarthy and his fear of alienating the Wisconsin demagogue's sizable mass of unreconstructed backers. Had Kennedy instructed Sorensen to register support for censure (through a Senate procedure known as pairing, in which two absent lawmakers declared positions on opposite sides of an issue), he would have spared himself much future agony. Initially, however, his decision not to do so had logic behind it. When the right-wing *Boston Post* ran a page 1 editorial blasting those New England lawmakers who voted against McCarthy as having acted "in accordance with the desires of the Kremlin," John Kennedy was not one of its targets.[44]

The comment he made to Chuck Spalding shortly before being wheeled into surgery was revealing: "You know," he said in a contemplative way, "when I go downstairs [after the operation], I know exactly what's going to happen. Those reporters are going to lean over my stretcher. There's going to be about ninety-five faces bent over me with great concern. And then every one of those guys is going to say, 'Now, Senator, what about McCarthy?' Do you know what I'm going to do? I'm going to reach for my back and I'm just going to yell, 'Oow,' and then I'm going to pull the sheet over my head and hope we can get out of there."[45]

The censure vote marked the effective end of Joe McCarthy's reign (though not the end of McCarthyism). He continued thereafter to make belligerent speeches on the Senate floor, but fewer and fewer colleagues heard them. With the Democrats having scored gains in the midterm elections and gained control of both houses of Congress, his clout was reduced. Even worse, to his mind, the press stopped paying attention. His alcoholism, already advanced at the time of the vote, became more severe, and he suffered bouts of deep depression. In May 1957, he died, succumbing to acute hepatitis brought on by the years of alcohol abuse. Robert Kennedy, loyal to the end, cried upon hearing the news and flew to Wisconsin for the funeral, while Joe Kennedy told McCarthy's widow how "shocked and deeply grieved" he was to learn of the senator's passing. "His indomitable courage in adhering to the cause in which he believed evoked my admiration. His friendship was deeply appreciated and reciprocated."[46]

V

Throughout the long postoperative ordeal, first in New York and then in Palm Beach, Jackie Kennedy was the picture of steadfast support, remaining at her husband's bedside more or less continually, serving as de facto chief nurse. "Jackie was magnificent with him," recalled journalist and friend Charlie Bartlett, who visited the hospital in November. "She had this almost uncanny ability to rise to the occasion. She sat with him for hours, held his hand, mopped his brow, fed him, helped him in and out of bed, put on his socks and slippers for him, entertained him by reading aloud and reciting poems she knew by heart, bought him silly little gadgets and toys to make him laugh, played checkers, Categories, and Twenty Questions with him." Chuck Spalding agreed. "She stepped right in and did everything humanly possible to see that he'd pull through. People who thought she was some flighty society girl realized they'd made a big mistake. Jackie was far from helpless." She plumped his pillows, brought him snippets of gossip about family and friends, and told him about the new movies generating the most buzz. She smuggled in his favorite candy. And she urged friends to come by the hospital as often as possible, knowing that such visits distracted him from the pain. "Jack is feeling lousy," she'd say. "Come on down."[47]

Even strangers were recruited to the cause. At an evening function in Manhattan that she attended with her sister, Lee, Jackie met the glamorous screen star Grace Kelly, who would soon win an Oscar for her role in George Seaton's *The Country Girl.* The two sisters asked Kelly to come with them to the hospital to cheer Jack up. She agreed, slipping quietly into the room and—at the sisters' suggestion—whispering in his ear, "I'm the new night nurse." Depending on the account, Kelly either did or did not don a nurse's outfit, and Kennedy either recognized her or stared blankly ahead, too drugged to comprehend anything. Kelly's own recollection was that he "recognized me at once and couldn't have been sweeter or more quick to put me at ease."[48]

Sometimes Jackie showed a different side. Priscilla Johnson, who had been a research assistant for the senator the previous spring and whom he sporadically pursued, came to the hospital on a weekend afternoon in November. Jackie was there. "She looked absolutely stunning in a black suit," Johnson remembered, "frolicking around the bed, smiling and laughing, eating Jack's meal, before she was to venture out to meet her old beau, John Marquand, for dinner." To the former assistant it seemed obvious that Jackie, so perfectly made up, so fetching and attractive, was baiting her husband, trying to make him a little jealous, and that it was working. "I realized then and there she was an actress, a really excellent actress. She loved him, and she wanted him to know what he had in her, to really feel it."[49]

In Palm Beach she carried on in her role as lead caretaker. Years later she joked of that Christmas of 1954 that it was a "horrible" affair. "We spent the whole time hovering around the heir apparent." Yet she was ever attentive, day after exhausting day, never complaining even as the hours grew long and her own sleep was cut short. Her husband remained frail, his weight below 130 pounds, and he suffered regular infections and spikes in his temperature. His wound, deep and suppurating, required constant attention, and it was Jackie who gave it, and without fuss. "Jackie cleaned the wound skillfully, gently, and calmly," Rose Kennedy subsequently said, "and made no comment about it to anyone." As she had done in New York, she bathed him and fed him, read to him and told him stories, and she now added a new activity: she got him to try oil painting, in the manner of his hero Churchill. Her efforts notwithstanding, he suffered bouts of enveloping gloom and bitterness. Friends such as Red Fay and Dave Powers and Lem Billings saw it when they visited him in Florida, and family members saw it up close. (It says something about the devotion Jack inspired in his friends that Fay stayed for ten days, and Billings for a month.) At times they feared he was losing the will to go on as he contemplated possibly having to give up his Senate seat.[50]

What rescued him, according to his wife, was the writing project he had first conceived the previous winter, on political courage and the true meaning of representative democracy. It was a natural fit for him: he was a student of history, for one thing, and moreover the phenomenon of courage in public affairs had fascinated him since his youth. At various points in 1954, acquaintances suggested nominees for a list of U.S. senators who had acted on principle even at the price of damage to their political careers. Arthur Krock suggested Robert Taft, while Ted Sorensen lobbied for the inclusion of fellow Nebraskan George Norris. In a book of orations, Kennedy read Daniel Webster's Seventh of March speech and the abolitionists' condemnation of it. Jackie's Georgetown course with Jules Davids in the spring of 1954 likely also played a role—Davids lectured dramatically to the students on the nation's political history, and in the evenings Jackie and Jack would discuss the themes and readings of the class. The senator's reading of another Herbert Agar book—*A Time for Greatness*, with its clarion call to Americans to lead the drive to a better and more just world—may have provided further inspiration.[51]

Now, in early 1955, the project gained momentum. It should be more than a magazine article, Kennedy determined; it should be a book, featuring profiles of senators representing different regions and political persuasions. Fifteen years had passed since the publication of *Why England Slept*, which had been a turning point in its author's young life; the new work would prove to be another milestone for him, not least for the deeper insight it would give him into his own political philosophy. As in the earlier book, Kennedy concerned himself here with the problem of the responsibilities of leadership in democratic society—in particular, what is a statesman to do if his constituents and his party advocate a course of action that he believes is dangerously mistaken?

Skeptics then and later wondered if the new book wasn't mostly an effort to make amends for his non-vote on McCarthy's censure. No doubt it was, in part, though it bears reiterating that he had conceived the study many months before the McCarthy crisis came to a head. At that time he had been too busy to give the project close attention; now, flat on his back on the Florida oceanfront, he had all the hours in the world. "Jack couldn't sleep for more than an hour or two at a time because the pain was so bad," his father remembered, "so he'd study to get his mind off the pain." Patricia's husband, Peter Lawford, not generally awed by the Kennedy men, was amazed by his brother-in-law's self-discipline and drive. "He was really ill with that back, but he fought his way through that, and . . . wrote the book while he was lying on his back."[52]

"This project saved his life," Jackie said. "It helped him channel all his energies while distracting him from pain."[53]

Her own role was critical, as the author would note in his preface: "This book would not have been possible without the encouragement, assistance and criticism offered from the very beginning by my wife Jacqueline, whose help during all the days of my convalescence, I cannot ever adequately acknowledge." Jackie read aloud to him when he was too weary to hold a book, taking detailed notes along the way, and she successfully lobbied to have him seek input from Professor Davids on some of the chapters.[54] She also coordinated on logistical matters with Ted Sorensen, who would be Kennedy's principal collaborator in the writing. From the senator's office in Washington, Sorensen worked with a coterie of clerical assistants who transcribed from Dictabelts, took dictation, and typed research materials and, later, sections of draft chapters. He also consulted with historians and other experts. Staff at the Legislative Reference Service of the Library of Congress sent cartons of books, some to Palm Beach, some to Sorensen in the Senate office.

Kennedy made the final choices about which figures to feature in the book. And although Sorensen took the lead role in drafting the bulk of the chapters, with significant input on some of them from Davids and Jim

Landis, the senator was responsible for the book's architecture, themes, and arguments. Sorensen, gifted though he was in so many ways, didn't have that capacity—at twenty-seven and with no personal political experience, he was too green, and moreover he knew far less about the details of U.S. history than did his boss. Kennedy was especially critical to the first and last chapters, as well as a big chunk of chapter 2, on John Quincy Adams—it was the Adams case that had first drawn him to the project, and he produced a lot of prose on Adams that never made it into the finished book. Often he worked while prone in bed, on heavy white paper in his loose, widely spaced hand; on better days, he was propped up on the patio or the porch. Some sections he dictated into a machine or to stenographers hired locally. On an almost daily basis, Sorensen recalled, Kennedy sent him instructions about "books to ship down, memoranda to prepare, sources to check, materials to assemble. More than two hundred books, journals, magazines, Congressional Records and old newspaper files were scanned, as well as my father's correspondence with Norris and other sources."[55]

"Politics is a jungle," Kennedy wrote in his notes, "torn between doing the right thing and staying in office—between the local interest & the national interest—between the private good of the politician & the general good." Moreover, "we have always insisted academically on an unusually high—even unattainable—standard in our political life. We consider it graft to make sure a park or a road, etc., be placed near property of friends—but what do we think of admitting friends to the favored list for securities about to be offered to the less favored at a higher price? . . . Private enterprise system . . . makes OK private action which would be considered dishonest if public action."[56]

"Enclosed pleased find the drafts for two chapters," Sorensen wrote to Kennedy on February 4. "These two chapters are of the approximate length intended; although undoubtedly you will want to introduce a more flowery style and greater historical detail (beyond that which was taught in Lincoln Central High School, the only American history I've ever had). I will say that this is the most gigantic undertaking we have ever gigantically undertaken; and I doubt whether Gibbon could have produced 'The Decline and Fall of the Roman Empire' in a proportionately brief time." The same day, Sorensen also shipped to Palm Beach biographies of Mississippi's Lucius Lamar and Missouri's Thomas Hart Benton. On February 14, he followed with draft chapters on John Tyler, who was a senator from

Virginia before he became vice president and president, and Sam Houston of Texas (only the latter made the final cut) and, under separate cover, "reference texts for your use in expanding and rewriting these drafts."[57]

The pace caused Kennedy to worry that they were moving too fast and risked producing a "second-rate" work; he wondered if they needed to take a step back and include more original research drawn from archival sources. But Sorensen pressed on, assuring his boss that the book would succeed or fail based on its broad interpretive claims and biographical richness, not on "whatever new, previously uncovered facts or facets we might include." This was no academician's work, after all, but a book by a statesman: "Even more important than the telling of these stories is the fact that a United States senator is telling them, telling them for their meaning and inspiration today, discerning the patterns in them and discussing in opening and concluding chapters the whole concept of political courage. No other Senator or author has done this."[58]

Gradually, a manuscript began to take shape, the work barely interrupted by Kennedy's return to New York in February 1955 for another operation. (Surgeons removed the metal plate as well as the screws that had been drilled into the bone to hold it in place. Then they replaced the shattered cartilage with a bone graft. The procedure seemed to work, but the patient was prescribed several more weeks of bed rest.) In April, Harper & Brothers, which had turned down *Why England Slept* in 1940 and which initially passed on this new work, offered a contract, with a $500 advance and with Evan Thomas II, the son of the socialist leader Norman Thomas, assigned as editor. In March and again in May, Sorensen traveled to Palm Beach, each time for ten days, to work with Kennedy on getting the draft chapters into shape.* "The way Jack worked," Sorensen later said, "was to take all the material, mine and his, pencil it, dictate the fresh copy in his own words, pencil it again, dictate it again—he never used a typewriter." On Sorensen's first visit, Kennedy was on his back throughout; by the second he was able to sit up and even take brief dips in the ocean.[59]

---

* Sorensen's wife was scheduled to give birth in the second week of March, but he told Kennedy he would gamble for the sake of the book. "My wife's intuition now tells her that this baby will not come early, and therefore if you desired my [presence in Palm Beach] during the first week in March, this would be no handicap." (Ted Sorensen to JFK, February 8, 1955, box 7, Ted Sorensen Papers.) Kennedy felt the matter was not urgent; Sorensen came later in the month, following the birth.

VI

The 266-page book that resulted features profiles of eight senators—John Quincy Adams, Daniel Webster, Thomas Hart Benton, Sam Houston, Edmund G. Ross, Lucius Quintus Cincinnatus Lamar, George Norris, and Robert A. Taft—who showed notable courage and risked their careers in taking political stances unpopular with their constituents, their parties, and in some cases their regions. Neither Kennedy nor Sorensen knew the historiography well enough to get much below the surface in any of the cases, and although they were helped in this regard by the counsel they received from Davids and Landis, some parts of the book have aged poorly.[60] Although Kennedy wrote powerfully about Lamar, who served as an officer in the Confederate army during the Civil War but later championed reconciliation between North and South, he missed the Mississippian's steadfast racism and white supremacist views. (In 1875, a year after eulogizing Northern abolitionist Charles Sumner, Lamar spoke of "the supremacy of the unconquered and unconquerable Saxon race.") In the same vein, the book embraced the then-common rendering of Reconstruction as a bleak time in which the defeated and debilitated South was further beaten down by a sinister mix of Northern reconstructionists (or carpetbaggers, as they were called), scalawags (Southern whites who collaborated with the reconstructionists), and "uppity" former slaves. This depiction, which took a dim view of Radical Republicans such as Thaddeus Stevens, was in line with prevailing scholarly accounts but would soon be undermined by a wave of studies providing a more nuanced assessment of the era.[61]

Profiles was hardly brilliant, in-depth history. Nor, given the cut-and-paste feel of some sections, could it be considered a stylistic triumph. Its principal contribution—both at the time of publication and today—lies in its broad interpretive claims, articulated most fully in the two chapters in which Kennedy's own imprint was greatest, namely, the first and the last. The introduction, candid and engaging, contains humorous asides reminiscent, in tone and style, of the college-age Kennedy writing to Lem Billings two decades before (including a heavy use of dashes): "If we tell our constituents frankly that we can do nothing, they feel we are unsympathetic to inadequate. If we try and fail—usually meeting a counteraction from other Senators representing other interests—they say we are like all the rest of the politicians. All we can do is retreat into the Cloakroom and weep on the shoulder of a sympathetic colleague—or go home and snarl at our wives." But the introduction's core message is serious. Its title is "Courage and Politics," but more than anything the chapter argues for the vital importance in a democracy of compromise, of having "the sense of things possible." The absolutist's condemnation of all compromise as immoral is shortsighted, Kennedy insists, for decisions of public policy often involve difficult choices, often mean choosing from a menu of lousy options.

> The fanatics and extremists and even those conscientiously devoted to hard and fast principles are always disappointed at the failure of their Government to rush to implement all of their principles and to denounce those of their opponents. . . . [But] some of my colleagues who are criticized today for lack of forthright principles—or who are looked upon with scornful eyes as compromising "politicians"—are simply engaged in the art of conciliating, balancing, and interpreting the forces and factions of public opinion, an art essential to keeping our nation united and enabling our Government to function. Their consciences may direct them from time to time to make a more rigid stand for principle—but their intellects tell them that a fair or poor bill is better than no bill at all, and that only through the give-and-take of compromise will any bill receive the successive approval of the Senate, the House, the President and the nation.[62]

For Kennedy, the compromise can be, should be, at the level of policy, not principle. "We can compromise our political positions," he writes, "but not ourselves. We can resolve the clash of interests without conceding our ideals." Idealists and reformers and dissenters in fact are crucial, because they prevent political situations from being about nothing but opportunism and expediency and careerism. Above all, "compromise need not mean cowardice. Indeed it is frequently the compromisers and conciliators who are faced with the severest tests of political courage as they oppose the extremist views of their constituents," as their loyalty to the nation triumphs "over all personal and political considerations."[63]

Not all of the eight men profiled in the remainder of the book were "compromisers and conciliators"; some were unyielding in their commitment to absolute principles. Nor, Kennedy informed his readers, did he agree with each historical stand. But all eight men had one thing in common, he insisted: they showed courage, in transcending narrow interests for what they saw as the greater good, in making the Senate "something more than a mere collection of robots dutifully recording the views of their constituents, or a gathering of time-servers skilled only in predicting and following the tides of public sentiment."[64]

Thus did John Quincy Adams ignore the narrow interests of Massachusetts and New England to support the Louisiana Purchase and the Embargo Act; and thus did Daniel Webster, also from Kennedy's home state, defy his constituents and his party in trumpeting nationalism over sectionalism in helping to broker the Compromise of 1850. Thomas Hart Benton, for his part, prevented Missouri from joining the seceding Southern states, while Sam Houston cast the lone vote among Southern Democrats against the Kansas-Nebraska Act of 1854. Edmund Ross of Kansas joined with six other Republicans to oppose the impeachment of Andrew Johnson, and Mississippi's Lucius Lamar sought, in the wake of Reconstruction, to encourage national unity over sectional strife. George Norris won acclaim for standing against the despotic rule of House Speaker "Uncle Joe" Cannon of Illinois, and Robert Taft, recently deceased, was commended for daring to oppose the Nuremberg Trials because of his belief that the U.S. Constitution prohibited ex post facto laws. Not selected for inclusion, Kennedy noted, were those legislators whose battles, however determined and impressive, were waged "with the knowledge that they enjoyed the support of the voters back home."[65]

The concluding chapter returns to the broader themes; it matters to us today for what it says about Kennedy's views on politics and leadership, and for serving as a kind of timeless antidote to the cynicism about politics and politicians that periodically courses through the American body politic. Representative democracy is hard work, he tells his readers, for unlike in an authoritarian system, leaders in a democracy cannot impose their will on society. "We, the people, are the boss, and we will get the kind of political leadership, be it good or bad, that we demand and deserve." Kennedy extols both compromise and courage (the courage he most favors tends to be that of moderates who resist extremists) and argues that it is on national issues—on matters of conscience that challenge party, regional, and constituent loyalties—"that the test of courage is presented." At the same time, Kennedy says his book is not intended to laud independence for the sake of independence, or to imply that there is on every policy issue a right side and a wrong side. "On the contrary," he writes, "I share the feelings expressed by Prime Minister Melbourne, who, when irritated by the criticism of the then youthful historian T. B. Macaulay, remarked that he would like to be as sure of anything as Macaulay seemed to be of everything."[66]

Kennedy then quotes Lincoln: "There are few things wholly evil or wholly good. Almost everything, especially of Government policy, is an inseparable compound of the two, so that our best judgment of the preponderance between them is continually demanded."[67]

Here the senator may have been influenced by an extended conversation he had at about this time with longtime friend David Ormsby-Gore. From his reading of American history, Kennedy told the Englishman, he had drawn the lessons that there were usually two sides to every serious political problem. The zealots of the left and right, in their constant demand for simple solutions, didn't grasp this fundamental point. "Now this didn't prevent him being capable of taking decisions," Ormsby-Gore said later of the conversation, "but it did always prevent him saying, 'I know that I have got nothing but right on my side and the other side is entirely wrong,' and he never would adopt that attitude. He said that one of the sad things in life, particularly if you were a politician, was that you discovered that the other side really had a very good case. He was most unpartisan in that way." According to Ormsby-Gore, Kennedy even wondered whether "he was really cut out to be a politician because he was so often impressed by the other side's arguments when he really examined them in detail. Of course, he thought nothing of them if they were just the usual sort of partisan speech attacking his position on something, but where he thought there was a valid case against his position, he was always rather impressed by the arguments advanced."

"He knew that if you were President of the United States or indeed had any position in public life, for good or evil, somebody had to make decisions and you had the responsibility of making decisions," Ormsby-Gore continued. "You did your best but you would be foolish to assume that you were omnipotent and all-seeing or that you were necessarily always right. The best you could hope for was that you were likely to be right more often than somebody else. It shows a considerable degree of humility in the conduct of human affairs. He felt that people who thought it was simple and that the answers were obvious were dangerous people."[68]

In July 1955, with the manuscript almost complete, Jack asked his sister Eunice and others for input on the title. He told them he had four possibilities in mind: "Men of Courage," "Eight Were Courageous," "Call the

Roll," and "Profiles of Courage." Responses varied, and Kennedy himself soon dropped "Men of Courage" from consideration. Other options considered and rejected included "The Patriots" and "Courage in the Senate." Ultimately, Evan Thomas and his colleagues at the publishing house made the call: it would be *Profiles in Courage*.[69]

That summer, Kennedy and Sorensen worked to incorporate suggestions from a range of academics, notably James MacGregor Burns, Arthur Holcombe (who had taught Kennedy at Harvard), Allan Nevins (who would also contribute a foreword), and Arthur M. Schlesinger Jr., who submitted four pages of single-spaced criticism in early July. (Kennedy had asked Schlesinger to be "ruthlessly frank in giving me your criticism, comments and suggestions, however major or however petty," and the historian obliged, calling the Webster chapter problematic and the Taft chapter wholly unpersuasive. "If statesmanship implies a capacity to see the real issues," he wrote with respect to the former, "then the architects of the Compromise [of 1850] were far from statesmen. Webster never saw either the political issue of Southern domination of the Union or the moral issue of slavery." As for Taft, his condemnation of the Nuremberg Trials, however defensible, took place outside the Senate, and moreover it was "hard to recollect Taft's doing anything else which required political courage." Kennedy tweaked both chapters in response, though not to Schlesinger's full satisfaction.) In early August, Kennedy informed Thomas that Sorensen would submit the finished version shortly, as soon as he received some final input from Nevins.[70]

VII

Sorensen would do the honors because by then Kennedy had decamped for a vacation in the South of France. Over the preceding months, his health had gradually improved. On March 1 he walked without crutches for the first time, and the next day he ventured to the beach, with Jackie and Dave Powers steadying him. There would be setbacks in the weeks thereafter, with long stints in bed, but the trend lines pointed in the right direction. He gained weight and grew steadily stronger. On May 23, 1955, after seven months away, he returned triumphantly to Washington. Family and friends were out in force at National Airport to greet his flight from Palm Beach, which also included Jackie and sister Jean. Later, on the Capitol steps, he posed for newsreel and TV cameramen, to the cheers of tourists and a delegation of southern textile workers who happened by. Inside the Senate Office Building, receptionists stood to applaud when the senator entered room 362, and he found his inner office crammed with waiting reporters. On his desk, among the letters and telegrams celebrating his return, was a giant fruit basket bearing a note that read "Welcome home," signed "Dick Nixon."[71]

One of the reporters asked about his upcoming thirty-eighth birthday. "I'm looking forward to it," he replied with a chuckle. "I'll certainly be glad to get out of my thirty-seventh year."

Would Ike run again?

"I don't know."

Wasn't the president's strength as formidable everywhere as it had been when he entered the White House?

"Well, I've been in a pretty limited area. I'll say that he seems to be standing up well in Palm Beach." Laughter all around.[72]

If Jackie hoped her husband would proceed with care, easing gently back into his routines, she was soon disappointed. At his direction, his staff arranged an ambitious schedule, starting with a commencement address at Assumption College, in Worcester, on June 3, followed by another graduation address at Boston College on June 5 and the Jefferson-Jackson Day dinner on June 9. On the sixteenth he attended the fifteenth reunion of his Harvard class.[73]

The big early event, though, occurred on June 10, when Kennedy hosted a picnic in Hyannis Port for close to three hundred state legislators and legislative assistants, including "secretaries" from the 1952 campaign but also many who had never been active for him. He greeted them in chinos, sweatshirt, and sneakers, looking youthful and energetic. It was a transparent attempt to show Massachusetts Democrats that he was back and healthier than ever, and it worked. "The thing I remember most about the event was that he was physically able to move around," Kenny O'Donnell remembered. "There were no crutches. They had softball games and so forth, and it was an excellent outing." Most important, to O'Donnell's mind, the senator's appeal to the rank and file hadn't dissipated one iota.

Jack Kennedy's magic was as solid as it ever had been. He was on his feet. He was healthy again, physically and mentally. The great attraction of the candidate was on display, and the fear that he might not return, that siding with Jack Kennedy was a risk, was finally put to rest. To many of these regular politicians who had eyed Jack with suspicion as an outsider, a rich kid, and a lightweight now saw something else. They saw their political future and the future of the party in Massachusetts. They knew now it was better to be on the winning side, and for the regulars that meant siding with Jack Kennedy.[74]

He was not, however, the same man. Close associates such as O'Donnell and Powers and Sorensen noticed that his long health ordeal had changed him, had made him more serious, more determined. Having long believed that he would not live past the age of forty-five, he felt enhanced pressure to achieve the goal, stated to his wife, of claiming his "place in history." Said journalist Joseph Alsop some years later, "I've always thought he did not begin to take his own career truly seriously, I mean to have any long range and high aim in his own career, until he went through his very serious illness in 1955. . . . Something very important happened inside him, I think, when he had that illness because he came out of it a very much more serious fellow than he was prior to it. He had gone through the valley of the shadow of death, and he had displayed immense courage, which he'd always had."[75]

This isn't quite right: Kennedy's "long range and high aim" was evident well before the middle of 1955—indeed, arguably from the first House race in 1946. But the depiction of a more serious, more focused political figure coming out of the harrowing surgery and aftermath rings true, as does the suggestion that Kennedy emerged from the tribulations with his reputation for physical courage further enhanced. In this way the episode actually boosted his public profile. Newspaper and magazine editors found the story irresistible, and the fact that Kennedy's misadventure came so soon after his high-profile society wedding made it all the more poignant. Photos of the senator entering the hospital, on crutches, while his devoted Jackie smiles bravely at his side played widely across the country, shaping the narrative of the handsome lawmaker and war hero who refused to give in to his ailments and ultimately vanquished them.[76]

To those who knew him well, the turnaround was stunning: eight months after almost dying in a New York hospital room and four months after it seemed he might never walk unaided again, his political career in all likelihood over, John F. Kennedy was back, by no means fully healthy but so much better than he had been, and on the cusp of becoming what he had not been up until now: a figure of national renown.

TWENTY-ONE

RISING STAR

O n the evening of September 23, 1955, Dwight D. Eisenhower, vacationing in Colorado, retired to bed early, as was his custom. He had played twenty-seven holes of golf that day, and upon leaving the course had complained of indigestion and heartburn. The discomfort subsided, but he ate sparingly at dinner and then turned in. At 1:30 A.M. he awoke with acute pain in his chest. Mamie Eisenhower took one look at her husband and determined it was serious. Physicians were summoned, and by the following afternoon the diagnosis was confirmed: the sixty-four-year-old president had suffered a heart attack.[1]

Frenzied speculation followed in every corner of the land. Would he live? Even if he did, would he be too weakened to remain in office, or at least to put up with the rigors of a reelection campaign a year later? If he did not run, who would be the Republican nominee? And what would it mean for the Democratic race? As if to underscore the national anxiety, on Monday the twenty-sixth the New York Stock Exchange took its steepest plunge since the outbreak of the Depression.[2] And small wonder: Eisenhower's popularity in mid-1955 was immense—and still growing. He had steered the economy through a brief recession and had brought fiscal balance back to Washington. His expansion of social security had benefited millions. Overseas, the truce Eisenhower had secured in Korea seemed to be holding, and he had avoided new troop commitments elsewhere. A tense crisis with China over some minuscule islands off the Chinese coast—Matsu and the chain known as Quemoy—had eased, at least for the moment. Superpower relations, meanwhile, were stable, and some observers even spoke of a thawing in the Cold War as the Soviet leadership, under Nikita Khrushchev, sought a lowering of East-West tensions. In May 1955 Khrushchev ended a ten-year impasse by agreeing to pull Soviet troops out of Austria (occupied by the Allies since 1945) and to allow that nation to become independent and neutral. In July there followed a four-power summit meeting in Geneva—the first one since Potsdam, a decade before—which, though it produced nothing of substance, seemed a harbinger of a less fractious world order.

Eisenhower returned from the Swiss city to a euphoric reception, his approval rating at 79 percent. According to James Reston of *The New York Times,* not normally a man given to rhetorical effusiveness, "the popularity of President Eisenhower has got beyond the bounds of reasonable calculation and will have to be put down as a national phenomenon, like baseball. The thing is no longer just a remarkable political fact but a kind of national love affair, which cannot be analyzed satisfactorily by the political scientists and will probably have to be turned over to the headshrinkers."[3]

Reston's language was music to the ears of Republican strategists, but it also spoke to a problem: much of the public chalked these positive developments up to Eisenhower personally, not the party he led. It followed that Republicans would be vulnerable without him. And indeed, polls in midyear showed that with any other standard-bearer the GOP would likely lose the presidency the following autumn, and perhaps hemorrhage seats in Congress as well. Accordingly, in the days leading up to the heart attack, party officials had been leaning hard on the president to announce his candidacy; afterwards, they chewed their fingernails and waited for a clear prognosis. Gradually, Eisenhower's condition improved, but he remained coy about his intentions. To press secretary James Hagerty he confided privately that none of his most likely Republican successors, including Vice President Richard Nixon, had what it took to lead the nation, while on the Democratic side the picture seemed to him equally grim— 1952 nominee and former Illinois governor Adlai Stevenson, New York governor Averell Harriman, and Tennessee senator Estes Kefauver, the three likely front-runners, simply "did not have the competency to run the office of President."[4]

An uncharitable assessment, and in any case several Democrats were suddenly liking their chances. Whereas in earlier weeks they had been content to tell Stevenson that he must carry the party's banner in the election, now they turned circumspect and quietly took soundings about their own prospects. Stevenson, recognizing the danger, worked to shore up support, including among southern party stalwarts who had been lukewarm to him in 1952.[5] The burst of activity did not escape the attention of the press, which now ramped up the discussion of potential candidates for the second slot on the Democratic ticket. Numerous names were floated, among them the junior senator from Massachusetts. Stevenson, though he had long been leery of Joseph Kennedy, finding him pushy and overbearing, could see the advantages of having the Ambassador's son as a running mate, even as he also considered him too young and inexperienced for the role. In particular, Jack Kennedy could counter Eisenhower's surprising strength (as reflected in the 1952 returns) among Catholic Democrats unhappy with Franklin Roosevelt and Harry Truman for failing to thwart Communist expansion in Eastern Europe and Asia. The Catholic vote was a weak spot for Stevenson—he knew it, everyone knew it. Nor did it help him with these voters that he was divorced, and that he struggled to connect with the blue-collar concerns that animated many of them. In addition, Kennedy would bring some geographic balance to the ticket, if not of the preferred southern variety. It all constituted a pretty formidable cluster of attributes, the Illinois man conceded.

II

Even so, the speculations about a Stevenson-Kennedy ticket were as yet scattershot and fragmentary, more notable in hindsight than they were at the time. But they were significant enough to get the attention of the Kennedy family, as well as Jack's senior aides. Already on September 12, eleven days *before* the president's heart attack, Ted Sorensen had written the senator in Cap d'Antibes to alert him to rumors that the Stevenson camp considered him an attractive potential running mate.[6] A few days before that, Joseph Kennedy, who was also in the South of France for his annual summer sojourn, sent a letter to son Teddy:

Last night we went to the Gala at Monte Carlo and Jack arrived early and dressed in my room. As usual, he arrived without his studs, with two different stockings and no underpants; so he walked off with a pair of brand new Sulka stockings of mine, a new pair of Sulka underpants of mine, and the last pair of evening studs I possessed. . . . He is back on crutches after having tried to open a screen in his hotel room, but if he hasn't any more brains than to try that, maybe he should stay on crutches. His general attitude towards life seems to be quite gay. He is very intrigued with the constant rumors that he is being considered for the Vice Presidency, which idea I think is one of the silliest I have heard in a long time for Jack.[7]

Jack was then in the second month of his European trip, begun immediately after Congress went into recess. Jackie had come, too, but in the early going the two were in separate locales. Over the previous months the marriage had shown renewed signs of strain as the closeness engendered by his illness and recovery wore off. Jack had resumed his long work hours and heavy speaking schedule, and Jackie spent much of her time house-hunting. In early July, while her husband was still stateside, she had set off for London, where her sister, Lee, and Lee's husband, Michael Canfield, lived in a chic apartment in upscale Belgravia. (Michael, the adopted son of Harper & Brothers publisher Cass Canfield, who would soon bring out Jack's book *Profiles in Courage*, served as private secretary to Winthrop W. Aldrich, the U.S. ambassador to the Court of St. James's.) The sisters were, as always, thick as thieves, delighting in each other's company and hitting the London social scene, the ultra-stylish Lee turning as many heads as her sister. At the end of July, Jackie and Lee traveled to Paris and from there to the Riviera, where Canfield, having rented a flat for them in Antibes, joined them.[8]

Jack, meanwhile, accompanied by Torby Macdonald, boarded the SS *United States* in New York and made for Le Havre, in Normandy, arriving on August 10. From there the two continued on immediately to Båstad, a coastal resort town in southwestern Sweden, where Jack had arranged to rendezvous with Gunilla von Post at the Hotel Skånegården. Since their abortive get-together the previous summer, they had exchanged letters, including during Kennedy's convalescence in Florida. He asked if she would come to the United States; she countered by saying he should visit her in Sweden. He relented, writing, "My plans are your plans." In another letter he said that although the trip would be "a long way to Gunilla—it is worth it." In July 1955, according to von Post, he called her and they firmed up their plan to meet in Båstad the following month. A confirmation letter soon followed, addressed to von Post at her parents' home in Stockholm—Gunilla's mother read it to her over the phone.[9]

"I rushed toward Jack, my heart pounding," she later wrote of the moment she first saw him on August 11, "and fell into his arms. We held each other tightly. I was so happy to see him. No words could express my feelings." She had an overpowering sense that he felt as strongly for her as she felt for him; why else would he travel all this way to be with her, at considerable risk to his health and his career? "I was relatively inexperienced," she went on, "and Jack's tenderness was a revelation. He said, 'Gunilla, we've waited two years for this. It seems almost too good to be true, and I want to make you happy.' For the first time, I could let go and luxuriate in the attentions of a man who not only respected and cared for me but clearly loved me. I fully trusted him."[10]

Macdonald, for his part, met a Swedish woman soon after arriving, and the quartet spent an idyllic week together motoring by rental car around Skåne, the country's southernmost province, which is dotted with old manor houses and churches, and which Kennedy thought reminiscent of Ireland and—along the coast—of Cape Cod. "What's that?" he would exclaim excitedly from behind the wheel about this or that landmark, and they would get out and have a look, he often relying on crutches. Gunilla introduced him to her friends and family, who were dazzled by this charming and handsome politician (a "senator," no less) from America. "He cast a spell on people that I've never quite seen before or since. And everyone—man, woman, child—was smitten, and happy to be near him." Gunilla's mother and father apparently approved of the adulterous romance, so long as marriage might be in the offing. At no point did Kennedy talk with Gunilla about his wife, but Macdonald did, murmuring to her that Jack was unhappy in his marriage and much freer and more himself around her than around Jackie. In Gunilla's telling, the glorious week ended with a traditional Swedish crayfish party at a grand estate near Ystad, followed by a night of tender romance and her suitor telling her, repeatedly, "I love you, Gunilla. I adore you. I'm crazy about you and I'll do everything I can to be with you."[11]

From Sweden, Kennedy flew to Nice to meet up with Jackie and the Canfields at Cap d'Antibes. The last time he was here, two years before, he had been with Gunilla, cooing in her ear in the nighttime breeze at Cap-Eden-Roc. Now, while he waited for Jackie to arrive, he wrote to Gunilla to suggest another meeting soon. The reunion with his wife, he said, would be "complicated by the way I feel now—my Swedish flicka [girl]. All I have done is sit in the sun and look at the ocean and think of Gunilla. . . . All love, Jack." The Kennedys and the Canfields soon joined up with William Douglas-Home and his wife, Rachel, for numerous days of lazing in the sun followed by evenings on the town. The Douglas-Homes took to Jackie immediately, appreciating her quick wit and intelligence. Asked later by biographer Sarah Bradford how the Kennedys got on with each other, William said it was hard to tell, because the marriage was not demonstrative. "Nothing with Jack would have been like that. So you wouldn't see them hugging and loving each other, holding hands, ever. There wasn't that kind of thing." Yet Jackie seemed happy with her husband, William Douglas-Home thought. "She wasn't demonstrative but she did love him, and they had this relationship which was fun, you'd have fun in their company, there'd be a lot of jokes and she used to tease him. It was good being with them. It was fun. But as I've said, they weren't a lovey-dovey couple."[12]

Jack certainly got plenty of reminders on the trip of how valuable Jackie could be to him in his dealings with world leaders. She translated for him during a meeting with senior French officials and won accolades from them and others for her elegance and her obvious familiarity with the country's history and art. "She had all the wit and the seductive charms of an eighteenth-century courtesan," Clare Boothe Luce later commented of Jackie's interactions with Old World luminaries. "Men just melted when she gazed at them with those gigantic eyes. The Europeans were not immune to this."[13]

According to von Post, Kennedy called her a few weeks later from Poland and said he had spoken with his father about divorcing Jackie so he could marry her, to which the elder Kennedy, he said, had responded, "You're out of your mind."[14] That Jack Kennedy might have said this to his Swedish lover on the phone is plausible; that he actually had such a conversation with his father is much less so. In the middle months of 1955 his political prospects were bright, brighter than they'd ever been before. The top rung of the ladder might even be within his reach at some point. Jack did not need his father to tell him that divorcing his young wife (of just two years, no less), especially after all the glowing press coverage their union had received, would almost certainly cause it all to fall apart. For a Catholic politician, whose church insisted on the inviolability of the marital vow, the risks were greater still. If father indeed spoke to son, he only stated what the son surely already knew.

Von Post's parents, sensing their daughter would likely be consigned to permanent mistress status, now intervened and compelled her to end the relationship. Soon thereafter, Gunilla became engaged to a Swede and in short order married. As he had with Inga Arvad after that relationship ended, Kennedy continued to keep in touch. "I had a wonderful time last summer with you," read one letter, penned on U.S. Senate stationery, in 1956. "It is a bright memory in my life—you are *wonderful* and I miss you."[15]

III

In early October 1955, Jack and Jackie Kennedy set sail for home, arriving in New York on the twelfth. Immediately, Jack headed for the Manhattan office of Dr. Janet Travell, an expert on pain management he had first visited a few months before. The muscle spasms in his lower left back had been bad on the trip, he told her, radiating out to his left leg and making him unable to put weight on it; he had been compelled to use crutches much of the time. He often could not reach his left foot to pull on a sock or sit in a low chair. Travell, in their earlier meeting, had determined that the left side of Kennedy's body was smaller than his right—the left side of his face was smaller, his left shoulder was lower, and his left leg significantly shorter. Astonishingly, in all the years of medical treatment, no previous doctor had ever detected the problem, which, with every step, caused a vacillating movement and generated strain in the spinal muscles. Upon initial diagnosis, Travell had prescribed lifts for Jack's left shoes and a lowered heel for his right, while also injecting him with procaine, more commonly known as Novocain. She now increased the dosage and suggested new exercises, then sent the patient on his way.

Kennedy found he liked Travell a great deal, liked the combination of her gentle woman's touch and her authoritative demeanor, backed by top credentials; in the weeks to come, he would regularly slip out of Washington for a day and fly up to have an appointment with her. She considered him a model patient—accepting of, or at least not resentful of, his condition, always game to try any regimen that seemed reasonable.[16]

Travell's efforts seemed to pay off. By the end of the year her patient was up to 168 pounds, his most ever, and he felt better than he had in a long time. His features had filled out, matured, as had his voice; he no longer looked or sounded younger than his years.

Jackie, for her part, suffered a physical setback of her own. On a fall weekend in Hyannis Port, she gamely agreed to play in the family's usual football scrimmage. Going out for a pass, she tripped and fell, crying out in pain. At

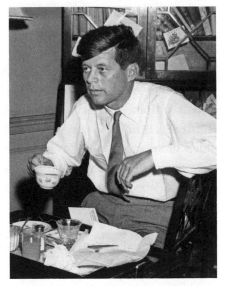

Back on the job in Washington, fall 1955.

New England Baptist Hospital, doctors confirmed an ankle fracture and kept her for five days, outfitting her with a cast below the knee. While recovering at her mother's Merrywood estate, in Northern Virginia, Jackie carried on the house hunt she had begun in the late spring before departing for Europe. Something kept bringing her back to Hickory Hill, a large three-story brick Georgian Colonial home in McLean, with guest quarters, stables, and a pool. The Potomac River ran nearby. She loved the tall trees and the rolling hills and the stables (she still liked to ride when circumstances permitted), and Jack was tickled by the historical connections: during the Civil War it had been General George B. McClellan's command post. They closed on the property for $125,000, and Jackie set about remodeling the main house extensively. Maybe, she thought, this could be the home that would make their marriage a happy one, where they could raise a family and live for the rest of their lives. Here, too, the close of 1955 brought happy news: Jackie found out she was pregnant.[17]

All the while that autumn, Dwight Eisenhower's heart attack and prognosis dominated the national headlines, with daily announcements marking his progress as he convalesced in Denver. On October 10 the president sat in the sun for a few minutes outside his Army hospital in Denver; on the fourteenth, his sixty-fifth birthday, he was photographed in a wheelchair on the hospital roof, looking relaxed and smiling. But the image belied the seriousness of his condition. Not until October 23 did he stand upright for the first time, and only on the twenty-sixth did he take unassisted steps—and then only a few feet across his bedroom. By November 11, forty-nine days after the heart attack, Eisenhower had improved sufficiently to be flown to Washington, where a large crowd greeted him at National Airport and others lined the streets en route to the White House. Even now he was weak, mostly screened from public view by his aides and doctors, and he spent the rest of 1955 at his home in Gettysburg, Pennsylvania. Only on January 9, 1956, did he resume his official duties in Washington—five months after departing the capital for his fateful summer holiday.[18]

Would he run for reelection? Political handicappers were uncertain as the year turned, which added intrigue in particular to the race for the Democratic nomination. (Republicans remained in stand-by mode.) Adlai Stevenson announced his candidacy on November 15, and Estes Kefauver followed on December 17. Averell Harriman waited in the wings, and there were well-founded rumors that Lyndon B. Johnson of Texas, the powerful Senate majority leader, looked to get in. This latter prospect intrigued Joe Kennedy. To his mind, Johnson would be a stronger candidate for the Democrats than any of the other possibilities, including Stevenson; though a healthy Eisenhower would likely best all of them, the margin would be narrower with Johnson at the top of the ticket. So the Ambassador devised a plan, one he laid out to Johnson ally and former FDR adviser Tommy Corcoran: if Johnson would declare his candidacy and promise to select Jack as his running mate, he, Joe Kennedy, would arrange financing for the ticket. Corcoran duly reported the offer to Johnson, who turned it down, claiming he wasn't running.[19]

Jack, it seems, never embraced the scheme, and it didn't surprise him that Johnson said no. To Jack's way of thinking, if the Texan coveted the nomination (and Jack had no doubt that he did), it made little sense for him to tie his hands in the way Joe Kennedy's offer demanded. For that matter, Lyndon Johnson was at best a long shot for the top spot—by Jack's calculation Adlai Stevenson remained the clear front-runner. Anyone seeking the number-two spot should focus his attention on him.

This was sound thinking on Jack's part. Stevenson may have lost in 1952, but he remained the titular head of the Democratic Party, deeply popular with many state leaders and rank-and-file members, and still the runaway favorite among the party's intellectuals. His loss in 1952, though admittedly lopsided, seemed in hindsight foreordained: no Democrat, in this line of reasoning, would have had a prayer of besting the popular Eisenhower, especially with the malaise of twenty straight years of Democratic rule and with the nation mired in an unpopular war in Korea. Even then, Stevenson had performed better than many gave him credit for—he racked up three million more votes nationally than Harry Truman had mustered in 1948. Since the election, moreover, Stevenson had only solidified his power position, giving well-received speeches around the country and winning accolades for his fundamental decency, his disavowal of bombast and banality, and his steadfast appeal to virtue and reason. "When demagoguery and deceit become a national political movement," he asserted in Miami Beach in early 1954, in pointed reference to Joseph McCarthy, "we Americans are in trouble; not just Democrats, but all of us."[20]

Jack saw the appeal of Stevenson and his message and shared his fundamental philosophy—Jack's own book, now deep in production, stressed the vital importance of rational, fact-based discourse in a democracy, and he shared the Illinoisan's affinity for blending poetry with power. He and Stevenson were not close allies, but in this period they got on well with each other.[21] And it mattered to him that Jackie admired Stevenson and wanted him for the top of the ticket, and that most of the friends the couple saw socially did, too. It intrigued Jack in this regard that the low-level buzz about a potential Stevenson-Kennedy ticket had not dissipated in the fall months; if anything, it had picked up.[22] Accordingly, he asked Ted Sorensen to undertake a study of the possible electoral benefits of having a Catholic vice presidential pick on the Democratic side. Sorensen took up the task eagerly, gathering a wide range of materials, journalistic as well as academic. He also went further, suggesting on November 22 that Kennedy endorse Stevenson at a high-profile news conference in Washington. Sorensen's rationale was twofold: an early public endorsement would bring Kennedy increased exposure and, "more important, provide an opportunity to clear up all doubts about your health, which is the one question I still hear frequently raised around here when your name is discussed as a possibility for the ticket."[23] (Jack's endorsement of Stevenson would come on March 8, 1956. He delayed the move, he told journalists, in order to give Stevenson the "best possible assist" in advance of the upcoming New Hampshire primary.[24])

Sorensen's seventeen-page study, completed in the winter of 1956 and titled "The Catholic Vote in 1952 and 1956," examined the results among Catholic voters in fourteen pivotal states in the North and the West, all of them previously Democratic, that had gone for Eisenhower over Stevenson in 1952 and, the report concluded, swung the election to the Republican. Using polling data, election returns, and academic research, Sorensen argued that the Catholic vote within those states had long been critical—without it, the Democrats would have lost the elections of 1940, 1944, and 1948. Moreover, Stevenson, in part because of his divorce and the perception of him as a liberal and an intellectual who was insufficiently strong on Communism, in 1952 had received lower percentages than Catholic Democratic candidates for the House and Senate in these states. For Sorensen, the conclusion was inescapable: if these traditionally Democratic voters could be brought back to the fold by means of a Catholic running mate for Stevenson, it could be decisive, combining with Democratic strengths in the South to bring the former Illinois governor success. Conversely, without these voters he had no realistic path to victory.

But what about Al Smith's defeat in 1928? Didn't that show the immense risk of having a Catholic on the ticket? Not remotely, the study said—1928 was a GOP year, a year for "dry" supporters of Prohibition. It wouldn't have mattered who the Democrats ran—he would have been vanquished. Of the states Smith lost, only four, all in the South, had been solidly Democratic in the years prior. Since then the picture had changed, and the Catholic vote now loomed more important than ever. Indeed, Sorensen suggested, in an indirect comment on the other potential vice presidential picks, Democratic chances in 1956 depended less on the farm vote or the southern vote than on reclaiming broad backing among Catholics.[25]

"Catholic voting strength is currently at its peak," Sorensen wrote, quoting pollster Samuel Lubell, "in view of the maturing of the offspring of the Italians, Czechs, and other former immigrant elements." Moreover, Sorensen stressed, ample research indicated that Catholics turned out to vote in greater proportions than did non-Catholics, a key point under any circumstances but especially given the nation's current population distribution: Catholics were particularly concentrated in fourteen crucial states with 261 votes in the electoral college (five fewer than were needed in 1956 to win the presidency).[26]

Even before Sorensen's study was completed, he and Kennedy quietly pushed its findings on sympathetic journalists. Fletcher Knebel, a witty and acerbic *Look* columnist who wrote political novels (including *Seven Days in May*) on the side, came away impressed after a meeting with the two men in February in which he received a rundown of the report. Kennedy, he wrote, had "all the necessary Democratic assets" in a vice president: good looks, youth, an outstanding war record, liberal policy positions, and exceptional vote-getting ability. His religion, moreover, far from being a liability in a national race, would be a boon, Knebel suggested, generating big turnouts in northern and eastern states with large Catholic populations.[27]

IV

There the matter might have rested, were it not for two other developments in early 1956 that served to raise Kennedy's stature. The first was the publication, in early January, of *Profiles in Courage*. In advance of the release, there had appeared a substantial excerpt in *The New York Times Magazine*, titled "The Challenge of Political Courage" and culled mostly from chapter 1, as well as shorter pieces in *The Boston Globe*, *Harper's*, *Reader's Digest*, and *Collier's*.[28] These prepublication efforts, vital in an age when glossy magazines were a hugely important source of information for the mass of Americans—*Reader's Digest* and *Collier's* had circulations of 10 million and 3.7 million, respectively—spurred advance orders of the book, and Kennedy received further encouragement from glowing reviews in prominent places. In a front-page assessment in *The New York Times Book Review*, political reporter Cabell Phillips gushed that it was "refreshing and enlightening to have a first-rate politician write a thoughtful and persuasive book about political integrity," featuring senators each of whom "at some moment of crisis staked his principles against the massed furies of bigotry, sectionalism, and conformity." An empathetic observer, the author was "no dilettante at his trade, but a solid journeyman full of ideals, but few illusions. His book is the sort to restore respect for a venerable and much abused profession."[29]

In a similar vein, *The Saturday Evening Post* praised Kennedy for recognizing "the necessity of compromise, to make democratic government work at all," and for understanding a senator's need to "act according to his own conscience regardless of what his constituents may think." According to the *Chicago Tribune*, it was "a remarkable book. . . . He writes brilliantly about a handful of American statesmen who, at crucial times in history, have displayed a rare kind of greatness."[30] Erwin D. Canham, writing in *The Christian Science Monitor*, cautioned that the author had better watch his step going forward, "for he has set up high standards of political integrity for comparison." But that, in its way, was a compliment to Kennedy, Canham went on: "That a U.S. senator, a young man of independent means with a gallant and thoughtful background, should have produced this study is as remarkable as it is helpful. It is a splendid flag that Senator Kennedy has nailed to his mast. May he keep it there." And so it went, with praise coming from *The Houston Chronicle* ("wholly engrossing"), the *Cleveland Plain Dealer* ("as fine a book as we are likely to get all year"), *The Wall Street Journal* ("a heartening and extremely spirited book"), and other papers across the nation.

In Boston, the City Council passed a resolution mandating that the School Committee incorporate *Profiles in Courage* as a central part of its history curriculum, and council member Gabriel F. Piemonte praised the volume as a "great lesson in democracy." In other cities, too, the book in short order became a staple on high school reading lists, in many places remaining there for years to come.[31]

A few dissonant voices could be heard. Charles Poore, in a review in *The New York Times*'s Books of the Times section, found it troubling that Kennedy lauded men who "showed their most conspicuous courage in defying the very forces that had chosen them for leadership." In his eloquent defense of the actions of Edmund G. Ross, for example, whose lonely vote in 1868 saved President Andrew Johnson from impeachment and thereby also upheld the Constitution, Kennedy had not taken "sufficient account of the enduring good sense of the American people as a whole who, as in the past, always will preserve constitutional government, no matter what the demagogues advocate in any passing time." Poore also wondered if it really was immaterial, as Kennedy claimed, whether another of his subjects, George Norris, was right or wrong on an issue, or only that Norris showed courage and was true to himself. Shouldn't the purpose to which the courage was put matter, too? "It almost urges us to admire courage as courage, no matter where it appears. And this has its repugnant aspects. . . . Our view of true courage, somehow, is inextricably woven into the fabric of the cause for which it is displayed." Poore nonetheless praised *Profiles in Courage* as "splendidly readable" and deeply impressive for having such an "extraordinarily varied" cast of characters. Kennedy, he wrote approvingly, "is a practical man as well as a connoisseur of idealists," a man who "appreciates Lord Melbourne's saying that he would like to be sure of anything as Macaulay seemed to be of everything."[32]

Sales were brisk from the start, and the book shot up the bestseller lists. It stayed there for many months. (Within three years it had sold 180,000 copies in hardback and half a million in paperback.) No longer could anyone consider John Kennedy just another freshman senator; now he was dubbed the unofficial historian of the upper chamber, and a respected champion of political integrity. With Soviet-led Communism posing a threat to the American way of life, the book affirmed for many readers the ability of democracy to triumph by producing leaders who put the national interest before selfish careerist ambition, who lived by the adage that no one has a monopoly on truth and therefore reasonable people can differ on the solutions to complex social and political problems. Foreign translations soon appeared, in languages from Hebrew to Japanese to Gujarati. On February 7, a month after publication, Kennedy was the featured speaker at the National Book Awards dinner in New York City, where he was photographed in the esteemed literary company of John O'Hara and W. H. Auden.[33]

Later, and especially after the book was awarded the 1957 Pulitzer Prize for Biography, critics would fault what they considered the deception of publishing a book under the name of a person who hadn't actually written it. Some were still leveling the charge decades after Kennedy's death.[34] The objection was largely baseless. For one thing, Kennedy had a bigger role in the writing, and certainly in the conception and framing of the book, than many of these analysts suggested; the book's broad themes and overarching structure were his. Friends who had visited in Florida attested to his hard work on the manuscript, as did secretaries who took his dictation, as did, with great vehemence, Jackie Kennedy.[35] (Without Sorensen or Jules Davids, Kennedy likely would have produced a similar book, if less felicitous in its prose; without Kennedy, on the other hand, *Profiles in Courage* would not have existed.) For another, it was standard practice for American politicians in midcentury—and later—to get significant assistance on books that appeared under their name alone. Everyone in Congress knew, for example, that *Crime in America*, a recent bestseller by Estes Kefauver, had mostly been written for him by his staff.[36]

Certainly it never occurred to Kennedy or Sorensen or anyone else involved in the project that they might be acting unethically, then or afterwards. Sorensen contributed mightily to the senator's speeches and articles; why should he not help write a book? Arguably, Kennedy should have refused the Pulitzer, but it's hard to imagine him (or anyone else in his position) actually doing so—such a move would have amounted to a self-declaration of fraudulence and possibly done lasting damage to his reputation. More to the point, in core respects Kennedy *was* the book's author. He himself never wavered from that conviction, and to the end of his days he would consider winning the Pulitzer perhaps the proudest moment of his life.[37]

V

Profiles in Courage paid immediate political dividends, elevating Kennedy's standing within a party already enamored of its seemingly erudite nominal head, Adlai Stevenson.[38] To Democratic leaders in Washington and to activists all across the nation, *Profiles* enhanced Kennedy's status as a rising star and a force to be reckoned with. (His insistence on having regional breadth in the book, with southerners well represented, now proved its worth.) He was further helped in this regard by the second notable development that spring, namely, his bruising, behind-the-scenes fight to wrest control of the Democratic Party organization in Massachusetts, the better to improve his standing with Stevenson. Here Kennedy's own long-term aloofness from the state party had left him on the outside looking in, which hardly mattered (the party as an organization had little actual power) except that its governing committee controlled the delegate selection process for the state's representation at the Democratic National Convention, set for Chicago in August.

In early March, soon after Eisenhower announced that he would stand for reelection, Kennedy attended a meeting of the committee to ask for its support. His prospects, he knew, were uncertain at best. The committee's chairman, a short, portly onion farmer and former tavern owner from central Massachusetts named William "Onions" Burke, was a protégé of James Michael Curley and a supporter of Joe McCarthy. More important,

Onions was a close ally of House Majority Leader John W. McCormack, who hailed from working-class South Boston and had come to Washington in 1928 and worked his way up in the leadership. Only Speaker of the House Sam Rayburn of Texas ranked higher. Though they were fellow Democrats and Irish Catholics, McCormack and Kennedy had never been close—McCormack distrusted cosmopolitan Ivy Leaguers, while Kennedy, though respectful of the older man, made it clear he did not consider him a role model. In addition, McCormack opposed Stevenson's presidential candidacy, seeking for himself a favorite-son designation in order to boost Averell Harriman and show the world that he, McCormack, spoke for the state's Democrats.[39]

McCormack was aided in this effort by Burke and John Fox, the rabidly McCarthyite publisher of *The Boston Post* who had backed Kennedy for the Senate in 1952 but had then turned on him for not standing by McCarthy. Fox, a Harvard man, also faulted Kennedy for failing to attack Harvard president Nathan Pusey, a favorite McCarthy target, whom Fox accused of coddling professors suspected of Communist sympathics. (To McCarthy and his acolytes, Harvard was "the Kremlin on the Charles.") When Kennedy refused Fox's urgings to join an alumni boycott of Harvard fundraising in retaliation, Fox pumped out editorials that condemned Kennedy and praised Burke and McCormack.[40]

Liberals in the state responded by rallying to Kennedy's side. The Americans for Democratic Action (ADA), in an action spearheaded by Harvard political scientist Samuel Beer (later to become president of the organization), joined in the campaign against Onions Burke, as did other progressive forces. According to Joseph Rauh, a founding member of the ADA and a tireless champion of civil rights, Jack Kennedy was now seen as "sort of a young liberal against the machine"—though probably, Rauh added, more anti-machine than liberal.[41]

The March meeting went poorly. Many of the party regulars, loyal to McCormack and resentful of the Kennedys for elbowing aside the state organization in the 1952 campaign, were disinclined to bend to the senator's wishes. Irritated by the defiance but outwardly calm, Kennedy knew that his own credibility in the state and nationwide would suffer grievous damage if his support for Stevenson was largely ignored by a Massachusetts delegation marching in lockstep with McCormack, Burke, and Fox. Kennedy thus proposed a deal in which half the delegates to the Chicago convention would back Stevenson and the other half would support

McCormack as the favorite-son candidate. Burke waved aside the proposal. He considered Kennedy a young upstart who should be put in his place. Then, in the state's primary in April, Burke orchestrated a successful write-in campaign for McCormack, who bested Stevenson easily. With the battle lines drawn, and with Burke up for reelection in May, Kennedy and his lieutenants worked every angle to get him ousted, using the kind of backroom politicking the senator generally avoided. (*Stay away from local politics*, his father had always warned him. It was a morass from which extrication would be all but impossible.) Aides gathered information on every committee member, whereupon Kennedy paid individual visits to many of them around the state, urging them to vote for his chosen candidate, ex–Somerville mayor John "Pat" Lynch. Burke's forces, meanwhile, worked to line up support for their man.[42]

The Burke team called a committee meeting in Springfield for Saturday, May 19, at 2:00 P.M. Kennedy's operation then called an official meeting of the committee to be held in the Bradford Hotel, a traditional meeting place just off Boston Common, for 3:00 P.M. on the same day. Burke's forces responded by rescinding their initial announcement and said *they* were calling a meeting for the Bradford at 3:00 P.M.

The Kennedy team perhaps should have taken a closer look at the calendar before setting the date: Jack's youngest sister, Jean, was getting married to Stephen Smith, the low-key and intelligent son of a large New York tugboat-and-barge-operating family, that same day at St. Patrick's Cathedral, in Manhattan. The senator was expected to be there as an usher, alongside brothers Bobby and Teddy. He flew to New York for the ceremony, then immediately caught the shuttle back to Boston so that he could be at the Bradford to greet committee members as they filed in. He made it in the nick of time, shaking hands in the lobby and vowing his support for Lynch. He then withdrew, prudently avoiding the raucous session that followed.

"We argued that Onions shouldn't be allowed to attend the meeting since he wasn't a member of the committee," recalled Larry O'Brien, a key player on Kennedy's side.

> To back up our ruling, we had two tough Boston cops guarding the door, one of whom had reportedly killed a man in a barroom fight. Burke arrived with some tough guys of his own. Just as the meeting was about to begin, he and his men charged out of the elevator and

broke past our guards. One of the leaders was Ed "Knocko" McCormack, the majority leader's two-fisted, three-hundred-pound younger brother. As shouting and shoving spread across the meeting room, I called the Boston police commissioner. He arrived minutes later.

"I'm O'Brien," I told him. "You've got to get those troublemakers out of here."

"One more word out of you, O'Brien," the commissioner replied, "and I'll lock you up." I hadn't known the commissioner was a McCormack man. The whole thing was a scene out of *The Last Hurrah* [a book and later a film depicting the no-holds-barred mayoral campaign of an unscrupulous politician modeled after James Michael Curley]. The two candidates for state chairman almost settled matters by a fistfight. There was shouting and confusion, and as the roll call began, one member who'd gotten drunk attempted to vote twice.[43]

When all the votes were counted, Kennedy's man Lynch had prevailed by a vote of 47–31. The senator, who, according to both Jackie Kennedy and Ted Sorensen, cared as much about this political fight as any in his career, had gained undisputed control of the state party and could now deliver a majority of the state's forty votes to Stevenson at the convention.[44] The victorious Kennedy hopped a plane to New York, where his sister's wedding reception at the Plaza Hotel was still going strong. Before departing Boston, he placed a call to Stevenson's campaign manager, James Finnegan, who expressed his delight at the outcome.[45]

Yet Kennedy seemingly took little joy in his win—the mudslinging by both sides, he told aides, had been unseemly and depressing. In a magazine article in late May and in a commencement address at Harvard two weeks later, he tried to reclaim loftier ground.[46] Drawing on arguments and examples developed in *Profiles in Courage* and echoing his remarks at the National Book Awards dinner, the Harvard address focused on what he described as the lamentable and seemingly deepening schism in the country between politicians and intellectuals.* "Instead of synthesis," he told the crowd of three thousand in Harvard Yard, a few feet from the

* The speech was substantially drafted for him, most likely by Sorensen. The best proof of that: in his handwritten edits, Kennedy crossed out a reference to the Harvard "campus" (which no Harvard man would have called it) and inserted "Yard."

dorm in which he lived freshman year, "clash and discord now character-
ize the relations between the two groups much of the time."

> The politician, whose authority rests upon the mandate of the popu-
> lar will, is resentful of the scholar who can, with dexterity, slip from
> position to position without dragging the anchor of public opin-
> ion. . . . The intellectual, on the other hand, finds it difficult to ac-
> cept the differences between the laboratory and the legislature. In
> the former, the goal is truth, pure and simple, without regard to
> changing currents of public opinion; in the latter, compromises and
> majorities and procedural customs and rights affect the ultimate de-
> cision as to what is right or just or good. And even when they realize
> this difference, most intellectuals consider their chief functions that
> of the critic—and politicians are sensitive to critics—(possibly be-
> cause we have so many of them). "Many intellectuals," Sidney Hook
> has said, "would rather die than agree with the majority, even on the
> rare occasions when the majority is right."

It would be imperative, Kennedy continued, for both sides to remember that American politicians and scholars claimed the same proud heritage. "Our Nation's first great politicians were also among the Nation's
first great writers and scholars. The founders of the American Constitution were also the founders of American scholarship. The works of Jefferson, Madison, Hamilton, Franklin, Paine, and John Adams—to name
but a few—influenced the literature of the world as well as its geography.
Books were their tools, not their enemies." Nor was this a temporary phenomenon, Kennedy added, for the link between the intellectual and the
politician in the United States lasted for more than a century. Thus, in the
presidential campaign a century before, in 1856, "the Republicans sent
three brilliant orators around the campaign circuit: William Cullen Bryant, Henry Wadsworth Longfellow, and Ralph Waldo Emerson. Those
were the carefree days when the eggheads were all Republicans."

He closed by reminding his audience that politicians and intellectuals
ultimately must commit to operating within a "common framework—
a framework we call liberty. Freedom of expression is not divisible into
political expression and intellectual expression." And the payoff for such
a common commitment could be great, he promised:

" 'Don't teach my boy poetry,' an English mother recently wrote the provost of Harrow. 'Don't teach my boy poetry; he is going to stand for Parliament.' Well, perhaps she was right—but if more politicians knew poetry and more poets knew politics, I am convinced the world would be a little better place in which to live on this commencement day of 1956."[47]

A VERY NEAR THING

John F. Kennedy's 1956 Harvard commencement speech received wide attention, inside and outside the press. *The New York Times* gave it prominent coverage, as did other papers. Fellow Democrats in Washington offered praise, none more extravagantly than Senate Majority Leader Lyndon B. Johnson, who called it "the most eloquent defense of politics and politicians that it has ever been my pleasure to read" and had it inserted into the *Congressional Record.*[1]

Political insiders speculating about the likely Democratic ticket for the fall election paid due attention. With two months to go until the Chicago convention, Adlai Stevenson was widely presumed to be the nominee, having gotten the better of Estes Kefauver in the key primaries and enjoying broader support among party leaders than any other potential standard-bearer. The former Illinois governor was increasingly intrigued by the prospect of Kennedy as his running mate, having seen the favorable publicity the Massachusetts man had garnered in recent months. And not merely from journalists—Connecticut governor Abraham Ribicoff led an effort by New England political leaders to get Kennedy on the ticket, a move supported also by Dennis J. Roberts, governor of Rhode Island, and others. Governor Luther Hodges of North Carolina, a moderate, had earlier indicated that having Kennedy on the ticket would be acceptable in the South. Several Stevenson advisers, among them Arthur M. Schlesinger Jr., also liked Kennedy for the second slot.[2] True, questions swirled about Kennedy's health and his youth. But he had two highly successful books to his credit and had shown himself to be an effective public speaker. He excelled on television. He projected a handsome, clean-cut, moderate image, was charmingly low-key and witty in his approach, and had a heroic war record to boot. His epic win against Henry Cabot Lodge in 1952 showed that he knew how to campaign and how to win. Even Kennedy's Catholicism could be an asset, blunting the effects of Stevenson's divorce and boosting vote totals in key states in the Midwest and the Northeast.[3]

Newton Minow, a friend and law associate of Stevenson's, had been in the audience for Kennedy's speech before the National Conference of Christians and Jews earlier in the year and had been mesmerized:

> I fell in love with Jack Kennedy immediately. I'd always admired him, but I was really taken with him. I was taken with his whole attitude, his whole appearance, his whole—He really sent me. I left that night and I said to [wife] Jo in the car, "You know, this would be the ideal candidate for Vice-President, with Adlai. This is a perfect match. He has what Adlai lacks. He has appeal to the Catholics. He will help on the divorce issue. He has appeal to young people, because of his youth. He has an appeal to a segment of the population that Adlai did very badly with in '52, the conservative Irish Catholic Democrats afraid of the soft-on-communism issue. He's perfect!"[4]

The religion issue cut both ways, however, and many seasoned observers urged Stevenson to be wary. Three-term Pittsburgh mayor David Lawrence, a power within the party and a Catholic, warned Stevenson that having a Catholic running mate would spell inevitable defeat in November. Speaker Sam Rayburn was similarly negative, as was, reportedly, Harry Truman. Small wonder that when Ted Sorensen's memorandum from earlier in the year began making the rounds among party insiders, Stevenson's people asked for copies. They wanted hard data. Sorensen, after feigning ignorance, made sure to comply with the request, though circumspectly, as the memo was no longer officially his own product—Kennedy, leery of having his aide perceived as promoting the issue, arranged for the party chairman of Connecticut, John Bailey, a strong backer, to assume responsibility for the document. The camouflage effort worked: thenceforth it would be known as the Bailey Memorandum.[5]

Did Jack Kennedy really want the vice presidential nomination? Early in the year he had disavowed the idea to Sorensen, calling it a nothing job that gave no role on policy, or on anything else of substance.[6] But the idea was growing on him, less out of a pining for the office than out of a sense of competition. All of the buzz that spring and summer was about the presidential ticket, and he wanted in on the action. Accordingly, at regular intervals he and Sorensen supplied Stevenson's office with updates on how the presidential nomination fight looked in Massachusetts and New England, and offered ideas on how best to turn back the Kefauver challenge nationally. On March 30, Sorensen called Minow at Kennedy's request to suggest that Stevenson use Kefauver's absentee record in "a vigorous way" in his speeches. On April 16, Kennedy wrote Minow to warn that Wyoming was in danger of slipping out of Stevenson's grasp. In May, as we've seen, after his successful battle to oust Onions Burke and gain control of the state party, Kennedy wasted no time in informing Stevenson of the fact. And in early June, after Stevenson thumped Kefauver in the California primary and effectively sewed up the nomination, Kennedy fired off a congratulatory telegram: "You have proven what many of us knew from the beginning and pointed the way to victory in August and November."[7]

Even the heartfelt opposition of his wife and his father did not deter Jack. Jackie wanted her husband to continue his convalescence in a less stressful mode, while Joseph Kennedy felt certain that a Stevenson-led ticket was doomed to lopsided defeat. Eisenhower was simply too strong. Polls showed him with a healthy lead over Stevenson, and moreover he had already defeated Stevenson once before. Thus, even if Jack won the vice presidential nomination (itself no sure thing), it would be no real victory; on the contrary, Joe believed, any Democratic rout would be blamed on Jack's Catholicism, which might scuttle his prospects for the presidency four or eight years down the road. "If you are chosen," he wrote his son, quoting Clare Boothe Luce approvingly, "it will be because you are a Catholic and not because you are big enough to do a good job. She feels that a defeat would be a devastating blow to your prestige."[8]

Jack was undaunted. Or at least he saw the merits in, as he put it to his father in a letter in late June, having "all of this churning up."[9] The vice presidential speculation kept his name before the national electorate, and that was all to the good. Plus he always relished a fight. A few weeks thereafter, Eunice, whose husband, Sargent Shriver, had just urged Jack's candidacy on Stevenson directly while flying with him from Cape Cod to Chicago, wrote her father that, absent the vice presidential nod and the name recognition it would generate, Jack didn't believe the Democrats would "select him as a presidential candidate any . . . time in the future." The Ambassador, ensconced in the South of France, had begun to soften in his opposition, especially after reports emerged that Dwight Eisenhower was experiencing new health problems. (In June the president had contracted ileitis and gone in for surgery, then remained in Walter Reed Army Medical Center for three full weeks.) If Ike couldn't run for reelection, that changed the equation dramatically, Joe believed, and he told friends he might have to return to America for the Democratic convention.[10]

The president's health was key. Joe continued to believe Eisenhower would coast to victory against Stevenson, and perhaps against any Democratic ticket. "I think Eisenhower is the most popular man that we have seen in our time and to make attacks on him in the coming campaign is to me a sure way to commit suicide," Joe wrote to Sargent Shriver from Èze-sur-Mer. "Oddly enough, as in Jack's case, when a man is ill and is putting up a good fight, it is almost impossible to generate a feeling against him. . . . Remember, Sarge, that you are going into an atmosphere where over 65 million persons are working and getting better pay than ever before. . . . So you have an economic condition that is excellent; you can't offer anything to anybody from laborer to capitalist that can persuade him that he can do better by [a Democrat]." In sum, the elder Kennedy told his son-in-law, "I believe that while Stevenson and Jack would certainly do better than last time, they will not win."[11]

To his son the Ambassador was more elliptical but still left his feelings clear. "I came to a couple of conclusions," he wrote to Jack in July:

> 1) Stevenson is going to nominate his own Vice President when he gets the nomination. 2) He's definitely worried about your health, and . . . that will be his excuse, if he wants it. 3) When you see what he wants the Vice President to do, you can decide how attractive it is. . . . If you make up your mind that you either don't want it or that you are not going to get it, before either of these things happen, you

should get out a statement to the effect that representing Mass. is one of the greatest jobs in the world, and there is lots to be done for your state and her people, and while you are most grateful for the national support offered you for the Vice Presidency, your heart belongs to Massachusetts.[12]

By the start of August, Eisenhower's condition had stabilized and he seemed set for the campaign. To Joe Kennedy that settled the matter, and the old man was perhaps fortunate that, on account of being overseas, he didn't have to read the new issue of *Time*, which put Jack at the top of the list of Democratic vice presidential candidates. "Trademarked by his boyishly unruly shock of brown hair, slim Jack Kennedy, 39, has looks, brains, personality, an attractive wife (who is expecting her first baby in October)," the magazine enthused. Kennedy's war record, as well as his "vote-getting ability in a pivotal state" and his "reputation as an able, independent-thinking, middle-of-the-road member of both the House . . . and the Senate," made him a top contender. On the debit side were Kennedy's Catholicism and his decision earlier in the year to side with the Eisenhower administration over his party in voting against full subsidization of American farmers by the federal government. Overall, the article said, Kennedy looked better positioned than ostensible front-runner Kefauver, who, with his overbearing approach, had "made too many enemies along the campaign trail."[13]

Not least, Kennedy seemed well positioned on a matter that threatened to cleave the party in two: civil rights. Over the prior two years, the insurgency against segregation had grown in intensity as activists demanded that African Americans have full access to the nation's institutions and prosperity. In 1954, a series of landmark cases testing segregation had culminated in the Supreme Court's unanimous *Brown v. Board of Education* ruling, which outlawed segregation in public schools. The following year, the court demanded that local school boards move "with all deliberate speed" to implement the decision. In August 1955, the gruesome killing in Mississippi of fourteen-year-old Emmett Till (for the alleged "crime" of whistling at a white woman) further galvanized the movement. And in December, black seamstress and NAACP activist Rosa Parks refused to give up her seat to a white man on a bus in Montgomery, Alabama. Parks's act of defiance prompted a yearlong bus boycott in

Montgomery organized by a new Baptist minister in town, the twenty-six-year-old Martin Luther King Jr.[14]

In his first nine years on Capitol Hill, Jack Kennedy had been a steadfast advocate on civil rights, with a blemish-free voting record. Now, however, in his tenth year, he subtly repositioned himself, hoping thereby to strengthen his vice presidential prospects. The Democrats were badly split between southern segregationists—who controlled key committees in both houses—and a group of liberal crusaders, centered in the Senate, who were determined to bring meaningful reform.[15] Stevenson, philosophically and intellectually in accord with the reformers but fearful of the electoral consequences of aligning with them, tried to finesse the issue, saying as little as he could about the *Brown* decision while hoping the party's platform committee could conjure up some kind of artful compromise. He also saw the need for a running mate who could appeal to both wings of the party, who would be tolerable to segregationists as well as to northern liberals.

Kennedy aimed to be that man. In the space of a few short weeks in the late spring and early summer, he attempted a delicate remolding of his political image, shifting to the right to make himself more palatable to the South while at the same time keeping on good terms with northerners, whose views on racial equality he shared. He cast himself as a civil rights gradualist who fully supported black betterment but thought that desegregation should occur step by step and with the voluntary acquiescence of southern municipalities. In effect, Kennedy followed the vague position of the Supreme Court in its "all deliberate speed" formulation—desegregation must occur, but the pace was open to discussion and compromise. This straddling didn't exactly endear him to many southern Democrats, but it nonetheless left him better positioned than the Tennessean Kefauver to win their support. Kefauver, in their eyes, had committed an act of betrayal by refusing to sign the "Southern Manifesto," a condemnation of the *Brown* decision as a "clear abuse of judicial power," signed by one hundred U.S. senators and representatives (ninety-six of them Democrats).[16]

On CBS's *Face the Nation* in early July, panelists grilled Kennedy on his stance and pushed him to indicate what Congress's role in desegregating schools ought to be. He bobbed and weaved, avoiding unambiguous statements, but left little doubt that it should be up to the courts, not lawmakers, to determine the pace of desegregation. Asked near the end of the program if the Democratic Party platform should endorse *Brown*, Kennedy constructed an adroit way of saying no: "Now it may be politically desirable, some people may feel, to reemphasize it. In my opinion, it is unnecessary because I accept it."[17]

II

When the Democratic convention opened at Chicago's International Amphitheatre on August 13, analysts in the party and the press identified several leading candidates for the number-two slot: in addition to Kefauver and Kennedy, they included Senators Hubert H. Humphrey of Minnesota, Albert Gore Sr. of Tennessee, and Lyndon Johnson of Texas, as well as New York City mayor Robert Wagner (also a Catholic) and W. Averell Harriman, governor of New York. Kefauver was the odds-on favorite going in, with Humphrey also attracting a lot of attention. (Johnson, most politicos speculated, preferred to remain majority leader and to set his sights on 1960.)

But now Jack Kennedy got one of those lucky breaks that periodically defined his career. Party chairman Paul Butler had commissioned a film about the history of the Democratic Party, by Hollywood producer and delegate Dore Schary, that would introduce the first evening's keynote address. Governor Edmund Muskie of Maine, a rising figure in the party, was asked to provide the narration but declined, whereupon Kennedy got the nod. He flew out to California in July to see a screening of the footage-only rough cut at the twenty-room Santa Monica beachfront home of his sister Patricia and her husband, Peter Lawford. (The house had been built in 1936 for film industry titan Louis B. Mayer.) Pleased by what he saw, Kennedy rehearsed the script, adding a few lines of his own, then went into a studio to record his voice-over. Schary was thrilled: "All of us who were in contact with [Kennedy] immediately fell in love with him because he was so quick and so charming and so cooperative, and obviously so bright and so skilled."[18]

The film was a smashing success, the high point of the convention's opening night. As the lights dimmed, the audience of eleven thousand heard Kennedy's New England voice fill the auditorium. The effect was electric. Schary, seated with the California delegation, recalled that the senator's personality "just came right out. It jumped at you on the screen. The narration was good, and the film was emotional. He was immediately a candidate. There was simply no doubt about that because he racked up the whole convention."[19] A press report said the film "sent the convention roaring for the first time." After it ended, Kennedy strode to the platform to take a bow and the roars came anew. Members of the Massachusetts delegation waved "Kennedy for President" placards and staged a brief but noisy favorite-son parade, and *The New York Times* proclaimed that "Senator Kennedy came before the convention tonight as a photogenic movie star."[20] But it was among the other states' delegates and, even more, the television viewing audience that the narration really mattered, in an instant raising his profile in a way nothing had ever done before—not his books, not his dramatic 1952 Senate win, not even his Pacific war heroics. He had reached a new level.

Stevenson, too, was impressed, but he remained uncertain at day's end about which way he would go on a running mate. When, during a late-evening cab ride, Newt Minow made an impassioned plea for Kennedy as the best choice, Stevenson launched into a recitation of all the

A star in Chicago: Jack confers with Jackie and
Eunice at the Democratic National Convention.

things he disliked about Joe Kennedy. "How can you blame the kid for his father?" Minow exclaimed. Stevenson fell silent for a moment, then murmured, "He's too young."[21]

The following day, Kennedy was the talk of the convention, mobbed wherever he went, on the streets and on the convention floor, an overnight sensation. Behind the scenes, though, all was not smooth. Eleanor Roosevelt, a formidable player in the party, had arrived in Chicago to proclaim her support of Stevenson's candidacy and extol her late husband's legacy; the Kennedy team, thinking she could boost Jack's chances of being tapped for the second slot, arranged for a half-hour meeting between the two at the storied Blackstone Hotel. It didn't go well. Mrs. Roosevelt was wary of Kennedy for what she saw as his father's tolerance of Nazis during the war, as well as Jack's failure to condemn Joseph McCarthy. Accounts of the meeting differ on the particulars, but all agree that the former First Lady placed the senator on the defensive over the McCarthy issue. When she pressed him on the matter, he reportedly said, "That was so long ago," and offered a meandering comment on Senate procedure. The reply "just wasn't enough of an answer for me, that's all," she reported afterwards, but Kennedy insisted "she must have misunderstood me because what I meant was that the bill of particulars against McCarthy was long before the censure movement. My position was that we couldn't indict a man for what happened before he was seated [for his new term, in January 1953]. If he was guilty of those things, the time to stop him was before he was seated . . . it was hardly a place or a basis for judgment."[22]

More likely, Roosevelt did not misunderstand Kennedy at all but merely saw his response for what it was: an evasive dodge on a matter he preferred not to confront.

III

On Wednesday, August 15, came more proof that Kennedy was having an outsize role in the convention. In a morning meeting, Adlai Stevenson asked him to deliver the main nominating speech before Thursday's presidential balloting. The offer came with a caveat: if northerners succeeded in pushing through a stronger civil rights plank in the party platform later that day, Stevenson would instead need a southerner to nominate him. Kennedy felt honored to be asked—this would mean yet more national attention for him, and on a critical day of the convention—but also came away disappointed, in that it probably meant he would not be the running mate. By tradition, one did not invite to give the nominating speech someone also under consideration for the second slot on the ticket. When Stevenson told Kennedy he wanted him to give the speech, Kennedy later reflected, "I asked him if that meant I was thereby being disqualified for the vice-presidential nomination and he said, no, not necessarily. So when Arthur [Schlesinger Jr.] came to see me that day, I told him I felt I should know whether or not I was being eliminated before I made the nominating speech, or at least before it happened. And that's when Arthur told me that nobody yet had been picked."[23]

It was true: Stevenson had not decided on a running mate. Prone to indecision at the best of times, he felt conflicted about the top three contenders. Kefauver, the consensus front-runner, had delegate strength and good organization and arguably deserved the nod, having won primaries in the spring. He had also gained national recognition for his chairmanship of a Senate committee whose hearings on organized crime attracted broad television coverage. But Stevenson disliked Kefauver, who had a reputation for heavy drinking and chronic extramarital dalliances, and he knew that many of Kefauver's Senate colleagues found him coarse and conniving, and too loquacious by half. Hubert Humphrey, a skilled orator and policy wonk with whom Stevenson had gotten on well in the past, represented the farm vote in the Midwest, which the ticket would need in the fall; he had arrived in Chicago expecting, on the basis of a conversation with Stevenson a few weeks prior, to get the nod.[24] But both Kefauver and Humphrey were suspect among southerners for their progressive stances on civil rights. Jack Kennedy, for his part, was a proven vote-getter with a heroic war record and abundant charm, a man who represented an important region of the country and had a reputation for centrism on policy issues. But there were the questions about his health, his youth, and his Catholicism. Trailing behind these three men in Stevenson's calculation were the other contenders: Johnson, Gore, Harriman, and Wagner.

That evening Ted Sorensen, still waiting for confirmation that Kennedy would give the nominating speech the following day, went over the draft Stevenson's aides had produced. He thought it terrible—"a wordy, corny, lackluster committee product," he subsequently said. He ran into Schlesinger, who would only say that the previous draft was worse. At one thirty in the morning, with the platform fight at last over and Kennedy authorized to give the speech, the senator and Sorensen met to discuss how to proceed. Kennedy would take the podium less than twelve hours later, at noon on August 16. He shared his aide's low opinion of the draft and told him, "We'll have to start over." Kennedy dictated the opening sentences and outlined the broad points, and instructed Sorensen to have a draft ready by eight o'clock in the morning. Sorensen worked through the night, then had a secretary type up the new version, jumped in a car, and took the draft over to Kennedy's hotel room. The senator "looked it over, rewrote some of it, cut out some things and added a few paragraphs, and by then it was so chopped up that we had to have it retyped because the TelePrompTer people were screaming for it. We gave them one copy and sent another copy to be mimeographed for the press."[25]

En route to the Amphitheatre, as his taxi sped down Michigan Avenue, Jack saw to his horror that parts of the typescript were illegible. He let loose a string of profanities—he was due on the stage in half an hour. In that instant he spotted a familiar face trying to hail a taxi: Tom Winship, a reporter from the *Boston Globe*. Kennedy told his driver to stop and pick up the reporter, who promptly agreed to help. After reaching the convention hall, Winship raced to the pressroom and typed two clear pages. The senator got the refreshed copy to the teleprompter with minutes to spare. As it happened, the teleprompter failed and Jack had to read from his notes, but the speech, while faulted by *The New York Times* for relying on a "cliché dictionary," was a hit with the delegates, especially a bit that slammed the GOP ticket of Eisenhower and Nixon as having one candidate who took the high road while the other traveled the low road. Chicago mayor Richard J. Daley came away deeply impressed, by both the content and the delivery: the young man from Massachusetts was a must for the ticket, he determined.[26]

Kennedy's stirring performance increased the buzz on the convention floor about his chances for the slot. Perhaps it also increased the buzz in Stevenson's head, for the candidate now shocked the political world by announcing, at 11:00 P.M., that he would throw the vice presidential nomination open to selection by the delegates, with the balloting to occur the following day, barely twelve hours later. Unbeknownst to all but a few insiders, he had in fact been chewing on this idea for some months—an open selection process, he reasoned, would be seen by the party activists and the public as an exciting, democratic move and an effective way to contrast his party's meeting with the Republican convention, slated for San Francisco the following week and likely to be tightly controlled. But Stevenson also went this route because he was torn, especially about Kefauver versus Kennedy: if he named Kefauver in place of Kennedy, he opened himself up to accusations of being anti-Catholic, a charge he could hardly afford in the coming campaign; but if he selected Kennedy, he risked alienating Kefauver's sizable number of delegates. Stevenson fully expected Kefauver to prevail in the open contest—his forces were better organized than were Kennedy's or Humphrey's—giving him the running mate he probably would have felt compelled to select anyway.

In an instant, the convention became a hive of frantic late-night activity as the contenders and their teams sprang into action. "No delegate could buy his own drink and no elderly lady could cross a Chicago street without help from an eager vice-presidential candidate," *Time* pithily reported.[27] Humphrey operatives were seen entering lakefront bars at 2:30 A.M. in search of delegates; Kefauver held a press conference at 4 A.M. The Kennedy operation, unprepared for this eventuality (notwithstanding fleeting back-channel rumors over the previous few days), had to decide how—and if—to respond. The senator, still ambivalent about the desirability of being on the ticket in the fall, chose quickly: he was in. His competitive spirit would not let him back away. "Call Dad and tell him I'm going for it," he instructed his brother Robert, then wisely left the room. The Ambassador, reached in Cap d'Antibes, was livid upon hearing the news, his blue language easily audible to the aides around Bobby. "Jack's a total fucking idiot, and you're worse!" he roared. A golden political career was being risked, and for nothing. The connection broke while he was in mid-rant, and Bobby thought the better of trying to call back. "Whew!" he said as he hung up, a wan smile on his face. "Is he mad!"[28]

Working through the night and the next morning, the Kennedy forces tried by any means available to drum up support for their man. They found a printer who would toil until dawn producing banners, placards, and leaflets. Jack, always his own best campaigner, met with state leaders and visited several state caucuses. His siblings Robert and Eunice paid calls on other delegations, as did John Bailey. Jack also got his brother-in-law Peter Lawford out of bed to try to secure the Nevada delegation. Inevitably, the team's lack of preparation showed. Powerful New York bosses Carmine DeSapio and Charlie Buckley, who controlled a fat heap of ninety-eight votes, were kept waiting in one of the Kennedy hotel rooms for half an hour without anyone knowing who they were. (When the candidate at last appeared, the two men told him they were pledged to Robert Wagner on the first ballot but might well switch to him on the second.) And when Kenny O'Donnell and Bobby Kennedy buttonholed Senator John L. McClellan of Arkansas to ask if he could help swing his state's delegation to their man, he gave them a powerful lesson—one they would never forget—in how politics at this level worked. It was not to him but to the governor, Orval Faubus, that they should be speaking, McClellan said, for governors always called the shots and controlled the delegates. Senators mattered far less.

"In the future," McClellan admonished them, "if one was interested in delegations and their votes, they better find out who has the power in the delegation and stop reading the newspapers. You can't just arrive at the convention and expect people to switch sides because your fella is so wonderful. You gotta do your homework, talk to the governors, the state reps, the party leaders, these people have been sized up, lined up, and courted for months. Just because you know a few high-profile, important fellas, a few senators or judges is not going to change things. Next time you gotta have this all done before you step off the train."[29]

And so it went, hour upon exhausting hour. Associated Press correspondent Jack Bell recalled, "At 5:00 A.M., I came across Kefauver doing a television recording in a corridor of the Conrad Hilton Hotel. Kennedy, rushing to another meeting, tripped over the power wires and almost fell into his rival." Sorensen, reflecting on the night, noted the total lack of sleep—and the frenzied confusion: "It was hectic, not very well organized, too many people packed into my bedroom who were just like me—green, completely green. I couldn't have been greener. I didn't talk to many people because I didn't know too many people." The candidate himself remembered the chaotic scene: "Everybody was running around. My sister Eunice worked on Delaware. I had breakfast with some of the California delegation. I went to a lot of caucuses. I got nothing from Ohio, of course, but I did talk to them. We got Virginia because Governor [John S.] Battle's son was in the Navy with me. And we got Louisiana because their delegation sat right next to ours and they had a lot of bright young fellows with whom we got real friendly."[30]

Bit by bit, Kennedy racked up support. He proved especially effective with southern delegates, many of whom viewed Kefauver as a turncoat on racial matters and liked what they saw as Kennedy's centrism on civil rights and his stated concern about foreign textile competition. His war experience spoke to them as well, as did his dignified and youthful bearing.

Still, as the nominations closed and the balloting opened, no one knew how things would go. Kennedy had New England as well as Virginia, Louisiana, and Georgia, and on a second ballot he could count on New York and, it was hoped, Illinois. But that left a huge swath of the country still open, and he was weak in the West. Some high-placed Catholic party leaders continued to insist that the country was not yet ready for a Catholic on the ticket, and many northern liberals, suspicious of Kennedy for his failure to cast a censure vote against Joe McCarthy as well as his criticism of Truman for the "loss of China" in 1949, stuck with Humphrey or Kefauver or Wagner. The nominating and seconding speeches for Kennedy were neither a hindrance nor much of a help—Connecticut governor Abraham Ribicoff gave a ringing, largely off-the-cuff nominating speech (privately, he noted the irony of a Jew pushing a Catholic for the ticket), while Florida senator and Kennedy pal George Smathers and House Majority Leader John McCormack (the latter, in Sorensen's words, "literally propelled toward the platform at the last minute by Bob Kennedy") delivered hasty seconding speeches that failed to leave much of an impression.[31]

IV

On the first ballot, Kefauver jumped out to an early lead, running especially strong in the Midwest and the West. But Kennedy showed strength in Georgia, Virginia, Louisiana, and Nevada. "This thing is really worth winning now," he told Sorensen as the two watched on television from Kennedy's hotel room, the candidate flopping on the bed in his undershorts. They were further cheered when Illinois delivered 46 of its 64 votes to him, but disappointed when Maine split its 14 votes. Kennedy cursed out loud when power brokers Michael DiSalle of Ohio and David Lawrence of Pennsylvania, both nervous about having a fellow Catholic on the ticket, mustered more than 100 of their 132 combined votes for Kefauver. The other contenders struggled to gain traction, and by the end of the first ballot it looked like a two-man race: Kefauver stood at 483 ½, and Kennedy came next with 304, followed by Gore at 178, Wagner at 162 ½, and Humphrey at 134 ½. A total of 687 were needed to claim the nomination.[32]

Kennedy aide Kenny O'Donnell had repaired to a bar across the street to watch the voting on television. He sensed something important happening as Kennedy gained support—the thing might actually be within reach. "Even more amazing was the assembled crowd of Chicago truck drivers, policemen and stock yard workers around us, all of them cheering, pounding on the bar and waving their beer glasses when another Kennedy vote was announced." O'Donnell hurried back to the convention floor.[33]

In round two, Kennedy picked up steam when Arkansas switched from Gore to him. By Illinois he led 155 to 82; by New Hampshire the margin stood at 271 ½ to 229 ½ in his favor. Then more good news: New Jersey and New York, both of which had backed Wagner in the first round, delivered 128 of their 134 combined votes to Kennedy. Suddenly the press scrum scrambled from Kefauver's corridor to Kennedy's, while on the convention floor there was bedlam as conventioneers marched up and down the aisles wearing placards and tooting horns, others standing on chairs, waving frantically for attention. Bobby Kennedy, John Bailey, and other Kennedy lieutenants roamed the Amphitheatre, shouting to delegations to come to their man. In his Stockyards Inn hotel room, however, the candidate was serene. "He bathed," Sorensen would write, "then again reclined on the bed. Finally we moved, through a back exit, to a larger and more isolated room."[34]

For a moment Kennedy surged way ahead, 402 ½ to 245 ½, only to see Kefauver pick up four state delegations and cut the margin to 416 ½ to 387. Oklahoma stayed with Gore ("He's not our kind of folks," the governor said of Kennedy), as did Tennessee, while Puerto Rico stuck with Wagner, even though he had withdrawn. The uncertainty in the hall increased. Then rose the imposing figure of Lyndon Johnson to announce that Texas proudly backed "the fighting Senator who wears the scars of battle, that fearless Senator . . . John Kennedy of Massachusetts!"[35] Pandemonium in the Kennedy camp—it seemed a harbinger of victory. Sargent Shriver burst into his brother-in-law's room and exclaimed, "Jack, you've got it!" Sorensen, too, reached out a hand of congratulation. The candidate waved them aside; he remained uncertain, even when the second round ended with him in the lead, 618 to 551½, which put him only 69 votes away from the magic 687.

His numbers grew still more when North Carolina cast half of its votes for Kennedy, and Kentucky switched its 30 votes from Gore to Kennedy. Only 39 votes separated Jack from a majority. Jackie, seated in the Kennedy box in the arena with other members of the family, started yelling enthusiastically, waving her "Stevenson for President" placard for all to see. In the hotel suite, her husband finished getting dressed and at last allowed that perhaps he should give thought to what he ought to say to the convention if nominated.

What happened next would be the subject of intense scrutiny and controversy. For suddenly the tide turned, as convention chairman Sam Rayburn recognized Tennessee. With the convention and the country hanging on every word, Albert Gore requested that his name be withdrawn as a candidate and his delegates released to "my colleague, Estes Kefauver." Kefauver supporters erupted in cheers. Oklahoma then switched its twenty-eight votes from Gore to Kefauver, and Minnesota and Missouri changed from Humphrey to Kefauver. Illinois and South Carolina tried to stem the onslaught by moving a few votes to Kennedy, but it was for naught. The Kennedy surge was over. More Kefauver votes followed, and he took the lead. "Let's go," said Kennedy, and he pushed through the throng in his corridor and brushed aside supporters who wanted him to stick it out to the end. Once in the Amphitheater he headed straight for the rostrum and was recognized by Rayburn.

Kennedy spoke movingly and gallantly and without notes:

> Ladies and gentlemen of this convention, I want to take this opportunity first to express my appreciation to Democrats from all parts of the country, north and south, east and west, who have been so generous and kind to me this afternoon. I think it proves, as nothing else can prove, what a strong and united party the Democratic party is.
>
> Secondly, what has happened today bears out the good judgment of Governor Stevenson in deciding that this issue should be taken to the floor of the convention. Because I believe that the Democratic Party will go from this convention far stronger for what we have done here today. And therefore, ladies and gentlemen, recognizing that this convention has selected a man who has campaigned in all parts of the country, who was worked untiringly for the party, who

will serve as an admirable running mate to Governor Stevenson, I hope that this convention will make Estes Kefauver's nomination unanimous. Thank you.[36]

He backed away, the hall cheering wildly, only to have Rayburn whisper in his ear that he should make a motion. Kennedy returned to the rostrum and moved that the convention nominate Kefauver by acclamation. The crowd roared anew, as the band swung into the "Tennessee Waltz."

V

If Adlai Stevenson had hoped to generate excitement by having the delegates choose his running mate, he certainly succeeded—beyond his wildest dreams. No American political convention since has matched those eighteen hours of August 16–17, 1956, for intrigue, high-stakes pressure, and sheer edge-of-your-seat suspense. In the following day's *New York Times*, Russell Baker described the unfolding drama as "a spectacle that might have confounded all Christendom in the old days," an epic political clash in an atmosphere shaken by "a shrieking pandemonium with 11,000 people on their feet and howling."[37]

Whether Stevenson got the outcome he wanted is another question. An aide who was with him as he watched the balloting on television from his suite in the Blackstone Hotel thought he saw Stevenson visibly slump as Kefauver achieved his majority.[38]

For John F. Kennedy, the nomination fight would in time be seen as hugely helpful. For one thing, he and his brother Robert and the rest of their team learned valuable lessons about how to wage battle on the convention floor—about the importance of having a superior communications strategy and knowing how to track delegate counts, about grasping even the finer points of convention rules. For another, they saw how Estes Kefauver's personal connection with a great many delegates had proved crucial. The Tennessean had been through a convention battle before, in 1952, and he learned then that there was no substitute for familiarity, for face-to-face interaction. Consequently, Kefauver had spent much time in the intervening years traveling the country, shaking hands, meeting people, chatting them up, often in his trademark coonskin cap (in honor of his pioneer forebears). Jack Kennedy hadn't done that kind of traveling, didn't have that same level of familiarity among people outside New England, and it made all the difference at the pivotal moment.[39]

Yet here, too, the Chicago experience would provide Kennedy with an immense boost. Even at the time, seasoned observers could see what the convention had done for him, especially in the new television age. (This was the first convention to have gavel-to-gavel coverage, and CBS and NBC each had more than three hundred employees on-site.) He had arrived in the Windy City as one of several contenders for the second spot on the presidential ticket, a rising leader in the party and a figure of intrigue on account of his youth, looks, and background, but not yet well known among the party's rank and file. He left five days later as a star.

The Kennedy camp could scarcely have scripted things better. On Monday, the opening day, Kennedy had narrated, to universal acclaim, the film that introduced the first keynote speech. On Thursday he had delivered an effective nominating speech for the party's presidential nominee, his handsome face and resonant voice beamed into living rooms all across the land. And on Friday he'd come within inches of winning the vice presidential balloting, then offered an impromptu concession, magnanimous and elegant and brief (it totaled 162 words), captured on television and raising his stature still more—in all parts of the nation. Kefauver had won the battle, but Kennedy, with his near miss, had captured the hearts of masses of Democrats. His surprising strength among southern delegates, meanwhile, seemed to strike a blow against the "Al Smith myth" that no Catholic could win national office. Best of all for him, as some could see already and others would soon determine, Kennedy would not be saddled with any responsibility for the drubbing Stevenson was likely to endure come November. Not for the first time in American politics and not for the last, a narrow defeat turned out to be the best possible result.

Arthur Schlesinger, the Stevenson insider, wrote to Kennedy on August 21 that "you clearly emerged as the man who gained most during the Convention. . . . Your general demeanor and effectiveness made you in a single week a national political figure. The [coming fall] campaign provides a further opportunity to consolidate this impression." Connecticut governor Abe Ribicoff, a staunch backer, told journalists, "We were

Kennedy at the rostrum, alongside Democratic Party chairman Paul Butler.

awful close," and "I am confident that Jack Kennedy has a great future ahead of him." According to *The Boston Globe*, Kennedy may have lost by "a whisker," but "he won the hearts of the Democratic convention delegates," who let out a "mighty roar of approval" any time his name was mentioned. Another article in the paper said he had come away from Chicago "with the greatest increase in stature" and predicted "that the increased stature Sen. Kennedy has achieved will someday put him in the way of opportunity, which sometimes knocks more than once in politics."[40]

Stevenson himself was effusive: "I had hoped to see you before you left Chicago, and left, may I say, a much bigger man than you arrived! If there was a hero, it was you, and if there has been a new gallantry on our horizon in recent years, it is yourself. I say with confidence that you couldn't have been half as disappointed about the Vice Presidency as my children were, and I *know* that they reflect the view of many."[41]

Kennedy would come to accept the view that the outcome in Chicago had served his purposes, but only later; in the initial hours after the tense battle in Chicago, he was morose. He had suffered his first major political reversal, and it stung. Back in his hotel suite, he grumbled to Jackie, Bobby, Eunice, and a few aides and friends about how close he had come and about friends who'd let him down. With cutting sarcasm he dictated an imaginary wire to fellow Catholic David Lawrence, Pittsburgh's mayor, who had earlier invited him to that city but also had urged Stevenson not to choose a Catholic for the second spot.[42]

"What impressed me was that Jack really showed more emotion than I'd really seen him display up to that point," George Smathers recalled of the scene, "and Jackie even shed some tears. I was just shocked that Jackie had taken it so seriously, felt so deeply about it. After all, the whole thing was only a twelve-hour operation." Yet what Smathers had long considered Kennedy's even-keeled nature soon reasserted itself: "He stood up on the corner of the bed and I kept wondering if he was going to fall and hurt himself. But he told everybody, 'Look, it's all over. We did great considering what time we had. I want to thank everybody.' And then he made some joke about my speech being cut off. But I knew he was hurt, deeply hurt. The thing is, he came so close. These Kennedys, once they're in something, they don't like to lose. But it was great the way he could joke about it."[43]

Robert Kennedy, who always felt things more deeply than did his older brother, took longer to cool down. "I sat right next to Bobby Kennedy [on the flight back to Boston]," said one delegate, "and he was bitter. He said they should have won and somebody had pulled something fishy and he wanted to know who did it."[44] Others wondered as well, then and afterwards, about the sudden shift to Kefauver just when Kennedy seemed to have the battle won, and whether shenanigans were involved.* Bobby also groused that if a large electronic tote board at the back of the hall had not been dismantled the night before, after Stevenson's nomination (no one thought it would be needed anymore), delegates would have seen how close Jack was to victory on the second ballot and put him over the top.

* One theory has it that Rayburn's antipathy toward Kefauver was outweighed by his opposition to having a Catholic on the ticket, and by his anger at the Massachusetts delegation for nominating Kennedy instead of his close friend John McCormack. So he resisted calling for a recess and a third ballot and instead recognized late second-ballot switches that he rightly expected would turn the tide. Another theory posits that Rayburn was hoodwinked—he recognized Tennessee at the key moment because he had been falsely told the state was switching to Kennedy. "I'll never forget that look on Rayburn's face as long as I live," the manager of Kefauver's floor operations reportedly said of Tennessee's announcement. "He was so shocked, he really lost his composure for a moment." (Martin, *Ballots and Bandwagons*, 402.)

VI

Exhausted from a mostly sleepless week in Chicago, his back pain unrelenting, Jack Kennedy returned to New England with Jackie. But he didn't stay: to her intense disappointment, he departed in short order for the South of France. Jackie was herself feeling spent after the hectic convention, and moreover she was eight months pregnant; she thought they should recuperate together, in anticipation of the coming baby. But Jack would not be deterred. Still smarting from his defeat, he reasoned that he could take his long-planned trip and still be back in time for the baby's birth. Jackie, rather than be by herself in his absence, opted to stay with her mother and stepfather at Hammersmith Farm.

Jack flew first to Paris and thence to the Riviera to see his father. "Jack arrived here very tired but I think very happy because he came out of the convention so much better than anyone could have hoped," the elder Kennedy wrote singer Morton Downey, a longtime friend and Cape Cod neighbor, on August 24. "As far as I am concerned, you know how I feel—if you're going to get licked, get licked trying for the best, not the second best. His time is surely coming!"[45] Father and son spent several days together, plotting—we can imagine—the next steps in Jack's political career, after which the son left for a weeklong sailing trip with the ubiquitous—and equally married—Torby Macdonald. Teddy Kennedy, now twenty-four, joined them as well. Details are sketchy, but a subsequent newspaper report suggested several bikini-clad young women were aboard.[46]

On August 23, a few days after arriving at her mother's Newport home, Jackie experienced severe cramps. She began to hemorrhage. Rushed to the Newport Hospital, she underwent an emergency cesarean. The baby was stillborn. Upon hearing of the emergency, Robert Kennedy went immediately to be with her, reaching her hospital bedside even before she had come to from her anesthetic. He made arrangements for the funeral of the baby, a girl the couple had intended to call Arabella. Bobby advised his parents not to tell Jack about what had occurred, on the theory that he would fly back immediately and find his wife so upset and angry at his absence that strains between them would become more severe. So Jack was initially told that Jackie felt poorly, with no mention of the stillbirth.[47]

Just how he responded when he was told this has never been made clear. The evidence is fragmentary. Some accounts claim that he packed his bags and made arrangements to return home as soon as possible; others say he hesitated, thinking he might continue his sail for a few more days.[48] According to the latter version, it was only when George Smathers (also in the South of France but not on the boating trip) reached him by phone and stressed the seriousness of the situation that he reconsidered. "If you want to run for president, you'd better get your ass back to your wife's bedside or every wife in the country will be against you," Smathers allegedly lectured him.[49] Whichever account is correct, the senator flew home, having learned of the stillbirth prior to departure. His anxiety deepened. Upon landing at Boston's Logan Airport, he snapped at a reporter who dared ask him an election-related question, then immediately boarded a private plane to Newport, where he asked his driver, "Can you get me to Newport Hospital in ten minutes?" Only by violating traffic laws, came the answer. "He was nervous," the driver said later, "and if the light would be yellow, he'd say, 'Go through it. I'll pay for all the tickets.' "[50]

Jack stayed by Jackie's side for two weeks. She was incensed by his obtuse neglect of her needs in favor of his own, and the strains in the marriage were evident to friends who visited, such as Lem Billings. After the stillbirth, "Jackie worried about whether she'd be able to have a baby," Billings told author Doris Kearns Goodwin, "and she blamed her problem on the crazy pace of politics and the constant demands to participate in the endless activities of the Kennedy family. The only answer, she decided, was to separate herself even more from the rest of the family, insisting even in the summer months that she and Jack have dinner by themselves instead of gathering at Joe Senior's house as everyone else in the family did." Of course, such action would not necessarily do anything to change Jack's behavior, as Jackie surely understood. She had long since come to the grim realization that, however different his worldview was from his father's, however different his politics, when it came to marital relations he was Joseph Kennedy's true heir.[51]

In September, with Jackie recovering at home, Kennedy took to the road to campaign for Stevenson, hitting twenty-six states and making 140 public appearances. Only the candidate and his running mate campaigned harder. To the Stevenson team's frustration, Kennedy insisted on setting his own itinerary, one that was national in scope rather than focused on the Northeast, as the campaign wanted. "Jack had his own invitations to speak around the country," a Stevenson aide remembered. "He pretty much ran his own campaign. There was a lot of mumbling about that."[52] But when Kennedy subsequently offered to cancel a series of engagements in Philadelphia, Indianapolis, and Cleveland in order to concentrate on getting the vote out in Massachusetts, Stevenson himself demurred, telling aides it was important to have Kennedy speak before the party's annual fundraising dinner in Philadelphia in late October. (The number of attendees was expected to top four thousand, which would make it the largest dinner ever held in the city.)[53]

Kennedy's speeches extolled Stevenson and urged audiences to turn out in force for the Democratic ticket in November. But he also delved into policy issues, sometimes in unexpected ways, as he went beyond simple Cold War shibboleths. In Los Angeles, for example, he suggested that Americans' fixation on Communism and the East-West struggle had caused them to lose sight of the "Asian-African revolution of nationalism" and the unshakable will of human beings everywhere to control their own destiny, free of colonial control. "In my opinion, the tragic failure of both Republican and Democratic administrations since World War II to comprehend the nature of this revolution, and its potentialities for good and evil, has reaped a bitter harvest today—and it is by rights and by necessity a major foreign policy campaign issue that has nothing to do with anti-Communism."[54]

Everywhere the response to Kennedy was overwhelming, with often glowing local press coverage. (He drew much bigger crowds than Kefauver.) In Louisville on October 4, Kennedy caused a near riot after a speech at Ursuline College when the coeds surged forward as he tried to make his way to a waiting automobile. "We love you on TV!" the women screamed. "You're better than Elvis Presley!" In San Francisco, a crowd of six hundred gave him repeated standing ovations. So it went, at stop after stop, Kennedy's energy never flagging. Even bad weather didn't faze him. After an event in Idaho, as a terrible storm fast approached, Kennedy learned that an overflow crowd awaited him in Reno. He refused to cancel, and found an intrepid pilot willing to take him and Ted Sorensen in a tiny single-engine aircraft. The trio took off in brutal conditions. The flight proved so harrowing that the pilot had to make five passes before he put the landing wheels on concrete, but the assembled audience got their speaker.[55] All the while, hundreds of speaking invitations flooded Kennedy's Senate office on a weekly basis, along with letters from all over the country—some in response to his Chicago performance, others to the baby's death. "People wrote of how they cried and how their children cried and how they prayed for him," Evelyn Lincoln remembered.[56]

Robert Kennedy, for his part, accepted Stevenson's invitation to join the campaign. In Stevenson's eyes, it would show Catholics and conservative Democrats that their views were represented at the upper level, while to Bobby it was a glorious chance to see how a presidential campaign should—or should not—be run. Schlesinger recalled seeing the young Kennedy always scribbling notes, sometimes in the rear of the plane or bus, sometimes sitting on a railroad track while Stevenson spoke from the back of a train. "Occasionally he revealed himself, but in a rather solitary way."[57] Always, he was watching, learning. Bobby was impressed by Stevenson's sense of humor and his "sparkle" in small groups in which the discussion centered on things that interested him. But overall he thought the candidate and the campaign operation a disaster. Stevenson spent too much time polishing his speeches in private and too little time cultivating politicians. He dithered endlessly over details, taking hours to discuss tactical questions that should have been handled in minutes, while ignoring vital strategic matters—how to win the Midwest, how to secure favorable press coverage, how to maximize voter turnout on Election Day. Too often he failed to connect with his audience, in part because of his habit of reading specially prepared texts instead of speaking extemporaneously—even on brief whistle-stops. This gave the impression of insincerity, Bobby believed, a deadly attribute in a candidate. Most egregious of all, he thought, Stevenson utterly missed the new and game-changing impact of television.

"People around Stevenson lost confidence in him," Bobby later wrote. "There was no sort of enthusiasm about Stevenson personally. In fact, to the contrary, many of the people around him were openly critical, which amazed me." In an interview, Bobby recalled, "I came out of our first conversation with a very high opinion of him. . . . Then I spent six weeks with him on the campaign and he destroyed it all." Others, too, noticed the problems, noticed how the candidate seemed less engaged than the last time around, his speeches less humorous and eloquent, his energy level a notch lower. The crowds still showed up at events, but there was a dutiful quality to their applause and their cheering. The candidate, torn between his need to hit the Republicans hard and his desire to project a more high-minded, noble image, too often landed in the muddled middle, stepping on his applause lines and articulating his strongest lines without conviction.[58]

Nor was Stevenson helped by developments beyond his control, and beyond America's shores. In October, tensions flared in Hungary, where a new revolutionary government, urged on by student protesters, announced the nation's withdrawal from the Warsaw Pact, the Soviet-led military alliance formed with Eastern European countries the year before. Soviet leaders rejected the action and, in early November, sent troops and tanks into Budapest and other locales, where they battled students and workers and ultimately put down the revolution. In Egypt, meanwhile, war erupted on October 29 when Israeli forces invaded the Sinai Peninsula, under a secret plan worked out with Britain and France. The operation was a reaction to Egyptian president Gamal Abdel Nasser's move, some months before, to nationalize the Suez Canal. As Israeli forces advanced, drawing closer to the canal, France and Britain, under the pretext of protecting the canal from the two belligerents, dispatched their own troops. American voters, preparing to go to the polls, wondered if their own leaders would feel compelled to join the fray, perhaps sparking a wider conflagration if the Soviets intervened as well.[59]

For a brief moment, Stevenson thought the twin global crises could play to his advantage. He'd always prided himself on his knowledge of foreign affairs and had been itching to refocus his speeches accordingly. (A few weeks before, the campaign had even made a five-minute film featuring him and Jack Kennedy conversing about the pressing issues of peace and security.[60]) Here was his eleventh-hour chance. Hardly had he cleared his throat, however, before it became obvious that voters were not inclined to take chances on a new commander in chief in the midst of international turmoil, especially when the incumbent was a military hero and the former supreme commander of Allied forces in Europe. Stevenson's claim that the Eisenhower-Nixon ticket could not be trusted to maintain America's alliance relationships or preserve its global credibility moved no one who was not already in the Democrat's corner.[61]

On Election Day, Stevenson and Kefauver were trounced by a margin of ten million votes, double Eisenhower's margin of four years before. The Democrat won only seven states—none in the North and only one (Missouri) outside of the old Confederacy. Among those who quietly cast a ballot for the incumbent: Robert F. Kennedy.[62]

VII

In later years, much speculation would swirl around the question of when John F. Kennedy made *the decision*—made his choice to seek the big prize four years later. No precise date can be given. Maybe he was inching toward it already in Chicago, in that electric moment on August 17 when he conceded to Kefauver. ("In this moment of triumphant defeat," James MacGregor Burns would write, "his campaign for the presidency was born."[63]) No doubt he and his father discussed the prospect at length in the South of France later that month. In early September, Sargent Shriver informed Evelyn Lincoln that Senator Kennedy had asked him to compile "a complete list of all the delegates and alternate delegates to the Democratic National Convention together with their home addresses," the theory being that many of the 1956 delegates would also be delegates the next time around. In late September, Kennedy told aides Kenny O'Donnell and Dave Powers that he'd "learned that you don't get far in politics until you become a total politician. That means you've got to deal with the party leaders as well as the voters. From now on, I'm going to be a total politician." Barnstorming the country on Stevenson's behalf—but not on his itinerary—suggested something as well, as did dispatching Bobby to observe the candidate's operation up close and take detailed notes on what he found.[64]

Immediately following the convention, during a long sail off the Cape, Kennedy revealingly contrasted himself with his party's standard-bearer: "The hell of it is, I love [the campaigning]. Not the fakery, but learning to talk to voters in their own language. Stevenson hates it. He's dying to be President, but he hates campaigning. That's the difference between us, and it's important."[65]

Two days after the election, Kennedy offered a further clue to his plans in humor-filled remarks before the Tavern Club, a venerable hangout for Boston Brahmins that had mostly barred Irish Catholics for years but would make him a member the following year. Poking gentle fun at his blue-blooded audience, Kennedy noted, "This is my first major speech in many months that has not begun with those stirring words, 'Fellow Democrats.' Those words would not only be inappropriate on this non-partisan occasion, they would also—I gather from looking around me—be as grossly inaccurate as any salutation could possibly be." Still, the senator went on, despite any partisan differences, he would, "like a tourist returned from a visit to Europe or Yellowstone Park who insists on showing his slides," offer the room his thoughts on the recent election. For, after all, "some of you may someday have the ill luck to participate in a national political campaign to the same extent that I did in this one. Indeed, there is always the danger that I may participate in another one myself."[66]

The climactic moment, one that would live forever in Kennedy family lore, came at Thanksgiving in Hyannis Port, after Jack and Jackie returned from a brief holiday in the Caribbean. On the Cape, the autumn light glittered in the quiet stillness. The Kennedy clan walked along the beach, accompanied only by the gulls circling overhead, then returned home for their traditional holiday feast. Following the clearing of the dishes, the senator and his father moved to the little study off the living room to talk about the future. Jack went first, laying out all the reasons why he shouldn't run: he was Catholic, he had yet to turn forty, he didn't have the support of the party leadership, he should bide his time. Joe listened intently, then calmly countered each claim. Back and forth they went as the dusk fell outside, each one respecting the other, each one holding his ground, until finally the younger man began to give way. The father offered his summation: "Just remember, this country is not a private preserve for Protestants. There's a whole new generation out there and it's filled with the sons and daughters of immigrants from all over the world and those people are going to be mighty proud that one of their own is running for President. And that pride will be your spur, it will give your campaign an intensity we've never seen in public life."

The son fell quiet, then looked up and smiled. "Well, Dad, I guess there's only one question left. When do we start?"[67]

ACKNOWLEDGMENTS

This book has been a long time in the making, and I've accumulated more intellectual debts than I can possibly repay. The greatest of these debts is to the superb archivists and librarians and other staff of the JFK Library, one of the crown jewels in our presidential library system. I would like to thank Karen Abramson, Alan Price, Rachel Flor, Steven Rothstein, James Roth, Stephen Plotkin, Michael Desmond, Nancy McCoy, Liz Murphy, Maryrose Grossman, Jennifer Quan, Matt Porter, and, in particular, Stacey Chandler and Abbey Malangone, for their abundant and adroit assistance. My thanks also to the talented and dedicated staff at numerous other repositories, in particular Judy Donald and Stephanie Gold of the Choate Rosemary Hall archives, Tim Driscoll of Harvard University Archives, and Rosalba Varallo Recchia of Princeton University's Seeley G. Mudd Library.

A tremendous group of research assistants have helped me on the book, in ways large and small. They include Nick Danby, Alice Han, Julie Leighton, Aroop Mukherjee, Usha Sahay, Ben Schafer, Jennifer See, Wright Smith, and Aliya Somani. Elizabeth Saunders and Luke Nichter kindly shared some of their research findings with me, as did Daniel Hart. Conversations over meals with David Nasaw and Nigel Hamilton were endlessly stimulating and instructive, and Sheldon Stern, whose knowledge of JFK's life and career runs about as deep as anyone's, provided steady guidance throughout. Ellen Fitzpatrick, with her vast knowledge of Kennedy and his times, was exceptionally helpful, as were Jill Abramson, David Starr, and Eddy Neyts. David Greenberg was a font of sagacious input at each step, and Geoff Ward, biographer extraordinaire, provided an important early boost. A leisurely stroll along Stockholm streets with Philip Bobbitt yielded conceptual and interpretive ideas that proved invaluable, while Rob Rakove, Chester Pach, and Zach Shore provided excellent aid at a late stage. To Stephen Kennedy Smith, always gracious and perceptive in discussing his uncle's life, my deepest gratitude. And special thanks to Ambassador Caroline Kennedy, who kindly let me quote from a poem to her father written by her mother.

Then there are the colleagues, near and far, who gave me critical readings of portions of the draft manuscript or, in some cases, individual chapters: David Greenberg, Will Hitchcock, Jill Lepore, Jeff Frank, Jill Abramson, Usha Sahay, Sheldon Stern, Jonathan Kirshner, Chester Pach, Ken Mouré, Greg Robinson, and Steve Atlas. Two intrepid souls, Laura Kalman and Jim Hershberg, read the entire text and provided incisive comments that helped greatly in my final rewrite.

I'm grateful to others for their assistance and observations: Eric Alterman, Chet Atkins, Gary Bass, Paul Behringer, Dag Blanck, Jim Blight, Bill Brands, Doug Brinkley, Heather Campion, Chris Clark, Campbell Craig, Brian Cuddy, Andreas Daum, Elizabeth Deane, E. J. Dionne, Margot Dionne, Aaron Donaghy, Charlie Edel, Jack Farrell, Dan Fenn, Susan Ferber, Tom Fox, Eliza Gheorghe, Doris Kearns Goodwin, the late Richard Goodwin, Deirdre Henderson, Mary Herlihy-Gearan, Michael Ignatieff, Matthew Jones, Michael Kazin, Paul Kennedy, Steven Kotkin, janet Lang, the late Jack Langguth, Chris Lydon, Megan Marshall, Priscilla Johnson McMillan, Diane McWhorter, Jamie Miller, David Milne, Tim Naftali, Dorine Neyts, Chris Nichols, Leopoldo Nuti, Tom Oliphant, Ken Osgood, Jane Perlez, Barbara Perry, Andrew Preston, Tom Putnam, Susan Ronald, Steve Schlesinger, Marc Selverstone, Emma Sky, Larry Tye, Chris Vassallo, Arne Westad, Ted Widmer, James Wilson, Philip Zelikow, and Erik Åsard.

At Harvard I'm fortunate to be part of a marvelously inspiring and engaging intellectual community, in the Department of History and in the policy school named for the subject of this biography: the John F. Kennedy School of Government. Heartfelt thanks, in particular, to Graham

Allison, Arthur Applbaum, David Armitage, Nick Burns, Ash Carter, Dara Cohen, Suzanne Cooper, Ashley Davis, Mark Elliott, Archon Fung, Mark Gearan, David Gergen, Doug Johnson, Alex Keyssar, Jim Kloppenberg, Jill Lepore, Charlie Maier, Erez Manela, Joe Nye, Richard Parker, Serhii Plokhy, Bob Putnam, Kathryn Sikkink, Moshik Temkin, Steve Walt, Calder Walton, Pete Zimmerman, and, most of all, the incomparable Karen McCabe. The Weatherhead Center for International Affairs provided a generous research grant. At Cornell University, my prior institutional home, big thanks to the gang at the Einaudi Center, especially Nishi Dhupa, Elizabeth Edmondson, and Heike Michelsen.

The team at Random House has demonstrated again that it's in a class of its own. Andy Ward and Marie Pantojan were virtuoso editors—deeply discerning, endlessly patient, ever supportive. On the production side, Loren Noveck and Will Palmer were masterful, and I'm indebted to Michelle Jasmine and Ayelet Gruenspecht for their expert efforts in publicity and marketing. To David Ebershoff, who encouraged me to pursue the project and signed it, thank you! In Britain, Daniel Crewe, the publishing director of Viking, showed early and steadfast enthusiasm. At John Hawkins & Associates, Warren Frazier is simply the consummate agent, a pro who combines smart, savvy, and exuberant in the best possible way.

This book would not have happened had it not been for Susan Kamil, the late and legendary publisher and editor in chief of Random House. From the start Susan was an irrepressible champion of the project, and I treasured our leisurely lunches at Harvest in Harvard Square when she came for visits, our conversations ranging far and wide but always coming back to the book trade she loved. The lunches will be no more, but I will cherish the memory of them always.

Friends and family undergird writing projects like this in ways that are harder to measure but no less vital. For their love and encouragement I'm deeply grateful to Richard and Robin Parker, Jonathan Kirshner, Esty Schachter, Robin Wilkerson, Steve Atlas, Ken Mouré, David Starr, Bertil and Tracy Jean-Chronberg, Tanya Meyer, Rohn Meijer, Tom and Karen Gilovich, Alan Lynch, and Julie Simmons-Lynch. Apologies to Julie (who read the entire draft) that we didn't go with her suggested title: *You Don't Know Jack*. Special thanks to my dear friends Kristen Rupert and John Foote, whose charming summer home in aptly named Friendship, Maine, provided a tranquil setting for feverish writing.

My wonderful daughter and son, Emma and Joe, provided constant support and affection, and Emma showed her sharp editorial eye on the preface. Warm thanks also to my siblings, Maria and Robert, and to our parents, who did not live to see this project completed but who thrilled at the news that their son would write an in-depth biography of an American president who was and is a deeply inspirational figure to many Scandinavians. Danyel, my lovely and brilliant and witty wife, read every word and gave fabulous feedback, on the big picture as well as the intricate details, while also providing love, devotion, laughter, and a regular supply of her matchlessly delicious Swedish baked goods. I dedicate this book to her.

NOTES

ABBREVIATIONS USED

1. Archives

AESP: Adlai E. Stevenson Papers, Seeley G. Mudd Manuscript Library, Princeton University, Princeton, New Jersey

AHC: American Heritage Center, University of Wyoming, Laramie, Wyoming

AKP: Arthur Krock Papers, Seeley G. Mudd Manuscript Library, Princeton University, Princeton, New Jersey

AMSP: Arthur M. Schlesinger Jr. Personal Papers, John F. Kennedy Presidential Library, Boston, Massachusetts

CBLP: Clare Booth Luce Papers, Library of Congress, Manuscript Division, Washington, D.C.

CBP: Clay Blair Papers, American Heritage Center, University of Wyoming, Laramie, Wyoming

CBSI: CBS Interviews, John F. Kennedy Presidential Library, Boston, Massachusetts

CCP: Clark M. Clifford Papers, Library of Congress, Manuscript Division, Washington, D.C.

CSA: Choate School Archives, Choate Rosemary Hall, Wallingford, Connecticut

DFPP: David F. Powers Personal Papers, John F. Kennedy Presidential Library, Boston, Massachusetts

FDRL: Franklin D. Roosevelt Presidential Library, Hyde Park, New York

GBP: George Ball Papers, Seeley G. Mudd Manuscript Library, Princeton University, Princeton, New Jersey

HCLP: Henry Cabot Lodge Jr. Papers, Massachusetts Historical Society, Boston, Massachusetts

HIP: Harold L. Ickes Papers, Library of Congress, Manuscript Division, Washington, D.C.

HMP: Henry Morgenthau Jr. Papers, Library of Congress, Manuscript Division, Washington, D.C.

HUA: Harvard University Archives, Harvard University, Cambridge, Massachusetts

JFK Pre-Pres: John F. Kennedy Pre-Presidential Papers, John F. Kennedy Presidential Library, Boston, Massachusetts

JFKL: John F. Kennedy Presidential Library, Boston, Massachusetts

JFKPOF: John F. Kennedy President's Office Files, John F. Kennedy Presidential Library, Boston, Massachusetts

JFKPP: John F. Kennedy Personal Papers, John F. Kennedy Presidential Library, Boston, Massachusetts

JPKP: Joseph P. Kennedy Personal Papers, John F. Kennedy Presidential Library, Boston, Massachusetts

JKOP: Jacqueline Bouvier Kennedy Onassis Personal Papers, John F. Kennedy Presidential Library, Boston, Massachusetts

KLBP: Kirk LeMoyne Billings Personal Papers, John F. Kennedy Presidential Library, Boston, Massachusetts

LC: Library of Congress, Washington, D.C.

MHS: Massachusetts Historical Society, Boston, Massachusetts

NARA: National Archives and Records Administration, College Park, Maryland

NAUK: National Archives of the United Kingdom, Kew, Richmond, Surrey, U.K.

OCF: Official and Confidential Files (J. Edgar Hoover), Record Group 65, National Archives and Records Administration, College Park, Maryland

RKP: Rose Fitzgerald Kennedy Personal Papers, John F. Kennedy Presidential Library, Boston, Massachusetts

TOP: Tip O'Neill Congressional Papers, John J. Burns Library, Boston College, Chestnut Hill, Massachusetts

TSP: Theodore C. Sorensen Personal Papers, John F. Kennedy Presidential Library, Boston, Massachusetts

2. Individuals

AES: Adlai E. Stevenson

FDR: Franklin D. Roosevelt

JFK: John F. Kennedy

JPK: Joseph P. Kennedy

JPK Jr.: Joseph P. Kennedy Jr.

KK: Kathleen "Kick" Kennedy

KLB: Kirk LeMoyne "Lem" Billings

RFK: Robert F. Kennedy

RK: Rose Kennedy

TS: Theodore "Ted" Sorensen

3. Newspapers

BG: Boston Globe

BP: Boston Post

NYT: New York Times

SEP: Saturday Evening Post

THC: The Harvard Crimson

WP: Washington Post

4. Oral Histories

Alastair Forbes OH, JFKL
Arthur Krock OH, CBP
Arthur Krock OH, JFKL
Barbara Ward OH, JFKL
Betty Coxe Spalding OH, CBP
Billy Sutton OH, JFKL
Charles Bartlett OH, JFKL
Charles Spalding OH, JFKL
David Powers extended OH, box 9,
   DFPP
David Powers OH, JFKL
Dore Schary OH, JFKL
Edmund Gullion OH, JFKL
Edward J. McCormack OH, JFKL
Fletcher Knebel OH, JFKL
Frank Morrissey OH, JFKL
George Taylor OH, JFKL
Gloria L. Sitrin OH, JFKL
Grace de Monaco OH, JFKL
Henry Cabot Lodge Jr. OH, JFKL
Hirsch Freed OH, JFKL
Hugh Fraser OH, JFKL
James Farrell OH, JFKL
Janet Auchincloss OH, JFKL
Janet Travell OH, JFKL
Jean McGonigle Mannix OH, JFKL
Joe DeGuglielmo OH, JFKL

John M. Bailey OH, JFKL
John Droney OH, JFKL
John Sharon OH, JFKL
John T. Burke OH, JFKL
Joseph Alsop OH, JFKL
Joseph Healey OH, JFKL
Joseph Rauh OH, JFKL
Kay Halle OH, JFKL
Kirk LeMoyne Billings OH, JFKL
Luella Hennessey OH, JFKL
Mark Dalton OH, JFKL
Patricia Kennedy Lawford OH,
   JFKL
Peter Lawford OH, JFKL
Peter Cloherty OH, JFKL
Phil David Fine OH, JFKL
Polly Fitzgerald OH, JFKL
Ralph Horton OH, CBP
Ralph Horton OH, JFKL
Samuel Bornstein OH, JFKL
Thomas Broderick OH, JFKL
Thomas "Tip" O'Neill OH, JFKL
Tony Galluccio OH, JFKL
Torbert Macdonald OH, JFKL
William Douglas-Home OH, JFKL
William O. Douglas OH, JFKL

NOTES

PREFACE

1. Prior to his arrival in Berlin, he had visited other German cities, including Munich and Hamburg. On the storm troopers, see Sandford, *Union Jack*, 53. And see also Lubrich, *John F. Kennedy Unter Deutschen*, 129–50.
2. On the German government's propaganda efforts, see Evans, *Third Reich in Power*, 695–96.
3. JFK to Lem Billings, August 20, 1939, printed in Lubrich, *John F. Kennedy Unter Deutschen*, 146–48. See also Leaming, *Jack Kennedy: Education*, 89; and O'Brien, *John F. Kennedy*, 96.
4. Shirer, *Berlin Diary*, 181–83; Kotkin, *Stalin: Waiting*, 661; "Greatest Surprise in Berlin," *The Scotsman*, August 22, 1939.
5. Ted Widmer, "Ich Bin Ein Berliner," *NYT*, June 25, 2013; Martin and Plaut, *Front Runner*, 127; McCarthy, *Remarkable Kennedys*, 81; *The American Weekly*, May 30, 1948.
6. JPK diary, March 12, 1939, box 100, JPKP.
7. The speech in full is on the website of the International Churchill Society, winston

churchill.org/resources/speeches/1939-in-the-wings/war-speech/, accessed February 8, 2020.

8. Second on the list is Dwight Eisenhower, with a 65 percent average rating. Harry Truman averaged 45 percent, and Lyndon Johnson 55 percent. Kennedy's was of course an abbreviated presidency, and thus he was not subject to the dip in ratings that typically occurs in the second term. For ex post facto popular views of Kennedy's performance, see Andrew Dugan and Frank Davenport, "Americans Rate JFK as Top Modern President," November 15, 2013, Gallup, https://news.gallup.com/poll/165902/americans-rate-jfk-top-modern-president.aspx. For the first set of figures, showing who claimed to have voted for Kennedy, see Manchester, *Glory and the Dream*, 890.

9. Dallek's valuable *An Unfinished Life* moves swiftly through the first two-thirds of Kennedy's life and is now almost two decades old. Herbert Parmet's perceptive two-volume effort, *Jack* and *JFK*, dates from the 1980s, when much archival material was still unavailable. Other useful works include O'Brien, *John F. Kennedy*; Burns, *John Kennedy*; Matthews, *Jack Kennedy*; Leaming, *Jack Kennedy: Education*; Perret, *Jack*; and Martin, *Hero for Our Time*. Not to be missed are the often penetrating early accounts by insiders: Schlesinger, *Thousand Days*; Sorensen, *Kennedy*; O'Donnell and Powers, *"Johnny"*; and O'Brien, *No Final Victories*. See also Sorensen's memoirs, *Counselor*. Several family portraits are likewise important, including Leamer, *Kennedy Men* and *Kennedy Women*; Maier, *Kennedys* and *When Lions Roar*; Collier and Horowitz, *Kennedys*; and, especially, Goodwin, *Fitzgeralds and the Kennedys*. Brief and useful introductions to JFK include Brinkley, *John F. Kennedy*; Burner, *John F. Kennedy*; and Ling, *John F. Kennedy*. Interpretive works, some of them polemical in tone, include Wills, *Kennedy Imprisonment*; Hersh, *Dark Side*; Hellman, *Obsession*; Hogan, *Afterlife*; and Brogan, *Kennedy*. Several biographies of Joseph Kennedy are key, starting with Nasaw's seminal effort, *Patriarch*. See here also Whalen, *Founding Father*; Kessler, *Sins of the Father*; and Koskoff, *Joseph P. Kennedy*. On Rose Kennedy, see Perry, *Rose Kennedy*; and Cameron, *Rose*. Rose Kennedy's own account *Times to Remember* is essential. In a special category is the extraordinary compendium of Joe Kennedy correspondence compiled by his granddaughter Amanda Smith, *Hostage to Fortune*. For a discerning and balanced overview of the historiography, see Michael Kazin, "An Idol and Once a President: John F. Kennedy at 100," *Journal of American History* 104 (December 2017): 707–26.

10. Highly important on the early years is Hamilton, *JFK: Reckless Youth*. Hamilton and I disagree on various aspects of these years, and abundant archival and other material has appeared in the almost three decades since the publication of his book, but I remain in his debt. Also valuable on the early years is Blair and Blair, *Search for JFK*.

11. Historian Barton J. Bernstein has written, "Scholars should adequately recognize that chief executives, like other people, develop attitudes, responses, and values well before reaching middle age or beyond. Those who enter the presidency are neither unformed nor fully formed, but they are usually largely formed." Barton J. Bernstein, "Understanding Decisionmaking, U.S. Foreign Policy, and the Cuban Missile Crisis: A Review Essay," *International Security* 25, no. 1 (Summer 2000): 134–64.

12. Especially valuable are the voluminous Joseph P. Kennedy Personal Papers, which until 2013 were accessible only by permission but which are now open to all. An extremely useful compendium, which includes perceptive interpretive essays, is Smith, *Hostage to Fortune*.

13. Schlesinger, *Life in the 20th Century*, 261.

14. "My husband was a romantic," Jackie Kennedy said a year after his death, "although he didn't like people to know that." *Look*, November 17, 1964.

15. Aide Richard Goodwin, who also worked for Lyndon Johnson, said many years later, "We all loved the guy, those of us who worked for him. The feelings were more intense than they were for Johnson." Richard Goodwin, interview with the author, October 16, 2016, Concord, MA.

16. "As a lifetime fan of comedy and American history," Conan O'Brien observes in a trenchant essay, "I have thought quite a bit about our truly funniest presidents, and I think we have had exactly two: Abraham Lincoln and John F. Kennedy. . . . The humor that resonates with me is . . . the sense of humor one needs in order to hold two opposing ideas at once: that our life here on earth is simultaneously beautiful and terribly sad. To wit, it is the humor of John F. Kennedy." Conan O'Brien, "Comedy as Worldview," in Smith and Brinkley, *JFK: A Vision for America*, 27–29.

17. Manchester, *Portrait of a President*, 49; JFK to Inga Arvad, n.d. (September 1943), printed in Sandler, *Letters*, 31–33; transcript of MBN radio address, November 14, 1951, box 102, JFK Pre-Pres.

18. He returned to the topic many times in the years thereafter. See, e.g., his speech at the University of Notre Dame on January 29, 1950. Transcript is in box 95, JFK Pre-Pres.

19. As Jill Abramson has put it, "a dolorous mood of 'what might have been' hangs over a good deal of writing about Kennedy." Jill Abramson, "Kennedy, the Elusive President," *NYT*, October 22, 2013. My thanks to Zach Shore for his input on this point.

CHAPTER 1: TWO FAMILIES

1. A half century later, the Kennedys would pay $55,000 to repurchase the house, refurnish it with everything from the original Victorian furniture to JFK's bassinet, and then turn the deed over to the federal government, to maintain as a national historic site: the birthplace of the thirty-fifth president. At the official dedication in 1969, Rose Kennedy stood on the front porch she had crossed as a newlywed and spoke briefly to the crowd of seven hundred gathered in front of her. "We were very happy here," she said, "and although we did not know about the days ahead, we were enthusiastic and optimistic about the future." Greg Wayland, "At His Birthplace in Brookline, Historians Preserve Stories of JFK's Early Years," WBUR News, May 25, 2017, www.wbur.org/news/2017/05/25/jfk-birthplace-brookline, accessed March 18, 2019.

2. Karr, *Between City and Country*, 189–90; Hamilton, *JFK: Reckless Youth*, 23–24.

3. The term is usually attributed to Oliver Wendell Holmes Sr. In his novel *Elsie Venner* (Boston, 1847), Holmes describes a young Bostonian: "He comes of the Brahmin caste of New England. This is the harmless, inoffensive, untitled aristocracy."

4. Rawson, *Eden on the Charles*, 162–67. On Brookline's rise in these years, see Karr, *Between City and Country*.

5. Some accounts suggest he traveled directly from New Ross to Boston, but it seems more likely he went via Liverpool. Passenger lists from the period show several Patrick, Pat, or P. Kennedys arriving in Boston on various dates, so it's impossible to be certain when he traveled, and by which route.

6. O'Connor, *Boston Irish*, 59.

7. Maier, *Kennedys*, 22; Miller, *Emigrants and Exiles*, 285.

8. Ó Gráda, *Ireland's Great Famine*, 14–16; Miller, *Emigrants and Exiles*, 283; Dolan, *Irish Americans*, 71–72.

9. Kerby Miller, "Emigration to North America in the Era of the Great Famine, 1845–1855," in Crowley, Smyth, and Murphy, *Atlas*, 214–27; Dolan, *Irish Americans*, 74; Kenny, *American Irish*, 94–95.

10. Ó Gráda, *Ireland's Great Famine*, 190–91, quoted in Dolan, *Irish Americans*, 74; Kenny, *American Irish*, 99.

11. Kenny, *American Irish*, 102; Woodham-Smith, *Great Hunger*, 238.

12. Kelly, *Graves Are Walking*, 252–89; Handlin, *Uprooted*, 50–52; Kenny, *American Irish*, 94–95; Whalen, *Founding Father*, 7–8. Herman Melville, who served as crew member on an emigrant ship, the *Highlander*, in 1849, wrote of the passengers' experience: "Stowed away like bales of cotton, and packed like slaves in a slave ship, confined in a place that during storm time must be closed against light and air, [unable to do any] cooking nor warm so much as a cup of water." Quoted in Kelly, *Graves Are Walking*, 271.

13. Nasaw, *Patriarch*, 5–6; Kelly, *Graves Are Walking*, 299.

14. It's possible they knew each other before departure or met on the voyage to America, but more likely they first laid eyes on each other in Boston. Rose Kennedy, in her memoirs, implies that Patrick and Bridget met after arriving in Boston. See *Times to Remember*, 20.

15. The first-last formulation is from Collier and Horowitz, *Kennedys*, 24.

16. Koskoff, *Joseph P. Kennedy*, 4. Other estimates are even lower; see Miller, "Emigration," in Crowley, Smyth, and Murphy, *Atlas*, 225.

17. Peterson, *City-State of Boston*, 572; Nasaw, *Patriarch*, 7. Ralph Waldo Emerson once wrote to his friend Henry David Thoreau to say how stunned he was to discover Irish laborers who regularly worked a fifteen-hour day for not more than fifty cents. O'Connor, *Boston Irish*, 100.

18. Handlin, *Boston's Immigrants*, 113.

19. O'Neill, *Rogues and Redeemers*, 4–5; O'Connor, *Boston Irish*, 60; Patrick Blessing, "Irish," in *Harvard Encyclopedia of American Ethnic Groups*, ed. Stephan Thernstrom (Cambridge, MA: Harvard University Press, 1980), 530.

20. O'Connor, *Boston Irish*, 61.

21. Miller, *Emigrants and Exiles*, 323–24.

22. Handlin, *Boston's Immigrants*, 186; O'Neill, *Rogues and Redeemers*, 11.

23. Anbinder, *Nativism and Slavery*, 87–94, 135–42; Puleo, *City So Grand*, 72–73.

24. Quoted in Anbinder, *Nativism and Slavery*, 266.

25. O'Neill, *Rogues and Redeemers*, 16.

26. Quoted in Burns, *John Kennedy*, 7.

27. Handlin, *Boston's Immigrants*, 91.

28. Nasaw, *Patriarch*, 8; Collier and Horowitz, *Kennedys*, 24.

29. Goodwin, *Fitzgeralds and the Kennedys*, 226; Collier and Horowitz, *Kennedys*, 24–25.

30. Whalen, *Founding Father*, 14–15.

31. From 1851 to 1921, that is to say, after the famine, as many as 4.5 million left Ireland, about 3.7 million of them going to the United States.

32. Dolan, *Irish Americans*, 147–49.

33. Collier and Horowitz, *Kennedys*, 27.

34. Duncliffe, *Life and Times*, 3; Collier and Horowitz, *Kennedys*, 31–32.

35. Leamer, *Kennedy Men*, 9.

36. Nasaw, *Patriarch*, 14.

37. Kessler, *Sins of the Father*, 12.

38. Nasaw, *Patriarch*, 13–14; Dallek, *Unfinished Life*, 15.

39. Nasaw, *Patriarch*, 13–14; Goodwin, *Fitzgeralds and the Kennedys*, 228.

40. Collier and Horowitz, *Kennedys*, 31–32. Koskoff, *Joseph P. Kennedy*, 15–16; Kessler, *Sins of the Father*, 16.

41. Whalen, *Founding Father*, 22.

42. Kessler, *Sins of the Father*, 16; Leamer, *Kennedy Men*, 12.

43. Whalen, *Founding Father*, 23–24; Nasaw, *Patriarch*, 19.

44. Nasaw, *Patriarch*, 21; Collier and Horowitz, *Kennedys*, 34.

45. "List of Secondary Schools, Universities and Colleges . . . from Which Students Have Entered Harvard College During the Years 1901–1920," Harvard University Archives (hereafter HUA).

46. Amory, *Proper Bostonians*, 292; Whalen, *Founding Father*, 31.

47. The class of 1910 was a golden one: in addition to Lippmann, it had poet T. S. Eliot, radical journalist John Reed, journalist Heywood Broun, poet Alan Seeger, theatrical stage designer Robert Edmond Jones, psychiatrist Carl Binger, and politicians Hamilton Fish III and Bronson Cutting.

48. Steel, *Walter Lippmann*, 12; Schlesinger, *Veritas*, 148; Nasaw, *Patriarch*, 23.

49. Koskoff, *Joseph P. Kennedy*, 19.

50. The story of the Yale game in which he earned his letter and also picked up the game ball would become controversial, a supposed sign of his bottomless and ruthless ambition, the argument being that the game ball should have gone to the winning Harvard pitcher. But teammates defended Joe on the grounds that he had made the final out at first base and therefore by custom was entitled to pocket the ball. See Nasaw, *Patriarch*, 24.

51. JPK Grade Card, UAIII 15.75.12 1910–1919, box 12, HUA.

52. Collier and Horowitz, *Kennedys*, 29; Cameron, *Rose*, 27.

53. RK, *Times to Remember*, 8; Goodwin, *Fitzgeralds and the Kennedys*, 61–68.

54. O'Brien, *John F. Kennedy*, 6–7.

55. Collier and Horowitz, *Kennedys*, 37; O'Donnell and Powers, *"Johnny,"* 58–59.

56. RK, *Times to Remember*, 6–7; Perry, *Rose Kennedy*, 15.

57. Cameron, *Rose*, 40.

58. Salinger quoted in Cameron, *Rose*, 53.

59. RK, *Times to Remember*, 28.

60. The specifics from the early period of the relationship are scarce. Only at the time of their wedding would Rose begin to document their relationship. Joe's assessments of the early years, meanwhile, are extremely limited and entirely retrospective.

61. RK, *Times to Remember*, 57–58. Three-quarters of a century later, as she neared ninety years of age, Rose would say, "I shall always remember Old Orchard Beach as a place of magic, for it was the place where Joe and I fell in love." Goodwin, *Fitzgeralds and the Kennedys*, 144.

62. C. F. Hennessey, "Prophecy for the Class of 1908," in R. J. Dobbyn to JPK, January 24, 1934, box 34, JPKP; RK, *Times to Remember*, 59; Nasaw, *Patriarch*, 21.

63. Goodwin, *Fitzgeralds and the Kennedys*, 184–89; Perry, *Rose Kennedy*, 23–28.

64. She did not get an earned degree, however, as the college would become accredited only in 1917. It bestowed an honorary doctorate on Rose in 1953 and now considers her its most notable alumna. Perry, *Rose Kennedy*, 31.

65. Nasaw, *Patriarch*, 28.

66. Quoted in Nasaw, *Patriarch*, 32.

67. Koskoff, *Joseph P. Kennedy*, 22–23.

68. Nasaw, *Patriarch*, 39.

69. Halley, *Dapper Dan*, 105–9; Kessler, *Sins of the Father*, 18. An excellent biography of Curley is Beatty, *Rascal King*.

70. The scholarship on the origins is massive. See, e.g., Clark, *Sleepwalkers*; MacMillan, *War That Ended Peace*; McMeekin, *July 1914*; Ferguson, *Pity of War*.

71. Rose Kennedy diary and wedding log, box 1, RKP. The Boston papers covered the wedding; see, e.g., *BP* and *BG*, October 8, 1914.

72. O'Brien, *John F. Kennedy*, 19.

CHAPTER 2: CHILDISH THINGS

1. A detailed assessment of this critical year is Stevenson, *1917*.
2. The more commonly asserted start date is 1941, the year in which Henry Luce published his seminal editorial "The American Century," to be discussed later in this book.
3. Hobsbawm, *Age of Extremes*, 4. See also Mazower, *Dark Continent*, ix–xx; Michael Neiberg, "The Meanings of 1917," *Journal of Military and Strategic Studies* 18 (2017).
4. Tocqueville, *Democracy*, 559.
5. Englishman William T. Stead's book *The Americanization of the World*, which appeared in 1902, predicted that America's economic and demographic strength would propel it to the forefront of world leadership.
6. Kennedy, *Rise and Fall*, 202; Tooze, *Deluge*, 14–15. On the rise of the United States in this period, see also Zakaria, *From Wealth to Power*.
7. Quoted in Thompson, *Woodrow Wilson*, 102.
8. The studies are numerous, but see Neiberg, *Path to War*, and Knock, *To End All Wars*. Also illuminating are O'Toole, *Moralist*, and Kennedy, *Will to Believe*.
9. Between 1914 and 1916, U.S. exports to France and Britain grew 265 percent, from $754 million to $2.75 billion. In the same period, largely on account of a British blockade of German ports, exports to Germany dropped by more than 91 percent, from $345 million to a mere $29 million.
10. Figures are from Paterson et al., *American Foreign Relations*, 292.
11. Goodwin, *Fitzgeralds and the Kennedys*, 271–72.
12. Goodwin, *Fitzgeralds and the Kennedys*, 272.
13. Page quoted in Kamensky et al., *People and a Nation*, 582. The trench warfare has spawned a huge literature. On the Somme fighting, see, e.g., Prior and Wilson, *Somme*. A superb study of anti-war thinking and activism in the United States is Kazin, *War Against War*.
14. Kennedy, *Over Here*, 12; LaFeber, *American Age*, 294.
15. Nasaw, *Patriarch*, 51–53.
16. JPK to Draft Board, February 18, 1918, box 37, JPKP.
17. On the war's final months, see, e.g., Strachan, *First World War*, 259ff; Stevenson, *Cataclysm*, 303–406.
18. Keynes, *Economic Consequences*, 297. On the legacy of the war, see Reynolds, *Long Shadow*.
19. See, e.g., Barry, *Great Influenza*; Crosby, *America's Forgotten Pandemic*; and Kolata, *Flu*.
20. Nasaw, *Patriarch*, 56–57; RK, *Times to Remember*, 151; Smith, *Hostage to Fortune*, 6.
21. Porter, *Greatest Benefit*, 484; Kamensky et al., *People and a Nation*, 585.
22. RK, *Times to Remember*, 73; Nasaw, *Patriarch*, 57.
23. Nasaw, *Patriarch*, 34.
24. Goodwin, *Fitzgeralds and the Kennedys*, 301–2; Cameron, *Rose*, 83.
25. Cott, *Grounding of Modern Feminism*.
26. Bailey, *From Front Porch*; Goodwin, *Fitzgeralds and the Kennedys*, 302.
27. Goodwin, *Fitzgeralds and the Kennedys*, 305–7; Beauchamp, *Joseph P. Kennedy Presents*, 29–30.
28. RK interview by Robert Coughlan, January 28, 1972, box 10, RKP; Perry, *Rose Kennedy*, 54.
29. Prior to one of the neighborhood outings, the governess got Jack dressed, then left him for a minute to get her coat and hat. While she was gone, he climbed through the nursery bathroom window. According to Edward Moore, "When the nurse returned she couldn't find him but she could hear his voice calling to some of his little friends in the street. She spied Jack and tried to coax him to come in, but he was having too much fun

to pay any attention to her. She called his mother and they tried to entice him in with candy and toys, but he refused to budge. They were afraid to go out and get him, because they thought he might try to fun [sic] away and fall off the roof. When he had all the fun he wanted out there he came in himself. Everyone was pretty much disturbed about it, because it was a 30 feet [sic] drop to the ground." Smith, *Hostage to Fortune*, 10.

30. Cameron, *Rose*, 82; RK, *Times to Remember*, 82–83.
31. Smith, *Nine of Us*, 68–69. Jack was christened at St. Aidan's. Rose was not present, as mothers were confined for three weeks then and she insisted on her children being christened as soon as possible.
32. RK, *Times to Remember*, 84–85.
33. JPK to Edward Place, July 2, 1920, box 21, JPKP. Earlier, Joe wrote: "Mrs. Kennedy and I feel that we can never repay you for the interest that you have taken in Jack. We would feel very badly to have the little fellow away for the period that we feel he must be, if we did not feel that he was under your care." JPK to Edward Place, March 4, 1920, box 21, JPKP.
34. Anna Pope to JPK, May 14, 1920, box 21, JPKP; Smith, *Hostage to Fortune*, 9; Nasaw, *Patriarch*, 63; O'Brien, *John F. Kennedy*, 26. In response to Sara Miller, Joe wrote, "As I have told you personally over the phone, Mrs. Kennedy and I feel we can never repay you for the interest you have taken in Jack. . . . It makes a great difference to us to know that he is so happy with you, and is getting along so very well under your treatment." JPK to Sara Miller, March 4, 1920, box 21, JPKP.
35. Kessler, *Sins of the Father*, 34; Whalen, *Founding Father*, 54.
36. The entrance is now at 51 Abbottsford Road.
37. RK, *Times to Remember*, 83.
38. RK, *Times to Remember*, 81.
39. RK diary, April 3, 1923, box 1, RKP.
40. RK diary, April 3, 1923, box 1, RKP; RK, *Times to Remember*, 94.
41. Perry, *Rose Kennedy*, 15; Kathryn Kish Sklar, "Victorian Women and Domestic Life: Mary Todd Lincoln, Elizabeth Cady Stanton, and Harriet Beecher Stowe," in *Women and Power in American History*, 3rd ed., ed. Kathryn Kish Sklar and Thomas Dublin (Upper Saddle River, NJ: Prentice Hall, 2009), 122, 128; Linda Kerber, "The Republican Mother," *American Quarterly* 28, no. 2 (summer 1976): 187–205.
42. Holt, *Care and Feeding*.
43. Watson, *Psychological Care*; O'Brien, *John F. Kennedy*, 39–40.
44. RK, *Times to Remember*, 7.
45. Cameron, *Rose*, 83, 85; RK, *Times to Remember*, 111.
46. Burns, *John Kennedy*, 22–23; Eunice Shriver interview, CBP.
47. Whalen, *Founding Father*, 57–58; Hamilton, *JFK: Reckless Youth*, 59.
48. RK diary, December 5, 1923, February 28, 1923, October 26, 1923, and September 11, 1923, box 1, RKP; Perry, *Rose Kennedy*, 61–62; Perret, *Jack*, 24.
49. RK diary, November 21, 1923, box 1, RKP; RK, *Times to Remember*, 97.
50. Flood, *Story of Noble and Greenough*, 79; Hamilton, *JFK: Reckless Youth*, 53.
51. Hamilton, *JFK: Reckless Youth*, 54–55.
52. Also on the team was another set of brothers, McGeorge and William Bundy. For the latter's recollection of being a classmate of Jack's, see Bird, *The Color of Truth*, 36.
53. Hamilton, *JFK: Reckless Youth*, 57; Bird, *The Color of Truth*, 36.
54. Myra Fiske OH, Dexter School, quoted in Hamilton, *JFK: Reckless Youth*, 57.
55. Quoted in Leamer, *Kennedy Men*, 35.
56. Rostow, *World Economy*, 210; Eckes and Zeiler, *Globalization*, 73.
57. On U.S. reluctance to face the challenges of world leadership in the interwar era, see

Tooze, *Deluge*; and Thompson, *Sense of Power*, chap. 3. The Eurocentered world as artificial is from Kennedy, *Rise and Fall*, 277. On Wilson and the League fight, see Cooper, *Breaking the Heart*; Ambrosius, *Woodrow Wilson*; and Nichols, *Promise*, chap. 6.

58. Whalen, *Founding Father*, 65–66; Collier and Horowitz, *Kennedys*, 42.

59. An excellent history of Prohibition is McGirr, *War on Alcohol*.

60. Okrent, *Last Call*, 366–71; Nasaw, *Patriarch*, 79–81. Nasaw did find a "Joseph Kennedy Ltd." involved in the liquor-smuggling trade, but the owner was a Vancouver-based Canadian whose given name was Daniel Joseph. See also Smith, *Hostage to Fortune*, xx.

61. "Mr. Kennedy, the Chairman," *Fortune*, September 1937.

62. Arthur Krock OH, JFKL; Whalen, *Founding Father*, 59.

63. Whalen, *Founding Father*, 58–59. Quoted in O'Brien, *John F. Kennedy*, 29. See also Beschloss, *Kennedy and Roosevelt*, 65.

64. RK, *Times to Remember*, 57; RK interview by Robert Coughlan, January 7, 1972, box 10, RKP.

65. RK, *Times to Remember*, 166; Hamilton, *JFK: Reckless Youth*, 62.

66. "Mr. Kennedy, the Chairman," *Fortune*, September 1937; Collier and Horowitz, *Kennedys*, 46–47; Kamensky et al., *People and a Nation*, 622.

67. Parmet, *Jack*, 11; Smith, *Hostage to Fortune*, 9.

68. Beauchamp, *Joseph P. Kennedy Presents*, 93–99; Nasaw, *Patriarch*, 100–102.

69. Quoted in Goodwin, *Fitzgeralds and the Kennedys*, 393–94.

70. Byrne, *Kick*, 19; Beauchamp, *Joseph P. Kennedy Presents*, 122–25.

71. Swanson, *Swanson on Swanson*, 356–57, 359. Though the family had moved to Riverdale, Rose returned to Boston to give birth.

72. Beauchamp, *Joseph P. Kennedy Presents*, 272–73; Nasaw, *Patriarch*, 144.

73. Swanson, *Swanson on Swanson*, 385–86.

74. Goodwin, *Fitzgeralds and the Kennedys*, 391–92; Perry, *Rose Kennedy*, 78; O'Brien, *John F. Kennedy*, 35. In *Marriage and Parenthood: The Catholic Ideal* (1911), Father Thomas Gerrard stated that sexual intercourse should be completed quickly.

75. Dallek, *Unfinished Life*, 23–24.

76. Swanson, *Swanson on Swanson*, 394. According to the book, Kennedy had sought permission from the Catholic Church to live apart from Rose and maintain a second home with Swanson.

77. Nasaw, *Patriarch*, 146–47; Higham, *Rose*, 110–11.

78. On June 3, Kennedy wrote to Joe Junior to commend him on how he had carried himself at the funeral. "Everybody says you were perfectly fine and handled yourself splendidly. I was terribly disappointed not to be there myself, but I was more than proud to have you as my own representative and delighted everybody liked you so much." JPK to JPK Jr., June 3, 1929, printed in Smith, *Hostage to Fortune*, 84.

79. Goodwin, *Fitzgeralds and the Kennedys*, 420; Kessler, *Sins of the Father*, 80–81.

80. Allen, *Only Yesterday*, quoted in Whalen, *Founding Father*, 106.

81. Leamer, *Kennedy Men*, 57; Goodwin, *Fitzgeralds and the Kennedys*, 391–92, 425–26.

82. Hamilton, *JFK: Reckless Youth*, 50.

83. RK, *Times to Remember*, 150; Parmet, *Jack*, 14.

84. Quoted in Burns, *John Kennedy*, 21.

85. Riverdale Country School scholarship report, June 7, 1929, box 20, JPKP; O'Brien, *John F. Kennedy*, 29.

86. "Plea for a Raise," n.d., box 1, JPKP. Jack signed the letter "John Fitzgerald Francis Kennedy." Mystified by the inclusion of "Francis," which was not part of his name, his mother could only surmise that Jack added the name of the kindly saint to increase his chances of getting his wish.

87. O'Brien, *John F. Kennedy*, 29.

88. Damore, *Cape Cod Years*, 19–21; Nasaw, *Patriarch*, 92.

CHAPTER 3: SECOND SON

1. RK interview by Robert Coughlan, January 7, 1972, box 10, RKP.

2. Goodwin, *Fitzgeralds and the Kennedys*, 351–52.

3. Collier and Horowitz, *Kennedys*, 60; Thompson and Meyers, *Robert F. Kennedy*, 64.

4. Parmet, *Jack*, 20; Luella Hennessey OH, JFKL. Lem Billings recalled, "But Jack, I can remember, was as fluent as Joe [Jr.] right from the time he was fifteen. The topics were always on a high level during the entire meal. This was a challenge—it was a challenge for me as a visitor. I felt it was much more important for me to read and to know what was going on so that, when I was at the Kennedys, I would be able to at least understand the topics at the table." KLB OH, JFKL.

5. Smith, *Nine of Us*, 54–55.

6. Leamer, *Kennedy Men*, 67.

7. Ralph Horton OH, JFKL; Leaming, *Jack Kennedy: Education*, 30.

8. "When he was home," Eunice later said, "[Mother] let him sort of take over." RK, *Times to Remember*, 148.

9. Smith, *Hostage to Fortune*, xxv; Goodwin, *Fitzgeralds and the Kennedys*, 351; Charles Laurence, "Grandpa Joseph's Letters Edited by Adopted Kin," *National Post*, January 13, 2001. As Amanda Smith notes, the volume of Kennedy family letter-writing picked up markedly at the start of the 1930s. "As the younger children learned to write and as Joe and Jack set off for boarding school (from which they were obliged to write home weekly), the volume of family correspondence grew dramatically. The children evidenced less care in saving letters received from their parents than did their parents in saving letters from them. Their father's correspondence with them survives largely because he dictated it and filed the letters he received from them along with the carbon copies of the letters he had sent. Their mother's correspondence, which at the time was often handwritten, appears to be less complete." Smith, *Hostage to Fortune*, 64.

10. Kennedy, *True Compass*, 40, 30–31.

11. Alfred Adler, *The Individual Psychology of Alfred Adler: A Systematic Presentation in Selections from His Writings*, ed. H. L. Ansbacher and R. R. Ansbacher (New York, Basic Books: 1956), 379–80, quoted in Leamer, *Kennedy Men*, 46; James quoted in Dorothy Rowe, *My Dearest Enemy, My Dangerous Friend: Making and Breaking Sibling Bonds* (London: Routledge, 2007), 87.

12. Kennedy, *True Compass*, 21; RK, *Times to Remember*, 120.

13. Burns, *John Kennedy*, 28.

14. JPK to JPK Jr., July 28, 1926, box 1, JPKP.

15. KLB OH, JFKL; Goodwin, *Fitzgeralds and the Kennedys*, 353.

16. RK, *Times to Remember*, 110–12; Smith, *Nine of Us*, 154.

17. Collier and Horowitz, *Kennedys*, 61.

18. RK, *Times to Remember*, 94; Parmet, *Jack*, 18–19.

19. Parmet, *Jack*, 19.

20. RK, *Times to Remember*, 192; McTaggart, *Kathleen Kennedy*, 10; JFK to RK, n.d., printed in Smith, *Hostage to Fortune*, 97; Kennedy, *True Compass*, 24.

21. Cameron, *Rose*, 101–2; KLB OH, JFKL.

22. John F. Kennedy, ed., *As We Remember Joe* (privately published, 1944), 3.

23. McTaggart, *Kathleen Kennedy*, 14; Kessler, *Sins of the Father*, 43; KLB OH, JFKL.

24. Quoted in Meyers, *As We Remember Him*, 6.

25. Seymour St. John, "JFK: 50th Reunion of 1000 Days," June 1985, CSA.

26. Quoted in Kennedy, *Fruitful Bough*, 210–11.
27. McTaggart, *Kathleen Kennedy*, 12; Damore, *Cape Cod Years*, 23; Cameron, *Rose*, 98–100.
28. Kennedy, *True Compass*, 33. At Christmastime in Bronxville, Jean Kennedy Smith related in her own memoir, each child could expect just one special gift, such as a doll, a game, or roller skates. Smith, *Nine of Us*, 47, 77.
29. KLB OH, JFKL.
30. Mary Pitcairn Davis interview, CBP; McTaggart, *Kathleen Kennedy*, 15; Leamer, *Kennedy Men*, 67.
31. Quoted in Burns, *John Kennedy*, 130.
32. Quoted in Perry, *Rose Kennedy*, 51. See also Larson, *Rosemary*, 43–59.
33. Perry, *Rose Kennedy*, 51–52; McTaggart, *Kathleen Kennedy*, 11.
34. RK interview by Robert Coughlan, January 24, 1972, box 10, RKP; Leamer, *Kennedy Men*, 47.
35. JPK to Rosemary Kennedy, November 13, 1929, box 1, JPKP; Nasaw, *Patriarch*, 153.
36. Whalen, *Founding Father*, 165.
37. From the Choate class of 1933, the school placed forty-six students at Yale, twenty at Princeton, eight at Williams, and three at Harvard. *Choate News*, January 28, 1933.
38. Years later, Jack would claim he was denied admission to Groton on account of his Catholicism. Brauer, *Second Reconstruction*, 13.
39. Wardell St. John to JPK, May 20, 1929, box 20, JPKP; JPK to Wardell St. John, April 20, 1929, CSA; JPK to Russell Ayers, May 1, 1929, printed in Smith, *Hostage to Fortune*, 83–84.
40. Russell Ayers to JPK, June 27, 1933, CSA; Housemaster (Ben Davis) report, June 1930, box 20, JPKP.
41. On June 20, 1930, Assistant Headmaster Wardell St. John wrote Rose that Jack had achieved a score of 124 on the Otis-Lennon School Ability Test, "which is nine or ten points above our School average." St. John predicted on that basis that Jack would do very well at Choate. He advised Mrs. Kennedy not to inform her son of his Otis score, as that might incline him to depend too much on his ability, which "in itself is never at all sufficient!" Wardell St. John to RK, June 20, 1930, box 20, JPKP.
42. Goodwin, *Fitzgeralds and the Kennedys*, 459; Hamilton, *JFK: Reckless Youth*, 85.
43. JFK to John Fitzgerald, n.d., box 4b, JFKPP.
44. JFK to RK, n.d., box 1, JFKPP; JFK to JPK and RK, n.d., box 1, JFKPP.
45. JFK to RK, n.d. (1930–31), box 1, JFKPP.
46. Nelson Hume to JPK, January 7, 1931, box 21, JPKP.
47. Stossel, *Sarge*, 24; Leamer, *Kennedy Men*, 65.
48. In his next report, the grades slipped a bit: English II, 86; History II, 77; Math II, 95; Latin II, 55; Science II, 72; Religion II, 75. Canterbury Record, box 1, JFKP.
49. JFK to JPK, n.d. (1930), box 5, JPKP; JFK to JPK, n.d., box 4b, JPKP.
50. JFK to JPK and RK, March 31, box 21, JPKP.
51. JFK to JPK and RK, postmarked March 5, 1931, box 21, JFKPP.
52. Hamilton, *JFK: Reckless Youth*, 87–88.
53. Wardell St. John to RK, June 24, 1931, box 20, JPKP; Bruce Belmore to Choate School, July 11, 1931, CSA; Hamilton, *JFK: Reckless Youth*, 88–89.
54. Meyers, *As We Remember Him*, 11.
55. George St. John to JPK, October 20, 1931, CSA; Clara St. John to RK, October 7, 1931, CSA.
56. Goodwin, *Fitzgeralds and the Kennedys*, 458; Seymour St. John and Richard Bode, " 'Bad Boy' Jack Kennedy," *Good Housekeeping*, September 1985. For the experience of another

Choate student in this period, the poet and publisher James Laughlin, see MacNiven, *Literchoor Is My Beat,* 28–29.

57. Quoted in St. John, "JFK: 50th Reunion"; Hamilton, *JFK: Reckless Youth,* 90.
58. Both letters quoted in St. John, "JFK: 50th Reunion."
59. St. John to JPK, October 20, 1931, CSA; Leamer, *Kennedy Men,* 76.
60. Leaming, *Jack Kennedy: Education,* 21. Said a classmate years later: "I recall that in our third form year teacher Ben Davis one day sent Jack out of French class to comb his hair. When he returned, it looked worse than ever. 'Le Petit Chou,' said Ben with a sigh. It looked worse than a head of cabbage." St. John, "JFK: 50th Reunion."
61. Ralph Horton OH, JFKL; KLB OH, JFKL; Perret, *Jack,* 33; Meyers, *As We Remember Him,* 15. See also Lem Billings's recollections in *The New Yorker,* April 1, 1961.
62. Horton OH, JFKL. In a different interview, Horton said, "Jack had an excellent mind, and it wasn't channeled into the type of work we were doing. He hadn't matured to channel it as he did in later years at Harvard." Horton OH, CBP.
63. Horton OH, CBP.
64. Blair and Blair, *Search for JFK,* 33; Horton OH, JFKL; KLB to RK, January 1972, box 12, RKP. The prime place of football in campus life can be seen in back issues of *The Choate News* from the period. Jack did, however, win praise for his effort on the junior squad: "Aggressive, alert and interested—Jack was a tower of strength on the line." Leinbach Football Juniors report, n.d. (fall 1933), Choate School Archives–Outline, box 1, JFKPP.
65. JFK to JPK, December 9, 1931, box 1, JFKPP.

CHAPTER 4: JACK AND LEM

1. Mrs. St. John to RK, Choate School Archives–Outline, box 1, JFKP.
2. RK, *Times to Remember,* 176–77.
3. JPK to JFK, April 12, 1932, box 1, JPKP.
4. Earl Leinbach to St. John, n.d. (1932), box 20, JPKP. Emphasis in original. Mae West story is in Hamilton, *JFK: Reckless Youth,* 94. The headmaster agreed that the young man was likable. In a letter to Joseph Kennedy in February 1932, he summarized Leinbach's efforts, then concluded: "Jack is so pleasantly optimistic and cheerful that he makes all of us want to help him. He challenges the best that's in us—and we're giving it, with full confidence in the outcome." George St. John to JPK, February 17, 1932, box 20, JPKP.
5. Earl Leinbach to St. John, n.d. (1932), box 20, JPKP. Emphasis in original.
6. George St. John to JPK, November 24, 1933, box 20, JPKP; George St. John to JPK, November 27, 1933, box 20, JPKP; St. John, "JFK: 50th Reunion."
7. George St. John to JPK, June 14, 1932, box 20, JPKP; Choate Summer Session Report in Algebra, September 3, 1932, box 20, JPKP; Choate Summer Session Report in French, September 4, 1932, box 20, JPKP. According to *The Choate News,* the summer session opened on August 8 with twenty boys; by the end, on September 19, the number had grown to forty-seven. *Choate News,* October 8, 1932.
8. St. John, "JFK: 50th Reunion"; Parmet, *Jack,* 31–32.
9. Rip Horton later said, "He was a very mediocre student. He did have one particular flair that stands out in my mind and that was a flair for writing. We used to have to submit essays two or three times a year and we had an English teacher by the name of Dr. Tinker. I can remember after we had submitted our essays, Dr. Tinker said to Jack Kennedy, 'Jack you have a very definite flair for writing. It's a career that you should think of pursuing when you graduate from school and college.' And it came as sort of a shock to me because I never considered Jack Kennedy a very outstanding student in any particular area." Horton OH, JFKL. A slightly different version is in Horton OH, CBP.

10. JPK to JPK Jr., November 21, 1933, box 1, JPKP; Parmet, *Jack*, 32; Smith, *Hostage to Fortune*, 113; Hamilton, *JFK: Reckless Youth*, 134.

11. JPK to George St. John, November 21, 1933, CSA. Kennedy also expressed his frustration in a letter to Joe Junior, who was now in London. "I wish you would write Jack and really set forth some ideas that will give him a sense of responsibility. . . . It will be too bad if with the brain he has he really doesn't go as far up the ladder as he should." JPK to JPK Jr., November 21, 1933, box 1, JPKP.

12. George St. John to JPK, November 27, 1933, CSA.

13. "Justice" (JFK English composition paper), April 1934, box 1, JFKPP; O'Brien, *John F. Kennedy*, 67–68. Niece Amanda Smith points to this paper in suggesting that Jack in this period outstripped Joe Junior in sensitivity and empathy. Smith, *Hostage to Fortune*, 113.

14. Kay Halle OH, JFKL; Churchill, *World Crisis*; Leaming, *Jack Kennedy: Education*, 22. Just when this encounter occurred is not clear. Barbara Leaming has it in late October 1932, while Nigel Hamilton places it in mid-1934. Also possible is early 1934, when we know Jack had an acute case of anemia. Much later, Halle, who knew Churchill and had turned down an offer of marriage from Churchill's son Randolph, compiled three volumes of Churchilliana.

15. Leaming, *Jack Kennedy: Education*, 22; Hellman, *Kennedy Obsession*, 14–15.

16. Nasaw, *Patriarch*, 134–35.

17. Whalen, *Founding Father*, 117–42; Beschloss, *Kennedy and Roosevelt*, 65–66. On Hoover, see Whyte, *Hoover*; and Kennedy, *Freedom from Fear*, chap. 3.

18. Kennedy himself is usually the source of the story. For contrasting assessments of its veracity, see Whalen, *Founding Father*, 49; and Nasaw, *Patriarch*, 55. See also Smith, *Hostage to Fortune*, 5–6.

19. Beschloss, *Kennedy and Roosevelt*, chap. 4; Nasaw, *Patriarch*, 167–84. See also Joe Kennedy's later explanation in McCarthy, *Remarkable Kennedys*, 58.

20. Whalen, *Founding Father*, 113; McCarthy, *Remarkable Kennedys*, 58.

21. See the astute analysis in Beschloss, *Kennedy and Roosevelt*, 266–76.

22. JPK to FDR, March 14, 1933, printed in Smith, *Hostage to Fortune*, 116. See also Beschloss, *Kennedy and Roosevelt*, chap. 4; Krock, *Memoirs*, 330.

23. Quoted in Beschloss, *Kennedy and Roosevelt*, 77.

24. Moley, *After Seven Years*, 286–89; *Newsweek*, September 12, 1960. On the Ireland offer, see JPK to JPK Jr., May 4, 1934, box 21, JPKP.

25. The idea may have come from economist and presidential adviser Raymond Moley, who reasoned that since Kennedy knew the loopholes, he could close them. Manchester, *Glory and the Dream*, 96.

26. Horton OH, CBP; KLB OH, JFKL.

27. On Joe Junior's Harvard Trophy, see *Choate News*, June 3, 1933.

28. Quoted in Parmet, *Jack*, 33.

29. KLB to RK, January 1972, box 12, RKP; Collier and Horowitz, *Kennedys*, 62. On February 24, 1933, *The Choate News* announced that Frederic Billings had been awarded the Pyne Honor Prize, Princeton's highest general distinction.

30. KLB OH, JFKL.

31. The theme of mutual dependence is ably laid out in Pitts, *Jack and Lem*.

32. Collier and Horowitz, *Kennedys*, 45; Pitts, *Jack and Lem*, 33, 30.

33. Quoted in David Michaelis, "The President's Best Friend," *American Heritage* 34 (June/July 1983), 16.

34. JFK to KLB, n.d. (April 1934), box 1, KLBP.

35. Quoted in Pitts, *Jack and Lem*, 21.

36. Pitts, *Jack and Lem*, 21.

37. St. John, "JFK: 50th Reunion"; KLB to RK, January 1972, box 12, RKP; KLB OH; Hamilton, *JFK: Reckless Youth*, 117. To his father, Jack wrote of Maher, "We are practically rooming with him which is more than we bargained for." JFK to JPK, n.d. (1934), box 5, JPKP.

38. Quoted in St. John, "JFK: 50th Reunion."

39. Larson, *Rosemary*, 69–70.

40. G. St. John to JPK, February 8, 1934, box 4, JFKPP; Clara St. John to JFK, February 6, 1934, excerpted in Choate calendar of JFK letters, box 21, DFPP. According to his biographer, the poet James Laughlin, three years ahead of Jack, felt from Mrs. St. John a degree of empathy and emotional support he did not get from his own mother. MacNiven, *Literchoor Is My Beat*, 28–29.

41. Jeffrey Laikind, "Life at Choate," *Choate Rosemary Hall Bulletin*, Spring 2017; McNamara, *Eunice*, 19.

42. C. St. John to RK, February 6, 1934, CSA. To Billings he wrote, after the worst was over, "It seems that I was much sicker than I thought I was, and am supposed to be dead, so I'm developing a limp and a hollow cough." JFK to KLB, February 1934, box 1, KLBP.

43. JFK to RK, April 21, 1934, printed in Smith, *Hostage to Fortune*, 129; Hamilton, *JFK: Reckless Youth*, 106.

44. JFK to Mr. and Mrs. St. John, March 4, 1934, excerpted in Choate calendar of JFK letters, box 21, DFPP; Choate report for House (Maher), n.d. (1934), box 20, JPKP.

45. Michaelis, "President's Best Friend," 15–16.

46. JFK to KLB, June 19, 1934, box 1, KLBP.

47. JFK to KLB, June 19, 1934, box 1, KLBP. Emphasis in original. His sign-off in another letter showed his affection for his friend: "Well, LeMoyne, I hope you are progressing. Will see you soon, Le Moyne ma Cherie (my darling, French) if I ever get out of the place alive. Yours till hell freezes over." JFK to KLB, June 18, 1934, box 1, KLBP.

48. JFK to KLB, June 27, 1934, quoted in Hamilton, *JFK: Reckless Youth*, 112.

49. Leamer, *Kennedy Men*, 89–90; Dr. Paul O'Leary to JPK, July 6, 1934, box 21, JPKP; JPK to G. St. John, September 15, 1934, JPKP; Dallek, *Unfinished Life*, 75.

50. O'Brien, *John F. Kennedy*, 64–65; Searls, *Lost Prince*, 58–59. For a dramatic description of one of Jack's come-from-behind victories, see Graham, *Victura*, 40–43.

51. Pitts, *Jack and Lem*, 21–22; David Walter, "Best Friend," *Princeton Alumni Weekly*, April 12, 2017.

52. JFK to KLB, June 27, 1934, quoted in Pitts, *Jack and Lem*, 22.

53. JFK to KLB, June 27, 1934, quoted in Pitts, *Jack and Lem*, 20.

54. JFK to KLB, June 23, 1933, KLBP; St. John, "JFK: 50th Reunion"; Collier and Horowitz, *Kennedys*, 65.

55. Recalled Rip Horton of Cawley: "I remember Jack dating Olive Cawley. She was a magnificent-looking girl, really beautiful. But I can remember we were not particularly effective with girls." Blair and Blair, *Search for JFK*, 34. Cawley, meanwhile, described Jack as smart, funny, and mischievous. "He was always surrounded by excitement. In the group that travelled together, Jack called the shots: where they would go, what they would do. His friends were the satellites, especially LeMoyne." O'Brien, *John F. Kennedy*, 63.

56. Pitts, *Jack and Lem*, 25.

57. Hamilton, *JFK: Reckless Youth*, 120; Pitts, *Jack and Lem*, 25.

58. Maher reported of Jack in November: "Matched only by his roommate, Billings, in sloppiness and continued lateness. All methods of coercion fail." By January 1935 the assessment had become harsher still: "I'm afraid it would be foolishly optimistic to expect

anything but the most mediocre from Jack. . . . For a year-and-a-half, I've tried everything from kissing to kicking Jack into just a few commonly decent points of view and habits of living in community life, and I'm afraid I must admit my own failure as well as his." Quoted in St. John, "JFK: 50th Reunion."

59. KLB to RK, January 1972, box 12, RKP.
60. Horton OH, CBP.
61. Horton OH, CBP; KLB OH, JFKL. Some accounts have it that the headmaster changed his mind about expulsion only after being persuaded to do so by Joe Kennedy.
62. St. John telegram to JPK, February 11, 1935, box 20, JPKP; JPK to St. John, telegram, February 15, 1935, CSA; KLB to RK, January 1972, box 12, RKP; KLB OH, 2:75, JFKL; Goodwin, *Fitzgeralds and the Kennedys*, 488.
63. KLB OH, 2:56–57, JFKL; Dallek, *Unfinished Life*, 40; Meyers, *As We Remember Him*, 16.
64. JPK to JFK, April 26, 1935, box 1, JPKP; JPK to JFK, December 5, 1934, box 1, JPKP.
65. Wardell St. John to JPK, March 18, 1935, box 20, JPKP; St. John, "JFK: 50th Reunion."
66. Parmet, *Jack*, 40; Paul Chase to Seymour St. John, July 28, 1983, CSA. One friend recalled this affability: "When we graduated from Choate we exchanged pictures as so many seniors do and the inscription on his picture of me was also, I think, indicative of his interest in political affairs. I remember it very well—I still have the picture. He signed it 'To Boss Tweed from Honest Abe, may we room together at Sing Sing.' He had a sense of humor about things." Horton OH, JFKL.
67. The letter concluded, "He isn't going to be at his best this evening or tomorrow or next day; he has too complex and entertaining a nature to enable him to bring all his best to bear in a mature way this week or next month. Jack needs time for his development. But if we can be patient, and have confidence, and hold Jack up steadily and wisely at the same time, we shall be playing our best part, and more and more we shall have the satisfaction of seeing him respond." G. St. John to JPK, November 27, 1933, CSA.
68. St. John, "JFK: 50th Reunion."

CHAPTER 5: FRESHMAN YEARS

1. In answer to the question of why he wished to come to Harvard, Jack offered a concise and handwritten answer (the form did not leave a lot of space), one stressing status and elite connections over academics: "The reasons that I have for wishing to go to Harvard are several. I feel that Harvard can give me a better background and a better liberal education than any other university. I have always wanted to go there, as I have felt that it is not just another college, but is a university with something definite to offer. Then too, I would like to go to the same college as my father. To be a 'Harvard man' is an enviable distinction, and one that I sincerely hope I shall attain." The explanation he gave to Princeton was nearly identical. The applications are in box 2, JFKPP.
2. Certificate of admission, Harvard College, July 17, 1935, box 20, JPKP.
3. Schlesinger, *Robert Kennedy*, 19. Kramnick and Sheerman, *Harold Laski*, 333–35.
4. Manchester, *Portrait of a President*, 185; Nasaw, *Patriarch*, 198; JPK to JPK Jr., February 14, 1934, box 1, JPKP. Wrote Rose of the decision: "The United States and most of the western world were in the grip of the Depression, and there were many revolutionary currents and ideas—Marxist and semi-Marxist—in the political atmosphere. . . . Therefore he [Joe Senior] wanted our son to understand the challenges he might be facing as put forth by a brilliant challenger, Professor Laski. He already had the same plan in mind for Jack. For after all, he said, 'these boys are going to have a little money when they get a little older, and they should know what the "have nots" are thinking and planning.' " RK, *Times to Remember*, 170–71.
5. JFK to JPK, December 4, 1934, box 1, JPKP.

6. Quoted in Lasky, *J.F.K.*, 70.

7. Perry, *Rose Kennedy*, 87; RK, *Times to Remember*, 200.

8. JPK to JFK, February 6, 1935, box 21, JPKP; Byrne, *Kick*, 40–41.

9. Quoted in Goodwin, *Fitzgeralds and the Kennedys*, 482.

10. Hamilton, *JFK: Reckless Youth*, 126; Michaelis, *Best of Friends*, 138.

11. JPK to KK, February 20, 1935, box 1, JPKP.

12. Byrne, *Kick*, 41.

13. RK diary notes, box 1, RKP; JFK to KLB, September 29, 1935, quoted in Pitts, *Jack and Lem*, 40.

14. RK diary notes, box 1, RKP.

15. On these developments, see, e.g., Kershaw, *Hitler: Hubris*, 531–73.

16. See, e.g., Throntveit, *Power Without Victory*; Knock, *To End All Wars*.

17. The literature is large, but see, e.g., Steiner, *Triumph of the Dark*, chap. 3; and Kershaw, *To Hell and Back*, chap. 5. For a survey of the entire troubled decade, see Brendon, *Dark Valley*.

18. For an interesting contemporaneous assessment of Laski, see Schlesinger, *Life in the 20th Century*, 197–99.

19. JFK to KLB, n.d. (October 1935), quoted in Pitts, *Jack and Lem*, 41–42.

20. JFK to KLB, October 21, 1935, box 1, KLBP. According to Herbert Parmet, Joe Kennedy helped make the late matriculation possible: "Bending to Jack's desire, his father used a contact to overcome the barriers to late admission. Lacking personal leverage with Princeton, Joe Kennedy turned to one with influence, Herbert Bayard Swope. The newspaperman talked Princeton's Dean Christian Gauss into some 'enlightened' flexibility. In mid-October, Jack's father received Swope's wire that Gauss had waived the rule prohibiting such late admissions 'in response to picture I painted young Galahad [*sic*] . . . Hurrah new tiger!' " Parmet, *Jack*, 42.

21. KLB to JFK, October 17, 1935, box 4b, JFKPP.

22. Quoted in Pitts, *Jack and Lem*, 42–43.

23. Torbert Macdonald OH, JFKL.

24. JPK to JFK, November 11, 1935, box 21, JPKP.

25. KLB to JFK, December 10, 1935, box 4B, JFKPP; Hamilton, *JFK: Reckless Youth*, 147.

26. Dr. William Murphy to JPK, November 30, 1935, box 21, JPKP; Murphy to JPK, December 16, 1935, box 21, JPKP; JPK to JFK, January 11, 1936, box 21, JPKP; JFK to JPK and RK, n.d. (January 1936), box 1, JPKP.

27. JFK to KLB, January 18, 1936, quoted in Hamilton, *JFK: Reckless Youth*, 149.

28. JFK to KLB, n.d. (January 1936), quoted in Hamilton, *JFK: Reckless Youth*, 148.

29. JFK to KLB, January 27, 1936, quoted in O'Brien, *John F. Kennedy*, 78.

30. JFK to KLB, January 27, 1936, quoted in Hamilton, *JFK: Reckless Youth*, 149.

31. JFK to KLB, n.d. (January 1936), quoted in Hamilton, *JFK: Reckless Youth*, 149.

32. JFK to KLB, n.d. (January 1936), quoted in Pitts, *Jack and Lem*, 45–46; Horton OH, JFKL.

33. Quoted in Hamilton, *JFK: Reckless Youth*, 205.

34. JFK to KLB, March 3, 1936, quoted in Hamilton, *JFK: Reckless Youth*, 153–54.

35. The initial notes were compiled by Kennedy's successor at the SEC, James Landis, and by another SEC associate, John J. Burns. Krock then fashioned the various bits into a polished manuscript.

36. JPK, *I'm for Roosevelt*, 3. "Dear Joe," FDR's thank-you note began, "I'M FOR KENNEDY. The book is grand. I'm delighted with it." Whalen, *Founding Father*, 186.

37. JFK to JPK, May 9, 1936, box 21, JPKP.

38. JFK to KLB, May 9, 1936, quoted in Collier and Horowitz, *Kennedys*, 67. Jack's physician

at Peter Bent Brigham had advised against the ranch sojourn, on the grounds that the young man would be too far away from medical assistance should he need it. Murphy to JPK, November 30, 1935, box 21, JPKP.

39. On this point, see Leamer, *Kennedy Men*, 100–101. The boasts were a standard feature of Jack's letters in this period.

40. JFK to KLB, May 25, 1936, quoted in Hamilton, *JFK: Reckless Youth*, 157.

41. RK, *Times to Remember*, 155.

42. Searls, *Lost Prince*, 94–99.

43. JFK handwritten reapplication letter, July 6, 1936, box 2, JFKPP.

44. Admissions dean to JFK, July 9, 1936, box 2, JFKPP. For a time, father and son gave thought to the idea of having Jack try to complete the four-year degree in three years. Wrote Mr. Kennedy to the dean of freshmen, Delmar Leighton: "Jack has a very brilliant mind for the things in which he is interested, but is careless and lacks application in those in which he is not interested. This is, of course, a bad fault. However, he is quite ambitious to try and do the work in three years." JPK to Leighton, August 28, 1936, box 20, JPKP. Nothing came of the idea.

45. Smith, *Harvard Century*, 124–31.

46. Parker, *John Kenneth Galbraith*, 43–44; Schlesinger, *Veritas*, 168, 181; Nell Painter, "Jim Crow at Harvard: 1923," *New England Quarterly* 44, no. 4 (December 1971).

47. Conant, *Man of the Hour*, 117–32; Lemann, *Big Test*, 39–52; Schlesinger, *Veritas*, 175–78.

48. White, *In Search of History*, 41.

49. White, *In Search of History*, 42–43.

50. Myrer, *Last Convertible*, 42.

51. White, *In Search of History*, 42; Schlesinger, *Life in the 20th Century*, 115. White's assessment of Schlesinger would in later years grow more mixed, a fact acknowledged by both men (see Schlesinger, 115). An excellent biography of Schlesinger is Aldous, *Imperial*.

52. Schlesinger, *Life in the 20th Century*, 108–12; Smith, *Harvard Century*, 125.

53. See the academic records in box 2, JFKPP.

54. James Farrell OH, JFKL; Blair and Blair, *Search for JFK*, 46.

55. JFK to KLB, October 21, 1936, quoted in Hamilton, *JFK: Reckless Youth*, 166; Gerald Walker and Donald A. Allan, "Jack Kennedy at Harvard," *Coronet Magazine*, May 1961, 85; Meyers, *As We Remember Him*, 22.

56. JFK to JPK, n.d. (1937), box 5, JPKP; "JFK's Harvard/Harvard's JFK" (exhibit), Lamont Library, Cambridge, MA, 2017; Walker and Allan, "Jack Kennedy at Harvard," 85; Graham, *Victura*, 50. In addition to *Guadalcanal Diary*, Tregaskis would also write an account of Jack Kennedy's wartime experience aboard PT 109.

57. Walker and Allan, "Jack Kennedy at Harvard," 85.

58. Galbraith, *Life in Our Times*, 53; Searls, *Lost Prince*, 98.

59. "JFK's Harvard/Harvard's JFK," Lamont Library; Hamilton, *JFK: Reckless Youth*, 175. The program for Freshman Smoker, with a full-page ad from the men's clothier J. Press, is in box 2, JFKPP. Joe Junior, who had run the event two years before, had lined up Rudy Vallée, the bandleader and actor.

60. Quoted in Parmet, *Jack*, 50; and Schlesinger, *Veritas*, 183.

61. JFK to KLB, January 27, 1937, box 1, KLBP.

62. Nigel Hamilton calls it "one of the most important documents of John F. Kennedy's early life." Hamilton, *JFK: Reckless Youth*, 170.

63. JFK, "Francis the First," box 1, JFKPP.

64. JFK, "Francis the First."

65. Hamilton, *JFK: Reckless Youth*, 170.
66. JPK to JFK, February 15, 1937, box 1, JPKP; JFK to KLB, n.d. (February 1937), box 1, KLBP.
67. Quoted in Perret, *Jack*, 51.
68. JFK European diary, 1937, box 1, JFKPP.
69. KLB OH, JFKL.
70. JFK European diary, July 8, 1937, box 1, JFKPP.
71. JFK European diary, July 9, 1937, box 1, JFKPP.
72. JFK European diary, July 10, 1937, box 1, JFKPP. Lem, who kept his own diary on the trip, wrote on July 10: "We are very careful to leave the car around the block & then apply for rooms looking as poverty stricken as possible." KLB diary, PX 93-34, AV Archives, JFKL. See also Maryrose Grossman, "Jack and Lem's Excellent European Adventure, Summer 1937," jfk.blogs.archives.gov/2017/10/18/jack-and-lems-excellent -european-adventure-summer-1937/.
73. JFK European diary, July 13, 1937, box 1, JFKPP; Perrett, *Jack*, 54.
74. Gunther, *Inside Europe*. On Jack quizzing the French about their defenses, see Billings's recollections in *The New Yorker*, April 1, 1961.
75. JFK European diary, July 19, 1937, box 1, JFKPP.
76. JFK European diary, July 25, 1937, box 1, JFKPP; Leamer, *Kennedy Men*, 132.
77. JFK European diary, July 26, 1937, box 1, JFKPP; KLB diary, July 26, 1937, PX 93-34, AV Archives, JFKL; Dallek, *Unfinished Life*, 50.
78. JFK European diary, July 26, 1937, box 1, JFKPP. Of Carcassonne, Jack wrote: "An old medieval town in perfect condition—which is more than can be said for Billings."
79. Hamilton, *JFK: Reckless Youth*, 184.
80. JFK European diary, August 1, 1937, box 1, JFKPP; Perret, *Jack*, 57.
81. JFK European diary, August 3, 1937, box 1, JFKPP.
82. JFK European diary, August 9, 1937, box 1, JFKPP.
83. Quoted in Pitts, *Jack and Lem*, 62–63.
84. JFK European diary, August 17, 1937, box 1, JFKPP. Lem wrote in his diary: "Hitler seems very popular here—you can't help but like a dictator when you are in his own country—as you hear so many wonderful things about him and really not too many bad things." KLB diary, August 17, 1937, PX 93-34, AV Archives, JFKL. For a German account of the visit, see Lubrich, *John F. Kennedy Unter Deutschen*, 55–127.
85. JFK European diary, August 18, 1937, box 1, JFKPP; Perret, *Jack*, 60–61.
86. JPK Jr. to JPK, April 23, 1934, printed in Smith, *Hostage to Fortune*, 130–32; JPK to JPK Jr., May 4, 1934, printed in Smith, *Hostage to Fortune*, 133–35.
87. JFK European diary, August 20, 1937, box 1, JFKPP.
88. KLB diary, August 27, 1937, PX 93-34, AV Archives, JFKL.
89. Dallek, *Unfinished Life*, 51.

CHAPTER 6: OUR MAN IN LONDON

1. JPK diary, February 23, 1938, box 100, JPKP.
2. *NYT*, February 11, 1938. Rose had planned for herself and the children to travel at the same time as her husband, but she came down with appendicitis and had to postpone her departure.
3. JPK to Felix Frankfurter, December 5, 1933, printed in Smith, *Hostage to Fortune*, 122; Nelson, *John William McCormack*, 222–23. On the donations, see Smith, *Hostage to Fortune*, 66; and *Newsweek*, September 12, 1960. David Nasaw gives a lower sum for the personal contribution: $15,000. Nasaw, *Patriarch*, 182–83.
4. Krock, *Memoirs*, 169–71; Beschloss, *Kennedy and Roosevelt*, 106.

5. Quoted in Brands, *Traitor to His Class*, 457. When a friend charged the administration with pursuing far-left policies, Kennedy shot back: "There has been scarcely a liberal piece of legislation during the last sixty years that has not been opposed as Communistic." Schlesinger, *Robert Kennedy*, 11.

6. Nasaw, *Patriarch*, 272.

7. Krock, *Memoirs*, 333; Koskoff, *Joseph P. Kennedy*, 114–15.

8. Roosevelt, *My Parents*, 208–10; Whalen, *Founding Father*, 214.

9. Beschloss, *Kennedy and Roosevelt*, 153–54; Roosevelt, *My Parents*, 208–10.

10. Henry Morgenthau Jr. diaries, December 8, 1937, vol. 101, HMP, LC; Nasaw, *Patriarch*, 273. According to Secretary of the Interior Harold Ickes, a key advocate of the appointment was Thomas Corcoran, a lawyer and close adviser to FDR. Corcoran, Ickes wrote in his diary, "had done everything that he could to bring about the appointment of Kennedy to London, his chief motive being that he wanted to get Kennedy out of Washington." Harold Ickes diary, December 18, 1937, HIP, LC.

11. *NYT*, December 9, 1937; Koskoff, *Joseph P. Kennedy*, 118; Collier and Horowitz, *Kennedys*, 81.

12. Boake Carter to JPK, December 28, 1937, box 90, JPKP; Nasaw, *Patriarch*, 275, 277. On the background to the *New York Times* story, see Arthur Krock private memo, December 23, 1937, box 31, AKP.

13. Beschloss, *Kennedy and Roosevelt*, 161; JPK to Jimmy Roosevelt, March 3, 1938, printed in Smith, *Hostage to Fortune*, 239; Whalen, *Founding Father*, 214–15.

14. On world developments in 1938, see, e.g., Steiner, *Triumph of the Dark*, chaps. 8–9; Kershaw, *To Hell and Back*, 303–34; Mitter, *Forgotten Ally*, 98–144. On the Austrian annexation, see Evans, *Third Reich in Power*, 646–64.

15. Smith, *Hostage to Fortune*, 226; Bailey, *Black Diamonds*, 337–38. By tradition, the U.S. ambassador selected some thirty American debutantes, from at least ten times that number of applicants, for presentation to the king and queen. Because the ambassador rarely knew the women in question, the process was bound to be arbitrary, not to mention time-consuming. Kennedy, after checking with superiors in Washington and the British government, amended the criteria so that thenceforth only American residents of Britain were eligible. Cynics wondered if he did it partly in order to boost the publicity for his own daughters.

16. Cutler, *Honey Fitz*, 279; Goodwin, *Fitzgeralds and the Kennedys*, 516. The feat even made the news in France. "M. Kennedy fait 'hole-in-one,'" one paper headlined it. Rose reiterated that Joe Junior and Jack were skeptical about the hole-in-one in a telegram dated March 17, 1948, box 2, JPKP. See also Swift, *Kennedys Amidst the Gathering*, 27.

17. Morison, *Three Centuries*, 476–79; Bunting, *Harvard*, 187–88; Schlesinger, *Life in the 20th Century*, 112.

18. George Taylor OH, JFKL; George Taylor, "A Seaman Remembers John F. Kennedy," *The Sea Breeze* 76 (July 1964); Gerald Walker and Donald A. Allan, "Jack Kennedy at Harvard," *Coronet Magazine*, May 1961, 82–95.

19. Walker and Allan, "Jack Kennedy at Harvard."

20. Parmet, *Jack*, 46; Macdonald OH, JFKL.

21. Macdonald OH, JFKL; O'Brien, *John F. Kennedy*, 85.

22. Hamilton, *JFK: Reckless Youth*, 205. Hamilton provides an excellent account of the ins and outs of the Spee story.

23. Renehan, *Kennedys at War*, 21.

24. Hamilton, *JFK: Reckless Youth*, 206–8.

25. JFK to JPK and RK, n.d. (April 1938), box 21, JPKP; JPK to JFK, May 2, 1938, box 21, JPKP; Hamilton, *JFK: Reckless Youth*, 209.

26. Arthur M. Schlesinger Jr., "Harvard Today," *Harvard Advocate*, September 1936, 20–24; Schlesinger, *Life in the 20th Century*, 120.

27. Schlesinger, *Life in the 20th Century*, 120.

28. JFK Academic Record 1937–1938, box 2, JFKPP.

29. To hear the recording, go to Colleen Walsh, "JFK Speaks from His Harvard Past," *Harvard Gazette*, May 9, 2017, news.harvard.edu/gazette/story/2017/05/earliest -recording-of-jfk-found-in-harvard-archives/.

30. Parmet, *Jack*, 49.

31. Quoted in O'Brien, *John F. Kennedy*, 80.

32. Schlesinger, *Life in the 20th Century*, 122–23; Leuchtenburg, *Shadow of FDR*, 64–65; Parker, *John Kenneth Galbraith*, 47–48.

33. Parmet, *Jack*, 55. According to Kenny O'Donnell and Dave Powers, Jack later told them he and his brother Joe met FDR during the 1936 campaign, in the company of their grandfather Honey Fitz. Roosevelt, Jack said, threw out his arms and cried, "El Duce Adelino!" in reference to the older man's theme song, "Sweet Adeline." O'Donnell and Powers, *"Johnny,"* 58.

34. *Washington Evening Star*, January 20, 1961; Goodwin, *Fitzgeralds and the Kennedys*, 507.

35. For varying interpretations of what happened, see Hamilton, *JFK: Reckless Youth*, 210; and Parmet, *Jack*, 45; RK, *Times to Remember*, 215; and Blair and Blair, *Search for JFK*, 54. According to his mother, Jack ruptured a spinal disc when he hit the ground at a bad angle. RK, *Times to Remember*, 215.

36. Dallek, *Unfinished Life*, 79–80; Hamilton, *JFK: Reckless Youth*, 227.

37. Cawley would go on to marry Thomas Watson Jr., the president of IBM and later U.S. ambassador to the Soviet Union, with whom she had six children. *Time* would name Watson one of the one hundred most influential people of the twentieth century.

38. KLB OH, JFKL.

39. KLB OH, JFKL.

40. Walker and Allan, "Jack Kennedy at Harvard."

41. O'Brien, *John F. Kennedy*, 84.

42. JPK unpublished diplomatic memoir, chap. 8, p. 10, box 147, JPKP.

43. Harold Ickes diary, July 3, 1938, HIP, LC; Whalen, *Founding Father*, 228–29.

44. Quoted in Swift, *Kennedys Amidst the Gathering*, 61.

45. Chamberlain held to the maxim that "it is always best to count on nothing from the Americans except words." Quoted in Reynolds, *From Munich*, 38.

46. In an early dispatch to Roosevelt, Kennedy summed up his early performance: "I think I have made a fairly good start here with the people and seem to be getting along reasonably well with the Government so far." JPK to FDR, March 11, 1938, box 10, PSF, FDRL. In his first letter as ambassador, which he wrote to Arthur Krock, Kennedy said the present world crisis would have to be solved via an economic settlement rather than a political one. JPK to Krock, 3/8/38, box 31, AKP.

47. JPK to Arthur Krock, March 28, 1938, box 31, AKP.

48. JPK unpublished diplomatic memoir, chap. 5, pp. 4–5, box 147, JPKP; Reston, *Deadline*, 66. A biography is Fort, *Nancy*.

49. JPK to Arthur Krock, March 21, 1938, box 31, AKP.

50. JPK unpublished diplomatic memoir, chap. 3, pp. 8–10, box 147, JPKP. See also Nasaw, *Patriarch*, 291–96. Of Kennedy's original version, Secretary of State Hull wrote to say that he thought "the tone of the speech is a little more rigid, and hence subject to possible misinterpretation, than would appear advisable at this precise moment." Hull to JPK, March 14, 1938, OF 3060, FDRL.

51. A standard account of these popular views is Cohen, *American Revisionists*. See also

Jonas, *Isolationism in America*. An excellent study of the longer history of isolationism, dating to the 1890s, is Nichols, *Promise*. See also Brooke L. Blower, "From Isolationism to Neutrality: A New Framework for Understanding American Political Culture, 1919–1941," *Diplomatic History* 38, no. 2 (2014): 345–76.

52. Langer and Gleason, *Challenge to Isolation*, 14, quoted in Olson, *Angry Days*, 28.

53. Berlin, *Personal Impressions*, 24.

54. Ernest Hemingway, "Notes on the Next War: A Serious Topical Letter," *Esquire*, September 1935. Hemingway would later sing a different tune, strongly supporting U.S. entry into the war against the Axis powers.

55. Walter Millis, *Road to War: America, 1914–1917* (New York: Houghton Mifflin, 1935).

56. Quoted in Evans, *American Century*, 286, 288.

57. Beard, *Open Door at Home*, 274, quoted in Milne, *Worldmaking*, 150–51.

58. Burns, *Crosswinds of Freedom*, 152; FDR quoted in Olson, *Angry Days*, 32. According to historian Warren Cohen, FDR's first administration marked "the only period in American history when the country might be fairly labeled isolationist." Cohen, *Nation*, 84.

59. Herring, *From Colony to Superpower*, 505–8.

60. Doenecke, *From Isolation to War*, 71; Nasaw, *Patriarch*, 294–95.

61. The literature is large, but see Self, *Neville Chamberlain*; Paul Kennedy, "Appeasement," in *The Origins of the Second World War Reconsidered*, ed. George Martel (New York: Routledge, 1999); Parker, *Chamberlain*; Donald Cameron Watt, "The Historiography of Appeasement," in *Crisis and Controversy: Essays in Honour of A.J.P. Taylor*, ed. Alan Sked and Chris Cook (London: Macmillan, 1976), 110–129; Andrew Barros et al., "Debating British Decisionmaking Toward Nazi Germany in the 1930s," *International Security* 34, no. 1 (Summer 2009): 173–98. A recent book-length examination is Bouverie, *Appeasing Hitler*, and there is in-depth treatment as well in Steiner, *Triumph of the Dark*. A summary of the strategic and economic case for appeasement is in Ferguson, *War of the World*, 319–30. On the Chiefs of Staff warning, see Watt, *How War Came*, 27.

62. *NYT*, June 23, 1938; Collier and Horowitz, *Kennedys*, 87. Page Huidekoper Wilson, secretary in the office, would later write that Kennedy "desperately wanted to have one more thing in common with John Adams: he wanted to be President of the United States." Wilson, *Carnage and Courage*, 16. See also Arthur Krock OH, CBP. For Kennedy's own interpretation of the issue, see JPK unpublished diplomatic memoir, chap. 9, pp. 3–4, box 147, JPKP.

63. Harold Ickes diary, July 3, 1938, HIP, LC. See also Henry Morgenthau Jr. diaries, August 30, 1938, vol. 140, HMP, LC.

64. *Chicago Tribune*, June 28, 1938; Beschloss, *Kennedy and Roosevelt*, 170–71; Leamer, *Kennedy Men*, 116–17. Though he was unwilling to recall Kennedy, FDR told Morgenthau some weeks later, "If Kennedy wants to resign when he comes back, I will accept it on the spot." Henry Morgenthau Jr. diaries, August 30, 1938, vol. 140, HMP, LC.

65. JPK unpublished diplomatic memoir, chap. 9, p. 7, box 147, JPKP.

CHAPTER 7: THE AMBASSADOR'S SON

1. Nasaw, *Patriarch*, 286.

2. O'Brien, *John F. Kennedy*, 90; *Life*, April 11, 1938; Swift, *Kennedys Amidst the Gathering*, 35–36.

3. *Times* (London), May 28, 1938, quoted in Renehan, *Kennedys at War*, 54–55; Goodwin, *Fitzgeralds and the Kennedys*, 540; Bailey, *Black Diamonds*, 338–40.

4. Collier and Horowitz, *Kennedys*, 67–68; RK, *Times to Remember*, 157.

5. Whalen, *Founding Father*, 212.

6. Larson, *Rosemary*, 105–10; Swift, *Kennedys Amidst the Gathering*, 49–50.

7. RK diary notes, box 1, RKP; RK, *Times to Remember*, 217.

8. Quoted in Beschloss, *Kennedy and Roosevelt*, 160.

9. Leamer, *Kennedy Men*, 118.

10. William Douglas-Home OH, JFKL; Leaming, *Jack Kennedy: Education*, 50.

11. Quoted in Swift, *Kennedys Amidst the Gathering*, 66–67. On Mitford, see also Thompson, *The Six*; and Mosley, *Mitfords*.

12. The topic of discussion was Churchill's son-in-law, Duncan Sandys, a military officer and an MP himself. Sandys had asked a question in Parliament that revealed sensitive national security information, and was ordered to appear before a military court. A Committee of Privileges was asked to rule on whether this was a breach of parliamentary privilege (they ruled that it was). A debate ensued in Parliament about several procedural aspects of this episode, with Churchill defending his son-in-law's actions.

13. Churchill, *Arms and the Covenant*; Leaming, *Jack Kennedy: Education*, 54–56.

14. Nasaw, *Patriarch*, 326; Riva, *Dietrich*, 469.

15. Hennessy OH, JFKL; O'Brien, *John F. Kennedy*, 92.

16. Overy, *Twilight Years*, 345–46; Perrett, *Jack*, 70.

17. JPK to Cordell Hull, August 31, 1938, printed in Smith, *Hostage to Fortune*, 270–72; Henry Morgenthau Jr. diaries, September 1, 1938, vol. 138, HMP, LC; Blum, *Morgenthau Diaries*, 518.

18. Quoted in James, *Europe Reborn*, 147.

19. Jackson, *Fall of France*, 116–17. See also Martin Thomas, "France and the Czechoslovak Crisis," *Diplomacy & Statecraft* 10, no. 2–3 (July 1, 1999): 122–59.

20. Joe Kennedy's own account of these weeks is in JPK unpublished diplomatic memoir, chaps. 13 and 14, box 147, JPKP. Quote to the Cabinet is in Roberts, *Storm of War*, 8.

21. Berg, *Lindbergh*, 355–62, 367–68; Hessen, *Berlin Alert*, 92–105; Hermann, *Lindbergh*, 199. For Lindbergh's high regard for Kennedy, see Lindbergh, *Wartime Journals*, 159.

22. JPK unpublished diplomatic memoir, chap. 15, pp. 3–5, JFKL; Mosley, *Lindbergh*, 229–30. A important older study on the aviator's views and actions in this period is Cole, *Charles A. Lindbergh*.

23. Lindbergh, *Wartime Journals*, 11, 72.

24. Ferguson, *War of the World*, 364; Berg, *Lindbergh*, 375. At no point would the Germans succeed in mass-producing an aircraft akin to the B-17 Flying Fortress, which the United States had in operation prior to the war.

25. Anne Morrow Lindbergh, in the introduction to the fifth volume of her letters and diaries, denied that her husband's advocacy had contributed significantly to the Munich deal. Lindbergh, *War Within and Without*, xvi.

26. JPK unpublished diplomatic memoir, chap. 15, p. 11, box 147, JPKP; Hull, *Memoirs*, 590.

27. Reynolds, *Summits*, 84–87; Kershaw, *To Hell and Back*, 330–31. A detailed history is Faber, *Munich, 1938*.

28. Kershaw, *Hitler: Nemesis*, 123–25; Whalen, *Founding Father*, 243.

29. Meyers, *As We Remember Him*, 23; Hamilton, *JFK: Reckless Youth*, 243. Many years later, now-Senator John F. Kennedy would write, "Personally I shall always remember my assignment in Professor Holcombe's class in government to examine a single Congressman for a year. The thought that some zealous and critical sophomore is now dissecting my own record in a similar class often causes me some concern." *Harvard Alumni Bulletin*, May 19, 1956, box 19, JPKP.

30. Charlie Houghton interview, CBP.

31. Quoted in Hamilton, *JFK: Reckless Youth*, 241–42.

32. JFK to KLB, October 20, 1938, quoted in Hamilton, *JFK: Reckless Youth*, 246.

33. Damore, *Cape Cod Years*, 50.

34. Blair and Blair, *Search for JFK*, 68–69, 75; Horton OH, CBP.

35. Dallek, *Franklin D. Roosevelt*, 166; Reynolds, *From Munich*, 39–40.

36. Quoted in Best, *Churchill*, 157.

37. Caquet, *Bell of Treason*, 149–50; Ferguson, *War of the World*, 363–64.

38. Kershaw, *To Hell and Back*, 333; Wark, *Ultimate Enemy*, 66–67. A nuanced assessment of the "war in 1938" counterfactual is in Steiner, *Triumph of the Dark*, 652–56. Another one is in Calvocoressi and Wint, *Total War*, 92–96.

39. JPK to Hull, February 17, 1939, in *Foreign Relations of the United States 1939* (Washington, DC: Government Printing Office, 1956), vol. 1, 16–17; Watt, *How War Came*, 79, 83; May, *Strange Victory*, 192.

40. JPK unpublished diplomatic memoir, chap. 18, pp. 1–4, box 147, JFKP. Arthur Krock offered soothing words: "I know what a wonderful job you have been doing, and I am highly indignant over the barrage of misrepresentations to which you have been subjected." Krock to JPK, October 6, 1938, AKP.

41. Beschloss, *Kennedy and Roosevelt*, 178–79; WP, October 22, 1938. Joe Junior, quick as always to jump to his father's defense, called Lippmann's claim "the natural Jewish reaction. . . . Either you have to be prepared to destroy the fascist nations . . . or you might as well try to get along with them. I know this is hard for the Jewish community in the U.S. to stomach, but they should see by now that the course which they have followed the last five years has brought them nothing but additional hardship." JPK Jr. draft memo, November 14, 1938, printed in *HTF*, 301–2.

42. Brands, *Traitor to His Class*, 496–500.

43. Beschloss, *Kennedy and Roosevelt*, 178–79; Whalen, *Founding Father*, 248; JPK unpublished diplomatic memoir, chap. 18, pp. 4–6, box 147, JPKP.

44. Evans, *Third Reich in Power*, 580–97; Kershaw, *Hitler: Hubris*, 131–53.

45. JPK to Charles Lindbergh, November 12, 1938, printed in Smith, *Hostage to Fortune*, 300–301.

46. Smith, *Hostage to Fortune*, 233–34; Leamer, *Kennedy Men*, 114–15; Swift, *Kennedys Amidst the Gathering*, 108–9. Karabel, *The Chosen*. Joseph Kennedy's foremost biographer, David Nasaw, came to the same conclusion regarding Kennedy's attitudes. "David Nasaw and 'The Patriarch,' Part 2," *City Talk*, CUNY TV, December 10, 2012, available at www.youtube.com/watch?v=Sb6PGqxw1GQ.

47. Whalen, *Founding Father*, 252; Leamer, *Kennedy Men*, 115; Koskoff, *Joseph P. Kennedy*, 281–82.

48. *NYT*, November 27, 1938; Collier and Horowitz, *Kennedys*, 97; Smith, *Hostage to Fortune*, 232–33. On the U.S. government's response to Kristallnacht, see also Wyman, *Paper Walls*, chap. 4. On the development of Nazi refugee policy, see Schleunes, *Twisted Road*.

49. RK diary notes, September 15, 1938, box 1, RKP.

50. JPK Jr. to Thomas Schriber, November 5, 1938, in Schriber interview, CBS interviews, JFKL; Searls, *Lost Prince*, 110.

51. JPK Jr. Note, November 21, 1938, printed in Smith, *Hostage to Fortune*, 303–4; JPK Jr. Note, December 10, 1938, printed in Smith, *Hostage to Fortune*, 305–6.

52. JFK to parents, n.d. (1938), box 56, JPKP; Hamilton, *JFK: Reckless Youth*, 249.

53. JFK to JPK, n.d. (1938), box 21, JFKPP.

54. Collier and Horowitz, *Kennedys*, 98.

55. Hamilton, *JFK: Reckless Youth*, 249.

56. Wheeler-Bennett, *Special Relationships*, 34–35; Swift, *Kennedys Amidst the Gathering*, 110; Leaming, *Jack Kennedy: Education*, 72–74.

CHAPTER 8: THE OBSERVER

1. Cordell Hull to JPK, March 7, 1939, box 172, JPKP; JPK unpublished diplomatic memoir, chap. 22, pp. 8–9, and chap. 23, pp. 1–3, box 147, JPKP; JPK to JPK Jr., March 9, 1939, box 2, JPKP; Nasaw, *Patriarch*, 374–75. On Pacelli's visit to Bronxville, see Smith, *Nine of Us*, 48–49.

2. JPK diary, March 12, 1939, box 100, JPKP; Kennedy, *True Compass*, 56.

3. Maier, *Kennedys*, 124; JPK unpublished diplomatic memoir, chap. 23, pp. 5–6, box 147, JPKP.

4. JFK to KLB, March 23, 1939, quoted in Hamilton, *JFK: Reckless Youth*, 257.

5. Quoted in Faber, *Munich, 1938*, 428.

6. Quoted in Overy, *1939*, 15. Three days before Hitler's occupation of Prague, Chamberlain had written, "I know that I can save this country and I do not believe that anyone else can." Quoted in May, *Strange Victory*, 192.

7. Churchill, *Gathering Storm*, 309; Kershaw, *Hitler: Hubris*, 174.

8. Bullitt to Hull, *Foreign Relations of the United States 1938* (Washington, DC: Government Printing Office, 1955), vol. I, 711–12; Steiner, *Triumph of the Dark*, 643–44.

9. Watt, *How War Came*, 185–86; Kershaw, *To Hell and Back*, 337.

10. JPK diary, March 30, 1939, box 100, JPKP; Watt, *How War Came*, 167–68.

11. She had sent him a telegram as he boarded the SS *Queen Mary*, bound for England: "Great golden tears too plentiful for very famous last words. Can only stay away from the hay. Goodbye darling. I love you." Frances Ann Cannon to JFK, February 25, 1939, box 4, JPKP.

12. JFK to KLB, March 23, 1939, quoted in Hamilton, *JFK: Reckless Youth*, 257.

13. Brownell and Billings, *So Close to Greatness*, 189–222; Mayers, *FDR's Ambassadors*, 132.

14. Etkind, *Roads Not Taken*, 188–89; Brownell and Billings, *So Close to Greatness*, 221–33.

15. JFK to KLB, April 28, 1939, quoted in Hamilton, *JFK: Reckless Youth*, 260; Leaming, *Jack Kennedy: Education*, 79.

16. JFK to KLB, April 6, 1939, quoted in Pitts, *Jack and Lem*, 73; Lindbergh, *Wartime Journals*, 174.

17. Kershaw, *Hitler: Nemesis*, 189; JFK to KLB, April 28, 1939, quoted in Hamilton, *JFK: Reckless Youth*, 262.

18. Overy, *Twilight Years*, chap. 8.

19. Cecil, *Young Melbourne*; Leamer, *Kennedy Men*, 135. A penetrating comparison is in Morrow, *Best Year*, 96–102.

20. Cecil, *Young Melbourne*, 8, 67, 260; Schlesinger, *Thousand Days*, 83; Nunnerly, *Kennedy and Britain*, 17–18.

21. Cecil, *Young Melbourne*, 61, quoted in Morrow, *Best Year*, 99.

22. Cecil, *Young Melbourne*, 76. Perhaps, too, some part of Kennedy identified with another figure in the book, the romantic poet Lord Byron, who carried on a torrid affair with Melbourne's wife, Lady Caroline. Charles "Chuck" Spalding, who met Jack the following year and would become one of his closest friends, recalled numerous conversations in the early going about Byron and his poetry. Collier and Horowitz, Kennedys, 175–76.

23. RK interview, CBS, quoted in Hamilton, *JFK: Reckless Youth*, 297–98.

24. JFK to Carmel Offie, May 11, 1939, box 19, JFKPP; JPK to JFK, telegram, May 24, 1939, box 2, JPKP. After the tour, Jack wrote thank-you notes to the various vice consuls at the U.S. embassies in the cities he visited. See box 19, JFKPP.

25. JFK to KLB, n.d (May 1939), quoted in Hamilton, *JFK: Reckless Youth*, 262–63.

26. In the Kennedy administration, Bohlen would become U.S. ambassador to France. For his role in midcentury U.S. diplomacy, see Isaacson and Thomas, *Wise Men*.

27. Some of the dates are hard to pin down. We know he arrived in Alexandria, Egypt, at 2:00 P.M. on June 4, traveling from Athens on a Romanian vessel, and departed soon thereafter for Cairo. From there he flew to Palestine. He arrived in Sofia on June 12, flew to Bucharest the following day, and arrived in Belgrade on June 16.
28. Burns, *John Kennedy*, 37–38; O'Brien, *John F. Kennedy*, 94.
29. JFK to JPK, n.d. (1939), box 4A, JFKPP; O'Brien, *John F. Kennedy*, 95.
30. Tom Segev, "JFK in the Land of Milk and Honey," *Haaretz*, October 19, 2012; *NYT*, June 3, 1939; Parmet, *Jack*, 64; Hoffman, *Anonymous Soldiers*, 97.
31. Kershaw, *To Hell and Back*, 338.
32. Milne, *Worldmaking*, 194–95; Reston, *Deadline*, 69–70; Steel, *Walter Lippmann*, 376; Nicolson, *Harold Nicolson Diaries*, 212–13.
33. On Joe Kennedy's failure to understand the change in British thinking, see Leaming, *Jack Kennedy: Education*, 83.
34. Ormsby-Gore interview, CBS, JFKL, quoted in Hamilton, *JFK: Reckless Youth*, 268; Nunnerly, *Kennedy and Britain*, 41.
35. Hamilton, *JFK: Reckless Youth*, 269.
36. Macdonald OH, JFKL; O'Brien, *John F. Kennedy*, 95.
37. Blair and Blair, *Search for JFK*, 72; Meyers, *As We Remember Him*, 28.
38. RK, *Times to Remember*, 251.
39. Kennan, *Memoirs 1925–1950*, 91–92. On Kennan's life and career, see Gaddis, *George F. Kennan*.
40. JPK Jr. to JPK, n.d. (August 1939), box 17, JPKP. The analysis of German propaganda efforts was largely accurate. See Evans, *Third Reich in Power*, 695–96.
41. *The American Weekly*, May 30, 1948; McCarthy, *Remarkable Kennedys*, 81.
42. Overy, *1939*, 19.
43. In Ian Kershaw's words, "the U-turn of all time." *Hitler, 1936–1945*, 206. See also Moorhouse, *Devil's Alliance*.
44. Evans, *Third Reich in Power*, 692–95; Roberts, *Storm of War*, 10; Gorodetsky, *Grand Delusion*, 10–13; Kotkin, *Stalin: Waiting*, 670–75.
45. See, e.g., Kotkin, *Stalin: Waiting*, chap. 11; Roberts, *Stalin's Wars*, chap. 2. On Chamberlain's dim view of working in concert with the Soviets, see also Bouverie, *Appeasing Hitler*, 335–38; Parker, *Chamberlain*, 347.
46. Georges Bonnet, the French foreign minister and an arch-appeaser, blamed the Poles for the invasion: it was their "stupid and obstinate attitude" that caused it, he said. Quoted in Quétel, *L'Impardonnable Défaite*, 195.
47. JPK unpublished diplomatic memoir, chap. 33, p. 2, box 148, JPKP. After a visit with Chamberlain on August 25, Kennedy wrote in his diary: "He looks like a broken man. He said he could think of nothing further to say or do. He felt that all his work had come to naught. 'I can't fly [to meet with Hitler] again because that was good only once.' " JPK diary, August 25, 1939, box 100, JPKP.
48. Reston, *Deadline*, 73.
49. Overy, *1939*, 69–110; Parker, *Chamberlain*, 336–42.
50. Quoted in Steiner, *Triumph of the Dark*, 1018.
51. JPK unpublished diplomatic memoir, chap. 34, pp. 1–2, box 148, JPKP.
52. JPK diary, September 3, 1939, printed in Smith, *Hostage to Fortune*, 365–67. Rose Kennedy shared her husband's reaction. Decades later she could still recall Chamberlain's "heartbroken, heartbreaking speech." RK, *Times to Remember*, 252.
53. The speech in full is at the International Churchill Society, winstonchurchill.org /resources/speeches/1939-in-the-wings/war-speech/. Chamberlain had not relished bringing Churchill into the government: in July 1939, he told Joe Kennedy that

Churchill "has turned into a fine two-handed drinker . . . his judgment has never proved to be good," and that if he had been in the Cabinet "England would have been at war before this." Now, however, the prime minister felt that Churchill was likely to cause less trouble inside the Cabinet than outside. Self, *Neville Chamberlain*, 386.

54. Overy, *1939*, 97.

55. Beschloss, *Roosevelt and Kennedy*, 190.

56. Kathleen Kennedy, "Lamps in a Blackout" (unpublished comment), September 1939, printed in Smith, *Hostage to Fortune*, 371–72; Swift, *Kennedys Amidst the Gathering*, 194.

57. *Time*, September 18, 1939; Whalen, *Founding Father*, 273; Sandford, *Union Jack*, 56–58; Macdonald OH, JFKL. See also the materials in box 19, JPKP.

58. JFK memo, September 8, 1939, box 17, JPKP.

59. JFK memo, September 8, 1939, box 17, JPKP; Hamilton, *JFK: Reckless Youth*, 286.

60. Brogan, *Kennedy*, 14.

CHAPTER 9: A HISTORY OF THE PRESENT

1. The poem first appeared in *The New Republic* on October 18, 1939. For context, see Mendelson, *Later Auden*. A book-length analysis is in Sansom, *September 1, 1939*.

2. JFK to JPK, September 22, 1939, box 2, JPKP. On the Winthrop suite, see Katie Koch, "A Room Fit for a President," *Harvard Gazette*, October 27, 2011, news.harvard.edu/gazette/story/2011/10/a-room-fit-for-a-president/.

3. Hershberg, *James B. Conant*, 116; Schlesinger, *Veritas*, 187; Conant, *Man of the Hour*, 161–63.

4. *THC*, November 11, 1939.

5. *THC*, October 16, 1939.

6. *THC*, September 26, 1939; September 28, 1939; October 3, 1939; and October 13, 1939.

7. *THC*, October 9, 1939.

8. See, e.g., Dallek, *Unfinished Life*, 59.

9. JFK to JPK, n.d. (1939), box 4B, JFK PP.

10. JPK to JPK Jr. and JFK, October 13, 1939, box 2, JPKP; JPK to Arthur Krock, November 3, 1939, box 31, AKP.

11. JPK to FDR, September 30, 1939, printed in Smith, *Hostage to Fortune*, 385–86.

12. Minute Sheet, October 12, 1939, FO 371/22827, NAUK; Beschloss, *Kennedy and Roosevelt*, 196.

13. Foreign Office to Washington, telegram, October 3, 1939, FO 371/22827, NAUK. See also Koskoff, *Joseph P. Kennedy*, 217–18.

14. King George diary entry, September 9, 1939, quoted in Swift, *Gathering*, 194.

15. JPK to Cordell Hull and FDR, September 11, 1939, box 3, Safe Files, FDRL; Hull to JPK, September 11, 1939, *Foreign Relations of the United States 1939* (Washington, DC: Government Printing Office, 1956), vol. I: 424; Farley, *Jim Farley's Story*, 198–99.

16. Beschloss, *Kennedy and Roosevelt*, 191; Moe, *Second Act*, 77–78.

17. *Time*, September 18, 1939; Whalen, *Founding Father*, 103.

18. *Time*, September 25, 1939; Olson, *Angry Days*, 71–72; Berg, *Lindbergh*, 397.

19. *Time*, September 25, 1939.

20. *NYT*, October 14, 1939, quoted in Brands, *Traitor to His Class*, 532.

21. Kurth, *American Cassandra*; Lepore, *These Truths*, 434, 468–70; Olson, *Angry Days*, 78–79.

22. Olson, *Angry Days*, 89; Meacham, *Franklin and Winston*, 50.

23. For the correspondence, see Kimball, *Churchill and Roosevelt*. See also Meacham, *Franklin and Winston*, 44–46.

24. JPK diary, October 5, 1939, box 100, JPKP; Nasaw, *Patriarch*, 415. On the Roosevelt-Churchill relationship, see Meacham, *Franklin and Winston*.

25. Koskoff, *Joseph P. Kennedy*, 249.

26. JPK Jr. to JPK, September 27, 1939, box 2, JPKP; Swift, *Kennedys Amidst the Gathering*, 200.

27. Eddie Moore wrote to Jack after one visit, "Your sister Rosie is wonderful." Moore to JFK, November 3, 1939, box 19, JPKP.

28. Larson, *Rosemary*, 122–24.

29. JPK to RK, October 11, 1939, printed in Smith, *Hostage to Fortune*, 393–94.

30. Isabel Eugenie to RK, December 20, 1939, box 26, JPKP (emphasis in original); Rosemary Kennedy to JPK, n.d. (April 1940), printed in Smith, *Hostage to Fortune*, 412.

31. Hamilton, *JFK: Reckless Youth*, 294.

32. Holcombe quoted in Hamilton, *JFK: Reckless Youth*, 295.

33. KK to JPK, September 26, 1939, printed in RK, *Times to Remember*, 256; "attractive girl" is on 256–57; Houghton interview, CBP; Treglown, *Straight Arrow*, 56.

34. JFK to KLB, December 7, 1939, box 1, KLBP.

35. Blair and Blair, *Search for JFK*, 80–81.

36. Paul Murphy to JFK, January 24, 1940, box 19, JPKP. See also Paul Murphy to JFK, April 26, 1938, box 19, JPKP; Paul Murphy to JFK, January 7, 1938, box 19, JPKP.

37. JFK, "Fascism" (fragment), box 4, JFKPP.

38. Government 4: Case 82, October 23, 1939, box 4, JFKPP.

39. League of Nations course paper, box 4, JFKPP.

40. See the recollection by Josephine Fulton, the wife of the Winthrop House janitor, in Hamilton, *JFK: Reckless Youth*, 301.

41. "I have decided to take as my subject," he wrote his father, "the turn from appeasement to war—tracing the change that came about in England that culminated in the war in Sept." JFK to JPK, n.d. (fall 1939), box 5, JPKP. A later letter to both parents acknowledged the size of the task: "Am just in the process of finding out how little I know." JFK to RK and JPK, n.d. (fall 1939), box 5, JPKP.

42. "Am really being kept busy now on my thesis," he wrote to Lem Billings in early December. JFK to KLB, December 7, 1939, box 1, KLBP.

43. Originally a staunch backer of appeasement, Lothian began to shift after the German takeover of Czechoslovakia in March 1939. "Up until then it was possible," he wrote to a friend that month, "to believe that Germany was only concerned with recovery of what might be called the normal rights of a great power, but it now seems clear that Hitler is in effect a fanatical gangster who will stop at nothing to beat down all possibility of resistance anywhere to his will." Butler, *Lord Lothian*, 227. Even after that point, however, indeed into 1940 and until his sudden death in Washington that June, he favored efforts to seek a negotiated settlement to the war.

44. JFK to James Seymour, January 11, 1940, box 1, JSP.

45. Seymour replied to Jack's cable the same day: "I am rushing this off so you will know the matter is in hand and shall notify you as soon as the material goes off." James Seymour to JFK, January 11, 1940, box 1, JSP. Murphy wrote to Jack on January 29, 1940: "I have today mailed parcel post a package containing pamphlets, magazines, and books which were forwarded to me by Jim Seymour. Will you kindly acknowledge receipt when they are delivered as Mr. Seymour is quite anxious about their safe arrival." Murphy to JFK, January 29, 1940, box 19, JFKPP.

46. Nasaw, *Patriarch*, 431; Collier and Horowitz, *Kennedys*, 83.

47. Whalen, *Founding Father*, 284; Koskoff, *Joseph P. Kennedy*, 231. "The president said that, as might be expected, Joe Kennedy was utterly pessimistic," Interior Secretary Harold

Ickes wrote in his diary. "He believes that Germany and Russia will win the war and that the end of the world is just down the road. I suspect that Joe has been worrying about his great fortune for a long time and the London atmosphere hasn't helped him any." Harold Ickes diary, December 10, 1939, HIP, LC.

48. Leamer, *Kennedy Men*, 147. On November 29, 1939, John Colville, assistant private secretary to the prime minister, recorded in his diary overhearing Kennedy at a dinner "talking about our inability to win the war. [At the same time], to the P.M. and the F.O. he poses as the greatest champion of our cause in the U.S." Colville, *Fringes of Power*, 35.

49. Schlesinger, *Robert Kennedy*, 33; Swift, *Kennedys Amidst the Gathering*, 227.

50. Harold Ickes diary, March 10, 1940, HIP, LC; Whalen, *Founding Father*, 286.

51. Clare Boothe Luce to JPK, May 26, 1939, box 93, CBLP; Morris, *Rage for Fame*, 340–41, 364; Nasaw, *Patriarch*, 379–80.

52. JPK to Arthur Krock, April 22, 1940, box 31, AKP.

53. Quoted in Davies, *No Simple Victory*, 82.

54. Dallek, *Franklin D. Roosevelt*, 215.

55. Langer and Gleason, *Challenge to Isolation*, 272.

56. Brands, *Traitor to His Class*, 537; Fullilove, *Rendezvous*, 31.

57. Hull, *Memoirs*, 740; Welles, *Sumner Welles*, 240–57.

58. Quoted in O'Brien, *John F. Kennedy*, 105–6.

59. Quoted in Dallek, *Unfinished Life*, 61.

60. Parmet, *Jack*, 69.

61. Gerald Walker and Donald A. Allan, "Jack Kennedy at Harvard," *Coronet Magazine*, May 1961, 92. After the incident, there appeared an unsigned note in Jack's college file: "We should make it clear to him that from now on any women in his room for any purpose have to be duly signed for and arranged for." *Newsweek*, August 9, 1971.

62. Hamilton, *JFK: Reckless Youth*, 315.

63. John F. Kennedy, "Appeasement at Munich," unpublished honors thesis, Harvard University, 1940, p. 91. The thesis is in box 2, JFKPP.

64. JFK, "Appeasement," 97–98.

65. JFK, "Appeasement," 147.

66. Hamilton, *JFK: Reckless Youth*, 317.

67. The revisionist school is ably described in the introductory essay in Self, *Neville Chamberlain Diary Letters*, 1–48.

68. JPK Jr. to JPK, March 17, 1940, box 2, JPKP.

69. Yeomans report, box 2, JFKPP; Friedrich report, box 2, JFKPP; Hamilton, *JFK: Reckless Youth*, 322.

70. JPK to JFK, August 2, 1940, box 2, JPKP.

71. Leaming, *Jack Kennedy: Education*, 80–81. The piece was a brief assessment of the bombing of Valencia. It appeared in the October 1939 issue.

72. Arthur Krock to Gertrude Algase, April 17, 1940, box 31, AKP; Hamilton, *JFK: Reckless Youth*, 322–23.

73. JPK unpublished memoir, chap. 43, p. 2, box 148, JPKP.

74. Beevor, *Second World War*, 79.

75. Quoted in Roberts, *Churchill*, 526–27.

76. A. J. P. Taylor, *The Second World War: An Illustrated History* (London: Hamish Hamilton, 1975), quoted in Davies, *No Simple Victory*, 83.

77. A provocative and engaging account is May, *Strange Victory*. See also Jackson, *Fall of France*. According to Joe Kennedy, Churchill told him on May 15 that the chances of the Allies winning were slight, and that he would not send more troops to aid the French,

given the strong likelihood that Britain would soon be attacked. JPK to FDR and Hull, May 15, 1940, box 3, Safe Files, FDRL.

78. Ferguson, *War of the World*, 390–91; Keegan, *Second World War*, 80–81.

79. JPK to RK, May 20, 1940, printed in Smith, *Hostage to Fortune*, 432–33; JPK to Hull, May 24, 1940, *Foreign Relations of the United States, 1940* (Washington, DC: Government Printing Office, 1958), III: 31–32. See also Kennedy, *Freedom from Fear*, 440.

80. Kershaw, *Fateful Choices*, 11–52; Lukacs, *Five Days*.

81. JPK to Hull, June 12, 1940, box 3, Safe Files, FDRL; JPK unpublished memoir, chap. 46, p. 6, box 149, JPKP. Churchill's assistant private secretary, John Colville, recorded in his diary on June 15, "Kennedy telephoned and Winston, becoming serious for a minute, poured into his ears a flood of eloquence about the part that America could and should play in saving civilisation. Referring to promises of industrial and financial support, he said such an offer 'would be a laughing-stock on the stage of history,' and he begged that 'we should not let our friend's (President R.) efforts peter out in grimaces and futility.'" Colville, *Fringes of Power*, 129.

82. JPK to JFK, May 20, 1940, box 2, JPKP; Leaming, *Jack Kennedy: Education*, 105.

83. Krock OH, JFKL; JFK, *Why England Slept*, 137. Emphasis in the original. See also Burns, *John Kennedy*, 43.

84. *THC*, June 9, 1940.

85. RK to JPK, June 24, 1940, printed in Smith, *Hostage to Fortune*, 446–47; Murphy to JFK, June 21, 1940, box 19, JPKP; JFK to JPK, n.d. (May 1940), box 4b, JFKPP. Yale Law School's letter of admission, dated May 14, 1940, is in box 20, JPKP.

86. Gertrude Algase to Alfred Harcourt, June 20, 1940, box 73, JFK Pre-Pres; Joel Satz to JFK, July 9, 1940, box 19, JPKP; Hamilton, *JFK: Reckless Youth*, 327.

87. Gertrude Algase to Arthur Krock, July 12, 1940, box 31, AKP.

CHAPTER 10: INTERLUDES

1. Marvin R. Zahniser, "Rethinking the Significance of Disaster: The United States and the Fall of France," *International History Review* 14 (May 1992): 252–76; Olson, *Angry Days*, 130.

2. *Life*, June 3, 1940.

3. Herring, *From Colony to Superpower*, 519–20; Kaiser, *No End*, 57–58.

4. Ketchum, *Borrowed Years*, 358.

5. Wheeler-Bennett, *Special Relationships*, 97; Olson, *Angry Days*, 128; *Time*, June 17, 1940.

6. Casey, *Cautious Crusade*; Doenecke, *Storm on the Horizon*; Herring, *From Colony to Superpower*, 520–22. On "America First," see also Churchwell, *Behold, America*.

7. Searls, *Lost Prince*, 172–73; Leamer, *Kennedy Men*, 152.

8. JPK to JPK Jr., July 23, 1940, box 2, JPKP; JPK Jr. to JPK, May 4, 1940, box 2, JPKP; Swift, *Kennedys Amidst the Gathering*, 214; Collier and Horowitz, *Kennedys*, 105.

9. Renehan, *Kennedys at War*, 158; KLB OH, JFKL.

10. JPK Jr. to JPK, August 23, 1940, box 2, JPKP; Renehan, *Kennedys at War*, 161.

11. Herzstein, *Henry R. Luce*, 155.

12. On the expansion in this period of what constituted "national security," see Andrew Preston, "Monsters Everywhere: A Genealogy of National Security," *Diplomatic History*, 38, no. 3 (2014): 477–500.

13. Henry R. Luce, "The American Century," *Life*, February 17, 1941. For assessments of the article and the concept, see Bacevich, *Short American Century*. For a different assessment of the concept, see Zunz, *Why the American Century?* On the 1940 nomination fight, see Lewis, *Improbable Wendell Willkie*, chap. 6; and Brinkley, *The Publisher*, 253–60.

14. Henry Luce OH, JFKL.

15. Henry Luce, foreword to *Why England Slept*, xix.

16. JFK to Luce, July 9, 1940, box 19, JPKP.

17. "Best Sellers of the Week," *NYT*, September 9, 1940; "Reader's Choice," *WP*, September 1, 1940. Until the early 1940s the *New York Times* bestseller list was a composite of top-selling books in a variety of big cities, Boston being one of them.

18. JFK, *Why England Slept*, xxiv.

19. FDR to JFK, August 27, 1940, box 74, JFK Pre-Pres; Hamilton, *JFK: Reckless Youth*, 336–37.

20. Quoted in Freedman, *Roosevelt and Frankfurter*, 590. Laski's letter, dated August 21, 1940, is in GB 50 U DLA/21, Papers of Harold Laski (and Frida Laski), Hull University Archives, UK. See also Hamilton, *JFK: Reckless Youth*, 333.

21. B. H. Liddell Hart to JFK, October 24, 1940, box 73, JFK Pre-Pres.

22. *New York Sun*, August 2, 1940; *New Republic*, September 16, 1940.

23. Brogan, *Kennedy*, 16.

24. Brogan, *Kennedy*, 19. See also Dallek, *Unfinished Life*, 65.

25. Schlesinger, foreword to *Why England Slept* (New York: Ishi Press, 2016), xiv. Schlesinger also writes, "The broad factual recounting of British attitudes in young Kennedy's book brilliantly captures the passivity of the British state" (xiii). See also Hellman, *Kennedy Obsession*, 22–27.

26. Bruce Hopper to JFK, September 5, 1940, box 73, JFK Pre-Pres.

27. Charles Spalding OH, JFKL; Blair and Blair, *Search for JFK*, 98–100. In late December 1940, Jack told his publisher he would not write another book at that time. JFK to Frank Henry, December 28, 1940, box 19, JPKP.

28. Arlene B. Hadley (registrar) to JFK, May 14, 1940, box 20, JPKP.

29. KLB OH, JFKL.

30. Dr. Vernon S. Dick to Dr. William P. Herbst, March 20, 1953, Travell files, JFKL; JFK to London Embassy, telegram, July 10, 1940, box 21, JPKP; Dr. Sara Jordan to JPK, July 12, 1940, box 21, JPKP.

31. JFK to JPK, telegram, July 10, 1940, box 21, JPKP; JFK to dean of admissions, Yale Law School, July 31, 1940, box 20, JPKP.

32. The invoice for the car purchase, totaling $1,329.51, including sales tax, is in box 20, JPKP. Various historical accounts say the car was green in color, but according to the invoice it was black.

33. Quoted in Hamilton, *JFK: Reckless Youth*, 350.

34. Hamilton, *JFK: Reckless Youth*, 351.

35. JPK to JFK, November 16, 1943, box 3, JPKP; JFK to JPK, n.d. (March 1940), box 5, JPKP.

36. *Stanford Daily*, October 30, 1940. As a student, he was entitled to deferment until at least July 1941.

37. Ralph Horton OH, JKFL; Blair and Blair, *Search for JFK*, 114.

38. Stansky, *First Day*. The house Kennedy rented is now the home of the Legoland Windsor Resort theme park.

39. Collier and Horowitz, *Kennedys*, 107.

40. Luce OH, JFKL.

41. In a letter to Jack in early August, he wrote, "The whole crux of the matter is, as I have said to you before, the strength of the German air force. . . . No country today can stand up unless it has air parity with another country, assuming that the other country can get its airplanes in to fight, which of course the Germans can do very easily now because they have practically all the bases up and down the whole west coast of Europe." JPK to JFK, August 2, 1940, box 2, JPKP.

42. JPK to JFK, September 10, 1940, box 4A, JFKPP.

43. JPK diary, October 19, 1940, box 100, JPKP; Arthur Krock private memo, December 1, 1940, box 1, AKP. On the twists and turns in the presidential election, see Moe, *Second Act*.

44. On October 16, 1940, Kennedy wrote in his diary, "Unless we handle our affairs with more vision than I think we are going to, we shall be getting ourselves deeper and deeper in the mud." JPK diary, box 100, JPKP. See also Nasaw, *Patriarch*, 485–86; and Whalen, *Founding Father*, 347–48.

45. Whalen, *Founding Father*, 231–33; Goodwin, *Fitzgeralds and the Kennedys*, 517; Swift, *Kennedys Amidst the Gathering*, 81.

46. Account of Ambassador's Trip to U.S. on Clipper, October 1940, box 100, JPKP; Arthur Krock private memo, December 1, 1940, box 1, AKP; Beschloss, *Kennedy and Roosevelt*, 216–19; Leamer, *Kennedy Men*, 155; Moe, *Second Act*, 295–99. When she learned of Kennedy's plan to endorse FDR, Clare Boothe Luce wrote him, "I want you also to know that I believe with all my heart and soul you will be doing America a terrible disservice. I know too well your private opinions not also to know that half of what you say (*if* you say it) you *really* won't believe in your heart." Clare Boothe Luce to JPK, October 28, 1940, box 100, JPKP.

47. *BG*, November 10, 1940.

48. "Apparently, Joe Kennedy is out to do whatever damage he can," Harold Ickes remarked in his diary. "The president said that, in his opinion, the interview obtained with Kennedy in Boston a couple of weeks ago was authentic, despite its subsequent denial by Kennedy." Harold Ickes diary, December 1, 1940, HIP, LC.

49. JPK to JFK, telegram, December 5, 1940, box 4A, JFKPP; Nasaw, *Patriarch*, 506–9; Leamer, *Kennedy Men*, 160.

50. JFK to JPK, December 6, 1940, box 4A, JFKP. Emphasis in original.

51. JFK to JPK, December 6, 1940, box 4A, JFKP.

52. JFK "supplementary note," n.d., box 5, JPKP.

53. Harriet Price to JFK, n.d., box 4B, JFKPP; Leamer, *Kennedy Men*, 162.

54. Even as Kennedy delivered the radio address, senior administration officials, including FDR, were not sure which way he would go. See Harold Ickes diary, January 19, 1941, HIP, LC. On the isolationist opposition in these weeks, much of it funded by Robert McCormick, see Smith, *Colonel*, 398–409.

55. See Edwards, *Edward R. Murrow;* and Cloud and Olson, *Murrow Boys*.

56. Searls, *Lost Prince*, 173; Collier and Horowitz, *Kennedys*, 112.

57. JFK passport file, box 6, JFKPP; RK, *Times to Remember*, 279.

58. Kaiser, *No End*, 200–204; Reynolds, *From Munich*, 126–30; Heinrichs, *Threshold of War*, 90.

59. Kershaw, *Hitler: Nemesis*, 393; Gorodetsky, *Grand Delusion*. For a summary of Hitler's motives in launching the invasion, see Ferguson, *War of the World*, 426–31.

60. *BG*, April 30, 1941; Searls, *Lost Prince*, 172–73.

61. Schoor, *Young John Kennedy*, 118; Searls, *Lost Prince*, 174.

62. See Hamilton, *JFK: Reckless Youth*, 398–41.

63. Collier and Horowitz, *Kennedys*, 113.

CHAPTER 11: IN LOVE AND WAR

1. Blair and Blair, *Search for JFK*, 111–13.

2. Report of Physical Exam, August 5, 1941, box 11A, JFKPP; Investigation Report, USNIS, September 10, 1941, box 11A, JFKPP; Perrett, *Jack*, 94.

3. Searls, *Lost Prince*, 181–82.

4. A biography is Farris, *Inga.*

5. Quoted in Farris, *Inga,* 3–4.

6. Arvad memoir in Ron McCoy Papers, quoted in Hamilton, *JFK: Reckless Youth,* 422; White interview at 423; Inga Arvad, "Did You Happen to See?" *Washington Times-Herald,* November 27, 1941.

7. Farris, *Inga,* 43; McTaggart, *Kathleen Kennedy,* 11, 62.

8. JFK to RK, n.d. (November 1941), box 21, JPKP.

9. JFK memo, "Dinner at Mrs. Patterson's," n.d. (November 1941), box 11, JFK Pre-Pres.

10. On the Newfoundland meeting and the Atlantic Charter, see, e.g., Wilson, *First Summit;* and Borgwardt, *New Deal,* part 1. Churchill recollection is quoted in Kennedy, *Freedom from Fear,* 496. See also Kimball, *Churchill and Roosevelt,* vol. 1, 299.

11. Cull, *Selling War,* 185; Schlesinger, *A Life,* 256–57; Lepore, *These Truths,* 482; Berg, *Lindbergh,* 425–29.

12. On the developments in these months, see, e.g., Hotta, *Japan 1941;* Heinrichs, *Threshold of War;* and Gillon, *Pearl Harbor.*

13. See, e.g., Stinnett, *Day of Deceit.* For a critique, see Rosenberg, *Date Which Will Live,* 158–62.

14. Schlesinger, *A Life,* 241–61; Olson, *Angry Days,* 426–27; JPK telegram to FDR, December 7, 1941, printed in Smith, *Hostage to Fortune,* 533.

15. FDR to Boettiger, March 3, 1942, Boettiger Papers, FDRL, quoted in Nasaw, *Patriarch,* 520.

16. Hamilton, *Mantle of Command,* 76–77.

17. Churchill, *Grand Alliance,* 539–40; Fenby, *Alliance,* 79–80.

18. Roberts, *Storm of War,* 193–94. For the provocative argument that Hitler's principal concern was never primarily Bolshevism, as has often been claimed, but "Anglo-America and global capitalism," see Simms, *Hitler.*

19. JFK to KLB, December 12, 1941, box 1, KLBP.

20. Writing decades later under her married name, Page (Huidekoper) Wilson would say of Arvad: "I didn't get the impression [in late 1941 and early 1942] that she was hiding any history of her life as a reporter in Germany." Wilson, *Carnage and Courage,* 170.

21. Hamilton, *JFK: Reckless Youth,* 427; Hardison Report, January 6, 1942, box 5, Hoover OCF.

22. Hardison Report, January 6, 1942, box 5, Hoover OCF, NARA; Ladd Memo for Hoover, January 17, 1942, box 5, Hoover OCF; McKee report for Hoover, February 3, 1942, box 5, Hoover OCF.

23. *Berlingske Tidende,* November 1, 1935, quoted in Farris, *Inga,* 137–38.

24. Kramer to Ladd, January 28, 1942, box 5, Hoover OCF; FDR to Hoover, May 4, 1942, quoted in O'Brien, *John F. Kennedy,* 120. The request for phone surveillance authorization is in a Hoover "Memo for the Attorney General," January 21, 1942, box 5, Hoover OCF. Hoover wrote, "The combination of these facts indicates a definite possibility that she may be engaged in a most subtle type of espionage activities against the United States."

25. Hardison Report, January 22, 1942, box 5, Hoover OCF.

26. Hardison Report, January 6, 1942, box 5, Hoover OCF.

27. *New York Daily Mirror,* January 12, 1942; Farris, *Inga,* 211–14. On Winchell's extraordinary reach in terms of readership, see Gabler, *Winchell.* According to Rose Kennedy, Jack was "completely mystified" by the sudden transfer to Charleston. RK to children, January 20, 1942, box 2, JPKP.

28. On March 4, 1942, Kennedy again lobbied FDR for a job: "I don't want to appear in the role of a man looking for a job for the sake of getting an appointment, but Joe and Jack

are in the service and I feel that my experience in these critical times might be worth something in some position. I just want to say that if you want me, I am yours to command at any time." JPK to FDR, March 4, 1942, printed in Smith, *Hostage to Fortune,* 541–42. On March 7, Kennedy wrote again. JPK to FDR, March 7, 1942, box 4A, JFKPP. Again, no significant offer materialized. Felix Frankfurter, in a diary entry in early 1943, would write, "I don't suppose it ever enters the head of a Joe Kennedy that one who was so hostile to the war effort as he was all over the lot, and so outspoken in his foulmouthed opposition to the President himself, barred his own way to a responsible share in the conduct of the war." Lash, *From the Diaries of Felix Frankfurter,* 237–38.

29. Hamilton, *JFK: Reckless Youth,* 447.
30. Inga Arvad to JFK, February 19, 1942, box 4A, JFKPP; Arvad to JFK, n.d. (1942), box 4A, JFKPP; Arvad to JFK, March 11, 1942, box 4A, JFKPP; S. K. McKee to J. Edgar Hoover, February 24, 1942, box 4, Hoover OCF.
31. Inga Arvad to JFK, n.d. (1942), box 4A, JFKPP.
32. Torbert Macdonald to JFK, n.d. (1942), box 4B, JFKPP; Farris, *Inga,* 204.
33. ARV Summary, February 3, 1942, box 5, Hoover OCF.
34. ARV Summary, February 3, 1942, box 5, Hoover OCF.
35. E. H. Adkins Report, February 9, 1942, box 5, Hoover OCF.
36. ARV Summary, March 2, 1942, box 5, Hoover OCF; Ruggles to the director, February 23, 1942, box 5, Hoover, OCF.
37. ARV Summary, March 6, 1942, box 5, Hoover OCF.
38. RK round-robin letter, February 16, 1942, printed in Smith, *Hostage to Fortune,* 539–40; KLB OH, JFKL.
39. RK, *Times to Remember,* 286; Byrne, *Kick,* 165.
40. Nasaw, *Patriarch,* 534–36. On the development of the procedure, and the roles played by Moniz and Freeman, see also Dittrich, *Patient H.M.,* 77–88. *New York Times* is quoted at 83.
41. Marguerite Clark, "Surgery in Mental Cases," *American Mercury,* March 1941; Waldemar Kaempffert, "Turning the Mind Inside Out," *SEP,* May 24, 1941; "Neurological Treatment of Certain Abnormal Mental States Panel Discussion at Cleveland Session," *Journal of the American Medical Association* 117, no. 7 (August 16, 1941); Larson, *Rosemary,* 161–62.
42. Walter Freedman and James Watts, *Psychosurgery: Intelligence, Emotion, and Social Behavior Following Prefrontal Lobotomy for Mental Disorders* (Springfield, IL: Charles C. Thomas, 1942), quoted in Dittrich, *Patient H.M.,* 84.
43. Nasaw, *Patriarch,* 534–36; Larson, *Rosemary,* 161; Perry, *Rose Kennedy,* 164–65.
44. Eunice Kennedy Shriver interview by Robert Coughlan, February 7, 1972, box 10, RKP. See also Smith, *Nine of Us,* 236.
45. Larson, *Rosemary,* 169–70.
46. Goodwin, *Fitzgeralds and the Kennedys,* 644; Leamer, *Kennedy Men,* 170.
47. Larson, *Rosemary,* 160–61, 179–80; McNamara, *Eunice,* 22, 58; JPK to JFK, November 16, 1943, box 3, JPKP; JPK to JPK Jr., February 21, 1944, box 3, JPKP. To his wife, Kennedy wrote in November 1942, "I stopped off to see Rosemary and she was getting along very nicely. She looks very well." JPK to RK, November 23, 1942, box 21, JPKP.
48. RK to children, December 5, 1941, box 55, RKP, JFKL. Her round-robin letter of January 20, 1942, gave no hint that anything was amiss. RK to children, January 20, 1942, box 21, JPKP.
49. Kennedy, *Times to Remember,* 286; Goodwin, *Fitzgeralds and the Kennedys,* 643. David Nasaw suspects that Rose had little say in the decision to operate, both because of the nature of the Kennedys' marriage and because of the custom at the time. He quotes

historian Janice Brockley's finding that mental health professionals in midcentury often recommended that fathers—thought to be more emotionally detached, more clearheaded—take the decision-making burden from their wives when it came to the treatment options for disabled children. Nasaw, *Patriarch*, 534.

50. JFK to KK, March 10, 1942, box 4A, JFKPP. Emphasis in original. He also mused about a conversation he'd had in Palm Beach with Lord Halifax, the former British foreign minister and now ambassador to Washington, over the Christmas holiday. Halifax had asserted, Jack jotted in notes of the conversation, that "if England had fought in 1938, she would have been licked immediately. As evidence he repeated the conversation that he had with Sir John Dill, chief of the British General Staff. He asked him whether he would rather have fought in 1938 or 1939. Dill thought for a moment and then said, 'I would rather have fought in 1940.'" Later in the conversation, Halifax dismissed Jack's suggestion that a grand alliance with the Soviet Union might have been possible, and explained why he was not the right person to succeed Chamberlain as prime minister in 1940. "Talk with Lord Halifax," n.d. (January 1942), box 11, JFK Pre-Pres.

51. Luce to JPK, February 5, 1942, box 4B, JFKPP. Taken aback by the letter, the elder Kennedy wrote to Jack, "Heaven knows, I don't want any pessimism of mine to have any effect on you, but I don't know how to tell you what I think unless I tell you what I think." JPK to JFK, February 9, 1942, box 2, JFKP.

52. JFK, draft article, n.d. (Feb. 1942), box 11, JFKPP. In a letter to Rip Horton, Jack showed again that he didn't share his father's pessimism. Musing on the themes of Greek tragedy, he concluded: "We can do something the Greeks couldn't—we can prevent the gloomy ending—it isn't inevitable—something can be done." JFK to Ralph Horton, n.d. (Feb. or March 1942), box 4b, JFKPP.

53. Clinical report, Chief of Bureau of Navigation to JFK, May 8, 1942, box 11A, JFKPP.

54. RK to JPK Jr., September 29, 1942, quoted in Goodwin, *Fitzgeralds and the Kennedys*, 647–48; Dallek, *Unfinished Life*, 76.

55. Farris, *Inga*, 283; ARV Summary of June 24, 1942, box 5, Hoover OCF; JFK to RK, n.d. (1942), box 2, JPKP. Arvad had moved to Reno, Nevada, for several weeks to secure a divorce from Fejos but had recently returned. The FBI had promptly resumed technical surveillance. Memo for the Director, June 16, 1942, box 4, Hoover OCF.

56. Goodwin, *Fitzgeralds and the Kennedys*, 635.

57. Schlesinger, *Robert Kennedy*, 16.

58. JFK, "For What We Fight" (speech), July 4, 1942, box 28, DFPP.

59. ARV Summary, July 24, 1942, box 5, Hoover OCF; Hamilton, *JFK: Reckless Youth*, 494.

60. Admiral Chester Nimitz said of the early developments after Pearl Harbor: "From the time the Japanese dropped those bombs on December 7th until at least two months later, hardly a day passed that the situation did not get more chaotic and confused and appear more hopeless." Quoted in Toll, *Pacific Crucible*, 129. On Japan's advances in these months, see also Calvocoressi and Wint, *Total War*, 722–37.

61. On the results at Midway, see Costello, *Pacific War*, 305–8; Toll, *Pacific Crucible*, 473–76.

62. JFK to KLB, n.d. (July 1942), box 1, KLBP.

63. Donovan, *PT 109*, 23.

64. Breuer, *Sea Wolf*, 108–9.

65. O'Brien, *John F. Kennedy*, 130.

66. JPK to JPK Jr., October 1, 1942, box 2, JPKP.

67. Dallek, *Unfinished Life*, 88.

68. Hamilton, *JFK: Reckless Youth*, 513.

69. Hamilton, *JFK: Reckless Youth*, 512.

70. Quoted in O'Brien, *John F. Kennedy*, 131.

71. David I. Walsh to John Fitzgerald, December 21, 1942, quoted in Goodwin, *Fitzgeralds and the Kennedys*, 648.

72. JFK to RFK, January 10, 1943, quoted in Schlesinger, *Robert Kennedy*, 54.

73. Pitts, *Jack and Lem*, 87–88; Dallek, *Unfinished Life*, 90. According to Rose, Jack was "quite ready to die for the U.S.A. in order to keep the Japanese and the Germans from becoming the dominant people in their respective continents, believing that sooner or later they would encroach on ours." RK to children, October 9, 1942, box 4a, JFKPP.

CHAPTER 12: OVERBOARD

1. Quoted in Hamilton, *JFK: Reckless Youth*, 530.

2. Buchan, *Pilgrim's Way*, 49–50. See also David Shribman, "Remembering a Forgotten Man and His Forgotten Book," *Toledo Blade*, May 28, 2017.

3. Buchan, *Pilgrim's Way*, 58; Sorensen, *Kennedy*, 14. In the same way, Arthur M. Schlesinger Jr., a White House aide during the Kennedy administration, would remark, "Only the unwary could conclude that his 'coolness' was because he felt too little. It was because he felt too much and had to compose himself for an existence filled with disorder and suffering." Quoted in Rubin, *Forty*, 252.

4. James Reed interview in Hamilton, *JFK: Reckless Youth*, 526–27; "Edgar Stephens Remembers JFK He Knew in Navy," *Albany Gazette* (MO), November 23 and 25, 1988, box 132, JFKPOF; Meyers, *As We Remember*, 39.

5. The literature is enormous. See, e.g., Beevor, *Stalingrad*; Glantz and House, *To the Gates*; Atkinson, *Army at Dawn*.

6. Hastings, *Inferno*, 256. Costello, *Pacific War*, 364.

7. Kennedy, *Victory at Sea*, chap. 8.

8. Spector, *Eagle Against the Sun*, 222–26.

9. Manchester, *Glory and the Dream*, 266; Hynes, *Soldiers' Tale*, 159–60.

10. Thomas, *Sea of Thunder*, 69. Before the war, Tulagi had been the capital of the British Solomon Islands Protectorate.

11. Toll, *Conquering Tide*, 202; JFK to KLB, May 6, 1943, quoted in Pitts, *Jack and Lem*, 97.

12. JFK to RK and JPK, received May 10, 1943, box 2, JPKP.

13. JFK to RK and JPK, n.d. (early May 1943), printed in Smith, *Hostage to Fortune*, 550–51; JFK round-robin letter, June 24, 1943, box 2, JPKP; Dallek, *Unfinished Life*, 91.

14. JFK to JPK and RK, May 14, 1943, box 2, JPKP.

15. JFK to Inga Arvad, n.d. (spring 1943), quoted in Stern, *Averting "The Final Failure,"* 37; JFK to RK and JPK, May 14, 1943, box 5, JFKPP. The letter to the parents concluded with a note of assurance for Rose: "P.S. Mother: Got to church Easter. They had it in a native hut and aside from having a condition read 'Enemy aircraft in the vicinity' it went as well as St. Pat's."

16. Quoted in Stern, *Averting "The Final Failure,"* 37–38.

17. On the PT boats and their service in the war, see Keating, *Mosquito Fleet*; and Whipple, *Small Ships*.

18. *Life*, May 10, 1943; JFK to KK, June 3, 1943, printed in Smith, *Hostage to Fortune*, 555–56.

19. Michener, *Tales of the South Pacific*, 52–53.

20. Donovan, *PT 109*, 21; Blair and Blair, *Search for JFK*, 204. A history of PT 109, from its launching in June 1942 to its destruction in 1943, is Domagalski, *Dark Water*.

21. "To Mother with love," he wrote on the card accompanying the flowers. "Love, Jack. Sorry I could not be there." Box 2, JPKP.

22. JFK to RK and JPK, May 15, 1943, box 2, JPKP. In another letter to his family, Jack wrote, "The living conditions here are rugged—nearly as rugged as Daly, and much

more rugged than me (or is it I, mother). We live on the boats, eat canned army rations (beans, fried spam) and go out nearly every night—try to grab a little sleep in the day. So far we have been lucky. The first night out they came the closest. We were well up in there and lying to, thinking this wasn't too tough, when suddenly I heard a plane, looked up and said it looks like one of our new ones to my exec. The next minute I was flat on my back across the deck. He had straddled us with a couple. The boat was full of holes and a couple of the boys were hit but are doing O.K." JFK to JPK and RK and siblings, n.d. (received August 10, 1943), box 21, JPKP.

23. JFK to KK, June 3, 1943, printed in Smith, *Hostage to Fortune*, 555–56.

24. JFK to RK and JPK, n.d. (early May 1943), printed in Smith, *Hostage to Fortune*, 550–51.

25. Goodwin, *Fitzgeralds and the Kennedys*, 649; Edward Oxford, "Ten Lives for Kennedy," *Argosy*, July 1960.

26. Renehan, *Kennedys at War*, 245.

27. The story of John F. Kennedy and PT 109 has been told many times. An early, highly sympathetic account that holds up quite well is Donovan, *PT 109*. The most recent book-length study, also favorable, is Doyle, *PT 109*. The incident also receives close attention in Hamilton, *JFK: Reckless Youth* (sympathetic); and Blair and Blair, *Search for JFK* (more critical). All were highly useful in preparing the account that follows. John Hersey's classic account in *The New Yorker*, titled "Survival" and published June 17, 1944 (and discussed in later chapters), though superseded by these later accounts, retains power.

28. Donovan, *PT 109*, 76–77.

29. JFK to JPK and RK and siblings, n.d. (received August 10, 1943), box 21, JPKP.

30. B. R. White and J. G. McClure, Memo to Commander, "Sinking of PT 109 and Subsequent Rescue of Survivors," August 22, 1943, box 22, JPKP; O'Brien, *John F. Kennedy*, 158.

31. White/McClure memo; Donovan, *PT 109*, 90.

32. Hersey, "Survival."

33. Hersey, "Survival"; JFK notes for a speech on PT 109, n.d. (fall 1945), box 96, JFK Pre-Pres; Blair and Blair, *Search for JFK*, 274; Doyle, *PT 109*, chaps. 6 and 7.

34. Barney Ross interview, CBSI, JFKL.

35. White/McClure memo; Doyle, *PT 109*, 115–16; Renehan, *Kennedys at War*, 264–65. In 2002, a National Geographic expedition led by deep-sea explorer Robert Ballard discovered the wreck of PT 109 about twelve hundred feet below the water's surface.

36. Quoted in Donovan, *PT 109*, 103.

37. Doyle, *PT 109*, 118; Donovan, *PT 109*, 105. In later years the island would become known as Kennedy Island.

38. Fay, *Pleasure of His Company*, 127. On the initial Fay-Kennedy interactions in Melville, see also Meyers, *As We Remember*, 39.

39. White/McClure memo.

40. Hersey, "Survival"; Donovan, *PT 109*, 109–11.

41. Blair and Blair, *Search for JFK*, 285–88; White/McClure memo.

42. White/McClure memo; Doyle, *PT 109*, 149–51. On Eroni Kumana and Biuku Gasa, who lived to be ninety-three and eighty-two, respectively, see also Rob Brown, "The Solomon Islanders Who Saved JFK," BBC, August 6, 2014, at www.bbc.com/news/magazine-28644830, accessed November 30, 2019.

43. Quoted in Goodwin, *Fitzgeralds and the Kennedys*, 657.

44. Jessica Contrera, "He Saved JFK's Life During WWII—With the Help of an SOS Carved on a Coconut," *WP*, August 23, 2018.

45. O'Brien, *John F. Kennedy*, 153–54; Doyle, *PT 109*, 105. Ensign William Battle, the skip-

per of another PT boat who later in life became U.S. ambassador to Australia during the Kennedy administration, claimed he wanted to go back into Blackett Strait during the day on August 2 but that the request was denied.

46. Blair and Blair, *Search for JFK*, 271; O'Brien, *John F. Kennedy*, 157; Doyle, *PT 109*, 294.

47. Quoted in Hamilton, *JFK: Reckless Youth*, 569.

48. Donovan, *PT 109*, 89; Bill Hosokawa, "John F. Kennedy's Friendly Enemy," *American Legion Magazine*, June 1965; Doyle, *PT 109*, 1–9.

49. Parmet, *Jack*, 107. Said William "Bud" Liebenow, who commanded PT 157, with respect to the 109 crew, "Not one of them ever had anything bad to say about JFK. And they are the ones who know." Quoted in Doyle, *PT 109*, 176. Bucky Harris, for his part, declared: "If it wasn't for him I wouldn't be here—I really feel that. I venture to say there are very few men who would swim out in that ocean alone without knowing what was underneath you. Brother, I wouldn't do it. . . . I thought he was great. Everybody on the crew thought he was top-notch." Quoted in Hamilton, JFK: *Reckless Youth*, 602.

50. Quoted in Hamilton, *JFK: Reckless Youth*, 610–11.

51. "Ten Lives for Kennedy," *Argosy*, July 1960. See also Donovan, *PT 109*, 124; and Stephen Plotkin, "Sixty Years Later, the Story of PT-109 Still Captivates," *Prologue* 35, no. 2 (Summer 2003).

52. Wills, *Kennedy Imprisonment*, 131. A more consistently sympathetic voice, that of Arthur Schlesinger Jr., said that Kennedy's "leadership, resourcefulness, and cheer until rescue came . . . [made] this . . . one of the authentic passages of heroism in the war." Schlesinger, *Thousand Days*, 82–83.

53. Louis Denfeld to Russell Willson, April 7, 1944, box 22, JPKP; A. P. Cluster to JPK, January 9, 1944, box 22, JPKP. Kennedy is the only president to have received either of these honors.

54. RK to children, August 25, 1943, box 2, JPKP. See also RK, *Times to Remember*, 293.

55. Nasaw, *Patriarch*, 557.

56. JFK to RK and JPK, August 13, 1943, box 2, JPKP.

57. *BG*, August 19, 1943; *NYT*, August 20, 1943; Nasaw, *Patriarch*, 557–58.

58. JFK to RK and JPK, n.d. (September 1943), box 5, JFKPP.

59. JFK to JPK, n.d. (September 1943), box 2, JPKP.

60. JFK to Inga Arvad, n.d. (September 1943), printed in Sandler, *Letters*, 31–33.

61. JPK to JPK Jr., August 31, 1943, box 2, JPKP.

62. JPK Jr. to parents, August 29, 1943, quoted in Goodwin, *Fitzgeralds and the Kennedys*, 662.

63. Searls, *Lost Prince*, 202–3; Blair and Blair, *Search for JFK*, 325.

64. RK, *Times to Remember*, 285.

65. Blair and Blair, *Search for JFK*, 337, 339–40. In a letter home, he made light of his new title: "Got promoted . . . —purely routine—and am now a full Lieutenant. (Mother, you can look that up on your little chart—it's the same as Captain in the Army.)" JFK to family, n.d. (received November 1, 1943), box 2, JPKP. Byron White co-authored the report on the PT 109 incident cited above. In 1962 Kennedy would nominate him for a seat on the U.S. Supreme Court, where he turned out to be more conservative than Kennedy and his advisers expected.

66. O'Brien, *John F. Kennedy*, 163, 164.

67. The malaria symptoms would continue to plague him. See JPK to JFK, February 10, 1948, box 3, JPKP.

68. JFK to RFK, November 14, 1943, in Donovan, *PT 109*, 152.

69. Fay, *Pleasure of His Company*, 130–31.

70. Hastings, *Inferno*, 422.

71. Blair and Blair, *Search for JFK*, 352; Hamilton, *JFK: Reckless Youth*, 638.
72. The story appeared in dozens of newspapers nationwide; e.g., "Tells Story of PT Epic: Kennedy Lauds Men, Disdains Hero Stuff," *BG*, January 11, 1944.
73. *BG*, January 11, 1944; Farris, *Inga*, 306.

CHAPTER 13: LOST PRINCE

1. Smith, *American Diplomacy*, 74; Meacham, *Franklin and Winston*, chap. 9. On Tehran's importance, see also Hamilton, *War and Peace*, part 3.
2. Butler, *Roosevelt*, xliii, liv; *NYT*, December 7, 1943.
3. Quoted in Budiansky, *Battle of Wits*, 243. On the symbiosis between the USSR's manpower contribution and America's productive might, see also Katznelson, *Fear Itself*, 17.
4. Quoted in Evans, *American Century*, 354.
5. Quoted in Harbutt, *Yalta 1945*, 131.
6. Quoted in Ash, *History of the Present*, 214.
7. Quoted in Kennedy, *Rise and Fall*, 347.
8. Evans, *American Century*, 346.
9. Evans, *American Century*, 346. See also Herman, *Freedom's Forge*; and Baime, *Arsenal of Democracy*. Inevitably, Paul Bunyan–type yarns made the rounds, such as the one about the woman who was invited to christen a new ship. She was escorted to an empty launching pad and handed a bottle of champagne. "But where is the ship?" she asked, bewildered. "You just start swinging the bottle, lady," a worker replied. "We'll have the ship there." Burns, *Crosswinds of Freedom*, 186.
10. Liddell Hart, *History of the Second*, 23; Kennedy, *Victory at Sea*, chap. 8.
11. Manchester, *Glory and the Dream*, 292.
12. Thompson, *Sense of Power*.
13. Dr. Paul O'Leary to Dr. Frank Lahey, January 18, 1944, box 21, JPKP; JFK to Clare Boothe Luce, January 11, 1944, Clare Boothe Luce Papers, LC.
14. Rose Kennedy diary note, n.d. (January 1944), printed in Smith, *Hostage to Fortune*, 573.
15. Spalding OH, JFKL; Hamilton, *JFK: Reckless Youth*, 640.
16. Blair and Blair, *Search for JFK*, 354–55; Rose Kennedy diary note, n.d. (January 1944), printed in Smith, *Hostage to Fortune*, 573. To her other children, however, Rose offered assurances that he was still the same Jack: "He wears his oldest clothes, still late for meals, still no money. He has even overflowed the bathtub, as was his boyhood custom, and I was the one who discovered it as the water came trickling down through the ceiling to my bath house below." RK to children, January 31, 1944, box 3, JPKP.
17. JFK to Inga Arvad, n.d. (September 1943), quoted in Leamer, *Kennedy Men*, 192–93; JFK to JPK and RK, September 1943, box 2, JFKPP.
18. Kennedy, *Freedom from Fear*, 712; Max Hastings, "Imagining the Unimaginable," *New York Review of Books*, May 10, 2018.
19. Betty Coxe Spalding OH, CBP; Blair and Blair, *Search for JFK*, 317–20, 364. A lengthy analysis of Hersey's article and its genesis is in Hellman, *Obsession*, chap. 2.
20. *BG*, February 12, 1944.
21. Blair and Blair, *Search for JFK*, 365–66.
22. Canellos, *Last Lion*, 23–24. Interestingly, research by historian Douglas Brinkley indicates that while in Miami, Kennedy may have made a stab at becoming a naval aviator. Records suggest he spent a number of days piloting Piper J-3 Cub floatplanes at the Embry-Riddle Seaplane Base. Brinkley, *American Moonshot*, 52.
23. Quoted in Parmet, *Jack*, 117–18.
24. JPK to JPK Jr., May 24, 1944, box 3, JPKP; Navy Department, Office of the Chief of

Naval Operations, "History of USS PT-109," n.d., box 132, President's Office Files, JFKL; *NYT*, June 12, 1944; Dallek, *Unfinished Life*, 101–2.

25. JFK to KLB, May 3, 1944, quoted in Hamilton, *JFK: Reckless Youth*, 646.

26. RK, *Times to Remember*, 265.

27. KK to JFK, July 29, 1943, box 2, JPKP. See also Bailey, *Black Diamonds*, 346–51. In addition to their main seat at Chatsworth, the family owned Hardwick Hall, in Derbyshire, Compton Place, in Eastbourne, Bolton Abbey, in Yorkshire, and Lismore Castle, in Ireland, as well as various townhouses in London.

28. Byrne, *Kick*, 218–25; *NYT*, May 7, 1944. A few weeks after the wedding, Joe Junior wrote to his parents that "Kick is terribly happy, and I think everything will work out very well." JPK Jr. to JPK and RK, June 23, 1944, box 3, JPKP.

29. JPK Jr. to RK, telegram, May 6, 1944, printed in Smith, *Hostage to Fortune*, 586; JPK to JPK Jr., May 24, 1944, box 3, JPKP.

30. JFK, *As We Remember Joe* (privately published, 1944), 54.

31. JFK to KLB, May 19, 1944, KLBP, quoted in Hamilton, *JFK: Reckless Youth*, 652.

32. Sorensen, *Kennedy*, 40.

33. Treglown, *Straight Arrow*, 90–91.

34. JFK to John Hersey, n.d. (1944), in Parmet, *Jack*, 119.

35. John Hersey, "Survival," *The New Yorker*, June 17, 1944.

36. JPK to JPK Jr., May 24, 1944, box 3, JPKP; Doyle, *PT 109*, 201–2.

37. Hellman, *Obsession*, 43.

38. JFK to KLB, February 20, 1945, quoted in O'Brien, *John F. Kennedy*, 171.

39. McTaggart, *Kathleen Kennedy*, 146.

40. JPK Jr. to JFK, August 10, 1944, box 4a, JFKPP.

41. RK, *Times to Remember*, 301.

42. Four days before, he had written to his eldest son, "The reason I haven't been writing you is that I have been expecting to hear the telephone ring any time and to hear that you were in Norfolk and were on your way home." JPK to JPK Jr., August 9, 1944, box 3, JPKP.

43. JPK Jr. to JPK and RK, August 4, 1944, box 3, JPKP.

44. Axelrod, *Lost Destiny*, 160ff; Olsen, *Aphrodite*. The U.S. Army Air Forces called its version of the effort Operation Aphrodite. On the V-weapons and their impact, see Tami Davis Biddle, "On the Crest of Fear: V-Weapons, the Battle of the Bulge, and the Last Stages of World War II in Europe," *Journal of Military History* 83, no. 1 (January 2019): 157–94; and Brinkley, *American Moonshot*, 31–39, 61–69.

45. Leamer, *Kennedy Men*, 211.

46. Leamer, *Kennedy Men*, 214; Searls, *Lost Prince*, 270–71.

47. See Krock, *Memoirs*, 348.

48. Hamilton, *JFK: Reckless Youth*, 661. See also Brinkley, *American Moonshot*, 53–58.

49. McNamara, *Eunice*, 69–70; JFK, *As We Remember*, 5. Part of the Navy Cross citation read, "For extraordinary heroism and courage in aerial flight as a pilot of a United States Liberator bomber on August 12, 1944. Well knowing the extreme dangers involved and totally unconcerned for his own safety, Lieutenant Kennedy unhesitatingly volunteered to conduct an exceptionally hazardous and special operations mission."

50. Whalen, *Founding Father*, 373; Goodwin, *Fitzgeralds and the Kennedys*, 693.

51. Krock, *Memoirs*, 348; Krock interview, Blair Papers.

52. Kennedy, *Times to Remember*, 302; Goodwin, *Fitzgeralds and the Kennedys*, 691. Chuck Spalding sent a touching condolence letter to Rose and Joe, in which he said he had not known Joe Junior well. Spalding to RK and JPK, September 2, 1944, box 4B, JFKPP.

53. McTaggart, *Kathleen Kennedy*, 175.

54. Byrne, *Kick*, 253; Bailey, *Black Diamonds*, 375–76.

55. Various items from this notebook, including Kick's letter, are in box SG64, JKOP. Kick wrote, "If Eunice, Pat, and Jean marry nice guys for fifty years they'll be lucky if they have five weeks like I did." See also Schlesinger, *Thousand Days*, 87.

56. JFK to KLB, February 20, 1945, quoted in O'Brien, *John F. Kennedy*, 176; Martin, *Hero for Our Time*, 41. Choate headmaster George St. John congratulated Jack on a "real tribute, a tribute with breadth of appeal, showing the many facets of Joe's personality." Lem Billings, who saw the two brothers up close and understood the nature of their relationship, was moved to say, "When two brothers are growing up and they are two years apart you aren't aware of a great love between them, but Jack's editing of Joe's memorial book was a real work of love." Hamilton, *JFK: Reckless Youth*, 704–5; KLB OH, JFKL.

57. JFK to JPK and RK, May 21, 1945, printed in Smith, *Hostage to Fortune*, 619–20; O'Donnell and Powers, *"Johnny,"* 44.

58. JFK, *As We Remember Joe*, 3–5; O'Brien, *John F. Kennedy*, 176–77.

59. On the disappearance of the thesis, see Searls, *Lost Prince*, 109.

60. Quoted in Thomas, *Robert Kennedy*, 48.

61. O'Donnell and Powers, *"Johnny,"* 45. Professor William G. Carleton of the University of Florida, who participated in an evening discussion at Palm Beach in the spring of 1941, later said, "It was clear to me that John had a far better historical and political mind than his father or his elder brother; indeed, that John's capacity for seeing current events in historical perspective and for projecting historical trends into the future was unusual." Quoted in Schlesinger, *Thousand Days*, 80.

62. JPK to Joe Kane, March 4, 1944, quoted in Savage, *Senator from New England*, 6.

63. Parmet, *Jack*, 2, 125; Sorensen, *Kennedy*, 15. Lem Billings went further: "Nothing could have kept Jack out of politics: I think this is what he had in him and it just would have come out, no matter what." Quoted in Brinkley, *Kennedy*, 22. Or, as sister Eunice put it three decades later, "It wasn't like he was headed to be a doctor and had to change his course. Nothing like that. He was very interested in politics. It was just a natural culmination of his interests." McNamara, *Eunice*, 82.

64. Bradley to Pardee, December 19, 1944, box 19, JPKP; JFK to KLB, February 20, 1945, quoted in O'Brien, *John F. Kennedy*, 179.

65. "Let's Try an Experiment in Peace," box 21, DFPP; Edward Weeks to JFK, April 17, 1945, box 73, JFK Pre-Pres; JPK to Henry Luce, February 15, 1945, box 19, JPKP. There's also a folder of materials pertaining to the article draft in box 19, JPKP.

66. JFK, "Let's Try an Experiment in Peace," box 21, DFPP; Sandford, *Union Jack*, 83.

67. Blair and Blair, *Search for JFK*, 365–67.

68. Blair and Blair, *Search for JFK*, 416.

CHAPTER 14: "POLITICAL TO HIS FINGERTIPS"

1. Smith, *Franklin Roosevelt*, 600–36; Richard J. Bing, "Franklin Delano Roosevelt and the Treatment of Hypertension: Matters at Heart," *Dialogues in Cardiovascular Medicine* 12, no. 2 (2007): 133–35. Roosevelt's health in his final months is ably explored in Lelyveld, *His Final Battle*.

2. On the war developments in these months, see, e.g., Beevor, *Second World War*, 586–727; and Davies, *No Simple Victory*, 116–27.

3. Plokhy, *Yalta*; Costigliola, *Roosevelt's Lost Alliances*, 232–53; Preston, *Eight Days*.

4. Perlmutter, *FDR and Stalin*; Adam Ulam, "Forty Years After Yalta: Stalin Outwitted FDR and the West Still Pays," *New Republic*, February 11, 1985.

5. See Dallek, *Franklin Roosevelt*, 541; Woolner, *Last Hundred Days*.

6. Burns, *Crosswinds of Freedom*, 212–17; Kimball, *Juggler*. FDR's strategic brilliance is a

theme of Hamilton's three-volume study of his role as commander in chief. See also Gaddis, *On Grand Strategy*, 280–88.

7. Leuchtenburg, *Shadow of FDR*.

8. Berlin, *Personal Impressions*, 31.

9. Gerhard Weinberg, a leading historian of the war, rejects this criticism. He notes that the U.S. "accepted about twice as many Jewish refugees as the rest of the world put together: about 200,000 out of 300,000." He then asks readers to consider "how many Jews would have survived had the war ended even a week or ten days earlier—and, conversely, how many more would have died had the war lasted an additional week or ten days." That latter number, Weinberg concludes, would be larger than the total number of Jews saved by the various rescue efforts of 1944–45. Gerhard Weinberg, "The Allies and the Holocaust," in *The Bombing of Auschwitz: Should the Allies Have Attempted It?*, ed. Michael J. Neufeld and Michael Berenbaum (New York: St. Martin's, 2000), 15–26.

10. Quoted in Manchester, *Glory and the Dream*, 353–54.

11. Halberstam, *Coldest Winter*, 172; Greenberg, *Republic of Spin*, chaps. 20 and 39.

12. JPK to KK, May 1, 1945, quoted in Smith, *Hostage to Fortune*, 615–18; Nasaw, *Patriarch*, 579; Whalen, *Founding Father*, 365. To Harry Truman, Kennedy was more pungent, at least according to Truman's much later recollection. "Harry, what the hell are you doing campaigning for that crippled son of a bitch that killed my son Joe?" Kennedy reportedly asked him in Boston in the early fall of 1944, a few weeks after Joe Junior's death. Miller, *Plain Speaking*, 199.

13. JPK to KK, May 1, 1945, printed in Smith, *Hostage to Fortune*, 615–18.

14. Roberts, *Twentieth Century*, 428.

15. Hamilton, *JFK: Reckless Youth*, 684; Blair and Blair, *Search for JFK*, 419–20.

16. JFK to KLB, February 20, 1945, quoted in Hamilton, *JFK: Reckless Youth*, 683.

17. An excellent history of the conference is Schlesinger, *Act of Creation*.

18. His father, after commending him on his articles, offered a suggestion: "I think you ought to consider from now on whether you want to write under the name of Jack Kennedy rather than John F. You are known as Jack everywhere, and I think it would be well to consider this." JPK to JFK, JPKP, May 21, 1945, box 3, JPKP.

19. "Kennedy Tells Parley Trends." *Chicago Herald-American*, April 28, 1945, box 23, JPKP; Blair and Blair, *Search for JFK*, 428. For his handwritten notes during the conference, including regarding veterans' views, see the loose notebook pages in box SF64, JKOP.

20. On Bretton Woods and its implications, see Steil, *Battle of Bretton*; Rauchway, *Money Makers*; Helleiner, *Forgotten Foundations*. On the worsening Soviet-American tensions in the first half of 1945, see Dobbs, *Six Months*.

21. "Yank-Russo Test Seen at Frisco," *Chicago Herald-American*, April 30, 1945, box 23, JPKP; "World Court Real Test for Envoys," *New York Journal-American*, May 2, 1945, box 23, JPKP.

22. As A. J. P. Taylor would put it: "In short, the British and Americans sat back, though not of malice aforethought, while the Russians defeated Germany for them. Of the three great men at the top, Roosevelt was the only one who knew what he was doing: he made the United States the greatest power in the world at virtually no cost." Taylor, *English History*, 577. I thank Jane Perlez for supplying me with this citation.

23. "Peace in Europe Spurs Parley," *New York Journal-American*, May 9, 1945; "Big Three Friction Menaces Peace," *New York Journal-American*, May 18, 1945. Both articles, as well as others Jack wrote that spring and summer, can be found in box 23, JPKP.

24. "Allied Parley Dismays Vets," *New York Journal-American*, May 7, 1945.

25. JFK to "Jim," box SG64, JKOP.

26. "Kennedy Tells Parley Trends," *Chicago Herald-American,* April 28, 1945; "Allied Parley Dismays Vets," *New York Journal-American,* May 7, 1945; "Small Nations Hit Big 5 Veto Rule," *New York Journal-American,* May 23, 1945.

27. Loose pages, in box SG64, JKOP.

28. Krock, *Memoirs,* 351.

29. Parmet, *Jack,* 133.

30. Blair and Blair, *Search for JFK,* 423–24.

31. On the liberation of Europe and its aftermath, see Hitchcock, *Bitter Road to Freedom.*

32. Churchill's private secretary noted in his diary on July 4 that even Labour leader Clement Atlee predicted a Tory majority of 30. Sandford, *Union Jack,* 87. On the difficult conditions in Britain, see Kynaston, *Austerity Britain,* chaps. 1–4.

33. "Churchill May Lose Election," *New York Journal-American,* June 24, 1945.

34. Leaming, *Jack Kennedy: Education,* 176; Blair and Blair, *Search for JFK,* 382. Fraser told a later interviewer, "Jack was a great listener—and a great questioner. He wanted to know the root cause of things. He was much more serious than he gave on." Hugh Fraser OH, JFKL.

35. Forbes lost to an Oxford-educated Tory bearing the name Sir Hugh Vere Huntly Duff Munro-Lucas-Tooth of Teanich, or, for short, Hugh Lucas-Tooth.

36. Alastair Forbes OH, JFKL; Hamilton, *JFK: Reckless Youth,* 709.

37. Barbara Ward OH, JFKL.

38. Sandford, *Union Jack,* 94.

39. *New York Journal-American,* July 10, 1945; diary entry, July 3, 1945, printed in *Prelude to Leadership,* 23–24.

40. Diary entry, June 21, 1945, printed in *Prelude to Leadership,* 9–10.

41. Diary entry, July 27, 1945, printed in *Prelude to Leadership,* 37–38.

42. Diary entry, June 29, 1945, printed in *Prelude to Leadership,* 11–14; diary entry, June 30, 1945, printed in *Prelude to Leadership,* 15–17.

43. "We Are a Republic," *New York Journal-American,* July 29, 1945, box 23, JPKP.

44. Diary entry, July 24, 1945, printed in Smith, *Hostage to Fortune,* 621.

45. An excellent biography is Hoopes and Brinkley, *Driven Patriot.*

46. Diary entry, n.d., printed in *Prelude to Leadership,* 49–50.

47. Diary entry, July 29, 1945, printed in *Prelude to Leadership,* 44.

48. Diary entry, July 29, 1945, printed in *Prelude to Leadership,* 46–47; diary entry, July 10, 1945, printed in *Prelude to Leadership,* 5–8.

49. Diary entry, July 28, 1945, printed in *Prelude to Leadership,* 41–42; diary entry, n.d., printed in *Prelude to Leadership,* 59; Diary entry, August 1, 1945, printed in *Prelude to Leadership,* 74.

50. Baime, *Accidental President.*

51. Diary entry, August 1, 1945, printed in *Prelude to Leadership,* 71–74; diary entry, June 30, 1945, printed in *Prelude to Leadership,* 15–17.

52. Blair and Blair, *Search for JFK,* 439; Seymour St. John, "Frankfurt, Germany, 1945," n.d., CSA. According to St. John, he and Jack proceeded to have lunch together at the officers' mess, whereupon they drove around the devastated city. "Jack was easy, alert, and interested, but he took no notes. I suspected that he was awaiting more sensational material from a more sensational source."

53. Neiberg, *Potsdam.*

54. Sexton, *Nation Forged,* 166, 169; Leffler, *Preponderance,* 5; Vine, *Base Nation,* 17–44. On the emergence and nature of the hegemonic U.S. position in the 1940s, see also Daniel J. Sargent, "Pax Americana: Sketches for an Undiplomatic History," *Diplomatic History* 42, no. 3 (2018): 357–76.

55. Sorensen, *Kennedy*, 15–16.
56. JFK to Harold L. Tinker, February 9, 1945, quoted in Sandford, *Union Jack*, 84.
57. United War Fund speech, October 8, 1945, box 28, DFPP.
58. James Forrestal to JFK, September 8, 1945, box 73, JFK Pre-Pres. On the end of the Pacific war, see Hasegawa, *Racing the Enemy;* and Frank, *Downfall.*

CHAPTER 15: THE CANDIDATE

1. On what Joe Kennedy may or may not have done on Curley's behalf, see, e.g., Nasaw, *Patriarch*, 593; Beatty, *Rascal King,* 456; Farrell, *Tip O'Neill,* 91. An alternative theory is that Curley decided on his own to give up his House seat and seek the mayoralty, and Joe Kennedy's money merely greased the subsequent victory.
2. As it happened, Massachusetts had no law that said a congressional representative must live in his or her district. Curley lived in Jamaica Plain, on the other side of Boston.
3. Charles Bartlett OH, JFKL.
4. Diary entry, January 27, 1946, printed in *Prelude to Leadership,* 79–83. Emphasis in the original.
5. A folder with requests for copies of the speech, titled "England, Germany, Ireland," and delivered on September 11, 1945, is in box 11A, JFKPP.
6. McNamara, *Eunice,* 83. Longtime aide Mark Dalton said of Kennedy as an orator during this first campaign, "The interesting thing about it was I discovered that he was extremely bright, and that in the back and forth of debate and repartee, like in the press conferences, he was excellent, but as an orator he did not have it." Mark Dalton interview, WGBH May 13, 1991.
7. Dallek, *Unfinished Life,* 124; O'Neill, *Man of the House,* 85.
8. O'Donnell and Powers, *"Johnny,"* 56.
9. Quoted in Blair and Blair, *Search for JFK,* 499.
10. Tony Galluccio OH, JFKL; Samuel Bornstein OH, JFKL. Powers: "After I worked with him for a week, I knew the secret if you were trying to explain his success was in two sentences: To meet him was to like him. And to know him was to want to help. These people, they looked at this man and they liked him right off." David Powers extended OH, box 9, DFPP.
11. Quoted in Goodwin, *Fitzgeralds and the Kennedys,* 708; Powers extended OH, box 9, DFPP.
12. Tony Galluccio OH, JFKL.
13. Thomas Broderick OH, JFKL. Billy Sutton, who often guided Jack around the district and spent more time with him than anyone else, noticed the same thing: "Well the campaign actually began early in the morning. He—for a fellow who was supposed to be injured during the war, he really wore me out." Billy Sutton OH, JFKL.
14. Manchester, *One Brief Shining Moment,* 36–37.
15. Peter Cloherty OH, JFKL.
16. George Taylor OH, JFKL.
17. Burns, *John Kennedy,* 66.
18. Joe DeGuglielmo OH, JFKL. John Droney, an attorney who assisted with the campaign, remembered, "I think the first time he ever made a speech in Cambridge was at the Kiwanis Club—it was only about a week after I met him. I noticed that all the waitresses waited to get his autograph, and I had never seen that before. He spoke on his war experiences. He spoke for about forty minutes; you could hear a pin drop. They waited after they were through work to see him and talk with him. And I think that that was the tipoff." John Droney OH, JFKL.
19. Goodwin, *Fitzgeralds and the Kennedys,* 712; O'Donnell and Powers, *"Johnny,"* 54–55. In an interview, Powers discussed how women reacted when he and Jack knocked on

triple-decker doors in Charlestown: " 'Oh he looks like such a fine boy—c'mon in, c'mon in.' And some of them wanted to fatten him up right away. They thought he looked too thin for a candidate. And our trouble was that they loved him so much that we were spending a little too much time in each house. They'd say, 'Oh now, why don't you have a cup of tea, a cup of coffee, or a glass of milk,' [and] in some places it'd be the Sullivans on the first floor and the Murphys on the second floor and the Dohertys on the top floor. And the next house would be almost the same and after a while he'd say, 'I feel like I was here before,' because they all treated him the same way and they all looked alike." Powers extended OH, box 9, DFPP.

20. Pitts, *Jack and Lem,* 98; Press release on John F. Kennedy's war record, June 1, 1946, box 28, DFPP; O'Donnell and Powers, *"Johnny,"* 50; Blair and Blair, *Search for JFK,* 540.

21. The two Russos apparently had faced off before, in a campaign in which there was also a *third* Joseph Russo. The City Council Russo had taken to telling voters, "Vote for the one in the middle." O'Donnell and Powers, *"Johnny,"* 62. And there were numerous instances in Boston politics of namesakes capitalizing on a famous name. In the 1950s, John F. Kennedy, a shop foreman in the Gillette razor factory in South Boston, twice won election as state treasurer simply by putting his name on the ballot, with no party support or campaigning. O'Donnell and Powers, *"Johnny,"* 62.

22. Mark Dalton OH, JFKL; Whalen, *Founding Father,* 399. The actual financial records from the campaign do not seem to survive.

23. Dalton OH, JFKL.

24. In the words of reporter and family friend Samuel Bornstein, "His father was in on every campaign and he planned a lot of things, but as far as I could determine, when you come right down to something specific, Jack Kennedy made the final decision." Samuel Bornstein OH, JFKL.

25. See O'Donnell and Powers, *"Johnny,"* chap. 2.

26. Dalton OH; McNamara, *Eunice,* 84.

27. Whalen, *Founding Father,* 401; Goodwin, *Fitzgeralds and the Kennedys,* 719.

28. Burns, *John Kennedy,* 68.

29. *Boston Herald,* June 19, 1946.

30. Quoted in Leamer, *Kennedy Men,* 237.

31. *Boston Traveler,* June 23, 1946; Hamilton, *JFK: Reckless Youth,* 770–71.

32. KK to JFK, July 13, 1946, box 4A, JFKPP.

33. Manchester, *Glory and the Dream,* 289.

34. William E. Leuchtenburg, "New Faces of 1946," *Smithsonian Magazine,* November 2006. A penetrating account of America in the year 1946 is Weisbrode, *Year of Indecision.*

35. Leuchtenburg, "New Faces"; Lichtenstein, *State of the Union,* chap. 3.

36. Patterson, *Grand Expectations,* 14.

37. Campaign speech, n.d., box 96, JFKPP.

38. According to Ted Kennedy (relying on sister Patricia's diary), Churchill stayed with the Kennedys in the Palm Beach house during his Florida visit. Kennedy, *True Compass,* 27–28. On the "long telegram," see Gaddis, *Strategies of Containment,* 18–22; and Craig and Logevall, *America's Cold War,* 69–73.

39. Harry S. Truman to Bess Truman, September 20, 1946, Family, Business, and Personal Affairs Papers, Family Correspondence File, Harry S. Truman Library.

40. Radio Speech on Russia, box 94, JFK Pre-Pres.

41. Independence Day Oration, July 4, 1946, box 94, JFK Pre-Pres.

42. Young Democrats of Pennsylvania speech, August 21, 1946, box 94, JFK Pre-Pres; Choate speech, September 27, 1946, box 94, JFK Pre-Pres; Seymour St. John, "September 28, 1946," CSA.

43. Tierney, *Self Portrait*, 141–42; Vogel, *Gene Tierney*, 101–10.
44. Tierney, *Self Portrait*, 143.
45. Tierney, *Self Portrait*, 152.
46. Blair and Blair, *Search for JFK*, 550; Hamilton, *JFK: Reckless Youth*, 778.
47. Blair and Blair, *Search for JFK*, 549; Tierney, *Self Portrait*, 147.
48. Blair and Blair, *Search for JFK*, 550–51.
49. Hamilton, *JFK: Reckless Youth*, 779–80.
50. Swope to JFK, November 6, 1946, box 5, JFKPP.

CHAPTER 16: THE GENTLEMAN FROM BOSTON

1. Arthur Krock OH, JFKL; Burns, *John Kennedy*, 71.
2. Morrow, *Best Years*, 182; Billy Sutton interview, WGBH, May 1991; Blair and Blair, *Search for JFK*, 587; McNamara, *Eunice*, 100.
3. Quoted in Blair and Blair, *Search for JFK*, 588–89.
4. Sandford, *Union Jack*, 89; Martin, *Hero for Our Time*, 49. The continuing romance with Tierney was reported on the gossip page of the New York *Daily News*, August 18, 1947. Ironically, the Tierney film then in American theaters was *The Ghost and Mrs. Muir*, about an impossible love affair.
5. Florence Pritchett to JFK, June 5, 1946, box 4B, JFKPP.
6. C. McLaughlin interview, CBP.
7. Martin, *Hero for Our Time*, 49–50.
8. Quoted in Blair and Blair, *Search for JFK*, 594.
9. Goodwin, *Fitzgeralds and Kennedys*, 722; Stossel, *Sarge*, 96.
10. Blair and Blair, *Search for JFK*, 593, 597; McNamara, *Eunice*, 100.
11. McNamara, *Eunice*, 102; Stossel, *Sarge*, 99. Joe Kennedy's real estate holdings included several large office buildings on Park Avenue in New York City as well as the gigantic Merchandise Mart in Chicago, which he bought in 1945 from the Marshall Field interests for an estimated $20 million and was second in size only to the Pentagon among the world's largest buildings.
12. Quoted in Stossel, *Sarge*, 100.
13. McNamara, *Eunice*, 102; Eunice Kennedy Shriver interview, CBP.
14. Krock OH, JFKL; JFK interview by James MacGregor Burns, March 22, 1959, quoted in Dallek, *Unfinished Life*, 136.
15. Sutton interview, CBP; Blair and Blair, *Search for JFK*, 582–83.
16. Quoted in Shaw, *JFK in the Senate*, 19.
17. John F. Kennedy, *John Fitzgerald Kennedy: A Compilation of Statements and Speeches Made During His Service in the United States Senate and House of Representatives* (Washington, DC: Government Printing Office, 1964), 10–11.
18. Burns, *John Kennedy*, 79; O'Brien, *John F. Kennedy*, 218.
19. Commenting on the episode, aide Mark Dalton said, "Jack was fearless. He would listen to you, and if he decided you were right, he would go with you. Everybody wanted him to sign the Curley petition." Dalton interview with Laurence Leamer, quoted in Leamer, *Kennedy Men*, 247.
20. Meyers, *As We Remember Him*, 50.
21. Quoted in Matthews, *Jack Kennedy*, 94. See also Frank, *Ike and Dick*, 200.
22. *McKeesport Daily News*, April 25, 1947. Fifteen years later, on October 13, 1962, President John F. Kennedy returned to McKeesport, mere days before the onset of the Cuban Missile Crisis. His remarks on that occasion began as follows: "The first time I came to this city was in 1947, when Mr. Richard Nixon and I engaged in our first debate. He won that one, and we went on to other things. We came here on that occasion to debate the

Taft-Hartley law, which he was for and which I was against. Since 1947, which was the first year of the 80th Congress, I have had an opportunity to examine with some care and some interest the record of the Republican Party, and I can tell you, in case you don't know it, that it is opposed, year in, year out, in the administration of Harry Truman in 1947, in the administration of Franklin Roosevelt in the 1930's, in the administration—in my administration." Remarks at City Hall, McKeesport, Pennsylvania, October 13, 1962, American Presidency Project, www.presidency.ucsb.edu/ws/index .php?pid=8951.

23. Stokes, *Capitol Limited.*

24. Nixon, *RN*, 42–43; Thomas, *Being Nixon*, 40; Farrell, *Richard Nixon*, 84. A more detailed account is in Matthews, *Kennedy and Nixon*, chap. 2.

25. William O. Douglas OH, JFKL; O'Neill, *Man of the House*, 85.

26. *Washington Star*, July 29, 1947, as cited in Perrett, *Jack*, 145. At the start of the year, Jack had been named one of the "nation's 10 outstanding young men of the year" by the U.S. Junior Chamber of Commerce. Others making the list included historian Arthur M. Schlesinger Jr., age thirty, who had won the Pulitzer Prize the previous year for his *Age of Jackson;* and Joe Louis, who, at age thirty-three, had been the heavyweight boxing champion for a decade. *Boston Herald*, January 20, 1947.

27. Craig and Logevall, *America's Cold War*, 76–80.

28. Nasaw, *Patriarch*, 607–8.

29. Craig and Logevall, *America's Cold War*, 82–83; *BP*, April 23, 1947, quoted in Perrett, *Jack*, 144.

30. On the Marshall Plan and its legacy, see Steil, *Marshall Plan*. That same June, Jack was elected a director at large of the Harvard Alumni Association. *New York Herald Tribune*, June 6, 1947.

31. Fredrik Logevall, "Bernath Lecture: A Critique of Containment," *Diplomatic History* 28, no. 4 (September 2004): 473–99. An important work, depicting a flexible Stalin open to a political settlement, is Naimark, *Stalin and the Fate*.

32. JPK to T. J. White, October 9, 1947, printed in Smith, *Hostage to Fortune*, 634. To his daughter Kick, Joe was equally gloomy. Truman's popularity had peaked and was sliding fast, he told her, and the U.S. economic outlook was poor. "We can produce so much more in this country than we can consume and there is no way that we can dispose of that surplus if all the world is going to be Communist dominated." JPK to KK, June 10, 1947, box 3, JPKP.

33. Parmet, *Jack*, 177–78; U.S. Congress, House, *Hearings*, 80th Cong., 1st sess., Vol. 1, 3585.

34. Anthony Eden to KK, January 10, 1948, quoted in Goodwin, *Fitzgeralds and the Kennedys*, 730; KK to JPK, September 4, 1947, box 21, JPKP; KK to JPK, September 18, 1947, box 21, JPKP. On Kick's relationship with Eden, see Leaming, *Kick*, 233–35.

35. JFK to James MacGregor Burns, August 25, 1959, box 129, JFKPOF, JFKL; Tubridy, *JFK in Ireland*, 30–31.

36. Byrne, *Kick*, 273–74; McTaggart, *Kathleen Kennedy*, 219.

37. Blair and Blair, *Search for JFK*, 640–41.

38. Barbara Ward OH, JFKL; Perrett, *Jack*, 147.

39. *BP*, February 1, 1948.

40. Leaming, *Jack Kennedy: Education*, 192.

41. Bailey, *Black Diamonds*, 420–25.

42. Sutton interview, WGBH; *BG*, May 14, 1948; Goodwin, *Fitzgeralds and the Kennedys*, 738–39. Sutton recalled the scene: "So they said, 'Well, we have no confirmation right now, but we'll call you back.' So he continued to talk about Ella Logan, what a great

voice. Then when the news came that the fatal accident happened, he, you know, his eyes filled up with tears. And, you know, when they say that the Kennedys never cry, don't believe that. They do. I saw him."

43. Leaming, *Jack Kennedy: Education*, 193; Alastair Forbes OH, JFKL.

44. KLB OH, JFKL; O'Brien, *John F. Kennedy*, 228; Burns, *John Kennedy*, 54. Among the letters of condolence that Jack received was a touching one from his future Senate opponent, Henry Cabot Lodge. See Lodge to JFK, May 14, 1948, reel 8, HCLP II.

45. Collier and Horowitz, *Kennedys*, 171–72.

46. Collier and Horowitz, *Kennedys*, 172; Leaming, *Jack Kennedy: Education*, 203.

47. Blair and Blair, *Search for JFK*, 624. Now and then, he'd also come up during the week. In 1947 he made a guest appearance in his former professor Arthur Holcombe's graduate seminar on American politics, and enjoyed the experience so much that it became an annual thing—he would come back to Harvard every year until he entered the White House. On another occasion he debated socialist leader Norman Thomas at Harvard Law School, on the question "How Far Should Our Government Go in Regulating Our Economy?" Thomas was known far and wide as a skilled debater, but according to observers Kennedy held his own. *THC*, March 19, 1949; Dalton interview, WGBH.

48. Blair and Blair, *Search for JFK*, 625. In the Boston press, too, there occurred much speculation in the fall of 1947 about a possible gubernatorial run the following year. See, e.g., *Boston American*, October 19, 1947; and *Boston Herald*, November 23, 1947. In June 1948 the rumors began anew.

49. Manchester, *Portrait of a President*, 189–90; O'Brien, *John F. Kennedy*, 364.

50. Bryant, *Bystander*, 25–26.

51. Asch and Musgrove, *Chocolate City*, chap. 10; Levingston, *Kennedy and King*, 11.

52. Bryant, *Bystander*, 27–28.

53. *Washington Daily News*, March 6, 1949; Bryant, *Bystander*, 28–29.

54. JFK to Stuart Symington, August 13, 1948, box 8, JFKPP.

55. Leaming, *Jack Kennedy: Education*, 197–98; Churchill; *Gathering Storm*.

56. Sandford, *Union Jack*, 127.

57. Craig and Logevall, *America's Cold War*, 91–95; Hitchcock, *Struggle*, 93–96.

58. Craig and Logevall, *America's Cold War*, 98–99; Kamensky et al., *People and a Nation*, 705.

59. Burns, *John Kennedy*, 93.

60. Quoted in Burns, *John Kennedy*, 80.

61. Speech transcript, January 30, 1949, box 95, JFK Pre-Pres. The speech was inserted into the *Congressional Record* on February 21, 1949. See also JFK, *Statements and Speeches*, 971–72; Shaw, *JFK in the Senate*, 25.

62. Goodwin, *Fitzgeralds and the Kennedys*, 745.

CHAPTER 17: RED SCARE

1. Only in the United States, among the Western powers, Eric Hobsbawm has written, was the "communist world conspiracy" a major aspect of domestic politics. Hobsbawm, *Age of Extremes*, 234, 236–37. On this point, see also Sam Tanenhaus, "The Red Scare," *New York Review of Books*, January 14, 1999.

2. Logevall, "Critique of Containment"; Storrs, *Second Red Scare*; Patterson, *Grand Expectations*, 204.

3. Oshinsky, *Conspiracy So Immense*, 49; Patterson, *Mr. Republican*, 446–47; Anthony Badger, "Republican Rule in the 80th Congress," in McSweeney and Owens, eds., *Republican Takeover*, 168.

4. Halberstam, *Best and the Brightest*, 108–9. See also Freeland, *Truman Doctrine*.

5. Halberstam, *Coldest Winter*, 173–74.

6. Halberstam, *Coldest Winter*, 212–13; Karabell, *Last Campaign*; McCullough, *Truman*, 710–19.

7. Taft quoted in Halberstam, *Fifties*, 57.

8. Acheson, *Present at the Creation*, 355–56; Halberstam, *Fifties*, 66.

9. Gaddis, *Strategies*, 87–106; Thompson, *Hawk and Dove*, chaps. 6, 7; May, *American Cold War Strategy*.

10. Thomas and Isaacson, *Wise Men*, 547. On Acheson, a standard biography is Beisner, *Dean Acheson*. But see also Hopkins, *Dean Acheson*; and Smith, *Dean Acheson*.

11. Tanenhaus, *Whittaker Chambers*, 224ff; Ambrose, *Nixon*, 205–6; Greenberg, *Nixon's Shadow*, 28–29. On the question of Hiss's guilt, see also Weinstein, *Perjury*; and White, *Alger Hiss's Looking-Glass Wars*.

12. McClellan, *Dean Acheson*, 221; Goldman, *Crucial Decade*, 134–35.

13. Quoted in Patterson, *Grand Expectations*, 195.

14. Two excellent biographies are Oshinsky, *Conspiracy So Immense*; and Tye, *Demagogue*. Though a draft of the Wheeling speech survives, it is not known whether McCarthy gave precisely this version, as there exists no record of the Wheeling speech. See also Doherty, *Cold War, Cool Medium*, 14.

15. Reedy quoted in Bayley, *Joe McCarthy and the Press*, 68. See also Schrecker, *Many Are the Crimes*, 242.

16. In Peter Viereck's marvelous words, "McCarthyism is the revenge of the noses that for twenty years of fancy parties were pressed against the outside window pane." Bell, *Radical Right*, 163. I thank David Greenberg for drawing this quote to my attention. See also Hofstadter, *Anti-Intellectualism*.

17. Richard Rovere's assessment from more than six decades ago retains power: McCarthy, he wrote, was "a great sophisticate in human relationships, as every demagogue must be. He knew a good deal about people's fears and anxieties, and he was a superb juggler of them. But he was himself numb to the sensation he produced in others. He could not comprehend true outrage, true indignation, true anything." Rovere, *Senator Joe McCarthy*, 60.

18. Oshinsky, *Conspiracy So Immense*, 185–90.

19. Bayley, *Joe McCarthy and the Press*, 68.

20. Halberstam, *Fifties*, 55.

21. The literature is large. See, e.g., Wells, *Fearing the Worst*; Cumings, *Korean War*; Stueck, *Rethinking*; Halberstam, *Coldest Winter*; Chen Jian, "Far Short of a Glorious Victory: Revisiting China's Changing Strategies to Manage the Korean War," *Chinese Historical Review* 25 (Spring 2018): 1–22.

22. Fried, *Men Against McCarthy*, 53–58; Barnet, *Rockets' Red Glare*, 309; Patterson, *Mr. Republican*, 445–46; Burns, *Crosswinds of Freedom*, 245.

23. The text of Smith's speech can be found at Teaching American History, teachingamericanhistory.org/library/document/declaration-of-conscience/, accessed October 27, 2019.

24. Oshinsky, *Conspiracy So Immense*, 163–65. See also Rebecca Onion, "We're Never Going to Get Our 'Have You No Decency?' Moment," *Slate*, July 26, 2018.

25. John P. Mallan, "Massachusetts: Liberal and Corrupt," *New Republic*, October 13, 1952.

26. RK to RFK and Ethel Kennedy, July 13, 1950, printed in Smith, *Hostage to Fortune*, 643–44; Damore, *Cape Cod Years*, 103; Parmet, *Jack*, 173–75.

27. Nasaw, *Patriarch*, 667; *New York Post*, January 9, 1961, quoted in Whalen, *Founding Father*, 427.

28. Halberstam, *Fifties*, 56; Mitchell, *Tricky Dick*, 170; Greenberg, *Nixon's Shadow*, 29–30; Farrell, *Richard Nixon*, 150–55.

29. He won 82.3 percent of the vote, against Republican Vincent J. Celeste's 17.2 percent.

30. Beatty, *Rascal King*, 501–5; Goodwin, *Fitzgeralds and the Kennedys*, 745–46.
31. "There's no question," Ted later wrote of his grandfather, "that I inherited this joy of people from him. I inherited the whole way I approach politics." Kennedy, *True Compass*, 78–79.
32. Kennedy and Billings quoted in Goodwin, *Fitzgeralds and the Kennedys*, 748.
33. Schlesinger, *Thousand Days*, 91; O'Brien, *No Final Victories*, 17.
34. Said Mark Dalton later, "I felt at the time that it would be bad for John to clash with Governor Dever because Dever was very well liked in the Democratic party and I thought that even if John were to defeat him that the wounds would be very great after a campaign like that." Dalton OH, JFKL.
35. Joseph DeGuglielmo OH, JFKL.
36. JPK, University of Virginia Law School Student Forum speech, December 12, 1950, box 256, JPKP. The folder includes the original draft of the speech as well as various research notes.
37. Nasaw, *Patriarch*, 637. "There is indeed a rising tide of isolationism in this country," Lippmann wrote. "It could carry with it a withdrawal that could take us very far, perhaps as far as Mr. Joseph P. Kennedy proposes—that is to say, to the positions we occupied in 1939." *WP*, December 19, 1950.
38. Schlesinger, *Robert Kennedy*, 69–71; Lind, *American Way*, 57.
39. JFK travel journal, box 11, JFKPP. Following the meeting, Jack summarized the discussion in a press conference in Belgrade. See *New York Herald Tribune*, January 26, 1951. See also JFK to JPK and RK, n.d. (January 1951), box 4, JPKP; and the U.S. embassy's summary in Belgrade telegram to DC, January 26, 1951, *FRUS, 1951*, Vol. IV, Part 2: 1701–1702.
40. JFK travel journal, box 11, JFKPP; Perrett, *Jack*, 163.
41. JFK travel journal, box 11, JFKPP; Leamer, *Kennedy Men*, 283.
42. JFK, Nationally Broadcast Speech on Radio Station WOR, February 6, 1951, box 95, JFK Pre-Pres; *New York Herald Tribune*, February 7, 1951. The entire transcript of the speech is in New York *Daily News*, February 7, 1951.
43. JFK testimony before SFRC, February 22, 1951, box 94, JFK Pre-Pres; *BG*, February 23, 1951. Two weeks prior, after Jack's radio address, the *Boston Traveler* had editorialized in favor of his assessment over the "gloomy defeatism" of his father. *Boston Traveler*, February 8, 1951.
44. *Boston's Political Times*, March 17, 1951, cited in Parmet, *Jack*, 220.
45. JFK speech, April 21, 1951, box 95, JFK Pre-Pres.
46. Matthews, *Bobby Kennedy*, 88.
47. When he took a trip to Latin America in late 1946, he annoyed his travel companion Lem Billings by never touching alcohol and showing scant interest in the local nightlife. Schlesinger, *Robert Kennedy*, 65.
48. Emerson Spies to Paul Murphy, June 7, 1948, box 11, JPKP.
49. Thomas, *Robert Kennedy*, 55.
50. Tye, *Bobby Kennedy*, 21–22.
51. Travel Journal Book 2, box 11, JFKL. Subsequent diary entries are from this source.
52. See the astute analysis in Leamer, *Kennedy Men*, 287.
53. Patricia Kennedy to RK, October 13, 1951, box 4, JPKP.
54. Pat, too, remarked on Nehru's penchant for speaking in generalities. "He was so very general or also said 'That is a very difficult question.'" Patricia Kennedy to RK, October 13, 1951, box 4, JPKP. Though Jack's diary speaks sympathetically of Nehru, Bobby's later recollection was that his brother disliked the Indian leader. See Guthman and Shulman, *Robert Kennedy*, 437.

55. He wrote upon his return to the United States: "When I visited a tin mine five miles outside Kuala Lumpur, the capital of Malaya at dusk, with the American manager, we were accompanied by an armoured car and a truck load of Malayan guards." Undated speech fragment (late 1951), box 96, JFK Pre-Pres.
56. JFK to JPK, October 26, 1951, box 4, JPKP.
57. Logevall, *Embers*, xi–xiv.
58. Logevall, *Embers*, xi–xiv.
59. 1951 Trips, Mid and Far East, travel diary, box 24, RFK Pre-Administration Personal Files, JFKL.
60. Jack at this point barely knew Gullion, but that did not keep him from being frank about his plans. As Gullion later related, "I asked him what he was going to do, what his plans were, and he said, 'Oh, I expect to go back and run for governor or for Senator.' . . . If you were out in Indochina and there was this extremely young man before you and he makes a statement of this sort and it certainly makes you think, Well, has he really got it in him. I thought he had great things in him." Edmund Gullion OH, JFKL. See also Topping, *On the Front Lines*, chap. 17.
61. Of the dinner, which had "flags, spotlights, bands," and was attended also by Emperor Bao Dai, Patricia wrote to her mother, "I must say it was most impressive." Patricia Kennedy to RK, October 24, 1951, box 4, JPKP.
62. Speech excerpt, n.d. (early 1952), box 96, JFK Pre-Pres.
63. RFK to JPK, October 24, 1951, box 4, JPKP.
64. It's often claimed that Jack received last rites on Okinawa, but I have found no evidence to that effect.
65. Guthman and Shulman, *Robert Kennedy*, 438.
66. Transcript of MBN radio address, November 14, 1951, box 94, JFK Pre-Pres.
67. Speech transcript, November 19, 1951, box 102, JFK Pre-Pres.
68. *Meet the Press*, December 3, 1951, transcript available at catalog.archives.gov/id/193106. The four panelists were Ernest Lindley, May Craig, James Reston, and Lawrence Spivak. Martha Rountree served as moderator. The twenty-one-minute video of the program, which shows a calmly confident and engaging lawmaker who already knows how to use the new medium of television, could be seen at view.yahoo.com/show/meet-the-presidents/clip/5682840/john-f-kennedy-december-2-1951 as of early 2020.
69. *The Boston Post* praised the performance: "He remained ahead of his questioners throughout the program, showed a balanced viewpoint, ready wit, and a keen sense of fair play." *BP*, December 3, 1951.
70. *BG*, November 20, 1951.
71. Quoted in Schlesinger, *Robert Kennedy*, 93.
72. Oshinsky, *Conspiracy*, 194–202; Patterson, *Grand Expectations*, 198.
73. "Weighed in the Balance," *Time*, October 22, 1951; Brinkley, *The Publisher*, 360–61.
74. Swanberg, *Luce*, 302.
75. Patterson, *Grand Expectations*, 202–3; Kabaservice, *Rule and Ruin*, 10; Hamby, *Man of the People*, 531–32.
76. In a speech before three hundred leaders of the Salvation Army at the end of November, Jack warned that American rearmament needed to be stepped up substantially, and that in Korea in particular the United States needed more airpower. *BP*, November 30, 1951.

CHAPTER 18: TWO BRAHMINS

1. Thomas "Tip" O'Neill OH, TOP.
2. Joseph Healey OH, JFKL; *BG*, April 7, 1952; O'Brien, *John F. Kennedy*, 239; O'Brien, *No Final Victories*, 26.

3. JPK to Cornelius Fitzgerald, October 22, 1951, box 220, JPKP.
4. John F. Royal to JPK, December 4, 1951, box 22, JPKP; JPK to Spivak, January 4, 1952, box 235, JPKP.
5. O'Donnell and Powers, *"Johnny,"* 82.
6. *NYT,* April 7, 1952; *BP,* April 7, 1952.
7. On Lodge and his political persona, see Brown, *Moderates,* 175–201; and Nichter, *Last Brahmin.*
8. Miller, *Henry Cabot Lodge,* 174; Whalen, *Kennedy Versus Lodge,* 49–51; Matthews, *Jack Kennedy,* 125.
9. Schlesinger, *Thousand Days,* 91; Leamer, *Kennedy Men,* 281–82.
10. Quoted in Nasaw, *Patriarch,* 657.
11. Quoted in Schlesinger, *Journals, 1952–2000,* 291. See also Brown, *Moderates,* 192–93; and Nichter, *Last Brahmin.*
12. Burns, *John Kennedy,* 102.
13. David Powers extended OH, box 9, DFPP.
14. O'Brien, *No Final Victories,* 11–14; O'Donnell, *Brotherhood,* 8–9.
15. Much later, this building would serve as the exterior for the hit television series *Cheers.*
16. Martin and Plaut, *Front Runner,* 161.
17. Quoted in Martin and Plaut, *Front Runner,* 176.
18. Shaw, *JFK in the Senate,* 36.
19. O'Donnell in Stein, *American Journey,* 41, quoted in Nasaw, *Patriarch,* 664; O'Donnell, *Irish Brotherhood,* 60–63. Dalton initially took a philosophical view of being shunted aside in favor of Bobby Kennedy: "It probably was a good decision that was made, because I found it very difficult, when I would give a decision, to have other people abide by the decision. But if a Kennedy made the decision, the people in the campaign would abide by it." Dalton OH, JFKL. In his later years, he became more bitter. See his interview with Laurence Leamer, in *Kennedy Men,* 295; and his interview for the PBS program *The Kennedys.* I'm grateful to Elizabeth Deane of WGBH for providing me with this transcript.
20. O'Donnell and Powers, *"Johnny,"* 86.
21. Quoted in Bzdek, *Kennedy Legacy,* 169.
22. Bzdek, *Kennedy Legacy,* 89; Laing, *Robert Kennedy,* 131.
23. Edward J. McCormack OH, JFKL; O'Brien, *Victories,* 27–30; Guthman and Shulman, *Robert Kennedy,* 441–43.
24. Powers extended OH, box 9, DFPP.
25. David Powers OH, JFKL.
26. John T. Burke OH, JFKL; Whalen, *Founding Father,* 423.
27. Bryant, *Bystander,* 34–35.
28. Kennedy speech, "Kennedy fights for civil rights," n.d., box 93, JFK Pre-Pres; Bryant, *Bystander,* 36.
29. Kennedy speech, "Kennedy fights for civil rights," n.d., box 93, JFK Pre-Pres; Bryant, *Bystander,* 36.
30. Powers extended OH, box 9, DFPP; Polly Fitzgerald OH, JFKL.
31. Polly Fitzgerald personal account, box 103, JFK Pre-Pres.
32. Quoted in Martin and Plaut, *Front Runner,* 169–70. See also *Berkshire Eagle,* September 8, 1952.
33. Martin and Plaut, *Front Runner* 168–9; Polly Fitzgerald OH, JFKL.
34. Parmet, *Jack,* 253; Martin and Plaut, *Front Runner,* 178. Lodge said in another interview, "I remember thinking at the time—and I think I probably said it—that we have a two-party system in America, that it was a good thing when the parties put up men of quality, that I realized that, of course, I was going to have an opponent, and that it was

in the public interest for him to be a fine man, as John Fitzgerald Kennedy was." Henry Cabot Lodge Jr. OH, JFKL.

35. Cabell Phillips, "Case History of a Senate Race," *New York Times Magazine,* October 26, 1952; Burns, *John Kennedy,* 113–14.

36. McCarthy, *Remarkable Kennedys,* 135; Collier and Horowitz, *Kennedys,* 162.

37. Whalen, *Kennedy Versus Lodge,* 83; Bryant, *Bystander,* 39–40. Columnist Joe Alsop said: "Well, what impressed me most was all the [Kennedy] girls. They were exactly like an old-fashioned, burlesque pony ballet, wonderfully good-looking girls, with their great long legs and great manes of hair, attacking the voters sort of en masse. It was an extraordinary performance, I'd never seen anything like it before in any campaign." Alsop OH, JFKL.

38. O'Brien, *No Final Victories,* 31–32.

39. Frank Morrissey OH, JFKL.

40. Martin and Plaut, *Front Runner,* 180.

41. Whalen, *Founding Father,* 424; Shaw, *JFK in the Senate,* 34; Savage, *Senator from New England,* 17–18.

42. An excellent biography is Patterson, *Mr. Republican.* A brief and incisive treatment is in Farber, *Rise and Fall,* chap. 1.

43. As early as July 1951, however, Joe Kennedy could write to Jack: "[Arthur] Krock also told me very confidentially that Chris Herter had a confidential talk with Eisenhower and that Eisenhower is definitely a candidate and wants the Republican nomination." JPK to JFK, July 13, 1951, box 4, JPKP.

44. On the GOP nomination fight, see, e.g., Hitchcock, *Age of Eisenhower,* chaps. 3–4; and Patterson, *Mr. Republican,* 509–34.

45. On the selection of Nixon, and Eisenhower's ambivalence, see Frank, *Ike and Dick,* 33–37.

46. Stevenson refused to strike back at these and other GOP attacks. In a speech before the American Legion on "The Nature of Patriotism," he said, "The tragedy of our day is the climate of fear in which we live, and fear breeds repression. Too often sinister threats to the Bill of Rights, to freedom of the mind, are concealed under the patriotic cloak of anti-Communism."

47. See Lodge, *Storm Has Many Eyes,* chap. 3.

48. Whalen, *Founding Father,* 425.

49. *Boston Herald,* August 23, 1952.

50. *Boston Herald,* September 9, 1952.

51. Ruth Karp to Francis Morrissey, September 5, 1952, box 102, JFK Pre-Pres; *BG,* September 17, 1952; *Waltham News Tribune,* September 17, 1952; Miller, *Henry Cabot Lodge,* 253. "Few Differences Bared in Kennedy-Lodge Debate," read the *Globe* headline. According to the accompanying article, the debate was delayed by thirty-five minutes as Kennedy supporters protested plans to make a wire recording of the debate for local broadcast, and distribution of a pro-Lodge pamphlet. Kennedy put the matter to rest when he allowed the recording.

52. Norris, *Mary McGrory,* 27–28; *BG,* September 17, 1952.

53. It is perhaps noteworthy that Jack himself wrote his substantial opening statement for the debate, judging by the handwritten version to be found in his papers, and that he focused substantially on foreign policy. See box 94, JFK Pre-Pres.

54. Whalen, *Kennedy Versus Lodge,* 89.

55. On a typical late-campaign day, October 21, Kennedy toured Fall River and its factories in the morning, and Taunton and its factories in the afternoon. That evening he appeared in a televised American Federation of Labor panel discussion, then hustled to

evening rallies in Brockton, Randolph, and Taunton. Campaign press release, October 21, 1952, box 25, DFPP.

56. Powers extended OH, box 9, DFPP.

57. *Time*, July 19, 1954.

58. Quoted in Wicker, *Shooting Star*, 110. See also Frank, *Ike and Dick*, 74–75.

59. *BG*, September 10, 1962; Whalen, *Kennedy Versus Lodge*, 145.

60. "Information from Sargent Shriver," September 19, 1952, box 47, AES; Stossel, *Sarge*, 109.

61. Collier and Horowitz, *Kennedys*, 187.

62. Phil David Fine OH, JFKL; Leamer, *Kennedy Men*, 303.

63. Fine OH, JFKL; Hirsch Freed OH, JFKL; Whalen, *Founding Father*, 426; Kessler, *Sins of the Father*, 337.

64. Whalen, *Founding Father*, 427–28. For JFK's denial, see his letter to Westbrook Pegler in 1958, quoted in Oshinsky, *Conspiracy So Immense*, 241. See also Pegler's harshly anti-Lodge column in the *New York Journal-American*, October 16, 1952. "This is the McCarthy bandwagon," Pegler wrote. "It is the best bandwagon in the whole campaign. Anyone who wants a ride ought to be man enough to ask Joe publicly." For the possibility that Kennedy over time may have sent much more money to McCarthy, see Tye, *Demagogue*, chap. 4. The amount cannot be known, since public reporting was not required in the period.

65. Nasaw, *Patriarch*, 668; Oshinsky, *Conspiracy So Immense*, 241.

66. An internal Lodge poll in September showed that Kennedy had made worryingly large gains in Boston. Lodge had carried the city by twenty thousand votes in 1946, but he was now projected to lose it by ninety thousand votes. Upper-income voters who generally leaned Republican were moving to Kennedy, an analyst noted. "PMS Analysis of Poll," September 5, 1952, reel 18, HCLP II.

67. *BG*, October 3, 1952, and October 23, 1952. The Lodge campaign prepared a tabulation of the two men's voting records in 1947 to 1952; it showed Kennedy with 179 votes "absent and not recorded" and Lodge with 58. "Absent and Not Recorded—The Kennedy-Lodge Record, 1947–1952," u.d. (fall 1952), reel 18, HCLP II.

68. Quoted in Greenberg, *Republic of Spin*, 281.

69. *BP*, October 25, 1952; Shaw, *JFK in the Senate*, 43–44; Whalen, *Founding Father*, 430–31. A later pro-Kennedy editorial in the *Post*, dated November 3, the day before the deadline, was titled "Jack Kennedy: All Man—100 % American."

70. O'Donnell transcripts re. Lodge, box 9, DFPP; Charles Worden to Lodge, November 8, 1952, quoted in Whalen, *Kennedy Versus Lodge*, 151.

71. Macdonald OH, JFKL; RK, *Times to Remember*, 327; O'Brien, *No Final Victories*, 36.

72. O'Donnell transcripts re. Lodge, box 9, DFPP.

73. Matthews, *Jack Kennedy*, 145.

74. O'Donnell, *Brotherhood*, 82.

75. Kenneth O'Donnell transcripts re. Lodge, box 9, DFPP.

76. See Robert Kennedy's recollection in Meyers, *As We Remember Him*, 59.

77. Whalen, *Kennedy Versus Lodge*, 157.

78. "Congressman John F. Kennedy gained more prestige by defeating Senator Henry Cabot Lodge last election day than any other winner in the entire country, with the one exception of President-Elect Eisenhower," wrote columnist Clem Norton. *Lynn Telegram-News*, November 16, 1952.

79. O'Donnell transcripts re. Lodge, box 9, DFPP; *Lynn Telegram-News*, November 16, 1952. For a Lodge adviser's post-election assessment, which listed several of these factors in explaining the outcome, see Sears to Shea, December 8, 1953, reel 8, HCLP II.

80. Schlesinger, *Robert Kennedy*, 96–98. Lodge himself placed primary blame for his defeat on fellow Republicans: "Lodge blamed Republicans, not JFK's early start: 'I have a view which I think I can substantiate. What lost me that election were the Republicans who were angry at me because of the defeat of Senator Robert A. Taft at the Convention.' " Lodge OH, JFKL.
81. O'Brien, *No Final Victories*, 27.
82. *SEP,* June 13, 1953.
83. O'Brien, *No Final Victories*, 31.
84. Comparing the rival campaigns' expenditures is not easy, but according to *The New York Times* they were not that far apart, at least in the final two months: "Each has large headquarters establishments in downtown Boston, with both paid and volunteer help. Each is producing bales of expensively printed literature. Each is making extensive use of local radio and television facilities. Kennedy has about 800 billboards around the state and Lodge about 500." Cabell Phillips, "Case History of a Senate Race," *New York Times Magazine*, October 26, 1952.
85. Transcript, *Meet the Press*, November 9, 1952, box 105, JFK Pre-Pres.
86. Powers extended OH, box 9, DFPP.

CHAPTER 19: JACKIE

1. It's possible they had a passing encounter on a train in 1948. See Michael Beschloss, introduction to *Jacqueline Kennedy: Historic Conversations on Life with John F. Kennedy, Interviews with Arthur M. Schlesinger, Jr., 1964*, ed. Michael Beschloss (New York: Hyperion, 2011), xx.
2. Meyers, *As We Remember Him*, 51; Spoto, *Jacqueline*, 75–76. Charlie Bartlett said later, "I used to see her up in East Hampton when she visited her father and then down in Washington. She always had these sort of English beaux and I must say they were not up to her." At the wedding, "I spent the whole evening trying to get Jackie Bouvier across this great crowd to meet John Kennedy." Andersen, *Jack and Jackie: Portrait*, 73.
3. In the curious, doubly negative phrase, presumably approved by Jackie prior to publication (for this was an authorized, soft-focus book, penned by a friend and published just after Jackie became First Lady, in 1961, which Jackie went through line by line prior to publication), she said, "Such a heartbreak would be worth the pain." Thayer, *Jacqueline*, 95. In Jackie's recollection no asparagus was served that evening.
4. Anthony, *As We Remember Her*, 71, quoted in Bradford, *America's Queen*, 58; Goodwin, *Fitzgeralds and the Kennedys*, 770.
5. Meyers, *As We Remember Him*, 64; O'Brien, *No Final Victories*, 42; Kennedy, *Historic Conversations*, 42.
6. *New York World-Telegram*, December 17, 1952.
7. Klein, *All Too Human*, 363.
8. In some of these respects Jackie resembled his late sister Kick, to whom he had been so close. (In other respects, the two women were sharply different.) See Leaming, *Mrs. Kennedy*, 29–30.
9. Klein, *All Too Human*, 183. On Jack Kennedy paying more attention to his attire during this time, see Powers extended oral history, box 9, DFPP, JFKL.
10. Spoto, *Jacqueline*, 83; Levingston, *Kennedy and King*, 18–19.
11. Kennedy, *Historic Conversations*, 27.
12. Andersen, *Jack and Jackie*, 105. Gore Vidal, a distant relation of Jackie's by marriage, spoke in similar terms: "If she hadn't married Jack she would have married someone else with money, although it wasn't likely she would have gotten someone as exciting as Jack in the bargain. When given a choice of glory or money, most people choose glory.

But not Jackie. She also wound up with plenty of the latter, of course, but she didn't need that like she needed to be rich." Andersen, *Jack and Jackie*, 106.

13. Kelley, *Jackie Oh!*, 30; Sorensen, *Kennedy*, 37; Andersen, *Jack and Jackie*, 112. Jack Kennedy quoted in Martin, *Hero for Our Time*, 76.

14. Martin, *Hero for Our Time*, 77.

15. Alastair Forbes OH, JFKL.

16. Collier and Horowitz, *Kennedys*, 190.

17. Quoted in Dallek, *Unfinished Life*, 193.

18. Collier and Horowitz, *Kennedys*, 191; Leaming, *Mrs. Kennedy*, 7.

19. Quoted in Andersen, *Jack and Jackie*, 60.

20. Leaming, *Mrs. Kennedy*, 7.

21. See her comments to Arthur M. Schlesinger Jr. in March 1964, printed in Kennedy, *Historic Conversations*. In later years, her views shifted and she became a strong advocate for women's rights and gender equality.

22. Leaming, *Untold Story*, 5; Spoto, *Jacqueline*, 53. A classmate recalled Jack Bouvier's visits to Miss Porter's: "What we liked to do was run around and shake our behinds at him because he was an absolute lecher, absolute ravening, ravenous lecher, and Jackie, of course, knew it, and it amused her, but I don't think she was aware—she might have been, she didn't miss anything—of the extent to which we were teasing her father and making fun of him. . . . He came through as this sort of cartoon example of a dirty old man and I don't know if Jackie ever realized the extent to which we felt he was." Ellen "Puffin" Gates quoted in Bradford, *America's Queen*, 27.

23. Perry, *Jacqueline Kennedy*, 27.

24. Spoto, *Jacqueline*, 61.

25. Baldrige, *Kennedy Style*, 12–13; Spoto, *Jacqueline*, 59.

26. A penetrating assessment of the year in France is Kaplan, *Dreaming in French*, 7–46. Andersen, *Jack and Jackie*, 85; Vidal, *Palimpsest*, 309–10. For a skeptical view of the elevator story, see, e.g., Bradford, *America's Queen*, 66–67.

27. Prix de Paris application materials, box 1, JKOP; Kaplan, *Dreaming in French*, 48–49. A later winner of the competition was Joan Didion.

28. *Washington Times-Herald*, April 21, 1953.

29. Burns, *John Kennedy*, 117–18.

30. Sorensen, *Kennedy*, 11–12.

31. Burns, *John Kennedy*, 118–19.

32. Leamer, *Kennedy Men*, 311.

33. Matthews, *Jack Kennedy*, 151–55. For a partial defense of Kennedy's "cutthroat approach to personnel," see Matthews, *Jack Kennedy*, 155.

34. Sorensen, *Counselor*, 97.

35. Sorensen, *Counselor*, 98–99. On January 12, Kennedy told the Mutual Broadcasting System's Reporters Roundup that he approved of some of McCarthy's conduct, but "I disapprove very strongly" of other actions of the Wisconsin senator, including the effort to go after alleged Communists on the faculties of private universities. *New Bedford Standard Times*, January 13, 1953.

36. Lasky, *J.F.K.*, 165. Kennedy's personal secretary, Evelyn Lincoln, said of Sorensen that he was a "quiet, reserved, quizzical intellectual," a tower of steadfast support who was "devoted, loyal and dedicated to the Senator in every way possible. Time meant nothing to him—he gave it all to the Senator." Lincoln, *My Twelve Years*, 18.

37. Oliphant and Wilkie, *Road to Camelot*, 4.

38. Shaw, *JFK in the Senate*, 123; Sorensen, *Counselor*, 113.

39. Evelyn Lincoln, "My Twelve Years with Kennedy," *SEP*, August 15, 1965; Sorensen,

Counselor, 114–15; Sorensen, *Kennedy,* 30. Jackie Kennedy would later say: "He never wanted to have people in the evening that he worked with in the daytime." Kennedy, *Historic Conversations,* 23–24.

40. Lincoln, "My Twelve Years with Kennedy."

41. Sorensen, *Kennedy,* 55–56.

42. John F. Kennedy, May 18, 1953, *Congressional Record,* 83rd Cong., 1st sess., 5054–5056; John F. Kennedy, May 25, 1953, *Congressional Record,* 83rd Cong., 1st sess., 5466. Many of the speeches can be found in box 893, JFK Pre-Pres.

43. John F. Kennedy, "What's the Matter with New England?" *New York Times Magazine,* November 8, 1953; John F. Kennedy, "New England and the South," *Atlantic Monthly,* January 1954; Shaw, *JFK in the Senate,* 69.

44. Quoted in Chernus, *Atoms for Peace,* 94.

45. See Osgood, *Total Cold War,* 71–74; and Bowie and Immerman, *Waging Peace.*

46. On the war's final phase and its resolution, see, e.g., Stueck, *Rethinking the Korean War,* chap. 6; and Foot, *Substitute for Victory.*

47. Schlesinger, *Imperial Presidency,* 134–35.

48. Wright Smith, "Too Many Generals: Eisenhower, the Joint Chiefs, and Civil-Military Relations in Cold War America," Senior Honors Thesis, Harvard University, 2017.

49. This is a theme in Craig and Logevall, *America's Cold War.*

50. Speech transcript, February 1, 1953, box 893, JFK Pre-Pres; Nye, *Soft Power.*

51. Gullion OH, JFKL; Collier and Horowitz, *Kennedys,* 193.

52. Logevall, *Embers,* 342–47.

53. L. P. Marvin to Priscilla Johnson, April 17, 1953, box 481, JFK Pre-Pres; Priscilla Johnson to JFK, April 23, 1953, box 481, JFK Pre-Pres; JFK to John Foster Dulles, May 7, 1953, box 481, JFK Pre-Pres.

54. Logevall, *Embers,* chap. 14; JFK, Amendment to Mutual Security Act of 1951, July 1, 1953, Compilation of JFK Speeches, JFKL; Dallek, *Unfinished Life,* 186.

55. *NYT,* July 2, 1953.

56. According to some accounts, the proposal came immediately before she left for London. See, e.g., Spoto, *Jacqueline,* 97–98. Yet another theory has Jack proposing at Martin's Tavern in Georgetown on the evening of June 24, but this seems unlikely, given that the formal press announcement was issued that day and the story was in the next morning's papers. More likely is that the couple celebrated their engagement at Martin's, a place they were known to frequent. *WP,* June 23, 2015.

57. The letter, to Joseph Leonard, an Irish priest with whom she exchanged regular letters over a period of fourteen years, is quoted in *WP,* May 13, 2014.

58. David Pitts, a perspicacious observer of the Jack-Lem relationship, concludes that Lem found it relatively easy to adjust to the marriage. Pitts, *Jack and Lem,* 137. See also KLB OH, JFKL.

59. Spalding quoted in Andersen, *Jack and Jackie: Portrait,* 104; and in Klein, *All Too Human,* 139–40. See also Bradford, *America's Queen,* 64.

60. Leaming, *Untold,* 34; Leaming, *Mrs. Kennedy,* 9.

61. Klein, *All Too Human,* 146–47; Martin, *Hero for Our Time,* 74.

62. To Father Leonard she sent a telegram: "Announcing Engagement to Jack Kennedy Tomorrow Letter Follows So Happy Love—Jacqueline." *Irish Times,* May 13, 2014.

63. David Powers extended OH, box 9, DFPP; Andersen, *Jack and Jackie,* 119; Paul F. Healy, "The Senate's Gay Young Bachelor," *SEP,* June 13, 1953.

64. Jacqueline Bouvier to RK, June 29, 1953, box 4, JPKP.

65. New York *Daily News,* June 25, 1953; *Boston Herald,* June 25, 1953; *NYT,* June 25, 1953.

66. Leamer, *Kennedy Men*, 317.

67. Lincoln, *Twelve Years*, 25; O'Brien, *John F. Kennedy*, 266.

68. JPK to Macdonald, July 22, 1953, box 4, JPKP, JFKL; Leamer, *Kennedy Men*, 317.

69. Von Post's account, which contains implausibly exact dialogue and other dubious-sounding details, is in her brief memoir, *Love, Jack*, 19–33.

70. Von Post, *Love, Jack*, 33; Leamer, *Kennedy Men*, 319.

71. McNamara, *Eunice*, 137; Bradford, *America's Queen*, 69–70. A few weeks before the wedding, Jack hosted an engagement reception in his sister's honor at his Washington residence. Among those in attendance: Vice President Richard Nixon and Democratic senators Stuart Symington, George Smathers, and Albert Gore. *BG*, April 30, 1953.

72. Fay, *Pleasure of His Company*, 154–55.

73. Martin, *Hero for Our Time*, 80.

74. Bradford, *America's Queen*, 71; Parmet, *Jack*, 261.

75. *NYT*, September 13, 1953.

76. *Providence Sunday Journal*, September 13, 1953, quoted in Bradford, *America's Queen*, 73.

77. *NYT*, September 13, 1953.

78. Janet Auchincloss OH, JFKL.

79. Quoted in Hunt and Batcher, *Kennedy Wives*, 152.

80. Fay, *Pleasure of His Company*, 141, 143.

81. Hess, *America's Political Dynasties*, 506.

82. The full poem is in box 20, JPKP, JFKL.

83. Anderson, *Jack and Jackie*, 131.

84. Adler, *America's First Ladies*, 135.

85. Parmet, *Jack*, 296–97. The excerpt read: "Whether I am on the winning side or the losing side is not the point with me; it is being on the side where my sympathies lie that matters, and I am ready to see it through to the end. Success in life means doing that thing than which nothing else conceivable seems more noble or satisfying or remunerative, and this enviable state I can truly say that I enjoy, for had I the choice I would be nowhere else in the world than where I am."

86. Anderson, *Jack and Jackie*, 133.

87. David Ormsby-Gore OH, JFKL.

88. Martin, *Hero for Our Time*, 95.

89. Quoted in Smith, *Grace and Power*, 7.

90. Anderson, *Jack and Jackie*, 139. Tip O'Neill was fascinated by the steady improvement in the speechmaking. In time, he said, Kennedy turned into a "beautiful talker." Thomas "Tip" O'Neill OH, TOP.

CHAPTER 20: DARK DAYS

1. Though some accounts claim that McCarthy was godfather to their oldest child, Kathleen, her actual godfather was Daniel Walsh, a professor at Manhattanville College of the Sacred Heart, Ethel's alma mater. Tye, *Bobby*, 46. In Ethel's view, McCarthy was "just plain fun. . . . He didn't rant and roar, he was a normal guy." Tye, *Bobby*, 35.

2. See Betty Beale's column in the *Washington Evening Star*, September 30, 1953. I thank Larry Tye for this citation. For Robert's role on the subcommittee and his relationship with McCarthy in this period, see Tye, *Bobby*, 24–36; and Thomas, *Robert Kennedy*, 64–68.

3. Sorensen, *Kennedy*, 59; O'Brien, *John F. Kennedy*, 272.

4. Sorensen, *Counselor*, 145.

5. O'Neill, *Man of the House*, 90.

6. Logevall, *Embers*, 341–52, 365–66, 398–402.

7. *The Pentagon Papers: The Defense Department History of Decisionmaking on Vietnam*, Sena-

tor Gravel Edition (Boston: Beacon, 1971), vol. I: 591–92; Cole, *Conflict in Indo-China*, 171.

8. Speech transcript, January 21, 1954, box 893, JFK Pre-Pres.

9. Memorandum for the Secretary of Defense, "Preparation of Department of Defense Views Regarding Negotiations on Indochina for the Forthcoming Geneva Conference," March 12, 1954, *Pentagon Papers* (Gravel ed.), vol. I: 449–50.

10. Memorandum of Discussion, 192nd Meeting of the NSC, April 6, 1954, *Foreign Relations of the United States, 1952–1954* (Washington, DC: Government Printing Office, 1982), vol. XIII, part 1, 1261.

11. Quoted in McMahon, *Major Problems in the History*, 121. See also Adams, *Firsthand Report*, 120.

12. Fredrik Logevall, "We Might Give Them a Few," *Bulletin of the Atomic Scientists*, February 21, 2016; Prados, *Operation Vulture*.

13. *Congressional Record*, 83rd Cong., 2nd sess., 4671–74. Evidently proud of his intervention, Kennedy sent a copy of his April 6 remarks to his party's titular head, Adlai Stevenson. JFK to Stevenson, April 12, 1954, box 47, AES; William McCormack Blair Jr. to JFK, April 14, 1954, box 47, AES.

14. Quoted in Fite, *Richard B. Russell*, 359.

15. Mann, *Grand Delusion*, 153.

16. *Atlanta Constitution*, April 21, 1954; speech transcripts, May 11, 1954, and May 28, 1954, box 647, JFK Pre-Pres; Parmet, *Jack*, 285–86.

17. Logevall, *Embers*, 481ff.

18. See the voluminous file of letters, many of them from outside Massachusetts, in box 647, JFK Pre-Pres.

19. *Brooklyn Eagle*, April 26, 1954; *NYT*, April 8, 1954. Lippmann's column ran under the title "Kennedy Destroys False Hopes." *BG*, April 12, 1954.

20. Quoted in Sorensen, *Kennedy*, 37.

21. To her Irish friend Father Leonard, she wrote in 1954, "I love being married much more than I did even in the beginning." Quoted in *WP*, May 13, 2014.

22. Evelyn Lincoln, "My Twelve Years with Kennedy," *SEP*, August 15, 1965; KLB OH, JFKL. "Violent" is in Dallek, *Unfinished Life*, 194.

23. Leaming, *Mrs. Kennedy*, 11.

24. Bradford, *American Queen*, 94–95.

25. Von Post, *Love, Jack*, 37ff.

26. Quoted in Burns, *John Kennedy*, 139.

27. Irwin Ross of the *New York Post* was in Kennedy's Senate office when McCarthy called him to ask how he planned to vote on Conant's nomination. Kennedy replied that he would vote in favor. After they hung up, Ross asked Kennedy what he thought of McCarthy. "Not very much. But I get along with him." Recalling the episode three years later, Kennedy suggested that the criticism of him for his handling of the Wisconsin man was unfair. "How many senators spoke out against McCarthy in states where it would have hurt them?" Ross described the encounter in an article three years later. *New York Post*, July 30, 1956.

28. *Boston Post* quoted in Burns, *John Kennedy*, 143.

29. Parmet, *Jack*, 302; Hitchcock, *Age of Eisenhower*, 145. Speaking with extreme care, Eisenhower said in early March, "There are problems facing this nation today of vital importance. They are both foreign and domestic in character. . . . I regard it as unfortunate when we are diverted from these grave problems—of which one is vigilance against any kind of internal subversion—through disregard of the standards of fair play recognized by the American people." *Time*, March 15, 1954.

30. Nichols, *Ike and McCarthy*; Frank, *Ike and Dick*, 82.

31. Matthews, *Jack Kennedy*, 177. In mid-August, the Ambassador insisted to some "pontificating," disdainful British dinner companions that McCarthy remained the strongest man in America next to Eisenhower, and asked them what they had against him. He then replayed the encounter with obvious relish in a letter to Bobby. JPK to RFK, August 15, 1954, box 4, JPKP.

32. *Time*, June 14, 1954; Parmet, *Jack*, 303–4.

33. McCarthy, *Remarkable Kennedys*, 150; Parmet, *Jack*, 308–9; Dallek, *Unfinished Life*, 196.

34. Goodwin, *Fitzgeralds and the Kennedys*, 774.

35. Dallek, *Unfinished Life*, 196.

36. Sorensen, *Counselor*, 127–28; Nelson, *John William McCormack*, 497.

37. *Time*, October 25, 1954; Burns, *John Kennedy*, 147–48; Matthews, *Jack Kennedy*, 184–87.

38. O'Brien, *No Final Victories*, 44 ; James A. Nichols, M.D., et al., "Management of Adrenocortical Insufficiency During Surgery," *Archives of Surgery* (November 1955): 737–40.

39. Goodwin, *Fitzgeralds and the Kennedys*, 774–75.

40. Arthur Krock OH, JFKL.

41. *BG*, November 6, 1954; *Time*, November 22, 1954.

42. Senator Prescott Bush (R-CT) offered one of the more eloquent arguments for censure: McCarthy, he declared, had "caused dangerous divisions among the American people because of his attitude and the attitude he has encouraged among his followers: that there can be no honest differences of opinion with him. Either you must follow Senator McCarthy blindly, not daring to express any doubts or disagreements about any of his actions, or, in his eyes, you must be a Communist, a Communist sympathizer, or a fool who has been duped by the Communist line." *Time*, December 13, 1954.

43. Sorensen, *Counselor*, 154.

44. *BP*, December 2, 1954, quoted in Parmet, *Jack*, 310–11. Parmet rejects the suggestion that Kennedy used his illness to avoid casting a vote (308).

45. Charles Spalding OH, JFKL.

46. Tye, *Bobby*, 48; Nasaw, *Patriarch*, 685.

47. Heymann, *Woman Named Jackie*, 170–71; O'Brien, *John F. Kennedy*, 282.

48. Grace de Monaco OH, JFKL. For differing accounts of what occurred, and who issued the invitation, see, e.g., Bradford, *America's Queen*, 98; and Andersen, *Jack and Jackie*, 145.

49. Priscilla Johnson McMillan interview with author, September 17, 2018, Cambridge, MA.

50. Kelley, *Jackie Oh!*, 143; Leaming, *Mrs. Kennedy*, 13; RK, *Times to Remember*, 353.

51. Agar, *Time for Greatness*; Parmet, *Jack*, 324–25.

52. Leaming, *Jack Kennedy: Education*, 221; Whalen, *Founding Father*, 442; Peter Lawford OH, JFKL.

53. Quoted in Adler, *Eloquent*, 39. See also Kennedy, *Historic Conversations*, 16.

54. Powers, too, would read aloud to Kennedy on his visits to Palm Beach. "I would think he had fallen asleep, and I'd stop reading," Powers remembered. "He would open his eyes and tell me to keep going. When I came to a line that he liked, he would stop me and tell me to read it again." O'Donnell and Powers, *"Johnny,"* 101. See also Perry, *Jacqueline Kennedy*, 44–45.

55. Sorensen, *Kennedy*, 67; Sorensen, *Counselor*, 146.

56. Quoted in Schlesinger, *Thousand Days*, 101.

57. TS to JFK, February 4, 1955, box 7, TSP; TS to JFK, February 14, 1955, box 7, TSP.

58. TS to JFK, February 14, 1955, box 7, TSP.

59. Parmet, *Jack*, 328. See also Kennedy's January 28, 1955 letter to Cass Canfield, the president of Harper and Brothers, in Sandler, *Letters*, 46–47.

60. Davids made an especially valuable contribution, in the form of memos he submitted on the individual senators being considered for inclusion, and on the overall organization. See TS to JFK, February 28, 1955, box 7, TSP.

61. Lamar quoted in Lemann, *Redemption*, 151. On Reconstruction, a standard account is Foner, *Reconstruction*. See also Bryant, *Bystander*, 48–49; and James Oakes, "An Unfinished Revolution," *New York Review of Books*, December 9, 2019.

62. JFK, *Profiles*, 4–5, 10.

63. JFK, *Profiles*, 18.

64. JFK, *Profiles*, 18.

65. JFK, *Profiles*, 222–23; Parmet, *Jack*, 322.

66. JFK, *Profiles*, 265, 222. For a contemporary examination of some of these themes, see Wilentz, *Politicians and the Egalitarians*; and see Charles Edel, "Why Is Political Courage So Rare?" *Washington Post*, March 12, 2018.

67. JFK, *Profiles*, 222.

68. David Ormsby-Gore OH, JFKL.

69. JFK to Eunice Shriver, July 26, 1955, printed in JFK, *Profiles*, "PS" section, p. 15; Parmet, *Jack*, 326.

70. TS to JFK, July 17, 1955, box 7, TSP; Schlesinger, *Letters*, 108–9, 112–18; JFK to Thomas, August 1, 1955, box 31, *Profiles in Courage* file, JFKL. Nevins, according to Sorensen, was "tremendously enthusiastic about the book, writing Mr. Canfield that he believes it will be extremely influential and well received, and that it adds still further to the stature of a Senator he has long admired." TS to JFK, August 12, 1955, box 7, TSP.

71. *BG*, May 24, 1955; Burns, *John Kennedy*, 169. This is now the Russell Senate Office Building.

72. O'Brien, *John F. Kennedy*, 283. On May 24, Kennedy received a warm welcome from colleagues on the Senate floor. See *NYT*, May 25, 1955.

73. Assumption College Commencement Address, June 3, 1955, box 12, Senate Files, JFK Pre-Pres.

74. O'Donnell, *Irish Brotherhood*, 140–43; Damore, *Cape Cod Years*, 145–46. See also Frank Morrissey to JPK, June 28, 1955, box 231, JPKP.

75. O'Donnell and Powers, *"Johnny,"* 103–4; Sorensen, *Counselor*, 145; Joseph Alsop OH, JFKL.

76. Leaming, *Jack Kennedy: Education*, 225.

CHAPTER 21: RISING STAR

1. Hitchcock, *Age of Eisenhower*, 280–85; Smith, *Eisenhower*, 674–79. A detailed account is Lasby, *Eisenhower's Heart Attack*.

2. Frank, *Ike and Dick*, 113.

3. *NYT*, August 29, 1955; Smith, *Eisenhower*, 670–71.

4. Hagerty, *Diary*, 240–46; Farrell, *Richard Nixon*, 239–40. To Dulles as well, Eisenhower voiced doubts that Nixon was presidential material. Frank, *Ike and Dick*, 125.

5. *NYT*, October 30, 1955.

6. TS to JFK, September 12, 1955, box 7, TSP. Sorensen may have been referring partly to a front-page article in *The Boston Globe* by Jim Colbert, which noted that "party leaders in the South have already been sounded about [Kennedy] and have declared that the Junior Senator from Massachusetts would be acceptable to them. Many Massachusetts Democrats who are not enthusiastic about Stevenson would be forced to revise their views if Kennedy were his running mate . . . Stevenson and Kennedy are far closer than

is generally realized." Colbert added that Stevenson himself had encouraged the reports. See Lasky, *J.F.K.*, 175. In the letter, Sorensen also updated Kennedy on the status of *Profiles in Courage*, noting that the production process was running smoothly and that all of the senator's corrections had been incorporated. In an earlier letter to Teddy, the Ambassador had indicated how he expected Kennedy men to behave, even married ones: "I haven't seen all those beautiful girls that everybody talks about being here in the South of France, but maybe when Jack arrives here next week he'll find them." JPK to EMK, August 15, 1955, box 4, JPKP.

7. JPK to Edward Kennedy, September 3, 1955, printed in Smith, *Hostage to Fortune*, 670–71.

8. Bradford, *America's Queen*, 103.

9. Von Post, *Dear Jack*, 54–59.

10. Von Post, *Dear Jack*, 63–64.

11. Von Post, *Dear Jack*, 68, 85.

12. Bradford, *America's Queen*, 105.

13. Andersen, *Jack and Jackie*, 154; Spoto, *Jacqueline*, 117.

14. Von Post, *Dear Jack*, 103.

15. Von Post, *Dear Jack*, 109; Leamer, *Kennedy Men*, 349.

16. Janet Travell OH, JFKL; Dallek, *Unfinished Life*, 212–13; Kennedy, *Historic Conversations*, 17.

17. Janet Auchincloss OH, JFKL; Spoto, *Jacqueline*, 118.

18. Hitchcock, *Age of Eisenhower*, 284–85; *NYT*, October 16, 1955; *WP*, November 12, 1955.

19. Dallek, *Lone Star Rising*, 490–91; Caro, *Years of Lyndon Johnson*, vol. 3, 646–47.

20. Stevenson quoted in Henry, *Eleanor Roosevelt*, 59. In October, historian Arthur Schlesinger Jr. told Stevenson that Harriman constituted the biggest threat to his nomination. "Bosses and Truman are against you; only voters are for you. But the bosses and Truman are less important than they were [in 1952]. . . . I think you should play boldly and from strength." Schlesinger Jr. to Stevenson, October 10, 1955, box P-23, AMSP.

21. See the warm letters and telegrams between them in box 47, AES. In later years, the relationship would become more fraught, a matter to be explored in volume 2 of this work.

22. See, e.g., C. R. Owens, "Politics & Politicians: Kennedy Views as 'Favorite Son at Chicago Parley,'" *BG*, November 20, 1955. The article said that although Kennedy would almost certainly not be the nominee, there had been talk of him for the vice presidential slot. See also Martin and Plaut, *Front Runner*, 27.

23. TS to JFK, November 22, 1955, box 7, Sorensen Papers, JFKL. Kennedy had already mused about the possibility, telling Stevenson himself on October 21 that he was preparing a statement pledging his support for Stevenson's candidacy. JFK to AES, October 21, 1955. See also Parmet, *Jack*, 338.

24. The announcement read in part: "I supported Adlai Stevenson for the nomination in 1952. I shall support him again in 1956. No other candidate in 1952 possessed his unique combination of qualifications for that most arduous of offices. In the intervening years, his intelligence, farsightedness, and temperate approach to difficult problems have not diminished nor been matched by any other potential nominee." Announcement of Senator Kennedy, March 8, 1956, box 47, EAS. Stevenson offered his thanks by telegram to Kennedy, March 12, 1956, box 47, AES.

25. "The Catholic Vote in 1952 and 1956," box 9, TSP.

26. "The Catholic Vote in 1952 and 1956," box 9, TSP. In the key state of New York, according to the report, Catholics made up an estimated 32 percent of the electorate; in Pennsylvania, 29 percent; in New Jersey, 39 percent; in California, 22 percent; in Massachusetts, 50 percent; in Michigan, 24 percent; and in Illinois, 30 percent.

27. Fletcher Knebel OH, JFKL; Knebel column, February 23, 1956, box 8, TSP. See also Knebel, "Can a Catholic Become Vice President?" *Look*, June 12, 1956.

28. *New York Times Magazine*, December 18, 1955; Shaw, *JFK in the Senate*, 129; Sorensen to JFK, September 12, 1955, box 7, TSP.

29. *NYT*, January 1, 1956.

30. *SEP*, February 18, 1956.

31. Parmet, *Jack*, 320–21.

32. *NYT*, January 7, 1956.

33. Parmet, *Jack*, 321–23; O'Brien, *John F. Kennedy*, 289; *Boston Herald*, February 9, 1956; Remarks at the National Book Awards Dinner, February 7, 1956, box 894, JFK Pre-Pres. Kennedy concluded his speech by calling on writers and politicians to join together: "Somehow we in the political world will have to find time to read more than the local newspapers and the latest Gallup Poll. And somehow you in the literary world must find time to devote increasing attention to the political issues of our day. . . . Could not politicians and intellectuals pool our forces to ask where we are going, what we are doing and why—to analyze our political directions and institutions—not in the rigid, traditional and emotional patterns of the Left or the Right, not in terms of political parties or personalities, but in the detached yet experienced view that only a combination of politics and scholarship can achieve? Let us forget our petty quarrels of the past and the present—and unite our talents for the challenge of the future."

34. The story of the Pulitzer Prize and the fallout from it will be discussed in more detail in volume 2 of this biography.

35. Gloria L Sitrin OH, JFKL; Jean McGonigle Mannix OH, JFKL; Kennedy, *Historic Conversations*, 59–61; Manchester, *One Brief Shining Moment*, 71; Oliphant and Wilkie, *Road to Camelot*, 82.

36. As Garry Wills later noted with respect to *Profiles in Courage*, "This kind of political production is normal, not only for an officeholder's speeches but his books. . . . There is no deception in this, because there is no pretense that the man signing his name did all or even most of the writing." Wills, *Kennedy Imprisonment*, 135. In Robert Dallek's view, "the final product was essentially Jack's." Dallek, *Unfinished Life*, 199. See also the unambiguous assessment in Sorensen, *Counselor*, 151.

37. Brogan, *Kennedy*, 35–36. As Sorensen would put it, "Of all the honors he would receive throughout his life, none would make him more happy than his receipt in 1957 of the Pulitzer Prize for biography." Sorensen, *Kennedy*, 68. See also Sorensen, *Counselor*, 151–52.

38. Of the two men Kennedy was by far the more bookish. Stevenson read relatively little, preferring to spend his time with people. Martin, *Adlai Stevenson of Illinois*, 476. Kennedy, according to his wife, read constantly. "He'd read walking, he'd read at the table, at meals, he'd read after dinner, he'd read in the bathtub, he'd read—prop open a book on his desk—on his bureau while he was doing his tie." Kennedy: *Historic Conversations*, 40–41.

39. A perceptive and massively detailed biography is Nelson, *John William McCormack*.

40. Oliphant and Wilkie, *Road to Camelot*, 28; Sorensen, *Kennedy*, 78.

41. Joseph Rauh OH, JFKL.

42. *BG*, May 8, 1956; *NYT*, May 8, 1956; O'Donnell and Powers, *"Johnny,"* 108–10; O'Donnell, *Brotherhood*, 146.

43. O'Brien, *No Final Victories*, 50; Nelson, *John William McCormack*, 513–15; *BG*, May 20, 1956.

44. Donald Malcolm, "The Man Who Wants Second Place," *New Republic*, July 30, 1956; Kennedy, *Historic Conversations*, 9–13.

45. Oliphant and Wilkie, *Road to Camelot*, 33–34. See also Schlesinger to Stevenson, n.d. (May 1956), box P-23, AMSP.
46. The article, "What My Illness Taught Me," appeared in the May 29 issue of *The American Weekly*. "I would not wish to exaggerate the compensation of being ill," he wrote. "It is better by far to be well. But if illness strikes, though we may grumble at first about the long days away from our normal work and routine—if we recognize the potential those long days make possible, we will realize that our disability—whatever its pains and discomforts—may in some ways have been a blessing in disguise."
47. Harvard Commencement Address, June 14, 1956, box 895, JFK Pre-Pres, JFKL; *NYT*, June 15, 1956. A version of the address was published in article form under the title "Brothers, I Presume?" in *Vogue*, April 1956. On the address, see also Drew Gilpin Faust, "A Common Cause," in Smith and Brinkley, *JFK: A Vision for America*, 69–70. That spring Harvard also granted him the honorary degree his father had so craved but failed to get.

CHAPTER 22: A VERY NEAR THING

1. *NYT*, June 15, 1956; *Christian Science Monitor*, June 22, 1956; Parmet, *Jack*, 355.
2. *NYT*, June 26, 1956; JFK to JPK, June 29, 1956, printed in Sandler, *Letters*, 53–54; Martin, *Adlai Stevenson*, 343.
3. According to Connecticut state party chair John Bailey, Ribicoff wrote to Kennedy in the spring, "Adlai is giving considerable thought to you for the second spot." Oliphant and Wilkie, *Road to Camelot*, 23.
4. Newton Minow OH, Columbia University, quoted in Parmet, *Jack*, 339. Kennedy's speech is in box 12, JFK Pre-Pres.
5. Sorensen, *Kennedy*, 81–82; Sorensen, *Counselor*, 160; John M. Bailey OH, JFKL.
6. Sorensen, *Counselor*, 169.
7. Newton Minow to AES, March 30, 1956, box 47, AES; JFK to Minow, April 16, 1956, box 47, AES; JFK to James Finnegan, May 2, 1956, box 47, AES; Stan Karson memo to AES, May 22, 1956, box 47, AES; JFK to AES, telegram, June 6, 1956, box 47, AES.
8. JPK to JFK, May 25, 1956, box 4, JPKP; Dallek, *Unfinished Life*, 205; Schlesinger, *Robert Kennedy*, 131.
9. JFK to JPK, June 29, 1956, box 4, JPKP.
10. Sargent Shriver to JPK, July 18, 1956, box 810, JFK Pre-Pres, JFKL; Eunice Shriver to JPK, August 1, 1956, box 4, JPKP; Dallek, *Unfinished Life*, 205–6.
11. JPK to Sargent Shriver, July 18, 1956, printed in Smith, *Hostage to Fortune*, 673–75.
12. JPK to JFK, July 23, 1956, box 4, JPKP.
13. *Time*, August 6, 1956.
14. On the challenges the party faced on the civil rights issue in the looming presidential campaign, see Schlesinger to Stevenson, June 11, 1956, box P-23, AMSP.
15. Levingston, *Kennedy and King*, 14–15.
16. Bryant, *Bystander*, 54–55.
17. Transcript of *Face the Nation*, July 1, 1956, box 12, TSP; Bryant, *Bystander*, 55–56.
18. Dore Schary OH, JFKL; Sabato, *Half-Century*, 34–35; Longley, *Gore*, 127–29.
19. Quoted in Goodwin, *Fitzgeralds and the Kennedys*, 782.
20. *NYT*, August 14, 1956. The title of the articles summarized the thrust: "Party's Film Aids Kennedy Drive."
21. Martin, *Hero for Our Time*, 109.
22. Martin, *Ballots and Bandwagons*, 416; Parmet, *Jack*, 368. According to *Time*, Roosevelt stressed in her appearances in Chicago that her late husband was "a man of moderation," and implied that Stevenson was the same. *Time*, August 27, 1956.
23. Martin, *Ballots and Bandwagons*, 394–95.

24. Offner, *Hubert Humphrey*, 117–18.

25. Martin, *Ballots and Bandwagons*, 396.

26. Tom Winship OH, JFKL, quoted in Oliphant and Wilkie, *Road to Camelot*, 42; *NYT*, August 17, 1956; O'Donnell and Powers, *"Johnny,"* 121.

27. Quoted in Caro, *Years of Lyndon Johnson*, vol. 3, 825.

28. O'Donnell and Powers, *"Johnny,"* 122; Mahoney, *Sons and Brothers*, 19.

29. Martin, *Ballots and Bandwagons*, 407; O'Donnell, *Brotherhood*, 166.

30. Lasky, *J.F.K.*, 187; Martin, *Ballots and Bandwagons*, 407–11. One supporter said afterwards, "Bobby Kennedy was supposed to be floor manager for Jack at that convention, but that's a lot of crap. There was no floor manager; there was just nobody in control. Everybody was out on his own, talking to anybody and everybody he could, and there was a helluva lot of overlapping." Martin and Plaut, *Front Runner*, 71.

31. Sorensen, *Kennedy*, 88.

32. Sorensen, *Kennedy*.

33. O'Donnell and Powers, *"Johnny,"* 123.

34. Sorensen, *Kennedy*, 89. An illuminating firsthand journalistic account is Thomas Winship, "Inside Senator's Room: What Kennedy Did, Said as Tide Came in, Ebbed," *BG*, August 18, 1956.

35. Caro, *Years of Lyndon Johnson*, vol. 3, 826–27.

36. A remarkable video survives of the concluding balloting and Kennedy's brief speech. See "Kennedy vs Kefauver '56," www.youtube.com/watch?v=wlIej3uTwHM.

37. *NYT*, August 18, 1956, quoted in Oliphant and Wilkie, *Road to Camelot*, 46.

38. The aide was Arthur Schlesinger Jr. See Oliphant and Wilkie, *Road to Camelot*, 52; Martin and Plaut, *Front Runner*, 107.

39. Gorman, *Kefauver*, 260; Matthews, *Jack Kennedy*, 209–10. Bobby Kennedy later spoke of encountering this personal attachment to Kefauver among the delegates in Chicago: "It really struck me that it wasn't the issues which matter. It was the friendships. So many people said to me they would rather vote for Jack, but that they were going to vote for Estes Kefauver because he had sent them a card or gone to their home. I said right there that we should forget the issues and send Christmas cards and go to their homes next time." Toledano, *RFK*, 142.

40. Dallek, *Unfinished Life*, 208; *BG*, August 18, 1956, and August 19, 1956. See also Caro, *Years of Lyndon Johnson*, vol. 4, 50.

41. AES to JFK, August 26, 1956, box 47, AES.

42. O'Donnell and Powers, *"Johnny,"* 124; Sorensen, *Kennedy*, 91–92.

43. Martin, *Hero for Our Time*, 120.

44. Martin, *Ballots and Bandwagons*, 453.

45. JPK to Morton Downey, August 24, 1956, printed in Smith, *Hostage to Fortune*, 677; Nasaw, *Patriarch*, 708.

46. O'Brien, *John F. Kennedy*, 322.

47. RK to Patricia Kennedy Lawford, August 26, 1956, box 4, JPKP.

48. For the former view, see, e.g., O'Donnell and Powers, *"Johnny,"* 125; Parmet, *Jack*, 383; Goodwin, *Fitzgeralds and the Kennedys*, 785; McCarthy, *Remarkable Kennedys*, 164. For the latter, see, e.g., Collier and Horowitz, *Kennedys*, 209; Reeves, *Question of Character*, 138.

49. Quoted in Perrett, *Jack*, 226. Smathers was not always the most reliable witness; he would make dubious claims regarding Kennedy's later relationship with Marilyn Monroe, to be examined in the second volume of this work.

50. O'Brien, *John F. Kennedy*, 323.

51. Matthews, *Jack Kennedy*, 212.

52. John Sharon OH, JFKL; Sorensen to James Finnegan, September 17, 1956, box 47, AES; Sabato, *Half-Century*, 39–40.

53. JFK to Finnegan, October 3, 1956, box 47, AES; Martin, *Adlai Stevenson*, 356. For Stevenson's initial invitation to the Philadelphia dinner, see AES telegram to JFK in Èze-sur-Mer, August 23, 1956, box 47, AES.

54. Speech transcript, September 21, 1956, box 895, JFK Pre-Pres; Muehlenbeck, *Betting on the Africans*, 35–36.

55. *BG*, October 26, 1956.

56. Goodwin, *Fitzgeralds and the Kennedys*, 786.

57. Schlesinger, *Robert Kennedy*, 134. Harrison Salisbury of *The New York Times* had a similar impression: "Bobby always seemed to be on the fringe of the crowd someplace. He was always watching what was going on." Stein, *American Journey*, 65–66.

58. Already in the spring, advisers had tried to coax Stevenson to change his campaigning style and speechmaking. See, e.g., Schlesinger Jr. to Stevenson, May 15, 1956, box P-23, AMSP.

59. On Suez, see Zelikow and May, *Suez Deconstructed;* and Nichols, *Eisenhower 1956*. In December, under U.S. pressure, British and French forces withdrew; in March 1957, again in response to American pressure, Israel relinquished control of the canal to Egypt.

60. The most pressing problems facing the nation, Kennedy said early in the film, were "peace and security." "Yet nowhere has the Republican Administration of Mr. Eisenhower and Mr. Nixon told us less or misled us more. Actually, Governor Stevenson, this adds up pretty much to what you've been saying, does it not?" Stevenson: "That's right. This administration has been using foreign policy for political purposes at home. It has been unwilling to admit its failures. It has refused to take people into its confidence. It has attempted to describe reverses as victories." Film transcript, September 17, 1956, box 47, AES. A longer transcript is in box 167, GBP.

61. McKeever, *Adlai Stevenson*, 388.

62. McKeever, *Adlai Stevenson*, 136. On November 18, Stevenson wrote to Kennedy: "I should have thanked you long before this. I can think of no one to whom we should all be more grateful than to you. And I am only sorry that I did not better reward you for your gallantry in action. I have confident hopes for your future leadership in our party, and I am sure you will help immeasurably to keep it pointed in a positive direction. With my boundless gratitude, and affection regards, Cordially, Adlai." AES to JFK, November 18, 1956, box 47, AES.

63. Burns, *John Kennedy*, 190.

64. Oliphant and Wilkie, *Road to Camelot*, 55; O'Donnell and Powers, *"Johnny,"* 125–26. With respect to the itinerary, Sorensen would later write: "I took over a briefcase filled with speaking invitations that had poured in from all over the country. I placed on his dining room table those I thought were of serious interest, arranging them by geography and date, trying to form a rough speaking schedule for the next several months, arranging them also in terms of priority and category—including political gatherings, universities and civic organizations. After a long night working out a tentative schedule, he casually uttered seven fateful words, 'You may as well come with me.'" Sorensen, *Kennedy*, 100.

65. Manchester, *One Brief Shining Moment*, 81.

66. Remarks at the Tavern Club, November 8, 1956, Speeches and Press Releases File, box 896, JFK Pre-Pres.

67. Kennedy, *True Compass*, 116; Goodwin, *Fitzgeralds and the Kennedys*, 787–88.

BIBLIOGRAPHY

Acheson, Dean. *Present at the Creation: My Years in the State Department.* New York: W. W. Norton, 1969.

Adams, Sherman. *Firsthand Report: The Story of the Eisenhower Administration.* New York: Harper & Brothers, 1961.

Adler, Bill. *America's First Ladies.* Lanham, MD: Taylor Trade Publishing, 2006.

———. *The Eloquent Jacqueline Kennedy Onassis: A Portrait in Her Own Words.* New York: William Morrow, 1994.

Agar, Herbert. *The Price of Union: The Influence of the American Temper on the Course of History.* New York: Houghton Mifflin, 1950.

———. *A Time for Greatness.* Boston: Little, Brown and Company, 1942.

Aldous, Richard. *Schlesinger: The Imperial Historian.* New York: W. W. Norton, 2017.

Allen, Frederick Lewis. *Only Yesterday: An Informal History of the Nineteen-Twenties, 1890–1954.* New York: Harper and Row, 1959.

Alsop, Joseph, and Robert E. Kintner. *American White Paper.* New York: Simon and Schuster, 1940.

Ambrose, Stephen E. *Nixon.* Vol. 1, *The Education of a Politician, 1913–1962.* New York: Simon and Schuster, 1987.

Ambrosius, Lloyd E. *Woodrow Wilson and the American Diplomatic Tradition.* New York: Cambridge University Press, 1987.

Amory, Cleveland. *The Proper Bostonians.* New York: E. P. Dutton, 1947.

Anbinder, Tyler. *Nativism and Slavery: The Northern Know Nothings and the Politics of the 1850s.* New York: Oxford University Press, 1992.

Andersen, Christopher P. *Jack and Jackie: Portrait of an American Marriage.* New York: William Morrow, 1996.

Anthony, Carl Sferrazza. *As We Remember Her: Jacqueline Kennedy Onassis in the Words of Her Family and Friends.* New York: HarperCollins, 1987.

Asch, Chris Myers, and George Derek Musgrove. *Chocolate City: A History of Race and Democracy in the Nation's Capital.* Chapel Hill: University of North Carolina Press, 2017.

Ash, Timothy Garton. *History of the Present: Essays, Sketches, and Dispatches from Europe in the 1990s.* New York: Penguin, 1999.

Atkinson, Rick. *An Army at Dawn: The War in North Africa, 1942–1943.* New York: Henry Holt, 2002.

Axelrod, Alan. *Lost Destiny: Joe Kennedy Jr. and the Doomed WW2 Mission to Save London.* New York: Palgrave Macmillan, 2015.

Bacevich, Andrew J., ed. *The Limits of Power: The End of American Exceptionalism.* New York: Metropolitan, 2008.

———. *The Short American Century: A Postmortem.* Cambridge, MA: Harvard University Press, 2012.

Bailey, Beth L. *From Front Porch to Back Seat: Courtship in Twentieth-Century America.* Baltimore: Johns Hopkins University Press, 1988.

Bailey, Catherine. *Black Diamonds: The Rise and Fall of an English Dynasty.* New York: Viking, 2007.

Baime, Albert J. *The Accidental President: Harry S. Truman and the Four Months that Changed the World.* Boston: Houghton Mifflin Harcourt, 2017.

———. *The Arsenal of Democracy: FDR, Detroit, and an Epic Quest to Arm an America at War.* Boston: Houghton Mifflin Harcourt, 2014.

Baldrige, Letitia. *In the Kennedy Style: Magical Evenings in the Kennedy White House.* New York: Doubleday, 1998.

Barnet, Richard J. *The Rockets' Red Glare: War, Politics, and the American Presidency.* New York: Simon and Schuster, 1990.

Barry, John M. *The Great Influenza: The Epic Story of the Deadliest Plague in History.* New York: Viking, 2004.

Bayley, Edwin R. *Joe McCarthy and the Press*. Madison: University of Wisconsin Press, 1981.

Beatty, Jack. *The Rascal King: The Life and Times of James Michael Curley, 1874–1958*. Reading, MA: Addison-Wesley, 1992.

Beauchamp, Cari. *Joseph P. Kennedy Presents: His Hollywood Years*. New York: Knopf, 2009.

Beevor, Antony. *The Second World War*. London: Weidenfeld & Nicolson, 2012.

———. *Stalingrad*. New York: Viking, 1998.

Beisner, Robert L. *Dean Acheson: A Life in the Cold War*. New York: Oxford University Press, 2006.

Bell, Daniel, ed. *The Radical Right: The New American Right*. Garden City, NY: Doubleday, 1964.

Berg, A. Scott. *Lindbergh*. New York: Berkley, 1999.

Berlin, Isaiah. *Personal Impressions*. London: Hogarth, 1980.

Beschloss, Michael. *Kennedy and Roosevelt: The Uneasy Alliance*. New York: W. W. Norton, 1980.

Best, Geoffrey. *Churchill: A Study in Greatness*. Oxford: Oxford University Press, 2003.

Bird, Kai. *The Color of Truth: McGeorge and William Bundy: Brothers in Arms*. New York: Simon and Schuster, 1999.

Blair, Joan, and Clay Blair Jr. *The Search for JFK*. New York: G.P. Putnam's Sons, 1976.

Blum, John Morton. *From the Morgenthau Diaries*. Vol. 1, *Years of Crisis, 1928–1938*. Boston: Houghton Mifflin, 1959.

Borgwardt, Elizabeth. *A New Deal for the World*. Cambridge, MA: Harvard University Press, 2007.

Bouverie, Tim. *Appeasing Hitler: Chamberlain, Churchill, and the Road to War*. London: Bodley Head, 2019.

Bowie, Robert R., and Richard H. Immerman. *Waging Peace: How Eisenhower Shaped an Enduring Cold War Strategy*. New York: Oxford University Press, 1998.

Bradford, Sarah. *America's Queen: The Life of Jacqueline Kennedy Onassis*. New York: Viking, 2000.

Brands, H. W. *Traitor to His Class: The Privileged Life and Radical Presidency of Franklin Delano Roosevelt*. New York: Doubleday, 2009.

Brauer, C. *John F. Kennedy and the Second Reconstruction*. New York: Columbia University Press, 1977.

Brendon, Piers. *The Dark Valley: A Panorama of the 1930s*. New York: Knopf, 2000.

Breuer, William B. *Sea Wolf: The Daring Exploits of Navy Legend John D. Bulkeley*. Novato, CA: Presidio, 1989.

Brinkley, Alan. *The Publisher: Henry Luce and His American Century*. New York: Knopf, 2010.

——. *John F. Kennedy: The American Presidents Series: The 35th President, 1961–1963*. Edited by Arthur M. Schlesinger Jr. and Sean Wilentz. New York: Times Books, 2012.

Brinkley, Douglas. *American Moonshot: John F. Kennedy and the Great Space Race*. New York: HarperCollins, 2019.

Brogan, Hugh. *Kennedy*. New York: Longman, 1996.

Brown, David Scott. *Moderates: The Vital Center of American Politics, from the Founding to Today*. Chapel Hill: University of North Carolina Press, 2016.

Brownell, Will, and Richard N. Billings. *So Close to Greatness: The Biography of William C. Bullitt*. New York: Macmillan, 1987.

Bryant, Nick. *The Bystander: John F. Kennedy and the Struggle for Black Equality*. New York: Basic Books, 2006.

Buchan, John. *Pilgrim's Way*. Boston: Houghton Mifflin, 1940.

Budiansky, Stephen. *Battle of Wits: The Complete Story of Codebreaking in World War II*. New York: Free Press, 2000.

Bunting, Bainbridge. *Harvard: An Architectural History*. Cambridge, MA: Belknap Press of Harvard University Press, 1985.

Burner, David. *John F. Kennedy and a New Generation*. New York: Pearson/ Longman, 2005.

Burns, James MacGregor. *The Crosswinds of Freedom: 1932–1988*. New York: Knopf, 2012.

——. *John Kennedy: A Political Profile*. New York: Harcourt, Brace, 1960.

Butler, J. R. M. *Lord Lothian*. London: Macmillan, 1960.

Butler, Susan. *Roosevelt and Stalin: Portrait of a Partnership*. New York: Knopf, 2015.

Byrne, Paula. *Kick: The True Story of JFK's Sister and the Heir to Chatsworth*. New York: HarperCollins, 2016.

Bzdek, Vincent. *The Kennedy Legacy: Jack, Bobby and Ted and a Family Dream Fulfilled*. New York: Palgrave Macmillan, 2009.

Calvocoressi, Peter, and Guy Wint. *Total War: The Story of World War II*. New York: Pantheon, 1972.

Cameron, Gail. *Rose: A Biography of Rose Fitzgerald Kennedy.* New York: G.P. Putnam's Sons, 1971.

Canellos, Peter S., ed. *Last Lion: The Fall and Rise of Ted Kennedy.* New York: Simon and Schuster, 2009.

Caquet, P. E. *The Bell of Treason: The 1938 Munich Agreement in Czechoslovakia.* New York: Other Press, 2018.

Caro, Robert. *The Years of Lyndon Johnson.* Vol. 3, *Master of the Senate.* New York: Knopf, 2002.

———. *The Years of Lyndon Johnson.* Vol. 4, *The Passage of Power.* New York: Knopf, 2012.

Casey, Steven. *Cautious Crusade: Franklin D. Roosevelt, American Public Opinion, and the War Against Nazi Germany.* Oxford: Oxford University Press, 2001.

Cecil, David. *The Young Melbourne: And the Story of His Marriage with Caroline Lamb.* London: Constable and Co., 1939.

Chernus, Ira. *Eisenhower's Atoms for Peace.* College Station: Texas A&M University Press, 2002.

Churchill, Winston. *Arms and the Covenant.* London: George G. Harrap & Co., 1938.

———. *The Gathering Storm.* New York: Houghton Mifflin, 1948.

———. *The Grand Alliance.* London: Cassell, 1950.

———. *The World Crisis.* 5 vols. New York: Scribner, 1923–31.

Churchwell, Sarah. *Behold, America: A History of America First and the American Dream.* London: Bloomsbury, 2018.

Clark, Christopher M. *The Sleepwalkers: How Europe Went to War in 1914.* London: Allen Lane, 2012.

Cloud, Stanley, and Lynne Olson. *The Murrow Boys: Pioneers on the Front Lines of Broadcast Journalism.* Boston: Houghton Mifflin, 1996.

Cohen, Warren I. *American Revisionists: The Lessons of Intervention in World War One.* Chicago: University of Chicago Press, 1967.

———. *A Nation Like All Others: A Brief History of American Foreign Relations.* New York: Columbia University Press, 2018.

Cole, Allan B., ed. *Conflict in Indo-China and International Repercussions: A Documentary History, 1945–55.* Ithaca, NY: Cornell University Press, 1956.

Cole, Wayne S. *Charles A. Lindbergh and the Battle Against American Intervention in World War II.* New York: Harcourt Brace Jovanovich, 1974.

Collier, Peter, and David Horowitz. *The Kennedys: An American Drama.* New York: Summit, 1984.

Colville, Sir John Rupert. *The Fringes of Power: 10 Downing Street Diaries, 1939–1955*. New York: W. W. Norton, 1985.

Conant, Jennet. *Man of the Hour: James B. Conant, Warrior Scientist*. New York: Simon and Schuster, 2017.

Cooper, John Milton. *Breaking the Heart of the World: Woodrow Wilson and the Fight for the League of Nations*. Cambridge, UK: Cambridge University Press, 2001.

Costello, John. *The Pacific War*. New York: Rawson, Wade, 1981.

Costigliola, Frank. *Roosevelt's Lost Alliances: How Personal Politics Helped Start the Cold War*. Princeton, NJ: Princeton University Press, 2012.

Cott, Nancy, F. *Grounding of Modern Feminism*. New Haven, CT: Yale University Press, 1987.

Cox Richardson, Heather. *To Make Men Free: A History of the Republican Party*. Boulder, CO: Basic Books, 2014.

Craig, Campbell, and Fredrik Logevall. *America's Cold War: The Politics of Insecurity*. Cambridge, MA: Belknap Press of Harvard University Press, 2009.

Crosby, Alfred W. *America's Forgotten Pandemic: The Influenza of 1918*. Cambridge, UK: Cambridge University Press, 2003.

Crowley, John, William J. Smyth, and Mike Murphy, eds. *Atlas of the Great Irish Famine*. New York: New York University Press, 2012.

Cull, Nicholas J. *Selling War: The British Propaganda Against American "Neutrality" in World War II*. New York: Oxford University Press, 1995.

Cumings, Bruce. *The Korean War: A History*. New York: Modern Library, 2010.

Cutler, John Henry. *Honey Fitz: Three Steps to the White House: The Life and Times of John F. (Honey Fitz) Fitzgerald*. Indianapolis: Bobbs-Merrill, 1962.

Dallek, Robert. *Franklin D. Roosevelt and American Foreign Policy, 1932–1945*. New York: Oxford University Press, 1979.

———. *Lone Star Rising: Lyndon Johnson and His Times, 1908–1960*. New York: Oxford University Press, 1991.

———. *An Unfinished Life: John F. Kennedy, 1917–1963*. New York: Back Bay Books, 2003.

Damore, Leo. *The Cape Cod Years of John Fitzgerald Kennedy*. Englewood Cliffs, NJ: Prentice-Hall, 1967.

Davies, Norman. *No Simple Victory: World War II in Europe, 1939–1945*. New York: Viking, 2007.

Dittrich, Luke. *Patient H.M.: A Story of Memory, Madness, and Family Secrets*. New York: Random House, 2016.

Dobbs, Michael. *Six Months in 1945: FDR, Stalin, Churchill and Truman—From World War to Cold War*. New York: Knopf, 2012.

Doenecke, Justus D. *Storm on the Horizon*. Lanham, MD: Rowman and Littlefield, 2000.

Doenecke, Justus D., and John E. Wilz. *From Isolation to War: 1931–1941*. Hoboken, NJ: Wiley-Blackwell, 2015.

Doherty, Thomas Patrick. *Cold War, Cool Medium: Television, McCarthyism, and American Culture*. New York: Columbia University Press, 2003.

Dolan, Jay P. *The Irish Americans: A History*. New York: Bloomsbury, 2008.

Domagalski, John J. *Dark Water: The Story of Three Officers and PT-109*. Havertown, PA: Casemate, 2014.

Donovan, Robert J. *PT 109: John F. Kennedy in World War II*. New York: McGraw-Hill, 1961.

Doyle, William. *PT 109: An American Epic of War, Survival, and the Destiny of John F. Kennedy*. New York: William Morrow, 2015.

Eckes, Alfred E., and Thomas W. Zeiler. *Globalization and the American Century*. Cambridge, UK: Cambridge University Press, 2003.

Edwards, Bob. *Edward R. Murrow and the Birth of Broadcast Journalism*. Hoboken, NJ: Wiley, 2004.

Engel, Jeffrey A., and Thomas J. Knock. *When Life Strikes the President: Scandal, Death, and Illness in the White House*. New York: Oxford University Press, 2017.

Etkind, Aleksandr. *Roads Not Taken: An Intellectual Biography of William C. Bullitt*. Pittsburgh: University of Pittsburgh Press, 2017.

Evans, Harold. *The American Century*. New York: Knopf, 1998.

Evans, Richard J. *The Coming of the Third Reich*. New York: Penguin, 2004.

———. *The Third Reich in Power, 1933–1939*. New York: Penguin, 2005.

Faber, David. *Munich 1938: Appeasement and World War II*. New York: Simon and Schuster, 2009.

Fanta, J. Julius. *Sailing with President Kennedy: The White House Yachtsman*. New Jersey: Sea Lore, 1968.

Farber, David. *The Rise and Fall of Modern American Conservatism*. Princeton, NJ: Princeton University Press, 2010.

Farley, James Aloysius. *Jim Farley's Story: The Roosevelt Years*. New York: Whittlesey House, 1948.

Farrell, John A. *Richard Nixon: The Life*. New York: Doubleday, 2017.

———. *Tip O'Neill and the Democratic Century*. Boston: Little, Brown, 2001.

Farris, Scott. *Inga: Kennedy's Great Love, Hitler's Perfect Beauty, and J. Edgar Hoover's Prime Suspect*. Guilford, CT: Lyons Press, 2016.

Fay, Paul B. *The Pleasure of His Company*. New York: Harper and Row, 1966.

Fenby, Jonathan. *Alliance: The Inside Story of How Roosevelt, Stalin and Churchill Won One War and Began Another*. New York: Simon and Schuster, 2006.

Ferguson, Niall. *The Pity of War: Explaining World War I*. New York: Basic Books, 1999.

———. *The War of the World: Twentieth-Century Conflict and the Descent of the West*. New York: Penguin, 2006.

Fite, Gilbert Courtland. *Richard B. Russell, Jr., Senator from Georgia*. Chapel Hill: University of North Carolina Press, 1991.

Flood, Richard T. *The Story of Noble and Greenough School 1886–1966*. Dedham, MA: Noble and Greenough School, 1966.

Foner, Eric. *Reconstruction: America's Unfinished Revolution, 1863–1877*. New York: HarperPerennial, 2014.

Foot, Rosemary. *A Substitute for Victory: The Politics of Peacemaking at the Korean Armistice Talks*. Ithaca, NY: Cornell University Press, 1990.

Fort, Adrian. *Nancy: The Story of Lady Astor*. London: Jonathan Cape, 2012.

Frank, Jeffrey. *Ike and Dick: Portrait of a Strange Political Marriage*. New York: Simon and Schuster, 2013.

Frank, Richard B. *Downfall: The End of the Imperial Japanese Empire*. New York: Random House, 1999.

Freedman, Max. *Roosevelt and Frankfurter: Their Correspondence*. Boston: Little, Brown, 1967.

Freeland, Richard M. *The Truman Doctrine and the Origins of McCarthyism: Foreign Policy, Domestic Politics, and Internal Security, 1946–1948*. New York: New York University Press, 1985.

Fried, Richard M. *Men Against McCarthy*. New York: Columbia University Press, 1976.

Fullilove, Michael. *Rendezvous with Destiny*. New York: Penguin, 2013.

Gabler, Neal. *Winchell: Gossip, Power, and the Culture of Celebrity*. New York: Knopf, 1994.

Gaddis, John Lewis. *George F. Kennan: An American Life*. New York: Penguin, 2011.

———. *On Grand Strategy*. New York: Penguin, 2018.

———. *Strategies of Containment: A Critical Appraisal of American National Security Policy During the Cold War*. New York: Oxford University Press, 2005.

Galbraith, John Kenneth. *A Life in Our Times: Memoirs*. Boston: Houghton Mifflin, 1981.

Giglio, James N. *John F. Kennedy: A Bibliography*. Westport, CT: Greenwood, 1995.

Gillon, Steven M. *Pearl Harbor: FDR Leads the Nation into War*. New York: Basic Books, 2011.

Glantz, David, and Jonathan House. *To the Gates of Stalingrad: Soviet-German Combat Operations, April–August 1942*. Lawrence: University Press of Kansas, 2009.

Goodwin, Doris Kearns. *The Fitzgeralds and the Kennedys: An American Saga*. New York: Simon and Schuster, 1987.

Gorman, Joseph Bruce. *Kefauver: A Political Biography*. New York: Oxford University Press, 1971.

Gorodetsky, Gabriel. *Grand Delusion: Stalin and the German Invasion of Russia*. New Haven, CT: Yale University Press, 1999.

Graham, James W. *Victura: The Kennedys, a Sailboat, and the Sea*. Lebanon, NH: ForeEdge, 2014.

Greenberg, David. *Nixon's Shadow: The History of an Image*. New York: W. W. Norton, 2003.

———. *Republic of Spin: An Inside History of the American Presidency*. New York: W. W. Norton, 2016.

Gunther, John. *Inside Europe: Again Completely Revised*. New York: Harper & Brothers, 1937.

Guthman, Edwin O., and Jeffrey Shulman, eds. *Robert Kennedy, in His Own Words: The Unpublished Recollections of the Kennedy Years*. New York: Bantam, 1988.

Hagerty, James Campbell. *The Diary of James C. Hagerty: Eisenhower in Midcourse, 1954–1955*. Bloomington: Indiana University Press, 1983.

Halberstam, David. *The Best and the Brightest*. 20th anniversary ed. New York: Random House, 1992.

———. *The Coldest Winter: America and the Korean War*. New York: Hyperion, 2007.

———. *The Fifties*. New York: Villard Books, 1993.

Halley, Patrick S. *Dapper Dan*. CreateSpace Independent Publishing Platform, 2015.

Hamilton, Nigel. *JFK: Reckless Youth*. New York: Random House, 1992.

———. *The Mantle of Command: FDR at War, 1941–1942*. New York: Houghton Mifflin Harcourt, 2014.

———. *War and Peace: FDR's Final Odyssey, D-Day to Yalta, 1943–1945.* Boston: Houghton Mifflin Harcourt, 2019.

Handlin, Oscar. *Boston's Immigrants: 1790–1880.* Cambridge, MA: Harvard University Press, 1979.

———. *The Uprooted.* Philadelphia: University of Pennsylvania Press, 2002.

Harbutt, Fraser J. *Yalta 1945: Europe and America at the Crossroads.* New York: Cambridge University Press, 2010.

Hasegawa, Tsuyoshi. *Racing the Enemy: Stalin, Truman, and the Surrender of Japan.* Cambridge, MA: Belknap Press of Harvard University Press, 2005.

Hastings, Max. *Inferno: The World at War, 1939–1945.* New York: Knopf, 2011.

Heinrichs, Waldo H. *Threshold of War.* New York: Oxford University Press, 1988.

Helleiner, Eric. *Forgotten Foundations of Bretton Woods: International Development and the Making of the Postwar Order.* Ithaca, NY: Cornell University Press, 2014.

Hellman, John. *The Kennedy Obsession: The American Myth of JFK.* New York: Columbia University Press, 1997.

Henry, Richard. *Eleanor Roosevelt and Adlai Stevenson.* New York: Palgrave Macmillan, 2010.

Herman, Arthur. *Freedom's Forge: How American Business Produced the Victory in World War II.* New York: Random House, 2012.

Herring, George C. *From Colony to Superpower: U.S. Foreign Relations Since 1776.* New York: Oxford University Press, 2011.

Herrmann, Dorothy. *Anne Morrow Lindbergh: A Gift for Life.* New York: Ticknor & Fields, 1992.

Hersh, Seymour. *The Dark Side of Camelot.* Boston: Little, Brown, 1997.

Hershberg, James. *James B. Conant: Harvard to Hiroshima and the Making of the Nuclear Age.* New York: Knopf, 1993.

Herzstein, Robert E. *Henry Luce, Time, and the American Crusade in Asia.* New York: Cambridge University Press, 2005.

———. *Henry R. Luce: A Political Portrait of the Man Who Created the American Century.* New York: Scribners, 1994.

Hess, Stephen. *America's Political Dynasties: From Adams to Clinton.* Washington, DC: Brookings, 2016.

Hessen, Robert. *Berlin Alert.* Stanford, CA: Hoover Institution, 1984.

Heymann, C. David. *A Woman Named Jackie.* New York: L. Stuart, 1989.

Higham, Charles. *Rose: The Life and Times of Rose Fitzgerald Kennedy*. New York: Pocket, 1995.

Hitchcock, William I. *The Age of Eisenhower: America and the World in the 1950s*. New York: Simon and Schuster, 2018.

———. *The Bitter Road to Freedom: A New History of the Liberation of Europe*. New York: Free Press, 2008.

———. *The Struggle for Europe: The Turbulent History of a Divided Continent, 1945–2002*. New York: Doubleday, 2003.

Hobsbawm, Eric. *Age of Extremes: A History of the World, 1914–1991*. New York: Pantheon, 1994.

Hoffman, Bruce. *Anonymous Soldiers: The Struggle for Israel, 1917–1947*. New York: Knopf, 2015.

Hofstadter, Richard. *Anti-Intellectualism in American Life*. New York: Knopf, 1963.

Hogan, Michael J. *The Afterlife of John Fitzgerald Kennedy: A Biography*. New York: Cambridge University Press, 2017.

Holt, L. Emmett, Jr. *The Care and Feeding of Children: A Catechism for the Use of Mothers and Children's Nurses*. New York: Appleton Century, 1935.

Hoopes, Townsend, and Douglas Brinkley. *Driven Patriot: The Life and Times of James Forrestal*. New York: Knopf, 1992.

Hopkins, Michael F. *Dean Acheson and the Obligations of Power*. Lanham, MD: Rowman & Littlefield, 2017.

Hotta, Eri. *Japan 1941: Countdown to Infamy*. New York: Knopf, 2013.

Hull, Cordell. *The Memoirs of Cordell Hull*. Vol. 1. New York: Macmillan, 1948.

Hunt, Amber, and David Batcher. *The Kennedy Wives: Triumph and Tragedy in America's Most Public Family*. Guilford, CT: Lyons Press, 2015.

Hynes, Samuel Lynn. *The Soldiers' Tale: Bearing Witness to Modern War*. New York: Penguin, 1997.

Immerwahr, Daniel. *How to Hide an Empire: A History of the Greater United States*. New York: Farrar, Straus and Giroux, 2019.

Isaacson, Walter, and Evan Thomas. *The Wise Men: Six Friends and the World They Made*. New York: Simon and Schuster, 1986.

Jackson, Julian. *The Fall of France: The Nazi Invasion of 1940*. Oxford: Oxford University Press, 2003.

James, Harold Douglas. *Europe Reborn: A History, 1914–2000*. Harlow, UK: Longman, 2003.

Jonas, Manfred. *Isolationism in America, 1935–1941*. Ithaca, NY: Cornell University Press, 1966.

Kabaservice, Geoffrey. *Rule and Ruin: The Downfall of Moderation and the Destruction of the Republican Party*. New York: Oxford University Press, 2012.

Kagan, Robert. *The World America Made*. New York: Knopf, 2012.

Kaiser, David. *No End Save Victory: How FDR Led the Nation into War*. New York: Basic Books, 2014.

Kamensky, Jane, et al. *A People and a Nation: A History of the United States*. 8th ed. Boston: Cengage, 2019.

Kaplan, Alice Yaeger. *Dreaming in French: The Paris Years of Jacqueline Bouvier Kennedy, Susan Sontag, and Angela Davis*. Chicago: University of Chicago Press, 2012.

Karabel, Jerome. *The Chosen: The Hidden History of Admission and Exclusion at Harvard, Yale, and Princeton*. Boston: Houghton Mifflin, 2005.

Karabell, Zachary. *The Last Campaign: How Harry Truman Won the 1948 Election*. New York: Knopf, 2000.

Karr, Ronald Dale. *Between City and Country: Brookline, Massachusetts, and the Origins of Suburbia*. Amherst: University of Massachusetts Press, 2018.

Kashner, Sam, and Nancy Schoenberger. *The Fabulous Bouvier Sisters: The Tragic and Glamorous Lives of Jackie and Lee*. New York: HarperCollins, 2018.

Katznelson, Ira. *Fear Itself: The New Deal and the Origins of Our Time*. New York: Liveright, 2013.

Kazin, Michael. *War Against War: The American Fight for Peace, 1914–1918*. New York: Simon and Schuster, 2017.

Keating, Bern. *The Mosquito Fleet*. New York: Putnam, 1963.

Keegan, John. *The Second World War*. London: Hutchinson, 1989.

Kelley, Kitty. *Jackie Oh!* Secaucus, NJ: Lyle Stuart, 1978.

Kelly, John. *The Graves Are Walking: The Great Famine and the Saga of the Irish People*. New York: Henry Holt, 2012.

Kennan, George, F. *Memoirs 1925–1950*. Boston: Little Brown, 1967.

Kennedy, David M. *Freedom from Fear: The American People in Depression and War, 1929–1945*. New York: Oxford University Press, 2001.

———. *Over Here: The First World War and American Society*. New York: Oxford University Press, 2004.

Kennedy, Edward M. *True Compass: A Memoir*. New York: Twelve, 2009.

Kennedy, Jacqueline, and Michael Beschloss. *Jacqueline Kennedy: Historic Conversations on Life with John F. Kennedy*. New York: Hyperion, 2011.

Kennedy, John F. *Prelude to Leadership: The Post-War Diary of John F. Kennedy*. Edited by Deirdre Henderson. Washington, DC: Regnery, 1997.

———. *Profiles in Courage*. 50th anniversary ed. New York: Harper Perennial, 2006. First published by Harper, 1956.

———. *Why England Slept*. New York: Wilfred Funk, 1961. First published 1940.

Kennedy, Joseph P. *I'm for Roosevelt*. New York: Reynal & Hitchcock, 1936.

Kennedy, Paul. *The Rise and Fall of the Great Powers: Economic Change and Military Conflict from 1500 to 2000*. New York: Random House, 1987.

———. *Victory at Sea*. New Haven, CT: Yale University Press, forthcoming 2021.

Kennedy, Rose Fitzgerald. *Times to Remember*. New York: Doubleday, 1974.

Kennedy, Ross A. *The Will to Believe: Woodrow Wilson, World War I, and America's Strategy for Peace and Security*. Kent, OH: Kent State University Press, 2009.

Kenny, Kevin. *The American Irish: A History*. Essex, UK: Pearson, 2000.

Kershaw, Ian. *Fateful Choices: Ten Decisions That Changed the World, 1940–1941*. New York: Penguin, 2007.

———. *Hitler, 1889–1936: Hubris*. New York: W. W. Norton, 2000.

———. *Hitler, 1936–1945: Nemesis*. New York: W. W. Norton, 2001.

———. *To Hell and Back: Europe 1914–1949*. New York: Penguin, 2015.

Kessler, Ronald. *Sins of the Father: Joseph P. Kennedy and the Dynasty He Founded*. New York: Warner, 1996.

Ketchum, Richard M. *The Borrowed Years, 1938–1941: America on the Way to War*. New York: Random House, 1989.

Keynes, John Maynard. *The Economic Consequences of the Peace*. New York: Harcourt, Brace, and Howe, 1920.

Kimball, Warren F. *Churchill and Roosevelt: The Complete Correspondence*. 3 vols. Princeton, NJ: Princeton University Press, 1984.

———. *Forged in War: Roosevelt, Churchill, and the Second World War*. New York: William Morrow, 1997.

———. *The Juggler: Franklin Roosevelt as Wartime Statesman*. Princeton, NJ: Princeton University Press, 1991.

Klein, Edward. *All Too Human: The Love Story of Jack and Jackie Kennedy*. New York: Pocket Books, 1996.

Knock, Thomas. *To End All Wars: Woodrow Wilson and the Quest for a New World Order*. Princeton, NJ: Princeton University Press, 1995.

Kolata, Gina. *Flu: The Story of the Great Influenza Pandemic of 1918 and the Search for the Virus That Caused It*. New York: Farrar, Straus and Giroux, 1999.

Koskoff, David E. *Joseph P. Kennedy: A Life and Times*. Englewood Cliffs, NJ: Prentice-Hall, 1974.

Kotkin, Stephen. *Stalin*. Vol. 2, *Waiting for Hitler*. New York: Penguin, 2017.

Kramnick, Isaac, and Barry Sheerman. *Harold Laski: A Life on the Left*. London: Hamish Hamilton, 1993.

Krock, Arthur. *Memoirs: Sixty Years on the Firing Line*. New York: Funk & Wagnalls, 1968.

Kurth, Peter. *American Cassandra: The Life of Dorothy Thompson*. Boston: Little, Brown, 1990.

Kynaston, David. *Austerity Britain, 1945–51*. New York: Walker, 2008.

LaFeber, Walter. *The American Age: U.S. Foreign Policy at Home and Abroad*. Vol. 2. New York: W. W. Norton, 1994.

Langer, William L., and S. Everett Gleason. *The Challenge to Isolation: The World Crisis of 1937–1940 and American Foreign Policy*. New York: Harper and Row, 1952.

Larson, Kate Clifford. *Rosemary: The Hidden Kennedy Daughter*. Boston: Mariner, 2015.

Lash, Joseph P. *From the Diaries of Felix Frankfurter*. New York: W. W. Norton, 1975.

Lasky, Victor. *J.F.K.: The Man and the Myth*. New York: Macmillan, 1963.

Leamer, Laurence. *The Kennedy Men: 1901–1963*. New York: William Morrow, 2001.

———. *The Kennedy Women: The Saga of an American Family*. New York: Villard, 1994.

Leaming, Barbara. *Jack Kennedy: Education of a Statesman*. New York: W. W. Norton, 2006.

———. *Jacqueline Bouvier Kennedy Onassis: The Untold Story*. New York: Thomas Dunne Books/St. Martin's, 2014.

———. *Mrs. Kennedy: The Missing History of the Kennedy Years*. Riverside, CA: Free Press, 2002.

Leffler, Melvyn P. *A Preponderance of Power: National Security, the Truman Administration, and the Cold War*. Stanford, CA: Stanford University Press, 1992.

Lelyveld, Joseph. *His Final Battle: The Last Months of Franklin Roosevelt*. New York: Knopf, 2016.

Lemann, Nicholas. *The Big Test: The Secret History of the American Meritocracy*. New York: Farrar, Straus and Giroux, 1999.

———. *Redemption: The Last Battle of the Civil War*. New York: Farrar, Straus and Giroux, 2006.

Lepore, Jill. *These Truths: A History of the United States*. New York: W. W. Norton, 2018.

Leuchtenburg, William E. *In the Shadow of FDR: From Harry Truman to Barack Obama*. Ithaca, NY: Cornell University Press, 2009.

Levingston, Steven. *Kennedy and King: The President, the Pastor, and the Battle Over Civil Rights*. New York: Hachette, 2017.

Lewis, David Levering. *The Improbable Wendell Willkie: The Businessman Who Saved the Republican Party and His Country, and Conceived a New World Order*. New York: Liveright, 2018.

Lichtenstein, Nelson. *State of the Union: A Century of American Labor*. Princeton, NJ: Princeton University Press, 2002.

Liddell Hart, Sir Basil Henry. *History of the Second World War*. London: Pan Books, 1973.

Lincoln, Evelyn. *My Twelve Years with John F. Kennedy*. New York: D. McKay, 1965.

Lind, Michael. *The American Way of Strategy*. New York: Oxford University Press, 2006.

Lindbergh, Anne Morrow. *War Within and Without: Diaries and Letters of Anne Morrow Lindbergh, 1939–1944*. New York: Harcourt Brace Jovanovich, 1980.

Lindbergh, Charles A. *The Wartime Journals of Charles A. Lindbergh*. San Diego: Harcourt Brace Jovanovich, 1970.

Ling, Peter John. *John F. Kennedy*. New York: Routledge, Taylor & Francis, 2013.

Lodge, Henry Cabot. *The Storm Has Many Eyes: A Personal Narrative*. New York: W. W. Norton, 1973.

Logevall, Fredrik. *Embers of War: The Fall of an Empire and the Making of America's Vietnam*. New York: Random House, 2012.

Longley, Kyle. *Senator Albert Gore, Sr.: Tennessee Maverick*. Baton Rouge, LA: LSU Press, 2004.

Lubrich, Oliver, ed. *John F. Kennedy Unter Deutschen: Reisetagebucher und Briefe, 1937–1945*. Berlin: Aufbau, 2013.

Lukacs, John. *Five Days in London, May 1940*. New Haven, CT: Yale University Press, 1999.

MacMillan, Margaret. *Paris 1919: Six Months That Changed the World*. New York: Random House, 2002.

———. *The War That Ended Peace: The Road to 1914*. New York: Random House, 2013.

MacNiven, Ian S. *Literchoor Is My Beat: A Life of James Laughlin, Publisher of New Directions*. New York: Farrar, Straus and Giroux, 2014.

Mahomey, Richard D. *Sons and Brothers: The Days of Jack and Bobby Kennedy*. New York: Arcade, 1999.

Maier, Charles. *Among Empires: American Ascendancy and Its Predecessors*. Cambridge, MA: Harvard University Press, 2006.

Maier, Thomas. *The Kennedys: America's Emerald Kings*. New York: Basic Books, 2003.

———. *When Lions Roar: The Churchills and the Kennedys*. New York: Crown, 2014.

Manchester, William. *The Glory and the Dream: A Narrative History of America, 1932–1972*. Boston: Little, Brown, 1974.

———. *One Brief Shining Moment: Remembering Kennedy*. Boston: Little, Brown, 1983.

———. *Portrait of a President*. Boston: Little, Brown, 1967.

Mann, Robert. *A Grand Delusion: America's Descent into Vietnam*. New York: Basic Books, 2001.

Martin, John Bartlow. *Adlai Stevenson and the World: The Life of Adlai E. Stevenson*. Garden City, NY: Doubleday, 1977.

———. *Adlai Stevenson of Illinois: The Life of Adlai E. Stevenson*. New York: Doubleday, 1976.

Martin, Ralph G. *Ballots and Bandwagons*. Chicago: Rand McNally, 1964.

———. *A Hero for Our Time: An Intimate Story of the Kennedy Years*. New York: Macmillan, 1983.

Martin, Ralph, and Ed Plaut. *Front Runner, Dark Horse*. New York: Doubleday, 1960.

Matthews, Chris. *Bobby Kennedy: A Raging Spirit*. New York: Simon and Schuster, 2017.

———. *Jack Kennedy: Elusive Hero*. New York: Simon and Schuster, 2011.

———. *Kennedy and Nixon: The Rivalry That Shaped Postwar America*. New York: Simon and Schuster, 1996.

May, Ernest R. *American Cold War Strategy: Interpreting NSC 68*. Boston: Bedford, 1993.

———. *Strange Victory: Hitler's Conquest of France*. New York: Hill and Wang, 2001.

Mayers, David Allan. *FDR's Ambassadors and the Diplomacy of Crisis: From the Rise of Hitler to the End of World War II*. Cambridge, UK: Cambridge University Press, 2013.

Mazower, Mark. *Dark Continent: Europe's Twentieth Century*. New York: Knopf, 1998.

McCarthy, Joe. *The Remarkable Kennedys, 1915–1980*. New York: Dial Press, 1960.

McClellan, David S. *Dean Acheson: The State Department Years*. New York: Dodd, Mead, 1976.

McCullough, David G. *Truman*. New York: Simon and Schuster, 1992.

McGirr, Lisa. *The War on Alcohol: Prohibition and the Rise of the American State*. New York: W. W. Norton, 2016.

McKeever, Porter. *Adlai Stevenson: His Life and Legacy*. New York: William Morrow, 1989.

McMahon, Robert J., ed. *Major Problems in the History of the Vietnam War*. Lexington, MA: D.C. Heath, 1990.

McMeekin, Sean. *July 1914: Countdown to War*. New York: Basic Books, 2013.

McNamara, Eileen. *Eunice: The Kennedy Who Changed the World*. New York: Simon and Schuster, 2018.

McSweeney, Dean, and John E. Owens, eds. *The Republican Takeover of Congress*. New York: St. Martin's, 1998.

McTaggart, Lynne. *Kathleen Kennedy: Her Life and Times*. New York: Doubleday, 1983.

Meacham, Jon. *Franklin and Winston: An Intimate Portrait of an Epic Friendship*. New York: Random House, 2003.

Mendelson, Edward. *Later Auden*. New York: Farrar, Straus and Giroux, 1999.

Meyers, Joan Simpson. *As We Remember Him*. New York: Atheneum, 1965.

Michaelis, David. *The Best of Friends: Portraits of Extraordinary Friendships*. New York: William Morrow, 1983.

Miller, Kerby A. *Emigrants and Exiles: Ireland and the Irish Exodus to North America*. New York: Oxford University Press, 1985.

Miller, Merle, ed. *Plain Speaking: An Oral Biography of Harry S. Truman*. New York: Berkley, 1974.

Miller, William J. *Henry Cabot Lodge: A Biography*. New York: Heineman, 1967.

Milne, David. *Worldmaking: The Art and Science of American Diplomacy*. New York: Farrar, Straus and Giroux, 2015.

Miscamble, Wilson. *From Roosevelt to Truman: Potsdam, Hiroshima, and the Cold War*. Cambridge, UK: Cambridge University Press, 2007.

Mitchell, Greg. *Tricky Dick and the Pink Lady: Richard Nixon vs. Helen Gahagan Douglas—Sexual Politics and the Red Scare, 1950*. New York: Random House, 1998.

Mitter, Rana. *Forgotten Ally: China's World War II, 1937–1945*. Boston: Houghton Mifflin Harcourt, 2013.

Moe, Richard. *Roosevelt's Second Act: The Election of 1940 and the Politics of War*. New York: Oxford University Press, 2013.

Moley, Raymond. *After Seven Years*. New York: Harper & Brothers, 1939.

Moorhouse, Roger. *The Devil's Alliance: Hitler's Pact with Stalin, 1939–1941*. New York: Basic, 2014.

Morison, Samuel Eliot. *Three Centuries of Harvard, 1636–1936*. Cambridge, MA: Harvard University Press, 1936.

Morris, Sylvia Jukes. *Rage for Fame: The Ascent of Clare Boothe Luce*. New York: Random House, 1997.

Morrow, Lance. *The Best Year of Their Lives: Kennedy, Johnson, and Nixon in 1948: Learning the Secrets of Power*. New York: Basic Books, 2005.

Mosley, Charlotte. *The Mitfords: Letters Between Six Sisters*. New York: Harper, 2007.

Mosley, Leonard. *Lindbergh: A Biography*. Garden City, NY: Doubleday, 1976.

Muehlenbeck, Philip E. *Betting on the Africans: John F. Kennedy's Courting of African Nationalist Leaders*. New York: Oxford University Press, 2012.

Myrer, Anton. *The Last Convertible*. New York: Putnam, 1978.

Naimark, Norman. *Stalin and the Fate of Europe: The Postwar Struggle for Sovereignty*. Cambridge, MA: Harvard University Press, 2019.

Nasaw, David. *The Patriarch: The Remarkable Life and Turbulent Times of Joseph P. Kennedy*. New York: Penguin Press, 2012.

Neiberg, Michael. *The Path to War*. New York: Oxford University Press, 2016.

———. *Potsdam: The End of World War II and the Remaking of Europe*. New York: Basic Books, 2015.

Nelson, Garrison. *John William McCormack: A Political Biography*. New York: Bloomsbury Academic, 2017.

Nichols, Christopher McKnight. *Promise and Peril: America at the Dawn of a Global Age*. Cambridge, MA: Harvard University Press, 2015.

Nichols, David Allen. *Eisenhower 1956*. New York: Simon and Schuster, 2011.

———. *Ike and McCarthy: Dwight Eisenhower's Secret Campaign Against Joseph McCarthy*. New York: Simon and Schuster, 2017.

Nichter, Luke A. *The Last Brahmin: Henry Cabot Lodge Jr. and the Making of the Cold War*. New Haven, CT: Yale University Press, 2020.

Nicolson, Nigel, ed. *Harold Nicolson Diaries and Letters*. London: Collins, 1966.

Nixon, Richard M. *RN: The Memoirs of Richard Nixon*. New York: Grosset & Dunlap, 1978.

Norris, John. *Mary McGrory: The First Queen of Journalism*. New York: Viking, 2015.

Nunnerly, David. *President Kennedy and Britain*. New York: St. Martin's, 1972.

Nye, Joseph S. *Soft Power: The Means to Success in World Politics*. New York: Public Affairs, 2004.

O'Brien, Lawrence F. *No Final Victories: A Life in Politics—From John F. Kennedy to Watergate*. Garden City, NY: Doubleday, 1974.

O'Brien, Michael. *John F. Kennedy: A Biography*. New York: St. Martin's Press, 2005.

O'Connor, Thomas H. *The Boston Irish: A Political History*. Boston: Northeastern University Press, 1995.

O'Donnell, Helen. *The Irish Brotherhood: John F. Kennedy, His Inner Circle, and the Improbable Rise to the Presidency*. Berkeley, CA: Counterpoint, 2015.

O'Donnell, Kenneth P., and David F. Powers. *"Johnny, We Hardly Knew Ye": Memories of John Fitzgerald Kennedy*. Boston: Little, Brown, 1972.

Offner, Arnold A. *Hubert Humphrey: The Conscience of the Country*. New Haven, CT: Yale University Press, 2018.

Ó Gráda, Cormac, ed. *Ireland's Great Famine*. Dublin: University College Dublin, 2005.

Okrent, Daniel. *Last Call: The Rise and Fall of Prohibition*. New York: Scribner, 2010.

Oliphant, Thomas, and Curtis Wilkie. *The Road to Camelot: Inside JFK's Five-Year Campaign*. New York: Simon and Schuster, 2017.

Olsen, Jack. *Aphrodite: Desperate Mission*. New York: Putnam, 1970.

Olson, Lynne. *Those Angry Days: Roosevelt, Lindbergh, and America's Fight over World War II, 1939–1941*. New York: Random House, 2014.

O'Neill, Gerard. *Rogues and Redeemers: When Politics Was King in Irish Boston*. New York: Crown Publishers, 2012.

O'Neill, Tip. *Man of the House: The Life and Political Memoirs of Speaker Tip O'Neill*. New York: Random House, 1987.

Osgood, Kenneth. *Total Cold War: Eisenhower's Secret Propaganda Battle at Home and Abroad*. Lawrence: University Press of Kansas, 2006.

Oshinsky, David M. *A Conspiracy So Immense: The World of Joe McCarthy*. New York: Oxford University Press, 2005.

O'Toole, Patricia. *The Moralist: Woodrow Wilson and the World He Made*. New York: Simon and Schuster, 2018.

Overy, Richard. *1939: Countdown to War*. New York: Allen Lane, 2009.

———. *Twilight Years: The Paradox of Britain Between the Wars*. New York: Penguin, 2010.

Parker, R.A.C. *Chamberlain and Appeasement: British Policy and the Coming of the Second World War*. New York: St. Martin's, 1993.

Parker, Richard. *John Kenneth Galbraith: His Life, His Politics, His Economics*. New York: Farrar, Straus and Giroux, 2015.

Parmet, Herbert S. *Jack: The Struggles of John F. Kennedy*. New York: Dial Press, 1980.

Paterson, Thomas G., et al. *American Foreign Relations: A History*. Vol. 1, *To 1920*. 8th ed. Stamford, CT: Cengage Learning, 2015.

Patterson, James T. *Grand Expectations: The United States, 1945–1974*. New York: Oxford University Press, 1996.

———. *Mr. Republican: A Biography of Robert A. Taft*. Boston: Houghton Mifflin, 1972.

Perlmutter, Amos. *FDR and Stalin: A Not So Grand Alliance, 1943–1945*. Columbia: University of Missouri Press, 1993.

Perret, Geoffrey. *Jack: A Life Like No Other*. New York: Random House, 2001.

Perry, Barbara Ann. *Jacqueline Kennedy: First Lady of the New Frontier*. Lawrence: University Press of Kansas, 2004.

———. *Rose Kennedy: The Life and Times of a Political Matriarch*. New York: W. W. Norton, 2013.

Peterson, Mark. *The City-State of Boston: The Rise and Fall of an Atlantic Power, 1630–1865*. Princeton, NJ: Princeton University Press, 2019.

Pitts, David. *Jack and Lem: John F. Kennedy and Lem Billings: The Untold Story of an Extraordinary Friendship*. Boston: Da Capo, 2009.

Plokhy, Serhii. *Yalta: The Price of Peace*. New York: Viking, 2010.

Porter, Roy. *The Greatest Benefit to Mankind: A Medical History of Humanity*. New York: W. W. Norton, 1997.

Prados, John. *The Sky Would Fall: Operation Vulture, the U.S. Bombing Mission in Indochina, 1954*. New York: Dial Press. 1983.

Preston, Diana. *Eight Days at Yalta: How Churchill, Roosevelt, and Stalin Shaped the Post-War World*. New York: Atlantic Monthly, 2020.

Prior, Robin, and Trevor Wilson. *The Somme*. New Haven, CT: Yale University Press, 2005.

Puleo, Stephen. *A City So Grand: The Rise of an American Metropolis, Boston 1850–1900*. Boston: Beacon, 2010.

Quétel, Claude. *L'Impardonnable Défaite: 1918–1940*. Paris: Lattès, 2009.

Rakove, Robert B. *Kennedy, Johnson, and the Nonaligned World*. New York: Cambridge University Press, 2012.

Rauchway, Eric. *The Money Makers: How Roosevelt and Keynes Ended the Depression, Defeated Fascism, and Secured a Prosperous Peace*. New York: Basic Books, 2015.

Rawson, Michael. *Eden on the Charles: The Making of Boston*. Cambridge, MA: Harvard University Press, 2010.

Reeves, Thomas C. *A Question of Character: A Life of John F. Kennedy*. New York: Free Press, 1991.

Renehan, Edward J., Jr. *The Kennedys at War*. New York: Doubleday, 2002.

Reston, James. *Deadline: A Memoir*. New York: Random House, 1991.

Reynolds, David. *From Munich to Pearl Harbor*. Chicago: Ivan R. Dee, 2001.

———. *The Long Shadow: The Great War and the Twentieth Century*. New York: Simon and Schuster, 2013.

———. *Summits*. New York: Basic Books, 2009.

Riva, Maria. *Marlene Dietrich: The Life*. New York: Knopf, 1993.

Roberts, Andrew. *Churchill: Walking with Destiny*. New York: Viking, 2018.

———. *The Storm of War: A New History of the Second World War*. London and New York: Allen Lane, 2011.

Roberts, Geoffrey. *Stalin's Wars: From World War to Cold War, 1939–1953*. New Haven, CT: Yale University Press, 2008.

Roberts, John Morris. *Twentieth Century: The History of the World, 1901 to 2000*. New York: Viking, 1999.

Roosevelt, James. *My Parents: A Differing View*. Chicago: Playboy Press, 1976.

Rosenberg, Emily S. *A Date Which Will Live: Pearl Harbor in American Memory*. Durham, NC: Duke University Press, 2003.

Rostow, W. W. *The World Economy: History and Prospect*. Austin: University of Texas Press, 1978.

Rovere, Richard H. *Senator Joe McCarthy*. New York: Harper & Row, 1959.

Rubin, Gretchen. *Forty Ways to Look at JFK*. New York: Ballantine, 2005.

Sabato, Larry. *The Kennedy Half-Century: The Presidency, Assassination, and Lasting Legacy of John F. Kennedy*. New York: Bloomsbury, 2013.

Sandford, Christopher. *Union Jack: John F. Kennedy's Special Relationship with Great Britain*. Lebanon, NH: ForeEdge, 2017.

Sandler, Martin W., ed. *The Letters of John F. Kennedy*. New York: Bloomsbury, 2015.

Sansom, Ian. *September 1, 1939: A Biography of a Poem*. New York: HarperCollins, 2019.

Savage, Sean J. *The Senator from New England: The Rise of JFK*. Albany: State University of New York Press, 2015.

Schlesinger, Andrew. *Veritas*. Chicago: Ivan R. Dee, 2007.

Schlesinger, Arthur M., Jr. *Journals, 1952–2000*. New York: Penguin Press, 2007.

———. *The Imperial Presidency*. Boston: Houghton Mifflin, 1973.

———. *The Letters of Arthur Schlesinger, Jr*. Edited by Andrew Schlesinger and Stephen C. Schlesinger. New York: Random House, 2013.

———. *A Life in the 20th Century*. New York: Mariner, 2002.

———. *Robert Kennedy and His Times*. Boston: Houghton Mifflin, 1978.

———. *A Thousand Days: John F. Kennedy in the White House*. Boston: Houghton Mifflin, 1965.

Schlesinger, Stephen C. *Act of Creation: The Founding of the United Nations*. Boulder, CO: Westview, 2003.

Schleunes, Karl A. *The Twisted Road to Auschwitz: Nazi Policy Toward German Jews, 1933–1939*. Urbana: University of Illinois Press, 1990.

Schoor, Gene. *Young John Kennedy*. New York: Harcourt, Brace and World, 1963.

Schrecker, Ellen. *Many Are the Crimes: McCarthyism in America*. Boston: Little, Brown, 1998.

Searls, Hank. *The Lost Prince: Young Joe, the Forgotten Kennedy*. New York: World, 1969.

Self, Robert C. *Neville Chamberlain: A Biography*. Burlington, VT: Ashgate, 2006.

———. *The Neville Chamberlain Diary Letters*. Vol. 4, *The Downing Street Years*. Burlington, VT: Ashgate, 2005.

Selverstone, Marc J. *Constructing the Monolith: The United States, Great Britain, and International Communism, 1945–1950*. Cambridge, MA: Harvard University Press, 2009.

Sexton, Jay. *A Nation Forged by Crisis: A New American History*. New York: Basic Books, 2018.

Shaw, John. *JFK in the Senate: The Pathway to the Presidency*. New York: Palgrave Macmillan, 2013.

Shirer, William L. *Berlin Diary: The Journal of a Foreign Correspondent, 1934–1941*. New York: Knopf, 1941.

Simms, Brendan. *Hitler: A Global Biography*. New York: Basic Books, 2019.

Smith, Amanda, ed. *Hostage to Fortune: The Letters of Joseph P. Kennedy*. New York: Viking, 2001.

Smith, Gaddis. *American Diplomacy During the Second World War, 1941–1945*. 2nd ed. New York: Knopf, 1985.

———. *Dean Acheson*. New York: Cooper Square, 1972.

Smith, Jean Edward. *Eisenhower: In War and Peace*. New York: Random House, 2012.

———. *FDR*. New York: Random House, 2007.

Smith, Jean Kennedy. *The Nine of Us: Growing Up Kennedy*. New York: Harper, 2016.

Smith, Richard Norton. *The Colonel: The Life and Legend of Robert R. McCormick, 1880–1955*. Boston: Houghton Mifflin, 1997.

———. *The Harvard Century: The Making of a University to a Nation*. New York: Simon and Schuster, 1986.

Smith, Sally Bedell. *Grace and Power: The Private World of the Kennedy White House*. New York: Random House, 2004.

Smith, Stephen Kennedy, and Douglas Brinkley, eds. *JFK: A Vision for America in Words and Pictures*. New York: Harper, 2017.

Sorensen, Theodore C. *Counselor: A Life at the Edge of History*. New York: Harper, 2008.

———. *Kennedy*. New York: Harper & Row, 1965.

Spector, Ronald H. *Eagle Against the Sun: The American War with Japan*. New York: Free Press, 1985.

Spoto, Donald. *Jacqueline Bouvier Kennedy Onassis: A Life*. New York: St. Martin's, 2000.

Stack, Robert. *Straight Shooting*. New York: Macmillan, 1980.

Stansky, Peter. *The First Day of the Blitz: September 7, 1940*. New Haven, CT: Yale University Press, 2007.

Stead, William T. *The Americanization of the World*. Whitefish, MT: Kessinger, 1901.

Steel, Ronald. *Walter Lippmann and the American Century*. Boston: Little, Brown, 1980.

Steil, Benn. *The Battle of Bretton Woods: John Maynard Keynes, Harry Dexter White, and the Making of a New World Order*. Princeton, NJ: Princeton University Press, 2013.

———. *The Marshall Plan: Dawn of the Cold War*. New York: Simon and Schuster, 2018.

Stein, Jean, ed. *American Journey: The Times of Robert Kennedy*. New York: Harcourt Brace Jovanovich, 1970.

Steiner, Zara. *The Triumph of the Dark: European International History 1933–1939*. Oxford: Oxford University Press, 2011.

Stern, Sheldon M. *Averting "The Final Failure": John F. Kennedy and the Secret Cuban Missile Crisis Meetings*. Stanford, CA: Stanford University Press, 2003.

Stevenson, David. *1917: War, Peace, and Revolution*. Oxford: Oxford University Press, 2017.

———. *Cataclysm: The First World War as Political Tragedy*. New York: Basic Books, 2004.

Stinnett, Robert B. *Day of Deceit: The Truth About FDR and Pearl Harbor*. New York: Free Press, 2000.

Stokes, David R. *Capitol Limited: A Story about John Kennedy and Richard Nixon*. Create Space Independent Publishing, 2014.

Stoll, Ira. *JFK, Conservative*. Boston: Houghton Mifflin Harcourt, 2013.

Storrs, Landon R. Y. *The Second Red Scare and the Unmaking of the New Deal Left*. Princeton, NJ: Princeton University Press, 2013.

Stossel, Scott. *Sarge: The Life and Times of Sargent Shriver*. Washington, DC: Smithsonian, 2004.

Strachan, Hew. *The First World War*. New York: Viking, 2003.

Stueck, William W. *Rethinking the Korean War: A New Diplomatic and Strategic History*. Princeton, NJ: Princeton University Press, 2002.

Swanberg, W. A. *Luce and His Empire*. New York: Scribner, 1972.

Swanson, Gloria. *Swanson on Swanson*. New York: Random House, 1980.

Swift, Will. *The Kennedys Amidst the Gathering Storm: A Thousand Days in London, 1938–1940*. Washington, DC: Smithsonian, 2008.

Tanenhaus, Sam. *Whittaker Chambers: A Biography*. New York: Random House, 1997.

Taraborrelli, J. Randy. *Jackie, Janet & Lee: The Secret Lives of Janet Auchincloss and Her Daughters Jacqueline Kennedy Onassis and Lee Radziwill*. New York: St. Martin's, 2018.

Taylor, Alan John Percivale. *English History, 1914–1945*. New York: Oxford University Press, 1965.

Thayer, Mary Van Rensselaer. *Jacqueline Bouvier Kennedy*. Garden City, NY: Doubleday, 1961.

Thomas, Evan. *Being Nixon: A Man Divided*. New York: Random House, 2015.

———. *Robert Kennedy: His Life*. New York: Simon and Schuster, 2000.

———. *Sea of Thunder: Four Commanders and the Last Great Naval Campaign, 1941–1945*. New York: Simon and Schuster, 2006.

Thompson, John A. *A Sense of Power: The Roots of America's Global Role*. Ithaca, NY: Cornell University Press, 2015.

———. *Woodrow Wilson*. London: Longman, 2002.

Thompson, Laura. *The Six: The Lives of the Mitford Sisters*. New York: St. Martin's, 2016.

Thompson, Nicholas. *The Hawk and the Dove: Paul Nitze, George Kennan, and the History of the Cold War*. New York: Henry Holt, 2009.

Thompson, Robert E., and Hortense Meyers. *Robert F. Kennedy: The Brother Within*. New York: Macmillan, 1962.

Throntveit, Trygve. *Power Without Victory: Woodrow Wilson and the American Internationalist Experiment*. Chicago: University of Chicago Press, 2019.

Tierney, Gene. *Self Portrait*. New York: Wyden, 1979.

Tocqueville, Alexis de. *Democracy in America*. Edited by J. P. Mayer and Max Lerner. New York: Harper and Row, 1966.

Toledano, Ralph de. *R.F.K.: The Man Who Would Be President*. New York: G. P. Putnam's Sons, 1967.

Toll, Ian W. *The Conquering Tide: War in the Pacific Islands, 1942–1944*. New York: W. W. Norton, 2015.

———. *Pacific Crucible: War at Sea in the Pacific, 1941–1942*. New York: W. W. Norton, 2012.

Tooze, Adam. *The Deluge: The Great War, America and the Remaking of the Global Order, 1916–1931*. New York: Penguin, 2014.

Topping, Seymour. *On the Front Lines of the Cold War*. Baton Rouge: Louisiana State University Press, 2010.

Treglown, Jeremy. *Mr. Straight Arrow: The Career of John Hersey, Author of Hiroshima*. New York: Farrar, Straus and Giroux, 2019.

Tubridy, Ryan. *JFK in Ireland: Four Days That Changed a President*. Guilford, CT: Lyons Press, 2011.

Tye, Larry. *Bobby Kennedy: The Making of a Liberal Icon*. New York: Random House, 2016.

———. *Demagogue: The Life and Long Shadow of Senator Joe McCarthy*. Boston: Houghton Mifflin Harcourt, 2020.

Ulyatt, Michelle A. *Theodore Sorensen and the Kennedys*. New York: Palgrave Macmillan, 2019.

Vidal, Gore. *Palimpsest*. New York: Random House, 1995.

Vine, David. *Base Nation: How U.S. Military Bases Abroad Harm America and the World*. New York: Metropolitan/Henry Holt, 2015.

Vogel, Michelle. *Gene Tierney: A Biography*. Jefferson, NC: McFarland, 2005.

Von Post, Gunilla. *Love, Jack*. New York: Crown, 1997.

Wark, Wesley K. *The Ultimate Enemy: British Intelligence and Nazi Germany, 1933–1939*. Ithaca, NY: Cornell University Press, 1985.

Watson, John B. *The Psychological Care of Infant and Child*. New York: W. W. Norton, 1928.

Watt, Donald Cameron. *How War Came: The Immediate Origins of the Second World War*. New York: Pantheon, 1989.

Weinstein, Allen. *Perjury: The Hiss-Chambers Case*. 2nd ed. New York: Random House, 1997.

Weisbrode, Kenneth. *The Year of Indecision, 1946: A Tour Through the Crucible of Harry Truman's America*. New York: Viking, 2016.

Welles, Benjamin. *Sumner Welles: FDR's Global Strategist*. New York: St. Martin's, 1997.

Wells, Samuel F. *Fearing the Worst: How Korea Transformed the Cold War*. New York: Columbia University Press, 2019.

Westad, Odd Arne. *The Cold War: A World History*. New York: Basic Books, 2017.

Whalen, Richard J. *The Founding Father: The Story of Joseph P. Kennedy*. New York: New American Library, 1964.

Whalen, Thomas J. *Kennedy Versus Lodge: The 1952 Massachusetts Senate Race*. Boston: Northeastern University Press, 2000.

Wheeler-Bennett, John. *Special Relationships: America in Peace and War*. London: Macmillan, 1975.

Whipple, Chandler. *Small Ships, Courageous Men*. Uncommon Valor Press, 2015.

White, G. Edward. *Alger Hiss's Looking-Glass Wars: The Covert Life of a Soviet Spy*. New York: Oxford University Press, 2004.

White, Mark J. *Kennedy: A Cultural History of an American Icon*. New York: Bloomsbury, 2013.

White, Theodore Harold. *In Search of History*. New York: HarperCollins, 1978.

Whyte, Kenneth. *Hoover: An Extraordinary Life in Extraordinary Times*. New York: Knopf, 2017.

Wicker, Tom. *Shooting Star: The Brief Arc of Joe McCarthy*. New York: Harcourt, 2006.

Wilentz, Sean. *The Politicians and the Egalitarians: The Hidden History of American Politics*. New York: W. W. Norton, 2016.

Wills, Garry. *The Kennedy Imprisonment: A Meditation on Power*. Boston: Little, Brown, 1982.

Wilson, Page. *Carnage and Courage: A Memoir of FDR, the Kennedys, and World War II*. Newburyport, MA: Skyhorse Publishing, 2015.

Wilson, Theodore A. *The First Summit: Roosevelt and Churchill at Placentia Bay, 1941*. Lawrence: University Press of Kansas, 1991.

Woodham-Smith, Cecil. *The Great Hunger: Ireland: 1845–1849*. New York: Harper and Row, 1962.

Woolner, David B. *The Last Hundred Days: FDR at War and at Peace*. New York: Basic Books, 2017.

Wyman, David S. *Paper Walls: America and the Refugee Crisis, 1938–1941*. Amherst: University of Massachusetts Press, 1968.

Zakaria, Fareed. *From Wealth to Power: The Unusual Origins of America's World Role*. Princeton, NJ: Princeton University Press, 1998.

Zelikow, Philip, and Ernest May. *Suez Deconstructed: An Interactive Study in Crisis, War, and Peacemaking*. Washington, DC: Brookings, 2018.

Zelizer, Julian E. *Arsenal of Democracy: The Politics of National Security—from World War II to the War on Terrorism*. New York: Basic, 2009.

Zunz, Olivier. *Why the American Century?* Chicago: University of Chicago Press, 1998.

PHOTO CREDITS

Page 121: *Copyright © John F. Kennedy Library Foundation.*
Page 125: *John F. Kennedy Presidential Library and Museum, Boston.*
Page 147: *John F. Kennedy Presidential Library and Museum, Boston.*
Page 149: *John F. Kennedy Presidential Library and Museum, Boston.*
Page 161: *© Spee Club Inc.*
Page 165: *John F. Kennedy Presidential Library and Museum, Boston.*
Page 177: *John F. Kennedy Presidential Library and Museum, Boston.*
Page 179: *Acme/John F. Kennedy Presidential Library and Museum, Boston.*
Page 188: *Bettmann/Bettmann Collection via Getty Images.*
Page 204: *John F. Kennedy Presidential Library and Museum, Boston.*
Page 218: *Copyright © John F. Kennedy Library Foundation.*
Page 263: *John F. Kennedy Presidential Library and Museum, Boston.*
Page 281: *Keystone/Hulton Archive via Getty Images.*
Page 286: *Copyright © John F. Kennedy Library Foundation.*
Page 296: *Bettmann/Bettmann Collection via Getty Images.*
Page 320: *Frank Turgeon/John F. Kennedy Presidential Library and Museum, Boston.*
Page 323: *Joel Benjamin/courtesy of the John F. Kennedy Presidential Library and Museum;
gift of Rose Kennedy.*
Page 335: *John F. Kennedy Presidential Library and Museum, Boston.*
Page 338: *John F. Kennedy Presidential Library and Museum, Boston.*
Page 355: *John F. Kennedy Presidential Library and Museum, Boston.*
Page 368: *John F. Kennedy Presidential Library and Museum, Boston.*
Page 371: *John F. Kennedy Presidential Library and Museum, Boston.*
Page 376: *John F. Kennedy Presidential Library and Museum, Boston.*
Page 409: *HUP Kennedy, John F. (1–3). Harvard University Archives.*
Page 415: *Hulton Archive/Archive Photos via Getty Images.*
Page 423: *John F. Kennedy Presidential Library and Museum, Boston.*
Page 438: *John F. Kennedy Presidential Library and Museum, Boston.*
Page 447: *Fox Photos/Hulton Archive via Getty Images.*
Page 455: *John F. Kennedy Presidential Library and Museum, Boston.*
Page 489: *Joel Benjamin/courtesy of the John F. Kennedy Presidential Library and Museum.*
Page 493: *John F. Kennedy Presidential Library and Museum, Boston.*
Page 497: *John F. Kennedy Presidential Library and Museum, Boston.*
Page 509: *Yale Joel/The LIFE Picture Collection via Getty Images.*
Page 515: *Yale Joel/The LIFE Picture Collection via Getty Images.*
Page 524: *Dick Sears/John F. Kennedy Presidential Library and Museum, Boston.*
Page 536: *ullstein bild Dtl./ullstein bild Collection via Getty Images.*
Page 541: *Bettmann/Bettmann Collection via Getty Images.*
Page 559: *Hy Peskin Archive/Archive Photos via Getty Images.*
Page 564: *MPI/Archive Photos via Getty Images.*
Page 565: *Toni Frissell/John F. Kennedy Presidential Library and Museum, Boston.*
Page 580: *Bettmann/Bettmann Collection via Getty Images.*
Page 588: *New York* Daily News *Archive/New York* Daily News *via Getty Images.*
Page 611: *John F. Kennedy Presidential Library and Museum, Boston.*
Page 631: *Howard Sochurek/The LIFE Picture Collection via Getty Images.*
Page 642: *John F. Kennedy Presidential Library and Museum, Boston.*

INDEX

Page numbers of photographs and their captions appear in italics.
Key to abbreviations: Lyndon Baines Johnson = LBJ; Jacqueline Bouvier Kennedy = JBK;
John F. Kennedy = JFK; Joseph Kennedy, Sr. = JPK Sr.; Joseph Kennedy, Jr. = JPK Jr.; Robert F.
Kennedy = RFK; Franklin Delano Roosevelt = FDR

ABOUT THE AUTHOR

FREDRIK LOGEVALL is Laurence D. Belfer Professor of International Affairs and professor of history at Harvard University. A specialist on U.S. foreign relations history and modern international history, he is the author or editor of nine books, most recently *Embers of War*, which won the Pulitzer Prize for History and the Francis Parkman Prize.

ABOUT THE TYPE

This book was set in Photina, a typeface designed by José Mendoza in 1971. It is a very elegant design with high legibility, and its close character fit has made it a popular choice for use in quality magazines and art gallery publications.